LEARNING CHINESE

汉语基础教材

Learning Chinese

A FOUNDATION COURSE IN MANDARIN

JULIAN K. WHEATLEY

YALE UNIVERSITY PRESS NEW HAVEN & LONDON

Publisher: Mary Jane Peluso
Editorial Assistant: Elise Panza
Project Editor: Timothy Shea
Manuscript Editor: Jamie Greene
Production Editor: Ann-Marie Imbornoni
Production Controller: Aldo Cupo
Designed by Nancy Ovedovitz
Maps by Bill Nelson
All photographs are by the author unless otherwise noted.
Set by Toppan Best-set Premedia Limited, Hong Kong.
Printed in the United States of America by Victor Graphics, Baltimore, Maryland.

ISBN: 978-0-300-14117-7
Library of Congress Control Number: 2009937463

A catalogue record for this book is available from the British Library.

This paper meets the requirements of ANSI/NISO Z39.48-1992 (Permanence of Paper).

10 9 8 7 6 5 4 3 2 1

Dedicated to
The Four Generations
四世同堂
and
honoring
The Pivot of the Four Quarters
四方之極

Learning Chinese comes with an extensive set of audio clips that serve as a personal guide to the Chinese language material in the book. These, as well as vocabulary lists (both Chinese-to-English and English-to-Chinese), keys to exercises, and other special features, can be found at the companion website **yalebooks.com/wheatley**.

汉语基础教材

CONTENTS

汉语基础教材

PREFACE

A. Ten basic features of *Learning Chinese*

1. Provides instruction in spoken and written Mandarin; no prior background assumed.
2. Serves as a comprehensive resource for the foundation levels of Chinese language study. *Learning Chinese* (first year) and the forthcoming companion volume (second year) cover approximately 200 class hours.
3. Includes sample schedules for all 200 hours of class study.
4. Presents rich content (based on the author's own experience learning Chinese) that is presented incrementally and in detail, is carefully sequenced, and builds toward dialogues or narratives that recapitulate important content.
5. Includes a variety of exercises and audio materials for self-study. The companion website, **yalebooks.com/wheatley**, provides a full set of audio clips, as well as comprehensive vocabulary lists, exercise keys, and other features.
6. Contains content that is easily transformed into class activities, and easily supplemented by online or other materials.
7. Includes conversational lessons and character lessons that can be used separately or together.
8. Includes conversational and character lessons that are related but not identical to each other, and which can be interleaved.
9. Teaches reading with both the traditional (Taiwan) and simplified (Mainland) character sets.
10. Teaches characters inductively, by emphasizing reading in context as much as possible.

《汉语基础教材》：十个主要特点

一、 供零起点学生口语和书面语学习的汉语入门教材。
二、 这是一套综合性的基础教材。共两册，第一册是初级水平，第二册是中级水平，大约需要修读200个课时。
三、 本教材附有200个课时的课程进度表实例。
四、 作者根据自己的汉语学习经历，精心编排话题，并以循序渐进的方式逐步开展，每课最后还编排了一段对话或叙述以重现该课的重要话题。内容充实，层次分明。
五、 为自学者提供多样化的书面练习及录音资料（见**yalebooks.com/wheatley**）。
六、 教材内容易转换成课堂活动，也便于通过网络或其他途径进行补充。
七、 会话教材与汉字教材可以分开使用，也可以相互配合使用。
八、 会话教材与汉字教材内容相关，但不互相依赖，自成体系。
九、 汉字教材以繁简汉字编写。
十、 识字教学采用归纳法，透过高重现率的篇章，使学习者能够在真实语境中自然学习。

B. Ten general principles for using *Learning Chinese*

1. Prepare before class, perform in class, and consolidate after class.
2. Move from simple to complex, from familiar to novel, and from rote to realistic.
3. Focus on typical interchanges, personalize them when possible, and compound them into longer conversations.
4. Recognize that Mandarin usage varies as much as English. Regard *Learning Chinese* as a guide, but accept additional input from teachers and your own observations.
5. Learn functional phrases rather than individual words; visualize interactions and match appropriate language; and act out scenarios from cues.
6. Distinguish character recognition from reading, and focus reading activities on comprehension.
7. Write characters to improve recognition ability, but utilize word processing programs to compose texts.

8. Consolidate conversational skills while studying the character units; consolidate character skills while studying the conversational units.
9. As much as possible, learn language in context rather than from lists. (But be mindful that lists can help with recall and review.)
10. Know the core, test the core (i.e., that practiced in class). For character material, test comprehension.

使用《汉语基础教材》的十个基本原则

一、 强调课前预习，课中练习以及课后复习。
二、 从简单到复杂，从陌生到熟悉，从机械操练到自然交际。
三、 先熟记典型的会话，再向个性化延伸，最后扩展为完整的会话。
四、 汉语表达同英语一样复杂多变，学生可将本教材作为用法指南使用，不仅应该听取老师的建议，自己也应勤于观察。
五、 与其只学习个别生词，不如学习如何使用词组，借助提示，摹拟实际交流情境，演练与之相匹配的表达方式。
六、 分清识字和阅读的不同，阅读活动最好以理解为主。
七、 通过书写汉字来提高辨认字形的能力，同时借助拼音输入软件来写作。
八、 学习汉字时，同时加强会话能力；学习会话时，同时加强汉字能力，互相促进。
九、 与其利用生字表、生词表学习，不如利用有上下文的课文学习。(生字表、生词表可用来回忆与复习。)
十、 掌握核心教材，测试核心教材。所谓核心教材指的是课堂教学中所使用的教材，至于汉字教材则主要用来测试理解能力。

汉语基础教材

GENESIS AND ACKNOWLEDGMENTS

Drafts for the first few lessons of *Learning Chinese: A Foundation Course in Mandarin* started to appear as many as seven years ago. Since that time, the whole course has been completely revamped at least twice, and then further revised and re-ordered an additional two or three times. The resulting work has been used in draft form for several years in the beginning and intermediate courses of MIT's regular Chinese language program; over the past few years, a version has also been made available to the public through MIT's OpenCourseWare.

It is not an exaggeration to say that everyone associated with MIT's Chinese language program over the years that *Learning Chinese* was being developed contributed in some way to the final product. Students and teachers gamely put up with earlier versions, some of which appeared only 'just-in-time'. In that regard, it helped to be writing in the new millennium, when pinyin and characters can be produced electronically, with proper formatting and illustrations, and then easily revised and delivered to students via course websites. It also helped to be at an institution with enthusiasm for novelty and experimentation.

Tong Chen (陈彤), who started at MIT when I first began there, provided the raw text that evolved into many of the conversations and narratives in the later units of the book, and both he and Jin Zhang (张锦), who joined our small group a few years later, also provided apt examples, noted mistakes, and made suggestions on the basis of their broad language teaching experience. Min-min Liang (梁敏敏), who taught in the program briefly and then returned as the book neared completion, edited some of the later units and scrupulously reported errors, typos, and other problems as she used the text in her intermediate Chinese classes, and Amy Liang (梁爱萍), who observed classes at both beginning and intermediate levels when the new materials were first being used and regularly joined me for late afternoon tea at a local café so that I could elicit examples from her and check correct usage.

Enrollments in Chinese classes increased regularly over the years that I was at MIT, so I am unlikely to be able to recall the names of all those students who deserve to be noted for contributions over and above the normal enthusiasm and resilience that almost all of our students brought to the task of learning Chinese. At the risk of omitting a few names, let me cite Kevin A. McComber, who carefully checked through a number of units and provided useful feedback, and Justin M. Paluska and Erwan M. Mazarico, who over the course of several semesters regularly sent me lists of typos and other infelicities that they noted in their perusal of the materials.

Thanks also go to: Li Yongyan (李咏燕), a linguist whom I first met in Nanjing, for gathering examples of nursery rhymes, jingles, and light verse from her friends for use in the 'Rhymes and rhythms' sections; and to Jordan Gilliland, who, as an undergraduate and graduate student at MIT, developed a program for inputting tone marks efficiently, and the multifaceted flashCube program that, among its many uses, allowed students to test themselves on the material in *Learning Chinese.*

I also wish to thank my colleagues at the National Institute of Education (NIE), at Nanyang Technological University in Singapore, particularly Goh Yeng-Seng (吴英成), head of the Asian Languages and Cultures Division, who invited me to join the Institute for a year, thus placing me in an ideal setting to check and revise *Learning Chinese* one more time. Thanks also go to my colleagues at NIE, particularly Yang Yanning (杨延宁) and Yang Ronghua (杨荣华), who read over much of the conversational material and suggested improvements, and Cheung Lin Hong (张连航), Xu Feng (徐峰), and Luo Qingming (罗庆铭), who patiently answered the many questions I posed to them.

Finally, I wish to acknowledge the people who made this enterprise possible in the first place, and in the last place. In the first place, they are the teachers who covered much of the same ground as *Learning Chinese* when I was an undergraduate student at Columbia University: Chih Ping C. Sobelman (蘇張之丙) and Roger Yeu (樂亦平). In the last place, they are the seven reviewers for Yale University Press, who took time out of busy schedules to evaluate a nearly eight-hundred-page manuscript, and the team at the Press itself, who nursed the project through to fruition. The reviewers are Dana Bourgerie (Brigham Young University); Stephanie Divo (Cornell University); Yeng-Seng Goh (National Institute of Education, Singapore); Carolyn Lee (Duke University); Victor Mair (University of Pennsylvania); Scott McGinnis (Defense Language Institute); and Madeline Spring (Arizona State University). The team at the Press are Mary Jane Peluso; Elise Panza; Ann-Marie Imbornoni; and in particular Jamie Greene, who asked all the difficult questions in the course of carrying out the unenviable job of formatting and editing the manuscript.

Even though I did not always take their advice, and frequently injected my own idiosyncratic views into the final product, the willingness of colleagues, students, and friends to discuss issues, offer advice and criticism, and assist with production has, obviously, made *Learning Chinese* a much better book than it would otherwise have been. After teaching Chinese for so long and, in the time-honored fashion of language teachers, preparing supplementary materials for fine textbooks written by others, I decided it was time to write my own so that I could indulge my own preferences. The result is this book. My hope is that there will be pleasure in it for both students and teachers.

> 子曰，知之者，不如好之者，好之者不如乐之者。
> *Zǐ yuē, zhī zhīzhě, bùrú hào zhīzhě, hào zhīzhě bùrú lè zhīzhě.*
>
> The Master [Confucius] said:
> ‘Knowing it is not as good as love for it; love for it is not as good as delight in it.’

汉语基础教材

INTRODUCTION

Goals and methods

The language

This is a course in Standard Chinese, a language that is often colloquially referred to as Mandarin. The origins of this language and its position in the Chinese-speaking world will be discussed below, in the section on linguistic background.

Variation

Given the geographic spread of Mandarin across the Chinese-speaking world, and its function as a lingua franca co-existing with regional and local languages, it is not surprising that it demonstrates a broad range of variation in pronunciation, word choice, grammar, and usage. Some speakers, by virtue of geographic origin or educational background, may claim to be arbiters of 'good' and 'bad' Mandarin, particularly in matters of pronunciation, where the educated speech of Beijing is generally considered to be standard. However, when it comes to the pronunciation of individual words, word choice, particular nuances of meaning, grammatical organization of sentences, or linguistic usage, Chinese displays a range of variation comparable to, or perhaps greater than, that of English, and such variation is only likely to grow as contact with foreigners increases and the Chinese language spreads beyond the borders of China.

Learning Chinese recognizes a standard sound system for Mandarin (as represented in the pinyin system of romanization) but otherwise accepts a broad range of usage, much of it conditioned by social or geographic factors. Where particular usage can be labeled (as, for example, 'Taiwan' or 'southern China'), it is. There may also be unlabeled linguistic material in *Learning Chinese* that is judged aberrant by teachers or other native speakers of the language. Such judgments should be noted, but they too may need to be revised as you continue to observe the language in its full richness, as it is actually spoken or written.

The audience

Though students who already have some ability in Chinese will, in many cases, find this course useful, it does not assume any prior background in the language. *Learning Chinese* is intended for a diverse audience, specialist and non-specialist alike, who need a course that not only guides them toward basic conversational and literary skills but also stimulates their curiosity about the linguistic setting of the language and the geography, history, and culture of the lands where it is spoken. *Learning Chinese* is intended to provide a solid foundation for further study of the language, whether in a specialized program of Chinese studies or in conjunction with work or further study in a Chinese-speaking environment.

A foundation

When you begin studying a language, a lot of time has to be spent familiarizing yourself with the 'code': the sounds, words, and organization of the language. There comes a point, after a year or two of (non-intensive) study, when you have acquired a critical mass of language material and, provided you remain observant and responsive to feedback, can start to learn effectively from direct interaction with native speakers. This is also the point at which the notion of immersion begins to make sense, and when going abroad to study the language in a completely immersive setting offers the maximum benefit. This textbook is designed to get you to that point. With the additional materials recommended within, it covers approximately 200 class hours—a year and a half to two years in a regular course of study.

Self-instruction

With help from a Chinese speaker, particularly in the early stages of language development, *Learning Chinese* can also serve as a manual for self-instruction. It introduces the language systematically; it has extensive explanations about usage, as well as suggestions about how to learn the material within; it provides a pathway for the inductive learning of both conversational and literary skills; and it comes with a selection of audio files and other materials that can be accessed electronically.

Goals summarized

Succinctly, the goals of *Learning Chinese* are: (a) a basic conversational competence, which means mastery of pronunciation and familiarity with a repertoire of useful conversational situations, including some, involving language and cultural issues, that allow you as a learner to explore topics of interest; (b) an understanding of the reading process and the properties of the character writing system so that you can begin to develop a reading competence by way of edited texts written in either the simplified or the traditional character set; (c) the ability to represent speech with the pinyin system of transcription, to write a selection of characters from one of the standard character sets, and to use reference materials, word processing, or other forms of electronic communication to continue to independently build language competence; and (d) a basic familiarity with those aspects of modern Chinese society and culture that specifically relate to language use.

Reaching the goals

You study a foreign language in order to learn how to converse with people of another culture, to read material written in the language of that culture, to be able to write the language down, to prepare spoken presentations, and, if you are very ambitious, to write letters, reports, or other forms of composition in that language. How should you proceed effectively to reach those goals? What should the focus of study be? The following is a brief attempt, in anticipation of a complete course of study, to answer these questions.

A. CONVERSATIONAL SKILLS When learning a foreign language, the conversational skills of listening and speaking are primary; the literary skills of reading and writing are secondary. In effect, conversational skills can be taught independently of reading and writing, but the latter are most effectively taught with reference to spoken language.

For the oral skills of speaking and listening, the objective—learning how to interact in context—is clear. If a colleague pokes his head in my office to ask, *Nǐmen yǒu sǎn ma?* (literally: 'You-all have umbrella question'), I can interpret his request not as an inquiry about possessions—'Do you own an umbrella?'—but as a request to borrow an umbrella—'Can you lend me an umbrella?'—because I know it's raining and he's going to meet his wife. So I respond, without much thought: *Yǒu, yǒu, yào yòng ma?* 'Sure, you want to use it?' Almost before the words are out of my mouth, I realize—for various reasons that involve the likelihood of his making such a request—that it is more likely he's asking if I need to borrow *his* umbrella: 'Do you need an umbrella?' Indeed, this is the case, for he then clarifies: *Bù, bù, wǒ pà nǐmen méiyǒu* 'No, I was afraid you [all] didn't have one.'

This example underscores the importance of situational context. Ultimately, it was context that led me to an interpretation of the speaker's intentions. It was also context that allowed me to figure out that 'You-all have umbrella question' meant 'Do you need an umbrella?' For the learner, the situational context is clearest during personal interactions; in other words, in conversation. *Learning Chinese* focuses on conversation from the start, with you, the learner, as a participant as much as possible. Conversation also involves instant feedback and a degree of overlapping content, so that listening skills support speaking and vice versa.

In *Learning Chinese,* content is organized into units of a dozen or more topics, each of which takes several weeks to complete. You will proceed as if on a guided tour, being introduced to relevant material, practicing short interactions, proceeding in overlapping waves, and culminating in one or more extensive dialogues that knit the various parts of the unit into a cohesive whole. This approach makes it possible to introduce a wealth of interconnected material that can form the basis of engaging conversations and interesting narratives.

For example, Unit 4 presents (among other things) time phrases, names and titles, introductions, and subjects of study. These can be practiced piecemeal during introductory classes; later, they are woven into a dialogue involving a Chinese businessman striking up a conversation with an overseas student (such as yourself) on a bus in Sichuan province. Within each lesson, topics are selected so you can build up a conversational repertoire that can be personalized, practiced, and extended from lesson to lesson.

B. READING AND CHARACTERS During conversation, you are trying to apprehend the intentions of the speaker; so, too, in reading, you are trying to interpret the intentions of the author, who had to imagine an audience and transform the language into written code. In English, the written code is based on letters and various grammatical conventions; in Chinese, it is based on characters and a different set of grammatical conventions.

For the literate, reading Chinese feels like a seamless process of extracting meaning from text: characters evoke words (or parts of words) and words evoke images that blend into meanings. However, when you are learning to read a language like Chinese, the reading process tends to resolve itself into two phases: recognizing the characters (which is actually a process of matching 'single-syllable' characters to what are often polysyllabic words) and then reading for comprehension. Because learning to recognize characters is so difficult, the problems of comprehension (over and above basic recognition of characters) sometimes receive less attention than they deserve.

The character units in *Learning Chinese* are intended to address both issues. To ease the burden of learning to recognize characters, the texts are composed of words and grammatical patterns that are familiar from the core units; the texts are also composed so that new characters appear with enough frequency, and in a sufficient range of contexts, to make it possible to retain and recall them through the process of reading alone. In addition, to ensure that reading proceeds smoothly from character recognition to comprehension, most of the readings are embedded in question-and-answer or comment-and-response formats that provide clear contexts for understanding.

The goal of the reading instruction in *Learning Chinese* is to foster an understanding of the reading process and develop basic reading skills in students with little or no prior experience in Chinese so that they may make the transition to graded reading materials already in print, beginning with such well-tested classics as *The Lady in the Painting* and *Strange Tales in a Chinese Studio* (both published by Yale University Press).

C. COMPOSITION Of the four essential language skills—listening, speaking, reading, and writing–the last (better called 'composition') is the most elusive, and after years of schooling, even native speakers often find written expression difficult. The problem stems from the lack of the sort of feedback that guides face-to-face interaction; not just linguistic features like stress and intonation, but facial expressions, gestural movements, and the physical context of the interaction, all of which help to monitor the communicative event. However, because writing persists, the good writer learns to tailor it to an imagined audience, providing more redundancy in the form of complete sentences, precise usage, and elaboration. This careful tailoring often depends on language intuition that only native speakers possess, and even the most fluent speakers of a learned language usually depend on native speakers to verify the accuracy of written work.

While learning to write well enough to serve even basic needs of written communication is a skill best left to higher levels of language learning, when conversational and reading skills are more advanced, composition can serve a useful purpose even at foundation levels. Because it is a productive skill, like speaking, composition can help with vocabulary growth, usage, grammar, and cohesion. In later units, *Learning Chinese* occasionally makes use of 'guided compositions', in which an outline of the content is given and the task is to incorporate it into a written text. Teachers may wish to add other written assignments, in the form of diary entries, biographical sketches, or personal letters (such as the one that appears in Unit 7).

Romanization versus characters

Even though written Chinese is generally a style of its own, rather different from spoken language, it is obviously possible to write out conversations and other spoken material using characters. Dramatic plays and the dialogue sections of novels and language textbooks are among the genres that record spoken language in this way. However, as you know, while the Chinese script is an efficient and aesthetically pleasing writing system for native speakers of the language, it has disadvantages for learners who need a way of representing pronunciation and keeping track of language material during the learning process. *Learning Chinese* separates the study of the language in general from the study of characters in particular. Conversational material is presented in the standard, phonetically based notation of the Chinese-speaking world, called Hanyu Pinyin, 'spelling the sounds of Chinese'. Utilizing Hanyu Pinyin for the core units ensures that the learning of spoken material is not conditioned by factors related to character acquisition; in effect, it means that dialogues and other spoken material can be more natural and extensive than would be possible if all the characters that represent them had to be learned at the same time.

Because *Learning Chinese* separates character reading (and writing) from other aspects of language learning, students who wish to study or review the spoken language without reference to characters can ignore, or postpone, the character units, while those with sufficient vocabulary and grammatical knowledge can alternatively study the character material alone.

Writing of characters

While learning to write, or reproduce characters, does help with recognition (and so, ultimately, with reading), it is not the case that you need to be able to write all characters from memory in order to be able to read them. A hint or two—the 'heart' sign in one character, a 'phonetic' element in another—will often be enough for the expectations arising from context to be confirmed. In recognition of this, the character material in *Learning Chinese* is organized primarily to develop reading skills. Information on how to write the graphs is included to draw attention to the general structure of characters, as well as to facilitate their reproduction. It is certainly useful to learn to write from memory a few hundred of the more common characters in order to absorb the general principles of character construction. It is also useful to be able to write personal information in characters so that you can sign in and sign out, fill out forms, and jot down your contact information. Otherwise, like most Chinese themselves nowadays, the bulk of your writing will make use of Chinese language word processing, which involves selecting from a set of character options—in other words, character recognition, not production. Thus, *Learning Chinese* takes the position that learning to write characters from memory is not a primary goal at foundation levels.

The simplified and traditional character sets

Without the requirement that characters be written from memory, the existence of two sets of Chinese characters (the simplified set used on the Mainland and in Singapore, and the traditional set associated with Taiwan and many overseas communities) becomes much less problematical. Both sets can be introduced simultaneously. Students note the relationship between the two forms, learn to read both in context (though *Learning Chinese* places more emphasis on the simplified set), and select one to write. We recommend following the Mainland majority and learning to write the simplified set, which is generally based on well-established written variants. Individuals are free to choose, but should be aware that while formal examinations tend to offer versions of both, Mainland study programs expect their students to be able to read simplified characters.

From textbook to classroom

The selection and ordering of topics in *Learning Chinese* is based on my own experience learning and teaching Chinese over several decades. It is guided by what the beginning student is likely to encounter in and out of the classroom setting, as well as by the need to provide a broad foundation of grammatical, lexical, and cultural information for future work in Chinese. It mixes practical topics, such as providing biographical information, buying train tickets, or giving toasts, with topics of general interest, such as geography, regional languages ('dialects'), and brand names. Such topics are easily enriched with online materials such as satellite maps, photographs, video clips, and advertisements. They are also easy to transform into effective classroom activities.

The language learner as explorer

It is my belief that, given the enormity of the task of learning a new language (which I sometimes liken to repairing a car while driving it, or renovating your house while still living in it), it is helpful to be as interested in the new language as it is to be fascinated by the new culture—of which language is a part. Unfortunately, writing about language tends to be dry and unnecessarily technical. Until now, there has been no 'Indiana Jones' for linguists. In *Learning Chinese*, we have not only made the language the focus of some conversations and narratives, but we have also frequently gone out of the way to comment on the history, structure, and delightful quirks that are scattered across the linguistic terrain. In my own experience, one of the main topics of conversation with Chinese friends all over the world has been the language itself, whether it be regional accents, local usage, or the Chinese equivalent of 'splat'. (Which is, incidentally, *biā*, a sound for which, officially at least, there is no character.) The other two common subjects of conversation are weather and, as you might expect, food; therefore, these two topics are also given some prominence in *Learning Chinese.*

Learning Chinese is exuberant rather than restrained. Its Chinese content is current and lively, with subjects that range from ordering food to bargaining, from religion to the Chinese school system. It is also larded with quotations, rhymes, popular culture, linguistic information, and historical and geographical notes. It is intended to be an intellectually stimulating resource for both students and teachers alike.

Basic geography

Names for China

The immediate source of the name 'China' is thought to be a Persian word[1], which appeared in European languages during the 16th or 17th century as a name for porcelain, that was then applied to the country from which the finest examples of that material came. If this is correct, then 'China' derives from 'china', not the other way around.

Another name, Cathay, now rather poetic in English but surviving as the regular name for the country in languages such as Russian ('Kitai'), as well as in the name of the Hong Kong–based airline Cathay Pacific, is said to derive from the name of the Khitan (or Qitan) Tartars, who formed the Liao dynasty in the north of China during the 10th century. The Liao dynasty was the first to make a capital in the region of modern Beijing.

The Chinese now call their country *Zhōngguó*, often translated as 'Middle Kingdom'. Originally, this name meant the central, or royal, state of the many that occupied the region prior to the Qin unification in 221 BCE. Other names were used before *Zhōngguó* became current. One of the earliest was *Huá* (or *Huáxià*, combining *Huá* with the name of the earliest dynasty, the *Xià*). *Huá*, combined with the *Zhōng* of *Zhōngguó*, appears in the modern official name of the country—as the following entries show.

The People's Republic of China (PRC)—*Zhōnghuá Rénmín Gònghéguó*
The PRC is the political entity proclaimed by Mao Zedong when he gave the inaugural speech ('China has risen again') at the Gate of Heavenly Peace (*Tiān'ānmén*) in Beijing on October 1, 1949. The PRC also claims sovereignty over Taiwan and all other regions currently controlled by the government in Taipei.

The Republic of China (ROC)—*Zhōnghuá Mínguó*
The ROC was the name of the political entity established in 1912, after the fall of the Manchu Qing dynasty, which took place the previous year. The man most responsible for the founding of the Republic was Sun Yat-sen (*Sūn Yìxiān* in Mandarin), and for this, he has earned the epithet 'Father of the Country'. Although he was named provisional president in 1911, fears for the unity of the country led to the appointment of Yuan Shih-k'ai (*Yuán Shìkǎi*), an important military and diplomatic official under the Qing, as the first president of the Republic in 1912. In 1949, the president of the Republic, Chiang Kai-shek (*Jiǎng Jièshí*), fled with the government to Taiwan and maintained the name Republic of China as part of his claim to be the only legitimate government of the whole of China. De facto control, however, has been limited to the

island of Taiwan, clusters of islands in the Taiwan Straits, the 'offshore islands' of Quemoy (*Jīnmén*) and Matsu (*Mǎzǔ*) close to the mainland, and some minor islands in the South China Sea and to the east of Taiwan. In recent years, even in formal contexts (such as on recent postage stamps), 'Taiwan' sometimes takes the place of 'Republic of China' as a name for the political entity.

Taiwan–*Táiwān*

Taiwan is some 210 kilometers off the coast of eastern China's Fujian province; its central mountains are just visible from the Fujian coast on a clear day. The Dutch colonized the island in the early 17th century, fighting off the Spanish, who had also established bases on the northern part of the island. The Dutch called the island Formosa, from the name *Ilha Formosa* 'beautiful island', given to it earlier by the Portuguese (who did not actually colonize it).

Taiwan's earliest inhabitants spoke Austronesian languages unrelated to Chinese, and indigenous groups such as the Ami, Paiwan, and Bunan (who still speak non-Chinese languages) are descendents of those early Taiwan Austronesians. By the 13th century, Chinese speaking Hakka and Fukienese—regional Chinese languages—had established small communities on the island. These were joined by refugees from the Ming after the fall of that dynasty on the mainland. The Qing dynasty annexed Taiwan in 1683, making it a province. In 1895, Taiwan, along with nearby islands such as the Pescadores group (*Pénghú Lièdǎo*), was ceded to Japan as part of the settlement of the Sino-Japanese war. It remained a Japanese colony until 1945, when it was returned to the Republic of China.

Under the Nationalist government, Mandarin (*Guóyǔ*) was made the official language of the country, while Taiwanese (*Táiyǔ*), a form of Southern Min spoken by the majority of its population, was suppressed. In recent years, however, Taiwanese has undergone a resurgence in public life.

Hong Kong—*Xiāng Gǎng*

Hong Kong lies within the Cantonese-speaking region of southern China. The English name derives from the Cantonese pronunciation of the place, 'Heung Gong', which means 'fragrant harbor' (*Xiāng Gǎng* in Mandarin). Hong Kong was formally ceded to the British in the Treaty of Nanking (*Nánjīng*), which was signed at the end of the Opium War in 1842 on a ship anchored in the Yangtze River, slightly to the east of Nanjing. The Kowloon Peninsula (*Jiǔlóng* 'nine dragons') was added in 1860 after the Second Opium War, and the New Territories (*Xīnjiè*), which includes islands and mainland territory, were leased to the British in 1898 for 99 years, making Hong Kong total slightly more than 1,000 square kilometers.

In 1984, well before the expiration of the New Territories lease, Prime Minister Margaret Thatcher and Chairman Deng Xiaoping formulated the Sino-British Joint Declaration, an agreement for the return of Hong Kong to Chinese sovereignty. In 1990, the principle of 'One Country, Two Systems' [*Yī Guó, Liǎng Zhì*] was formulated: Hong Kong would retain its laws and a high degree of political autonomy for 50 years. At midnight on July 1, 1997, Hong Kong became a Special Administrative Region [*Tèbié Xíngzhèngqū*] of China, which guaranteed it autonomy within the PRC in all but foreign affairs and defense.

Historically, Hong Kong has been settled by a number of distinct Chinese groups. These include the Bendi ('locals'), who emigrated during the Song dynasty (10th–13th century) after being driven from their homes in north China; the Tanka, fisherfolk who lived on boats and are thought by some to be the descendents of the non-Han Yue people; the Hokla, early immigrants from Fujian; the Hakka, who ended up mostly in less fertile parts of the New Territories; and numerous clans and people from nearby Cantonese-speaking regions, as well as other parts of China. Despite its small size, Hong Kong has more successfully preserved the traces of many traditional Chinese social forms and practices than have many other parts of the Chinese-speaking world.

Macau—*Àomén*

Sixty kilometers to the west of Hong Kong, across the Pearl River estuary, is *Àomén*, known in English as Macau. The Chinese and English names have different sources. *Àomén*, means, literally, 'gate to the inlet'; but the Portuguese name, 'Macao' (English Macau), is said to derive from the name of a revered local temple, called 'Maagok' in Cantonese (*Māgé*), dedicated to Matsu, a goddess worshipped by fishermen and sailors[2].

The peninsula of Macau was settled by the Portuguese in 1557, and was administered by them for over 400 years, though the question of who held sovereignty was not resolved[3] until 1999, when it reverted completely to Chinese territory. The two small islands of Coloane and Taipa were added to the territory in the middle of the 19th century, and later connected to the Macau peninsula by bridges. Recently, the islands have been joined by landfill, and the central portion has become the site of the Cotai Strip, envisioned as an Asian version of the Las Vegas strip—only larger. Macau is the only place in China where gambling is legal.

Chinese lands; Chinese overseas

Informally, the two Chinese political entities are often referred to as Mainland China (*Zhōngguó Dàlù*)—or simply 'the Mainland'—and Taiwan, rather than the PRC and the ROC. The occasional need to talk about a single Chinese entity, consisting of the Chinese mainland plus Hong Kong and Taiwan, has recently given rise to a term, *Liǎng'àn Sāndì* ('two-shores three-lands').

Chinese who live outside the *Liǎng'àn Sāndì* can be classified as *Huáqiáo*, generally translated as 'Overseas Chinese'. In its broadest sense, *Huáqiáo* can apply simply to ethnic Chinese living outside the *Liǎng'àn Sāndì*, regardless of how assimilated they are to local cultures. More typically, however, it has a narrower application, referring to Chinese who retain features of Chinese culture in their adopted homelands and who keep ties with the motherland. There is another term, *Huáyì* ('Chinese-hem [of a robe]; frontier') that is applied to ethnic Chinese born overseas, e.g., *Měiguó Huáyì* 'Chinese Americans', etc.

Nationalists and Communists

After the establishment of the PRC in 1949, it was customary to distinguish the two political entities by their only extant political parties, the Communist Party (*Gòngchǎndǎng*), abbreviated CCP, and the Nationalist Party (*Guómíndǎng*, or Kuomintang), the KMT. Hence, 'the Communist government', 'the Nationalist leaders', etc. Recent changes in Taiwan and on the Mainland make neither term appropriate. In 2000, the Nationalists lost to Chen Shui-bian and the Democratic Progressive Party, though they returned to power in 2008 with the election of the KMT candidate, Ma Ying-jeou (*Mǎ Yīngjiǔ* in Mandarin). Meanwhile, on the Mainland, the Communist Party, though retaining its institutional position in the government, has become less of a dominating force in political life.

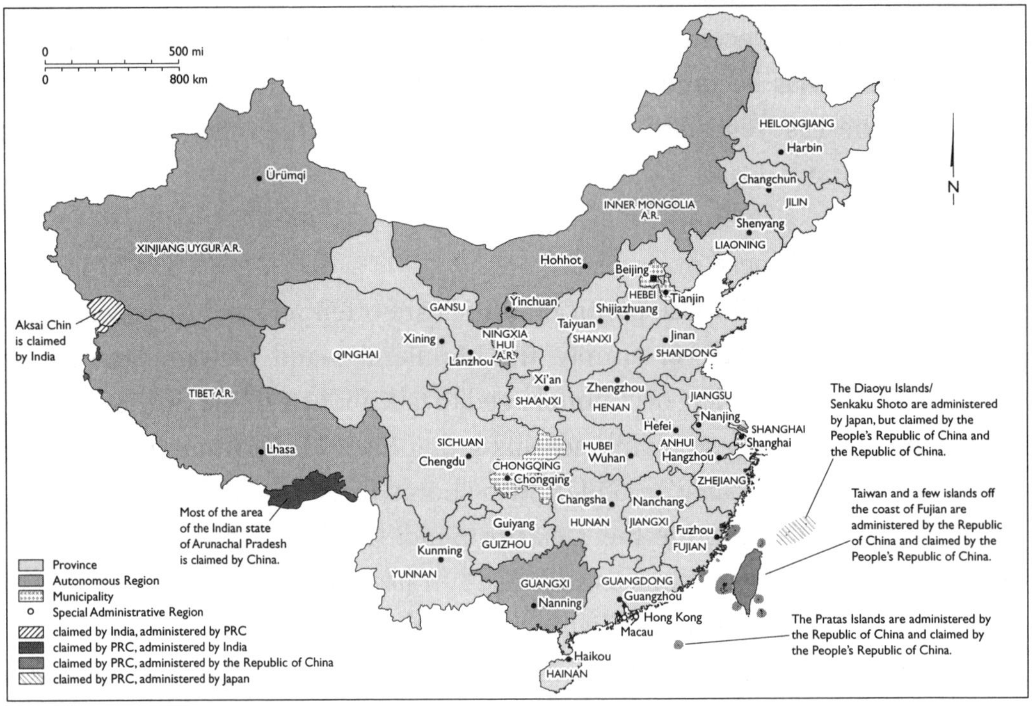

Liǎng'àn Sāndì

Peking, Beijing, and Peiping

One of the curious consequences of the political differences between the PRC and the ROC is that they have different names for the city formerly known to the English-speaking world as Peking. For the PRC, the capital is *Běijīng* 'northern capital', the city that has been the capital for all but brief periods since 1422, when Emperor Yong Le of the Ming dynasty moved the government north from *Nánjīng* 'southern capital'. However, in 1927, the Nationalists under Chiang Kai-shek, having little real power in the north and under threat from the Japanese, made Nanjing their capital and restored the name Běipíng (Peiping) ('northern-peace') that the northern city possessed before becoming capital in the 15th century. Officially, the Nationalists retained the name *Běipíng* even after the Japanese conquered the city of Nanjing, and continued to do so after Beijing reverted to the capital in 1949 under the PRC.

The spelling 'Peking' is probably a reflection of the Cantonese pronunciation of the name Beijing, in which the initial of the second syllable is pronounced with a hard 'k' sound. Representations of Cantonese pronunciation were often adopted by the British as official postal spellings (cf. Nanking for *Nánjīng* and Chungking for *Chóngqìng*). Though most foreigners now spell the name of the city, in Mandarin pinyin transcription, as Beijing, the old spelling and pronunciation survive to this day in certain proper names, such as Peking University (still the official English name of the institution) and Peking duck. The transcription, Beijing, is not without its problems either, since speakers who do not know the pinyin system tend to make the 'j' sound more foreign or exotic by giving it a French quality: [bay-zhing]. As you will soon learn, the actual standard pronunciation is closer to [bay-džing].

Linguistic background

Chinese

One of the consequences of the long duration of Chinese history is that the term 'Chinese' has come to have a wide range of applications. It can refer to the earliest records, written on oracle bones, and dated to the second millennium BCE. It can refer to the languages in the Sinitic branch—the 'Sino' of the Sino-Tibetan family—which includes not only the standard language but regional languages ('dialects') such as Cantonese and Hokkien. (In this sense, Chinese is to the modern Chinese languages as Romance is to the modern Latin languages French, Spanish, Italian, and so on.) Finally, in its most narrow sense, it can refer to the modern standard language, often called Mandarin by English speakers.

Mandarin and Chinese

When the Portuguese began to have extensive contact with China in the late 16th and early 17th centuries, they adapted the word 'mandarin' (itself adapted to Portuguese from Indian and other sources) to refer to Chinese officials; hence modern meanings such as 'powerful official; member of a powerful group'. They also used it for the language spoken by such officials, called *Guānhuà* in Chinese, 'the speech of officials'. *Guānhuà* was the name given to specialized speaking practices, based on northern Chinese, which served as a lingua franca among officials and members of other educated classes who might come from different parts of China and speak mutually unintelligible Chinese in their home regions.

Guānhuà can be regarded as the precursor of the modern standard language. In English, the name 'Mandarin' has survived the transformation from specialized language to the modern standard, but the name *Guānhuà* has not. The Chinese term only survives in the specialized terminology of linguists, who use the term *Běifāng Guānhuà Tǐxì* 'northern Guanhua system [of dialects]' to refer to the northern dialect grouping that includes Mandarin and other distinct dialects now spoken over a vast stretch of territory in the north, west, and southwest of China. Western linguists often refer to this grouping as the Mandarin dialects, using 'Mandarin' in a generic sense. The Mandarin dialects stand in contrast to other dialect groupings, such as the Cantonese or Fujianese.

Strange as it may seem, the Chinese-speaking world has no single term for modern standard Chinese, or Mandarin. In the PRC, it is officially called *Pǔtōnghuà* ('the common language'), a term with a legacy dating back to the early part of the 20th century; in Taiwan, it is called *Guóyǔ* ('the national language'), a term dating to at least 1918; while in Singapore, it is called *Huáyǔ* ('the language of the *Huá*')—*Huá* being an ancient name for the Chinese people. In ordinary speech, other terms are often used: *Hànyǔ* ('language of the Han'), for example, or *Zhōngwén* ('Chinese-language').

Mainlanders tend to find it strange that English speakers refer to the standard language as Mandarin. Norman (1988: 136) recommends using the term Standard Chinese or, when possible, just Chinese, and keeping Mandarin for the dialect grouping. In certain contexts, Chinese will suffice, but at times it will be ambiguous, for it does not rule out Cantonese, Shanghainese, and other so-called 'dialects'. The longer term, Standard Chinese, is awkward, and assumes that there is only one standard, which makes it difficult to talk about differences in, say, Taiwan and Mainland Mandarin. So, in *Learning Chinese,* if the simple term 'Chinese' is not sufficient, we fall back on the venerable term 'Mandarin', taking heart from the usage of such eminent Chinese as Yuen Ren Chao, who wrote a much-loved textbook called *Mandarin Primer* (1948), and more recently, Singapore's Lee Kwan Yew, who wrote a volume describing his own study called *Keeping My Mandarin Alive* (2005).

The origins of spoken Mandarin

Historically, a majority of the Chinese population spoke regional or local languages and was illiterate. For them, there was no general medium of communication across regional lines. For the educated, *Guānhuà* served in a limited way as a spoken medium, while Classical Chinese, the language of administration, education, and high culture (see below), served as a written medium. By the 19th century, it was clear that the lack of a spoken norm that could serve the communicative needs of all classes across the country was a major obstacle to the modernization of China, and eventually efforts were made to identify a suitable medium and promote it as the standard. *Guānhuà* was an obvious candidate. However, by the 19th century, it had become strongly associated with the educated speech of Beijing, putting southerners at a disadvantage. Classical Chinese, though it had no regional bias, was a highly stylized written language with ancient roots that made it an unsuitable basis for a national spoken medium.

After various interesting, but completely impractical, attempts to establish a hybrid language to balance regional differences (particularly between north and south) the Chinese language planners settled on a northern strategy: promoting the pronunciation of the *educated speech* of the capital, Beijing, but incorporating material from a broad range of other sources as the basis of usage. Thus, words with wide distribution were adopted over northern or Beijing localisms, for example. The spoken standard also absorbed material from written sources that introduced words and phrasing from the important economic and cultural region of the Lower Yangtze Valley (*Shànghǎi* to *Nánjīng*) as well as words for modern concepts first coined in Japanese.

Norms and variation

Though both Taiwan and the PRC have always agreed on the educated Beijing standard for pronunciation, geographical distance, political separation, and cultural divergence have resulted in the emergence of two norms for spoken usage, as a comparison of dictionaries from Taiwan and the PRC will demonstrate. These differences, though still moderate in scope, extend from the pronunciation of particular words to grammar and usage.

Even within the emerging norms of Standard Chinese (Mainland and Taiwan versions), enormous variety exists at the local level. The case of Taiwan is illustrative. There, *Guóyǔ* (Mandarin) is not the first language of much of the population. The most common first language is *Táiyǔ* (Taiwanese), a Southern Min language that is very similar to the Southern Min spoken in the province of Fujian across the Taiwan Straits. (Until the success of the 'Speak Mandarin' movement, Southern Min was also the language of most Singapore Chinese; elsewhere in Southeast Asia, it remains an important language in Chinese communities.)

With so many in Taiwan speaking *Táiyǔ* as a first language, it is not surprising that the Mandarin spoken there is often influenced by the pronunciation, grammar, and usage of Taiwanese. The result is a unique Taiwanese Mandarin. The same phenomenon occurs elsewhere, of course, so that no matter where you are in China, Mandarin heard on the street will generally have local features. Native speakers quickly get used to these differences, just as English speakers get used to regional accents of English. Learners will typically find the variation disruptive, and they will need time and experience to adjust to it.

Though there are probably more and more Chinese who speak some variety of Mandarin as their first language, and whose speech is close to the appointed norms, it is still true that the majority of Chinese speak more than one variety of Chinese, and for many of them the standard speech represented in this textbook would be a second language. A few years ago, *USA Today* published statistics on the 'world's most common languages, ranked by population that uses each as a first language'. Mandarin was listed first, with 885 million speakers (followed by Spanish with 332 million and English with 322 million). The figure for Mandarin does not include those who speak Cantonese or one of the other regional languages, but it must include a large number of speakers whose Chinese would be difficult to understand by someone familiar only with the Beijing standard.

When describing the best Chinese language, Chinese speakers tend to focus on pronunciation, praising it as *biāozhǔn* 'standard'. For this reason, native Chinese speakers, who tend to be effusive in their praise in any case, will sometimes flatter a foreigner by saying he or she speaks the language better than they do. By 'better', they mean with a better approximation to the standard, educated accent. Apart from language classrooms, the most *biāozhǔn* Mandarin is heard on the broadcast media, in schools, and in the speech of young, educated urban Chinese.

Regional languages and minority languages

There are seven major dialect groupings of Chinese, including the geographically extensive Mandarin group (divided into southwestern, northwestern, and northern regions) mentioned earlier. Of the others, Cantonese (*Yuè*), Shanghainese (*Wú*), Fukienese or Hokkien (*Mǐn*), and Hakka (*Kèjiā*) are the best known. (*Yuè*, *Wú*, and *Mǐn* are Chinese linguistic designations, while Hokkien and Hakka are the regional pronunciations of the names *Fújiàn* and *Kèjiā*, respectively.) All represent groupings of diverse dialects thought to share a common origin. Even within each group, the varieties are not necessarily mutually intelligible. Cantonese, for example, includes dialects such as Hoisan (*Táishān*) which are quite distinct from the standard dialect.

In many respects, the dialect groupings of Chinese—represented by Cantonese, Shanghainese, Hakka, etc.—are different languages. They are not, after all, mutually intelligible, and they have their own standard speeches (Guangzhou for Cantonese, Suzhou for Shanghainese, etc.). In linguistic terms, they are often said to be comparable to Dutch and German or Spanish and Portuguese. However, unlike those European languages, the Chinese 'dialects' share a written language and identify with a common culture. Recently, the term 'topolect', a direct translation with Greek roots of the Chinese term *fāngyán* ('place-language'), has gained currency as a more formal term for what are generally called 'regional languages' in this book. So we may speak of Cantonese as the standard language within the Cantonese (or *Yuè*) grouping, and varieties such as Hoisan (*Táishān*) as dialects within Cantonese.

Regional languages should be distinguished from the languages of the non-Chinese (non-Han) ethnic groups—such as the Mongolians, Tibetans, or Uighurs—that make up about 8–9 percent of the total population of China. There are 56 officially recognized ethnic minorities in China, almost all of them with their own languages or language groups.

A *Bái* couple in their finery, *Dàlǐ*, *Yúnnán* (photograph by Jordan Gilliland)

Standard Written Chinese

Standard Written Chinese (or written Mandarin) is the language of composition, learned in school and used by all educated Chinese regardless of the particular variety or regional language that they speak. A Cantonese, for example, speaking Taishan Cantonese at home and in the neighborhood, speaking something closer to standard Cantonese when he or she goes to Guangzhou, and speaking Cantonese-flavored Mandarin in certain formal or official situations, is taught to write a language that is different in terms of vocabulary, grammar, and usage from both Taishan and standard Cantonese. Even though he or she would read it aloud with Cantonese pronunciation, it would in fact be more easily relatable to Mandarin in lexicon, grammar, and in all respects *other than pronunciation*.

From Classical Chinese to modern written Chinese

Written language always differs from spoken, for it serves quite different functions. In the case of Chinese, the difference was, until the early part of the 20th century, extreme. Until then, most written communication, and almost all printed matter, was written in a language called *Wényán* 'literary language', and generally known in English as Classical Chinese. As noted earlier, it was this language that served as a medium of written communication for the literate classes, much as Latin served as a medium for communication among educated classes in medieval Europe.

Classical Chinese was unlikely ever to have been a close representation of a spoken language. It is thought to have had its roots in the language spoken some 2,500 years ago in northern China. That language, though still Chinese in the sense that it is ancestral to modern Chinese languages, would have differed quite significantly in sound, grammar, and vocabulary from any form of modern Chinese. Though Classical Chinese can be regarded as a different language from the modern, it was written in characters that have retained their basic shape to the present day, and these serve to preserve the connection between ancient and modern words whose pronunciation and grammatical context is radically different. While spelling differences (that reflect changes in pronunciation), as well a high degree of word replacement, make Old English texts almost completely opaque to modern readers, ancient Chinese texts continue to look familiar to Chinese readers despite the changes that have taken place in the intervening years. Educated Chinese can read them aloud in modern standard pronunciation, say, or in Cantonese or Hokkien. Without knowledge of the grammar and vocabulary of Classical Chinese, they may not fully understand them, but enough words—and, indeed, sayings and phrases—

have survived to modern times to make the writings of Confucius (6th–5th century BCE) or the poems of Li Po (8th century CE) superficially accessible to the modern reader of Chinese.

Classical Chinese is still used for certain kinds of formal or ritual writing, much as Latin is used for diplomas and certain kinds of inscriptions in Western countries. It has also served as a source of words, quotations, allusions, and even style for the modern language, both written and spoken, but relatively few people read the classical language well, and only a few specialists are still able to write it fluently.

Since Classical Chinese was not based on an accessible spoken language, facility in composition required memorizing large samples to act as models. Once learned, the classical language would tend to channel expression in conservative directions. Citation was the main form of argument; balance and euphony were crucial elements of style. These features did not endear it to the modernizers, and they sought to replace it with a language closer to the modern spoken version. They had a precedent, for all through Chinese history there had in fact been genres of writing known as *Báihuà* ('white—plain or vernacular—language') that were rich in colloquial elements. Such genres were not highly regarded or considered worthy of being literary models, but they were well known as the medium of the popular Ming and Qing novels, such as *Dream of the Red Chamber* (also called the *The Story of Stone*), *Journey to the West* (also known as *Monkey King*), or the *Romance of the Three Kingdoms.* Though it retained classical elements, *Báihuà* provided the early model for a more colloquial standard written language.

Because norms within the newly emerging written language varied, and led to problems of consistency and clarity, some advocated a return to Classical Chinese as the written standard. If it could have shed some of its stylistic affectations (such as the high value put on elaborate or archaic diction), Classical Chinese might have developed into a modern written norm much as Classical Arabic has become the written norm of the Arabic-speaking world. Classical Chinese, however, was too closely associated with conservatism and insularity at a time when China was looking to modernize. Nevertheless, a new written norm does not arise overnight, and for at least the first half of the 20th century, a number of different styles across the range of classical to colloquial coexisted and vied for dominance. Following the revolution of 1949, written styles in Taiwan and the PRC diverged. In the PRC, political and other factors favored a more colloquial written style, whereas in Taiwan, the influence of classical styles has remained stronger.

Characters

The earliest extensive examples of written Chinese date from late in the second millennium BCE. These are the so-called oracle bone inscriptions (*jiǎgǔwén*), inscribed or painted on ox bones and the bottom plate (the carapace) of tortoise shells. This early writing made use of characters whose forms differed in appearance but can still be directly related to modern characters. During the Qin dynasty (221–206 BCE), the script was modified and standardized as part of the reform of government administration. The resulting style, known as the 'little seal' (*xiǎo zhuàn*), is still used on official seals (or 'chops'). At first glance, little seal characters look quite unlike the modern versions, but a native reader can often discern the correspondences.

A script known as *lìshū* came into extensive use during the Han dynasty (202 BCE–220 CE). Individual strokes in the *lìshū* style are described as having a 'silkworm's head and swallow's tail'. It is still used occasionally for writing large characters. The modern script, the kind generally used for printed matter, is based on the *kǎishū* 'model script' that has been in use since before the period known as the Southern and Northern Dynasties (5th and 6th centuries). Other varieties of script were developed for handwriting (*xíngshū* 'running script') and calligraphy (*cǎoshū* 'grass script'). Illustrations of the development of Chinese script can be found at websites such as Simon Ager's 'Omniglot': www.omniglot.com/writing/chinese_evolution.htm.

Traditional and simplified characters

In the past, simpler and more complex versions of characters have often coexisted. In many cases, the more complicated were used for formal correspondence, and the simpler were used for personal communications. In the 1950s, however, as part of a program to promote literacy in the PRC, a set of simpler characters, most of them based on attested forms, were promoted as a general standard for all printed matter. Singapore adopted the new forms for most purposes, but Taiwan, Hong Kong, and most overseas communities kept the traditional forms; as a result, both types of (formal) characters are now in use in the Chinese-speaking world. In English, they are usually referred to as 'traditional' and 'simplified'. The two types are illustrated below, using the phrase *Zhōngguórè* 'fascination with Chinese' ('middle-kingdom-hot'), roughly pronounced [joong-kwoh-ruh].

Traditional	Simplified
中國熱	中国热
Zhōngguórè	*Zhōngguórè*

The three characters cited illustrate the differences nicely. Many characters have only one form (like *zhōng*); many show slight differences (like *rè*); others (like *guó*) show significant differences but are easily relatable. Relatively few—no more than a few dozen—are completely different, and most of those are commonly encountered. So the differences between the two sets of characters are not as significant as might be imagined. A native speaker sees the relationship between the two fairly easily and, using context, moves from one to the other without much difficulty. Students generally write only one style, but they should be comfortable reading either.

Homophony

Characters represent syllable-length words (or rather, morphemes—the smallest meaningful units of language). Since, in Chinese, these units are short, the chance of homophony is relatively high, more so than in English. In English, words pronounced the same are often written the same, as is the case for the 'pens' of 'pig pen' and 'ink pen'. It is also common in English for different words of identical pronunciation to be written differently, such as 'to', 'too', and 'two'. Written Chinese is more comparable to the latter case: words with the same pronunciation but different (and unrelated) meanings are written with different characters. A syllable such as *shi* can be written dozens of ways, depending on the meaning, as the Chinese linguist Yuen Ren Chao demonstrated in a tour de force whose title was:

> 施 氏 食 獅 史
> *Shī shì shí shī shǐ*
> ('[Shi] clan eat lion story')
> 'The tale of how *Shī* of the *Shì* clan ate the lion.'

Chao's tale continues for another 100 or so characters, all pronounced *shi* in one of the four tones. It is written in the very concise prose of Classical Chinese, which is normally read out with modern sound values; so while it is just intelligible as written language, it is completely unintelligible as spoken. However, written in modern Chinese, many of the words would be disyllabic (*shī* 'lion', for example, would be *shīzi*), and the result would probably be intelligible. However, Chao's exercise makes the point nicely: characters represent words—units of sound and meaning—and letters represent sounds only.

Transcribing sound in characters

Characters are sometimes used only for their sound values, with the usual meanings ignored. In this way, Chinese characters can be used to transcribe foreign sounds. So, just as English speakers use Roman letters to write Chinese, Chinese speakers sometimes use Chinese characters to write English (or other languages). Here is an example from a very simple Chinese-English teaching manual from the Mainland (with Chinese written in simplified characters, and English written in the Romanized system of transcription that you will soon learn). See if you can figure out what English sentence is represented.

> 艾姆搜普利丝得吐斯衣油厄根。
> *Ài-mǔ sōu pǔ-lì-sī-dé tǔ sī-yī yóu è-gēn.*

Characters are regularly used for their syllabic value, in this way, to transliterate personal names, names of places, and sounds: 莎士比亚 *Shāshìbǐyà* 'Shakespeare'; 密西西比 *Mìxīxībǐ* 'Mississippi'. Because characters can only be used for syllabic units, the match is not usually as good as it would be in an alphabetic system, which can match a symbol to each consonant and vowel sound.

Pictograms, ideograms, logograms

Because some Chinese characters derive from attempts to represent objects pictorially, they are sometimes called 'pictograms'. However, as you will see in the character units, the majority of modern characters do not derive directly from pictorial representations; even in those cases which do, changes in the form of graphs brought about by processes of standardization and writing reform over the centuries have generally obscured any representational origins. That is not to say that Chinese characters do not have certain aesthetic qualities that can be exploited in poetry and art; it is just that these qualities do not necessarily play a significant role in ordinary reading or writing.

Because the form of characters is not determined by sound, graphs can be borrowed for their meaning and given an entirely different pronunciation. So, for example, the character 山 *shān*, which originated as a representation of a mountain, can be borrowed into Japanese to represent 'yama', the Japanese word for 'mountain'. (The same property is found in Arabic numerals: the graph '8' is read 'eight' in English, 'osiem' in Polish, 'tám' in Vietnamese, and so on.) This property of characters, together with the pictorial origins of many of the simple graphs, has given rise to the notion that Chinese characters somehow represent meaning directly without the mediation of words, hence the term 'ideogram'. This misconception is a result of viewing characters as single entities, outside of normal contexts. In running texts (in Chinese, Japanese, or even Classical Chinese), it is quite clear that readers have to identify words and contexts that are linguistic, not just in the realm of thought, in order to perceive meaning. Neither the term 'pictogram' nor 'ideogram' applies to Chinese characters.

Writing systems are better named according to the units that they encode. Thus, the English writing system basically encodes specific sounds (phonemes), though there are some word symbols as well (e.g., &, $, %). Chinese basically encodes words, though characters may sometimes be called upon to represent

Selling New Year scrolls, *Táiběi*

syllables. Using technical names, English writing is primarily phonographic, and Chinese is primarily logographic.

Representing the sounds of Chinese

Alphabetic systems for writing Chinese date back at least to the 16th century. Most have made use of Roman letters, and are therefore called Romanizations (often written with a capital letter). We can illustrate some of the systems, using the compound word for 'Chinese [spoken] language':

Wade-Giles	Chūngkuó huà
Yale	Jūnggwó hwà
National Romanization	Jong-guo huah
Hànyǔ Pīnyīn	Zhōngguó huà
Zhùyīn Fúhào	ㄓㄨㄥ ㄍㄨㄛˊ ㄏㄨㄚˋ

The Wade-Giles system (named for its originator Thomas Wade, a professor of Chinese at Cambridge University at the turn of the 19th century, and Herbert

A. Giles, a consular officer and, later, Wade's successor at Cambridge who incorporated the system into his dictionary) was used for many years in library catalogues and in most English-language publications on China. It is known for distinguishing the plain initial consonants from the aspirated (*g* from *k*, *d* from *t*, etc., in the pinyin system) by use of an apostrophe: *kuo* versus *k'uo*, for example, or *chung* versus *ch'ung*. (This is phonetically quite sensible since both sounds are voiceless in Chinese.)

The Yale system grew out of work performed by the U.S. War Department during World War II and was used in the Yale textbook series, familiar to several generations of students of Chinese. As much as possible, it used the values of English letters to represent Chinese pronunciation, so it is the most transparent of all the Romanization systems (for speakers of English). National Romanization, a system that had official status in China during the 1930s, incorporates tone in the spelling (notice that there are no tone marks above the vowels), which makes it invaluable for learning and retaining tones. *Hànyǔ Pīnyīn* is the official system of the PRC and has been accepted by most of the rest of the world, including, recently, Taiwan.

Finally, *Zhùyīn Fúhào* ('indicating-sounds transcription'), the last of the systems illustrated, is colloquially called *Bopo mofo* after the first four letters of its alphabet. It has a longer history than pinyin, based on a system created in 1919 called *Zhùyīn Zìmǔ* ('indicating-sounds alphabet') that was intended to serve as a full-fledged writing system. It was inspired by the Japanese 'kana' system, whose symbols derive from characters rather than Roman letters. *Bopo mofo* symbols have the advantage of appearing Chinese and not suggesting any particular English (or other language's) sound values. In Taiwan, children, as well as many foreign students, learn to read with materials in which *Bopo mofo* is written vertically to the right of corresponding characters to indicate pronunciation.

Hànyǔ Pīnyīn

Pīnyīn ('spelling the sound') was developed and officially adopted by the PRC in the 1950s, and it is now used in textbooks, dictionaries, reference sources, computer input systems, and on road and shop signs in Mainland China. In recent years, some schools in China have been encouraging children at certain stages in their education to write essays in pinyin to improve composition and style, and it is not unlikely that its functions will continue to expand in the future.

It is sometimes claimed that pinyin (or any other such system of transcribing the sounds of Mandarin) cannot serve as a full-fledged writing system because the degree of homophony in Chinese is such that some reference to characters is necessary for disambiguation. This is certainly true in the case of the *shi* story cited earlier, and it might be true for Classical Chinese in general. However, it is certainly not true for texts written in colloquial styles. *Anything that can be understood in speech can be written and understood in pinyin.* Many people e-mail successfully in pinyin without even indicating the tones! The question is, using pinyin, how far one can stray from colloquial speech and still be understood. Written styles range from the relatively colloquial to the relatively classical, but if the latter can be understood when read aloud, then they can presumably be understood when written in pinyin.

> 百花齐放，百家争鸣
> 百花齊放，百家爭鳴
> *Bǎihuā qífàng, bǎijiā zhēngmíng!*
> 'Let a hundred flowers blossom and a hundred schools of thought contend!'
> ('100-flowers together-blossom, 100-schools [of thought] contend')

Key Terms

- Peoples Republic of China (PRC)
- The Mainland
- The Republic of China (ROC)
- Taiwan
- Hong Kong (*Xiāng Gǎng*)
- *Běijīng* (Peking)
- *Běipíng* (Peiping)

Qīng (Manchu) dynasty (1644–1911)
Míng (Han) dynasty (1368–1644)
Yuán (Mongol) dynasty (1271–1368)

1842
1912
1949

Máo Zédōng
Chiang Kai-shek (*Jiăng Jièshí*)
Sun Yat-sen (*Sūn Yìxiān*)

Chinese
Guānhuà (officials' language)
Mandarin
Guóyŭ (national language)
Pŭtōnghuà (ordinary language)

Standard Chinese
Classical Chinese (*Wényán*)
Báihuà (vernacular written Chinese)
Táiyŭ (Taiwanese Minnan)
Taiwanese Mandarin

Hànyŭ Pīnyīn
Wade-Giles
Zhùyīn Fúhào (*Bopo mofo*)

lingua franca
dialects
regional languages
  Cantonese
  Fujianese (Hokkien)
  Kejia (Hakka)
  Shanghainese

oracle bone inscriptions (*jiǎgǔwén*)
little seal characters (*xiǎozhuàn*)
model script (*kǎishū*)
traditional characters (*fántǐzì*)
simplified characters (*jiǎntǐzì*)

homophony
pictograms
ideograms
logograms

NOTES

1. Endymion Wilkinson, *Chinese History: A Manual,* Harvard-Yenching Monograph Series 32, revised and enlarged edition (Cambridge, MA: Harvard University Press, 2000), p. 753.

2. B. V. Pires, "Origin and Early History of Macau", in R. D. Cremer, ed., *Macau: City of Commerce and Culture* (Hong Kong: UEA Press, 2000), p. 11.

3. Ibid, p. 15.

Further reading and references

Chao, Yuen Ren. *Mandarin Primer.* Cambridge, MA: Harvard University Press, 1948.

Chen, Ping. *Modern Chinese.* Cambridge: Cambridge University Press, 1999.

DeFrancis, John. *The Chinese Language: Fact and Fantasy.* Honolulu: University of Hawai'i Press, 1984.

DeFrancis, John, ed. *ABC Chinese-English Dictionary.* Honolulu: University of Hawai'i Press, 1999.

Erbaugh, Mary S., ed. *Difficult Characters: Interdisciplinary Studies of Chinese and Japanese Writing.* Pathways to Advanced Skills, publication series volume VI. National Resource Center, The Ohio State University, 2002.

Hannas, William C. *Asia's Orthographic Dilemma.* Honolulu: University of Hawai'i Press, 1997.

Newnham, Richard. *About Chinese.* Penguin Books, 1971.

Norman, Jerry. *Chinese.* Cambridge Language Surveys. Cambridge: Cambridge University Press, 1988.

Ramsey, Robert S. *The Languages of China.* Princeton, NJ: Princeton University Press, 1987.

Wilkinson, Endymion. *Chinese History: A Manual.* Harvard-Yenching Monograph Series 52. Harvard University Asia Center, revised and enlarged, 2000.

In the Imperial Palace, *Běijīng*

SOUNDS AND SYMBOLS

The writer was required at school to read his lessons aloud sixty times; that was for reading books in his own language.
—Yuen Ren Chao, talking about himself in *Mandarin Primer* (Harvard University Press, 1961)

This lesson serves as an introduction to the pronunciation of standard Chinese (Mandarin) and to the Hanyu Pinyin transcription system ('pinyin'). Pinyin will represent pronunciation and be your written code for conversational or 'sayable' material in Chinese. This lesson introduces the whole system but pays particular attention to those elements that you will need in order to actually use the language in the next lesson, that is, tones, initials, and certain 'rhymes'. The units that follow this lesson will provide you with actual language (transcribed and, in many cases, recorded for you). You will be able to refer back to this lesson both to confirm information and to flesh out the system. As you proceed through the units, you will be learning to relate sound to symbol so that you can accurately read out and write down the Chinese language samples that you will be practicing.

Contents

To learn to speak a language, you need to master its sounds. This is not easy. It requires changing habits of articulation that were deeply internalized during the first few years of your life and are now quite automatic. It also requires learning to pay attention to sounds that may have no particular importance in your native language but are crucially important in the new one. What is more, while you are establishing these new habits, you have to hold on to the old. Eventually, you will learn to switch between two systems, but while you are learning, there is bound to be interference from the first language (which will likely be English for most users of this book). In the early stages of language learning, recordings will help, but the critical role will be played by your teachers, who have advice, know the pitfalls, and can provide timely feedback.

As you learn Chinese, you need to be able to write down the new language, not simply in an ad hoc fashion, but in a way that allows you to have an unambiguous record of the pronunciation. As you know, Chinese has an aesthetically pleasing but mnemonically challenging character writing system. Even though many characters do offer phonetic hints to those who know where to look, they offer no information about pronunciation at all to the learner. To cite a particularly clear case: 木 is pronounced *mù*, 林 is *lín*, and 森 is *sēn*. The graphs are additive; the sounds are not. Of course, English is not completely reliable either; words like 'lead' can be pronounced [leed] or [led], and the three spellings 'to,' 'too,' 'two' all have the same sound. However, words written in an alphabetical system almost always provide some sort of phonetic hint that helps in the recovery of sound. (Exceptions in English would be signs such as + or & that offer no help to the uninitiated; they are, in fact, functionally like characters.)

The solution for the learner is a system of transcription that represents the sounds of Chinese with relatively few symbols and uses them consistently, so that—unlike English—words can be pronounced reliably. The Introduction (p. xlix) mentioned a number of such systems used for Chinese in the past, many of them with virtues. The official system, used for textbooks, for reference works, on signs, and for computer input, is Hanyu Pinyin, which means, literally, 'Chinese spelling of sounds'. It was developed in the mid-1950s in China, under the guidance of the venerable *Zhōu Yǒuguāng*, who, at the time of this writing, was still alive and working at the age of 103.

Běijīng metro station sign, including characters and pinyin (the latter without tones)

0.1 Syllable components

0.1.1 Sound versus symbol (letter)

From the start, it is important to make a distinction between sound and the representation of sound. In pinyin, for example, *jī* represents a sound like [jee] (with 'level tone'), *qī* represents [chee]. Neither is hard (for English speakers) to imitate, but the way the latter is represented—with a 'q' (and no subsequent 'u')—is counterintuitive and difficult to remember at first. On the other hand, pinyin *r* represents a sound that, for many speakers of standard Chinese, is a blend of the 'r' of 'run' with the 's' (pronounced [ž]) of 'pleasure' (or the 'j' of French *je*)—in other words, an 'r' with friction. This sound may be difficult for non-Chinese speakers to produce well, but associating it with the symbol 'r' is less problematical. So, as you learn pinyin, you may encounter problems of pronunciation on the one hand, and problems of transcription on the other. It is important to keep the distinction clear.

0.1.2 The syllable

When introducing the sounds of standard Chinese, it is useful to begin with the syllable, a unit whose prominence is underscored by the one-character-per-syllable writing system. The *spoken* syllable in Chinese is traditionally analyzed in terms of an initial consonant sound and a rhyme, the latter being everything other than the initial. Chinese schoolchildren, when focusing on pronunciation, often read syllables (which are usually also meaningful units) in an exaggerated initial-rhyme division: tuh + ù = *tù* 'hare', luh + óng = *lóng* 'dragon', etc.

The *written* pinyin syllable (as opposed to the spoken syllable) can also be usefully analyzed in terms of an initial (C_i) and a rhyme. The rhyme, in turn, contains vowels (V), tones (T) written above the vowels, medials (M), and endings (E). Of these, only the vowel is always present (as, for example, in the sentence-final particle that is simply an untoned *a*). All possible pinyin syllables can be represented by the following formula (with V underlined as the only obligatory unit); there are so few options for M (medials) and E (endings) that they can be usefully listed in our formula.

INITIAL		RHYME				
				T		
C_i	+	M	+	$\underline{V}$	+	E
		|				|
		i, u, ü		i, o (but o+o = ou) and n, ng		

Examples (which you need not know how to pronounce yet):

Vowel:	a
Vowel/Tone:	ā, è
Initial + Vowel/Tone:	tā, bǐ, kè, shū
Initial + Medial + Vowel/Tone:	xiè, zuò, duì, xué, jiù, nüé
Initial + Vowel/Tone + Ending:	lèi, hǎo, hěn, máng
Initial + Medial + Vowel/Tone + Ending:	jiāo, jiàn, jiǎng

There are 21 pinyin **initial consonants.** They are usually presented in a chart of representative syllables, arranged in rows and columns (see section 0.3.1). Whether the initials are written with a single consonant letter (*l*, *m*, *z*) or several (*sh*, *zh*), they all represent only one sound unit (or phoneme). Chinese has no initial clusters—consonant blends—of the sort represented by 'cl' or 'sn' in English.

There are six possible (written) **vowels**: *a*, *e*, *i*, *o*, *u*, and *ü* (the last a 'rounded high front' vowel, as in German *über* or the last vowel of French *déjà vu*). Vowels can be preceded by **medials** (*i*, *u*, *ü*) and followed by **endings**, two of which are written with vowel symbols (*i*, *o*) and two with consonants (*n*, *ng*). There is actually a third (written) vowel ending that can occur after the main vowel (in addition to *i* and *o*), and that is *u*. When the main vowel is *o*, the ending *o* is written *u* to avoid the misleading combination 'oo'. Thus, to cite words from Unit 1, one finds *hǎo* and *lǎo* (both with *a*+*o*), but instead of 'dōo' or 'zhōo' (*o*+*o*), you get *dōu* and *zhōu* (both with *u*).

Notice that the inventory of consonant endings in Chinese is small—there are only *n* and *ng*. Regional languages, such as Cantonese, have more (-p, -t, -m, etc.). The English name of the Chinese frying pan, the 'wok', is derived from a Cantonese word with a final [k] sound; its standard Chinese counterpart, *guō*, lacks the final consonant. In historical terms, standard Chinese has lost most final consonants, while Cantonese has preserved them. Surnames often demonstrate this same distinction between the presence and absence of a final consonant in standard Chinese and Cantonese: Lu/Luk, Ye/Yip, for example (see Unit 4, Appendix 2 for more examples).

Tones are a particularly interesting feature of the Chinese sound system and will be discussed in more detail below. For now, we note that stressed syllables may have one of four possible tones, indicated by the use of diacritical marks written over the main vowel (V). Unstressed syllables, however, do not have tonal contrasts; their pitch is, for the most part, conditioned by that of surrounding syllables.

Because medials, vowels, and some endings are all written with vowel letters, pinyin rhymes may have strings of two or three vowel letters, such as: *iu*, *iao*, *uai*. This can be confusing, particularly with 'opposites' such as *iu*/*ui*, *ie*/*ei*, and *uo*/*ou*, which represent quite different sounds. Later, there will be exercises that focus on such vowel combinations.

By convention, the tone mark is placed on the vowel proper, not on the medial or ending, as in: *lèi, jiāo, zuò*. As a rule of thumb, look to see if the first of two vowel letters is a possible medial. If it is, then the following vowel letter is the core vowel, which receives the tone mark; if it is not, then this first letter is the core vowel: *liè, zhǎo, xué, dōu, jiào*.

Exercise 1

Without trying to pronounce the syllables, place the tone marks provided over the correct letter of the pinyin representations.

xie (ˋ) jiang (ˇ) dui (ˋ) hao (ˇ) lian (ˇ) gui (ˋ) zhou (ˉ) qiao (ˊ)

One sound that is not shown in the syllable formula given above is the final 'r' sound. It is represented, not surprisingly, by *r* in pinyin, and is obligatory in a few words with the written *e*-vowel, such as *èr* 'two'. In northern varieties of standard Chinese, a common word-building suffix, appearing mostly in nouns and favored by some speakers and regions more than others, is also represented by a final *r*: *diǎnr, huàr, bànr, huángr*. The final *r* often blends with the rest of the syllable according to rather complicated rules that will be discussed in detail in later lessons.

0.2 Tones

Words in Chinese are pronounced with a regular tonal contour, much like the stress patterns that distinguish the English verb 'reCORD' from the noun 'REcord'. In Chinese, the word *lǎoshī* 'teacher', for example, is pronounced $_{\text{lao}}$shi ('low' followed by 'high'). In English terms, this is like having to say TEAcher rather than teaCHER or TEACHER (with both syllables stressed) each time you say the word. The presence of tones in Chinese is often cited as another of those lurid features that make the language unique and difficult to learn; but tones are, in fact, not unique to Chinese and probably no more difficult to learn than stress or intonation is for learners of English.

As noted earlier, there are four basic tones in Mandarin. This is far fewer than some of the regional Chinese languages. Cantonese, for example, is usually analyzed as having four tones on two levels, plus one, for a total of nine. Mandarin also differs from many of the regional languages in having a predilection for words with (non-initial) toneless syllables: *shūshu* 'uncle'; *xíngli* 'luggage'.

0.2.1 The four tones

It is difficult to learn to produce or even recognize tones from descriptions, though we will use the descriptive terms 'high (and level)', 'rising', 'low', and 'falling' as a way of referring to them. These terms are only suggestive of the actual shape of the tone, but they do underscore the symmetry of the system: a high and a low, a rising and a falling. In modern Chinese, though the tones have formal names (that can only be rationalized by reference to earlier stages of the language), it is common practice to refer to them numerically by using the numbers 1–4 (*yī, èr, sān, sì*) and the word for sound, *shēng* [shuhng]: *yīshēng, èrshēng, sānshēng, sìshēng*. (Toneless syllables are called *qīngshēng* 'light-toned'.) In English, we can also refer to the tones as 'first', 'second', 'third', and 'fourth'. As noted earlier, in pinyin, tones are indicated by marks placed over the main vowel letter.

Tones

ā	high	first	*yīshēng*
á	rising	second	*èrshēng*
ǎ	low	third	*sānshēng*
à	falling	fourth	*sìshēng*
a	context dependent		*qīngshēng*

0.2.2 Tone concepts

To learn to produce tones, it is useful to *conceive* of them in particular ways. The first tone, for example, which has a high and level contour, can be thought of as **sung out**, because singing a syllable in English usually results in a sustained level pitch similar to the high tone. The second tone, which rises from mid-low to high, can be associated with **doubt** or **uncertainty**: 'Did you say "tea"? "milk"? "Mao"? "Wang"?' The third tone is the subject of the next paragraph, but the fourth tone, which falls from very high to low, can usefully be associated with **list final** intonation: 'One, two, three (all rising), and *four*!' For many people, the fourth tone contour is also associated with **certainty**: 'I said "*Wèi*"' or 'It's late.'

0.2.3 The low tone

You will notice that the pinyin symbol for the low tone is v-shaped, suggesting a contour that falls, then rises. In isolation, it does indeed fall and rise: *hǎo* 'be good'; *wǒ* 'I; me'; *jiǎng* 'speak; explain'. In close conjunction with a following syllable (other than one with the same low tone, as shown below), it tends to have a low, non-rising pitch.

If you can find a Chinese speaker to model the following phrases (from Unit 1), try listening for the relatively low pitch in the low-toned syllable, *hěn* [huhn] 'very; quite', that appears at the beginning of the following phrases.

hěn gāo	'tall'
hěn máng	'busy'
hěn lèi	'tired'

For most speakers, a low-toned syllable in the *second* position of a phrase will also stay low, without much of a rise. Again, if you can find a speaker to model the following phrases, see if you agree that the second syllable is primarily low.

shūfǎ	'calligraphy'
tuántǐ	'group'
kànfǎ	'point of view'

For learners, regarding the third tone as 'low', before learning that it rises in certain contexts, produces better results than learning it as a falling-rising pitch and only canceling the final rise in certain contexts. So we will refer to the third tone as 'low', and to produce it, you aim low and add the final rise only when the syllable is isolated.

0.2.4 Toneless syllables

Syllables in initial position in Mandarin almost always have one of the four tones, but those following a toned syllable can be toneless. In Chinese, such syllables have *qīngshēng* 'the light tone'. In this respect, Mandarin contrasts with some regional Chinese languages such as Cantonese, in which almost all syllables are toned, regardless of their position in the word.

Mandarin toneless syllables are of two types: those which never have full tones and those which can have tones but may become toneless after a stressed syllable. The question particle, *ma*, is an example of the first: *Máng ma*? 'Are [you] busy?' The final *ma* never has a tone. Other common examples are the many compound words with iambic stress pattern such as *xíngli* 'luggage' and *shūfu* 'to be comfortable'. The second type will be discussed in Unit 2, after you have examples to refer to.

0.2.5 The tone chart

The chart below uses twelve of the most common surnames to illustrate the four tones. In Chinese, the surname is the first component of the full name, not the last (e.g., *Lǐ* in *Lǐ Liánjié*—Jet Li's Chinese name). In the chart, the four tones are characterized in terms of their pitch contours (high and level, rising, etc.) as well as by the four heuristic concepts (sung out, doubt, etc.) that will help you to produce them correctly.

TONE:	1	2	3	4
	Zhōu	*Wáng*	*Lǐ*	*Wèi*
	Zhāng	*Máo*	*Kǒng*	*Dù*
	Gāo	*Chén*	*Mǎ*	*Zhào*
Description:	high, level	rising	low (with rise)	falling
Concept:	sung out	doubt (?)	low	finality (!)

Exercise 2

The following short sentences consist of the pronoun *tā* 'he; she', the verb *xìng* [sying] 'to be surnamed', and one of the twelve surnames presented above. Keeping your tone concepts in mind and, ideally, with feedback from a Chinese speaker, focus on the different tones of the surnames while pronouncing the sentences.

Tā xìng Zhāng.	'His/Her surname is Zhang.'
Tā xìng Máo.	
Tā xìng Wèi.	
Tā xìng Wáng.	
Tā xìng Kǒng.	
Tā xìng Zhōu.	
Tā xìng Dù.	
Tā xìng Gāo.	
Tā xìng Mǎ.	
Tā xìng Chén.	
Tā xìng Zhào.	
Tā xìng Lǐ.	

0.2.6 An aside on the history of Chinese tones

Tone systems as complex as those of Chinese are a feature of dozens of languages spoken in China and adjoining regions of mainland Southeast Asia, including the national languages of Burma, Thailand, and Vietnam. One tends to think of tone as being primarily a matter of pitch—like notes in a song. Pitch is controlled by stretching or loosening the vocal chords in the throat, rather like what happens when you stretch or loosen the mouth of a balloon. Tone is often more than just pitch. Even in standard Chinese, it is also associated with length; the rising tone, for example, is noticeably shorter than the high, level tone. In Southeast Asian languages, such as standard Vietnamese and Burmese,

Special attention to the rising tone, *Chéngdū*

tone involves quality of voice as well as pitch (and length), so descriptions of tones may include terms like 'breathy' or 'creaky'. The term 'tone', therefore, covers a complex set of features.

While tones may be a more or less permanent feature of the region, tone systems may appear, evolve, or even disappear within particular languages. Evidence from ancient Chinese rhyme tables and other sources indicates that the various Chinese tonal systems evolved from an earlier system which, like the current standard, also consisted of four tones. The modern Mandarin pronunciation of the names of the four ancient tones are: *píng* 'level', *shǎng* 'rising', *qù* 'going', and *rù* 'entering'. The last was found only with checked syllables, those ending with stopped consonants such as 'k', 't', and 'p', which, as noted earlier, are no longer found in Mandarin, but survive in Cantonese and other regional Chinese languages. This four-tone system evolved differently in different dialect groups. In standard Cantonese, for example, the four-tone system split into two sets of four tones each, with one set relatively higher than the other; an additional distinct tone derived from another split, providing a total of nine distinctive tones.

You may feel fortunate that the Mandarin dialects did not undergo the same development as Cantonese. In Mandarin, the ancient four-tone system remained as four tones, but they underwent a redistribution. Words with the *rù* tone, for example, are no longer a distinctive set in Mandarin; they have joined with words whose tones were originally *píng*, *shǎng*, or *qù*. The *rù*-toned words were distinguished mainly by the final stopped consonants ('p', 't', 'k'), and once those were lost, the *rù* tone was no longer distinct from the other three tones.

In another Mandarin development, *píng*-toned words split into two groups and formed two of the four modern tones, first tone (high and level) and second tone (rising), a development that is reflected in the names of those tones in modern Chinese, *yīnpíng* and *yángpíng*. *Yīnpíng* arose from *píng*-toned syllables with *yīn*—or voiced initial consonants; *yángpíng* arose from *píng*-toned syllables with *yáng*—or voiceless initials. So the modern tones that you find in the standard language, though still four in number, are neither pronounced the same way nor found on the same words as in the four-tone system that existed some 1,500 years ago.

A more detailed discussion of both the historical development of tone in Chinese and the tonal systems found in other varieties of Chinese can be found in books such as Norman (1988), listed at the end of the Introduction.

0.3 Initial consonants

First, note that many pinyin letters are pronounced similarly to their English equivalents; the *l* in *lǎo*, for example, is very like the English 'l', and the pinyin *f, s, n,* and *m* all have more or less the same values in Chinese and English scripts. Unfortunately, such cases are liable to make you think of English even when pinyin letters have values that are rather different. Below is a table of symbols that represent all possible initial consonants of Chinese. Following

Chinese custom, they are presented with a particular set of vowels and ordered from front of the mouth (labials) to back (velars and glottals).

0.3.1 The consonant chart

First, letters *w* and *y*, which do appear initially in pinyin (e.g., the numbers *wǔ* 'five' and *yī* 'one'), are treated as special cases of medial *u* and *i*, respectively, in initial position. Thus, instead of 'ī', one finds *yī*; instead of 'ǔ', *wǔ*; instead of 'iě', *yě*; instead of 'uǒ', *wǒ*; etc. This will be discussed again in detail later.

Second, the vowels conventionally placed with the different classes of initials to make them pronounceable turn out to be some of those that have quite idiosyncratic values for speakers of English. Thus, the *o* in the first line of the table below is not pronounced like the English long vowel 'o' but more like the vowel sound in the word 'paw'; the *e* in the second line is pronounced [uh]; the *i* in the third and fourth lines represents a continuation of the initial into a buzz (e.g., *zi* [dzz]; *zhi* [jrr]), but in the fifth line it represents the more expected [ee] (e.g., *ji* [jee]). The vowel sounds will be discussed in §0.4 below, but for now, you can use the hints provided in the far right column of the chart and imitate your teacher or the audio. You should learn to declaim (for sound) and write (for symbol) this table, line by line, as soon as possible: *bo po mo fo, de te ne le*, etc.

	PLACE OF ARTICULATION		(I)	(II)	(III)	(IV)	CONSONANT HINT	VOWEL HINT
(1)	lips		*bo*	*po*	*mo*	*fo*		[waw]
(2)	tongue tip at teeth	ˆ	*de*	*te*	*ne*	*le*		[uh]
(3)	flat tongue at teeth	_	*zi*	*ci*	*si*		[dsz/tsz/ssz]	not [ee]
(4)	tongue tip raised	!	*zhi*	*chi*	*shi*	*ri*		[r], not [ee]
(5)	spread lips	⟨ ⟩	*ji*	*qi*	*xi*			[ee]
(6)	back of tongue high		*ge*	*ke*	*he*			[uh]

0.3.2 Notes on the consonant chart

COLUMNS I AND II In English, the distinction between sounds typically written 'b' and 'p' or 'd' and 't' is usually said to be one of voicing (vocal chord vibration): with 'b' and 'd', voicing begins relatively earlier than with 'p' and 't'. However, in Chinese, the onset of voicing of the column I consonants is different from that of English. The sound represented by *b* in pinyin is actually between the English [b] and [p]; that represented by *d* is between the English [d] and [t], etc. This is why the Wade-Giles system of Romanization (mentioned in the Introduction) uses 'p, p'' (i.e., p, p-apostrophe) rather than 'b, p' (T'aipei rather than *Taibei*). In phonetic terms, both *b* and *p* are voiceless in pinyin, but the first is unaspirated while the second is aspirated (that is, accompanied by a noticeable explosion of air). Being aware of this will help you to adjust to what you hear; in fact, the English letters 'b', 'd', and 'g' are not highly voiced by most speakers (compared to their equivalents in, say, French and Spanish), so if you pronounce them 'lightly' in Chinese, you will not have too strong an accent. Contrast: *bo/po, de/te, ge/ke*; and *zi/ci, zhi/chi, ji/qi*.

ROW 1 These consonants are 'labials', or those whose pronunciation involve the lips. The pinyin *o* (not *ou*) only appears after the labials (*bo po mo fo*) and is, for many English speakers, pronounced like [aw] in 'paw'. Everywhere other than after labial consonants, the same sound is written *uo*. Thus *bo, po, mo,* and *fo* rhyme with *duo, tuo, nuo,* and *luo* (the latter set not shown in the table above). In other words, *o* by itself always equals *uo* (and never *ou*). Apparently, the creators of pinyin felt that, following labial initials, it was not necessary to indicate the labial onset with 'u'. It will be important to keep the sound of *o/uo* separate from that of *ou*. The last (*ou*) rhymes with both syllables of the English exclamation 'oh no'.

ROWS 3, 4, AND 5—THE CRUCIAL ROWS! With *z, c,* and *s* in row 3, the tongue is tense but flat and touching the back of the teeth near the gum line. The letter *i*, following row 3 initials, is *not* pronounced [ee]; it simply represents a continuation of the consonant sound. So, for *zi, ci,* and *si*, think [dzz], [tsz], and [ssz] (as indicated in the far left column). English does not have consonant sounds comparable to the first two row 3 initials, *z* and *c*, except across root boundaries: pads, cats. In German and Russian, though, similar sounds do occur at the beginning of words, such as in German *zehn* [dz-] 'ten', or Russian *cená* [ts-] 'price'. The latter example, also written with a 'c', demonstrates the Russian influence on the creators of pinyin.

With *zh, ch, sh,* and *r* in row 4, the tongue is pulled back and the tip is raised toward the roof of the mouth (on or near the rough area behind the teeth known as the alveolar ridge) in what is called a retroflex position. When preceding vowels without lip rounding (all but *o* or *u*), including *i* as in the table (*zhi*, etc.), the lips are tight and slightly spread, which allows teachers to see and hear whether the retroflex series is being pronounced correctly. As with the row 3 initials, the letter *i* in this position represents only a buzz. So, for *zhi, chi, shi,* and *ri*, think [jr], [chr], [shr], and [rr]. In English, an 'r' following a consonant will often produce the retroflex articulation of the tongue that is characteristic of the row 4 consonants. Another way to ensure that your tongue is in the correct position for those initials is to match *zh* to the 'dr' of 'drill', *ch* to the 'tr' of 'trill', *sh* to the 'shr' of 'shrill', and *r* to the 'r' of 'rill'.

Finally, with *j, q,* and *x* of row 5, the tongue is positioned like the 'yie' in English 'yield'. This time, the letter *i* is pronounced [ee], so for *ji, qi,* and *xi*, think [jyee], [chyee], and [syee]. Later, you will see that row 5 initials are followed only by the written vowels *i* and *u*. The first will always be pronounced [ee] in this context; the second will always be pronounced [ü]. Every time you encounter row 5 initials, think *i* is [ee] and *u* is [ü].

THE INITIAL *R* OF ROW 4 Pronunciation of the letter 'r' varies considerably among languages: the Scots trill their tongue tips; the Parisians flutter their uvulas; the Spanish flap their tongues; and the well-known American television interviewer, Barbara Walters, pronounces it like a cross between [r] and [w]. The Chinese *r* is different again; it has a little bit of a buzz to it. Like *zh, ch,* and *sh*, it is retroflex (with tongue pushed back and tip raised) so it resembles the initial sound of English 'rill' or 'ridge', but it also has friction like the 's' in 'pleasure' (or French *je* 'I'). You will observe considerable variation in the quality of the Chinese *r*, depending on the following vowel and on the particular speaker. Examples: *rén, rè, rù, ràng, ruò, ròu, rì.*

Exercise 3

Try pronouncing the following syllables, randomly selected from the initials in rows 3, 4, and 5. Know your chart of initials before you try this!

qī	*sǐ*	*zhī*	*zì*	*jī*	*qī*	*sì*	*rì*	*chī*
xī	*shì*	*cì*	*zhǐ*	*qí*	*sī*	*chǐ*	*jí*	*xí*

Now try pronouncing these well-known Chinese names.

Cí Xǐ (last empress)	*Qí Báishí* (famous calligrapher)	*Lǐ Shízhēn* (16th-century herbalist from *Qizhou*)	*Qízhōu*	*Zhāng Zǐyí* (actress)

0.3.3 An expanded chart of initials

The conventional chart of initial consonants exhibits a rather restricted and idiosyncratic set of rhymes. We can make the chart more comprehensive by adding one or two lines to each row, as follows. (Unfortunately, because not all combinations of rhyme and tone are possible, this version of the chart requires you to shift tone in certain cases.)

	(I)	(II)	(III)	(IV)
(1)	*bō*	*pō*	*mō*	*fō*
	bān	*pān*	*mān*	*fān*
(2)	*dé*	*tè*	*né*	*lè*
	duō	*tuō*	*nuó*	*luó*
	dài	*tài*	*nài*	*lài*

	(I)	(II)	(III)	(IV)
(3)	*zī*	*cī*	*sī*	
	zǎo	*cǎo*	*sǎo*	
(4)	*zhī*	*chī*	*shī*	*rī*
	zhuō	*chuō*	*shuō*	*ruò*
	zhōu	*chōu*	*shōu*	*ròu*
(5)	*jī*	*qī*	*xī*	
	jù	*qù*	*xù*	
	jiān	*qiān*	*xiān*	
(6)	*gē*	*kē*	*hē*	
	gān	*kān*	*hān*	

0.4 Rhymes

A table showing all possible rhymes follows below. It is too long and complicated to be quickly internalized like the chart of initials, but you can practice reading the rows aloud with the help of a Chinese speaker. You can also map your progress through the rhymes by circling syllables, or adding meaningful examples, as you learn new words.

The table is organized by main vowel (*a, e, i, o, u, ü*), and then within each vowel by medial (*i, u,* and *ü*) and final (*i, o/u, n, ng*). The penultimate column, marked, 'w/o C_i' (i.e., 'without initial consonant'), lists syllables that lack an initial consonant (with the rarer ones placed in parentheses) and thus begin with a (written) vowel or medial (the latter always represented with an initial *y* or *w*). The final column provides pronunciation hints. Asterisks (*) following certain row numbers indicate sets that require special attention. Final *r*, whose special properties were mentioned above, is treated separately.

			UNTONED EXAMPLES						W/O C_1	PRONUNCIATION HINT
The *a* rhymes	(1)	a	*ta*	*cha*	*da*	*ma*	*ba*	*la*	*a*	
	(2)	a-i	*tai*	*chai*	*dai*	*mai*	*bai*	*zai*	*ai*	
	(3)	a-o	*tao*	*chao*	*dao*	*pao*	*zao*	*rao*	*ao*	
	(4)	a-n	*tan*	*ran*	*zhan*	*can*	*lan*	*pan*	*an*	
	(5)	a-ng	*dang*	*sang*	*zhang*	*mang*	*lang*	*zang*	*ang*	
	(6)	i-a	*jia*	*qia*	*xia*				*ya*	
	(7)	i-a-o	*jiao*	*qiao*	*xiao*				*yao*	
	(8)*	**i-a-n**	***jian***	***qian***	***xian***				***yan***	[yen]
	(9)	i-a-ng	*jiang*	*qiang*	*xiang*				*yang*	
	(10)	u-a	*hua*	*gua*	*zhua*	*shua*			*wa*	
	(11)	u-a-i	*chuai*						(*wai*)	
	(12)	u-a-n	*huan*	*guan*	*zhuan*	*shuan*	*cuan*		*wan*	
	(13)	u-a-ng	*huang*	*guang*	*zhuang*	*shuang*			*wang*	[wahng]
The *e* rhymes	(14)	e	*zhe*	*che*	*she*	*re*	*le*		*e*	[uh]
	(15)	e-i	*zhei*	*shei*	*lei*	*fei*	*bei*		(*ei*)	[(h)ay]
	(16)	e-n	*zhen*	*shen*	*fen*	gen	*men*		*en*	[uhn]
	(17)	e-ng	*leng*	*sheng*	*ceng*	*deng*	*zheng*		(*eng*)	[uhng]
	(18)	i-e	*jie*	*xie*	*lie*	*mie*			*ye*	[yeh]
	(19)*	**u-e**	***jue***	***que***	***xue***	***nüe***	***lüe***		***yue***	[yüeh]

The [ee]	(20a)	i	*li*	*bi*	*ti*			*yi*	[yee]
rhymes	(20b)	i	*ji*	*qi*	*xi*			*yi*	[yee]
	(21)	i-n	*jin*	*qin*	*xin*	*lin*	*bin*	*yin*	[yeen]
	(22)	i-ng	*jing*	*qing*	*xing*	*ling*	*bing*	*ying*	[yeeng]
	23)*	**u-i**	***dui***	***gui***	***shui***	***rui***	***chui***	***wei***	[way]
The 'buzzing'	(24)*	**i**	***zi***	***ci***	***si***				[dzz, tsz . . .]
i rhymes	(25)*	**i**	***zhi***	***chi***	***shi***	***ri***			[jr, chr . . .]
The *o* rhymes	(26)*	**o**	***bo***	***po***	***mo***	***fo***			[-waw]
	(27)	u-o	*duo*	*tuo*	*guo*	*shuo*	*zuo*	*wo*	[waw]
	(28)*	**o-u**	***zhou***	***zou***	***dou***	***hou***	***chou***	***ou***	[oh]
	(29)	o-ng	*zhong*	*dong*	*long*	*zong*			
	30)	i-o-ng	*jiong*	*qiong*	*xiong*			*yong*	
The [oo]	(31)	u	*shu*	*lu*	*zhu*	*zu*	*cu*	*wu*	[woo]
rhymes	(32)*	**u-n**	***shun***	***lun***	***zhun***	***kun***	***cun***	***wen***	[wuhn]
	(33)*	**i-u**	***jiu***	***qiu***	***xiu***	***liu***	***diu***	***you***	[yeo]
The *ü* rhymes	(34)*	**u**	***ju***	***qu***	***xu***	***lü***	***nü***	***yu***	[yü]
	(35)*	**u-n**	***jun***	***qun***	***xun***			***yun***	[yün]

0.4.1 Notes on the *i* and *u* rhymes and C_i

Recall that, in the C_i chart presented earlier, the row 4 C_i (*zh, ch, sh, r*) are distinguished from the row 5 C_i (*j, q, x*) by position of the tongue. In terms of English sounds and spellings, the distinction between 'j', 'ch', and 'sh' depends upon tongue position—'dr, tr, shr' (*zhi, chi, shi*) versus the 'y' of 'yield' (*ji, qi, xi*). This difference, even if appreciated, seems, nonetheless, very slight. Indeed, it would be much more difficult to perceive if the vowels following these initial consonants were identically pronounced. But they never are!

Note that row 5 C_i initials (*j, q, x*) are *only* followed by the medial sounds (not the written letters) [ee] and [ü], written *i* and *u*, respectively. Here are some examples (which can be read with a level tone).

> *ji, jie, jian, qi, qie, qian, xi, xie, xian; ju, jue, jun, qu, que, qun, xu, xue, xun.*

Row 3 and row 4 C_i, on the other hand, are *never* followed by the medial sounds [ee] or [ü].

> *zhi, zi, zhu, zu, zhan, zan, chi, ci, chu, cu, chan, chen,* etc.

Because the creators of pinyin let *i* and *u* each represent two different sounds, this complementary distribution is obscured: the vowels of *ji* and *zhi* look alike, but they do not sound alike; the same is true for *ju* and *zhu*. Therefore, if you hear [chee], it must be written *qi*, for the sound [ee] never follows *ch*; if you hear [chang], it must be written *chang*, for *q* can only be followed by the sound [ee]. This may sound complicated—and it is—but there is plenty of practice to come, beginning with Exercise 4.

0.4.2 The value of the letter *e*

The value of *e* also violates the expectations of English speakers. It is pronounced [uh] in all contexts (*zé, dēng, chén*), except after a written *i* or *u*, when it is pronounced [eh] (*xiē, niē, xuē*), or before a written *i*, when it is pronounced [ay] as in the English word 'way' (*lèi, bèi, zéi*).

Exercise 4

The following syllables all contain the written vowels *i* and *u*. Practice reading them clearly, with a single tone. As with all the exercises in this lesson, repeat this procedure daily, thinking of the relationship between initial and rhyme, until you feel confident.

chi qi xie qu chu chun jia qin cu qu shun

qun shu ju ci xu zi zhu shi xi xia qu

Exercise 5

Practice reading the following syllables containing pinyin *e*.

chén wèi zhēn xiē bèn rén lèi rè běi jiè è lěng zéi chē bié

Now try pronouncing the following proper names, all of which contain pinyin *e*, *ei*, or *ie*.

Zhōu Ēnlái (premier)	*Máo Zédōng* (chairman)	*Jiǎng Jièshí* 'Chiang Kai-shek'	*Héběi* (province)
Lǐ Dēnghuī (former Taiwan president)	*Éméi shān* 'Emei Mountain'	*Lièníng* 'Lenin'	*Sòng Měilíng* (wife of Chiang Kai-shek)

0.4.3 The *o* rhymes: *ou* versus *uo*/*o*

On early encounters, it is easy to confuse pinyin rhymes that are spelled similarly, such as *ou* and *uo*. This can lead to some pronunciation problems that are very difficult to correct later, so you need to make sure you master them early. The rhyme *ou*, with the leading *o*, is pronounced like the name of the English letter 'o', rhyming with 'know'. The rhyme *uo*, on the other hand, with the trailing *o*, is pronounced like the vowel sound in 'paw'. However, as you now know, after the row 1 C_i, *uo* is spelled *o*: *bo, po, mo,* and *fo* rhyme with *duo, tuo, nuo,* and *luo*.

Exercise 6

Try pronouncing these names and words that contain *o*.

Bōlán 'Poland'	*Sūzhōu* (city near Shanghai)	*Mòxīgē* 'Mexico'
luòtuo 'camel'	*Zhāng Yìmóu* (film director)	*Zhōu Ēnlái* (premier)
luóbo 'radish'	*Guō Mòruò* (20th-century writer)	*bōluó* 'pineapple'

Try pronouncing the following list of single syllables with *o*.

mōu tuō bō fǒ zhōu duō pò dōu zuò fǒu luó ròu

0.4.4 The *ü* rhymes

Section 0.4.1 (after the list of rhymes) makes the point that many of the *ü* rhymes are revealed by the type of initial consonant. Following row 5 initials (*j, q, x*), *u* is always pronounced the same as *ü*; following any other initial, it is pronounced [oo]. This results in distinct pronunciations (with any particular tone) for: *zhu/ju, chu/qu,* and *shu/xu*, but similar pronunciations for *pu, fu, du, ku,* and *hu*. However, the sound [ü] also occurs after the initials *n* and *l*, as well as those of row 5. In these cases, *ü* may contrast with *u*, and the difference has to be shown on the vowel, not on the initial. Examples include: *lù* 'road' versus *lǜ* 'green'; *nǔ* 'crossbow' versus *nǚ* 'female'. In addition to being a core vowel, *ü* also occurs as a medial. Again, when it follows row 5 initials, it is written as *u*: *jué, quē, xuě*; but following *l* or *n*, it is written as *ü*: *lüèzì* 'abbreviation'; *nüèji* 'malaria'. In the latter cases, it is redundant, since there is no contrast between *üe* and *ue*.

0.5 Miscellany

0.5.1 Tonal shifts

Before leaving the survey of sounds and notation, we need to return to the subject of tone, and take note of the phenomenon of tonal shifting (called 'tone sandhi' by linguists). It turns out that in certain contexts, Chinese tones undergo shifts from one to another. (In standard Chinese, the contexts where this occurs are very limited; in regional languages such as Hokkien, such shifts are much more pervasive, affecting almost every syllable.) We will mention these shifts here, and then practice producing them more systematically in later lessons.

0.5.2 Low-tone shift

If two low tones (tone 3) appear consecutively *in the same phrase*, the first tone is pronounced with a rising tone: *

3 + 3	→	2 + 3 *
low + low	→	rising + low
hěn + hǎo	→	hén hǎo 'good'
hěn + lěng	→	hén lěng 'cold'
Lǐ + lǎoshī	→	Lí lǎoshī 'Professor Lee'

hén hǎo *

It is, of course, possible to have three or more low tones in a row, but such cases will be considered later.

0.5.3 Two single-word shifts

There also exist a few more idiosyncratic shifts that involve only single words. The negative, *bu*, is usually pronounced with a falling tone except when it is followed by another falling tone, in which case it shifts and is pronounced with a rising tone: *bù hǎo* 'not well', but *bú lèi* 'not tired'. In the latter case, the result is a trajectory like the sides of a mountain, up then down, and students in the past have kept track of this shift by calling it the 'Fuji shift' (after Mount Fuji, which is, of course, in Japan, not China). Below, *bu* is shown in combination with some adjectival verbs (called stative verbs in Chinese grammatical tradition); these sets (involving stative verbs from the conversational material in Unit 1) should be repeated regularly until fully internalized.

	bù gāo	'not tall'
	bù máng	'not busy'
	bù hǎo	'not well'
Tone shift:	*bú lèi*	'not tired'
	bú è	'not hungry'
	bú rè	'not hot'
	bú cuò	'not bad'

Another single-word shift involves the numeral *yī* 'one'. In counting, and in many compounds, it is level toned (*yīshēng*): *yī, èr, sān, sì* 'one, two, three, four'. When *yī* is grammatically linked to a subsequent 'measure word', it adopts the same tonal shift as *bu*, rising before a falling tone (*yí fèn* 'a copy'), but falling before any other tone (*yì bāo* 'a pack').

	yì zhāng	'a [table]'
	yì tiáo	'a [fish]'
	yì běn	'a [book]'
But:	*yí fèn*	'a copy [of a newspaper]'

Note that the low tone shift (*hěn* + *hǎo* = *hén hǎo*) applies to any word (or syllable) that fits the grammatical condition (located within a phrase); but the shift from falling to rising affects only a few words, most commonly *bu* and *yi*.

0.5.4 The apostrophe

In certain contexts, an apostrophe appears between the syllables of a compound written in pinyin: *Xī'ān* (a city in China); *hǎi'ōu* 'seagull'; *chǒng'ài* 'to dote on'. The apostrophe is used when a syllable beginning with a vowel letter (*a, e, o*) is preceded (without a space) by another syllable; in other words, where the syllable boundary is ambiguous. By convention, the apostrophe is only used when the trailing syllable begins with a vowel; a word like *yīngān*, with two potential syllable divisions (*yīn-gān, yīng-ān*), is always to be interpreted as *yīn+gān*, never *yīng+ān* (which would be *yīng'ān*).

0.5.5 Interaction of tone and intonation

You may wonder whether a tonal language like Chinese, in which pitch adheres to individual syllables (with some accommodation across syllables), permits intonational pitch movements of the sort associated with contrast, denial, correction, and other kinds of emotional speech in English: 'That's a HIGH tone?!' *Nà shi PÍNGshēng ma?*

It turns out that Chinese (and other tonal languages) do have intonation contours, but rather than obliterating the word tones, they envelope them, exaggerating the pitch contours of key words, while narrowing the pitch contours of others. In the example above, *píng* is louder and its pitch rises to an exaggerated height, while the other syllables are diminished with shorter but nonetheless distinctive contours. You will have plenty of opportunities to practice superimposing intonation over tone as you work through the material in the core units.

People often ask about singing in tonal languages. Surely melody must obliterate word tone, or else you would have to choose your words to fit the melody and songs would resemble speech. The famous Chinese linguist Yuen Ren Chao (who provided the epigraph that began this lesson) considered this question in an article published in 1956 and concluded that, while the melodies of certain traditional song forms accounted for word tone, modern Chinese songs did not. Certainly, that is the way it appears. In the well-known folksong whose title translates as 'The Couple Returning Home' (夫妻双双把家还 *Fūqī shuāngshuāng bǎ jiā huán*), the first two lines begin with fourth-tone words (树 *shù* 'tree' and 绿 *lǜ* 'green'), yet the first is distinctly high in the melody, and the second is distinctly low. However, it should be noted that Wong and Diehl (2008) reached a different conclusion for Cantonese, which has a richer tone system than standard Chinese.

0.6 Writing connected text in pinyin

Unlike earlier systems of Chinese phonetic notation, some of which were intended as full-fledged auxiliary writing systems that could co-exist with (or even replace) characters, pinyin was intended as an adjunct system to indicate pronunciation and provide a means for alphabetical organization. For this reason, the rules and conventions for writing connected text in pinyin were not well defined at first. However, increasing use of computers for the input and production of text and in everyday communication, as well as the proliferation of contact between China and the rest of the world, has put a premium on the use of pinyin. Nowadays, in addition to its use in pedagogical materials such as this textbook, pinyin is widely used in e-mails, for word processing input, for Web and e-mail addresses, and to complement characters on advertisements, announcements, and menus (particularly those intended for an international audience in China and abroad).

In 1988, the State Language Commission issued a document with the translated title of "The Basic Rules for Hanyu Pinyin Orthography" and, with a few minor exceptions, this textbook conforms to those proposed rules. (The *ABC Chinese-English Dictionary*, cited at the end of the Introduction, contains a translation of this document as an appendix.) Only two general points need to be mentioned here. First, basic English punctuation practices hold. Sentences begin with capital letters, as do proper nouns, and they end with periods. Other punctuation marks are used more or less as they are in English.

Second, words, not syllables, are enclosed by spaces. Thus, 'teacher' is written *lǎoshī*, not *lǎo shī*. Characters, by contrast, which always represent syllable-length units, are evenly spaced regardless of word boundaries. Of course, defining what a word is can be problematic, but pinyin dictionaries or glossaries can usually be relied upon to make those decisions for us. Other conventions, such as the use of the hyphen, will be noted in this book when needed. When you write pinyin, it should follow this format:

> *Gémìng bú shì qǐngkè chīfàn.*
> 'Revolution isn't [like] inviting guests over for a meal.'
> ('revolution not be invite-guests eat-meal')
>
> —Mao Zedong

Writing pinyin in this way makes it readable. In fact, when e-mailing characters is restricted by technical problems, pinyin is an acceptable substitute (even without tone marks) so long as the above orthographical conventions are observed, as in: *Geming bu shi qingke chifan.*

Tiějú Lane, *Kūnmíng* (now demolished): the sign reads *zhǐ shēng yíge háizi hǎo* 'just have one child'. Not only is the pinyin written without tones or word breaks, but *shēng* is written 'shen' and *ge* is written 'gou', unintentionally reflecting local pronunciation.

0.7 Recapitulation

This completes our survey of the sounds and transcription of Chinese. Already, you should be able to pronounce the names of Chinese people and places considerably better than the average television and radio newscaster or announcer. Exercise 7 reviews what you have covered in this lesson.

Exercise 7

Write out the formula for all possible pinyin syllables; list the medials; list the finals. Correctly place the tone marks given in the parentheses over each of the following syllables.

xue (´)   bei (¯)   sou (¯)   jie (`)   bie (´)   suo (ˇ)

List (or recite) twelve surnames, grouped by tone.

Write out the table of initial consonants. How many rows are there? Which rows are particularly problematic? What sounds can follow the row 5 initials? How are those sounds written in pinyin?

Pronounce the following sets of syllables, being careful to contrast each pair.

Tone 1:	*qī/cī, xī/sī, jī/zī, qū/cū, xū/sū, jū/zū*
Tone 2:	*zú/zhú, cí/chí, jí/zhí, xí/shí, shú/sú, qí/chí*
Tone 3:	*zhě/lěi, gě/gěi, kě/fěi, chě/děi*
Tone 4:	*biè/bèi, liè/lèi, miè/mèi, niè/nèi*
Tone 1:	*pō/pōu, bō/duō, luō/lōu, tuō/pō, mō/luō, tuō/tōu*

Pronounce the following personal and place names.

Zhōu Ēnlái (premier)	*Máo Zédōng* (chairman)	*Jiǎng Jièshí* 'Chiang Kai-shek'	*Cáo Yǔ* (20th-century playwright)
Lǐ Dēnghuī (former Taiwan president)	*Lǐ Xiāngjūn* (Ming dynasty beauty)	*Sòng Měilíng* (wife of Chiang)	*Wáng Zhìzhì* (basketball player)
Dèng Xiǎopíng (post-Mao leader)	*Zhū Róngjī* (premier)	*Lǐ Xiǎolóng* 'Bruce Lee'	*Cáo Cāo* (Three Kingdoms period warlord)

Běijīng (capital)	*Xī'ān* (city in Shaanxi)	*Guǎngzhōu* (city in Guangdong)	*Zhèngzhōu* (city in Henan)
Sìchuān (province)	*Jiāngxī* (province)	*Chóngqìng* (city in western China)	*Chǔxióng* (city in Yunnan)

Apply the tone-change rules to the following phrases.

hěn lěng 'cold'	*bù gāo* 'not tall'	*lǎobǎn* 'boss'	*bù guì* 'cheap'	*lǎo Lǐ* 'old Lee'	*yī běn* 'one book'
bù hǎo 'not good'	*yǔsǎn* 'umbrella'	*bù duì* 'wrong'	*nǐ hǎo* 'hello'	*bù cuò* 'not bad'	*yī fèn* 'one copy'

Read aloud the sets listed below. Each set of three syllables follows the pattern 'rising, rising, falling', like the usual list intonation of English 'one, two, three', or 'boats, trains, planes'; *lá, wéi, jìn*! Note that in this exercise, not all syllables are actual Chinese words with the cited tone.

lá	*wéi*	*jìn!*
láo	*tái*	*dù!*
sóu	*sí*	*mìng!*
zí	*xiá*	*qìng!*
ní	*zhí*	*hòu!*
lái	*duó*	*zhèn!*
fó	*qí*	*cì!*
xíng	*cuó*	*shì!*
móu	*guó*	*shòu!*
rén	*béi*	*zhà!*

3. Chart of initials.
Row1: bō pō mō fō
bān pān mān fān
Row2: dé tè né lè
duō tuō nuó luó
dài tài nài lài
Row3: zī cī sī
zǎo cǎo sǎo
Row 4: zhī chī shī rī
zhuō chuō shuō ruò
zhōu chōu shōu rōu
Row5: jī qī xī
jù qù xù
jiān qiān xiān
Row6: gē kē hē
gān kān hān

Coda

Chinese who studied English during the early years of the People's Republic of China can often remember their first English sentence, because in those days textbook material was polemical and didactic, and lesson content was carefully chosen for content and gravity. Let *your* first sentences also carry some weight and be appropriate for the endeavors you are about to begin.

> 種瓜得瓜，種豆得豆。
> *Zhòng guā dé guā, zhòng dòu dé dòu.*
> '[You] reap what you sow.'
> ('plant melon get melon, plant bean get bean')

> 不入虎穴，焉得虎子。
> *Bú rù hǔxué, yān dé hǔzǐ.*
> 'Nothing ventured, nothing gained.'
> ('not enter tiger-lair, how get tiger-cub')

NOTES

a. *xīguā* 'watermelon'
b. *dòuzi* 'beans; peas'
c. *lǎohǔ* 'tiger'

Zàijiàn.	'Good-bye.' ('again-see')
Míngtiān jiàn.	'See you tomorrow!' ('tomorrow see')

Beijing road sign

1. Zhòng guā dé guā, zhòng dòu dé dòu.
("Plant melon, get melon. Plant bean, get bean.")
* You reap what you sow!

2. Bú rù hǔxué, yān de hǔzǐ.
('not enter tiger-lair, how get tiger cub?')
* Nothing ventured, nothing gained!

THE CORE UNITS

Unit 1

Qiān lǐ zhī xíng shǐ yú zú xià.
'A long journey begins with a single step.'
('1,000 mile journey begins with foot down')
—Lǎozǐ

This is the first lesson in which you actually begin to use the language, starting with simple questions and responses about states (e.g., 'Are you tired?' / 'Not very.') and events (e.g., 'Have you eaten?' / 'Yes, I have.'). In the course of presenting these simple interactions, you will be introduced to a range of verbs, pronouns, methods of asking 'yes/no' questions, and ways of answering affirmatively or negatively. You will also learn how to count, give dates, greet, and take your leave. In the first four units, you will be paying special attention to pronunciation and becoming more familiar with pinyin.

Contents

1.1 Conventions

The previous lesson on sounds and symbols provided the first steps in learning to associate the pinyin transcription of Chinese language material with accurate pronunciation. The task will continue as you start to learn to converse by listening to conversational material while reading it in the pinyin script. However, in these early units, it will be all too easy to fall back into associations based on English spelling, and so, occasionally (as in the previous overview), Chinese cited in pinyin will be followed by phonetic hints in brackets, such as: *máng* [mahng] or *hěn* [huhn]. These are only intended to alert you to potential problems and remind you of what you have been hearing on the audio and from your teachers.

Where needed, you will be provided with an idiomatic English translation of Chinese material in addition to a word-for-word gloss in parentheses. The latter takes you deeper into the world of Chinese linguistic concepts and allows you to better understand how meanings are composed. The following conventions are used to make the presentation of this information as clear as possible.

Parentheses (. . .)	enclose literal meanings, e.g.: *Máng ma?* ('be+busy Q')
Plusses (+)	indicate both meanings combined in the Chinese word, e.g., *nín* ('you+POL'). Also used to distinguish, in certain cases, two particles, both pronounced *de* but written with different characters. See §2.8.3, e.g., *shuō+de hěn hǎo.*
Capitals (Q)	indicate grammatical notions, e.g., Q for 'question'; POL for 'polite'. In cases where there

	is no easy label for the notion, the Chinese word itself is cited in capitals, with a fuller explanation to appear later: *Nǐ ne?* ('you NE?')
Spaces ( )	appear around words, e.g., *hěn hǎo* versus *shūfu*. Spaces are also used instead of + in glosses, e.g., *hǎochī* ('be good-eat') rather than ('be+good-eat')
Hyphens (-)	are used in standard pinyin transcription to link certain constituents, e.g., *dì-yī* 'first' or *mǎma-hūhū* 'so-so'. In the English glosses, hyphens indicate the meanings of the constituent parts of Chinese compounds: *hǎochī* ('be good-eat').
Brackets [ ]	indicate pronouns and other material that is obligatorily expressed in one language but not in the other, e.g., *Máng ma?* 'Are [you] busy?' In definitions, brackets enclose notes on style or other relevant information, e.g., *bàng* 'be good; super' [colloquial]. Finally, brackets also enclose phonetic hints and other indications of pronunciation other than pinyin, e.g., *hěn* [huhn].
Angle brackets ⟨ ⟩	indicate optional material: ⟨*Nǐ*⟩ *lèi ma?* means that either *Nǐ lèi ma?* or *Lèi ma?* are both possible.
Tildes (~)	indicate variant(s).

1.2 Pronunciation

1.2.1 Word Pairs

To get your vocal organs ready to pronounce Chinese, it is useful to contrast the articulatory settings of Chinese and English by pronouncing pairs of words selected for their similarity of sound. Thus, *kǎo* 'to test' differs from English 'cow' not only in tone, but also in vowel quality.

(1)	*kǎo*	cow	(2)	*xìn*	sin	(3)	*shòu*	show
	hǎo	how		*qín*	chin		*zhōu*	Joe
	nǎo	now		*jīn*	gin		*sǒu*	so
	chǎo	chow[-time]		*xìn*	seen		*ròu*	row
	sǎo	sow['s ear]		*jīn*	Jean		*dōu*	[s]tow
	bǎo	[ship's] bow		*lín*	lean		*tóu*	toe

(4a)	*pō*	paw	(4b)	*duō*	[s]to[r]e	(5)	*bízi*	beads
	bō	bo[r]e		*tuō*	to[r]e		*lǐzi*	leads
	mō	mo[r]e		*luō*	law		*xízi*	seeds

1.2.2 Falling and level tones

Recall the chart of initials: *bo, po, mo, fo,* etc., and particularly rows 3, 4, and 5. Practice reading aloud the following syllable combinations with the falling tone (fourth tone). Note that they all contain the shifting *i* rhyme.

qi zi chi ri ci ji shi si xi zhi ci qi ji xi si chi

Hint: the best way to approach this task is to let the buzzing vowel (as in *zi* and *zhi*) be the default, and scan for the [ee] rhymes of row 5—*ji, qi,* and *xi.*

Now pronounce row 3 and 4 initials with the level tone (first tone), unless otherwise indicated, with the *ao, ou,* and *uo* rhymes.

chao shuo zao ròu zhuo zhao ruò shou rào suo cao zuo zhou

1.3 Numbers (cardinal and ordinal)

This section contains information that can be practiced daily in class by counting or giving the day's date.

1.3.1 The numbers 1–10

yī	*èr*	*sān*	*sì*	*wǔ*	*liù*	*qī*	*bā*	*jiǔ*	*shí*
1	2	3	4	5	6	7	8	9	10

1.3.2 Beyond 10

Higher numbers are regularly formed around *shí* 'ten' (or multiples of ten), with following numbers additive (*shísān* 'thirteen', *shíqī* 'seventeen') and preceding numbers multiplicative (*sānshí* 'thirty', *qīshí* 'seventy').

shíyī	*shí'èr*	*shísì*	*èrshí*	*èrshíyī*	*èrshí'èr*	*èrshísì*	*sānshí*	*sānshíyī*
11	12	14	20	21	22	24	30	31

1.3.3 The ordinal numbers

Ordinals are formed with a prefix, *dì* (which, by pinyin convention, is attached to the following number with a hyphen).

dì-yī	*dì-èr*	*dì-sān*	*dì-sì*	*dì-wǔ*
'first'	'second'	'third'	'fourth'	'fifth'

Later in the lesson, the ordinals can be practiced by class members reporting on order or placement; who is first, second, third, and so on: *Wǒ shi dì-yī; Wǒ shi dì-èr*; etc.

1.3.4 Dates

Dates are presented in 'contracting' order in Chinese, with year listed first (*nián* [nien]), then month (*yuè* [yu-eh]), and finally day (*hào* [how]). Years are usually presented as a string of digits (that may include *líng* 'zero') rather than as a single figure: *yī-jiǔ-jiǔ-liù nián* '1996'; *èr-líng-líng-sān nián* '2003'. Months are formed regularly with numerals: *yīyuè* 'January', *èryuè* 'February', *shí'èryuè* 'December'.

èrlínglíngsān nián bāyuè sān hào	August 3, 2003
yījiǔbāwǔ nián èryuè shíbā hào	February 18, 1985

NOTES

a. Among northern Chinese, *yīyuè* often shows the *yi* tone shift when the month is followed by the day: *yíyuè sān hào*. With older speakers, the numbers *qī* 'seven' and *bā* 'eight', both level-toned words, sometimes adopt the same shift when used in dates (and in some other contexts) prior to a fourth-tone word: *qíyuè liù hào; báyuè jiǔ hào*.

b. In the written language, *rì* 'day' (a much simpler character) is often used in place of *hào*. Thus, *bāyuè sān rì* (八月三日), which would be written and read out as such, would tend to be spoken as *bāyuè sān hào* (which, in turn, could be written verbatim as 八月三号).

1.3.5 The celestial stems

Just as English sometimes makes use of letters rather than numbers to indicate a sequence of items, so Chinese sometimes makes use of a closed set of words with fixed order known as *shígān* 'the ten stems' or *tiāngān* 'the celestial stems' for counting purposes. The ten stems have an interesting history, which will be discussed in greater detail along with information on the Chinese calendar in a later unit. For now, they will be used in much the same way that, in English, Roman numerals or letters of the alphabet are used to mark subsections of a text, or turns in a dialogue. The first four or five of the ten are much more common than the others, simply because they occur early in the sequence. (Chinese people will be impressed if you can recite all ten!)

The ten celestial stems (*tiāngān*)

jiǎ	*yǐ*	*bǐng*	*dīng*	*wù*	*jǐ*	*gēng*	*xīn*	*rén*	*guǐ*
甲	乙	丙	丁	戊	己	庚	辛	任	癸
A	B	C	D	E	F	G	H	I	J

1.4 Stative verbs

The verb is the heart of the Chinese sentence. Young urban speakers of Chinese may slip material from English or other languages into the noun position in a sentence (*Wǒ yǒu* lab. 'I have a *lab.*'), and nouns with foreign origins, such as *jítā* 'guitar', have been incorporated into the language as a result of persistent contact with other cultures. Very rarely, however, does a foreign language influence the verb position in Chinese.

Some comparisons with English also reveal the centrality of the verb to the Chinese sentence scheme. In Chinese, where the context makes the participants clear, verbs do not need to be anchored with pronouns, as they do in English.

Jiǎ:	*Máng ma?*	'Are [you] busy?'
Yǐ:	*Hěn máng.*	'[Yes, I] am.'

In English, 'am' is not a possible response to the question 'Are you busy?' A pronoun is required, such as, 'I am.' However, in the English answer, the verb 'to be busy' does not need to be repeated: 'I am' rather than 'I am busy.' Chinese behaves oppositely from English, as our example shows. Pronouns are often *not* expressed when the context makes the reference clear. On the other hand, verbs tend to be *reiterated* in the answer. Moreover, in Chinese, there is no need to anticipate the verb with a confirmation ('yes') or denial ('no'): *Shūfu ma?/Hěn shūfu.* 'Are you comfortable?'/'Yes, I am.'

1.4.1 Types of verbs

As you encounter words in Chinese, you will find that it is useful to categorize them into groups and subgroups (traditional parts of speech and their subclasses), such as nouns (including subtypes such as countable and noncountable), verbs (including subtypes such as transitive and intransitive), pronouns (including personal and demonstrative), and adverbs (including those of manner and degree). Such categories capture useful generalizations about how words behave. An adverb, for example, will always appear before a verb (or other adverb).

It is also useful to be able to talk about the components of a sentence: subjects, predicates, adverbials, modifiers, etc. A general schema for the sentence *Hěn máng* would be simply a predicate consisting of an adverb (*hěn*) and a verb (*máng*). It is not necessary to be adept at using the linguistic nomenclature, but it is useful to be able to understand the notion of classes of words and positions within sentence structure so that generalizations can be noted.

For Chinese verbs, it will be useful to distinguish a number of classes. In this lesson, we will focus on two. One resembles adjectives in English and many other languages: *hǎo* 'be good', *máng* 'be busy', *è* 'be hungry'. As the English glosses show, these words do not require an additional form of the verb 'to be' ('are, am, is', etc.) when they are used as predicates in Chinese: *Lèi ma?/Hěn lèi.* 'Are [you] tired?' / '[I] am.' The difference is shown by translating the

Chinese words as 'be+tired', 'be+good', etc. Because such words convey states rather than actions, they are called 'stative verbs', abbreviated as SV. Strictly speaking, SVs should always be glossed as 'be+adjective' (when they function as predicates), but once the notion is familiar, we will often fall back on the more convenient practice of glossing them with English adjectives: *máng* 'busy'; *shūfu* 'comfortable'.

Another general class of verbs involves actions: *chī* 'to eat'; *xǐ* 'to wash'; *zǒu* 'to walk; leave'. These will simply be called action verbs, abbreviated V_{act}.

1.4.2 Questions and positive responses

You can begin by learning to ask questions with SVs and to give either positive or negative responses. Assuming that the context makes explicit (subject) pronouns unnecessary, then one way to ask 'yes/no' questions is to add the final question particle *ma* to the proposal.

Hǎo ma?	'Are [you] well?'
Máng ma?	'Is [she] busy?'
Lèi ma?	'Are [you] tired?'
È ma?	'Is [he] hungry?'
Kě ma?	'Are [you] thirsty?'
Jǐnzhāng ma?	'Are [they] nervous?'
Shūfu ma?	'Are [you] comfortable?'
Lěng ma?	'Are [you] cold?'
Rè ma?	'Is [it] hot?'
Gāo ma?	'Is [she] tall?'
Duì ma?	'Is [it] correct?'

NOTES

a. *Lèi* rhymes with 'say'; *duì* (and *wèi*) rhyme with 'way'.

b. *è* [uh]; cf. *rè* [ruh] and *hěn* [huhn]

c. *jǐnzhāng* [jeen-j!ahng]; *shūfu* [sh!oofoo]—! reminds you to raise the tip of your tongue toward the roof of your mouth.

Positive responses repeat the verb, usually with an adverb. The default adverb, when no other is chosen, is *hěn* 'very'. However, in contexts such as these, *hěn* does little more than support the positive orientation of the sentence, and so is best left untranslated. SVs such as *duì* 'correct', which do not permit gradients, do not occur with degree adverbs such as *hěn*.

Máng ma?	*Hěn máng.* '[Yes, I] am.'
Kě ma?	*Hěn kě.* '[Yes, I] am.' (Apply the tone rule!)
Gāo ma?	*Hěn gāo.* '[Yes, she] is.'
Duì ma?	*Duì.* '[Yes, it] is.'

Notice that, unlike English, where the typical positive answer indicates affirmation with 'yes' before going on to answer the question, Mandarin has only the direct answer.

1.4.3 Negative responses

Negative responses are usually formed with *bù* 'not the case'. Recall that the tone is conditioned by that of the following syllable.

Máng ma?	*Bù máng.* '[No, I]'m not.'
Kě ma?	*Bù kě.* '[No, I]'m not.'
Gāo ma?	*Bù gāo.* '[No, she]'s not.'
Duì ma?	*Bú duì.* '[No, it]'s not.'

As with positive answers, Chinese has no direct equivalent to 'no', but simply offers a negated verb.

A less abrupt negative (but, again, not used with *duì*) is formed with *bú* (with tone shift) plus *tài* 'too; very'.

bútài — less abrupt "no"

Hǎo ma?	*Bú tài hǎo.* '[No,] not very.'
Máng ma?	*Bú tài máng.* '[No,] not too.'
Lèi ma?	*Bú tài lèi.*
È ma?	*Bú tài è.*

NOTE

Negative questions with *ma*, such as *Nǐ bú lèi ma?* 'Aren't you tired?', will be dealt with in a later unit. While such questions are easy to form in Chinese, the responses follow patterns unfamiliar to speakers of English.

1.4.4 V-not-V questions

Another way to form 'yes/no' questions is to present the verb and its negative, as though offering both options. The negative, *bu,* in these constructions is often toneless in normal speech, for example: *hǎo bù hǎo* is usually pronounced *hǎo bu hǎo*, or even *hǎo bu hao.* While V-*ma* questions slightly presuppose an answer congruent with the question, that is, positive for positive questions, negative for negative questions, V-not-V questions are neutral. At this stage, you can regard the two as essentially equivalent.

Rè ma?	*Hěn rè.*
Rè bu rè?	*Hěn rè.*
Lěng ma?	*Bù lěng.*
Lěng bu lěng?	*Bú tài lěng.*

Other examples:

Duì bu duì?	*Duì.*
Hǎo bu hǎo?	*Hěn hǎo.* (Apply the tone rule!)
Máng bu máng?	*Bù máng.*
Lèi bu lèi?	*Hěn lèi.*
È bu è?	*Bú tài è.*
Kě bu kě?	*Hěn kě.* (Apply the tone rule!)
Lěng bu lěng?	*Hěn lěng.* (Apply the tone rule!)
Rè bu rè?	*Bú tài rè.*
Jǐn⟨zhāng⟩ bu jǐnzhāng?	*Bù jǐnzhāng.*
Shū⟨fu⟩ bu shūfu?	*Bù shūfu.*

NOTE

With two-syllable SVs, the second syllable of the first, positive part of V-not-V questions often gets elided, as indicated by ⟨ ⟩ in the last two examples.

1.4.5 Three degrees of response

You can respond to the two kinds of 'yes/no' questions positively, neutrally, or negatively. The typical neutral response makes use of the adverb *hái* (or, before other adverbs, *háishi*) 'still; yet': *hái hǎo* 'so-so; [I]'m okay (still okay)'.

Questions and responses involving SVs (*hǎo, máng, lèi, è, kě, lěng, rè, gāo, shūfu, jǐnzhāng, duì*)

YES/NO QUESTIONS		RESPONSES		
MA	V-NOT-V	+	O	–
Lèi ma?	*Lèi bu lèi?*	*Hěn lèi.*	*Hái hǎo.*	*Bú lèi.* *Bú tài lèi.*
Jǐnzhāng ma?	*Jǐn bu jǐnzhāng?*	*Hěn jǐnzhāng.*	*Hái hǎo.*	*Bù jǐnzhāng.* *Bú tài jǐnzhāng.*

1.5 Time and tense

1.5.1 Today, yesterday, and tomorrow

Speakers of English and other European languages take the verbal category of tense for granted: speaking of the past generally requires the past tense. For Chinese (as well as many other languages), this is not so. Time words, such as *jīntiān* 'today', *zuótiān* 'yesterday' (both of which share the root *tiān* 'sky; day'), or dates, may be added to simple sentences containing SVs without any change to the form of the verb, or any other addition to the sentence.

Zuótiān lěng ma? 'Was [it] cold yesterday?'	*⟨Zuótiān⟩ bú tài lěng.*
Zuótiān rè bu rè? 'Was [it] hot yesterday?'	*⟨Zuótiān⟩ hěn rè.*
Zuótiān hěn máng ma? 'Were [you] busy yesterday?'	*⟨Zuótiān⟩ hěn máng.*
Jīntiān lèi bu lèi? 'Are [you] tired today?'	*⟨Jīntiān⟩ hái hǎo.*
Èrshíbā hào lěng ma? 'Was it cold on the 28th?'	*⟨Èrshíbā hào⟩ hěn lěng.*

Note the differences in word order between the English and the Chinese in the previous examples.

Lěng ma? Hěn lěng.	*Was* it cold? It *was* cold.
Zuótiān lěng ma?	Was it cold *yesterday*?

The appearance of a time word such as *míngtiān* 'tomorrow' (or a date) can be sufficient to indicate that an event is certain to occur in the future—something that is also true of English.

Wǒ míngtiān hěn máng. 'I'm busy tomorrow.'

However, at times, Chinese does require some additional acknowledgment of the fact that, unlike the past and present, the future is uncertain. Thus, in talking about future weather, the word *huì* 'can; will; likely to' is, in many cases, added to the statement of futurity: *Míngtiān huì hěn lěng ma? / Míngtiān bú huì tài lěng.* 'Will [it] be cold tomorrow?' / 'No, tomorrow won't be that cold.' *Huì*, while it does correspond to the English 'will' in this example, is not actually as common as the latter. For the time being, you should be cautious about talking about future states.

1.5.2 *Le*: small word, big role

Rather than the static notion of past versus present (or, more accurately, past versus non-past), Chinese is more sensitive to a dynamic notion of 'phase' or 'change'. For example, if a speaker wishes to underscore the relevance of a *new situation*, he or she can signal it by the addition of the sentence-final particle *le*.

Zuótiān bù shūfu, jīntiān hǎo le. '[I] didn't feel well yesterday, but [I]'m better today.'

In this case, the English has no word that can be said to correspond to the Chinese *le*. In other contexts, however, the sense of *le* might be conveyed by the use of words such as 'become', 'now', or '[not] anymore'.

An explicit contrast between an earlier situation (*zuótiān*) and a current one (*jīntiān*) typically triggers this use of *le*. But it is also possible to state the situation before and after *without* underscoring the change with a final *le*.

Zuótiān hěn lěng, jīntiān hěn rè. 'Yesterday was cold; today's quite hot.'

Unlike tense in English, which appears under conditions that can be explicitly stated (including 'time before the time of speaking'), 'change of state' is more a question of interpretation. Sometimes the change will loom large in the mind of the speaker (or writer); sometimes it will not. Even notions such as 'change of state' or 'new situation' are only partial views of the overall function of *le* in Mandarin discourse. In §1.7.2 below, for example, you will see that, with V_{act}, *le* takes on a different complexion. Eventually, you will gain some insight into how the different functions of *le* relate, but at this point, it is best to proceed incrementally, distinguishing functions as they are encountered.

This is a good time to introduce some additional words that can signal prior and current time.

Earlier:

yǐqián	'formerly; before; used to [be]' ('take as before')
cóngqián	'before; in the past' ('from-before')
běnlái	'originally; at first' ('root-come')

Current:

xiànzài	'now; at present' ('current-now')
zuìjìn	'recently; lately' ('most-near')
mùqián	'at present; currently' ('eyes-before')

Examples:

Yǐqián hěn jǐnzhāng, xiànzài hǎo le.	'[I] was nervous before, but [I]'m okay now.'
Xiànzài bú è le!	'[I]'m not hungry anymore!'
Yǐqián bù shūfu.	'[It] used to be uncomfortable.'
Jīntiān rè le!	'[It]'s gotten hot today!'
Zuótiān hěn lèi, jīntiān hěn máng.	'Yesterday [I] was tired [and] today [I]'m busy!'
Běnlái hěn máng, xiànzài hǎo le.	'[I] was busy at first, but [I]'m okay now.'
Mùqián hěn lěng, hěn bù shūfu.	'[It]'s quite cold at present; [it] doesn't feel very nice.'

Běnlái hěn lěng, zuìjìn rè le.	'[It] used to be cold, but lately [it]'s hotter.'
Cóngqián wǒ bù shūfu, zuìjìn hái hǎo.	'I wasn't comfortable before, but recently [I]'ve been okay.'

NOTE

Observe that it is the *new situation* that is associated with *le*, not the original state. The presence of *le* generally cancels out the need for a supporting adverb, such as *hěn*.

1.6 Pronouns

As many of the examples above show, Chinese often manages to keep track of people (or things) relevant to a situation without the use of pronouns. However, pronouns are available where context alone might be insufficient, or where it might otherwise be more appropriate to use one. The set of personal pronouns in Chinese is relatively simple and regular. They are presented in the following table, with notes following.

	CHINESE PERSONAL PRONOUNS		ENGLISH PERSONAL PRONOUNS	
	SINGULAR	COLLECTIVE	SINGULAR	PLURAL
First person	*wǒ*	*wǒmen*	'I; me'	'we; us'
Second person	*nǐ, nín*	*nǐmen*	'you, you [polite]'	'you [all]'
Third person	*tā*	*tāmen*	'he, she, [it]; him, her'	'they; them'

NOTES tā refers to people - or animals treated like people

a. *Tā* tends to refer to people (or to animals being treated as if they were people) rather than to things. On those occasions when *tā* is used to refer to things, it is more common in object position, so it is more likely to occur in the Chinese equivalent of the sentence 'put it away' than in 'it's in the drawer'. Chinese sometimes uses a demonstrative (*zhè* 'this' or *nà* 'that') where English has 'it', but it often has no explicit correspondence at all.

b. The form *nínmen* ('you+POL-MEN') is rare, but does sometimes occur in letters or formal speech. The *-men* suffix (not usually toned, though sometimes cited in isolation with a rising tone) is most often found with pronouns, as shown. With nouns designating people, it can also occur as a 'collective': *lǎoshī* 'teacher', *lǎoshīmen* 'teachers'. Even in such cases, *-men* should not be thought of as a plural marker, for it never combines with numerals: *sān ge lǎoshī* 'three teachers'.

c. Mandarin speakers from Beijing and the northeast also make a distinction (found in many languages) between *wǒmen* 'we' (that collectively includes the speaker, addressee, and others) and *zán* or *zánmen* (pronounced 'zámen', as if without the first 'n') 'the two of us; we'. The latter includes the speaker and the person spoken to, but excludes others. For example: *Zánmen zǒu ba!* 'Let's leave [us, but not the others]', a phrase worth storing away as a prototype example for *zánmen*.

1.6.1 Names

Where the identification or status of a person requires more than a pronoun, Chinese has recourse to personal names or names and titles (cf. §1.9.1). Chinese students often refer to each other either by personal name (at least two syllables), or by surname (*xìng*) prefixed by a syllable such as *xiǎo* 'young'. Thus, *Liú Guózhèng* may be addressed by friends as *Guózhèng* or *xiǎo Liú*; *Lǐ Dān*, as *Lǐ Dān* (full name of two syllables) or *xiǎo Lǐ*.

1.6.2 The particle *ne* and the adverb *yě*

The particle *ne*, placed after subject nouns, has a number of uses. It may signal a pause for reflection, something particularly useful for learners.

Zuótiān ne, zuótiān hěn rè.	'Yesterday . . . yesterday was hot.'
Tā ne, tā hěn jǐnzhāng.	'[As for] him, he's quite anxious.'

The particle may also be used to signal follow-up questions. The response to a follow-up question often contains the adverb *yě* 'also; too; as well'. Recall that adverbs are placed before verbs (including SVs) or other adverbs (such as *bu*).

Jiǎ: *Jīntiān lèi ma?*
Yǐ: *Hěn lèi, nǐ ne?*
Jiǎ: *Wǒ yě hěn lèi.*

Jiǎ: *Jīntiān rè bu rè?*
Yǐ: *Hěn rè.*

Jiǎ:	*Zuótiān ne?*
Yǐ:	*Zuótiān yě hěn rè.*
Jiǎ:	*Nǐ jǐnzhāng ma?*
Yǐ:	*Bù jǐnzhāng le. Nǐ ne?*
Jiǎ:	*Wǒ háishi hěn jǐnzhāng.*
Yǐ:	*Ng.*
Jiǎ:	*Xiǎo Wáng zuótiān bù shūfu.*
Yǐ:	*Jīntiān ne?*
Jiǎ:	*Jīntiān hǎo le.*
Yǐ:	*Ng.*

NOTES

a. *Háishi* 'still'; cf. §1.7.1

b. Spoken Chinese makes use of a variety of interjections. *Ng* (with pronunciation ranging from a nasalized [uh] to [n]) is one of them. On the falling tone, it indicates agreement or, as in the above example, understanding.

Exercise 1

Write down and recite what you would say under the following circumstances; be prepared to shift roles.

1. Ask your classmate if he was busy yesterday.
2. Note that it's quite cold today.
3. Remark that it's gotten cold today.
4. Find out if young Li is nervous.
5. Respond that she is [nervous].
6. Say that you are too.
7. Say you didn't feel well yesterday.
8. Say that you're better now.
9. Tell your friend that you're not very hungry.

10. Tell her that you're okay today, but you were quite nervous before.
11. Ask your friend if she's thirsty [or not].
12. Find out if your classmate is comfortable.
13. Say that you're not hungry anymore.
14. Say that she was wrong.

1.7 Action verbs

While SVs attribute emotional or physical states to people or things, action verbs (V_{act}) involve actions, such as eating or going to class. V_{act} are often subdivided into 'transitive', those that generally presuppose an object ('read → a book'; 'eat → a meal'); and 'intransitive', those that do not presuppose an object ('walk'; 'kneel'). However, languages differ as to how this distinction is actually realized. In English, for example, when the verb 'to eat' means 'to eat a meal', there is the option of either not expressing an object ('When do we eat?'), or using the generic noun 'meal' ('We had a meal earlier').

Chinese adopts a different strategy. In comparable sentences, rather than not mentioning an object for lack of a particular one, Chinese provides a generic object like 'meal': *chīfàn* 'to eat; to have a meal'. The core meaning of *fàn* is 'cooked rice', but in conjunction with *chī*, it implies 'food' or 'meal'. When a particular kind of food is mentioned, *fàn* is replaced by specific words: *chī miàn* 'to eat noodles'; *chī báifàn* 'to eat [white] rice'; *chī bāozi* 'to eat dumplings'; *chī zǎodiǎn* 'to eat breakfast', etc.

Another case in which Chinese provides a generic object, where English has either an intransitive verb or one of a number of specific options, is *xǐzǎo* 'to bathe; to take a bath/shower'. *Xǐzǎo* is composed of the verb *xǐ* 'to wash' and *zǎo*, an element that no longer has independent status, but is treated like an object. While English uses an intransitive verb 'to bathe' or a specific object 'to take a bath', Chinese provides a generic object, *zǎo*. When a specific object is needed, it substitutes for *zǎo*: *xǐ yīfu* 'to wash clothes'; *xǐ liǎn* 'to wash one's face'; *xǐ shǒu* 'to wash one's hands'.

The following table gives verbs and verb + objects for events that tend to happen in the course of a day. (Polite inquiries about bathing are appropriate in tropical or sub-tropical climates.)

VERB	OBJECT	V-O
zǒu 'to leave'		
qǐlái 'to get up; to rise'		
shuì 'to sleep'	*jiào* (bound form)	*shuìjiào* 'to go to bed; to sleep'
chī 'to eat'	*fàn* 'cooked rice'	*chīfàn* 'to eat; to have a [proper] meal'
xǐ 'to wash'	*zǎo* (bound form)	*xǐzǎo* 'to bathe; to take a bath,' etc.
kàn 'to look at'	*bào* 'newspaper'	*kànbào* 'to read the paper'
shàng 'to ascend' }	*kè* 'class'	*shàngkè* 'to teach a class; to attend class'
xià 'to descend' }		*xiàkè* 'to finish class; to get out of class'
shàng 'to ascend' }	*bān* 'job; shift'	*shàngbān* 'to go to work; to start work'
xià 'to descend' }		*xiàbān* 'to get out of work'

1.7.1 Negative statements

With V_{act}, the plain negative with *bu* usually indicates intention.

Wǒ bù zǒu.	'I'm not leaving.'
Tāmen bù xǐzǎo.	'They're not going to bathe.'
Tā bù chī le.	'He won't eat anymore.'

Such declarations, while possible, are in fact more likely to be cast in some less abrupt form, using verbs such as *yào* 'to want' or *xiǎng* 'to feel like; to think'. We will get to such verbs quite soon, but at this stage, rather than talking about intentions, we will focus on whether events have happened or not. In such cases, the negation is formed with the negative of the verb *yǒu* 'to have; to exist'. This is *méiyǒu*, or simply *méi*. (*Yǒu* is the one verb in Mandarin whose negative is not formed with *bù*—the one *irregular* verb, you could say.)

Méi chīfàn.	'[We] didn't eat; [we] haven't eaten.'
Méiyǒu xǐzǎo.	'[I] didn't bathe; [I] haven't bathed.'
Méi shàngbān.	'[She] didn't go to work; [she] hasn't started work.'

Since the action verbs introduced in this lesson involve events that can be expected to take place regularly over the course of the day, the adverb *hái* (or *háishi* before other adverbs) 'still; yet' is common in negative answers. *Hái* ⟨*shi*⟩ is frequently accompanied by the sentence-final particle *ne*, which generally conveys a tone of immediacy or suspense (as well as being associated with follow-up questions, cf. §1.6.2).

Hái méi chīfàn ne.	'[We] haven't eaten yet.'
Hái méiyǒu xǐzǎo ne.	'[I] haven't bathed yet.'
Hái méi shàngbān.	'[She] hasn't started work yet.'

1.7.2 V_{act} with *le*

V_{act} may also appear with *le*. As noted in §1.5.2, *le* with SVs signals a change of state, or a newly relevant state: *jīntiān hǎo le*. With V_{act}, the function of *le* is more diffuse, or at least it seems so from a learner's perspective. *Le* with V_{act}, much as it does with SVs, may signal a newly relevant situation or phase. But with V_{act}, the initiation or conclusion of the action may be of relevance.

Initiation:

Zǒu le.	'[They]'re off.'
Chīfàn le.	'[They]'ve started [eating].'
Shàngkè le.	'Class is starting.'

Conclusion:

Zǒu le.	'[They]'ve gone; [they] left.'
Chīfàn le.	'[We]'ve eaten; [we] ate.'
Shàngkè le.	'[They]'ve gone to class; [they] went to class.'

'Conclusion' may seem like another way of saying 'past tense', but there are reasons for avoiding any identification of *le* with [past] tense. You have already seen that, with SVs, the past situation is not that which is marked with *le*, but the current one: *Zuótiān bù shūfu, jīntiān hǎo le*. You will also see many other cases where past tense in English does not correspond to the presence of *le* in Chinese. More to the point: injecting the notion of past tense into our description of *le* suggests a static function quite at odds with that other, well-established dynamic function of *le*, to signal a particular relevance of an event to the current discourse—the story line that is being advanced.

For the time being, then, note that *le* has two faces: it signals the current relevancy of a new state or situation (in this case, *le* can appear with the negative *bù*).

Lěng le.	'[It]'s gotten cold.'
Bù lěng le.	'[It]'s not cold anymore.'
Bù chī le.	'[They]'re not eating anymore.'

The particle *le* can also signal the current relevance of a completed event (in which case it is negated by *méi* ⟨*yǒu*⟩).

Shàngkè le.	'Class is beginning; [they]'ve gone to class.'
Hái méi⟨*yǒu*⟩ *shàngkè ne.*	'[They] haven't gone to class yet.'

Confusion about the several senses of *le* with V_{act} can often be resolved by the addition of an adverb, such as *yǐjīng* 'already'.

Tāmen yǐjīng zǒu le.	'They've already left.'
Wǒ yǐjīng chīfàn le.	'I've already eaten.'
Yǐjīng xiàbān le.	'[He]'s already quit [for the day].'

1.7.3 Questions

Actions can be questioned with the question particle *ma*.

Chīfàn le ma?	'Have [you] eaten [a meal]?'
Xǐzǎo le ma?	'Have [you] bathed?'
Shàngbān le ma?	'Has [she] started work?'

Actions can also be questioned with the V-not-V pattern, with the negative option reduced to *méiyǒu* (or just *méi*).

Chīfàn le méi⟨yǒu⟩?
Xǐzǎo le méi⟨yǒu⟩?
Shàngbān le méi⟨yǒu⟩?

1.7.4 Summary of *le* patterns

POSITIVE	NEGATIVE
Rè le. 'It's gotten warm.'	*Bú rè le.* 'It's not warm anymore.'
Chī le. '[We]'ve started eating.'	*Wǒ bù chī le.* 'I'm not eating anymore.'
⟨Yǐjīng⟩ zǒu le. '[He]'s ⟨already⟩ left.'	*⟨Hái⟩ méi⟨yǒu⟩ zǒu ⟨ne⟩.* '[She] hasn't left ⟨yet⟩.'
Tāmen ⟨yǐjīng⟩ chīfàn le. 'They've ⟨already⟩ eaten.'	*Tāmen hái méi⟨yǒu⟩ chīfàn ⟨ne⟩.* 'They haven't eaten ⟨yet⟩.'

1.7.5 Mini-conversations

Sections 1.1–1.7 present a considerable amount of information. The best way to internalize it is to practice short dialogues built around questions. Here are some examples. (The near synonyms *kěshi* and *dànshi*, used in the following two conversations, are both comparable to English 'but'.)

DIALOGUE A

Jiǎ:	*Xǐzǎo le ma?*	'Have [you] bathed?'
Yǐ:	*Xǐ le, kěshì hái méi chīfàn.*	'I have, but I haven't eaten yet.'
Jiǎ:	*È ma?* But	'Hungry?'
Yǐ:	*Hěn è, nǐ ne?*	'Sure am; and you?'
Jiǎ:	*O, wǒ . . . wǒ yǐjīng chī le.*	'Oh, me . . . I've already eaten.'
Yǐ:	*Xiǎo Bì ne?* already	'And young Bi?'
Jiǎ:	*Yǐjīng zǒu le, shàngbān le.*	'[She]'s gone, [she]'s at work.'
Yǐ:	*O, shàngbān le!* work	'Oh, [she]'s gone to work!'

DIALOGUE B

Jiǎ:	*Jīntiān hěn rè.*	'It's hot today.'
Yǐ:	*Ng, hěn rè. Nǐ chīfàn le ma?*	'Yeah, sure is. Have you eaten?'
Jiǎ:	*Hái méi, wǒ bú è.*	'Not yet, I'm not hungry.'
Yǐ:	*Jǐnzhāng ma?*	'Anxious?'
Jiǎ:	*Xiànzài hǎo le—dànshì yǐqián hěn jǐnzhāng!*	'[I]'m fine now—but I was before!'
Yǐ:	*Chén Bó yǐjīng zǒu le ma?*	'Has Chen Bo already left?'
Jiǎ:	*Yǐjīng zǒu le, shàngkè qu le.*	'Yes, he has, he's gone to class.'

NOTE

Shàngkè qu le, with a toneless *qù* 'go' indicating motion away, is more idiomatic than just *shàngkè le.*

1.8 Conventional greetings

1.8.1 The addition of *guò* (untoned)

Questions about eating are often used 'phatically', to be sociable rather than to seek actual information. There are a number of variants on the basic *Chīfàn le ma* that may serve this purpose. A particularly common variation used with verbs that describe regularly occurring events (such as having meals and going to work) involves the addition of a post-verbal *guò* (usually untoned), whose root meaning is 'to pass by, over, through'. *Guò* can occur in both the question and in responses (positive and negative), but it can also be dropped from the responses, as demonstrated below.

Chīguo ⟨fàn⟩ le ma? {
Chī⟨guo⟩ le.
Hái méi ⟨chī⟨guo⟩⟩ ne.

1.8.2 Reductions

In context, utterances are likely to be reduced along the following lines: *méiyǒu* → *méi*; *chīfàn* → *chī* (however, *xǐzǎo* does not reduce to *xǐ*, since *xǐ* alone means 'to wash' rather than 'to bathe'). Thus, the following are all possible—though the more elliptical questions are likely to produce more elliptical answers. (The English glosses for the responses only suggest the differences. Notice that, in English, forms of 'have' can substitute for 'eat' or 'eat one's meal'.)

Chīfàn le ma?	*Chīfàn le.* 'I've eaten my meal.'
Chīguo fàn le ma?	*Chīguo fàn le.* 'I've had my meal.'
Chī le ma?	*Chī le.* 'I have.'
Chīguo le ma?	*Chīguo le.* 'I've had it.'
Chīfàn le méiyǒu?	*Hái méi chī fàn ne.* 'I haven't eaten my meal yet.'
Chīguo fàn le méiyǒu?	*Hái méi chìguo ne.* 'I haven't had my meal yet.'
Chīfàn le méi?	*Hái méi chī ne.* 'I haven't eaten yet.'
Chīguo fàn le méi?	*Hái méi chìguo ne.* 'I haven't had it yet.'
Chī le méi?	*Hái méi ne.* 'Not yet.' *Méiyǒu.* 'No.' *Méi.* 'No.'

Typical expanded and reduced forms of questions and answers

ENGLISH MEANING	EXPANDED FORM	REDUCED FORM
Done?	*Chīfàn le ma?*	*Chī le ma?*
Done?	*Chīguo fàn le ma?*	*Chīguo le ma?*
Done [or not]?	*Chīfàn le méiyǒu?*	*Chī le méi?*
Done [or not]?	*Chīguo fàn le méiyǒu?*	*Chīguo le méi?*
Done.	*Chīfàn le.*	*Chī le.*
Done.	*Chīguo fàn le.*	*Chī le.*
Not done.	*Méiyǒu chīfàn.*	*Méi chī.*

Exercise 2

Ask and answer as indicated.

1. Read the paper? / Not yet.
2. Started work? / Yes, I have.
3. They've gone? / No, not yet.
4. Was it cold? / No, not very.
5. Have [they] finished work yet? / Yes, [they] have.
6. [We]'re not nervous anymore. / [You] were yesterday.
7. [I]'ve eaten. / Are [you] still hungry?
8. Bathed? / Yes, it was nice [comfortable].
9. Are they out of class yet? / Not yet.
10. Thirsty? / Not anymore.
11. Hungry? / Not anymore, I've eaten.
12. Has class started? / Not yet.
13. Nervous? / I am now!
14. Young Wang's in bed? / Yes, he's already in bed.
15. Are they up? / Yes, but they haven't eaten yet.

What would you say? (Use pronouns where necessary.)

1. Ask your friend if she's eaten yet. (three different ways)
2. Announce that she's already left work [for the day].
3. Explain that it was cold yesterday, but that it's gotten hot today.
4. Announce that she hasn't gone to class yet.
5. Explain that they've bathed, but they haven't eaten.
6. Explain that you were all unwell yesterday, but today you're fine.
7. Explain that the first's already gone, but the second and third still haven't.
8. Explain that it was warm yesterday, and that it is today as well.

1.9 Greeting and taking leave

1.9.1 Names and titles

Because even perfunctory greetings tend to involve a name and title, you need to have some rudimentary information about forms of address before being introduced to the language of greeting and leave taking. Below are five common Chinese surnames, followed by a title which means, literally, 'teacher', and the SV *hǎo*, which in this context serves as a simple acknowledgment. *Lǎoshī*, which has no exact correspondence in English, can be applied to both males and females, as well as to all ranks of teachers.

Zhāng lǎoshī hǎo.	'Hello, Professor Zhang.'
Wáng lǎoshī hǎo.	
Lǐ lǎoshī hǎo.	[with tone shift]
Zhào lǎoshī hǎo.	
Chén lǎoshī hǎo.	

1.9.2 Hello

Using specialized greetings such as 'hi' or *bonjour* to acknowledge or confirm the value of a relationship on every encounter is not a universal feature of cultures. The practice seems to have crept into Chinese relatively recently. Whereas in the past, people might have acknowledged your presence by asking where you were going or if you had eaten (that is, if they said anything at all to a stranger), urban Chinese today often make use of phrases like *nǐ hǎo* in ways similar to English 'hi' or 'hello'. Most people would probably regard *nǐ hǎo* as the prototypical neutral greeting, but other options are listed below.

Nǐ hǎo!		'Hi! Hello!'
Nín hǎo!	[deferential]	'How do you do?'
Hei!	[exclamation]	'Hey! Hi!'
Hǎo!		'Hi! Hello!'
Hǎo ma?		'You well?'
Nǐ hǎo a!	[informal]	'How're you doing?'
Dàjiā hǎo.	[to a group]	'Hello, everyone.' ('big-family well')

A version of 'good morning', based on the verb *zǎo* ('be+early'), has been in common usage in Taiwan for some time and is now becoming more common on the Mainland as well.

Zǎo!	'Morning!' ('be+early')
Zǎo ān.	'Good morning.' ('early peace')
Nǐ zǎo.	
Nín zǎo.	

Expressions comparable to English 'good afternoon' or 'good evening' are also starting to be used in modern China. Thus, *xiàwǔ* 'afternoon' and *wǎnshàng* 'evening' are used in the expressions *xiàwǔ hǎo* 'good afternoon' and *wǎnshàng hǎo* 'good evening'. *Wǎn ān* 'good night' ('late peace'), used as a sign-off at the end of the day, has a longer pedigree and is now commonly used by staff in larger hotels, for example.

In general, greetings of the sort listed above are used more sparingly than their English counterparts. Colleagues or classmates passing each other, for example, are less likely to use a formulaic greeting such as *nǐ hǎo*, though relative cultural novelties such as fast food restaurants and toll booths may encourage broader use. In general, though, a greeting to someone of higher status should be preceded by a name, or a name and title (as in §1.9.1).

1.9.3 Good-bye

Many cultures have conventional phrases for taking leave. Often, blessings serve this purpose (e.g., 'bye', from 'good-bye', supposedly derived from the phrase 'God be with you'). Below are several Chinese variations of 'good-bye', beginning with the standard, *zàijiàn* ('again-see').

Zàijiàn.	[neutral]	'Good-bye.' ('again-see')
Yìhuǐr ~ yíhuìr jiàn.	[friendly]	'See [you] soon.' ('awhile see')
Míngtiān jiàn.	[neutral]	'See [you] tomorrow.' ('tomorrow see')
Huíjiàn.	[informal]	'See [you] later; bye.' ('return-see')

Huítóu jiàn.	[friendly]	'See [you] shortly.' ('return-head see')
Màn zǒu.	[friendly]	'Take it easy.' ('slowly walk')

NOTES

a. The addition of final *r* to a written pinyin syllable represents a complex series of phonetic effects that will be considered more fully later. In the case of *yìhuǐr* ~ *yíhuìr*, the final *r* affects the quality of the preceding vowel, so that it is pronounced '*yìhuěr* ~ *yíhuèr*' rather than '*yìhuǐr* ~ *yíhuìr*'. The usual prescription applies: listen to your teacher or to the audio.

b. The alternate pronunciation *yíhuìr* may be more common in dialects found in southern China.

c. Students and other urban youth of all kinds often end a series of farewells with the English-influenced expression *baibai*.

d. As with greetings, when saying good-bye to an older person or a person of rank, it is normal to mention name and title first, e.g., *Wèi lǎoshī, zàijiàn.*

1.9.4 Bon voyage

This is a good time to familiarize yourself with a few phrases that are used to wish people well when they leave on a journey, or to greet them when they arrive. The most common expression for *bon voyage* is:

Yílù-píng'ān. ('Whole-journey peaceful.')

This expression applies to almost any journey, whether by air, ship, or bus. *Yílù-shùnfēng* ('whole-journey favorable-wind') has much the same meaning, but it is not used for journeys by air. Chinese people are generally superstitious about the effect of words, and many would usually deem it ill-advised to mention the word *fēng* 'wind' before a flight. Notice that both expressions contain four syllables, a favored configuration in the Chinese lexicon.

In greeting someone returning from a long journey, instead of the question 'How was the flight/journey/voyage?', Chinese people generally utter a variant of an expression that reflects the traditional discomforts of travel.

⟨Lù shàng⟩ xīnkǔ ba? 'Tough journey, huh?' ('⟨road on⟩ bitter BA')

An analysis of these expressions is provided above, but at this stage, they should simply be memorized (by repetition) and kept in storage for greeting visitors or seeing people off.

Yílù-píng'ān!

1.9.5 Smoothing the transitions

A. PRIOR TO ASKING A QUESTION In more formal situations, questions are often prefaced with the expression *qǐngwèn* ('request-ask'), idiomatically equivalent to 'may I ask' or 'excuse me'. *Qǐngwèn* may also be preceded by a name and title.

Qǐngwèn, nǐ chīfàn le ma?	'Excuse me, have you eaten?'
Zhào lǎoshī, qǐngwèn, nín è bu è?	'Professor Zhao, mind if I ask: are you hungry?'

Qǐng 'request; invite' also occurs in the common phrase *qǐng zuò* 'have a seat' ('invite sit') and the expression *qǐng jìn* 'won't you come in' ('invite enter').

B. PRIOR TO LEAVING In the normal course of events, a simple good-bye is often too abrupt for closing a conversation. One way to smooth the transition is to announce that you have to leave before you say good-bye. Here are four ways to accomplish this, all involving the verb *zǒu* 'to leave; to go'. These expressions are complicated to analyze; some notes are provided below, but otherwise, they should be internalized as units.

Hǎo, nà wǒ zǒu le.	'Okay, I'm off then.' ('okay, in+that+case, I leave LE')
Hei, wǒ gāi zǒu le.	'Say, I should be off.' ('hey, I should leave LE')
Hǎo, nà jiù zhè yàng ba, zǒu le.	'Okay then, that's it, [I]'m off!' ('okay, in+that+case, then this-way BA, leave LE')
Bù zǎo le, wǒ gāi zǒu le.	'[It]'s late, I'd better be off.' ('not be+early LE, I should leave LE')

NOTES

a. *gāi* / *yīnggāi* 'should; must'; *nà* 'in that case; well; then'; *jiù* 'then'; *ba* (particle associated with suggestions); *le* ([here] signals a new situation)

b. Taking leave obviously involves a broad range of situations, including seeing someone off on a journey (which, in China, is an extremely important event). The four options included in this section are acceptable for closing an informal conversation.

1.10 Tones

1.10.1 Tone combos (the first six)

Tones are easier to perceive and assimilate in pairs. Four tones form sixteen possible combinations of two, but because of the previously discussed restriction on combinations of low tones (3 + 3 = 2 + 3), only fifteen pairs are distinctive. The six sets below are mostly comprised of words you have already encountered. They should be memorized so that they can be recited by number (typically as part of warm-up activities at the beginning of class): *dì-yī*: *lǎoshī*, *jǐnzhāng*; *dì-èr*: *xǐzǎo*, *hěn hǎo*, etc.

(1)	*lǎoshī*	(2)	*xǐzǎo*	(3)	*zàijiàn*
	jǐnzhāng		*hěn hǎo*		*kànbào*
(4)	*bú rè*	(5)	*hěn máng*	(6)	*bù gāo*
	bú lèi		*hěn nán*		*shàngbān*

NOTE

hěn nán 'difficult'

Tones in combination tend to accommodate each other to some degree, though not to the point of shifting to another tone. In the above sets, the most salient adjustment is probably that of 4 + 4 (*zàijiàn*), where the tone of the first syllable is not as steeply falling as that of the last. The first of the two is sometimes referred to as the 'modified fourth tone'.

1.10.2 Tone lock

In these first weeks of learning Chinese, you may find yourself unable to pronounce a tone, even unable to mimic your teacher—a situation that might be called 'tone lock'. Tone lock can occur for many reasons, but a common one for beginners is that you will often be tentative, and tentativeness in English is accompanied by a rising contour. This is fine if you are trying to say a name, such as *Wáng*, with rising tone. However, it won't work if you want to say *Wèi*, with a falling tone. Other frustrating conditions may occur: you may hear rising as falling, and falling as rising (flip-flop); your falling tone may refuse to fall ('fear of falling'), your level tone may refuse not to fall ('fear of flying'). Regardless of the symptoms, the best cure is to take a figurative step back and make use of your tone concepts: level is 'sung out', rising is 'doubtful', low is 'low' (despite the contoured symbol), and falling is 'final' or 'confident'.

1.10.3 The first 'rule of three'

If you find that the tonal cues, 'sung out', 'doubt', 'low', and 'final' do not serve you well, there are others that have been used in the past. Walter C. Hillier, in his 1953 *English-Chinese Dictionary* (London: Routledge and Kegan Paul Ltd.), proposed 'languid assertion' for the first tone, 'startled surprise' for the second, 'affectionate remonstrance' for the third, and 'abuse' for the fourth. Whatever the label, the important point is to follow the rule of three: develop a concept for each tone, know what tone each word has, and monitor yourself when you speak.

1. Conceptualize the tones ('sung out', etc.).
2. Learn tones with each word (e.g., *hǎo* has a low tone).
3. Monitor your speech.

Exercise 3

Read out the following sets (recall your tone concepts).

1.	*dá*	*dǎ*	*dā*	*dà*	5. *bù*	*bǔ*	*bú*	*bù*
2.	*kǒu*	*kòu*	*kōu*	*kòu*	6. *jīn*	*jín*	*jǐn*	*jìn*
3.	*pán*	*pàn*	*pān*	*pán*	7. *guō*	*guǒ*	*guó*	*guò*
4.	*wèi*	*wěi*	*wéi*	*wēi*	8. *hǎi*	*hái*	*hāi*	*hài*

Tone shifts: Read the following sequences aloud, and write the missing tones that indicate tone shifts.

1.	*bu máng*	*bu è*	7.	*yi tào*	*yi tiáo*
2.	*bu lèi*	*bu shì*	8.	*yi kuài*	*dì-yi*
3.	*bu jǐnzhāng*	*bu kě*	9.	*yi wèi*	*yi zhāng*
4.	*bu hǎo*	*bu cuò*	10.	*yi běn*	*yi kè*
5.	*hen hǎo*	*hen máng*	11.	*hen zǎo*	*hen wǎn*
6.	*hen lèi*	*hen nán*	12.	*hái hǎo*	*hen kě*

NOTE

hěn wǎn 'late'

Learners often feel the tones that are the most difficult to distinguish are the rising and the low. Here is a discrimination exercise that focuses on these two. In the disyllabic words below, the final syllables all contain either a rising tone or a low tone. Have a Chinese speaker read each of them to you twice (from the characters); then see if you can correctly identify the missing tone in the pinyin versions of the words.

1. 英勇	2. 天才	3. 当年	4. 大米	5. 英语
6. 橡皮	7. 书法	8. 黑板	9. 加强	10. 冰球
11. 号码	12. 重叠	13. 开展	14. 开头	15. 多余
16. 孙女	17. 天然	18. 跳舞	19. 构成	20. 思想

1. *yīngyong*	2. *tiāncai*	3. *dāngnian*	4. *dàmi*	5. *Yīngyu*
6. *xiàngpi*	7. *shūfa*	8. *hēiban*	9. *jiāqiang*	10. *bīngqiu*
11. *hàoma*	12. *chóngdie*	13. *kāizhan*	14. *kāitou*	15. *duōyu*
16. *sūnnü*	17. *tiānran*	18. *tiàowu*	19. *gòucheng*	20. *sīxiang*

Practice reading out these syllables, all of which contain pinyin *o* as the main vowel.

duō	*dōu*	*fó*	*kuò*	*còu*	*zhōu*	*zhuō*	*zǒu*	*zuò*
bó	*guó*	*ruò*	*shòu*	*gòu*	*shuō*	*suǒ*	*pó*	*yǒu*

Read out the following syllables that contain the *ui* or *iu* rhymes.

guì	*shuí*	*ruì*	*chuī*	*zuì*	*duì*	*(wèi)*
liú	*niú*	*xiū*	*qiú*	*diū*	*jiǔ*	*(yǒu)*
guǐ/jiǔ		*liù/duì*		*cuì/qiú*		*liú/shuí*

1.11 Summary

MAIN PATTERNS

Nǐ lèi ma?	+	*Hěn lèi.*
	o	*Hái hǎo.*
	–	*Bú tài lèi.*

Nǐ máng bu máng?	+	*Hěn máng.*
	o	*Hái hǎo.*
	–	*Bú tài máng.*
Nǐ chīfàn le ma?	+	*Chī le.*
Nǐ chīfàn le méiyou?	–	*Hái méi ne.*
Nǐ chīguo fàn le ma?	+	*Chī⟨guo⟩ le.*
Nà, jiù zhè yàng ba.		*Hǎo, jiù zhè yàng!*
Zhāng lǎoshī hǎo.		*Wáng Jié, zàijiàn.*

CONVERSATIONAL SCENARIOS

GREETINGS →	DEVELOPMENT (QUESTIONS, ASSUMPTIONS, COMMENTS) →	LEAVING
Nǐ hǎo.	*máng / lèi / rè / jǐnzhāng . . .*	*Hǎo, zàijiàn, míngtiān jiàn.*
Wèi lǎoshī hǎo.	*zuótiān / jīntiān / xiànzài . . .*	*Chén lǎoshī, zàijiàn.*
Zǎo.	*xǐzǎo / chīfàn / shàngkè / qǐlái . . .* *hěn / yǐjīng / hái méi / yě / bú tài* *Nǐ ne? / Xiǎo Zhōu ne?*	*Míngtiān jiàn.* *Màn zǒu.*

1.12 Rhymes and rhythms

Rote learning, very highly prized in traditional and even modern China, and highly valued at other times in our own past, is no longer generally considered a beneficial educational method in the West. Outside class, however, people still learn parts for plays and often recall song lyrics, advertising jingles, and slogans without much self-conscious effort. We will take advantage of these predilections by providing some suitable Chinese rhymed and rhythmic material at the end of each of the core units. This material ranges from doggerel to poetry, from jingles to nursery rhymes, and from satirical verse to songs and poems. It has been selected for ease of recall, and eventually it will form a useful repertoire that can be tapped for information about pronunciation, vocabulary, and grammatical patterns. It also provides something to recite when you are asked to 'say something in Chinese' or when you are in China and are asked to sing or perform for an audience. Closer to home, you may be asked to atone for being late to class by reciting some short piece in front of your classmates.

The first rhyme—a nursery rhyme—tells the story of a young entrepreneur and his struggle to set up a business. The word-for-word gloss provided will guide you toward the meaning.

Dà dùzi

Dà dùzi,	('big tummy')
kāi pùzi,	('open shop')
méi běnqián,	('not+have, root-money')
dàng kùzi.	('pawn trousers')

The second—also a nursery rhyme—has a shifting rhythm but a more mundane subject matter: the tadpole, denizen of village ponds and urban drainage systems.

Xiǎo kēdǒu

Xiǎo kēdǒu,	('small tadpole')
shuǐ lǐ yóu,	('water in swim')
xìxì de wěiba,	('tiny DE tail')
dàdà de tóu.	('big DE head')

Unit 2

Yù bù zhuó, bù chéng qì.
'Jade isn't useful until it's carved.'
('jade not carve, not become implement')
—A saying, in classical style, that conveys the importance of discipline and perseverance in achieving success. The root meaning of *qì* (器) is 'vessel', that is, something that has a practical use. Its extended meanings include 'utensils' and 'talent'.

In this unit, you will continue to add to your repertoire of linguistic material needed for the first major dialogue, 'At the Airport', which is presented toward the end of this unit. New material includes more adverbs and stative verbs, a set of nouns with associated words called measures (that make nouns countable), demonstratives ('this' and 'that'), and various modifiers (e.g., 'your', 'today's'). Identity ('is'), existence ('there is'), and location ('is at') are also introduced so that it will be possible to talk about people and places. Of course, pronunciation (including tones) and pinyin continue to receive considerable attention throughout this unit.

Contents

2.1 Pronunciation

2.1.1 Articulatory settings

As previously discussed, contrast the following sets of Chinese and English words to properly set the articulatory positions of your mouth and tongue for Chinese speech.

(1)	*lèi*	lay	(2)	*lái*	lie
	méi	May		*shāi*	shy
	zhèi	Jay		*mài*	my
	bēi	bay		*pái*	pie
	péi	pay		*bái*	buy
	fēi	Fay			
(3)	*chū*	chew	(4)	*dízi*	deeds
	shū	shoo		*tóuzi*	toads
	shén	shun		*měicì*	mates
	chāo	chow		*xízi*	seeds
	zhōu	Joe		*qícì*	cheats
	shòu	show		*bǐcǐ*	beets (or beats)

2.1.2 The *e*, *i*, and *u* rhymes

Review the table of initials in section 0.3.1, paying special attention to rows 3, 4, and 5. Recall that in the pinyin system, the letters *i* and *u* have two discrete pronunciations depending on the preceding initial: *qi* versus *chi*, *qu* versus *chu*. In the following exercise (definitions are provided to satisfy curiosity), we add a third variable represented by *e*: *chi* (pronounced with the mouth and lips relatively close together) versus *che* (pronounced with the mouth open wider). Like the previous pronunciation exercises, this activity should be performed daily until it is familiar and comfortable.

qìchē	'automobile'	*cèshì*	'to survey'	*qíqū*	'rugged'
shèjì	'design'	*shùcí*	'numeral'	*zhīchū*	'expenditure'
rèqì	'steam'	*xǔkě*	'to permit'	*xūxīn*	'reserved'
chūqù	'go out'	*záshí*	'omnivorous'	*jūjī*	'to snipe at'
cèjì	'sidelights'	*zérèn*	'duty'	*zìchí*	'self-restraint'
cíqì	'porcelain'	*júcù*	'cramped'	*zhīzhū*	'spider'

2.2 Adverbs

In the first unit, you were introduced to a number of words classified as adverbs: *hěn*, *bù*, *yě*, *hái/háishi*, and *yǐjīng*. It is difficult to characterize the general function of adverbs beyond rather abstract notions like 'degree', 'amount', or 'manner', but they can be defined as words that are positioned before, and semantically linked to, a verb or other adverb.

2.2.1 *Tài* with *le*

Tài, used only in negative sentences in the first unit (*bú tài lèi*), is also commonly used in positive sentences, where it is frequently found with a final *le*: *Tài hǎo le.* 'Great!'; *Tài jǐnzhāng le.* '[I]'m real anxious!'; *Tài nán le.* '[It]'s too difficult!' *Le*, in this context, conveys a sense of excess (cf. English 'exceedingly busy') and, as such, can be regarded as a special case of the notion of a *new situation* introduced in Unit 1. Notice that negative sentences with *tài* often suggest moderation rather than excess, so they do not attract final *le* in the same way: *bú tài hǎo*.

2.2.2 Other adverbs

Below are examples of other common adverbs: *dōu* 'all', *gèng* 'even more', *bǐjiào* (colloquially pronounced *bǐjiǎo*) 'rather; quite; fairly', and *zǒngshi* 'always'.

dōu 'all'

Tāmen dōu hěn è.	'[They]'re all hungry.'
Dōu duì.	'[They]'re all correct.'
Dōu méi chī ne.	'None [of them] has eaten [yet].'

gèng 'even more'

Xiànzài hěn lěng, kěshì yǐqián gèng lěng.	'[It]'s cold now, but [it] was even colder before.'

bǐjiào 'quite'

Wǒ jīntiān bǐjiào máng.	'I'm fairly busy today.'
Zuótiān bǐjiào rè.	'Yesterday was fairly warm.'

zǒngshi 'always'

Xuéshēng zǒngshì hěn máng, hěn lèi; dànshì lǎoshī gèng máng, gèng lèi.	'Students are always busy and tired, but teachers are even more so.'

2.2.3 Intensifying or backing off

A. *FĒICHÁNG* 'VERY; ESPECIALLY; UNUSUALLY' Rather than answer a 'yes/no' question about a state of being with a neutral positive response (*Nǐ lèi ma? / Hěn lèi.*), you may want to intensify your answer. *Fēicháng,* an adverb whose literal meaning is 'not-often', is one of a number of options.

Jīntiān fēicháng rè!	'[It]'s really hot today!'
Fēicháng hǎo!	'[It]'s unusually good!'

B. ADVS *TǏNG* AND *MÁN* ~ *MǍN* AS INTENSIFIERS Some mention needs to be made here of two adverbs that are very common in certain phrases of colloquial speech. One is *tǐng,* whose core meaning is actually 'straight; erect', but which, as an ADV, carries the force of English 'very' or 'really'. The other is *mán,* which has a low-tone variant of *mǎn.* The pronunciation variants probably reflect a blend of two different roots that have come to have the same meaning in adverbial position: *mán* (蛮), with a core meaning of 'fierce', and *mǎn,* with a core meaning of 'full'. In adverbial position, both mean 'very; entirely; utterly'. The convergence in meaning was probably abetted by the fact that both are pronounced *mán* when the low-tone rule applies in common phrases such as *mán hǎo*, obscuring any nuances of difference.

Exclamations with *mán* or *tǐng* often occur with a final *de* (sometimes referred to as 'situational *de*', to distinguish it from particles also pronounced *de* but with quite different functions.)

Tǐng hǎo de.	'Perfect; great!'
Mán hǎo de.	'[That]'s great!'

Here are some common collocations, roughly glossed to convey the tone of the Chinese; *mán* is given in the second (rising) tone, but you may find that some speakers say *mǎn* in contexts where the third (low) tone is permitted.

Tǐng bú cuò de.	'Not bad!'
Tǐng shūfu.	'[It]'s quite comfortable.'
Tǐng yǒu yìsi de!	'How interesting!'
Mán hǎochī de!	'[It]'s delicious!'
Mán piàoliang.	'[She]'s real attractive.'
Mán bú cuò de!	'[That]'s pretty darn good!'
Mán bú zàihū.	'[He] doesn't give a darn.'

C. *-JÍLE* 'EXTREMELY' Another option to intensify meaning is the suffix *-jíle,* which directly follows SVs (and is therefore not an adverb). This suffix is a compound of *jí* 'the extreme point; axis' (cf. *Běijí* 'North Pole') plus *le*. It is quite productive and can follow almost any SV to mean 'extremely SV'.

Hǎojíle!	'Excellent!'
Tiānqì rèjíle!	'The weather's extremely hot!'

D. *YǑU ⟨YÌ⟩DIǍNR* 'KIND OF; A BIT' Rather than intensifying your answer, you may want to back off and answer 'kind of; rather; a bit'. An appropriate construction for this purpose is *yǒu ⟨yì⟩diǎnr* + SV ('have a bit-SV'), a phrase that appears in the adverbial slot and can be interpreted as a complex adverbial. The *yì* of *⟨yì⟩diǎnr* is often elided (hence the ⟨ ⟩). Taiwan and some southern Mandarin regions, where the final *r* is not usual, might say *yǒu yìdiǎn* + SV, without the *-r*. Like the English 'a bit', this construction conveys a sort of inadequacy; thus, *tā yǒu yìdiǎnr gāo* 'he's a bit tall' suggests that his height is problematical. Note the presence of *yǒu* 'have' in the Chinese, which has no direct correspondence in the English equivalent.

Wǒ jīntiān yǒu ⟨yì⟩diǎnr máng.	'I'm kind of busy today.'
Jīntiān yǒu ⟨yì⟩diǎnr rè.	'[It]'s rather hot today.'
Wǒmen yǒu ⟨yì⟩diǎnr è.	'We're a bit hungry.'

Summary of adverbs (and other expressions of degree)

ADV	ENGLISH EQUIVALENT	EXAMPLE WITH SV	EXAMPLE WITH V_{ACT}
bù	'not'	*bú lèi*	*bú shàngbān*
yě	'too; also'	*yě hěn lèi*	*yě chī le*
hái ~	'still'	*hái hǎo*	*hái méi zǒu ne*
háishi		*háishi hěn lèi*	
dōu	'all'	*dōu hěn gāo*	*dōu shuìjiào le*
yǐjīng	'already'		*yǐjīng zǒu le*
tài	'very; too'	*tài máng le; bú tài máng*	
hěn	'very'	*hěn lèi*	
tǐng, mǎn ~ mán	'very; really'	*mán bú cuò*	
gèng	'even more'	*gèng rè*	
bǐjiào ~ bǐjiǎo	'rather; relatively'	*bǐjiào lěng*	
zǒngshì	'always'	*zǒngshì hěn máng*	
fēicháng	'extremely; very'	*fēicháng lěng*	

SPECIAL CONSTRUCTION	ENGLISH EQUIVALENT	EXAMPLE WITH SV	EXAMPLE WITH V_{ACT}
jíle	'very; extremely'	*hǎojíle*	
yǒu ⟨yì⟩diǎnr	'kind of; rather; a bit'	*yǒu diǎnr guì*	

2.2.4 Conjunctions

Conjunctions are words that combine linguistic units in either an equal partnership, as in the case of English 'and' or 'but' (coordinating conjunctions), or in a skewed partnership, as in the case of English 'if' and 'because' (subordinating conjunctions). In Chinese, there is no precisely comparable word to English 'and' that connects sentences; this function is often served by the adverb *yě*.

Zuótiān wǒ bù shūfu, jīntiān yě bú tài hǎo.	'I wasn't very well yesterday, and [I]'m not too well today, either.'
Zuótiān hěn rè, jīntiān yě hěn rè.	'[It] was hot yesterday, and [it]'s hot today, too.'

As noted earlier, conjunctions *kěshi* and *dànshì* (the latter more common outside of northern China) correspond to English 'but' or 'however'. A third word, *búguò*, can also be mentioned here. Though its range of meaning is broader than that of the other two, its meaning and usage have considerable overlap with them, and it can also be translated as 'but; however'.

	Tāmen hái méi chīfàn, kěshì dōu bú è.	'They haven't eaten, but [they] aren't hungry.'
	Wǒ chīfàn le, dànshì hái méi xǐzǎo.	'I've eaten, but [I] haven't bathed yet.'
	Tā zǒu le, búguò jīntiān bú shàngbān.	'She's left, but [she]'s not going to work today.'
Cf.:	*Tā zǒu le, búguò jīntiān méi shàngbān.*	'She's gone, but [she] didn't go to work today.'

2.3 More SVs

Here are some additional SVs that can be used in the patterns introduced in the first two units.

Of people:

yán	'strict'
lìhai	'formidable; tough'

Of tasks:

nán	'difficult'
róngyì	'easy'

Of things:

hǎochī	'nice [to eat]'
hǎotīng	'nice [sounding]'
guì	'expensive'

Of people or things:

qīngchu	'clear'
hǎokàn	'nice [looking]'
piàoliang	'pretty'
qíguài	'strange; odd; surprising'

Of situations:

xíng	'be okay; be satisfactory; [it]'ll do'

Several of these SVs can be applied to people, such as *lǎoshī* 'teachers' and *xuéshēng* 'students'; others, as noted, are more likely to apply to things, such as *Zhōngwén* 'Chinese language', *Rìwén* 'Japanese', or *dōngxi* '[physical] things'.

2.3.1 Questions with *zěnmeyàng* 'how [is it]'

The question word *zěnmeyàng* (pronounced [zěmyàng], without the first 'n') is used to ask questions corresponding to 'how is X?' *Zěnmeyàng* is also used as an informal greeting, rather like English 'how's it going?'

Jīntiān zěnmeyàng?	'How is [it] today?'
Hěn rè.	'[It]'s hot.'
Rìwén zěnmeyàng?	'How's Japanese [class]?'
Hěn nán! Lǎoshī hěn yán.	'[It]'s difficult! The teacher's strict.'

2.3.2 Short dialogues with *zěnmeyàng*

Lǎoshī zěnmeyàng?	'How's the teacher?'
Hěn lìhài, tā fēicháng yán.	'[She]'s formidable; she's really strict.'

Tā zěnmeyàng?	'How is he?'
Hěn lèi, shuìjiào le.	'[He]'s tired, [he]'s gone to bed.'
Tāmen zěnmeyàng?	'How are they doing?'
Bù shūfu, méi shàngkè.	'[They]'re not well, [they] weren't in class.'
Zhōngwén zěnmeyàng?	'How's Chinese [class]?'
Bù nán yě bù róngyì.	'[It]'s not difficult, nor is [it] easy.'
Zěnmeyàng? Hǎochī ma?	'How is [it]? Good?'
Hái kěyǐ.	'[It]'s okay.'
Guì bu guì?	'Is [it] expensive?'
Bú tài guì, hái xíng.	'Not too—[it]'s reasonable.'
Tiānqì zěnmeyàng?	'How's the weather?'
Zuótiān fēicháng lěng, kěshì jīntiān hǎo le.	'Yesterday was very cold, but today's okay.'

2.3.3 *Juéde* 'to feel; to think'

Zěnmeyàng may be combined with, or may elicit, the verb *juéde* 'to feel; to think' to form a more specific question about internal states.

Xiànzài nǐ juéde zěnmeyàng?	'How do you feel now?'
Wǒ juéde bù shūfu.	'I'm not feeling well.'
Wǒ hěn jǐnzhāng.	'I'm nervous.'
Wǒ juéde hěn lèi.	'I feel quite tired.'
Hái xíng.	'Okay.'

2.3.4 *Zěnmeyàng* as a greeting

Responses to *zěnmeyàng* as an informal greeting include the following:

Zěnmeyàng?

Hái hǎo. '[I]'m fine.'
Hái xíng. '[I]'m okay.' ('still alright')
Hái kěyǐ. 'Passable.' ('still be+possible')
Bú cuò. 'Not bad.' ('not be+erroneous')
Mǎmǎ-hūhū. 'So-so.'
Lǎo yàngzi. 'The usual.' ('old way')

NOTES

a. *Kěyǐ* is a modal verb meaning 'may; be acceptable'.

b. *Cuò* is an SV meaning 'to be wrong; to be mistaken'.

c. *Mǎmǎ-hūhū* is a complex SV that is formed by repetition of the parts of the SV *mǎhu* 'to be casual; careless'.

Exercise 1

Perform a dialogue between the two students, Máo Dàwéi and Lǐ Lìsān, along the following lines.

Máo Dàwéi:	Hi, *Lìsān*!
Lǐ Lìsān:	Hello, *Dàwéi*. How're you feeling today?
Máo Dàwéi:	Tired. How about you?
Lǐ Lìsān:	I'm a bit tired too—I still haven't eaten. How about you—hungry?
Máo Dàwéi:	No, I already ate.
Lǐ Lìsān:	Was it good?
Máo Dàwéi:	It was okay. How're your teachers? Strict?
Lǐ Lìsān:	Very! They're formidable! Chinese is tough!
Máo Dàwéi:	But Japanese is even harder.
Lǐ Lìsān:	They're both hard! . . . Well, I must be off.
Máo Dàwéi:	Okay, see you later.
Lǐ Lìsān:	Okay, bye, take it easy.

2.4 Nouns and modification

This section begins with some additions to your repertoire of inanimate nouns. You will have a chance to practice using these words in context later in this unit (as well as in subsequent units).

yàoshi	'keys'
yǎnjìng	'glasses' ('eye-mirror')
shū	'books'
shūbāo	'backpack' ('book-bundle')
hùzhào	'passport'
xíngli	'luggage'
xié⟨zi⟩	'shoes'
màozi	'cap; hat'
yīfu	'clothes'
⟨yǔ⟩sǎn	'umbrella' ('rain umbrella')
bǐ	'pen'
qiānbǐ	'pencil' ('lead-pen')
bǐjìběn	'notebook' ('pen-note-book')
shǒujī	'cell phone' ('hand-machine')
xìnyòngkǎ	'credit card' ('credit-card')
qiánbāo	'wallet' ('money-pack')
dōngxi	'[physical] things'
tiānqì	'weather' ('sky-air')
bào⟨zhi⟩	'newspaper' ('report-paper')
zìdiǎn	'dictionary' ('character-records')
zìxíngchē	'bicycle' ('self-go-vehicle')
dānchē	'bicycle' ('unit-vehicle')
chēzi	'small vehicle; car'
qìchē	'car; automobile'

2.4.1 Measure words

A discussion of nouns leads to the subject of 'measure words'. In English, one can divide nouns into those that can be directly counted (river → three rivers) and those that are usually contained or otherwise delimited by 'measures' before they are counted (water → three buckets of water).

Directly counted:	book → two books
Measured:	wine → ten bottles of wine

It is true that the examples in the second column can be counted directly if one is counting varieties of wines, soups, or teas: e.g., 'Name three wines', which means 'name three types of wine'. Usually, however, such nouns need to be measured out. In Chinese (as well as in many other regional languages, including Thai, Vietnamese, and Burmese), all nouns are considered non-countable and are measured through the use of another noun-like word. (The vocabulary in these examples is only for illustration.)

shū	→	*sì běn shū*	*jiǔ*	→	*shí píng jiǔ*
'book'	→	('four spine book') 'four books'	'wine'	→	('ten bottle wine') 'ten bottles of wine'
yú	→	*yì tiáo yú*	*tāng*	→	*sì wǎn tāng*
'fish'	→	('one length fish') 'a fish'	'soup'	→	('four bowl soup') 'four bowls of soup'
bǐ	→	*sān zhī bǐ*	*chá*	→	*sān bēi chá*
'pens'	→	('three stub pen') 'three pens'	'tea'	→	('three cup tea') 'three cups of tea'

Often, a distinction is made between 'measures' and 'classifiers'. The phrases on the right all involve measures, which serve to portion out a substance that is otherwise not naturally bound; all the examples are, in fact, liquids. Chinese often uses measures where English would use them, as the examples show. Classifiers, on the other hand, are rare in English, though a good example might be 'block' in the phrase 'a block of apartments'. Classifiers serve to classify nouns according to various physical dimensions. For example, *tiáo* is a classifier typically used for sinuous things, such as roads, rivers, and fish.

yì tiáo lù	'a road'	*wǔ tiáo yú*	'five fish'
sān tiáo hé	'three rivers'	*sì tiáo tuǐ*	'four legs'

Rather than maintain the sometimes subtle distinction between classifiers and measures, both will be simply referred to as 'measure words' or 'measures', abbreviated as M. Before you encounter measure words in sentences, it will be useful to practice them in phrases.

We begin with the default M, *gè* (often toneless), that appears with many personal nouns, including *rén* 'person' and *xuéshēng* 'student'. Note that, when combined with an M, the number 'two' (but not a number ending in 2, such as 12 or 22) is expressed as *liǎng* ('pair of') rather than *èr*. Also, when measure words are used in context, nouns may sometimes be omitted, as in the example *liǎng ge* 'two [of them]'.

Recall that the tone of *yī* 'one' is level when counting or clearly designating the numeral one. However, pronunciation shifts to either a falling or rising tone when *yī* is used in conjunction with a following M. Similarly, the basic tone of *gè* is falling (hence *yí gè*), so even though *gè* is often toneless in common usage, it still elicits the shift before 'losing' its tone: *yí ge*. The following sets should be recited regularly until familiar.

yí ge rén 'one person'	*liǎng ge rén* 'two people'	*sān ge rén* 'three people'	*wǔ ge rén* 'five people'	*shí ge rén* 'ten people'
yí ge xuéshēng 'one student'		*liǎng ge xuéshēng* 'two students'		*sān ge xuéshēng* 'three students'
yí ge 'one of them'	*liǎng ge* 'two of them'	*sān ge* 'three of them'	*sì ge* 'four of them'	*wǔ ge* 'five of them'
dì-yī ge 'the first [one]'	*dì-èr ge* 'the second'	*dì-sān ge* 'the third'	*dì-sì ge* 'the fourth'	*dì-wǔ ge* 'the fifth'

Notice that the ordinal numbers are treated as unitary words, so *yī* in *dì-yī* does not shift tone before (intrinsically falling-toned) *ge*; nor does the *èr* of *dì-èr* shift to *liǎng* before *ge*.

Another particularly useful M is *kuài* 'lump; chunk; piece', which is often used in the context of money (*qián*) and as a replacement for *yuán*. The *yuán* is the basic unit of Chinese currency known as *Rénmínbì* (RMB) ('people's currency'), and both *yuán* and *kuài* are generally translated as 'dollar'.

yí kuài qián	*liǎng kuài qián*	*sān kuài qián*	*wǔ kuài qián*	*shí kuài qián*
yí kuài	*liǎng kuài*	*sān kuài*	*wǔ kuài*	*shí kuài*

2.4.2 Possessive pronouns

In English, possessive pronouns have a relatively complicated relationship to the basic personal pronouns (I, my, mine; she, her, hers), but in Chinese, possessive pronouns are formed in a perfectly regular fashion by the addition of the possessive marker *de*: *wǒ* 'I' → *wǒ de* 'my; mine'. The full system is illustrated below.

wǒ de	*wǒmen de*	'my; mine'	'our; ours'
nǐ de	*nǐmen de*	'your; yours'	'your; yours' (plural)
tā de	*tāmen de*	'his; her; hers'	'their; theirs'

These may combine with nouns, as follows.

wǒ de zìdiǎn	'my dictionary'
tā de hùzhào	'her passport'
wǒmen de xíngli	'our luggage'
wǒ de xié⟨zi⟩	'my shoes'
nǐ de dōngxi	'your things'

The possessive marker *de* may also link noun modifiers to other nouns, as follows.

xuéshēng de shūbāo	'students' bags'
lǎoshī de shū	'teachers' books'
Zhāng lǎoshī de yǎnjìng	'Professor Zhang's glasses'
zuótiān de tiānqì	'yesterday's weather'
jīntiān de bào⟨zhǐ⟩	'today's newspaper'

NOTE

Since the plain noun in Chinese can refer to one item or many, phrases such as *xuéshēng de shūbāo* could also correspond to English '[the] students' bag', '[a] student's bag', etc. Rather than give all options for every example, we will, in general, choose one to stand for all.

2.4.3 Demonstrative pronouns

Demonstrative pronouns ('this' and 'that') and words that indicate location ('here' and 'there') are shown in the chart below. Examples in context will follow later in the unit.

PROXIMATE	DISTAL	QUESTION
zhè ~ *zhèi* 'this'	*nà* ~ *nèi* 'that'	*nǎ* ~ *něi* 'which'
zhèr ~ *zhèlǐ* 'here'	*nàr* ~ *nàlǐ* 'there'	*nǎr* ~ *nǎlǐ* 'where'

NOTES

a. The forms *zhèi*, *nèi*, and *něi* tend to be found in combination with a subsequent M. Therefore, you might encounter *zhè* or *zhèi ge* 'this [one]' and *nà* or *nèi ge* 'that [one]'.

b. In northern Chinese, where both forms of the location words occur, the *r* forms are more colloquial, while the *lǐ* forms are more formal. Speakers of most other Mandarin dialects tend to eschew the *r* suffix and either merge the location words with the demonstrative pronouns (pronouncing *zhèr* as *zhè*, *nàr* as *nà*, and *nǎr* as *nǎ*) or use *zhèlǐ*, *nàlǐ*, and *nǎlǐ* (pronounced *nálǐ*). Note that the distal forms differ from the question forms only in tone: *nà*/*nǎ*; *nèi*/*něi*.

c. When used before a pause, *nà* is often translated in English as 'well; so; then; in that case'.

Nà, wǒmen zǒu ba.	'Well, let's go then.' ('so we leave BA')
Nà, nǐ de xíngli ne?	'So how about your luggage then?' ('so your luggage NE')

Exercise 2

Provide Chinese equivalents for the following phrases and sentences.

my wallet	three teachers	their clothes
her glasses	two people	the newspaper for July 4th
his things	four students	Professor Zhang's passport
yesterday's paper	two dollars	her bicycle

2.5 Identity

Statements such as 'Today's Monday', 'I'm Oliver', or 'She's an engineer' involve identity or category. In English, the primary verb that serves to identify or categorize is 'to be' (whose forms include 'is', 'are', 'was', etc.). In Chinese, the same relationship is sometimes expressed by simple juxtaposition, with no explicit linking verb. Dates, for example, can simply be juxtaposed to days, as follows.

Jīntiān jiǔyuè bā hào.	'Today's the 8th of September.'
Zuótiān qī hào.	'Yesterday was the 7th.'
Míngtiān jiǔ hào.	'Tomorrow's the 9th.'

However, the addition of an adverb, such as *bù*, requires a verb. In such cases, *shì* (usually untoned) must be expressed.

Jīntiān bú shi bā hào, shi jiǔ hào.	'It's not the 8th today, it's the 9th.'

An untoned *shì* can also be present in positive sentences.

Jīntiān ⟨shi⟩ jiǔyuè shí hào.	'Today's September 10th.'
Míngtiān ⟨shi⟩ Zhōngqiū Jié.	'Tomorrow's the Mid-Autumn Festival.'

Naming and other kinds of identification sometimes omit *shì* in fast speech, but it can usually be heard as a toneless whisper (similar to 'sh').

Tā shi Wáng Shuò, wǒ de lǎoshī.	'He's Wang Shuo, my teacher.'
Wǒmen shi xuésheng, tā shi lǎoshī.	'We're students, he's a teacher.'
Zhè shi jīntiān de bào.	'This is today's paper.'
Shi nǐ de yàoshi ma?	'Are [these] your keys?'
Bú shi wǒ de sǎn, shi tā de.	'[That]'s not my umbrella, [it]'s his.'
Tāmen dōu shi xuésheng.	'They're all students.'

Don't forget that *shì* is not required with SVs, as demonstrated in the following example.

Xuésheng zǒngshì hěn lèi, duì bu duì?	'The students are always tired, right?'

2.5.1 Questions

Now we can introduce the question words *shéi* (often pronounced *shuí* outside the northern Mandarin area) 'who, whom' and *shénme* 'what' (which, like *zěnme*, is pronounced [shéme], without the 'n'). Whereas, in English, question words generally appear at the head of the sentence, in Chinese they remain 'in place', as comparison of the Chinese and English equivalents listed below will show.

Tā shi shéi ~ shuí?	'Who's that?'
Tā shi wǒ de lǎoshī.	'That's my teacher.'
Nà shi shénme?	'What's that?'
Nà shi wǒ de hùzhào.	'That's my passport.'
⟨Shi⟩ shéi ~ shuí de yàoshi?	'Whose keys are [these]?'
⟨Shi⟩ wǒ de—xièxie.	'[They]'re mine—thanks.'
⟨Shi⟩ shéi de xíngli?	'Whose luggage [is this]?'
⟨Shi⟩ wǒmen de.	'[It]'s ours.'
Zhè shi shéi de?	'Whose is this?'
Shi wǒ de.	'[It]'s mine.'
Shéi shi dì-yī ge?	'Who is the first?'
Tā shi dì-yī ge.	'He's the first.'
Dì-èr ge ne?	'And the second?'
Tā shi dì-èr ge.	'She's the second.'

2.5.2 Hedging your answer

Frequently, when asked about identity, the answer is less than certain, so you may want to hedge your reply with a word like *hǎoxiàng* 'seems like' ('good-resemble'). The following short interchanges involve trying to guess the contents of a series of wrapped packages (or things in a bag) by feeling them.

Dì-yī gè shi shénme?	'What's the first?'
Dì-yī gè hǎoxiàng . . . shi yàoshi.	'The first seems like . . . keys.'
Zhè shi shénme?	'What's this?'
Hǎoxiàng . . . shi shū.	'Seems like a . . . book.'
Nà, zhè shi shénme?	'Well, what's this?'
Hǎoxiàng shi xiézi.	'Seems like shoes.'

2.5.3 Naming

Naming is also a form of identification. In fact, if you were to go around the classroom naming all your *tóngxué* 'classmates', you could do so with the verb *shì*, as follows.

Nà shi Máo Xiān'ān.	'That's Mao Xian'an.'
Nà shi Léi Hànbó.	'That's Lei Hanbo.'
Nà shi Lǐ Dān.	'That's Li Dan.'
Nà hǎoxiàng shi Luó Zhìchéng.	'Looks like that's Luo Zhicheng.'
Nǐ shì bu shi Luó Zhìchéng?	'Are you Luo Zhicheng?'
Tā shi Léi Fēng!	'He's Lei Feng!'

Exercise 3

Provide Chinese for the following question and answer exchanges.

Q: Is it the 29th today?
A: No, it's the 30th.

Q: Is this your umbrella?
A: No, that's Professor Zhang's.

Q: Who's first?
A: Seems like Wang Jie is first and Liu Guozheng is second.

Q: Are you all students?
A: Yes, we're all Professor Wei's students.

Q: Is that your bike?
A: No, it's Lei Feng's.

2.6 Names and titles

People's names are not always introduced by *shì*. In some contexts, more specialized verbs must be used, such as *xìng* 'to be surnamed' (which also functions as a noun meaning 'surname') and *jiào* 'to be named; to be called'. Before we illustrate the use of such verbs, we should add to the brief remarks that were made earlier about names and titles.

2.6.1 Names

Some common English names are directly transliterated into Chinese, for example, *Yuēhàn Shǐmìsī* 'John Smith'. Note that the English word order of given name before surname is retained. Students of Chinese are usually given Chinese names, typically based on their surnames (if there are enough syllables) or full names, and these conform to the Chinese form of two or three syllables. In such cases, Chinese custom, with surname before given name, is followed. (In all but the first example below, English surnames are reduced to single syllables in the Chinese, as shown by the bold type.)

Wèi Délì	'Paul **Wheatley**'
Táng *Lìlì*	'Lily **Tom**lin'
Máo *Xiān'ān*	'Anne **Mau**boussin'
Léi *Hànbó*	'Robert **Le**onhardt'
Lǐ *Dān*	'David **Li**ppmann'

Such names are practically indistinguishable from actual Chinese names, such as:

Cuī Lín	*Kāng Yǒuwéi*	*Yuán Shào*	*Zhèng Chénggōng*
Zhèng Hé	*Máo Qílíng*	*Wáng Lì*	*Bái Sùzhēn*

2.6.2 *Xìng*

Chinese names consist of a surname, or *xìng*, in initial position, followed by a given name or *míngzi* ('name-characters'). *Xìng* are usually—but not always—single syllables. As a verb, *xìng* is almost always used when asking for, or responding with, someone's surname.

Tā xìng shénme?	'What's her surname?'
Tā xìng Huáng.	'She's surnamed Huang.'
Xìng Wáng?	'Wang?'
Bú shi xìng Wáng, tā xìng Huáng.	'No, not Wang, she's named Huang.'

When addressing someone directly, the honorific expression *guìxìng* ('worthy-surname') (cf. *guì* 'expensive') can be used with or without a pronoun to ask that person's surname.

⟨*Nín*⟩ *guìxìng?*	'May [I] ask your surname?'
Wǒ xìng Wèi.	'I'm surnamed Wei.'

2.6.3 *Jiào*

In much of the English-speaking world, where informality tends to be considered a virtue, the shift from surname to given name can proceed very quickly. However, in Chinese professional settings, address is likely to persist as *xìng* plus title for a longer period of time. Under normal levels of politeness, then, you would question someone using *xìng*, not *míngzi*. However, in the appropriate context, it is possible to seek a third party's full name. In such cases, the verb *jiào* 'to be called' is used. *Jiào* can take either the person or the word *míngzi* as its subject; and it takes as its object at least two syllables of a name, never a single syllable (for example, *jiào Qílíng* 'named Qiling'). Below are some options, first for *Lǐ Xiāngjūn*, a three-syllable name, then for *Zhèng Hé*, with only two.

Tā jiào shénme míngzi? — *Tā jiào Lǐ Xiāngjūn.*
Tā de míngzi jiào shénme? — *Tā ⟨de míngzi⟩ jiào ⟨Lǐ⟩ Xiāngjūn.*

Tā jiào shénme míngzi? — *Tā jiào Zhèng Hé.*
Tā de míngzi jiào shénme? — *Tā ⟨de míngzi⟩ jiào Zhèng Hé.*

2.6.4 Asking and giving a name

Typically, in face-to-face interaction, one person asks politely for a surname and, in many cases, the response will be a surname only. However, when the individuals involved have a more or less matched status, the surname is often followed by the full name. The following is a good model for the foreign student to copy.

Q: *⟨Nín⟩ guìxìng?*
A: (Bái Sùzhēn) *Wǒ xìng Bái, jiào Bái Sùzhēn.*
A: (Xǔ Xiān) *Wǒ xìng Xǔ, jiào Xǔ Xiān.*

2.6.5 Titles

You are already familiar with the title *lǎoshī* 'teacher'. Here is a short selection of other titles to add to your list. All these titles may follow a *xìng*, though some can be used alone under certain conditions. *Xiānshēng* 'mister' ('first-born') is the generic title for adult males. In Taiwan and overseas Chinese communities, married women are often addressed with the husband's surname plus *tàitai* (etymologically related to the adverb *tài*). *Tàitài* is less commonly used in mainland China, though. *Xiǎojie* 'Miss; Ms' ('small older-sister') used to be a common title for unmarried women up to a certain age, but its use has declined for various reasons. Indeed, on the mainland, if no professional title (such as *lǎoshī*) is available, the most common options for addressing women are to use the full name and/or *míngzi*, or to simply avoid any form of address. *Shīfu* 'craftsman', often translated as 'master', has shifted in its usage in the last few decades, but it has been traditionally used to address male blue-collar workers. Finally, *jīnglǐ* 'manager' is a professional title for males or females, of the sort that might appear on a business card. Note the order of surname before title in the following examples.

SURNAME	GIVEN NAME	TITLE	
Wèi	⟨*Bóyáng*⟩	*lǎoshī*	'Professor'
Shí	⟨*Jìlóng*⟩	*xiānsheng*	'Mr.'
Wáng	⟨*Guóbǎo*⟩	*shīfu*	'master'
Zhōu	⟨*Lǐ*⟩	*jīnglǐ*	'manager'

2.6.6 *Shì* with names

As noted above, while surnames alone can only be introduced with the verb *xìng*, full names can be introduced with *shì* as well as *jiào*. In fact, unlike the other two verbs, *shì* can also introduce name and title. The *shì* option identifies one of a known group and, as such, is often appropriate to a classroom setting.

Tā shi Lǐ Guānghuī; tā shi Wáng Shuò; tā shi Táng Bīn; wǒ shi Wèi lǎoshī.

Dì-yī ge shi Xiāo Míngzuǒ, dì-èr ge shi Lǐ Míng, dì-sān ge shi Xiè Jìng.

Nǐ shì bu shi Zhāng xiānsheng?	'Are you Mr. Zhang?'
Zhè shi Dù shīfu.	'This is Master Du.'
Wǒ shi Wáng lǎoshī; tāmen dōu shi wǒ de xuéshēng.	'I'm Professor Wang and these are my students.'
Chén jīnglǐ shi Běijīng rén.	'Manager Chen is from Beijing.'

Exercise 4

Write, and say aloud, how people with the various names listed below might respond to the question ⟨*Nín*⟩ *guì xìng?* Assume informal settings.

1. *Liáng Xìnghàn*
2. *Lín Fēng*
3. *Wáng Yǔyàn*
4. *Xiè Huìmín*

5. *Lǐ Bó*
6. *Sītú Guāng*
7. *Lǐ Yǒngyàn*
8. *Sīmǎ Xuān*
9. *Zhōu Yǔ*
10. *Bái Guóróng*
11. *Ōuyáng Pèishān*

Paraphrase the following in Chinese, being careful to follow customary Chinese word order.

1. I'm a teacher.
2. Who's she?
3. Her surname's *Sòng*, her full name's *Sòng Měilíng.*
4. Hi, my name's *Lǐ Dān.*
5. Who's he? / He's my teacher.
6. That's *Zhōu Lì.*
7. His surname's *Chén*; full name, *Chén Bó.*
8. And him? / His surname's *Xǔ*; full name, *Xǔ Xiān.*
9. This is master *Wèi.*
10. Her name's Smith (*Shǐmìsī*).

2.7 Location and existence

In English, *location* is expressed with the same verb as *identity* (or *category*): the verb 'to be' (conjugated 'is', 'am', 'are', etc.). Chinese, however, uses entirely different verbs. Identity is signaled by *shì* and location is signaled by *zài* 'to be at'.

Identity:	*Tā shi xuésheng.*	'She's a student.'
Location:	*Tā zài Běijīng.*	'She's in Beijing.'

2.7.1 Some Chinese place names

The Chinese name for China is *Zhōngguó* ('middle kingdom'), a name which dates back to the time when it was designated as the ruling principality among many that owed it fealty. The Chinese are then called *Zhōngguórén* ('Chinese-people').

Administrative units of the People's Republic include provinces (省 *shěng*), prefectures (地 *dì*), counties (县 *xiàn*), townships (乡 *xiāng*), and villages (村 *cūn*). Of these, the county is the unit with the longest historical continuity, dating back some 2,500 years. In modern Mainland China, the highest administrative level–the provincial level–contains 33 divisions: 22 provinces (with Taiwan considered a 23rd), five autonomous regions, four municipalities (cities ruled by the central government—*Běijīng, Shànghǎi, Tiānjīn*, and *Chóngqìng*), and two special autonomous districts (*Xiāng Gǎng* 'Hong Kong' and *Àomén* 'Macau').

Taiwan, which administers the island of *Táiwān* and the Pescadores Islands (*Pēnghú*), as well as thirteen small, scattered offshore islands, has a slightly different administrative structure. It has two centrally administered cities: the capital *Táiběi* 'Taipei' and the southwestern city of *Gāoxióng* 'Kaohsiung'.

The chart below lists important Chinese cities. They can be located in terms of their province (using the verb *zài*) or in terms of their proximity to another place (using the *lí* pattern that follows in §2.7.2).

QUADRANT	CITY	'IS IN'	PROVINCE
NW	*Xīníng*	*zài*	*Qīnghǎi* ⟨*shěng*⟩
NW	*Wūlǔmùqí*		*Xīnjiāng*
N	*Hūhéhàotè*		**Nèiménggǔ*
NE	*Shěnyáng*		*Liáoníng*
NE	*Chángchūn*		*Jílín*
NE	*Hā'ěrbīn*		*Hēilóngjiāng*
W	*Lāsà*		**Xīzàng*
C	*Xī'ān*		*Shǎnxī*
E	*Nánjīng*		*Jiāngsū*
E	*Guǎngzhōu*		*Guǎngdōng*
SW	*Guìlín*		**Guǎngxī*
SW	*Chéngdū*		*Sìchuān*
SW	*Kūnmíng*		*Yúnnán*

NOTES

a. The asterisks (*) before *Nèiménggǔ* 'Inner Mongolia', *Xīzàng* 'Tibet', and *Guǎngxī* indicate that they are autonomous regions—*zìzhìqū*—not *shěng*.

b. *Shěnyáng* was formerly called by its Manchu name, Mukden.

c. The names of two provinces are distinguished by only tone: *Shānxī* ('mountains-west'), which is west of the province of *Shāndōng* ('mountains-east'), and *Shǎnxī* ('pass-west'), which is often Romanized as 'Shaanxi' to distinguish it from *Shānxī*. *Shǎnxī* is located even farther west than *Shānxī*.

d. *Guǎngzhōu* was, and often still is, called Canton in English, a name that actually derives from the name of the province, *Guǎngdōng*.

2.7.2 Proximity

Relative proximity of one place to another can be expressed by a construction that involves the word *lí* '[away] from', and the SVs *jìn* 'to be close' and *yuǎn* 'to be far'. Notice the difference in word order from English.

PLACE 1	*LÍ* + PLACE 2	PROXIMITY
Běijīng Beijing	*lí Guǎngzhōu* ('from Canton')	*hěn yuǎn / hěn jìn.* ('very far/close.')

USAGE

Tiānjīn lí Běijīng bǐjiào jìn.	'Tiānjīn is relatively close to Beijīng.'
Xī'ān zài Shǎnxī, lí Běijīng bǐjiào yuǎn.	'Xi'an is in Shaanxi, quite far from Beijing.'
Xīníng lí Chéngdū hěn jìn ma?	'Is Xining near Chengdu?'
Bú jìn, Xīníng lí Lánzhōu hěn jìn.	'No, it's not; it's close to Lanzhou.'
Xī'ān lí Běijīng hěn yuǎn, dànshì Xīníng gèng yuǎn.	'Xi'an is far from Beijing, but Xining is even farther.'

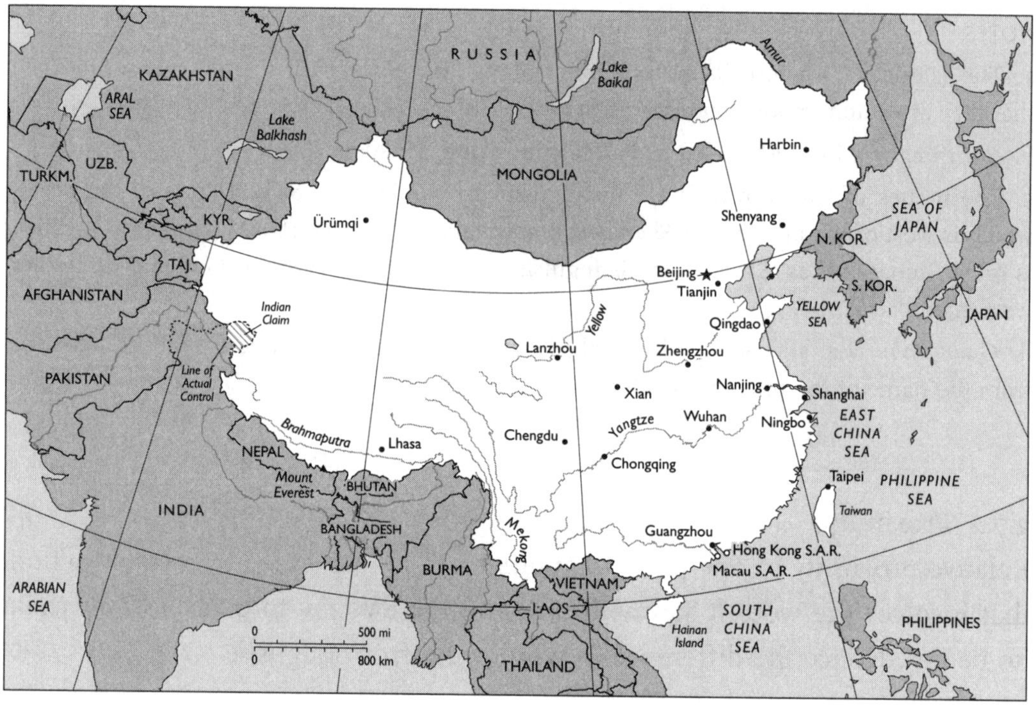

2.7.3 *Zài* 'be+at'

In certain contexts, *zài* may appear without an object, typically when it means 'to be at home' or as a euphemism for 'to be alive': *tā bú zài* 'he's not at home' or 'he's passed away' (the latter meaning is more often used with *le—bú zài le*—since such information is likely to be news). Usually, *zài* is followed by words or phrases that indicate location. However, just what constitutes a location is not always obvious. Place names are obvious locations, as the examples in §2.7.1 show. Other examples include the following words introduced earlier in this unit.

zài *zhèr* ~ *zhèlǐ* 'here'
nàr ~ *nàlǐ* 'there'
nǎr ~ *nǎlǐ* 'where'

Most nouns need to be followed by one of a number of position words, such as *shàng* 'on' or *lǐ* 'in', before they can be locations and thereby act as objects to *zài*.

zài	*fēijī shàng* 'on the plane'
zài	*shūbāo lǐ* 'in [my] bookbag'

However, some common words for places do not always require position words such as *shàng* or *lǐ*. Sometimes, additional position words are optional or add a slight nuance of meaning.

zài	*jiā* ⟨*lǐ*⟩ 'at home'
	cāntīng ⟨*lǐ*⟩ 'in the cafeteria'
	jīchǎng 'at the airport'

Before pronouns can act as objects of *zài*, they need support from one of the location words, such as *zhèr* ~ *zhèlǐ*: *zài wǒ zhèr* ('at me here'); *zài tā nàr* ('at her there'). English expresses this same notion more naturally with the verb 'to have'.

Qǐngwèn, jīntiān de bào zài nǎr ~ nǎlǐ?	'Excuse me, where's today's paper?'
Zài wǒ zhèr ~ wǒ zhèlǐ.	'I have it.'
Xíngli ne?	'And the luggage?'
Xíngli zài tā nàr.	'He has the luggage.'

2.7.4 *Zài* as a main verb and as a co-verb

Zài may be used as a main verb (as in §2.7.1 and below), but it can also introduce a location and appear prior to another verb, in which case it is called a co-verb (CV) in Chinese grammatical tradition.

A. EXAMPLES OF *ZÀI* AS A MAIN VERB

Qǐngwèn, Mǎ lǎoshī zài ma?	'Excuse me, is Professor Ma here?'
Mǎ lǎoshī xiànzài zài Yúnnán.	'Professor Ma is currently in Yunnan.'
Yàoshi zài nǎr?	'Where are the keys?'
Zài nàr. / Zài tā nàr.	'[They]'re over there. / She has [them].'

Nánjīng lí Héféi bú tài yuǎn, kěshì Nánjīng zài Jiāngsū, Héféi zài Ānhuī.	'Nanjing's not far from Hefei, but Nanjing's in Jiangsu, [and] Hefei's in Anhui.'
Wǒ de hùzhào zài nǐ nàr ma?	'Do you have my passport?'
Bú zài wǒ zhèr!	'I don't have [it]!'
Nǐ de xíngli zài nǎr?	'Where are your bags?'
Hái zài fēijī shàng.	'[They]'re still on the airplane.'

B. *ZÀI* AS A CO-VERB Co-verbs are similar to main verbs in that they allow direct modification by adverbs, but they frequently correspond to prepositions in English.

Xuéshēng zǒngshì zài cāntīng chīfàn.	'Students always eat in the cafeteria.'
Wǒmen zài fēijī shàng shuìjiào.	'We slept on the plane.'
Zài jiā lǐ chīfàn bǐjiào hǎo.	'It's better to eat at home.'

In such cases, the *zài* phrase expresses the location of an action. Later, you will see that *zài* phrases also follow certain verbs (where *zài* is usually untoned): *shēng zai Běijīng* 'born in Beijing'.

2.7.5 The verb *yǒu* 'to have'

The verb *yǒu* (with the 'irregular' negative *méiyǒu* or simply *méi*) was encountered in the previous unit as the negative counterpart of *le* with action verbs: *Chīfàn le méiyǒu?* Used alone, as a main verb, it conveys possession and existence.

Possession:

Wǒ yǒu sān ge hùzhào.	'I have three passports.'
Wǒ méiyǒu sǎn.	'I don't have an umbrella.'
Xuéshēng dōu yǒu zìdiǎn.	'The students all have dictionaries.'

Existence:

Wǒ méiyǒu xíngli.	'I don't have any baggage.'
Nánjīng méiyǒu dìtiě.	'There's no subway in Nanjing.'
Chēzi lǐ yǒu yīfu, yě yǒu shūbāo.	'There are clothes and bookbags in the car.'

Location and existence: A summary

Identity; category	*(bú) shì*	*Nà shi jīntiān de bào.* / *Tā shi lǎoshī.*	is	That's today's paper. / She's a teacher.
Location	*(bú) zài*	*Chéngdū zài Sìchuān.*	is in	Chengdu's in Sichuan.
Existence	*(méi)yǒu*	*Ruìlì méiyou jīchǎng.*	[there] is /are	There's no airport in Ruili.
Possession	*(méi)yǒu*	*Wǒ méiyou hùzhào.*	have	I don't have a passport.
Proximity	*lí . . . (bú) jìn / (bù) yuǎn*	*Tiānjīn lí Běijīng bù yuǎn.*	is close to / is far from	Tianjin isn't far from Beijing.

Exercise 5

Render the following short exchanges in idiomatic Chinese. (Hint: Chinese would probably not make use of the verb *yǒu* in dialogues A and C.)

DIALOGUE A

Jiǎ: Where's the paper please?
Yǐ: Yesterday's?
Jiǎ: No, today's.
Yǐ: Sorry, I don't have it.
Jiǎ: You had it earlier.
Yǐ: But I don't have it now.

DIALOGUE B

Jiǎ: Have you eaten yet?
Yǐ: I have.
Jiǎ: Oh, you've already eaten!
Yǐ: Yes, in the dorm.
Jiǎ: Is your dorm far from here?
Yǐ: It's kind of far.

DIALOGUE C

Jiǎ: Whose bookbag?
Yǐ: Not mine, I don't have a bookbag.
Jiǎ: Is it Lǐ Dān's?
Yǐ: No, I have Lǐ Dān's.
Jiǎ: Is it Liú Míng's?
Yǐ: No, he's not out of bed yet.
Jiǎ: Then it's Sūn Hào's.
Yǐ: Is it?

2.8 Miscellany

2.8.1 Welcome

In China, shops and other business establishments often station formally dressed *yīngbīn xiǎojie* ('welcome-guest girls') at main entrances to welcome customers with formal greetings–*huānyíng guānglín* ('welcome illustrious-presence')–or thanks–*xièxie guānglín* ('thanks illustrious-presence'). Both expressions make use of the formal word *guānglín* 'visitors; customers'. The same message is often written on the welcomers' sashes, on the doors, and on walls and counters within.

The dialogue at the end of this unit contains a less formal expression of welcome that makes use of the verbs *huānyíng* 'to welcome' and *lái* 'to come'.

With the verb *lái*, destinations (rather than locations per se) can follow directly without any equivalent of the English preposition 'to': *lái Běijīng, lái Guǎngzhōu.* Notice that, in English, the people being welcomed—'you'—are not mentioned, while in Chinese, they are (*nǐmen*).

Huānyíng nǐmen lái Chéngdū! 'Welcome to Chengdu!'

In Chinese settings, explicit thanks are usually reserved for favors that go beyond the expected. However, in some contexts (such as airports), an expression of gratitude in response to a welcome is not inappropriate. Such expressions involve the verbs *xiè* 'to thank'—frequently repeated as *xièxie*—and the verb *jiē* 'to meet; join'. Word order is the same as English, but Chinese eschews linking words such as 'to' and 'for'. ('Thank you for coming to meet us' appears in Chinese as simply 'thank you come meet us'.)

Xièxie nǐmen lái jiē wǒmen. 'Thanks for coming to meet us.'

Huānyíng nǐmen!

2.8.2 Particles

In addition to *ma* and *ne*, there are two other common final particles which have been encountered in the first two units. One is the particle *a*, which, among its diverse functions, lends a hearty tone to statements or exclamations, and also slightly softens the abruptness of questions.

Lěng a!	'Wow, [it]'s cold!'
Máng a!	'Busy, huh?!'
Shéi a?	'Who [is it]?'

The other is the particle *ba*, which is associated with *suggestions* or *consensus*.

Zǒu ba.	'Let's go.'
Nà hǎo ba.	'That's fine then.'
Shàngchē ba.	'Let's board the bus.'

2.8.3 Praise

Chinese will praise a foreigner's efforts to speak their language (called *Zhōngwén* or *Hànyǔ*), and will typically make use of an expression involving the verb *shuō* 'to speak' (or, in southern Mandarin, *jiǎng*) followed by the particle *+de*. If you wonder whether this *+de* is the same as the possessive *de* introduced earlier in this unit, the answer is that it is not. This *+de* is followed by SV expressions (that is, an adverb plus a SV): *shuō+de hěn hǎo*. The possessive *de* is followed by a noun (*wǒ de shūbāo*), or it has the potential to be followed by a noun (*wǒ de [shūbāo]*). Were meaning and distribution not sufficient evidence for positing two different *de* particles, we should cite the fact that they are also written with different characters, 的 (*wǒ de*) and 得 (*shuō+de*), respectively. In order to make the distinction clear (and prepare you for writing different characters), we will write the former as *de* and the latter as *+de*, a mild departure from pinyin conventions. You should do the same.

Zhōngwén shuō+de hěn hǎo.
Zhōngwén jiǎng+de hěn hǎo. } '[You] speak Chinese very well.'

The modest and polite response is that, in fact, you don't speak at all well.

Shuō+de bù hǎo
Jiǎng+de bù hǎo. } '[I] speak very poorly.'

The latter can be preceded by the (often repeated) expression *nǎlǐ*, which is the more formal word for 'where', but which is also used to deflect praise, as if questioning its basis.

Nǎlǐ, nǎlǐ, shuō+de bù hǎo. *Nǎlǐ, nǎlǐ, jiǎng+de bù hǎo.*	'Nah, [I] speak very poorly.'

When you see more examples, you will find that nothing can separate the combination *shuō+de*. Therefore, if *Zhōngwén* (or *Hànyǔ*) is mentioned, it cannot directly follow *shuō*, but needs to be cited first, as shown in the examples above. Since Chinese are so gracious about praising one's feeble efforts to speak their language, it is good to familiarize yourself with this exchange early. For now, though, practice it only as it appears, and only with the verb *shuō*, or its southern Mandarin counterpart, *jiǎng*.

2.9 Dialogue: At the airport

Given the need to restrict vocabulary and structures, the following dialogue cannot be regarded as completely natural, but it serves as a good model for some of the material that has been introduced in the first two units.

Situation: Professor Wang (W) has come to the airport with a university driver to meet half a dozen international students who are arriving in China to continue their study of Chinese. The students all have Chinese names as well as their English ones. One of them, Dawei (Dw), spots Professor Wang holding a sign and walks over to introduce himself; some of the others follow and introduce themselves too. (X designates any student, or several.)

Dw:	*Nín hǎo, wǒ shi Máo Dàwéi.*	'How are you, I'm Mao Dawei.'
W:	*O, Máo Dàwéi, wǒ shi Wáng lǎoshī.*	'Oh, Mao Dawei, I'm Professor Wang.'
An:	*Wáng lǎoshī, nín hǎo! Wǒ shi Lǐ Ānnà.*	'Professor Wang, how are you? I'm Li Anna.'
W:	*Lǐ Ānnà, nǐ hǎo.*	'Li Anna, how are you?'
Ym:	*Wáng lǎoshī, wǒ shi Xiǎolín Yóuměi.*	'Professor Wang, I'm Xiaolin Youmei.'

W:	*Xiǎolín Yóuměi, nǐ hǎo. Hǎo, sān ge rén le.*	'Xiaolin Youmei, hi. Okay, [that's] three.'
Ym:	*Hái yǒu tā—tā xìng Kǒng, jiào Kǒng Měi.*	(pointing) 'And her too—her name is Kong, she's called Kong Mei.'
W:	*Hǎo, Kǒng Měi, nǐ hǎo! Sì ge rén le. Nǐ ne?*	'Fine, how are you Kong Mei? [That's] four then. And [who are] you?'
Jf:	*Wǒ shì Bái Jiéfēi.*	'I'm Bai Jiefei.'
W:	*Bái Jiéfēi, nǐ hǎo . . . Nà hǎo, huānyíng nǐmen lái Běijīng!*	'Bai Jiefei, hi ...' 'Okay, then, welcome to Beijing!'
All:	*Xièxie, xièxie nǐmen lái jiē wǒmen.*	'Thanks; thank you for coming to meet us.'
W:	*Zhè shì Gāo shīfu.*	'This is Mr. Gao.'
All:	*Gāo shīfu, nín hǎo.*	'Mr. Gao, how are you?'
Gāo:	*Èi, nǐmen hǎo, nǐmen hǎo. Zhōngwén shuō+de hěn hǎo!*	'Ah, how are you, how are you?' '[You] speak Chinese very well!'
All:	*Nǎlǐ, nǎlǐ, shuō+de bù hǎo!*	'Nah, we don't speak very well.'
W:	*Nǐmen hěn lèi ba.*	'You're probably tired.'
X:	*Bù, bú tài lèi, hái hǎo.*	'No, not too tired, [we]'re okay.'
W:	*È ma? Chīfàn le ma?*	'Are [you] hungry? Have [you] eaten?'
X:	*Bú è, zài fēijī shàng chī le.*	'No, [we]'re not hungry, [we] ate on the airplane.'
W:	*Nà, nǐmen de xíngli ne?*	'And your bags?'
X:	*Zài zhèr: yī, èr, sān, sì, wǔ, liù. Dōu zài zhèr.*	'[They]'re here: one, two, three, four, five, six.' '[They]'re all here.'
W:	*Nà hǎo, wǒmen zǒu ba. Shàng chē ba.*	'Fine, let's go then. All aboard!'
X:	*Hǎo, hǎo.*	'Okay.'

W:	*Jīntiān yǒu diǎnr rè, nǐmen rè ma?*	[Aboard the minibus.] '[It]'s kind of hot today; are you hot?'
X:	*Bù, bú rè, hái hǎo. Wǒmen dōu hěn shūfu.*	'No, [we]'re not, [we]'re fine. We're all comfortable.'
W:	*Xíngli, hùzhào, sǎn dōu yǒu ma?*	'[You] have [your] bags, [your] passports, umbrellas?'
X:	*Dōu yǒu, dōu yǒu, xièxie.*	'[We] have them all, thanks.'
W:	*Hǎo, nà wǒmen zǒu ba.*	'Fine, so . . . let's go then!'
X:	*Běijīng hěn yuǎn ma?*	'Is Beijing far?'
W:	*Bù, lí zhèr bù yuǎn—hěn jìn!*	'No, it's not far from here—quite close!'

This model conversation is quite ambitious. All of its vocabulary is fairly new, of course, and it also introduces quite a few grammatical patterns and features. A bold beginning, though, has the advantage of providing interesting material with which to work from the start. To make the dialogue more manageable, it can be divided into four sections. The first includes introductions of all the people; the second deals with welcoming the students; the third concerns finding out how they are; and the fourth follows them to the minibus for the drive to Beijing. Get familiar with the scenario first, then visualize the conversation. You should be able to re-enact it 'in your head' more or less as presented before trying it out with partners.

Exercise 6

Paraphrase the following in Chinese.

1. Okay, that's three people.
2. Who's the first person? The second?
3. That's it then, I'm off.
4. It's late, I should be going.

5. We've all eaten, we ate on the plane.
6. We're not hungry, we're fine.
7. Welcome to [. . .].
8. Thanks for coming to meet us.
9. That's it then, see you tomorrow.
10. Okay, bye, take it easy.
11. How about you—you thirsty?
12. That looks like my umbrella.

Comment that

1. you haven't eaten yet.
2. they haven't left yet.
3. she hasn't had her shower yet.
4. he hasn't got out of class yet.
5. you haven't read the day's paper yet.
6. you were tired yesterday, but today you're fine.
7. you're not nervous anymore.
8. you were cold on the plane, but you're fine now.
9. they've already gone to bed.

AIRPORTS AND AIRLINES China has invested heavily in infrastructure projects over the last few decades, including the construction of new airports (*jīchǎng*) and the reconstruction of older ones. Some of the better known airports are Capital (*Shǒudū*) in Beijing, *Báiyún* ('white clouds') in Guangzhou, and *Hóngqiáo* and *Pǔdōng* in Shanghai. *Pǔdōng*, which like so many of the new airports is far from the city center, is served by a mag-lev (magnetic levitation) train, officially called a *cíxuán fúchē* ('magnet-suspend float-vehicle'), but colloquially referred to as a *diàncíchē* ('electromagnetic-vehicle') or as the *cífú*. It reaches a top speed of 430 kilometers an hour during its seven–eight minute run between the airport and its city terminus at the outlying Long Yang Road subway station (龙阳路).

Hángkōng gōngsī 'airlines' ('aviation company') are proliferating and consolidating in China. Here is a list of some of the larger Chinese airlines for you to practice reciting.

Zhōngguó Hángkōng Gōngsī	'Air China'
Zhōngguó Dōngfāng Hángkōng Gōngsī	'China Eastern Airlines'
Zhōngguó Běifāng Hángkōng Gōngsī	'China Northern Airlines'
Zhōngguó Xīběi Hángkōng Gōngsī	'China Northwest Airlines'
Zhōngguó Nánfāng Hángkōng Gōngsī	'China Southern Airlines'
Zhōngguó Xī'nán Hángkōng Gōngsī	'China Southwest Airlines'
Shēnzhèn Hángkōng Gōngsī	'Shenzhen Airlines'
Xīnjiāng Hángkōng Gōngsī	'Xinjiang Airlines'
Yúnnán Hángkōng Gōngsī	'Yunnan Airlines'
Xiàmén Hángkōng Gōngsī	'Xiamen Air'
Gǎng Lóng Hángkōng Gōngsī	'Dragonair' ['Hong Kong-dragon . . .']
Guó Tài Hángkōng Gōngsī	'Cathay Pacific'
Cháng Róng Hángkōng Gōngsī	'Eva Air'

Arriving at *Xīníng*, the capital of *Qīnghǎi*

2.10 Reflections: What have you learned?

2.10.1 Words

Most, but not all, multisyllabic Chinese words are, historically at least, compounds: *lǎoshī* ('old-teacher') (with 'old' having the respectful connotations of 'venerable'); *xǐzǎo* ('wash-bathe'); *hǎoxiàng* ('good-likeness').

2.10.2 Meaning

When learning a foreign language, particularly a language that is linguistically and culturally distant from one's native tongue, you quickly learn about the difficulties of translation. This is true for sentences as well as for words. *Hái hǎo*, for example, as a response to *Lèi bu lèi?* is composed of two words that, in other contexts, mean 'still' and 'be+good'. However, 'still good' does not make sense as a translation. 'Not too' or 'No, I'm fine' are closer to the Chinese sense, a fact we can only know from understanding how the Chinese functions in its context, then seeking an English expression that serves the same function (or has the same meaning in the context). As translators will tell you, this can be difficult to do, and in some cases nearly impossible without extensive circumlocution.

For learners, it is not enough to know the meaning of the sentence in context; learners want, and need, to understand the role of sentence parts—words—in the formation of that meaning. One reason for this is that word meanings, or glosses, are more abstract and thus more stable. 'Good' (or 'be good') is abstracted from the meaning of the word in specific contexts (where it may be translated variously as 'be well', 'be okay', 'hello', or 'nice'). That is why, in addition to citing a meaning appropriate to the context, word meanings in parentheses are also provided: e.g., *Hái hǎo* '[I]'m okay.' ('still be + good').

Providing word-for-word glosses serves another purpose. It takes us into the world of the foreign language and reveals conceptual differences that help to define the other culture. The fact that *chīfàn* 'to have a meal' (and, by extension, in other contexts 'to make a living') is composed of *chī* 'to eat' and *fàn* 'cooked rice' reveals the role of that staple in the Chinese diet. It is a moot point whether translators should try to capture that fact by translating *chīfàn* as ('eat-rice') rather than simply 'eat' or 'have a meal'. What do you think?

2.11 Pinyin notes and practice

2.11.1 Toneless syllables

As you have observed, particles like *ma* and *ne* are never written with a tone mark. Words such as *shì*, on the other hand, may be pronounced with tone in some cases and without tone in others: *Shì ma?* 'Is [that] so?'; *Bú shi.* '[No, it]'s not!' Clearly, tones cannot be written for the particles; but what about the second group? This section reviews the types of *qīngshēng* syllables and considers the question of how the optional tones should be represented in pinyin.

1. Particles such as *ma, ne, le,* and *ba* are never toned, so we can only write them with *qīngshēng.*
2. Many words show *qīngshēng* in the final syllable: *shūfu* 'comfortable'; *wǒmen* 'we; us'. On the evidence of compounds and other relatable expressions, these toneless syllables often turn out to have fully toned versions: *shūfu* has an adverbial form, *shūshufúfú,* in which final *fú* appears with a rising tone. Dictionaries, however, list words such as *wǒmen* and *shūfu* without a tone on the second syllable, and we will do the same.
3. Certain words (syllables) are toned in some contexts and toneless in others: *bú lèi* but *hǎo bu hǎo.* We will follow pronunciation in such cases, including the tone in contexts where it is pronounced, but omitting it in appropriate grammatical contexts.
4. Finally, the incidence of *qīngshēng* varies with the rate and formality of speech as well as the region (with the north and northeast being particularly susceptible to toneless syllables). Thus, in fast speech, *jīntiān* 'today' may be pronounced *jīntian,* without tone on *tian.* In these cases, we will often write the full tone, using current dictionaries as our guide.

For students' purposes, the general rule is: you are always safe in writing the word in its lexical, careful, slow speech form, as for example: *wǒmen, shūfu, hǎo bù hǎo, jīntiān.*

WRITING CHANGED TONES In this text, we do not write the changed tone for combinations of low tones; we write *hěn hǎo* and apply the rule. This accords with the standard rules for writing pinyin entries in dictionaries or in continuous text. We do make an exception in writing the changed tones for *bu* and *yi*, however: *bù gāo* but *bú lèi*; *yì zhāng* but *yí ge*.

2.11.2 A pinyin quirk

Standard pinyin writes *shénme*, *zěnme* 'how', and *zánmen* 'we [inclusive]' with a medial 'n' that is not reflected in the pronunciation. This compares to other systems of transcription, such as Yale which writes 'shéme'; National Romanization, which writes 'sherme' (with the 'r' representing the rising tone); and Zhuyin Fuhao, which writes ㄕㄜˊㄇㄜ˙ (i.e., 'shé me'). The reason pinyin writes a silent *n* in these words has to do with the characters that represent them. The first syllable of *shénme*, *zěnme*, and *zánmen* are written with characters that are, in other contexts, pronounced *shèn*, *zěn*, and *zán* respectively. While one is tempted to rectify the system and simply write 'shéme', 'zěme', and 'zámen' in conformity with actual pronunciation, pinyin is now regarded as the standard transliteration in the Chinese-speaking world. We should accept it as it is, if for no other reason than the fact that reference materials, as well as computer input systems, are based on pinyin.

2.11.3 Tone combos (the next six)

Recall the prototype examples of the six sets of tone combos presented in Unit 1: *lǎoshī, hái hǎo, zàijiàn, bú rè, hěn máng, bù gāo*. Now we will add six more combos—the first three all beginning with level-toned syllables—for a total of twelve.

(7)	*Kūnmíng*	(8)	*jīchǎng*	(9)	*chīfàn*
	Zhōngwén		*Wēiruǎn*		*qī hào*
	huānyíng		*Qīnghǎi*		*tiānqì*
(10)	*Héféi*	(11)	*qǐngwèn*	(12)	*zìdiǎn*
	Yúnnán		*hǎokàn*		*dìtiě*
	tóngxué		*yǎnjìng*		*Hànyǔ*

NOTE

tóngxué 'classmate'; *dìtiě* 'subway'

Exercise 7

Place the tone marks over the following words. (You may need to review the lesson on sounds and symbols.)

Level tone:	jie	qiao	nao	jiu	cui
Low tone:	zei	pou	shao	xiao	bie
Rising tone:	xue	bei	tuo	zhui	liao

Now focus on the problematical initials—those found on lines 3, 4, and 5 of the initial chart. You can assign level tone to them, and practice reading down.

ti	ta	dang		dou	dao
ci	ca	zang	si	zou	zao
chi	cha	zhang	shi	zhou	zhao
qi	qia	jiang	xi	jiu	jiao

2.12 Summary

tài . . . le	*Tài máng le. (Bú tài máng.)*
Adverbs	*Zǒngshì hěn máng hěn lèi; gèng máng; yǒu yìdiǎnr lěng;* etc.
SVs	*Hěn nán; Bù hǎochī; Hěn lìhai.*
Zěnmeyàng	*Jīntiān zěnmeyàng? Nǐ juéde zěnmeyàng?*
Nouns	*yàoshi, xíngli, dōngxi, zìxíngchē,* etc.
M words	*èrshí ge ⟨xuéshēng⟩; sān kuài ⟨qián⟩*
DE	*wǒ de zìdiǎn; zuótiān de bào*
Demonstratives	*zhè ~ zhèi; zhèr ~ zhèlǐ*
Identity	*Jīntiān qī hào; Dōu shi wǒ de xuéshēng.*

Question words	*shéi, shénme, nǎr ~ nǎlǐ, guìxìng, zěnmeyàng*
Naming	*Tā xìng Zhāng, jiào Zhāng Démíng; tā shi Zhāng Démíng.*
Titles	*Wèi lǎoshī; Gāo shīfu; Zhōu jīnglǐ*
Location	*Xíngli dōu zài zhèr; Dōu zài wǒ zhèr.*
Location with V	*Wǒmen zài fēijī shàng chī le.*
Proximity	*Tiānjīn lí Běijīng hěn jìn.*
Possession	*Wǒ méiyǒu qián.*
Existence	*Nánjīng méiyǒu dìtiě.*
Welcome	*Huānyíng nǐmen lái Běijīng. / Xièxie nǐmen lái jiē wǒmen.*
Particles	*Shàngchē ba. Shéi a?*
Praise	*Zhōngwén shuō+de hěn hǎo! / Nǎlǐ, nǎlǐ, shuō+de bù hǎo.*
Airports	*Zhōngguó Hángkōng Gōngsī; jīchǎng*
Qīngshēng	*xíngli; zǒu ba*

2.13 Rhymes and rhythms

First, a short rhyme that gives you practice with measure words: *zhī* (written with a different character from the *zhī* used with *bǐ* 'pen') is the M for animals such as chickens (*yì zhī jī*) and, as below, frogs; *zhāng* is the M for flat things such as tickets, tables, maps, and lawns, as well as mouths; *tiáo* is the M for sinuous objects. *Yǎnjīng* 'eye' is tonally distinct from *yǎnjìng* 'glasses'; eyes are counted by way of the default M, *gè*. *Dàshēng* ('big-sound') is 'loud'; *xiǎoshēng* is the opposite.

Yì zhī qīngwā

Yì zhī qīngwā, yì zhāng zuǐ,	('one frog, one mouth')
liǎng ge yǎnjīng, sì tiáo tuǐ.	('two eyes, four legs.')
Nǐ shuō:	('You say it:')
Shuō dàshēng yìdiǎnr:	('Say it louder:')
Shuō xiǎoshēng yìdiǎnr:	('Say it softer:')

The second rhyme praises the virtues of big feet, over bound feet presumably.

Dà jiǎo

Dà jiǎo dà, dà jiǎo dà,	('Big feet big, big feet big,')
yīntiān xiàyǔ bú hàipà;	('cloudy fall-rain not fear;')
dà jiǎo hǎo, dà jiǎo hǎo,	('big feet good, big feet good,')
yīntiān xiàyǔ shuāibùdǎo.	('cloudy fall-rain slip-not-fall.')

Finally, here are two *ràokǒulìng* 'tongue twisters', with traditional characters included to show how the phonetic components of Chinese characters provide visual support.

媽媽騎馬，馬慢，媽媽罵馬。
Māma qímǎ, mǎ màn, Māma mà mǎ.
('Mom rides horse, horse slow, Mom scolds horse.')

妞妞牽牛，牛佞，妞妞扭牛。
Niūniu qiān niú, niú nìng, Niūniu niǔ niú.
('Niuniu leads ox, ox cunning, Niuniu wrenches ox.')

Unit 3

Zǐyuē: Xué ér shí xí zhī, bú yì yuè hū?
'The Master said, "To learn and in due time, rehearse it: is this not also pleasurable?"' ('Master states: study and timely review it, not also pleasing Q')
—Opening lines of the *Analects* of Confucius

Unit 3 provides the basis for additional personal talk on place of origin and geographic location. It also provides rudimentary language for showing hospitality toward guests, offering them refreshment, and engaging in small talk; for finding out about prices and making purchases; and for talking about classes and courses. The last set of tone combos is presented toward the end of the unit.

Contents

3.1 Pronunciation

The sounds symbolized as *z* and *c* in pinyin (in row 3 of the initial chart) can be problematical for speakers of English, since they do not appear in initial position in English words. The word 'tsunami' for example, though represented in English dictionaries with the foreign 'ts' sound/spelling, is often anglicized and pronounced as 'sunami' by English speakers. Tsunami is a Japanese word, usually written 津波 ('shallows-wave') in Japanese; the Chinese equivalent is *hǎixiào*, written 海啸 ('sea-roar').

The row 4 initials—the retroflex consonants [!]—also present difficulties for English speakers. In fact, they present difficulties for southern Chinese speakers as well who, in colloquial speech, generally pronounce words with standard Mandarin *zh, ch,* and *sh* with *z, c,* and *s,* respectively. Standard Mandarin is unique to the region in having both the dental (row 3) and retroflex (row 4) series. Regional Chinese languages such as Cantonese and Hakka, and some Southeast Asian languages such as Thai and Vietnamese, usually have one or the other of the series, but not both.

The following sets focus on lines 3 and 4 of the initial consonant chart. Read them across, assigning a single tone; [!] reminds you to bunch your tongue and raise the tip to the retroflex position.

1.	*cū*	*tū*	*ch!ū*	*sū*	*zū*	*dū*	*zh!ū*	
2.	*tā*	*cā*	*sā*	*chā*	*sh!ā*			
3.	*zhé*	*dé*	*zé*	*cè*	*tè*	*chè*	*sè*	
4.	*duō*	*zuō*	*zh!uō*	*tuō*	*cuō*	*ch!uō*	*suō*	*sh!uō*
5.	*tóu*	*còu*	*chòu*	*zh!ōu*	*zoǔ*	*dōu*	*sǒu*	*shòu*

3.2 Amount

3.2.1 Larger numbers

As you know, numbers in Chinese are logical and regular: 11 is 10–1, 12 is 10–2; 20 is 2–10, 30 is 3–10, 41 is 4–10–1, etc. Higher numbers, also quite regular, are based on *bǎi* '100', *qiān* '1,000', and *wàn* '10,000'.

èrshíyī	*èrshí'èr*	*sānshí*	*sānshí'èr*	*jiǔshíjiǔ*	*yìbǎi*
21	22	30	32	99	100
yìbǎi wǔshísān	*bābǎi sānshí*	*yìqiān*	*yíwàn*	*yìbǎiwàn*	
153	830	1,000	10,000	1,000,000	

NOTES

a. Notice the use of the apostrophe to clarify syllable boundaries in those cases where a final vowel of one syllable meets an initial vowel of another: *shí'èr*. In large numbers, pinyin includes spaces between numbers built around a particular multiple of ten, *yìbǎi bāshíbā* '188'.

b. You will have more need, in later units, to use large numbers when the subject is population. In Chinese, there is a root for 10,000 (*wàn*), but not for a million. The latter is based on *wàn* and represented by *bǎiwàn* 'one million' (100 × 10,000).

3.2.2 Some more measure phrases

Drinks can be measured with *bēi* 'cup; glass' or *píng* 'bottle'. *Bēizi* 'cups' and *píngzi* 'bottles', however, are measured with *gè*. Books are measured with *běn* 'root; stem'. Vehicles, including bicycles, are measured with *liàng*; however, in Taiwan Mandarin, bicycles are often measured with *jià* 'frame'.

yì bēi chá	*liǎng bēi kāfēi*	*sān bēi qìshuǐ*	*sì bēi*
'one cup of tea'	'two cups of coffee'	'three glasses of soda'	'four cups [of it]'
yì píng píjiǔ	*liǎng píng kělè*	*sì píng jiǔ*	*sān píng*
'one bottle of beer'	'two bottles of cola'	'four bottles of wine'	'three bottles [of it]'
yí ge bēizi	*liǎng ge píngzi*	*sān ge bēizi*	*sì ge*
'one cup'	'two bottles'	'three cups'	'four [of them]'

yì běn shū 'one book'	*liǎng běn zìdiǎn* 'two dictionaries'	*sān běn shū* 'three books'	*shí běn* 'ten [of them]'
yí liàng chēzi 'one cart, small vehicle'	*liǎng liàng qìchē* 'two automobiles'	*yí liàng zìxíngchē* 'one bicycle'	*sān jià dānchē* 'three bicycles'

3.3 Nationality

3.3.1 Country names

Zhōngguó	*Rìběn*	*Yìnní*	*Yìndù*	*Hánguó*
Àodàlìyà	*Jiānádà*	*Měiguó*	*Mòxīgē*	*Éguó*
Fǎguó	*Yīngguó*	*Déguó*	*Yìdàlì*	*Xībānyá*

Some country names—mostly those with a history of independence and national power—are composed of a single syllable plus *guó* 'country; nation', on the model of *Zhōngguó* 'China' ('middle-country'). For these countries, the first syllable is chosen for its sound as well as meaning: *Měiguó* 'United States' ('beautiful-country'); *Yīngguó* 'England; Great Britain' ('hero-country'); *Fǎguó* 'France' ('law-country'); *Déguó* 'Germany' ('virtue-country'); *Tàiguó* 'Thailand' ('peace-country').

Countries with deep historical ties to China retain their old names. Japan is *Rìběn* ('sun-root'), a reflection of the fact that, from the Chinese perspective, Japan lies in the direction of the sunrise. The Chinese name is, in fact, the source of both the Japanese names for their own country, Nippon (formal) and Nihon (informal), as well as the English name, Japan. All reflect regional variants of earlier pronunciations of the word *Rìběn*, written 日本. Vietnam is *Yuènán*, also a name originally derived from a Chinese origin: *Yuè*, the name of an ethnic group, and *nán* 'south'. Most other countries are simply transliterated: *Jiānádà, Yìdàlì, Fēilǜbīn, Yìndù*. City names, except for those in Japan and Korea, are almost all transliterated: *Zhījiāgē, Bèi'ěrfǎsītè, Tèlāwéifū*. A few are translated rather than transliterated: *Yánhúchéng* ('salt-lake-city'). A more extensive list of country and city names, with English equivalents, is provided in the appendix to this unit.

3.3.2 Asking about nationality

rén 'person'	*guó* 'country'	*dìfang* 'place'
Zhōngguó rén 'a Chinese'	*Zhōngguó* 'China'	*shénme dìfang* 'what place'

There are several ways to ask about nationality, all of them involving the verb *shì*. Recall that *nǎ* and *něi* represent the same word, as do *nà* and *nèi*; the first members of each pair (*nǎ, nà*) tend to be 'free' forms, while the second (*něi, nèi*) tend to be bound to measures, for example, *nǎ* but *něi ge*. You may also hear the *nǎ* and *nà* forms used in combination with measure words as well: *nǎguó* rather than *něiguó*.

1. *Nǐ shi něiguó [~ nǎguó] rén?* ('you be which-country person')
2. *Nǐ shi nǎr ~ nǎlǐ de ⟨rén⟩?* ('you be where DE person')
3. *Nǐ shi shénme dìfang rén?* ('you be what place person')
4. *Nǐ shi ⟨cóng⟩ shénme dìfang lái de?* ('you be from what place come one')

Options 2–4 do not, strictly speaking, ask about nationality, but about place, and can be answered with a city, town, or country name. Notice that option 4 presents two alternatives. With *cóng* 'from', the question is, strictly speaking, about the country of residence or where you were born. Without *cóng*, it could simply mean 'Where do you [happen to have] come from?'

The responses to these questions generally take the same form as the question.

Nǐ shi ⟨cóng⟩ shénme dìfang lái de?	'Where are you from?'
Wǒ shi ⟨cóng⟩ Rìběn lái de.	'I'm from Japan.'
Nǐ shi něiguó rén?	'Which country are you from?'
Wǒ shi Hánguó rén.	'I'm from Korea.'

Occasionally in conversation, people will ask about nationality using the more formal word *guójí* 'nationality'.

	Nǐ de guójí shi shénme?	'What's your nationality?'
	Wǒ shi Měiguó guójí.	'I'm American.'
	Nǐ shi shénme guójí?	'What's your nationality?'
	Wǒ de guójí shi Jiānádà.	'My nationality is Canadian.'
Or:	*Wǒ shi Jiānádà rén.*	'I'm Canadian.'

3.3.3 Foreigners
'Foreign' in Chinese is *wàiguó* ('outside-country'); 'foreigners' are *wàiguó rén.* Foreigners in general are often called *yángrén. Yáng* actually means 'seas', but with implications of 'overseas'. In China, foreigners of European ancestry are generally called *lǎowài* 'venerable foreigners', and a commonly heard exclamation is *Ei, nǐ kàn, lǎowài lái le!* 'Hey, look, here comes the foreigner!' In southern China, local equivalents of the Cantonese term *guailo* 'ghost people' (incorporated in regional Mandarin as *guǐlǎo*) are used much like *lǎowài.* The presence of the rather respectable first word *lǎo* makes such terms acceptable. In Singapore, Caucasians are called *angmo* 'red hair' (Hokkien for Mandarin *hóngmáo*), a term that is also fairly innocuous. *Yáng guǐzi* 'foreign devils', however, is regarded as rather disparaging; one recent and widely used Chinese dictionary gives its definition as [translated] 'an archaic term of disparagement for Westerners who invaded our country'. Even though it may occasionally be used in a tongue-in-cheek manner to refer to oneself, it is generally better to avoid its use altogether.

3.3.4 Have you been there? V + *guò*
Talking about nationality or place of origin is likely to lead to questions about prior travel, so it is a worthwhile digression to introduce the basics of the verb suffix *guò* (often without tone in this usage) prior to a more detailed exposition in a later unit. Here, we will concentrate on two exchanges, the first involving the verb *qù* 'to go' and the second involving the verb *chī* 'to eat'.

Nǐ qùguo Zhōngguó ma?		'Have you [ever] been to China?'
+	*Qùguo.*	'[I] have.'
–	*Méi⟨yǒu⟩ qùguo.*	'[I] haven't.'

Nǐ chīguo hǎishēn ma?		'Have you [ever] eaten sea cucumber?'
+	*Chīguo.*	'[I] have.'
–	*Méi⟨yǒu⟩ chīguo.*	'[I] haven't.'

Note that responses to questions with *guò* retain the *guò* in both negative and positive responses. The negative response, like those with *le*, is formed with *méi⟨yǒu⟩* 'hasn't; haven't'.

'Experiential' *guò* should remind you of a construction that you encountered in Unit 1. There, you learned several ways to ask if someone had already had their meal, one way involving final *le* and another that involved both a post-verbal *guò* and a final *le*: *Nǐ chīguo fàn ⟨le⟩ ma?* / *Chī⟨guo⟩ le.* 'Have you eaten? / I have.' Clearly, the question does not mean 'Have you *ever* eaten?', along the lines of *Nǐ chīguo hǎishēn ma?* 'Have you [ever] eaten sea cucumber?' (Note that, in English, the two questions also have the same form: 'Have you eaten?' 'Have you eaten sea cucumber?') How can you be sure which meaning is meant? Pay attention to context, but also notice that only in the greeting is there a strong possibility of a final *le* after *guò*.

Here are some short dialogues that incorporate this new experiential usage of *guò*.

(1)	*Nǐ shi Zhōngguó shénme dìfang lái de?*	'Where in China are you from?'
	Wǒ shi Xī'ān rén.	'I'm from Xi'an.'
	Xī'ān, wǒ qùguo Xī'ān. Xī'ān hěn yǒumíng!	'Xi'an, I've been there. Xi'an's famous!'
	Shì ma?	'Is it?'
(2)	*Nǐ shi Měiguó rén ba?*	'I take it you're American.'
	Bù, wǒ shi Jiānádà rén.	'No, I'm from Canada.'
	⟨Nǐ shi⟩ Jiānádà shénme dìfang rén?	'Where in Canada [are you from]?'
	Wēngēhuá. Nǐ qùguo ma?	'Vancouver. Have you been?'
	Méi qùguo, kěshì hěn xiǎng qù.	'No, but I'd love to go.'

NOTES

a. *hěn yǒumíng* ('quite have-name'); *Xiǎng* literally means 'to think; to think of', but can often, as here, also be used to indicate intention, as in 'want to; feel like'.

b. In dialogue number 1, it is modesty that leads the Chinese speaker to respond so unassumingly, even though he probably feels that Xi'an, with 2,500 years of history, is very famous. Modesty of speech is reinforced by classical texts such as the *Analects*, a collection of aphoristic sayings attributed to Confucius: 'The virtuous man is restrained in speech but excessive in actions' (君子耻其言而过其行 *Jūnzǐ chǐ qí yán ér guò qí xíng* 'gentleman shames his words and excesses his actions'). 'He who speaks without modesty will find it difficult to get things done' (其言之不怍，则为之也难 *Qí yán zhī bú zuò, zé wéi zhī yě nán* 'his saying it not modest, then doing it also difficult'). The submissive virtues of humility and restraint, and reserve and modesty act to reduce strain and tensions within complex social units, and their importance even in earliest times in China comes as no surprise. Over the centuries, they have been refracted through the lens of philosophical and moral writings, such as the *Analects*, until they have become second nature, part of the rules of etiquette and social interaction. Of course, modesty and restraint have been seen as virtues throughout the English-speaking world as well, but the difference is that, in modern times at least, there is a degree of tension between being modest and being assertive, particularly in competitive contexts such as the job market. In China, modesty remains quite conventional: a degree of diffidence, such as responding to praise with *nǎli, nǎli*, or denigrating one's abilities as a cook or calligrapher will earn admiration, and put people at ease.

3.3.5 More on proximity

Cóng should be distinguished from *lí*, which has a similar meaning and occupies the same place in sentence structure. While *cóng* is associated with movement, *lí* is associated only with distance and with the adjectives *jìn* 'near' and *yuǎn* 'far'.

Tā cóng Dàlián lái de; Dàlián zài Liáoníng shěng, lí Běijīng bù yuǎn.	'She's from Dalian; Dalian's in Liaoning province, not far from Beijing.'

An actual distance may be substituted for *jìn* and *yuǎn*. Distances in Chinese are measured in *lǐ* 'Chinese mile', equivalent to half a kilometer (or a third of a mile), or in *gōnglǐ* 'kilometers', but usually not in English miles (*Yīnglǐ*). All are measure words, so 100 kilometers would be *yìbǎi gōnglǐ*. The noun *lù* 'road' can, in certain cases, be added to the measure phrase, optionally mediated by *de*: *yìbǎi gōnglǐ* ⟨*de*⟩ *lù* '100 kilometers [of road]'. Since mileage is a noun, a verb still has to be provided, and in Chinese it is usually *yǒu* 'have' (unlike English, which uses 'is'). Distances are often approximate, of course, so it is also useful to learn the adverb *dàgài* 'approximately'.

Jīchǎng lí wǒ de jiā yǒu wǔ gōnglǐ ⟨*lù*⟩.	'The airport is five kilometers from my house.'
Xīníng lí Xī'ān dàgài yǒu yìqiān gōnglǐ—hěn yuǎn.	'Xining is about 1,000 kilometers from Xī'ān—[it]'s a long way off.'
Wǒ de jiā lí huǒchēzhàn yǒu liǎng lǐ lù–bú tài yuǎn.	'My house is two Chinese miles from the station–not so far.'

3.4 The cardinal directions: NSEW

Most of the cardinal directions should already be familiar to you from place names (as well as from airline names). *Běijīng* is literally the 'northern capital', since *běi* means 'north'. During several historical periods, *Nánjīng* ('southern capital') served as the capital of China. The capital of Japan, Tokyo, is actually the Japanese pronunciation of the characters that, in Mandarin, are pronounced *Dōngjīng* ('eastern capital'). There is no *Xījīng* ('western capital'), but the city of *Xī'ān* ('western-peace') and the Chinese name for Tibet, *Xīzàng* ('western-repository'), both contain the word *xī* 'west'. Also relevant is *Pǔdōng* ('*[Huáng]-pǔ*-east'), the name of the district in Shanghai directly east of the Huángpǔ River and home to the country's tallest skyscrapers. The old city across the river from *Pǔdōng* is called *Pǔxī* ('*[Huáng]-pǔ*-west').

The four cardinal directions are conventionally ordered either *dōngnán-xīběi* 'E-S-W-N' (rotating clockwise around the compass) or *dōngxī-nánběi* 'E-W-S-N'. The ordering of the directions in Chinese reflects the primacy of the east-west axis, a primacy that is underscored in the names of the diagonal quadrants, which are the reverse of English: *dōngběi* 'northeast' ('east-north'), *dōngnán* 'southeast' ('east-south'), *xīběi* 'northwest' ('west-north'), and *xīnán* 'southwest' ('west-south'). *Dōngběi* (capitalized) is also the name of the northeast region of

China that includes the three provinces of *Hēilóngjiāng* ('black-dragon-river'), *Jílín*, and *Liáoníng*. Historically, this was the area colonized by Japan prior to World War II and, at the time, referred to (in English) as 'Manchuria'. This region was home to the *Mǎnzú* 'Manchu' people, who ruled China during the Qing dynasty from 1644–1912.

Although Beijing and Tianjin might be considered to be in northeastern China, they are usually described as being in the north, *zài běibiānr*, with *dōngběi* reserved for cities that are actually in the *Dōngběi* region. The northwestern region, including *Xīnjiāng* and *Qīnghǎi*, is referred to as *Dàxīběi* 'The Great Northwest'; while the southwestern region, including *Yúnnán*, *Sìchuān*, and *Guìzhōu*, is called the *Xī'nán*.

Generally speaking, directions require two syllables to function as nouns, so the diagonals may stand alone: *Jílín zài dōngběi*; *Kūnmíng zài xī'nán*. However, individual direction words need to combine with either *biān⟨r⟩* 'side; bank', *miàn* 'face', *bù* 'part', or *fāng* 'side; region'.

Bāotóu zài běibù.	'Baotou's in the north.'
Tiānjīn zài běibiān.	'Tianjin's to the north.'
Tàiyuán zài běimiàn.	'Taiyuan's to the north.'
Dàtóng zài běifāng.	'Datong's in the northern region.'

The options differ slightly. *Fāng*, in particular, refers not to relative direction, but to a quadrant of the country: *běifāng* 'the northern region' or 'the North'; *nánfāng* 'the southern region' or 'the South'. *Xīfāng* and *dōngfāng* not only mean 'the western region' and 'the eastern region', respectively, but also 'the West' (or 'the Occident') and 'the East' ('the Orient'). Constructions with *bù* (a combining version of *bùfen* 'part') refer to position within a whole; constructions with *biān⟨r⟩* and *miàn* are the least restricted, simply indicating a direction. So, the southern province of *Guǎngdōng* is *zài nánbù* (since it is within China) as well as *zài nánbiān⟨r⟩* or *nánmiàn*. *Yuènán* 'Vietnam'—a separate country—is, strictly speaking, only *zài nánbiān⟨r⟩* or *nánmiàn*, not *zài nánbù* (at least, with reference to China).

Central regions can be referred to with *zhōngbù* (*zhōng* 'middle', as in *Zhōngguó* and *Zhōngwén*).

Wǔhàn zài zhōngbù.	'Wuhan is in the center [of the country].'
Chóngqìng yě zài zhōngbù ma?	'Is Chongqing in the middle as well?'

Location within the country is expressed with the larger unit first, unlike the English order: *zài Zhōngguó běibù* 'in the north of China' ('in China north-part'). There is usually the option of inserting a possessive *de* between the country of reference and the direction (i.e., *zài Zhōngguó de běibù, zài Zhōngguó de běibiān*). The possessive *de* makes a subtle difference, and reveals the source of the Chinese word order as a possessive (or more accurately, an attributive) construction: 'in China's north'.

Běijīng zài Zhōngguó ⟨de⟩ běibù.	'Beijing's in the north of China.'
Niǔyuē zài Měiguó ⟨de⟩ dōngběi.	'New York's in the northeast of the U.S.'
Yuènán zài Zhōngguó ⟨de⟩ nánbiānr.	'Vietnam is south of China.'

The table shows the various constructions involving the cardinal directions, arranged around the central *zhōngbù*. Within each square, *biān⟨r⟩* options are outermost, *bù* options are innermost, and the four *fāng* quadrants are in between.

Summary of cardinal directions

xīběi⟨biānr⟩ ***xīběi⟨bù⟩***	*běibiānr ~ -miàn* *[běifāng]* ***běibù***	*dōngběi⟨biānr⟩* ***dōngběi⟨bù⟩***
xībiānr ~ -miàn *[xīfāng]* ***xībù***	***zhōngbù***	***dōngbù*** *[dōngfāng]* *dōngbiānr ~ -miàn*
xīnán⟨bù⟩ *xīnán⟨biānr⟩*	***nánbù*** *[nánfāng]* *nánbiānr ~ -miàn*	***dōngnán⟨bù⟩*** *dōngnán⟨biānr⟩*

Exercise 1

In class, translate the following geographic facts aloud. Then, at home, write the same.

> *Tiānjīn* is in the north of China, about 100 kilometers from *Běijīng*. *Shěnyáng* is in the northeast, not far from *Běijīng* either. *Shěnyáng* is in *Liáoníng*. *Chéngdū* is in the middle of *Sìchuān*. *Chóngqìng* is south of *Chéngdū*, but it's not in the southern part of *Sìchuān*; it's a *zhíxiáshì* ('centrally administered municipality'). *Kūnmíng* is in *Yúnnán*. *Yúnnán* isn't *Yuènán*. *Yúnnán* is a part of China, but *Yuènán* isn't part of China—it's southwest of China.

DIALOGUE A At a reception, *Jiǎ*, a student in London, finds himself next to *Chén Yuè*, a Chinese graduate student (female), and initiates a conversation in Chinese.

Jiǎ:	*Qǐngwèn, nín guìxìng?*	'May I ask your name?'
Ch:	*Wǒ xìng Chén, jiào Chén Yuè.*	'My name's Chen, Chen Yue.'
Jiǎ:	*Chén Yuè, nǐ shi Zhōngguó lái de ba.*	'Chen Yue, you're from China, I take it.'
Ch:	*Shì, wǒ shi Zhōngguó rén.*	'Right, I am Chinese.'
Jiǎ:	*Zhōngguó shénme dìfang rén?*	'Where in China are you from?'
Ch:	*Chángchūn.*	'Changchun.'
Jiǎ:	*O, Chángchūn. Nà, Chángchūn zài Dōngběi, shì bu shi?*	'O, Changchun. Now, Changchun's in the Northeast, isn't it?'
Ch:	*Shì, zài Jílín shěng.*	'Yes, in Jilin province.'
Jiǎ:	*Lí Běijīng bǐjiào yuǎn ba.*	'Quite far from Beijing, right?'

Ch:	*Ng, lí Běijīng hěn yuǎn, dàgài yìqiān gōnglǐ!*	'Yes, quite far from Beijing—about 1,000 kilometers!'
Jiǎ:	*O, shì hěn yuǎn!*	'Oh, [that] IS a long way!'

DIALOGUE B *Léi Hànbó*, an overseas student, thinks he recognizes *Zhāng Yīng* from an encounter earlier in the week.

Léi:	*Nín shì bu shi Zhāng Yīng?*	'Are you Zhang Ying?'
Zh:	*Wǒ shi Zhāng Yīng.*	'Yes, I'm Zhang Ying.'
Léi:	*Zhāng Yīng, wǒ shi Léi Hànbó, Wèi lǎoshī de xuéshēng.*	'Zhang Ying, I'm Lei Hanbo, Professor Wei's student.'
Zh:	*O, Léi Hànbó, nǐ hǎo. Nǐ shi Měiguó rén ba?*	'O, Lei Hanbo, how are you. You're American, right?'
Léi:	*Shì, wǒ shi Měiguó Bōshìdùn rén.*	'Yes, I'm an American from Boston.'
Zh:	*O, Bōshìdùn. Bōshìdùn hěn yǒumíng!*	'O, Boston. Boston's quite well known!'
Léi:	*Shì ma?*	'Really?'

DIALOGUE C *Jiǎ*, a foreigner, and *Yǐ*, a Chinese, are looking at a series of numbered illustrations of political leaders in an old copy of *China Reconstructs*. *Jiǎ* is asking questions about who's who.

Jiǎ:	*Nà, dì-yī ge shi Máo Zédōng ba.*	'Well, the first [one] is Mao Zedong, I take it.'
Yǐ:	*Shì, dì-yī ge shi Máo Zédōng.*	'Yes, the first [one] is Mao Zedong.'
Jiǎ:	*Máo Zédōng shi Húnán rén ba?*	'Mao Zedong's from Hunan, right?'
Yǐ:	*Shì, shi Húnnán rén.*	'Yes, [he]'s from Hunan.'
Jiǎ:	*Nà, dì-èr ge ne?*	'And the second [one]?'
Yǐ:	*Dì-èr ge shi Zhōu Ēnlái.*	'The second [one] is Zhou Enlai.'
Jiǎ:	*O, Zhōu Ēnlái. Tā shi shénme dìfāng rén?*	'Oh, Zhou Enlai. Where's he from?'

Yǐ:	*Zhōu Ēnlái ne, tā shi Huái'ān rén.*	'Zhou Enlai, he's from Huai'an.'
Jiǎ:	*Huái'ān ne, zài Jiāngsū, shì bu shi?*	'Huai'an, [that]'s in Jiangsu, isn't it?'
Yǐ:	*Shì, zài Jiāngsū, lí Shànghǎi bù yuǎn.*	'Yes, in Jiangsu, not far from Shanghai.'
Jiǎ:	*Dì-sān ge ne?*	'The third [one]?'
Yǐ:	*Dì-sān ge, nà shi Péng Déhuái.*	'The third [one], that's Peng Dehuai.'
Jiǎ:	*Péng Déhuái a, tā shi cóng shénme dìfāng lái de?*	'Peng Dehuai, where's [he] from?'
Yǐ:	*Péng Déhuái hǎoxiàng yě shì Húnán rén ba.*	'Seems like Peng Dehuai's also from Hunan.'

Dì-yí ge shì Máo Zédōng.

3.5 Yes and no

As observed throughout the first two units, where English tends to include 'yes' or 'no' in response to simple questions, Chinese often answers the same questions by simply reiterating the verb, or verbal parts, in positive or negative form, as the case may be. Agreement can be emphasized by the addition of an initial *duì* 'to be correct', though disagreement frequently requires a more subtle expression than the judgmental *bú duì* 'wrong'.

Hǎotīng ma?	'Do you like [the music]?'
⟨Duì⟩, hěn hǎotīng.	'Yes, [it] sounds very good.'
Xǐzǎo le ma?	'Have [you] bathed?'
Hái méi ne.	'No, not yet.'
Tāmen yǐjīng shuìjiào le ma?	'Are they in bed already?'
⟨Duì⟩, yǐjīng shuì le, kěshì Léi Bīn hái méi ne.	'Yes, [they] are, but Lei Bin's still up.'
Léi Bīn a, Léi Bīn shi shéi?	'Lei Bin? Who's Lei Bin?'
Léi Bīn shi tāmen de tóngxué.	'Lei Bin's their classmate.'
O, míngbai.	'Oh, I see.'

Though sentences with *shì* confirm a stated situation, initial *duì* is available for emphasis. Sentences with *bù* ~ *bú shì* deny a stated situation.

(1)	*Nǐ shi dì-yī ge ma?*	'You're the first?'
	Duì, wǒ shi dì-yī ge.	'Yes, I am.'
	Nà, tā shi dì-èr ge ma?	'And . . . she's second?'
	Bù, tā shi dì-sān ge.	'No, she's third.'
	Shì ma?	'Is that so?'
	Shì, dì-sān ge shi tā.	'Yes, she's third.'
(2)	*Tā shi Měiguó rén ba.*	'He's American, I take it.'
	Duì.	'Right.'
	Tā àiren yě shi ma?	'His spouse too?'
	Bú shì, tā shi Zhōngguó rén.	'No, she's Chinese.'
	A, míngbai.	'Oh, I see!'

3.5.1 Negative questions

So far, so good. With ordinary 'yes-no' questions, reiterating the verb in the positive confirms (with or without an initial *duì*); reiterating it in the negative denies. Negative questions, however, are not quite so straightforward. Negative questions convey a change in expectations: 'Haven't you eaten?' (I would have thought you had, but apparently you haven't.) Negative questions expect a negative answer: 'Haven't you eaten?' / 'No, I haven't'. In Chinese, as in English, it is still possible to reiterate the verb—in the negative—to confirm the new expectation. But while English generally responds to a negative question with 'no' (anticipating the negative verb), Chinese responds with *duì* 'correct' (confirming the negative statement).

Nǐ hái méi chīfàn ma?	'Haven't you eaten yet?'
⟨Duì⟩, hái méi ne.	'No, not yet.'

Tāmen bú shi Měiguó rén ba?	'They're not Americans, right?'
⟨Duì⟩, tāmen bú shi Měiguó rén.	'No, they're not.'

It is this incongruence between English and Chinese that gives rise to the observation that Chinese (along with Japanese and other regional languages) has no equivalent to English 'yes' and 'no'.

What if, in the last example, contrary to expectations, the people in question turned out to be Americans after all? In that case, the responses in both Chinese and English are less predictable. Typically, Chinese would change the value of the verb to positive and put emphasis on it: *Tāmen SHÌ Měiguó rén.* An introductory negative—*bù*—would also indicate the change of expectations.

Tāmen bú shi Měiguó rén ba?	'They're not Americans, are they?'
Bù, bù, tāmen SHÌ Měiguó rén.	'Yes, they are.'

Here again, while the English 'yes' matches the positive verb ('they are Americans'), Chinese *bù* (or *bú shi*) denies the anticipated answer ('it's not the case that they aren't Americans').

Nà bú shi nǐ de hùzhào ma?	'That's not your passport?'
Duì, bú shi wǒ de.	'No, it's not.'
Bù, bù, SHÌ wǒ de.	'Yes, it is.'

3.5.2 Tag questions

Sometimes, it is appropriate to indicate doubt, or seek confirmation through the use of tag questions. The addition of questions formed with *shì* or *duì* to the end of a sentence serves such a function.

Sūzhōu zài Jiāngsū, duì ma?	'Suzhou's in Jiangsu, correct?'
Duì a, Sūzhōu zài Jiāngsū.	'[That]'s the case, Suzhou's in Jiangsu.'
Tā shi Yīngguó rén, shì bu shi?	'He's British, right?'
Bú shì, tā shi Jiānádà rén.	'No, he's Canadian.'
Nǐ de sǎn, shì bu shi?	'[This] is your umbrella, isn't it?'
Shì, xièxie.	'[It] is, thanks.'
Tā shi Dài Sīyí, duì bu duì?	'That's Dai Siyi, right?'
Duì, shi Dài Sīyí.	'Right, Dai Siyi.'

3.5.3 Is it the case that . . . ?

Shì bu shi can also be inserted before sentence elements to seek confirmation.

Zhènjiāng shì bu shi zài Ānhuī?	'Is Zhenjiang really in Anhui?'

Stressed *shì* may then appear in a positive answer to confirm that 'it is indeed the case that'.

Shì a, Zhènjiāng shì zài Ānhuī.	'Yes, it IS [in Anhui].'

But *shì* would not appear in the negative, since nothing is being confirmed.

Bù, Zhènjiāng zài Jiāngsū, lí Nánjīng bù yuǎn.	'No, it isn't. Zhenjiang's in Jiangsu, not far from Nanjing.'

When adverbial modifiers are present, inserting *shì bu shi* becomes the only way to form a V-not-V question.

Zhèr de lǎoshī shì bu shi zǒngshì hěn lèi?	'Is it the case that the teachers here are always tired?'
Tāmen shì hěn lèi, kěshì xuéshēng bú shi gèng lèi ma.	'They ARE quite tired, but aren't students even more tired?'
Tāmen shì bu shi dōu yǐjīng qǐlái le?	'Is it the case that they're ALL up already?'
Bù, xiǎo Liáng hái méiyǒu qǐlái, tā yǒu yìdiǎnr bù shūfu.	'No, young Liang isn't up yet, he's not very well.'

Exercise 2

Provide Chinese equivalents for the following.

'Your dad (*bàba*) is German, right?'
'Yes, but my mother (*māma*) is American, so I have both U.S. and German nationalities.'

'Is it the case that Nanjing isn't far from Shanghai?'
'That's right, it isn't that far away, about 200 kilometers.'

'Aren't they Chinese?'
'No, they're not. None of them is. Two of them are Korean, and two are Thai.'

'Isn't that your umbrella?'
'No, it's not mine. I think it's the teacher's.'

'Is Tianjin near Beijing?'
'Yes, it is. It's about 180 kilometers from Beijing.'

3.6 Thanks and sorry

3.6.1 Responses to thanking

Thanking is not quite as perfunctory in Chinese as in English. In English, thanks are often given after making a purchase or when a waiter serves a dish or brings a drink. In Chinese, such transactions are more likely to be acknowledged with just *hǎo* 'fine'—if anything. Explicit thanking is not common, but when an action is worthy of thanks, then in informal or colloquial situations, *xièxie* or *duōxiè* (the latter, under the influence of Cantonese) suffices, while in more formal situations, the verb *gǎnxiè* 'to feel thanks' can be used: *Tài gǎnxiè le* 'Thank [you] so much!' Responses to *xièxie* (or *gǎnxiè*), corresponding to English 'you're welcome', vary considerably in Chinese. The main ones are listed below, along with their literal meanings.

Xièxie ⟨*nǐ*⟩.	'Thanks.'
Bú xiè.	'You're welcome.' ('not thank')
Bú yòng xiè.	('not use thanks')
Bú kèqi	('not be+polite')
Bié kèqi.	('don't be+polite')
Bú yào kèqi.	('not want be+polite')
Bú yòng kèqi.	('not use be+polite')
Béng kèqi. [northern]	('not use be+polite')
Yīnggāi de!	('should DE')

NOTES

a. The core meaning of *yòng* is 'to use' and *yào* is 'to want', but in the above contexts, the meanings of both are closer to 'to need'. *Béng* is a telescoped version of *bú+yòng*.

b. *Kèqi* is composed of roots for 'guest' and 'air; spirit', so the literal meaning is, roughly, 'adopt the airs of a guest'. *Kè* appears in expressions such as *qǐngkè* 'entertain guests; to treat [by paying]' ('invite-guests') and words like *kèrén* 'guest' ('guest-person') and *kètīng* 'living room; parlor' ('guest-hall'). *Qì* appears in words such as *tiānqì* 'weather' and *qìfēn* 'atmosphere'.

Tā hěn kèqi.	'She's / he's very polite.'
Nǐ bié kèqi, wǒ qǐngkè.	'Don't worry, I'm treating.'

c. *Yīnggāi de*, containing the modal verb *yīnggāi* 'should; ought' (cf. *gāi*), is a common response to a serious expression of gratitude. *Xièxie nǐ lái jiē wǒ!* / *Yīnggāi de!* 'Thanks for coming to meet me! / It's the least I could do!'

When someone fills your glass when you are conversing at a meal, or at other times when you might want to indicate appreciation without actually saying anything, you can tap the index finger, or the index and middle fingers on the table to express thanks. The practice is said to represent, with bent fingers, the act of bowing.

3.6.2 Sorry

Regret for minor infractions or potential shortcomings is most commonly expressed as *duìbuqǐ*, an expression built on the root *duì* 'to face squarely' (and hence 'to be correct'), plus the suffix *bùqǐ* ('not-rise', here suggesting 'not-worthy'). The typical response makes use of the culturally significant noun, *guānxi* 'connections'.

Duìbuqǐ!	'Sorry!' (I didn't hear, understand, etc.)
Méi guānxi.	'Never mind.'
Duìbuqǐ, lǎoshī, wǒ lái wǎn le.	'Sorry, sir, I'm late.' ('I come late LE')
Méi guānxi.	'Never mind.'

In a more serious context, regret may be expressed as *hěn bàoqiàn* '[I]'m very sorry' ('embrace shortcomings').

3.6.3 Refusal

No matter whether you are stopping by someone's home or office, or staying for a longer visit, your host will usually serve you tea or soft drinks, often together with some fruit or other snacks. Depending on the situation and the degree of imposition, it is polite to ritually refuse one or more time(s). Then, if you ultimately accept, you should consume them without showing desperation (just as you would in other countries and cultures). Some useful phrases for ritual refusals are provided below.

hē	*yòng*	*yào*	*mǎi*	*máfan*
'drink'	'use'	'want'	'buy'	'to bother; go to the trouble of'

OFFERS

Lǐ Dān, hē yì bēi chá ba.	'Li Dan, why don't you have a cup of tea.'
Zhāng lǎoshī, hē diǎnr shénme?	'Professor Zhang, what'll you have to drink?'

RESPONSES

Bú yòng le, bú yòng le.	'No need, I'm fine.' ('not use LE')
Bú yòng kèqi le!	'Don't bother!' ('not use politeness LE')
Bié máfan le.	'Don't go to any trouble.' ('don't bother LE')

Often, phrases can be used in combination and 'pile up': *Bú yòng le, bié máfan le, wǒ bù kě le!*

More abrupt refusals are appropriate when there is a perceived violation, as when merchants try to tout goods on the street.

Guāngdié, guāngpán!	'CDs, DVDs!'
Bú yào, bú yào!	'Not interested!' ('not want')
Bù xiǎng mǎi!	'Not interested!' ('not want buy')
Méi xìngqù!	'Not interested!' ('not have interest')

NOTE

Note the words for CD and DVD in the above example: *guāngdié* ('laser-small plate') and *guāngpán* ('laser-large plate'). *Guāng*, in this context, is short for *jīguāng* 'laser' ('excited-light'). These are good examples of how Chinese makes use of already existing lexical material to coin new words. Many street salesmen, however, will simply use the English terms 'CD' and 'DVD'.

3.6.4 Don't

The several responses to thanking and apologizing actually provide examples of the three main words of negation, *bù, méi, bié* 'don't'. The last is usually used in imperative statements and can be combined with the verb *wàng* 'to forget; to leave behind'.

Nǐ de sǎn, bié wàng le. 'Your umbrella, don't forget [it]!'
O, duì, xièxie. 'Oh, right, thanks!'
Bú xiè. 'You're welcome.'

Nǐ de píbāo, bié wàng le! 'Don't forget your wallet!'
O, tiān a, wǒ de píbāo! Duōxiè, duōxiè! 'Oh, heavens, my wallet!' 'Many thanks!'
Bú yòng kèqi. 'You're welcome.'

Exercise 3

Provide Chinese exchanges along the following lines.

'Excuse me, where is the office?'
'The office is upstairs.'

'Don't forget your passport!'
'Oh, heavens, my passport, thanks.'
'You're welcome!'

'Your bookbag, don't forget [it].'
'Yikes, thanks!'
'You're welcome.'

'Have some tea!'
'No, I'm fine, thanks.'

'What'll you have to drink?'
'You have tea?'

'Have some coffee.'
'Sorry, I don't drink coffee.'

3.7 Things to drink

Traditionally, Chinese quenched their thirst with soup (often simply the water used to boil vegetables) or, if they could afford it, tea. For formal occasions, there were varieties of *jiǔ*, alcoholic drinks made from grains such as rice and millet.

Today, soup, tea, and boiled water (*kāishuǐ*) are still the predominant beverages, but with increasing affluence and foreign commercial influence, drinking practices are changing, particularly in urban areas. Iced drinks, which were traditionally regarded as unhealthy, are now common. Soy milk drinks are popular, and even cow's milk is gaining acceptance (despite widespread lactose intolerance). With the rise of upscale restaurants and cocktail bars, alcohol drinking practices are changing too. A Franco-Chinese joint enterprise is producing wines made with grapes under the Dynasty (*Cháodài*) label. Brandies and whiskeys are also gaining popularity.

Foreign wines and spirits (*yángjiǔ*) are drunk in different fashion in China. Grape wines, for example, are sometimes mixed with carbonated drinks, or are watered down and drunk with meals. Spirits, served in small glasses or cups, are typically more compatible with the Chinese custom of toasting than are grape wines served in larger containers.

Non-alcoholic:

chá	'tea'
kāfēi	'coffee'
kāishuǐ	'boiled water'
kělè	'cola'
qìshuǐ	'carbonated drinks; soda'
guǒzhī	'fruit juice'
júzi zhī	'orange juice'
níngméng shuǐ	'lemonade'
niúnǎi	'milk'
dòujiāng	'soybean milk'
kuàngquánshuǐ	'mineral water' ('mineral-spring-water')
Kěkǒu kělè	'Coca-Cola'
Bǎishì kělè	'Pepsi'
Xuěbì	'Sprite' ('snow-azure')
Qī Xǐ	'7 Up'

Alcoholic:

yángjiŭ	('foreign-wine'); any foreign alcoholic drinks, both wines and spirits

Milder wines and beers:

píjiŭ	'beer'
zhāpí / shēngpí	'draft beer'
mĭjiŭ	'rice wine'
pútaojiŭ	'wine' ('grape-wine')
hóngjiŭ	'red wine'
hóngpútaojiŭ	'red wine' ('red-grape-wine')
báipútaojiŭ	'white wine'
huángjiŭ	'rice wine' ('yellow-wine')
Shàoxīngjiŭ	a smooth rice wine from *Shàoxīng* in *Zhèjiāng* province, often served hot

Spirits:

báijiŭ	generic white spirit, with high alcohol content
liángshijiŭ	generic name for wines made from grains
gāoliang⟨jiŭ⟩	a white spirit made from *gāoliang* 'sorghum'
Máotái⟨jiŭ⟩	the most famous of Chinese liquors, from *Máotái* in *Guìzhōu* province
Wŭliángyè	('five-grains-liquid'); a popular grain liquor with a medicinal taste

The syllable *pí* in *píjiŭ* derives from the English word 'beer', while *jiŭ* is a generic word for alcoholic drinks. Nowadays, there are a large number of popular beers in China, for example: *Yànjīng píjiŭ* (from *Yànjīng*, an old name for *Bĕijīng*), *Shànghăi píjiŭ*, *Wŭxīng píjiŭ* ('five star'), *Xuĕlù píjiŭ* ('snow deer'), and *Qīngdăo píjiŭ* (named after the city of *Qīngdăo* in *Shāndōng*). The *Qīngdăo* Company was originally a German brewery, established in Shandong's German concession.

Typically, soft drinks are served cold in China (albeit sometimes at a slightly higher price), but if not, you can request a cold one by saying *bīng de* ('ice one') or *yào bīng de* ('want ice one'). Generally, ice is not added to drinks. To be sure, however, you may want to add *bú yào bīngkuài* ('not want ice cubes') or, more politely, *qǐng bié jiā bīngkuài* ('request don't add ice cubes'). At fast food restaurants (Chinese or Western), you might anticipate the question of where you are going to eat the meal by saying: *zài zhèr chī* 'for here' ('at here eat'), *qǐng dǎbāo* 'please wrap [it]' ('request hit-wrap)', or *yào názǒu* 'to go' ('want take-go').

Exercise 4

Following the model above, practice ordering drinks in succinct language, stating the item first, and then the amount, for example: *Niúnǎi, yì bēi.* 'A glass of milk.'

1. a glass of Coke (Check to see if they have cold ones.)
2. a bottle of orange juice
3. two bottles of cold beer
4. two cups of tea and a cup of boiled water
5. two bottles of mineral water
6. two mugs of draft beer (Check first to see if they have it.)
7. two cups of coffee with milk, to go
8. two bottles or glasses of soda (First ask what kinds they have.)

DIALOGUE *Huáng Jūrén* (male) hears a knock on the door and recognizes his friend, *Zhèng Chūnhuá*. He addresses her with the personal form *xiǎo* plus the last syllable of her *míngzi*.

Hg:	*Shéi a?*	'Who is it?'
Zh:	*Wǒ shi Zhèng Chūnhuá.*	'I'm Zheng Chunhua.'
Hg:	*O, Xiǎohuá, qǐngjìn, qǐngzuò.*	'Oh, Xiaohua, come on in, have a seat.'
Zh:	*Xièxie. Ài, jīntiān rè jíle!*	'Thanks. Gosh, it's so hot today!'

Hg:	*Ng. Nà nǐ hē yìdiǎnr shénme? Yǒu kělè, níngméng shuǐ, píjiǔ.*	'Sure is. What'll you have to drink? There's cola, lemonade, beer.'
Zh:	*Bú yòng le, bú yòng le.*	'No need. [I'm fine.]'
Hg:	*Nǐ bié kèqi. Hē ba!*	'Relax. Have something!'
Zh:	*Hǎo, nà lái ⟨yì⟩ bēi lǜchá ba.*	'Okay, I'll have a cup of green tea, then.'
Hg:	*Hǎo, lǜchá . . . Nǐ zuìjìn zěnmeyàng?*	'Okay, green tea . . . How are you doing these days?'
Zh:	*Hái kěyǐ. Zuótiān yǒu diǎnr bù shūfu, dànshì xiànzài hǎo le.*	'I'm okay. I didn't feel too well yesterday, but I'm okay now.'
Hg:	*Nǐ tài máng le!*	'You're too busy!'
Zh:	*Shì yǒu diǎnr máng! Nǐ yě shì! Xuéshēng zǒngshì hěn máng, hěn lèi a!*	'I am a bit! You too! Students are always tired and busy!'

NOTES

a. Other teas: *lóngjǐng chá* '[a type of] green tea'; *wūlóng chá* 'oolong tea'; *júhuāchá* 'chrysanthemum tea'; *[Yīngguó] nǎichá* ('[English] milk-tea')

b. *zuìjìn* 'recently; these days'

3.8 Why; because [there's a lot of]; so

If someone says that he or she is tired or anxious, you will want to find out why. *Wèishénme* 'why', is made up of *wèi* 'for [the sake of]' and *shénme* 'what'. The response will often be introduced with *yīnwèi* 'because'. *Suǒyǐ* 'so' introduces the consequences. Before you can respond to this question, you will need some additional vocabulary. The following nouns all relate to classwork.

kǎoshì	*gōngkè*	*zuòyè*	*bàogào*	*shíyàn*
'test; exam'	'assignments'	'homework'	'reports'	'experiments'

NOTE

Kǎoshì and *shíyàn* are also two-syllable verbs meaning 'to do a test' and 'to do an experiment'. 'To test someone's ability in a subject' is simply *kǎo*: *Yīnggāi kǎo tāmen de Zhōngwén* '[We] should test their Chinese'. For now, concentrate on the use of these words as nouns.

DIALOGUES

Jīntiān zěnmeyàng?	'How are [you] today?'
Yǒu kǎoshì, suǒyǐ yǒu yìdiǎnr jǐnzhāng.	'[I] have a test, so [I]'m a bit nervous.'
Nǐ wèishénme jǐnzhāng?	'Why are you nervous?'
⟨Yīnwei⟩ míngtiān yǒu kǎoshì.	'⟨Because⟩ [I] have a test tomorrow.'
Shénme kǎoshì?	'What kind of test?'
Zhōngwén kǎoshì.	'A Chinese test.'

A LOT OF *Duō* (a word to be carefully distinguished from *dōu* 'all') is an SV meaning 'much; many; lots'. Its opposite, *shǎo* 'few; not many', is also common as an adverb meaning 'seldom; rarely'. *Duō* has some rather idiosyncratic properties. For example, it may modify nouns directly or be mediated by *de*, but to do so (with or without *de*), it requires the presence of at least a modifying adverb, such as *hěn*.

yǒu hěn duō ⟨de⟩ gōngkè	'lots of assignments'
yǒu hěn duō ⟨de⟩ kǎoshì	'lots of tests'
yǒu hěn duō ⟨de⟩ zuòyè	'lots of homework'

Instead of *hěn*, the two more or less synonymous adverbs *zhème* 'in this way; so; such' and *nàme* 'in that way; so; such' can also be used in conjunction with both *duō* and *shǎo*.

zhème duō gōngkè	'such a lot of assignments'
nàme duō bàogào	'so many reports'

Duō and *shǎo* can also be used as predicates—that is, main verbs. English finds the literal translation of the construction awkward ('exams are numerous'), preferring instead an existential 'there is/are' or a possessive 'we have'.

Shíyàn duō bu duō?	'Are there lots of experiments?'
Gōngkè bǐjiào duō.	'There are relatively many assignments.'
Bàogào yě hěn duō.	'[We] also have lots of reports.'
Zuòyè gèng duō.	'There is even more homework.'
Kǎoshì bù shǎo.	'[I] have quite a number of tests.'
Zuòyè wèishénme nàme shǎo?	'How come so little homework?'

Reference can be made to a class or course by simply presenting it at the head of the sentence as a 'topic'.

Zhōngwén zuòyè hěn duō.	'Chinese [class] has a lot of homework.'
Rìwén zuòyè duō, dànshì kǎoshì shǎo.	'Japanese [class] has a lot of homework, but few tests.'

Sentences of the above type can usually be re-formed with *yǒu* 'have', which makes them resemble common English constructions.

Zhōngwén yǒu hěn duō zuòyè.	'Chinese has lots of homework.'
Rìwén méiyǒu nàme duō kǎoshì.	'Japanese does not have so many tests.'
Zhōngwén, zuótiān yǒu kǎoshì, jīntiān yǒu bàogào.	'[We] had a test in Chinese yesterday, [and] today we have a report.'

Expressing 'lots of' or 'much'

Yǒu Zhōngwén zuòyè.	'[We] have Chinese homework.'
Yǒu hěn duō Zhōngwén zuòyè.	'There's a lot of Chinese homework.'
~ Zhōngwén zuòyè hěn duō.	'Chinese has lots of homework.'
Yǒu zhème duō Zhōngwén zuòyè.	'There's so much Chinese homework!'
Yǒu nàme duō Zhōngwén zuòyè.	'There's so much Chinese homework!'

Exercise 5

Paraphrase the following sentences in Chinese.

1. Explain that students have lots of homework each day so they're always tired.
2. Ask why Japanese [class] doesn't have many tests.
3. Explain that there are no classes tomorrow because it's May 1st.
4. Explain that your Chinese teacher is quite strict, and that you have lots of tests.
5. Explain that you didn't have any homework yesterday.
6. Ask why they have so many reports.
7. Explain that you feel quite nervous today because you have a test.
8. Explain that you have lots of tests, and even more assignments.
9. Explain that Chinese [class] isn't hard, but it has lots of homework.
10. Ask why they all have so many keys.

NOTE

May 1st is *Guójì Láodòng Jié* 'International Labor Day', celebrated in both the PRC and the ROC. Recently, to reduce overcrowding at scenic and historical sites, holiday schedules in the PRC have been reorganized, with the May Day holiday being reduced from a week to a three-day weekend.

3.9 Money

G. E. Morrison wrote a book called *An Australian in China*, about his journey across southwest China to northern Burma at the very end of the 19th century. In it, he described how he managed his money.

> Money in Western China consists of solid ingots of silver, and copper cash. The silver is in lumps of one tael or more each, the tael being a Chinese ounce and equivalent roughly to between 1400 and 1500 cash. . . . From Hankow to Chungking my money was remitted by draft through a Chinese

> bank. . . . I carried some silver with me; the rest I put up in a package and handed to a native post in Chungking, which undertook to deliver it intact to me in Yunnan city, 700 miles away, within a specified period. . . . Money is thus remitted in Western China with complete confidence and security. (Morrison 1902: 95)

Round coins (often bearing a *niánhào* or 'reign name') with square holes in the middle (traditionally, round objects are symbolic of heaven, square objects of earth) were used in China as early as several centuries BCE. In later times, these coins came to be known as *qián* 'cash; money'. Carried in strings of 1,000, they were the prevalent medium of exchange for small purchases. Morrison, as he notes, also carried lumps of silver which were useful for larger transactions. Silver was valued in *liǎng*, a unit of weight that is often translated as 'tael' in English, from Malay *tahil*. Originally, sixteen *liǎng* composed one *jīn*, translated in English by another term from Malay, the 'catty'. Nowadays, one *jīn* is divided into ten *liǎng* rather than sixteen. Paper money, reimbursable for silver (at least during those historical periods with a well-managed economy), has been in circulation in China for well over 1,000 years.

MODERN CURRENCIES Nowadays, currency in Mainland China is the *Rénmínbì* ('people's-currency'), abbreviated in English as 'RMB'. Its basic unit is the *yuán* (¥), colloquially called *kuài* and translated as 'dollar' or 'Chinese dollar'. Smaller denominations include the *jiǎo* (colloquially called *máo*) worth ten cents and the *fēn* worth one cent, which is, nowadays, hardly ever seen. In speech, ¥1.25 is *yí kuài liǎng máo wǔ* ('one dollar two dimes five'), rather than ('one dollar twenty-five cents'). Bills have values of one, two (rare), five, ten, fifty, and one hundred *yuán*. Coins are for small values only, including one *yuán*, five *máo* (fifty cents), and one *máo* (ten cents).

During the height of the communist period, foreign currencies were exchanged not for RMB, but for *wàihuìjuàn* 'Foreign Exchange Certificates' or simply 'FEC'. FEC were denominated like RMB and had the same official value, but since FEC were required for the purchase of foreign goods, they gained value on unofficial 'black' markets. FEC were officially abandoned in the early

1990s. Interestingly, some of the abandoned FEC ended up in neighboring Burma (Myanmar), which adopted the FEC system for a number of years.

In Taiwan (the Republic of China, or ROC), the unit of currency is the *Xīn Táibì*, called the 'new Taiwan Dollar' in English and abbreviated $NT. Like its Mainland counterpart, it is also called the *yuán* (*kuài* colloquially), with smaller units called *jiǎo* (*máo*) and *fēn*. Hong Kong also retains its own currency, called *Gǎngbì*, or Hong Kong Dollar in English (HK$). Macau's currency is the Pataca (abbreviated MOP$), divided into 100 Avos. It is roughly equivalent in value to the Hong Kong Dollar.

In Unit 2, you learned that money, *qián*, is counted with *kuài* 'yuan; dollar'. In fact, in formal language, *yuán* itself is the measure word, so that *yí kuài qián* is usually written (and sometimes spoken) as *yì yuán* (一元/一圆; both characters are used, but the former is more common).

3.9.1 Dollars and cents

Currency is subdivided into the following units (which are all measure words).

INFORMAL, SPOKEN WORD	LITERAL MEANING	FORMAL, WRITTEN WORD	VALUE
kuài	('lump; piece')	*yuán* ('round')	1.00
máo	('hair; small amount')	*jiǎo*	0.10
fēn	('part')	*fēn*	0.01

Note that *qián* is the noun—*kuài, máo, fēn,* etc. are measure words by which *qián* is counted.

yí kuài qián	*liǎng kuài qián*	*sān kuài qián*	*wǔ kuài qián*	*shí kuài qián*
yí kuài	*liǎng kuài*	*sān kuài*	*wǔ kuài*	*shí kuài*
RMB 1	RMB 2	RMB 3	RMB 5	RMB 10

liǎng máo	*bā máo*	*sān fēn* ⟨*qián*⟩	*jiǔ fēn* ⟨*qián*⟩	*liǎng máo wǔ*
RMB 0.20	RMB 0.80	3 cents	9 cents	25 cents

NOTE

Yuán and *jiǎo* are primarily written forms that appear on currency, menus, and bills. In spoken language, *kuài* and *máo* are more commonly used; however, in certain formal settings like hotels and banks, *yuán* and *jiǎo* are sometimes spoken: *sì yuán wǔ jiǎo* '¥4.50'.

Exercise 6

Practice citing the following prices until you can do so fluently and comfortably.

1.	0.30	11.	25.00
2.	0.50	12.	11.85
3.	1.00	13.	35.00
4.	1.40	14.	39.95
5.	2.00	15.	19.35
6.	0.85	16.	0.15
7.	0.95	17.	0.75
8.	3.60	18.	1.85
9.	9.95	19.	99.00
10.	15.00	20.	102.00

3.9.2 How many?

A. *DUŌSHAO* The opposites *duō* 'many' and *shǎo* 'few' combine to form the question word *duōshao* 'how many' (with *qīngshēng* on the second syllable).

Jīntiān yǒu duōshao xuéshēng? 'How many students today?'
Yǒu èrshísān ge. 'Twenty-three.'
Zuótiān ne? 'And yesterday?'
Zuótiān yǒu èrshísì ge! 'Twenty-four, yesterday.'

Duōshao qián? 'How much money?'
Liǎng kuài. '¥2.00.'

B. *JǏ GE?* When the expected number is low, the question word is not *duōshao*, but *jǐ* + M. Smaller than expected numbers and amounts may attract the adverb *zhǐ* 'only'.

Yǒu duōshao xuéshēng?	'How many students are there?'
Yǒu èrshísì ge.	'Twenty-four.'
Yǒu jǐ ge lǎoshī?	'How many teachers are there?'
Zhǐ yǒu yí ge.	'Only one.'
Nǐ yǒu jǐ kuài qián?	'How much [money] do you have?'
Wǒ zhǐ yǒu yí kuài.	'I have only a dollar.'
Wǒ de jiā lí jīchǎng zhǐ yǒu sān gōnglǐ.	'My house is only three kilometers from the airport.'
Nà hěn jìn!	'That's close!'

C. PRICES Prices can be asked with *duōshao* (usually without a measure word) or *jǐ* + M. The item in question can be placed first, with the sense of 'cost' left implicit.

Bǐjìběn duōshao qián?	'How much are notebooks?'
Yǔsǎn jǐ kuài qián?	'How many dollars for an umbrella?'

When items are sold by particular amounts, Chinese will use an appropriate M.

Sān kuài bā yí ge.	'¥3.80 each [for one].'
Wǔ máo yí fèn.	'¥0.50 each [per newspaper].'
Shí'èr kuài sān yì běn.	'¥12.30 each [per notebook].'

3.9.3 Making a purchase

In China, shopping and buying often take place under adverse conditions—markets can be noisy and crowded, vendors often have strong local accents, and tickets are often sold through small windows jammed with customers. Therefore, it pays to reduce grammatical complexity and speak in short, sharp phrases. We will start with food and drink. To the drink vocabulary introduced earlier, we can add some fruit. (For health reasons, many Chinese peel fruit before eating, and many even peel grapes.)

píngguǒ	*xiāngjiāo*	*xīguā*	*mángguǒ*	*chéngzi*
'apples'	'bananas'	'watermelons'	'mangoes'	'oranges'
↓	↓	↓	↓	↓
yí ge	*yí ge*	*yí ge*	*yí ge*	*yí ge*
	yí chuàn	*yí piàn (kuài)*		

Such fruits are purchased whole (*yí ge*), as parts (*yí piàn* 'a slice', *yí kuài* 'a piece'), or as bunches (*yí chuàn* 'a bunch; a cluster'). They can also be bought by weight, typically measured by the *jīn* in China.

yì jīn	'a catty'	½ kilogram, or 1.1 pounds
yì liǎng	'a tael'	ten *liǎng* in one *jīn*
yì gōngjīn	'a kilogram'	two *jīn*, or 2.2 pounds
yí bàng	'a pound'	

NOTES

a. Not so long ago, the *liǎng* was $1/16$ of a *jīn* (hence the term 'Chinese ounce').

b. People say *èr liǎng* 'two taels', rather than the awkward *liǎng liǎng*.

OTHER ITEMS

	bǐnggān	*miànbāo*	*gāodiǎn*	*miànjīnzhǐ*	*bīngjilín*
	'cookies'	'bread'	'pastries'	'tissues'	'ice cream'
M:	*bāo*	*gè*	*kuài*	*bāo*	*gēn*

NOTES

a. *Bǐng* is the generic word for *tortilla* or pancake-like foods; *gān* means 'dry'.

b. *Gāo* is a generic word for 'cake'; *diǎn* is 'a bit' or 'a snack'.

c. *Bīngjilín* is also pronounced *bīngqilín* and *bīngjilíng* (*jilín* ~ *qilín* deriving from English 'cream'). Ice cream is commonly available on a stick (*yì gēn*), in tubs (*yì xiǎobēi*), and in cartons (*yì hé*).

Duōshao qián yì jīn?

Exercise 7

What would you say to purchase the following items in the amounts indicated?

Work with a partner, if possible, with one of you buying and the other selling. The buyer should begin with a perfunctory (but friendly) greeting, then state the item—pointing to it if possible—and the quantity needed. The seller is likely to volunteer the price (per unit, if relevant), and the buyer can then repeat it to himself, or for confirmation, and close with: *Hǎo, jiù zhèiyàngr ba*. You would be expected to bargain a bit at street stalls–less so in shops. For now, you are buying small things and you won't lose much! (Prices given may need some adjusting.)

Item	Quantity	Price per unit
1. apple	1	0.70 each
2. bananas	1 bunch	2.50 for a bunch
3. apples	1 jin	1.50 per jin
4. biscuits	1 pack	4.00 a pack
5. spring water	1 bottle	2.00 a bottle

Item	Quantity	Price per unit
6. cola	2 bottles	5.00 for two bottles
7. bread	1 loaf	4.00 a loaf
8. buns	3	1.50 for three
9. orange juice	1 bottle	2.75 a bottle
10. watermelon	1 slice	0.80 per slice
11. watermelon	whole	1.80 per jin
12. cigarettes	1 pack	5.00 per pack
13. bananas	2	0.60 for two
14. tissue	2 packs	3.00 per pack
15. ice cream	1 tub	1.75 per tub
16. *Mènglóng*	1 stick	6.00 per stick

NOTE

Mènglóng is the Chinese translation of 'Magnum', the name of a Wall's [brand] chocolate covered vanilla ice cream, one of a number of 'popsicles' widely sold at street stands and small shops throughout China.

3.10 Other numbered sets

3.10.1 Telephone numbers

Asking about someone's *diànhuà hàomǎ* 'telephone number' makes use of the question words *duōshao* or *shénme.*

⟨Nǐ de⟩ diànhuà ⟨hàomǎ⟩ shi duōshao?
⟨Nǐ de⟩ diànhuà ⟨hàomǎ⟩ shi shénme? } 'What's your phone number?'

Local phone numbers in major Mainland Chinese cities generally have seven or eight digits (i.e., 3 + 4 or 4 + 4). Area codes begin with 0 and are followed by two or three digits. To state phone numbers, you need to know that 'zero' is *líng*, and that on the Mainland (but not Taiwan), the number 'one' (in strings of numbers, such as telephone numbers) is spoken *yāo* rather than *yī.*

Wǒ jiā lǐ de diànhuà shi (bāliùyāolíng) liù'èrwǔliù-jiǔ'èrsānsān. Wǒ de shǒujī shì (yāosānliùbā) yāosìbā sānqī'èrbā. Wǒ zài shuō yì biān: (yāosānliùbā) yāosìbā sānqī'èrbā.

'My home phone is (8610) 6256-9233. My cell is (136) 8148-3728. I'll repeat it ('I again say one time'): (136) 8148-3728.'

Diànhuà ('electric-speech') is the word for an ordinary telephone, but in China people are more likely to talk about their *shǒujī* 'mobile phone' ('hand-machine'). A variation on *shǒujī* is *xiǎolíngtōng* ('small-lively-communicator'), a cheap mobile phone that can be used only in a single locale. (*Xiǎolíngtōng* are now being phased out and will not be supported after 2010.)

3.10.2 Days of the week

The traditional Chinese lunar month was divided into three periods (*xún*) of ten days each. However, when the Gregorian calendar was adopted, the term *lǐbài* (itself a compound of *lǐ* 'ceremony; reverence' and *bài* 'pay respects'), which had been adapted by Christians to mean 'worship', was used to name days of the week. Today, *xīngqī* ('star-period') is preferred in print, at least on the Mainland, but *lǐbài* continues as a common colloquial form. The days of the week are formed by the addition of numerals, beginning with *yī* for Monday. Interestingly, the week (according to the calendar) begins with Monday in China, not Sunday.

lǐbàiyī	*xīngqīyī*	'Monday'
lǐbài'èr	*xīngqī'èr*	'Tuesday'
lǐbàisān	*xīngqīsān*	'Wednesday'
lǐbàisì	*xīngqīsì*	'Thursday'
lǐbàiwǔ	*xīngqīwǔ*	'Friday'
lǐbàiliù	*xīngqīliù*	'Saturday'
lǐbàitiān	*xīngqītiān*	'Sunday'
lǐbàirì	*xīngqīrì*	'Sunday' (alternate form)

Since the variable for days of the week is a number, the question is formed with *jǐ* 'how many': *lǐbàijǐ* ~ *xīngqījǐ* 'what day of the week'. Notice that there is conveniently no *lǐbàiqī* or *xīngqīqī* to confuse with *lǐbàijǐ* and *xīngqījǐ*.

'Daily' can be expressed as *měitiān* 'everyday'. A period of time covering several consecutive days can be expressed with *cóng* 'from' and *dào* 'to': ⟨*cóng*⟩ *lǐbàiyī dào* ⟨*lǐbài*⟩*sì* '⟨from⟩ Monday to Thursday'.

Jīntiān lǐbàijǐ?	'What's the day today?'
Jīntiān lǐbàiyī.	'[It]'s Monday.'
Míngtiān lǐbài'èr, shì bu shi?	'Tomorrow's Tuesday, isn't it?'
Shì, zuótiān shi lǐbàitiān.	'Yes, yesterday was Sunday.'
Lǐbài'èr yǒu kǎoshì ma?	'Is/was there an exam on Tuesday?'
Yǒu, dànshì lǐbàisān méiyǒu kè.	'Yes, but there are no classes on Wednesday.'
Xīngqīsì hěn máng.	'[I]'m busy on Thursday.'
Xīngqīwǔ xíng ma?	'Will Friday work?'
Měitiān dōu yǒu kè ma?	'Do [you] have class every day?'
Bù, xīngqīyī dào ⟨*xīngqī*⟩*sì dōu yǒu, dànshì xīngqīwǔ méiyǒu.*	'No, Monday to Thursday [I] do, but not on Friday.'

NOTE

Recall that when giving dates (e.g., *jīntiān xīngqīyī*), *shì* is often omitted if no adverbs are present. In the negative, *shì* would appear as support for the adverb *bù*: *Jīntiān bú shì xīngqīyī.*

3.10.3 Days of the month

Days of the month are formed, quite regularly, with *hào*, which in this context means 'number'.

Jīntiān jǐ hào?	'What's the date today?'
Èrshísān hào.	'The 23rd.'
Èrshíwǔ hào hěn máng—yǒu Zhōngwén kǎoshì.	'[We]'re busy on the 25th—there's a Chinese test.'

NAMES OF THE MONTHS The names of the months are also quite regular, formed with the word *yuè* 'moon; month' (often expanded to *yuèfèn*) preceded by a number: *sānyuè* 'March,' *liùyuèfèn* 'June', *shíyīyuè* 'November'. As with the other date elements, the question is formed with *jǐ* 'how many'.

Jīntiān jǐyuè jǐ hào?	'What's the date today?'
Jīntiān liùyuè èrshí'èr hào.	'Today's June 22nd.'
Shíyuè sān hào yǒu kǎoshì.	'There's a test on October 3rd.'
Shíyuè yī hào shi Guóqìngjié suǒyǐ méiyǒu kè.	'October 1st is National Day so there are no classes.'

NOTE

Guóqìngjié 'National Day' ('nation-celebration-festival') is a non-traditional holiday, celebrated on October 1st to mark the founding of the PRC.

Notice that dates and days of the week, such as *xīngqīliù* and *shíyuè sān hào*, behave like other 'time when' phrases, such as *jīntiān* and *měitiān*, in preceding the verbs with which they are associated.

3.10.4 Siblings

The collective term for brothers and sisters is *xiōngdì-jiěmèi*. *Xiōng* is an archaic equivalent of *gēge* 'older brother'; but the other syllables are all single-syllable reflections of the appropriate independent words for siblings: *dìdi* 'younger brother', *jiějie* 'older sister', and *mèimei* 'younger sister'.

Nǐ yǒu xiōngdì-jiěmèi ma?	'Do you have any brothers or sisters?'
Yǒu ⟨yí⟩ ge dìdi, yí ge mèimei.	'[I] have a younger brother and a younger sister.'
Yǒu méiyǒu xiōngdì-jiěmèi?	'Do [you] have any brothers or sisters?'
Wǒ zhǐ yǒu ⟨yí⟩ ge jiějie.	'I only have an older sister.'
Hǎoxiàng nǐ yǒu ⟨yí⟩ ge gēge, duì ma?	'Seems like you have an older brother, right?'
Méiyǒu, zhǐ yǒu ⟨yí⟩ ge jiějie.	'No, only an older sister.'

NOTE

In object position, the *yí* of *yí ge* is often elided, as indicated by ⟨*yí*⟩ *ge*.

3.10.5 *Yígòng* 'altogether; in all'

Yígòng is an adverb meaning 'all together; in all', but because it is more versatile than prototypical adverbs such as *yě* and *dōu*, it is classified as a 'moveable adverb'. Moveable adverbs, unlike regular ones, can sometimes appear without a following verb.

Jīntiān yígòng yǒu duōshao xuéshēng?	'How many students today?'
Yígòng yǒu shíqī ge.	'There are seventeen altogether!'
Yígòng duōshao qián?	'How much money altogether?'
Yígòng yìqiān liǎngbǎi kuài.	'Altogether, ¥1,200.'

Exercise 8

Express the following in Chinese.

1. Give your phone number.
2. Give the date.
3. Find out how many students there are today altogether.
4. Explain that you have a younger brother and an older sister.
5. Explain that there's an exam on October 30th.
6. Explain that you only have one dollar.
7. Explain that you're feeling quite anxious because you have so many exams!
8. Explain that you have an exam every day from Monday to Thursday.

3.11 Courses and classes

3.11.1 Subjects of study

Subjects of study—courses—frequently end in *xué* 'study; learning' (cf. *xuéshēng*); however, when a subject consists of two or more syllables, *xué* is optional.

shùxué	'mathematics' ('numbers-study')
lìshǐ⟨xué⟩	'history'
wùlǐ⟨xué⟩	'physics' ('things-principles')
jīngjì⟨xué⟩	'economics'
wénxué	'literature' ('language-study')
gōngchéng⟨xué⟩	'engineering'
guǎnlǐxué	'management'

Tǐyù 'physical education' is more 'sports' than a subject of study, so it is not usually combined with *xué*.

3.11.2 Talking about classes

A. CLASSES, COURSES, SESSIONS Many words function as both nouns and measure words. For example, *kè* can be a noun meaning 'subject; course' or a measure word meaning 'lesson'. Measure words only appear after numbers (or demonstratives) and are optionally followed by nouns: *yí ge ⟨xuéshēng⟩*; *zhèi ge rén, yí kuài ⟨qián⟩*. When there is no number (or demonstrative), there will be no measure words.

Jīntiān méiyǒu kè.	'[I] don't have class today.'
Kè hěn nán.	'The course/class is tough.'
Méiyǒu píjiǔ le.	'[We]'re out of beer!'

Nouns may be counted with different measures, each conveying slightly different nuances. *Kè*, as a noun meaning 'subject; class', for example, can be counted with *mén* (whose root meaning is 'door') when the sense is 'a course' and with *jié* (root meaning 'segment') or *táng* (root meaning 'hall') when the meaning is 'a class session'.

	KÈ	TÁNG	JIÉ	MÉN	BĀN
as Noun	'subject'	'hall'	'segment'	'door'	'session; class'
as Measure	'lesson'	'class'	'class'	'course/ subject'	[scheduled trip on bus, etc.; flight]

The following examples illustrate the various functions of the five words listed across the top of the above table. The first interchange contains *mén* as a M and *kè* as a N, the second, *kè* as a N and *táng* as a M, etc.

M: *mén*; N: *kè*	*Zhèi ge xuéqī, nǐ yǒu jǐ mén kè?*	'How many courses do you have this term?'
M: *mén*; N: *kè*	*Wǒ yǒu sì mén kè.*	'I have four.'
N: *kè*	*Jīntiān hái yǒu biéde kè ma?*	'Do [you] have other classes today?'
M: *táng*	*Hái yǒu liǎng táng.*	'I still have two more.'
M: *jié*	*Jīntiān yǒu jǐ jié?*	'How many [classes] today?'
N: *kè*	*Jīntiān méiyǒu kè.*	'I don't have any classes today.'
M: *jié*	*Nà, míngtiān ne, míngtiān yǒu jǐ jié?*	'Well, what about tomorrow, how many [classes] tomorrow?'
M: *jié*	*Míngtiān zhǐ yǒu yì jié: shùxué.*	'Tomorrow, I just have one—mathematics.'
N: *kè*	*Jīntiān yǒu kè, kěshì míngtiān méiyǒu!*	'There's class today, but not tomorrow.'
M: *kè*	*Zhè shi dì-yī kè.*	'This is the first lesson.'
M: *kè*	*Yígòng yǒu sānshí kè.*	'There are thirty lessons altogether.'

In addition to the noun form of *kè* 'class', the noun *bān*, whose root meaning is 'shift' or 'session' (cf. *shàngbān* 'to go to work'), is also relevant to the subject of taking classes. Large sessions (or lectures) are *dàbān*, and small sessions (or sections) are *xiǎobān*. These are counted with the general M, *gè*.

Yígòng yǒu wǔ ge bān, liǎng ge dàbān, sān ge xiǎobān.	'[There are] five sessions altogether: two lectures and three sections.'

Like *kè*, *bān* can also function as a measure word, but not for classes. *Bān* is a common M for trips of regularly scheduled transport, such as buses and airplanes: *Xīngqīyī-sān-wǔ yǒu yì bān.* 'There's a flight/bus/train on Monday, Wednesday, and Friday.'

B. 'TAKING' CLASSES In the examples above, 'taking a class' was construed as 'having a class': *yǒu wǔ mén kè.* However, you should be aware that just as English allows the option of saying 'how many courses do you have' and 'how many courses are you taking', so Chinese also offers options with *shàng* 'take' ('attend') and *xiū* 'take' ('cultivate'). The latter is used particularly in Taiwan.

Nǐ zhèi ge xuéqī shàng / yǒu / xiū jǐ mén kè?	'How many courses are you taking this semester?'
Wǒ shàng / yǒu / xiū wǔ mén.	'I'm taking five.'

3.11.3 Moveable adverbs: *dāngrán; yídìng*

A. DĀNGRÁN 'OF COURSE' *Dāngrán*, like *yígòng*, is classified as a moveable adverb, because some of the positional requirements of typical adverbs (such as preceding a verb) are relaxed.

Lǐbàiwǔ yǒu kè ma?	'Are there classes on Friday?'
Dāngrán, měitiān dōu yǒu kè.	'Of course, there are classes every day.'
Yǒu zuòyè ma?	'Any homework?'
Dāngrán yǒu zuòyè, měitiān dōu yǒu zuòyè.	'Of course there's homework, there's homework every day!'

B. *YÍDÌNG* 'FOR CERTAIN; FOR SURE'

Xīngqīliù yídìng méi kè ma?	'Is [it] certain that there's no class on Saturday?'
Xīngqīliù, xīngqītiān yídìng méiyǒu kè.	'For certain there are no classes on Saturday and Sunday.'

Yídìng is especially common in the negative, *bù yídìng* 'not necessarily', when it often stands alone. Frequently, *bù yídìng* can be followed by a comment beginning with *yǒude* 'some', literally meaning 'there are some of them [which]'.

Kǎoshì dōu hěn nán ma?	'Are the tests all difficult?'
Bù yídìng. Yǒude hěn nán, yǒude bù nán!	'Not necessarily. Some are difficult, some aren't!'
Xuéshēng yídìng hěn lèi ma?	'Are students necessarily always tired?'
Bù, lǎoshī hěn lèi, xuéshēng bù yídìng.	'No, teachers are tired, students aren't necessarily.'

Exercise 9

Express the following statements in Chinese.

1. In all, you're taking five courses this semester, and they're all hard.
2. In Beijing, November isn't necessarily cold but July is certainly hot.
3. You have lots of classes on Tuesday and Thursday, but only one on Wednesday.
4. The lecture has 120 students, but the sections only have 12.
5. The mathematics teacher isn't too strict, but the tests are hard.
6. You don't have any more classes today.
7. You were nervous yesterday, but you're okay today.
8. The physics teacher is very strict, so you're nervous in class.

3.11.4 Question words as indefinites

Question words in Chinese have two roles: they can function in questions (corresponding to the English question words 'who', 'what', 'where', etc.), and they can function as indefinites (corresponding to English 'anyone', 'anything', 'anywhere', etc.) So, *shénme*, in addition to its interrogative use, can also mean 'anything' in a non-interrogative context. The fuller sense is often 'anything in particular'.

Méi shénme wèntí.	'[I] don't have any questions [in particular].'
Méi shénme gōngkè.	'[We] don't have any homework [in particular].'
Xièxie nǐ lái jiē wǒ.	'Thanks for coming to pick me up.'
Méi shénme. Hěn jìn!	'[It]'s nothing. [It]'s close by!'
Duìbuqǐ, nǐ xìng shénme, wǒ wàng le.	'Sorry, what's your name—I've forgotten.'
Méi shénme. Wǒ xìng Zōu.	'That's all right. My surname's Zou.'

Many more examples of question words used as indefinites will be encountered in later units.

3.12 Dialogue: Courses and classes

Jiǎ and *Yǐ* are classmates at school, chatting over breakfast before going to class.

Jiǎ:	*Èi, nǐ hǎo, jīntiān zěnmeyàng?*	'Hi, how are you? How's it going today?'
Yǐ:	*Hái hǎo, hái hǎo.*	'Fine, fine.'
Jiǎ:	*Nǐ jīntiān máng bu máng?*	'You busy today?'
Yǐ:	*Hěn máng!*	'I am!'
Jiǎ:	*Wèishénme?*	'How come?'
Yǐ:	*Yīnwèi yǒu kǎoshì.*	'Because I have a test.'
Jiǎ:	*Yǒu shénme kǎoshì?*	'What test?'
Yǐ:	*Zhōngwén kǎoshì.*	'A Chinese [language] test.'

Jiă:	*Nà míngtiān ne?*	'Well how about tomorrow?'
Yǐ:	*Míngtiān méiyǒu. Míngtiān hái hǎo.*	'None tomorrow. Tomorrow's fine.'
Jiă:	*Yǒu gōngkè ma?*	'Do [you] have any homework?'
Yǐ:	*Yǒu, dāngrán yǒu.*	'Sure, of course [we] do.'
Jiă:	*Zhōngwén, gōngkè duō bu duō?*	'Is there a lot of homework in Chinese?'
Yǐ:	*Hěn duō, kěshì hěn yǒuyìsi!*	'There's a lot, but it's interesting!'
Jiă:	*Hěn nán ba!*	'It must be difficult!'
Yǐ:	*Bú tài nán, hái hǎo.*	'It's not so bad, it's fine.'
Jiă:	*Nǐ hái yǒu shénme biéde kè?*	'What other classes do you have?' ('you still have what other classes')
Yǐ:	*Jīntiān hái yǒu wùlǐ, shùxué, míngtiān yǒu lìshǐ.*	'I still have physics and math today, tomorrow I have history.'
Jiă:	*Zhōngwén měitiān dōu yǒu ma?*	'Do you have Chinese every day?' ('Chinese daily all have Q')
Yǐ:	*Xīngqīyī dào sì dōu yǒu, xīngqīwǔ méiyǒu.*	'Every day [from] Monday to Thursday, not on Friday.' ('Monday to Thursday all have, Friday not-have')
Jiă:	*Zhèi ge xuéqī yígòng shàng sì mén kè ma?*	'You're taking four courses altogether this semester?' ('this M term altogether take four M courses Q')
Yǐ:	*Yígòng shàng wǔ mén, hái yǒu tǐyù. Kěshì tǐyù méi shénme zuòyè.*	'Five altogether; there's PE as well. But PE doesn't have any homework.'
Jiă:	*Wǔ mén kè, yídìng hěn lèi!*	'Five courses, [you] must be tired!'
Yǐ:	*Hái kěyǐ.*	'[I] manage.'

Variations of *Nǐ jīntiān máng bu máng?* include:

Jīntiān nǐ jǐn⟨zhāng⟩ bù jǐnzhāng?	'Are you nervous today?'
Jīntiān nǐ lèi bu lèi?	'Are you tired today?'
Jīntiān hǎo ma?	'Are things okay today?'
Nǐ shū⟨fu⟩ bù shūfu?	'Are you comfortable?'

Variations of *Yǒu kǎoshì* include:

Yǒu gōngkè.	'There's / [we] have homework.'
Yǒu zuòyè.	'There's / [we] have an assignment.'
Yǒu bàogào.	'There's / [we] have a report.'
Yǒu shíyàn.	'There's / [we] have a lab.'

Exercise 10

Here are some sentences written by students learning Chinese. Identify and explain the likely mistakes; then correct them.

1. *Wǒmen hái méi chī le.
2. *Méiyǒu kǎoshì míngtiān.
3. *Zhōu, nǐ è bu è?
4. *Míngtiān yǒu shénme kǎoshì? / Míngtiān méiyǒu.
5. *Chī fàn le ma? / Hái méi ne? / Wǒ yě. ('Me neither!')
6. *Tā hěn hǎochī.
7. *Míngtiān shémme kǎoshì nǐ yǒu?

3.13 Sounds and pinyin

3.13.1 Tone combos (the final three sets)

(13)	*kāfēi*	(14)	*bù nán*	(15)	*Táiwān*
	fēijī		*dàxué*		*Chéngdū*
	cāntīng		*shùxué*		*zuótiān*

3.13.2 Initials

Recall that in the chart of initial sounds and symbols in Unit 1 (p. 13), rows 3 and 4 are in complementary distribution with row 5. The following groupings provide a summary. Review them by reading the examples aloud. Exercise 11 provides additional review of initials and rhymes.

(3, 4)	*i* (never [ee])		*u* ([oo], never [yu])	
	zì	*zhì*	*zū, zūn*	*zhǔ, zhǔn*
	cì	*chì*	*cū, cūn*	*chū, chūn*
	sǐ	*shǐ*	*sū, sūn*	*shù, shùn*
	rì			*rù, rùn*
(5)	i ([ee] only)		u ([yu], never [oo])	
	jī, jiē, jiān		*jū, juē, juān*	
	qì, qiè, qiàn		*qù, què, quàn*	
	xī, xiē, xiān		*xū, xuē, xuān*	

Exercise 11

Write lines 3, 4, and 5 of your initial chart (z, c, s, etc.) on a sheet of paper. Then, as your teacher recites a list like the one below, identify the initial involved:

xiě, chū, xī, qǔ, sū, shǔ, zhǔn, jūn, xián, cì, shuài, xǔ, cái, shì, xǐ, shùn

Read the following sets down; they all contain open 'o' rhymes.

dōu	*zhuō*	*gòu*	*tuō*	*lóu*	*pǒ*	*zǒu*	*shuō*	*ròu*	*mó*
duō	*zhōu*	*guò*	*tōu*	*luó*	*pǒu*	*zuǒ*	*shōu*	*ruò*	*móu*

Now, practice reading the following aloud, by row.

1.	*rè*	*lè*	*hé*	*è*	*kě*
2.	*rén*	*bèn*	*hěn*	*gēn*	*mén*
3.	*mèng*	*lěng*	*pèng*	*gèng*	*fěng*

4.	*zhāng*	*cháng*	*pàng*	*tàng*	*ràng*
5.	*hǎo*	*zhào*	*pǎo*	*mǎo*	*zǎo*
6.	*xiè*	*bié*	*jiè*	*tiē*	*liè*
7.	*lèi*	*bēi*	*méi*	*fēi*	*zéi*
8.	*lái*	*tài*	*mǎi*	*pái*	*zài*

3.14 Summary

Numbers	*yìbǎiwàn* (~ *yībǎiwàn*)
M words	*yì bēi chá; yí ge bēizi*
Nationality	*Nǐ shi něi guó rén? Tā shi cóng shénme dìfang lái de?*
Ever been?	*Nǐ qùguo Zhōngguó ma? / Méi qùguo.*
Miles away	*Jīchǎng lí wǒ jiā zhǐ yǒu sān lǐ ⟨lù⟩.*
NSEW	*Běijīng zài Zhōngguó běibiānr; Wúhàn zài zhōngbù.* *Yuènán zài Zhōngguó de nánbiānr.*
Confirmation	*Nǐ shi dì-yī ma? / Shì de; Tā bú shi Měiguó rén ba. / Shì.* *Jīntiān shì hěn rè!*
Tag questions	*Nǐ de sǎn, shì bu shi?*
Thanks	*Xièxie. / Bié kèqi.*
Sorry	*Duìbuqǐ. / Méi guānxi.*
Refusal	*Hē yìdiǎnr shénme? / Bú yòng le, hái hǎo.*
Don't forget	*Nǐ de sǎn, bié wàng le.*
Why?	*Wèishénme hěn máng? / Yīnwèi yǒu hěn duō kǎoshì.*
Lots of	*Zhōngwén zuòyè hěn duō; Zhōngwén yǒu hěn duō zuòyè.*
How many?	*Yǒu duōshao xuéshēng? Jǐ ge lǎoshī?* *Duōshao qián? / Liǎng kuài.*
Prices	*Píngguǒ duōshao qián yì jīn?*
Telephone	*Nǐ de diànhuà shi duōshao?*
Weekdays	*Lǐbàiwǔ méiyǒu kè.*
Siblings	*Yǒu xiōngdì-jiěmèi ma?*
Altogether	*Yígòng yǒu / shàng / xiū jǐ mén kè?*
Classes	*Jīntiān hái yǒu jǐ táng kè?*
Any	*Méi shénme wèntí.*
Other	*Hái yǒu shénme biéde kè?*

Exercise 12

Read each row aloud and then provide a distinguishing phrase for each word. For example, for the first set: *Wǒ bù shūfu; Gāo shīfu, hǎo; Shùxué hěn nán ba; nǐ de shūbāo.*

1.	*shūfu*	*shīfu*	*shùxué*	*shūbāo*
2.	*lǎoshī*	*kǎoshì*	*lìshǐ*	*kěshì*
3.	*gōngkè*	*kèqi*	*yígòng*	*gōnglǐ*
4.	*xīngqīyī*	*xīngqījǐ*	*xíngli*	*xìng Lǐ*
5.	*měitiān*	*tiānqì*	*zìdiǎn*	*tǐng hǎo*
6.	*zàijiàn*	*zuìjìn*	*jǐnzhāng*	*zài zhèr*
7.	*qián*	*xiānshēng*	*hǎoxiàng*	*xuéshēng*
8.	*xìng*	*xíng*	*xíngli*	*qǐng*
9.	*xiànzài*	*xǐzǎo*	*zǒngshi*	*hǎochī*
10.	*búguò*	*bú guì*	*bù gāo*	*bǐjiào*
11.	*cóngqián*	*cāntīng*	*gōngjīn*	*gāodiǎn*
12.	*qùguo*	*chīguo*	*qí ge*	*kèqi*

3.15 Rhymes and rhythms

Dàtóu

Dàtóu, dàtóu, ('Big-head, big-head,')
xiàyǔ, bù chóu; ('falls-rain, not worry;')
biérén yǒu sǎn, ('other-people have umbrella,')
wǒ yǒu dà tóu. ('I have big head.')

Sheila Yong, formerly at Boston University, made up an equally good version.

Tūtóu, tūtóu, ('Bald-head, bald-head,')
dà fēng, bù chóu; ('big wind, not worry;')
biérén luàn fà, ('other-people messy hair,')
wǒ béng shūtóu! ('I no+need comb-head!')

Sānlúnchē	
Sānlúnchē, pǎo+de kuài,	('three-wheel-vehicle, runs +DE fast,')
shàngmiàn zuò ⟨yí⟩ ge lǎo tàitai;	('top-side sits old woman;')
yào wǔ máo, gěi yí kuài,	('[driver] wants five dimes, [she] gives a dollar,')
nǐ shuō qíguài bù qíguài?	('you say strange or not?')

Appendix: Countries and nationalities

Appending *rén* to the end of a country name regularly names the nationality of people from that country.

COUNTRIES (*GUÓJIĀ*)

China	*Zhōngguó*
Taiwan	*Táiwān*
Singapore	*Xīnjiāpō*
Indonesia	*Yìnní*
Vietnam	*Yuènán*
Thailand	*Tàiguó*
Malaysia	*Mǎláixīyà*
Myanmar (Burma)	*Miǎndiàn*
India	*Yìndù*
Bangladesh	*Mèngjiālā*
Pakistan	*Bājīsītǎn*
Afghanistan	*Āfùhàn*
Iran	*Yīlǎng*
Iraq	*Yīlàkè*
Israel	*Yǐsèliè*
Japan	*Rìběn*
(South) Korea	*Hánguó*
(North) Korea	*Cháoxiǎn*
Philippines	*Fēilǜbīn*

Australia	*Àodàlìyà*
New Zealand	*Xīn Xīlán*
South Africa	*Nánfēi*
Nigeria	*Nírìlìyà*
Egypt	*Āijí*
USA	*Měiguó*
Canada	*Jiānádà*
Mexico	*Mòxīgē*
Brazil	*Bāxī*
Argentina	*Āgēntíng*
England/UK	*Yīngguó*
Ireland	*Ài'ěrlán*
France	*Fǎguó* (some: *Fàguó*)
Spain	*Xībānyá*
Germany	*Déguó*
Italy	*Yìdàlì*
Greece	*Xīlà*
Russia	*Éguó* (some: *Èguó*)

CITIES (*CHÉNGSHÌ*)

Beijing	*Běijīng*
Shanghai	*Shànghǎi*
Hong Kong	*Xiāng Gǎng*
Shenyang	*Shěnyáng*
Guangzhou	*Guǎngzhōu*
Shenzhen	*Shēnzhèn*
Beidaihe	*Běidàihé* (a resort on the coast near Beijing)
Qingdao	*Qīngdǎo*
Tianjin	*Tiānjīn*
Chongqing	*Chóngqìng*

Xi'an	*Xī'ān*
Nanjing	*Nánjīng*
Kunming	*Kūnmíng*
Guilin	*Guìlín*
Lhasa	*Lāsà*
Jakarta	*Yǎjiādá*
Hanoi	*Hénèi*
Ho Chi Minh City/Saigon	*Húzhìmíng Shì/Xīgòng*
Bangkok	*Màngǔ*
Kuala Lumpur	*Jílóngpō*
Yangon	*Yǎngguāng*
Delhi	*Délǐ*
Kolkata/Calcutta	*Jiā'ěrgēdá*
Mumbai/Bombay	*Mèngmǎi*
Dhaka	*Dákǎ*
Karachi	*Kālǎchī ~ Kǎlāqí*
Kabul	*Kābù'ěr*
Tehran	*Déhēilán*
Baghdad	*Bāgédá*
Tel Aviv	*Tèlāwéifū*
Tokyo	*Dōngjīng*
Osaka	*Dàbǎn*
Seoul	*Hànchéng ~ Shǒu'ěr*
Manila	*Mǎnílā*
Sydney	*Xīní*
Melbourne	*Mò'ěrběn*
Perth	*Bōsī*
Auckland	*Àokèlán*
Cairo	*Kāiluó*
Boston	*Bōshìdùn*
New York	*Niǔyuē*

Philadelphia	*Fèichéng*
Washington, D.C.	*Huáshèngdùn*
Chicago	*Zhījiāgē*
Houston	*Xiū ~ Háosīdùn*
Dallas	*Dálāsī*
Salt Lake City	*Yánhúchéng*
Los Angeles	*Luòshānjī*
San Francisco	*Jiùjīnshān*
London	*Lúndūn*
Manchester	*Mànchèsītè*
Glasgow	*Gèlāsēgē*
Belfast	*Bèi'érfǎsītè*
Dublin	*Dūbólín*
Paris	*Bālí*
Rome	*Luómǎ*
Athens	*Yádiǎn*
Moscow	*Mòsīkē*

NOTES

a. *Korea.* North Korea is called *Cháoxiǎn*, a Chinese version of what is usually rendered 'Choson' or 'Joseon' in English, the name of the Korean dynasty that came to an end in 1910. South Korea is called *Hánguó* (with rising-toned *Hán*, distinct from the *Hàn* of *Hànrén* 'Chinese'). *Hánguó* is a traditional name, historically applied to kingdoms on the southern and western parts of the Korean peninsula. In the recent past, the Chinese have also called Korea *Gāolì* after the ancient Koryo or Goryeo dynasty that is also the source of the English name. Paradoxically, the capital of South Korea, Seoul, was until very recently called *Hànchéng* in Chinese, the town on the *Hàn* River (not *Hán*). Nowadays, Seoul is usually transliterated as *Shǒu'ěr*.

b. *Russia. Éluósī* or *Éguó* on the Mainland, but often *Èguó* in Taiwan. The USSR was called *Sūlián* (with *Sū* from *Sūwéi'āi* 'Soviet' + *lián* 'unite').

c. Earlier versions of the names of Chinese cities, such as Canton, Chungking, Nanking, and Peking, reflect spelling conventions adopted by the British and probably based on Cantonese pronunciation. In the Wade-Giles transcription, which still has some currency, the distinction between (pinyin) *b, d, g* and *p, t, k*, etc. was represented as p, t, k and p', t', k', respectively. In common practice, the apostrophes were omitted; hence Peking, Taipei, and Tao Te Ching (the

Taoist classic), rather than pinyin Beijing, Taibei, and Dao De Jing (the Daoist classic). The name 'Canton' is based on the name of the province, *Guǎngdōng*, rather than the city, *Guǎngzhōu*.

d. *Philadelphia. Fèichéng. Chéng* is 'city' (originally 'wall', a characteristic feature of cities). *Fèi* is a rendering of the first syllable of Philadelphia.

e. *Washington, D.C.* Though usually called *Huáshèngdùn*, the city is also sometimes referred to as *Huáfǔ* 'national capital' in Chinese newspapers in the United States.

f. *San Francisco.* The Cantonese name, pronounced *Sānfānshì* (*shì* 'city') in Mandarin, is obviously a transliteration of the English. The commonly used Mandarin name, *Jiùjīnshān* ('old gold mountain'), is a reference to Gold Rush days, when many Chinese migrated to California from the southern provinces.

g. *Paris and Bali.* If Paris is *Bālí*, you may wonder what the Chinese name for the Indonesian island of Bali is. It's also (usually) *Bālí*. The distinction is made by adding *dǎo* 'island' to the latter: *Bālídǎo*; cf. *Hǎinándǎo* 'Hainan Island' (off the southern coast of China).

Unit 4

Hŭ sĭ liú pí, rén sĭ liú míng.
('Tiger dies leaves skin, person dies leaves name')
—Classical Chinese saying

This is the culminating unit of the first third of *Learning Chinese*. It continues with some of the earlier themes, such as existence, location, modification, and study. It also introduces, in detail, new topics such as clock time, names, titles, and introductions, and ends with a long dialogue that makes use of much of the material presented in the first third of the book. Near the end of the unit, the first of a number of sections on food and eating appears. Though some details still remain, your mastery of the sounds of Mandarin and the pinyin system for their transcription should be nearly complete by the end of this unit.

Contents

4.1 Tone contrasts

Practice the following tonal contrasts by reading the columns of paired words. Pause between each member of the pairs so as to keep their tonal contours distinct.

(1) first versus second		*(2) first versus fourth*		*(3) second versus third*	
cōng	*cóng*	*cū*	*cù*	*chú*	*chǔ*
cuō	*cuó*	*cūn*	*cùn*	*chóu*	*chǒu*
jiā	*jiá*	*jiāng*	*jiàng*	*jiáo*	*jiǎo*
qiān	*qián*	*qī*	*qì*	*qíng*	*qǐng*
tiān	*tián*	*tōng*	*tòng*	*tú*	*tǔ*
mō	*mó*	*niē*	*niè*	*miáo*	*miǎo*
xiā	*xiá*	*xiāng*	*xiàng*	*shéng*	*shěng*
shāo	*sháo*	*zāng*	*zàng*	*zháo*	*zhǎo*

4.2 Existence and location

4.2.1 Places

fànguǎn⟨r⟩	*tǐyùguǎn*	*túshūguǎn*	*lǚguǎn*
'restaurant'	'gymnasium'	'library'	'hotel; hostel'
('food-hall')	('PE-hall')	('map-book-hall')	('travel-hall')

shūdiàn 'bookstore' ('book-shop')	*shāngdiàn* 'shop; store' ('trade-shop')	*fàndiàn* 'hotel' ('food-shop')	*xǐshǒujiān* 'lavatory' ('wash-hands-room')
cèsuǒ 'restroom; toilet' ('leaning-place')	*zhāodàisuǒ* 'guest house' ('reception-place')	*bàngōngshì* 'office' ('do-work-room')	*yínháng* 'bank' ('silver-business')
dìtiě 'subway' ('ground-iron')	*huǒchēzhàn* 'train station' ('train-station')	*sùshè* 'dormitory' ('lodge-inn')	*cāntīng* 'cafeteria' ('food-hall')

NOTES

a. Several generic words for various kinds of buildings or rooms are found in the final position in a number of these compounds: *jiān, guǎn, suǒ, shì, diàn*, etc. Because these forms only occur in compounds (at least in modern Mandarin), it is difficult to give them distinct meanings, so the syllable glosses provided above are only suggestive.

b. *Cèsuǒ* ('leaning-place'), the standard word for 'restroom', is commonly used to refer to public toilets, and is often found on signs; *xǐshǒujiān* ('wash-hands-room') is the term commonly used in public buildings and hotels.

c. In spoken language, *fànguǎn⟨r⟩* is often a generic term for 'restaurant', along with *cānguǎn* and *càiguǎn* (neither with the final, optional *r*). Dining halls or cafeterias at universities or businesses are usually called *cāntīng*. However, other terms, including several that contain the word *jiǔ* 'wine', also appear in restaurant names. These include *fànzhuāng* ('food-place of business') for large restaurants, and *jiǔjiā* ('wine-house') and *jiǔlóu* ('wine-building'), which are common in Hong Kong. Words for 'hotel' also vary. *Lǚguǎn* ('travel-hall') is a generic term for small, local hotels. *Kèzhàn* ('guest-shelter') is used for inns in picturesque regions such as *Lìjiāng* in northwest Yunnan province. Large hotels of the sort deemed suitable for foreigners are often referred to as *jiǔdiàn* ('wine-shop') or *fàndiàn* ('food-shop'). Both terms suggest that such hotels were originally known for their bars or fancy restaurants; indeed, *jiǔdiàn* can still refer to pubs and *fàndiàn* to restaurants in parts of the country. Chinese government offices, universities, and even businesses often have *zhāodàisuǒ* 'hostels' ('reception-places') at their disposal, with basic amenities for official (non-paying) or other (paying) guests. *Bīnguǎn* 'hotel' is yet another term that is sometimes used for hotels; one of Beijing's more famous hotels is *Yǒuyì Bīnguǎn* 'Friendship Hotel' in the northwest of the city.

4.2.2 Locations

Earlier, you encountered a number of position words, such as *shàng* 'on' and *lǐ* 'in', that could be attached to nouns to form location phrases following *zài* 'be at': *zài fēijī shàng* 'aboard the airplane', *zài sùshè lǐ* 'in the dormitory'.

When position words are used alone (directly after *zài*), with no reference noun, they must be combined with suffixes *miàn⟨r⟩* 'face; facet', *biān⟨r⟩* 'border; side', or (more colloquially) *tou* (which, in its toned form, *tóu*, means 'head'): *zài fēijī shàng* 'on the airplane', but *zài shàngmian⟨r⟩*, *zài shàngbian⟨r⟩*, or *zài shàngtou*, all 'on top; above; on board'. The choice of the two-syllable position word is not ruled out by the presence of a reference noun. Rhythmic considerations play a role, with a single-syllable noun being more likely to attract a single-syllable position word; thus, *jiā lǐ* 'in the house' rather than *jiā lǐtou*, and *shān shàng* 'on the hill' rather than *shān shàngtou*. However, keep in mind that this is a natural tendency rather than a hard and fast rule.

The repertoire of position words, together with their possible suffixes, is presented in the following table.

Position words

COMBINING FORM	ROUGH MEANING	+ *MIÀN⟨R⟩*	+ *TOU*	+ *BIĀN⟨R⟩*	OTHER
shàng	'on; above'	*shàngmian*	*shàngtou*	*shàngbianr*	
xià	'under; below'	*xiàmian*	(*xiàtou*)	(*xiàbianr*)	*dǐxia*
qián	'in front; before'	*qiánmian*	*qiántou*	*qiánbianr*	
hòu	'behind; after'	*hòumian*	*hòutou*	*hòubianr*	
lǐ	'in; inside'	*lǐmian*	*lǐtou*	(*lǐbianr*)	*nèi*
wài	'outside'	*wàimian*	*wàitou*	*wàibianr*	
zuǒ	'left'			*zuǒbiānr*	
yòu	'right'			*yòubiānr*	
páng	'next to; beside'			*pángbiānr*	
dōng	'east'	*dōngmiàn*		*dōngbiānr*	

COMBINING FORM	ROUGH MEANING	+ *MIÀN⟨R⟩*	+ *TOU*	+ *BIĀN⟨R⟩*	OTHER
nán	'south'	*nánmiàn*		*nánbiānr*	
xī	'west'	*xīmiàn*		*xībiānr*	
běi	'north'	*běimiàn*		*běibiānr*	
	'vicinity'				*fùjìn*
	'among; between'				*zhōngjiān*

NOTES

a. Though *dǐxia* is more common than *xiàmian* and the other *xià* combinations, this may be a product of the slight difference in meaning between *xià* 'below; lower' and *dǐxia* 'underneath'; thus, *shān xià* 'at the foot of the mountains' but *chēzi dǐxia* 'underneath the car'.

b. While *lǐ* and its compounds are used for 'in; inside', *nèi* (with no compound forms) usually has a more abstract sense of 'within': *guónèi* 'within the country' (versus *guówài*); *shìnèi* 'in town' (versus *shìwài*).

c. *Biān⟨r⟩*, untoned in most combinations, is fully toned in *pángbiān* 'next to'.

d. *fùjin* 'nearby' ('connect-near'), as in *zhèr fùjìn* 'around here' or *sùshè fùjìn* 'in the vicinity of the dormitory'

e. *zhōngjiān* 'among; between' ('middle-space'), as in *zài tāmen zhōngjiān* 'among them' or *dàshān zhōngjiān* 'in the mountains'. *Zhōng* alone ('middle', as in *Zhōngguó* 'middle-kingdom') can also be used as a position word, as in phrases such as *jiā zhōng* 'within the family', or *shān zhōng* 'in the heart of the mountains'; but *zhōng* is less common than *lǐ*, so it is not included in the table. Finally, this is a good place to introduce another compound containing *zhōng*: *zhōngxīn* 'center' ('middle-heart'). Unlike *zhōngbù* 'the center of; the middle of' or *zhōngjiān* 'between', *zhōngxīn* usually designates a place (a center) rather than a location relative to other things. You will encounter *zhōngxīn* in this lesson in phrases such as *xuéshēng zhōngxīn* 'student center' and *shì zhōngxīn* 'town center'.

To practice using these words and phrases, focus on noun and position combinations that are particularly common. Here are some examples, along with some other phrases that can indicate location (after *zài*).

lóushàng 'upstairs' ('building-on')	*lóuxià* 'downstairs' ('building-below')	*shānshàng* 'on the mountain' ('mountain-on')	*shísìhào lóu lǐ* 'in building #14' ('14-number building-in')

fùjìn	*chénglǐ*	*chéngwài*	*gébì*
'in the vicinity'	'in town'	'out of town'	'next door'
('attach-near')	('city-inside')	('city-outside')	('separate-wall')

4.2.3 Existence versus location

As noted in Unit 2, the verb *yǒu* indicates existence as well as possession. Existential sentences ('there is/are') in Chinese have the order: Location + *yǒu* + item.

LOCATION	YǑU	ITEM	
Zhèr ~ Zhèlǐ	*yǒu*	*diànhuà*	*ma?*
⟨Zhèr ~ Zhèlǐ⟩	*méiyǒu*	*⟨diànhuà⟩.*	

Note that although *zài* is not usually present, the types of phrases that can indicate locations in this pattern are the same as those that typically follow *zài*, that is, places (*Běijīng*), position words (*qiántou, zuǒbianr*), or combinations of noun and position words (*jiā lǐ, shì zhōngxīn*).

Shànghǎi yǒu dìtiě, *kěshì Nánjīng méiyǒu.*	'There's a subway in Shanghai, but not in Nanjing.'
Zuǒbianr yǒu yí ge diànhuà.	'There's a phone on the left.'
Huǒchēzhàn zài shì zhōngxīn ma?	'Is the train station in the town center?'
Fùjìn yǒu liǎng ge huǒchēzhàn: *yí ge zài shì zhōngxīn,* *yí ge zài chéngwài.*	'There are two train stations in the vicinity: one's in town, one's out of town.'

In many cases, a question about existence will elicit a response about location. Location, as noted earlier, is conveyed by a pattern built around *zài*, with the object to be located mentioned before the position word: *zài chéngwài* 'out of town'.

ITEM	ZÀI	LOCATION
Diànhuà	*zài*	*nǎr?*
⟨Diànhuà⟩	*zài*	*lóushàng.*

USAGE

Zhèr yǒu xǐshǒujiān ma?	'Is there a lavatory here?'
Yǒu, xǐshǒujiān zài hòutou.	'Yes there is; the lavatory's in the back.'
Qǐngwèn, yǒu méiyǒu cāntīng?	'Excuse me, is there a cafeteria?'
Yǒu, zài gébì.	'Yes, there is, [it]'s next door.'
Wèi lǎoshī de bàngōngshì ne?	'And [where's] Professor Wei's office?'
Zài lóushàng.	'Upstairs.'

Qǐngwèn, dìtiě zài nǎli?

Zhèr fùjìn yǒu fànguǎnr ma?	'Are there any restaurants around here?'
Yǒu, lí zhèr bù yuǎn.	'There are, not far away.'
Qǐngwèn, dìtiě zài nǎlǐ?	'May I ask where the subway is, please?'
Dìtiě ne, dìtiě zài qiánmian—bù yuǎn.	'The subway, the subway's ahead—not far.'
Zhèr fùjìn yǒu cèsuǒ ma?	'Is there a restroom around here?'
Lóuxià hǎoxiàng yǒu.	'I believe there's one downstairs.'
Liúxuéshēng sùshè zài nǎr?	'Where's the foreign students' dorm?'
Liúxuéshēng sùshè zài Xuéshēng Zhōngxīn pángbiānr.	'The foreign students' dorm is next to the Student Center.'
Shūdiàn zài nǎr?	'Where's the bookshop?'
Shūdiàn dōu zài chéng lǐ.	'The bookshops are all in town.'
Qǐngwèn, diànhuà zài nǎr?	'May I ask where the phone is?'
Diànhuà ne, diànhuà zài nàr, zài zuǒbiānr.	'The phone's over there—on the left.'

NOTE

Liúxuéshēng 'overseas students' ('remain-students') are students studying abroad.

4.2.4 Comfort stations

Traditionally, as expected from a society where the majority of the people are farmers and human waste is an important fertilizer, Chinese have generally been less prone than English speakers to create euphemisms about human waste products and the places where they are deposited. As noted above, the most common term for the latter is *cèsuǒ*. However, hotels and upscale restaurants are more prone to euphemisms such as *xǐshǒujiān* 'lavatory' or *guànxǐshì* 'washroom'; the urban middle classes, particularly in Taiwan and overseas communities, might also use *huàzhuāngjiān* 'powder room' ('make up-room') or *wèishēngjiān* ('hygiene-room'). (A reduced form of the last, *wèi*, is standard in house listings, e.g., *sānshì liǎngwèi* 'three rooms, two bathrooms' or *sānfáng liǎngwèi* 'three rooms, two bathrooms'.) In the countryside, you are also likely to hear *máofáng* 'outhouse' ('thatched-house').

Qǐngwèn, cèsuǒ zài nǎr?	'Where's the toilet, please?'
Zài hòubianr de yuànzi lǐ.	'In the backyard.'
Qǐngwèn, zhèr yǒu méiyǒu cèsuǒ?	'Excuse me, is there a toilet [around] here?'
Cèsuǒ ne, hǎoxiàng zài lóuxià.	'A toilet . . . [I] believe it's downstairs.'
Qǐngwèn, zhèr yǒu xǐshǒujiān ma?	'Excuse me, is there a lavatory here?'
Xuéshēng Zhōngxīn yīnggāi yǒu.	'There should be one in the Student Center.'

The actual bowl—the commode—is *mǎtǒng* ('horse-tub') or *gōngtǒng* ('public-tub'). The acts are *sāniào* 'to piss' ('release urine'), *niàoniào* 'to urinate', or more euphemistically, *xiǎobiàn* ('small-convenience'), which can function as a noun as well as a verb. Its larger complement is, unsurprisingly, *dàbiàn* 'excrement' (as a noun) or 'to defecate' (as a verb). The less euphemistic version is *lā shǐ* 'to shit' ('pull shit'). While it is interesting to know the gritty details, as a novice, you should probably limit yourself to questions about location, as illustrated above. If someone needs to know more detailed information, then *xiǎobiàn* and *dàbiàn* are appropriate: *qù xiǎobiàn, qù dàbiàn.*

4.2.5 Verbs of development and life: *shēng, zhǎng, zhù*

In examples seen thus far, *zài* phrases have preceded their associated verbs: *zài fēijī shàng chī*. However, such is not always the case. With some verbs (such as *fàng* 'to put'), the *zài* phrase appears after the verb (as a destination). Some verbs also allow both a pre- and post-verbal position of *zài* phrases. This is true of the common verbs *shēng* 'to be born', *zhǎng* 'to grow up', and *zhù* 'to live; to reside'. Because the pre-verbal position has grammatical consequences that will not be properly introduced until a later unit, we will focus on the post-verbal position, which is quite appropriate for making some introductory biographical comments. Practice the following examples and then make up statements that suit your own situation; keep repeating until fluent.

Tā shēng zài Běijīng, yě zhǎng zài Běijīng, kěshì xiànzài zhù zài Xī'ān.	'She was born in Beijing and grew up in Beijing, but now she lives in Xi'an.'
Wǒ shēng zài Duōlúnduō, zhǎng zài Niǔyuē, xiànzài zhù zài Jiùjīnshān.	'I was born in Toronto; I grew up in New York; and now I live in San Francisco.'

4.3 Time phrases

4.3.1 Topic—comment

As noted earlier, words and phrases that convey the time when something takes place ('today', 'at three o'clock') appear before their associated verbs.

Tā zuótiān bù shūfu, kěshì jīntiān hǎo le.	'He wasn't well yesterday, but he's okay today.'

Such 'time when' phrases may appear before the subject, as well as after it.

Zuótiān tā zěnmeyàng?	'How was she yesterday?'
Zuótiān tā bù shūfu, hěn lèi, yě hěn jǐnzhāng, suǒyǐ méiyǒu qù shàngkè.	'Yesterday, she didn't feel well, [she] was tired and nervous, so [she] didn't go to class.'
Lǐbàiwǔ wǒmen dōu méiyǒu kè.	'None of us has class on Fridays.'
Xiètiān-xièdì!	'Thank heavens!'

The difference—position before or after the subject—has to do with what you are talking about. Typically, first position in a Chinese sentence introduces the topic, and what follows is a comment on that topic. (In English, the difference is often inferred from context alone, rather than represented by word order or emphasis.)

Zuótiān tā zěnmeyàng?	'[About yesterday:] How was he yesterday?'
Zuótiān tā bù shūfu, jīntiān hǎo le.	'He wasn't well yesterday, [but] he's fine today.'
Tā zuótiān zěnmeyàng?	'[About him:] How was he yesterday?'
Tā zuótiān juéde bù shūfu, hěn lèi, yě hěn jǐnzhāng.	'He didn't feel well yesterday; [he] was tired and anxious.'

4.3.2 Clock time

A. THE HOURS Clock times are also 'time when' phrases, often appearing in conjunction with *jīntiān, zuótiān*, or with words for divisions of the day such as the following, based on the roots *zǎo* 'early', *wǔ* 'noon', and *wǎn* 'late'.

zǎoshàng	*shàngwǔ*	*zhōngwǔ*	*xiàwǔ*	*wǎnshàng*
'morning'	'mid-morning'	'noon'	'afternoon'	'evening'

Like English, where the term 'o'clock' derives from 'of the clock', clock time in Chinese is based on the word *zhōng* 'clock' (originally 'bell'). *Zhōng* is measured out by *diǎn* 'dots; points' (cf. *yìdiǎn* 'a bit') to form phrases such as *jiǔ diǎn zhōng* (reducible to *jiǔ diǎn*) 'nine o'clock'. Time is questioned with *jǐ*: *Jǐ diǎn zhōng?* 'What time is [it]?' In asking or giving clock time, *le* is often present in final position, suggesting 'by now'. Complex time phrases in Chinese are ordered, like dates, from large units to small: *zǎoshàng jiǔ diǎn* 'nine in the morning'; *míngtiān xiàwǔ sān diǎn* 'tomorrow afternoon at three'.

Xiànzài jǐ diǎn ⟨zhōng⟩ le?	'What time is it now?'
Shí diǎn.	'[It's] 10:00.'
Zǎoshàng jiǔdiǎn dào shídiǎn yǒu kè.	'[I] have a class from 9 to 10 in the morning.'
Zhōngwén kè ⟨shi⟩ jiǔdiǎn dào shídiǎn.	'Chinese class is 9–10.'

B. DETAILS *Fēn* 'divide; a part' is used for minutes (as well as cents), and *miǎo* is used for seconds. Both are also measure words (so they can be counted directly).

jiǔ diǎn shí fēn	9:10
shí'èr diǎn líng sì	12:04
sān diǎn sānshíwǔ fēn	3:35
liù diǎn shíwǔ fēn	6:15

The half hour is either *sānshí fēn* 'thirty minutes' or *bàn* 'half', placed after the measure word *diǎn*.

Xiànzài jiǔ diǎn bàn le.	'It's now 9:30.'
Xiànzài jiǔ diǎn sānshí fēn le.	'It's now 9:30.'

'Quarter to' and 'quarter past' are expressed with *kè* ('a cut')—from the notch that marked the measuring stick on old water clocks: *yí kè* 'quarter'. 'Quarter past' is expressed by adding *yí kè* (some say *guò yí kè*) to the hour; 'quarter to' is expressed by saying *chà yí kè* 'less by one quarter' either before or after the (coming) hour.

jiǔ diǎn ⟨*guò*⟩ *yí kè*	'quarter past nine'
chà yí kè shí diǎn	'quarter to ten'
shí diǎn chà yí kè	'quarter to ten'

In general, time past the half hour can be expressed as a lack, using *chà* + the appropriate number of minutes, placed either before or after the approaching hour.

chà wǔ fēn shí diǎn	'five to ten'
shí diǎn chà wǔ fēn	'five to ten'
chà yí kè sì diǎn	'quarter to four'
sì diǎn chà yí kè	'quarter to four'

Clock time: A summary

DAY AND SEGMENT		TO	HOUR	MINUTES (TO/AFTER)	⟨O'CLOCK⟩
jīntiān	*zǎoshàng*		*yī diǎn*	*líng wǔ fēn*	*⟨zhōng⟩*
zuótiān	*shàngwǔ*		*liǎng diǎn*	*shí fēn*	
míngtiān	*zhōngwǔ*		*shí'èr diǎn*	*shíwǔ fēn ~ ⟨guò⟩ yíkè*	
	xiàwǔ		*sì diǎn*	*èrshíwǔ fēn*	
	wǎnshàng		*qī diǎn*	*sānshí fēn ~ bàn*	
		chà shí fēn	*jiǔ diǎn*	*chà shí fēn*	
		chà yíkè	*shí'yī diǎn*	*chà yíkè*	
			Jǐ diǎn		*⟨zhōng⟩?*

In colloquial language, *wǎnshàng* extends until bedtime, even if it's very late. Similarly, *zǎoshàng* is when you get up, even if it's very early.

> *Wǒ wǎnshàng liǎng diǎn shuìjiào, zǎoshàng shí diǎn qǐlai, cóng shàngwǔ shíyī diǎn dào xiàwǔ sì diǎn yǒu kè.*

> *Tiānwén kè shi xīngqīsì wǎnshàng shíyī diǎn dào liǎng diǎn.* 'Astronomy ('heaven-inscription') class is Thursday evenings, 11 to 2 A.M.'

When required, more specialized time words are available, of course: *yèli* 'in the night', *bànyè* 'at midnight; late at night', *língchén* 'very early in the morning; before dawn', *qīngzǎo* 'early morning', *dàqīngzǎo* 'very early'.

C. BUYING TRAIN TICKETS It is possible to buy tickets through hotels (*fàndiàn*) or through one's work unit (*dānwèi*) a few days in advance, and most travelers choose the former and pay a small service fee, *shǒuxùfèi* ('procedure-fee'). Buying at the station is more difficult. There, you generally have to work your way up to a small ticket window and state your needs (such as time and destination) succinctly, along the lines indicated below. Tickets are counted with

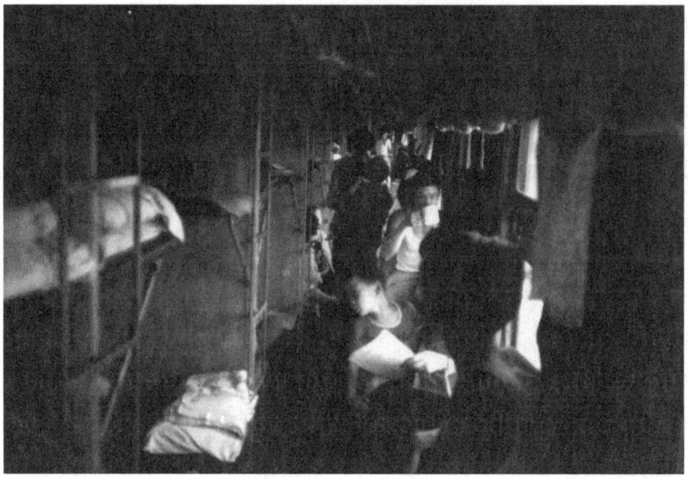

Yìngwò, nǐ juéde shūfu ma?

zhāng, the measure word for flat things (tables, maps, photographs, etc.). Tickets are usually one-way, so that is not a variable. On short-distance express trains, such as the one from *Shànghǎi* to *Nánjīng* (stopping at *Sūzhōu, Wúxī,* and *Zhènjiāng*), there is an option between soft seat (first class) and hard seat. On long-distance inter-city trains, there are commonly four types of tickets that provide seats, plus a fifth 'standing-room only' type.

yìngzuò ~ *yìngxí* 'hard seat'	*yìngwò* 'hard berth'	*zhànpiào* 'standing ticket'
ruǎnzuò ~ *ruǎnxí* 'soft seat'	*ruǎnwò* 'soft berth'	

Zhànpiào are sold (often for the same price) when *yìngzuò* ~ *yìngxí* tickets are sold out. Berths are four to a cabin (*ruǎnwò*), or six to a section (*yìngwò*), with egress to toilets, washrooms, and sometimes a dining car by way of a corridor along the station side of the carriage. A team of service staff (*fúwùyuán*) keep the cabins clean, make beds, sell snacks and reading matter, and on some lines even rent out portable TVs and other electronic equipment for the duration of the journey.

Here is a breakdown of the information that needs to be provided when buying a train ticket.

PLACE	TIME	TYPE	NUMBER
Chéngdū	*shàngwǔ jiǔ diǎn*	*ruǎnwò*	*liǎng zhāng*

Exercise 1

Practice buying tickets according to the specifications indicated.

1.	*Xīníng*	4:00 this afternoon	hard berth	1
2.	*Xī'ān*	8:00 tomorrow morning	soft seat	2
3.	*Hūhéhàotè*	7:00 this evening	soft berth	3
4	*Lánzhōu*	2:30 this afternoon	hard seat	1
5.	*Hā'ěrbīn*	7:00 tomorrow morning	soft seat	2
6.	*Guìlín*	3:25 this afternoon	hard berth	1
7.	*Chóngqìng*	7:00 P.M. on July 7	soft berth	4

4.3.3 Time of events (meals)

Meals are named by time of day added to roots such as *fàn* 'rice; food; meals', *cān* 'meal', or, in the case of breakfast, *diǎn* 'snack'.

'breakfast'	'lunch'	'dinner'
zǎofàn	*zhōngfàn*	*wǎnfàn*
zǎocān	*zhōngcān*	*wǎncān*
zǎodiǎn		

Recall that it is possible to express some uncertainty about time with the adverb *dàgài* 'approximately; probably'. In addition to this, other 'hedging' words include *yěxǔ* 'maybe; probably; possibly' and *chàbuduō* 'approximately' ('less-not-much').

For now, it will only be possible to ask generic questions, such as 'At what time do you eat breakfast?' Questions about specific events in the past introduce a number of complications that will be dealt with later. In addition to *měitiān* 'every day', it will be useful to learn the following expressions, all built on *cháng* 'often', that deal with habitual events.

cháng ~ chángcháng	'often'
píngcháng	'usually'
jīngcháng	'frequently; often; regularly'
tōngcháng	'generally; normally'

USAGE

(1)	*Zhōngguó rén píngcháng jǐ diǎn chī zǎofàn?*	'What time do Chinese usually eat breakfast?'
	Dàgài liù dào qī diǎn ba. Měiguó rén ne?	'About 6:00 to 7:00. How about Americans?'
	Měiguó rén ne, jīngcháng jiǔ diǎn shàngbān. Yěxǔ qī diǎn bàn, bā diǎn chī zǎofàn.	'Americans generally start work at 9:00. So maybe they eat breakfast at 7:30 [or] 8:00.'
(2)	*Xuéshēng ne, yīnwèi hěn máng, chángcháng zhǐ hē kāfēi bù chī zǎodiǎn.*	'Students, because they are so busy, often just drink coffee and don't eat breakfast.'
	Zhōngguó xuéshēng hěn shǎo shi zhèi yàngr. Zhōngguó xuéshēng tōngcháng chī zǎofàn.	'Chinese students are rarely like that. Chinese students regularly eat breakfast.'
	Tāmen chī shénme?	'What do they eat?'
	Chī xīfàn, miàntiáo⟨r⟩.	'Rice porridge, noodles.'
(3)	*Jǐdiǎn shàngkè? Jǐdiǎn xiàkè?*	'What time does class start? What time do [you] get out of class?'
	Wǒmen chàbuduō shí diǎn shàngkè shíyī diǎn xiàkè.	'We start class at about 10:00 and end at 11:00.'

(4)	*Chīguò zǎofàn le méi?*	'Have you eaten breakfast?'
	Hái méi ne.	'Not yet.'
	Nǐ bú shi jiǔ diǎn yǒu kè ma? Zěnme hái méi chī zǎofàn ne?	'Isn't it the case that you have class at 9:00? How come you haven't eaten breakfast yet?'
	Ai, wǒ bù xiǎng chī, wǒ hē kāfēi jiù xíng le.	'I don't feel like [eating], I'll just have coffee [and that'll be fine].'

NOTES

a. *Xīfàn* ('watery-rice') is a kind of porridge or gruel, to which many people add pickles, preserved meats, vegetables, and other items. It is similar to what is often called *zhōu* in southern China.

b. *Miàntiáo* ('wheat[flour]-lengths') is a generic term for noodles.

c. *Nǐ bú shi* 'Isn't it the case that . . .'

d. *xiǎng* 'to think; to feel like'

4.3.4 Business hours

bàngōng shíjiān	'office hours'
yíngyè shíjiān	'business hours'

Most urban communities in China operate on international business hours, often with adjustments for a longer lunch break than is the norm in most English-speaking countries. Business hours (banks, offices) vary with region, but are typically Monday–Friday, 8:30–5:30. Shops often keep much longer hours and stay open on the weekend. Lunch breaks can last from 12:00 to 1:30 or even 2:00. Any sort of official meeting usually begins punctually. Here, more for reference at this point, are some basic queries about business hours.

Yíngyè shíjiān jǐ diǎn dào jǐ diǎn?	'What are [your] business hours?'
Nǐ jǐ diǎn kāimén?	'When do you open?'
Jǐ diǎn guānmén?	'When do [you] close?'

NOTES

a. *kāimén* ('open-door')

b. *guānmén* ('close-door')

4.3.5 Time zones (*shíqū*)

It comes as a surprise for many people to learn that China operates on a single time zone, eight hours in advance of Greenwich Mean Time (and, conveniently, 12 hours in advance of Eastern Standard Time in the United States, at least when daylight savings is not in effect). The far west of China is relatively sparsely populated, so this system causes minimal disruption. Places like Xinjiang, farthest to the west, often follow 'local time' for shop hours and Beijing time for things like train schedules. For a period beginning in 1986, there was a daylight-savings shift called *xiàshízhì* ('summer-time-system'), but this was found to be impractical and was abandoned in 2003.

The word *shíchā* can mean both 'time difference' and 'jet lag'. The noun *chā* is related to the verb *chà* 'to lack', as in *chàbuduō*.

Shíchā hěn lìhai.	'The time lag / jet lag is bad!'
Wǒ háishi hěn lèi—yīnwèi shíchā.	'I'm still tired—because of the time lag.'

Exercise 2

Ask or explain the following.

1. What time do you bathe?
2. I generally bathe in the morning at 6:00 or 7:00.
3. I don't eat any breakfast, I just have some tea.
4. But I usually eat lunch and dinner; lunch at noon, dinner at 7:00.
5. We start class at about 2:00 and end at 3:00.
6. I have two classes today, one at 10:00 and one at 2:00.
7. The lecture is at 9:00, the section is at 10:00.
8. From 2:00 to 4:00 this afternoon, we're having a Chinese test.

9. I've bathed already, but I haven't eaten yet.
10. Do you always eat breakfast? / Not necessarily.
11. What time do you close, please?
12. Have you ever been to *Xīchāng*? It's in Sichuan, about 400 kilometers from *Chóngqìng*.

4.4 DE revisited

As noted in Unit 2, the addition of *de* turns a noun into an attribute of another noun, serving a function similar to the possessive use of the apostrophe or prepositions such as 'of' in English. In the following examples, note that many of the nouns could be singular or plural, e.g., 'student's homework' or 'students' homework'

Zhāng xiānshēng de xíngli	'Mr. Zhang's luggage'
Mǎ shīfu de dìdi	'Master Ma's younger brother'
xuéshēng de zuòyè	'students' homework'
jīntiān de bàozhǐ	'today's newpaper'
zhèi ge xīngqītiān de piào	'tickets for this Sunday'
sān suì de nǚháir	'a three-year-old girl'
yǐqián de lǎoshī	'a former teacher'
Shìjiè Bēi de xiāoxi hěn yǒuyìsi.	'The news about the World Cup is quite interesting.'
Yǒu shénme Àoyùnhuì de xiāoxi ma?	'Any news on the Olympics?'

NOTES

a. *nǚháir* 'girl' ('female-child')

b. *Shìjiè Bēi* 'World Cup'; cf. *Ōuzhōu Bēi* 'Euro Cup'; *Àoyùnhuì* 'Olympics' ('Ol[ympic]-sports-meeting')

c. *xiāoxi* 'report; news'

Defining or disambiguating words, or identifying the character associated with a particular syllable, often involves *de* in its function of linking attributes to nouns.

Něi ge 'shēng'?	'Which *sheng*?'
Shēngrì de shēng.	'The *sheng* of *shengri* ('birthday').
Dōngnánxīběi de xī ma?	'The *xi* of *dongnan-xibei*?'
Bù, xiāoxī de xī	'No, the *xi* of *xiaoxi*.'
Wǒ xìng Lù.	'My [sur]name's *Lu*.' (路)
Dàlù de lù ma?	'The *lu* of *dalu*?' (陆；大陆)
Bù, mǎlù de lù.	'No, the *lu* of *malu*.' (路；马路)
Mǎlù de lù shì bu shi zǒulù de lù?	'Is the *lu* of *malu* the *lu* of *zoulu*?' (马路；走路)
Duì, shi zǒulù de lù.	'That's right, the *lu* of *zoulu*.'
Zǒulù de lù zěnme xiě?	'How do you write the *lu* of *zoulu*?'
Shi zhèi yàngr xiě: 路; yígòng 13 ge bǐhuà. Lù nèi ge zì nǐ yǐjīng xuéguo ma?	'This way: 路; thirteen strokes in all. Have you already learned the character for road?'
Xuéguo, kěshì wàng le.	'[We]'ve studied [it], but [I]'ve forgotten [it].'

NOTES

a. *mǎlù* 'main road' ('horse-road')

b. *zǒulù* 'to walk' ('walk-road')

4.4.1 Where the noun head is omitted

In many cases, the noun following *de* is implied, in which case it can be glossed as 'the one/thing associated with'. In some cases, this form without the head noun is more natural.

Zhè shi tā de xíngli.	→	*Zhè shi tā de.*
'This is his luggage.'		'This is his.'

Shi xuéshēng de zuòyè ma? 'Is it the students' homework?'	→	*Shi xuéshēng de ma?* 'Is [it] the students'?'
Nà shi zuótiān de bào. 'That is yesterday's newspaper.'	→	*Nà shì zuótiān de.* 'That's yesterday's.'
Tā shi IBM de ma? *Bù, tā shi Wēiruǎn de.*		'Is she from IBM?' 'No, she's from Microsoft.'
Xìng Máo de yě shi lǎoshī ma?		'Is the person named Mao also a teacher?'
Wǒ bú tài qīngchu.		'I'm not sure.'
Xìng Zhào de shi lǎobǎn, xìng Lǐ de shi tā qīzi.		'The person named Zhao is the boss; the one named Li is his wife.'

4.4.2 Where *de* does not appear

A. COUNTRY NAMES Expressions like *Zhōngguó rén, Zhōngwén lǎoshī,* or *Běijīng dìtú* 'Beijing map' do not usually require an intervening *de.* The rule is that country (and language) names may be directly attributed to following nouns.

B. PRONOUNS WITH KIN TERMS While *tā de lǎoshī* requires *de, tā dìdi* usually omits it. Why? The rule is that pronouns (only!) tend to attach directly to kin terms.

	Zhè shì wǒ de péngyou.	'This is my friend.'
But:	*Zhè shì wǒ dìdi.*	'This is my younger brother.'
	Zhè shì wǒ de lǎoshī.	'This is my teacher.'
But:	*Zhè shì wǒ shūshu.*	'This is my uncle.'
	Zhè shì Chén lǎoshī de jiějie.	'This is Professor Chen's older sister.'
But:	*Zhè shì tā jiějie.*	'This is her older sister.'

C. SVs WITHOUT MODIFIERS SV phrases such as *hěn hǎo, hěn hǎokàn, bù hǎochī, nàme guì,* and *hěn hǎotīng* are generally followed by *de* when they modify a noun.

bù hǎokàn de dìfang	'an unattractive place'
hěn hǎochī de Zhōngguó cài	'delicious Chinese food'
nàme yuǎn de dìfang	'such a distant place'
bù hǎotīng de yīnyuè	'horrible sounding music'

Bare (unmodified) SVs (especially single-syllable ones) may be so closely associated with a following noun that *de* does not intercede—or at least, it is not required. Such combinations verge on becoming compound words. Compare the following examples.

	lǎo péngyou	'old friends'
But:	*hěn hǎo de péngyou*	'good friends'
	hǎo cài	'good food'
But:	*bù hǎochī de cài*	'food that's not good'
	dà yú	'big fish'
But:	*nàme dà de yú*	'such a big fish'

A similar distinction is possible with some combinations of nouns. Combinations that are particularly salient have formed tightly bound compounds, with no intervening *de*: *yúdǔ* 'fish stomach', *mǎchē* 'horse cart'. These would appear as entries in dictionaries. Combinations that are less salient form descriptive phrases whose parts are connected with *de*: *xiàng de bízi* 'an elephant's nose' (there is no specialized word for 'trunk [of an elephant]' in Chinese); *sùshè de dàmén* 'the main door of the dormitory'. These phrases would not appear as entries in dictionaries.

D. *DUŌ* AND *SHǍO* AS ATTRIBUTES As noted in Unit 2, *duō* and *shǎo* are exceptional as SV attributes in *requiring* a modifying adverb, such as *hěn*, and *not requiring* a connecting *de*.

Tā yǒu hěn duō Zhōngguó péngyou.	'He has lots of Chinese friends.'
Zhèi ge dìfang wèishénme yǒu nàme duō rén?	'How come this place has so many people?'
Nǐ yǒu zhème duō xíngli!	'You have such a lot of luggage!'

E. USAGE OF *DE* SEVERAL TIMES IN THE SAME PHRASE Finally, when *de* might appear several times in the same phrase, the first occurrence is often omitted.

wǒ ⟨de⟩ péngyou de lǎoshī	'my friend's teacher'

Sometimes, having more than one *de* in the same phrase is unavoidable. The presence of several in the following sentence is just as awkward as the several occurrences of the English 'of' in the translation.

Wǒ mèimei de xiānshēng de lǎoshī shi wǒ shūshu de tàitai.	'The teacher of the husband of my younger sister is the wife of my uncle.'

Exercise 3

1. Explain that big ones aren't necessarily tasty, and small ones aren't all bad.
2. Introduce your good friend, *Liú Shíjiǔ.*
3. Ask her if the keys belong to her.
4. Explain that your bags aren't here; they're still on the plane.
5. Explain that he's not your brother; you don't have a brother.
6. Explain that she's the boss's wife.
7. Explain that his older brother's wife is your Chinese teacher.
8. Announce that there's a report on the Olympics in yesterday's paper.
9. Ask how he feels about present-day music. (*yīnyuè*)
10. Explain that you don't usually drink coffee in the morning.
11. Ask how to say 'tomato' in Chinese; then ask how it's written.

4.5 Names in detail

Some basic information about names and titles was presented in Units 1 and 2. This section discusses this information in more detail.

4.5.1 The form of names

Chinese names are usually either two or three syllables long.

Wáng Mǎng	*Lǐ Péng*	*Liú Bāng*
Dù Fǔ	*Cuī Jiàn*	*Jiāng Qīng*
Dèng Xiǎopíng	*Lǐ Dēnghuī*	*Lǐ Guāngyào*
Jiāng Zémín	*Zhū Róngjī*	*Máo Zédōng*

Names of four or more syllables are usually foreign.

Zhōngcūn Yángzǐ	(Japanese name)
Yuēhàn Shǐmìsī	John Smith

Notice that two-syllable *xìng*, like two-syllable *míngzi*, are, by convention, written without spaces.

4.5.2 *Xìng*

Xìng, or surnames, are rather limited in number. An expression for 'the common people' *lǎobǎixìng* ('old hundred names') suggests that there are only 100 *xìng*; there are, in fact, considerably more (*bǎi* in that expression was not intended literally). Most Chinese *xìng* are single syllables (*Zhāng, Wáng, Lǐ*), but a few are two syllables (*Sīmǎ, Ōuyáng, Sītú*). *Sīmǎ*, you should know, was the *xìng* of China's first major historian, *Sīmǎ Qiān* (145–86 BCE), who wrote the *Shǐ Jì*, a history of China from earliest times to the time when he lived, during the Han dynasty.

The character primer called the *Bǎijiāxìng* 'Multitude of Family Names' ('100-family-names'), which first appeared in the 10th century, includes more than 400 single-syllable surnames and some 40 double-syllable names. In modern times, rare surnames would enlarge those numbers, but relatively few surnames account for a large percentage of the population. It has been estimated that 20 surnames account for about 50 percent of the population; indeed, the surname *Lǐ* alone may account for as many as 100 million people. Some *xìng* have distinct meanings, such as *Bái* 'white' and *Wáng* 'king'. Others, however, are (now) just names, such as *Wú* (also the name of several historical states). Some names are homophonous, differing only in character (e.g., *Lù*—路, 陆—as cited in an earlier example); while others differ only in tone (e.g., *Wáng* and *Wāng*).

4.5.3 Other names

In addition to their public names (*xìng*), Chinese traditionally had (and some still have) a number of other names, including the *zì*, a disyllabic name taken (mostly by males) for use outside the family, and *hào*, an adult nickname (again, mostly taken by males). Still other names were given in infancy (*rǔmíng* or *xiǎomíng*), in childhood (*míng*), or, at the other extreme, after death (*shìhào*). In modern times, the *míng* and the *zì* combine to form the *míngzì* 'given name'. The *rǔmíng* is still common, as for example, *xiǎobǎo* 'little treasure'.

It is worth examining the first lines of traditional biographical entries to see how names are cited. Here are two examples, one about a modern political leader, *Dèng Xiǎopíng*, from an exhibit in the Hong Kong Museum of History; the other, from an entry in the *Cí Hǎi* ('word sea'), one of the more comprehensive modern Chinese-to-Chinese dictionaries. The latter introduces Confucius, who lived in the 6th and 5th centuries BCE. Both entries are rendered in pinyin, with underscoring and highlighting to make the correspondences clearer.

(1) *Dèng Xiǎopíng* <u>*yuánmíng*</u> *Dèng Xiānshèng,* <u>*xuémíng*</u> *Dèng Xīxián, 1904 nián 8 yuè 22 rì chūshēng . . .*
('Deng Xiaoping <u>former name</u> Deng Xiansheng, <u>school [formal] name</u> Deng Xixian, 1904 [year] August 22 [day] born . . .')

(2) *Kǒngzǐ (**gōngyuánqián** 551–gōngyuánqián 479): Chūn Qiū **mòqī**, sīxiǎngjiā, zhèngzhìjiā, jiàoyùjiā, Rújiā de **chuàngshǐzhě**.* <u>*Míng Qiū, zì Zhōngní*</u>*.* ***Lǔguó** Zōuyì (**jìn** Shāndōng Qūfù dōngnán) **rén**.*

> 'Confucius (**BCE** 551–BCE 479): **End of** the Spring and Autumn Period; a philosopher, statesman, educator and **founder of** the Confucian School. His 'ming' was Qiu, his 'zi' was Zhongni. He was **a man** from Zouyi in **the state of Lu** (**near** modern southeast Qufu in Shandong).'

4.5.4 *Míngzi* ('name-character')

Given names, *míngzi*, are more numerous than *xìng* and are often selected for their meaning (along with the appearance of their characters): *Cài Qiáng* ('Cai strong'); *Cài Pǔ* ('Cai great'); *Cáo Hóng* ('Cao red'); *Lín Yíxī* ('Lin happy-hope'); *Zhāng Shūxiá* ('Zhāng virtuous-chivalrous'); *Luó Jiāqí* ('Luo family-in+good+order'). In many cases, it is possible to guess the gender of a person from the meanings of his or her name. For your information, of the six names mentioned in this paragraph, the third, fourth, and fifth are female, and the first, second, and sixth are male.

It is common practice to incorporate generational names in the *míngzi* by assigning a particular syllable (often chosen from a poem) to each generation. For example, *Máo Zédōng*'s younger brothers were *Máo Zémín* and *Máo Zétán*; his younger sister was *Máo Zéhóng*. All contain the syllable *zé* (泽). Such practices allow people from the same district to determine—and remember—kinship when they meet.

4.5.5 Usage

At pre-arranged meetings, people will often introduce themselves and immediately present a business card. People usually take the cards, glance at them to confirm the name, and note the title so that it can be used in address. At other times, people may wait to be introduced. If you ask a stranger for his or her name (say, someone seated next to you on a train) you would—as noted in Unit 2—use the polite form, *guìxìng*, often with the deferential pronoun *nín*. Often, the response would supply you with both the *xìng* and *míngzi*.

[Nín] guìxìng? *Wǒ xìng Liú, jiào Liú Shíjiǔ.*

In Taiwan, and sometimes on the Mainland, people may answer with more humble forms.

Taiwan:	*Guìxìng? / Bìxìng Wèi.*	'Shabby surname Wei.'
Mainland:	*Guìxìng? / Miǎn guì, xìng Wèi.*	'Dispense with the *guì*, [my] surname [is] Wei.'

4.6 Years

4.6.1 Dates

As noted in §1.3.4, years are usually expressed as strings of single digits (rather than large numbers) placed before *nián* 'year'. The only exception is the millennium year, 2000, which is sometimes expressed as 'two thousand' (making it, at a stretch, potentially ambiguous with 2,000 years [in duration]).

2002	*èrlínglíng'èr nián*
1998	*yījiǔjiǔbā nián*
1840	*yībāsìlíng nián*
2000	*èrlínglínglíng nián* or *liǎngqiān nián*

The question word used to elicit a year is *něi nián* 'which year'. (Recall that *něi* is the combining form of *nǎ* 'which', just as *nèi* is the combining form of *nà*.) Asking about dates in the past, however, introduces some grammatical features that will be presented in a later unit.

In the Republic of China (Taiwan), years are numbered formally from the establishment of the Republic, with 1912 as year 1. Here are the dates on two newspapers, one from the Mainland, and one from Taiwan.

Zhōngguó Dàlù [PRC]	*Táiwān* [ROC]
èr líng líng èr nián	*jiǔshíyī nián*
shíyuè	*shíyuè*
èrshíyī rì	*èrshíyī rì*
xīngqīyī	*xīngqīyī*

Observe the years: the Mainland newspaper reads 2002, but the Taiwanese newspaper reads 91. If you subtract the latter from the former, you get 1911—the date of the fall of the Qing dynasty and the establishment of a republic (*gònghéguó*). In Chinese, the official name of Taiwan is still *Zhōnghuá Mínguó*

'The Republic of China' [ROC]; the Mainland is called *Zhōnghuá Rénmín Gònghéguó* 'The People's Republic of China' [PRC]. In order to translate the ROC date into the Gregorian calendar date used in the PRC, you must add 1,911 years. In speech, the ROC year is only used on formal occasions in Taiwan, but it is still usual in official writing.

4.6.2 Historical notes on dating

In Unit 1, you were introduced to a set of ten terms of fixed order, the *tiāngān* or 'heavenly stems', which the Chinese use to designate members of a sequence. Traditionally, these *tiāngān* were used in combination with another set of twelve, known as the *dìzhī* 'the earthly branches'. The two sets formed a cycle of sixty *gānzhī*.

tiāngān (10)	甲	乙	丙	丁	戊	己	庚	辛	任	癸		
	jiǎ	*yǐ*	*bǐng*	*dīng*	*wù*	*jǐ*	*gēng*	*xīn*	*rén*	*guǐ*		
dìzhī (12)	子	丑	寅	卯	辰	巳	午	未	申	酉	戌	亥
	zǐ	*chǒu*	*yín*	*mǎo*	*chén*	*sì*	*wǔ*	*wèi*	*shēn*	*yǒu*	*xū*	*hài*

A sequence of sixty is achieved by combining the two sets in pairs, 甲子 *jiǎzǐ*, 乙丑 *yǐchǒu*, 丙寅 *bǐngyín*, and so on until the tenth, 癸酉 *guǐyǒu*, at which point the *tiāngān* begin again while the *dìzhī* continue: 甲戌 *jiǎxū*, 乙亥 *yǐhài*, 丙子 *bǐngzǐ*. After six repetitions of the *tiāngān* and five of the *dìzhī*, ending on 癸亥 *guǐhài*, all sixty possible combinations of the two sets will have been used, and the cycle begins again.

The *gānzhī* sets have been dated to at least the Shang dynasty (1523–1028 BCE) on oracle bone inscriptions, when they were apparently used to count days (Wilkinson: 176). However, the sets, individually as ten or twelve, or in combination as a set of sixty, also came to designate other temporal units, such as years and hours. The sixty *gānzhī* were used to specify the dates of specific historical events. This was done by indicating the ruling emperor, either by name or, more usually, by reign name (*niánhào*), and then by counting from the first year of his reign using the *gānzhī* pairs.

Reign names (several were often used over a single reign) were chosen for their auspicious meanings. The better-known emperors are often remembered only by their reign names. Thus, *Kāngxī* 'vitality and brilliance' is the reign name of the great Qing emperor who ruled from 1661 to 1722. The well-known dictionary compiled during his reign is referred to, in English, as the Kangxi Dictionary. It contains almost 50,000 entries, and is still sold in Chinese bookshops. Kangxi's grandson, the *Qiánlóng* emperor (another reign name), is also well known in the West. His long and eventful rule from 1736 to 1796 just exceeded a sixty-year *gānzhī* cycle. Some historical events are still commonly referred to by their *gānzhī* names, e.g., the *Xīnhài Gémìng* 'the 1911 Revolution' (*xīnhài* being year 48 of the cycle).

The twelve *dìzhī* were also used to designate time of day, each one assigned a two-hour period from 11 P.M. to 1 A.M. These 'hours' (or *shí*) also correlated with the *shēngxiào*, or the twelve animals of the zodiac (see below). The first *dìzhī*, *zǐ* (子), linked to the first animal, *shǔ* 'rat', and represented the *shí* from 11 P.M. to 1 A.M. The second, *chǒu* (丑), linked with *niú* 'ox' and represented the *shí* from 1 A.M. to 3 A.M. This pattern continued through the entire *dìzhī*. The five *shí*, or 'hours', that fall in the night (at least in the most populated regions) were also called the *wǔgēng* 'five changes'. In cities, daytime 'hours' were announced by rhythmic beats from the official drum (*gǔ*), often lodged in drum towers (*gǔlóu*) of the sort that survive in cities such as Xi'an and Beijing. The drumming would then be repeated in more distant neighborhoods.

In addition to the *dìzhī*, time was also kept by means of water clocks or 'clepsydra' (a word derived from Greek roots for 'steal' and 'water'). Water clocks measured time by the flow of water through a small aperture. Chinese water clocks traditionally divided the day into 100 equal divisions, called *kè*. The root meaning of *kè* is 'to inscribe', suggesting markings on a gauge; the usage survives in modern language for 'quarter past' and 'quarter to' the hour, *yíkè*. One *kè* represented 14.4 minutes, or approximately 1/8 of the two-hour periods represented by the *dìzhī* (or 1/100 of a day).

In 1912, the Republic of China officially adopted the Gregorian calendar, and named that year as year 1 of the new era (so 2004 is year 93). In the modern era, Chinese have sometimes dated from the birthdate of *Huángdì* 'Yellow Emperor', one of the five mythical founding emperors. At the beginning of the Republic, this date was fixed as 4,609 years before the Republic, i.e., 2698 BCE.

4.6.3 Age

In English, age and duration are both given in years ('three years old', 'for three years'), but a distinction between the two is made in Chinese. Years of duration are counted with *nián* (originally 'harvest' or 'harvest year'): *sān nián* 'three years'; *sānshí nián* 'thirty years'. Years of age are counted with *suì* (originally used for the planet Jupiter, with a revolution of twelve Earth years, and later used for the yearly cycle of seasons). Thus: *shíbā suì* 'eighteen years old', *èrshíyī suì* 'twenty-one years old', *jiǔ suì* 'nine years old'.

Asking about the age of adults, one can safely use the following expression.

Tā duō dà le?	('She how big by + now?')
Tā èrshíbā ⟨suì⟩ le.	'She's twenty-eight ⟨years old⟩.'

The addition of the noun *niánjì* 'age' makes the expressions a little more formal, and therefore more appropriate for a direct inquiry.

Nǐ duō dà niánjì?	('You how big age?')
Tā niánjì duō dà le?	('She age how big by + now?')

As the examples show, age can be expressed without a verb, much like dates, and *shì* can be omitted in cases where there is no adverbial modification. When there is adverbial modification, then a verb will usually appear. Where an age is being rejected, as in the following example, the verb will be *shì*.

Tā bú shi sìshí suì, tā shi shísì suì.	'She's not forty, she's fourteen.'

Otherwise, when a verb has to be supplied for an adverbial modifier, it is usually *yǒu*.

Tā duō dà?	'How old is he?'
Tā zhǐ yǒu bā suì.	'He's only eight.'

With children, it is possible to ask about age directly using the basic expression *Nǐ jǐ suì?* 'How many years old are you?' There are also deferential ways of asking about the age of older people. Sometimes, using the respectful form of address for the elderly, *lǎorénjiā*, will convey sufficient deference.

⟨*Lǎorénjiā*⟩ *jīnnián duō dà niánjì?*	'⟨Kind sir⟩, may I ask how old [you] are this year?'

Other expressions have the tone of English 'May I ask your age, sir?'

⟨*Lǎorénjiā*⟩ *guìgēng?*	('⟨venerable-sir⟩ worthy-age?')
⟨*Lǎorénjiā*⟩ *gāoshòu?*	('⟨venerable-sir⟩ long-life?')

One additional point: age is frequently given as an approximation, in which case *lái* can be inserted between the number (typically a multiple of ten) and the measure word *suì*.

Tā duō dà?	'How old is she?'
Tā ⟨*yǒu*⟩ *wǔshí lái suì.*	{ 'She's about fifty.' 'She's fifty-something.'

NOTES

a. Notice that *duō* in *duō dà* functions as a question word meaning 'to what degree'.

b. *Le* often appears with expressions of age in the sense of 'so far; by now'; however, the restrictive adverb *zhǐ* is not compatible with a final *le*.

c. *Suì* can safely be omitted when the number is larger than a single digit: *èrshíbā* ⟨*suì*⟩.

4.6.4 The animal signs

At times, it may be inappropriate to ask someone directly about his or her age, but it is nevertheless important to know roughly how old a person is so as to be able to use proper levels of deference. Thus, Chinese often ask about one's zodiac sign instead, and infer age from the response. Birth signs, called *shēngxiào* ('born-resemble') or *shǔxiàng* ('belong-appearance'), are the twelve animals associated with the Chinese zodiac, beginning with the rat and ending with the pig. For reference, two recent cycles are noted here.

shǔ	*niú*	*hǔ*	*tù*	*lóng*	*shé*
rat	ox	tiger	hare	dragon	snake
1984	1985	1986	1987	1988	1989
1996	1997	1998	1999	2000	2001

mǎ	*yáng*	*hóu*	*jī*	*gǒu*	*zhū*
horse	goat	monkey	chicken	dog	pig
1990	1991	1992	1993	1994	1995
2002	2003	2004	2005	2006	2007

Comments about birth signs generally make use of the verb *shǔ* 'to belong to': *Wǒ shǔ mǎ, tā shǔ tù!* 'I'm the horse [year], she's the hare.' So, to discover a person's age, you can ask:

Qǐngwèn, nǐ ⟨shi⟩ shǔ shénme de?	'What's your animal sign, please?'
Wǒ ⟨shi⟩ shǔ lóng de.	'I'm the year of the dragon.'

NOTES

a. The pattern with *shi* and *de* above literally translates as ('you be belong [to] what one'), which suggests a permanent status rather than a fleeting one; however, people do ask the question in its leaner form as well: *Nǐ shǔ shénme?*

b. In 2005, a person born in the year of the dragon is possibly 17, 29, 41, etc. In most cases, the correct choice will be obvious.

Though, traditionally, they have played a relatively small role in casting horoscopes and predicting the future, in recent years, particularly in more cosmopolitan places such as Hong Kong, the zodiac signs have come to play a more important role in the matching of couples for marriage, as well as in other social activities.

4.6.5 Year in school or college

'Year' or 'grade' in school or college is *niánjí* (listen for the subtle difference with *niánjì* 'age', introduced in the previous section). *Niánjí* is a compound consisting of *nián* 'year' and *jí* 'level'. Different levels are expressed as *yīniánjí* 'first year (freshman)'; *èrniánjí* 'second year (sophomore)', etc. The question, 'which level', is formed with *jǐ* 'how many; how much'; hence, *jǐniánjí* 'what year'.

Q:	*Qǐngwèn, nǐ shi jǐniánjí de ⟨xuéshēng⟩?*	'Excuse me, [may I ask] what grade you're in?'

A:	*Wǒ shi sìniánjí de ⟨xuéshēng⟩.*	'I'm a fourth-year student.'
	Wǒ shi Qīnghuá sānniánjí de xuéshēng.	'I'm a third-year student at Tsinghua.'
	Wǒ bú shi xuéshēng.	'I'm not a student.'
	Wǒ shi yánjiūshēng.	'I'm a graduate student.'

NOTES

a. Tsinghua University, located in northwestern Beijing, is one of China's top universities.

b. *Yánjiūshēng* ('research-student') is equivalent to 'graduate student' in American English and 'post-graduate student' in British English.

4.7 Studying and working

4.7.1 Vocabulary

zhuānyè	N	'a major; a specialty; a discipline' ('special-study')	[PRC]
zhǔxiū	N or V	'a major; to major in' ('main-study')	[Taiwan]
dúshū	V + O	'to study; to attend school' ('read-book')	
niànshū	V + O	'to read; to study' ('read-book')	
xuéxí	V	'to study; to learn; to emulate' ('study-review')	[PRC]
xué	V	'to study; to learn; to imitate'	
shàngxué	V + O	'to attend school; to go to school' ('attend-school')	
kāixué	V + O	'to start school' ('begin-school')	
gōngzuò	N or V	'a job; to work; to have a job' ('work-make')	
gànhuó⟨r⟩	V + O	'to be doing something; to work' ('do-livelihood')	[PRC]
bìyè ~ jiéyè	V + O	'to graduate' ('conclude-undertaking')	

In later units, you will discover that the difference between a two-syllable verb such as *xuéxí* or *gōngzuò* and a verb + object (V + O) such as *gànhuó⟨r⟩* or *bìyè* is that the latter combination is much less stable. With V + O constructions, the object can be detached from the verb: *Gàn shénme huó ne?* 'What's [he] doing?'

4.7.2 Major; specialization

A major subject of study, or a specialization, is *zhuānyè* ('special-study') or, particularly in Taiwan, *zhǔxiū* ('main-study'); the latter can also be a verb meaning 'to specialize; to major'.

Nǐ de zhuānyè/zhǔxiū shi shénme?	'What's your specialty/major?'
Shi wùlǐ⟨xué⟩.	'It's physics.'
Shi yīnyuè⟨xué⟩.	'It's music.'

4.7.3 To study

There are a number of verbs used for studying and learning, with differences in usage between the Mainland and Taiwan. One set includes the verbs *xué* and *xuéxí* 'to study; to learn'; the latter is rarely used in Taiwan. *Xuéxí* is often used for the activity of studying (expressed as *niànshū* in Taiwan).

Dàjiā dōu zài nǎr?	'Where is everyone?'
Dōu zài túshūguǎn xuéxí ~ niànshū; míngtiān yǒu kǎoshì.	'They're in the library studying; there's a test tomorrow.'

In many contexts, both the single and (except in Taiwan) disyllabic forms are possible.

Xuéshēng dōu yīnggāi xué⟨xí⟩ wàiyǔ, bú duì ma?	'Students should all study foreign languages, no?'
Ng, dōu yīnggāi xué!	'Yes, they should!'

However, there are some examples when *xué* is preferred. Consider the following, both of which translate as 'learn' rather than 'study'.

Zhōngwén hěn nán xué ba.	'Chinese must be tough to learn.'
Yǒu diǎnr nán, kěshì fēicháng yǒu yìsi.	'It is a bit, but it's fascinating!'
Tā hěn cōngmíng, xué +de hěn kuài.	'She's quite bright—[she] learns fast.'

Xuéxí also means 'to emulate' and is usually introduced by *xiàng* 'towards'.

Xiàng Léi Fēng tóngzhì xuéxí! { 'Learn from Comrade Lei Feng!' / 'Emulate Comrade Lei Feng!' }

NOTE

Léi Fēng is a well-known 'labor hero' who died in an accident in 1962, after dedicating his brief life to the Communist Party and the people.

When the question 'What are you studying?' is not about what you happen to be studying at the moment, but rather what field of study you are committed to, then the question (and answer) is usually cast as a nominalization, i.e., ('you be one [de] who studies what'). (Cf. *Nǐ ⟨shi⟩ shǔ shénme de?* in §4.6.3.)

Nǐ shì xué shénme de?	'What are you studying?'
Wǒ shi xué wùlǐxué de.	'I'm studying physics.'

4.7.4 *Zài* + verb 'action in progress'

Talking about school versus work often leads to comments that express ongoing action, such as 'she's still in school' or 'he's working now'. So here we take a brief detour to consider how to express continuous and ongoing action in Chinese.

It turns out that *zài* 'be at' not only occurs with noun objects to form location phrases (*zài bàngōngshì* 'in the office'; *zài wàitou* 'outside') and post-verbal phrases (*tā shēng zài Sūzhōu*), but it also occurs in the adverb position, before a verb, to emphasize an action in progress, often in conjunction with a final *ne*, which suggests a level of immediacy and engagement.

Tā chī zǎofàn le ma?	'Has she eaten breakfast?'
Hái méi ne, tā hái zài xǐzǎo ne.	'No, not yet, she's still showering.'
Zhāng Héng zài nǎr?	'Where's Zhang Heng?'
Tā zài kànbào ne.	'He's reading the paper.'
Duìbuqǐ, wǒ hái zài chīfàn ne.	'Sorry, I'm still eating.'
Nǐ ⟨zài⟩ chī shénme ne?	'What are you eating?'
Zhōu Shuǎng qǐlai le ma?	'Is Zhou Shuang up?'
Hái méi ne, tā hái zài shuìjiào ne.	'No, not yet, he's still sleeping.'

Ongoing action need not always be explicitly marked with *zài*; sometimes the final *ne* suffices to suggest that the action is in progress.

Nǐ chī shénme ne?	'What are you eating?'
Chī táng ne.	'Candy ~ sweets.'
Nǐ kàn shénme ne?	'What are you reading?'
Kàn Shìjiè Bēi de xiāoxi ne!	'An article on the World Cup.'

4.7.5 Studying; being in school

Studying, in the sense of being in school (or college), is expressed by one of a set of words that includes the synonymous verb + object compounds *dúshū* and *niànshū* 'to be studying' ('study-books'). The two also overlap with *shàngxué*, another verb + object which has the sense of 'being in school; studying' as well as 'starting school'—at the beginning of the day. In the following interchange, all three V + O combinations are acceptable.

Jiǎ:	*Nǐ mèimei duō dà le?*	'How old is your sister?'
Yǐ:	*Èrshíqī.*	'Twenty-seven.'
Jiǎ:	*Tā hái zài dúshū ma?*	'Is she still in school?'
Yǐ:	*Duì, tā hái zài dúshū, shi dàxué de xuéshēng, zài Qīnghuá Dàxué xué yīxué de.*	'Yes, she is, she's a university student, studying medicine at Tsinghua University.'

However, in the following exchange, where the sense is 'to go to school; to begin school for the day', *shàngxué* is more likely.

Měitiān jǐ diǎn ⟨qù⟩ shàngxué?	'What time does [he] go to school?'
Tā měitiān qī diǎn bàn qù shàngxué.	'He goes to school every day at 7:30.'

The verb *kāixué* means 'to begin the term at a school (or university)'. The first syllable, *kāi*, is also found in other common words, such as *kāihuì* 'to hold/attend a meeting' and *kāichē* 'to drive [a vehicle]'.

Wǒmen jiǔyuè èr hào kāixué.	'We start classes on September 2nd.'
Zhōngguó xuéshēng yě shi jiǔyuèfèn kāixué.	'Chinese students start in September, too.'
O, Zhōngguó dàxué yě shi jiǔyuèfèn kāixué ma?	'Oh, Chinese universities also begin in September?'
Shì de.	'That's right.'

4.7.6 Work

Students, of course, will eventually graduate and get jobs. When this is the case, the exchange in the previous section might read:

Jiǎ:	*Nǐ mèimei duō dà le?*	'How old is your sister?'
Yǐ:	*Èrshíqī.*	'Twenty-seven.'
Jiǎ:	*Tā hái zài dúshū ma?*	'Is she still in school?'
Yǐ:	*Tā bìyè le, tā gōngzuò le.*	'She's graduated, she's working.'
Jiǎ:	*Shénme gōngzuò?*	'What sort of job?'
Yǐ:	*Tā shi gǎo diànnǎo de.*	'She does computing.'

NOTE

Gǎo is a verb with a broad range of meanings, including 'to do; to make; to manage; to deal with; to set up; to pick up'.

OTHER EXAMPLES

Jiǎ:	*Tā zài shénme dìfang gōngzuò?*	'Where does he work?'
Yǐ:	*Tā zài bǎoxiǎn gōngsī gōngzuò.*	'He works in an insurance company.'

Jiă:	*Nĭ zhăo shéi?*	'Who are you looking for?'
Yĭ:	*Zhăo xiăo Féng—Féng Xiăoquán.*	'Young Feng—Feng Xiaoquan.'
Jiă:	*Tā zài gànhuó ne, zài cāngkù.*	'He's working, in the warehouse.'
Yĭ:	*Zhème wăn hái zài gànhuó ne?*	'So late [and] he's still at work?'
Jiă:	*Ng, tā shìr ~ shìqing tài duō le!*	'Yup, he's got too much [to do].'

4.7.7 College and department

Establishing a person's department (*xì*) or school or university (*dàxué*) makes use of the question word *nĕi* (*nă*) and the general measure word *gè*: *nĕi ge xì*; *nĕi ge dàxué*. There are two ways to ask about university and department. The first uses *zài*.

Nĭ shi zài nĕi ge dàxué?	'Which university are you at?'
Nĭ shi zài nĕi ge xì?	'Which department are you in?'

The other does not use *zài*, but rather the nominalizing pattern with *shi* and final *de*, along the lines of the earlier statements of a major: *wŏ shi xué wùlĭ de* 'I study physics'.

Nĭ shi nĕi ge dàxué de?	'Which is your university?'
Nĭ shi nĕi ge xì de?	'Which is your department?'

So, for example:

Jiă:	*Qĭngwèn, nĭ shi nĕi ge dàxué de?*	'Which university are you at?'
Yĭ:	*Wŏ shi Bĕijīng Dàxué de.*	'I'm at Peking University [*sic*].'
Jiă:	*O, Bĕi Dà; nà nĭ shi xué shénme de?*	'Oh, Bei Da; so what are you studying?'
Yĭ:	*Wŏ shi xué guănlĭxué de.*	'I'm studying management.'
Jiă:	*Zài nĕi ge xì?*	'In which department?'
Yĭ:	*Zài Jīngjì xì.*	'Economics.'

NOTE

The older spelling and associated English pronunciation is retained in the official English name of *Běijīng Dàxué,* Peking University; *Qīnghuá Dàxué* also retains the old spelling in its English name, Tsinghua. Many, but not all, university names in China have a short form, made up from the first and third syllables of the name: *Běijīng Dàxué* → *Běi Dà*. *Qīnghuá Dàxué,* however, is simply called *Qīnghuá* for short.

Exercise 4

Explain:

that you are [years old].
that you're at [university/school].
that you're a [grad/undergrad].
that you're a [grade-level] student there.
that you study [major].
that you're in the [subject] department.
that you are taking [number] of subjects this semester; [list].
that you have [number] of classes today.
that you have classes today at [time] and [time].
that you have classes every day except Wednesday.
that you were born and grew up in San Franciso, but now you live in Seattle.

4.8 Forms of address

In general, Chinese pay a lot of attention to forms of address, a fact that reflects the importance of status in Chinese society. It is useful to make a distinction between forms of address that replace names of strangers (e.g., 'sir', 'miss', 'buddy', 'dude') or intimates (e.g., 'sis', 'dad', 'auntie') and, on the other hand, titles that can occur with surnames (e.g., 'Mr.', 'Mrs.', 'Professor').

4.8.1 Forms of address used instead of names

For foreigners, the safest course may be to avoid forms of address entirely when speaking to strangers, particularly to women, and to simply begin with *qǐngwèn* 'may I ask [you]' or the more courtly expression *láojià* 'excuse me; may I bother you'. (This latter phrase is more commonly used in northern China and by older speakers.) Otherwise, *xiānsheng* 'sir' may be used to address adults of the salaried classes, and *shīfu* 'master' (*lǎo shīfu* for older people) can be used to address blue-collar workers (used mostly for males, but occasionally for females as well). Male shopkeepers can be addressed as *lǎobǎn*, which is similar in tone to English 'boss' (of a shop or small business). *Tóngzhì* 'comrade', common during the communist period, was never an appropriate term of address for foreigners to use to Chinese. (Nowadays, it is current among urban male homosexuals.)

Xiānsheng, jièguāng, jièguāng	'Sir, can I get through?' ('borrow light')
Láojià ~ qǐngwèn, xǐshǒujiān shì bu shi zài zhèi lóu?	'Excuse me, is the restroom on this floor?'
Shīfu, qǐngwèn, Pān yuànzhǎng de bàngōngshì zài nǎr?	'[Excuse me] sir, could you tell me where Dean Pan's office is?'
Lǎobǎn, yǒu méiyǒu bǐjìběn?	'Sir, do you have any notebooks?'

In Chinese, as in English, there is sometimes no perfectly appropriate way to address a female stranger. *Xiǎojie* 'Miss' (pronounced *xiǎojiě* if, for reasons of emphasis, the final syllable gets its full tone) had some currency in the past, and may still survive as a form of address in Taiwan and in overseas communities. However, it is now rare on the mainland, possibly because the term has been contaminated by association with expressions such as *sānpéi xiǎojie* ('three [ways]-keep+company girls'). Occasionally, people may use terms such as *dàjiě* 'big sister' or even *gūniáng* 'young lady; daughter', but such usage is not widespread.

Chinese, like many cultures, often uses kin terms for address where no actual relationship exists, in the same way that English-speaking children often use the terms 'uncle' and 'aunt' for adults of their parents' generation. In

China, usage varies greatly with region and age of speaker, but some typical examples are listed below, more for reference at this point than for usage. Unless otherwise stated, these terms are not generally used as titles (that is, not in association with a *xìng*).

shūshu	'uncle (father's younger brother)'; used by a child to a male of his or her parents' age
dàshū	same meaning as *shūshu*; used by adult speakers rather than by children
āyí	'auntie; nanny'; a child, and sometimes a young adult, to a woman of his or her parents' age
bófù	'uncle (father's elder brother)'; a young adult addressing the father of a good friend
bómǔ	'aunt (wife of father's elder brother)'; a young adult addressing the mother of a good friend
lǎorénjia	'sir'; a respectful term of address to elderly men of status
dàye	'uncle' (*yéye* 'paternal grandfather'); used to address older men with no particular status, therefore less respectful than *lǎorénjia*
dàmā; dàniáng	'madam (father's elder brother's wife)'; to elderly female acquaintances. *Dàmā* is more commonly used in northern China; *dàniáng* is more common to southern China; usage overlaps with *āyí*.
dàshěnr	'auntie'; commonly used in the countryside as an affectionate term for a female acquiantance of one's mother's age; can also be used after a *xìng* as: *Wáng shěnr* 'Aunt(ie) Wang'
xiǎo dì; xiǎo mèi⟨r⟩	'little brother; little sister'; used by some to address young waiters or other attendants, or for younger acquaintances

xiǎo péngyou	'little friend'; adult to child
gērmen	'brothers' ('elder brother-plural'); used by young men amongst themselves (cf. English 'man; buddy; dude; brother')

4.8.2 General titles

Most of the non-professional titles have been mentioned in earlier units, so we will only summarize them here.

	AS TITLE	GENERAL MEANINGS	EXAMPLE	USAGE NOTES
xiānsheng	'Mr.'	'[other's] husband'	*Wáng xiānsheng*	general
lǎoshī	'Mr.; Ms.'	'teacher'	*Wáng lǎoshī*	general
shīfu	'Master'		*Gāo shīfu*	Mainland
tàitai	'Mrs.'	'[other's] wife'	*Wáng tàitai*	Taiwan
fūrén	'Mrs.; Lady'	'[other's] wife'	*Wáng fūrén*	general
nǚshì	'Ms.'		*Téng nǚshì*	mostly written
xiǎojie	'Miss'	'young woman'	*Téng xiǎojie*	not Mainland

NOTES

a. Titles such as *xiānsheng* can also follow full names: *Wáng xiānsheng; Wáng Nǎi xiānsheng.* For a time, *xiānsheng* was also used as a deferential title for older and eminent professors—male or female; this usage now seems rare.

b. *Lǎoshī* can be used to refer to oneself, e.g., to students: *Wǒ shì Liú lǎoshī.* Though the expression *lǎoshī hǎo* does occur as a passing greeting or acknowledgment, a more considered greeting, such as one that includes the *xìng*, is more appropriate: *Wèi lǎoshī hǎo.*

c. *Tàitai* 'Mrs.' ('great; grand') and *fūrén* 'Lady' are both used with a husband's *xìng. Téng Wǎntíng* (female), married to *Xú Fēng zhǔrèn* 'Director Feng Xu', could be addressed as *Xú tàitai* or *Xú fūrén*, if appropriate.

d. *Fūrén* is a common form of address for wives of officials and others with high status, e.g., *Zhū Róngjī fūrén.* Margaret Thatcher, former prime minister of the UK, is called *Dài Zhuō'ěr fūrén* or *Sàqiè'ěr fūrén* (as well as *Tiě Niángzǐ* 'The Iron Lady').

e. *Nǚshì*, a formal term for 'Miss' or 'Ms.', is used with the woman's own *xìng. Nǚshì* might be starting to fill the gap left by the decline of *xiǎojie*, but, at present, the preferred form of address for women without professional titles seems to be the full name or *míngzi* (when appropriate). In certain regions, *jiě* 'older sister' is appended to the *xìng* and used between good friends: *Hóngjiě* 'sister Hong'.

4.8.3 Other terms

There are a number of other terms that are considered 'forms of address' but they are those which beginning students, and foreigners in general, are less likely to encounter. Here are two examples, using the surname *Chén*. Later, if you get a chance to work in a Chinese enterprise, you can observe the variety of titles and forms of address in more detail.

Chén lǎo used to address older people (male or female) of some eminence

Chén gōng used to address engineers or others who have, or had, positions in industry; *gōng* is short for *gōngchéngshī* 'engineer'

4.8.4 Professional titles

Professional titles are job titles, the sort that would be printed on a business card. They are used when first meeting someone and during introductions, but such titles are likely to soon be replaced by something less formal such as *lǎoshī*, *xiānsheng*, or even a full name (*xìng* + *míngzi*). Here is a selection of professional titles.

jiàoshòu 'professor' ('teaching-instruct'); *Zhōu jiàoshòu*; *ZhàoYuánrèn jiàoshòu*. Nowadays, on the mainland, teachers of all ranks are usually addressed, and often address each other, as *lǎoshī*. *Jiàoshòu* is more likely to be used in formal settings, such as introductions, when it is important to indicate rank explicitly.

jīnglǐ 'manager [of a company, etc.]'; *Qián jīnglǐ*

zhǔrèn 'director; head; chairperson [of a company, academic department, etc.]' ('main-official+post'); *Liào zhǔrèn*

dǒngshì 'director; trustee'; *Huáng dǒngshì*

zǒngcái	'director-general; CEO' ('overall-rule'); *Cáo zǒngcái*
dǎo	short for *dǎoyǎn* 'director [of films or plays]'; Zhāng Yìmóu, the film director, could be addressed as *Zhāng dǎo* (or less often as *Zhāng dǎoyǎn*).

Appending *zhǎng* to the end of a noun denotes the meaning 'head of; chief of' the associated noun.

xiàozhǎng	'principle of a school'	(*xiào* 'school')
yuànzhǎng	'dean; director of hospital'	(*yuàn* 'public facility')
huìzhǎng	'president of an association'	(*huì* 'association')
tíngzhǎng	'presiding judge'	(*tíng* 'law court')
chǎngzhǎng	'head of a factory'	(*chǎng* 'factory')
bùzhǎng	'minister; head of a section'	(*bù* 'board; ministry')
tīngzhǎng	'governmental dept. head'	(*tīng* 'hall')
chùzhǎng	'government section chief'	(*chù* 'office')
kēzhǎng	'department head'	(*kē* 'section')
shěngzhǎng	'governor'	(*shěng* 'province')
shìzhǎng	'mayor'	(*shì* 'city')

zǒngtǒng 'president'
Example: *Àobāmǎ zǒngtǒng (Kèlíndùn, Bùshí)*

zhǔxí 'chairman' ('main-seat')
Example: *Máo zhǔxí*

The titles on this list can be prefixed with *fù* 'vice; deputy; associate'; however, while *fù* might appear on a business card as part of the description of a person's rank, office, or function, it is not usually used in direct address. Thus, a Mr. Lee who is a *fùzhǔrèn* 'associate director' would be introduced and addressed simply as *Lǐ zhǔrèn*. A variety of possible *fù* titles are listed below.

fùjiàoshòu	'associate professor'	*fùxiàozhǎng*	'vice principal'
fùzhǔrèn	'associate director'	*fùshìzhǎng*	'vice mayor'
fùjīnglǐ	'deputy manager'	*fùzǒngtǒng*	'vice president'

One way to practice using titles is by greeting imaginary guests at the beginning of every class (or tutorial session): 'Our Dean, named Luo.' *'Luó Yuànzhǎng hǎo.'* 'Mr. Sima, head of a screw and bolt factory.' *'Sīmǎ chǎngzhǎng, nín hǎo.'* (See exercise 5 below.)

4.8.5 From title to prefix

As friendships among Chinese develop, there comes a point when address shifts from the relatively formal *xìng* + title to other forms, including full name, *míngzi*, or *hào* 'nickname'. One of the possibilities, common among males, makes use of the prefix *lǎo* 'old; venerable'. Instead of *Wáng xiānsheng*, friends might address *Wáng* as *lǎo Wáng* (nicely translated in Yuan and Church's *The Oxford Starter Chinese Dictionary*, as 'my pal [*Wáng*]'). The factors that condition this shift involve age, relative status, and other aspects of the relationship. Because it involves a degree of camaraderie that is not easily extended to non-locals, foreigners should probably wait for an explicit invitation before making such a shift.

In Cantonese-speaking areas, the equivalent of *lǎo* is *ā*, and so in southern regions (as well as in many communities of Southeast Asian Chinese), this prefix has been incorporated into Mandarin, e.g., *ā Bāo* = *lǎo Bāo, ā Méi* = *lǎo Méi.* During the years of his presidency in Taiwan, Chen Shui-bien (*Chén Shuǐbiǎn*) was frequently referred to as *ā Biǎn.*

Another prefix, *xiǎo*, is used before a *xìng* as a term of endearment for young adults, particularly women (*xiǎo Bì* 'young Bi') or in contrast to someone else with the same surname who is older or has other features (size, maturity) that set her or him apart.

Finally, it should be noted that intimates will sometimes use *xiǎo* in front of the last syllable of a given name; thus, *Chén Bó* might be addressed as *xiǎo Bó*, rather than *lǎo Chén, xiǎo Chén*, or *Chén Bó.*

FULL NAME	SEX	INFORMAL	INTIMATE	WITH TITLE (FORMAL)
Bái Sùzhēn	female	*xiǎo Bái*	*xiǎo Zhēn*	*Bái lǎoshī*
Zhāng Dàmíng	male	*lǎo Zhāng*	*xiǎo Míng*	*Zhāng jīnglǐ*
Liáng Àimín	female	*xiǎo Liáng*	*xiǎo Mín*	*Liáng zhǔrèn*

Exercise 5

Greet or address the following people appropriately.

Example: A teacher named *Zhào*: *Zhào lǎoshī, nín hǎo.*

1. A middle-aged, married woman whose husband's surname is *Bái*:
2. A young woman named *Guō Měifāng*:
3. The wife of an important official named *Zhū*:
4. A CEO named *Dèng*:
5. The eminent Professor *Xú*:
6. A company's deputy manager, named *Qián*:
7. A school principal, surnamed *Yuán*:
8. An elderly man seated on a park bench; an elderly woman:
9. Your bus driver, named *Zhào*:
10. Your teacher's husband, whose surname is *Huáng*:

4.9 Introductions

Making introductions usually involves names and titles (*Zhào Fāngfāng, Chén lǎoshī*), pointing words (*zhè, nà*), set expressions of greeting (*nǐ hǎo*), and, often, some explanation of the connection, usually provided in a phrase such as *zhè shi wǒ de lǎoshī* 'this is my teacher'. A host may use the disyllabic verb, *jièshào* 'to introduce', to express his or her intention to introduce someone, as shown below.

Zhāng lǎoshī, wǒ gěi nǐ jièshào jièshào! Zhè shi . . .	'Professor Zhang, let me introduce you! This is . . .'

Notice how *gěi* shifts in meaning from its core sense of 'to give' to 'for [your benefit]' when it is subordinated to the main verb, *jièshào*. Instead of *zhè shi*, the polite measure word for people, *wèi*, will often be used: *zhèi wèi shi . . .*

4.9.1 Relational information

To keep things manageable, you can provide information specific to personal relationships in the following format.

Zhè ⟨wèi⟩ shi wǒ ⟨de⟩ . . .	'This is my . . .'

A. WITH *DE*

Zhè ⟨wèi⟩ shi wǒ de lǎoshī.	'This is my teacher.'
wǒ de Zhōngwén lǎoshī.	'my Chinese teacher.'
wǒ de xuéshēng.	'my student.'
wǒ de tóngxué.	'my classmate.'
wǒ de péngyou.	'my friend.'
wǒ de lǎo péngyou.	'my good friend.'
wǒ de lǎobǎn.	'my boss.'
Zhāng lǎoshī de xuéshēng.	'Professor Zhang's student.'

B. USUALLY WITHOUT *DE*

Zhè shi wǒ fùqin.	'This is my father.'
wǒ bà⟨ba⟩.	'my dad.' (intimate)
wǒ mǔqin.	'my mother.'
wǒ mā⟨ma⟩.	'my mom' (intimate).
wǒ gēge.	'my older brother.'
wǒ dìdi.	'my younger brother.'
wǒ jiějie.	'my older sister.'
wǒ mèimei.	'my younger sister.'
wǒ àirén.	'my spouse.' (not used in Taiwan)
wǒ zhàngfu.	'my husband.' (neutral)
wǒ lǎogōng.	'my husband.' (neutral)
wǒ xiānsheng.	'my husband.' (formal)
wǒ qīzi.	'my wife.' (neutral)
wǒ lǎopo ~ lǎopó.	'my wife.' (informal)
wǒ xífur.	'my wife.' (regional)
wǒ tàitai.	'my wife.' (formal; Taiwan)

4.9.2 A note on words for husband and wife

In Chinese, as in English, words for 'spouse' go in and out of fashion. The use of *lǎogōng* for 'husband', for example, was probably influenced by films and television programs from Hong Kong and Taiwan, so the term is current among younger urban people on the mainland. The female version of *lǎogōng*, *lǎopó*, is also quite common, though for some it has a slightly jocular (and, some would add, disrespectful) tone, along the lines of English 'my old lady'. (The male equivalent would be *lǎotóuzi* 'my old man'.) Terms such as *qīzi* 'wife' and *zhàngfu* 'husband' are fairly neutral.

Máo Zédōng yǒu sì ge qīzi.	'Mao had four wives.'
Máo Zédōng yǒu sì ge lǎopó.	(more informal)

Nèirén 'wife' ('within-person') has a humble, intimate tone. Southerners often use *xífur*, a variant of *xífù* 'daughter-in-law', for wife: *Sǎozi shi gēge de xífur.* 'Saozi is the wife of one's elder brother.' *Sǎozi*, then, means 'sister-in-law'.

The PRC used to promote the use of *àirén* ('love-person') as an egalitarian term for 'spouse' (husband or wife), and the phrase *zhè shì wǒ àirén* is still current on the mainland. The term causes some giggles among non-Mainlanders, for in Taiwan, *àirén* sometimes has the meaning of 'sweetheart'. (*Aìrén* is not the normal word for 'lover', however; that is *qíngrén* ('feelings-person'), the word used for the Chinese title of the French film *The Lover*, for example.)

Another term that has come into vogue in informal situations on the mainland is *nèiwèi* for 'spouse' ('that-one'), which derives from the phrase *wǒmen jiā de nèiwèi* ('our family DE that-one'). Sometimes, it combines with a plural possessive pronoun even when the reference is singular: *wǒ* ~ *wǒmen nèiwèi* 'my husband/wife'. Thus: *Nǐ(men) nèiwèi zěnmeyàng?* 'How's your husband/wife?'

Foreigners, though they may hear intimate or familiar terms, should be careful not to use them unless their relationship warrants it!

4.9.3 Responses

A typical response to an introduction makes use of an appropriate title with the surname, followed by a conventional expression of greeting.

Ò, Qí lǎoshī, nín hǎo ma? 'Oh, Professor Qi, how are you?'

After being introduced to someone of eminence, an accepted response is *jiǔyǎng* ('long+time-look+up+to'), often repeated as *jiǔyǎng jiǔyǎng* '[I]'ve heard a lot about you'. Sometimes *dàmíng* 'great name' is added: *jiǔyǎng dàmíng.*

Ò, Qí lǎoshī, jiǔyǎng, jiǔyǎng. 'Oh, Professor Qi, [I'm] honored to meet you.'

Children, and sometimes young adults, may show respect by addressing elders as *shūshu* 'uncle' or *āyí* 'auntie': *Shūshu hǎo.* 'How are you, uncle?'

In English, we feel the need to confirm the worth of meeting someone by saying 'nice to meet you', either after an introduction or at the end of an initial meeting, before taking leave. Traditionally, Chinese had an expression *xìnghuì* ('fortunate-meet'), which was used as a more formal acknowledgment of a meeting, and was often heard in the same context as *jiǔyǎng*.

Ò, Qí lǎoshī, jiǔyǎng, jiǔyǎng, xìnghuì, xìnghuì. 'Oh, Professor Qi, [I've] heard so much about you, [I'm] honored.

Nowadays, *xìnghuì* is more often heard on television dramas than in the real world. Instead, people in the more cosmopolitan cities, particularly when they are talking to foreigners, will use the phrase *hěn gāoxìng rènshi nǐ* ('very happy know you') or *hěn gāoxìng jiàndào nǐ* ('very happy see you') in more or less the same situations as English 'nice to meet you'. The response may have a slightly different emphasis, expressed in the word order: *Rènshi nǐ, wǒ yě hěn gāoxìng!* 'Happy to meet you too! / My pleasure!'

À, Qí lǎoshī, hěn gāoxìng rènshi nǐ. 'Oh, Professor Qi, nice to meet you.'

4.9.4 Dialogues

You (*Wèi*) are introducing your friend *Chén Huībó* (male) to your classmate, a student from China named *Cài Wénjiā* (female). You get *Cài*'s attention by calling out her name, and as you guide her toward *Chén*, you explain who he is. *Cài* then (re)states her full name, and the two acknowledge each other.

Wèi:	*Cài Wénjiā, wǒ gěi nǐ jièshào jièshào; zhè shi wǒ de péngyou, Chén Huībó.*	'Cai Wenjia, let me introduce you; this is my friend, Chen Huibo.'
Cài:	*Chén Huībó, nǐ hǎo; wǒ shi Cài Wénjiā.*	'Chen Huibo, how are you? I'm Cai Wenjia.'
Chén:	*Cài Wénjiā, nǐ hǎo ma?*	'Cai Wenjia, how are you?'

Next is a relatively formal introduction between strangers sharing a train cabin. (Hng = *xìng Huáng de, jiàoshòu*; Zh = *xìng Zhōu de, jīnglǐ*.) Note the word for business card, *míngpiàn* ('name-slice').

Hng:	*Ei, nín hǎo ma, wǒ xìng Huáng, zhè shì wǒ de míngpiàn. Nín guìxìng?*	'Hi, how are you? My [sur] name's Huang; this is my card. What's your [sur]name?'
Zh:	*(Looking at the card.) O, Huáng lǎoshī, nín hǎo. Wǒ jiào Zhōu Bǎolín—wǒ de míngpiàn.*	'Oh, Professor Huang, how are you? My name's Zhou Baolin—my card.'
Hng:	*(He too looks at the card.) A, Zhōu jīnglǐ, nín hǎo. O, nín shì Wēiruǎn de! Wēiruǎn hěn yǒumíng a!*	'Ah. Manager Wang, how do you do? Oh, you're with Microsoft! Microsoft's famous!'
Wáng:	*Hái xíng ba!*	'I guess [if you say so]!'

NOTE

Wēiruǎn de 'of ~ from Microsoft' ('tiny-soft DE')

Exercise 6

Complete the following conversation using conventions of introductions. *Liáng Mínmǐn* meets *Dèng Lìlì* (both female teachers) and introduces her student *Mǎ Yán* (male). Fill in *Dèng Lìlì*'s responses.

Liáng: *Nín hǎo, wǒ xìng Liáng, jiào Liáng Mímǐn.*

Dèng: ______________________________

Liáng: *Dèng Lìlì, nǐ hǎo. Zhè shì Mǎ Yán, wǒ de xuéshēng.*

Dèng: ______________________________

Mǎ: *Dèng lǎoshī, hǎo. Rènshi nǐ, wǒ yě hěn gāoxìng.*

Translate the following introductions into Chinese.

1. Miss *Chén*, this is my classmate *Wáng Bīnbīn*.
2. This is my good friend *Bì Xiùqióng*.
3. This is my younger sister, *Chén Xiùxiù*.
4. Professor *Gāo*, I've heard so much about you.
5. Let me introduce you–this is Manager *Wáng*, he's with Microsoft.
6. This is *Lǐ Dàwéi*, he's been to China, and he's studying Chinese.

Dào Miányáng le ma?

4.10 Dialogue: On the bus to *Miányáng*

Méi Tàidé (Theo Meyering), a foreign student traveling by bus from *Chéngdū* to *Miányáng* (about 111 kilometers to the northeast), is attempting to read the local paper. The man sitting next to him, surnamed *Ōuyáng*, who has been watching him for a while, breaks into conversation.

Ōu-y:	*Kàndedǒng ma?*	'Can you read [it]?'
Méi:	*Néng kàndǒng yìdiǎnr.*	'I can read a bit.'
Ōu-y:	*Hànzì hěn duō ya!*	'Chinese has a *lot* of characters!'
Méi:	*Shì, tài duō le!*	'Yes, too many!'
Ōu-y:	*Wǒ xìng Ōuyáng—zhè shì wǒde míngpiàn.*	'My name's Ouyang—here's my card.'
Méi:	*A, Ōuyáng xiānsheng . . . Ōuyáng, jīnglǐ, nín hǎo! Hěn gāoxìng rènshi nín.*	'Oh, Mr. Ouyang . . . Manager Ouyang, hello! Nice to meet you.'
Ōu-y:	*Zhè shi wǒ àirén, Xiāo Měifāng.*	'This is my wife, Xiao Meifang.'
Méi:	*Nín hǎo. Wǒde míngzi shi Theo Meyering, Méi Tàidé: Tàiguó de Tài, Déguó de Dé. Duìbuqǐ, xiànzài wǒ yǐjīng méiyǒu míngpiàn le.*	'Hello. My name's Theo Meyering, Mei Taide: the tai of Taiguo, the de of Deguo. I'm sorry, I'm already out of business cards.'
Xiāo:	*Méi Tàidé, Méi xiānsheng, nǐ hǎo. Nǐ Zhōngwén jiǎng+de zhēn bàng!*	'Mei Taide, Mr. Mei, hello.' 'You speak Chinese *really* well!'
Méi:	*Nǎlǐ, nǎlǐ, jiǎng+de mǎmǎhūhū. Wǒ hái zài xué ne, wǒ zài Sìchuān Dàxué xuéxí.*	'Nice of you to say so [but] I speak poorly. I'm still studying [it]—I'm studying at Sichuan University.'
Ōu-y:	*Qǐngwèn nǐ shì cóng nǎ ge guójiā lái de?*	'May I ask what country you're from?'

Méi:	*Wǒ shi Hélán rén; wǒ shēng zài Hélán. Kěshì xiànzài wǒ shi Měiguó Mìxīgēn Dàxué de xuéshēng.*	'I'm from Holland; I was born in Holland. But at present, I'm a student at the University of Michigan.'
Ōu-y:	*O, Mìxīgēn Dàxué, hěn yǒumíng. Nǐ shì jǐniánjí de xuéshēng?*	'Oh, the University of Michigan, it's famous. What year are you?'
Méi:	*Wǒ shi sìniánjí de.*	'I'm a senior.'
Ōu-y:	*Nǐ shi Zhōngwén xì de ma?*	'Are you in the Chinese department?'
Méi:	*Bù, wǒ shì Jīngjì xì de, wǒ xué Zhōngguó jīngjì. Ōuyáng xiānsheng, nín zài Chángchūn gōngzuò a?*	No, I'm in economics, I'm studying Chinese economics. [So] you work in Changchun, Mr. Ouyang?'
Ōu-y:	*Duì, wǒ zài Chángchūn gōngzuò, búguò wǒ shi Shěnyáng rén.*	'Yes, I work in Changchun, but I'm from Shenyang.'
Méi:	*Dōu zài Dōngběi, duì ba?*	'Both in the Northeast, right?'
Ōu-y:	*Duì, Chángchūn zài Jílín shěng, Shěnyáng zài Liáoníng. Shěnyáng lí Běijīng bù yuǎn.*	'That's right, Changchun is in Jilin province, Shenyang is in Liaoning. Shenyang isn't far from Beijing.'
Měi:	*Shěnyáng hěn dà, shì bu shi?*	'Shenyang's big, isn't it?'
Ōu-y:	*Shì, yǒu chàbuduō wǔbǎiwàn rén . . . Nǐ chīguò zhōngfàn le ma?*	'It is, it has about five million inhabitants . . . Have you had lunch?'
Méi:	*Chī le, zài Chéngdū chī le.*	'I have—in Chengdu.'
Ōu-y:	*Nǐmen zhōngfàn dōu chī sānmíngzhì, shì bu shi?*	'You eat sandwiches for lunch, right?'
Méi:	*Bù yídìng. Kěshì zài Zhōngguó, wǒ dāngrán chī Zhōngguó fàn.*	'Not necessarily. But in China, I eat Chinese food of course.'

Ōu-y:	*Zhōngguó fàn nǐ chīdeguàn ma?*	'Are you accustomed to eating Chinese food?'
Méi:	*Dāngrán chīdeguàn, zài Hélán, zài Mèiguǒ, wǒ yě chángcháng chī Zhōngguó fàn . . . Dào Miányáng le ma?*	'Of course I am, I often eat Chinese food in Holland and in the United States. . . . Is this Mianyang?'
Ōu-y:	*Hái méi dào ne. Zhè shì Déyáng. Wǒmen zài zhèr xiàchē. Dàgài yì diǎn bàn dào Miányáng.*	'Not yet. This is Deyang. We get off here. [You] get to Mianyan at about 1:30.'
Méi:	*Oh, nǐmen zài Déyáng xiàchē?*	'Oh, you get off at Deyang?'
Ōu-y:	*Duì, wǒ yǒu ge jiějie zhù zài Déyáng.*	'Yes, I have an older sister living in Deyang.'
Méi:	*Nǐmen de xíngli duō bu duō?*	'Do you have a lot of bags?'
Ōu-y:	*Bù duō–zhǐ yǒu yí jiàn. Hǎo, wǒmen xiàchē le. Zàijiàn!*	'No, just one. Okay, we're getting off. 'Good-bye!'
Méi:	*Hǎo, zàijiàn, zàijiàn!*	'Okay, good-bye!'

NOTES

a. *kàndedǒng* 'can understand [by reading]' ('look-able+to-understand'). *Kàndedǒng* is an example of what is sometimes known as the 'potential construction', which involves an action (*kàn*) and result (*dǒng*) and an intervening *de* 'able to' or *bù* 'unable to'. Thus: *kànbudǒng* 'cannot understand [by reading]'. Other examples: *chīdeguàn*, appearing later in this dialogue, 'be in the habit of eating' ('eat-get-accustomed'); and earlier, in the rhyme at the end of Unit 2, *shuāibudǎo* 'won't fall down' ('slip-not-fall'). The response to Ouyang's question might have been *kàndedǒng* 'I do', but *Méi* is more modest and wishes to use *yìdiǎnr* 'a little'. *Kàndedǒng* or *kànbudǒng* do not permit gradations–either you do or you don't; so the response with *yìdiǎnr* has to be *néng kàndǒng yìdiǎnr* 'can understand a bit'.

b. *néng* 'able to; can'; not usually used for learned abilities

c. *Ōuyáng* is an example of one of the forty or so disyllabic surnames. *Tā xìng Ōuyáng. Méi Tàidé* re-addresses him with *jīnglǐ* after reading his business card.

d. *Xiāo Měifāng*: Notice how *Méi Tàidé* refrains from addressing *Ōuyáng*'s wife with a title or her name. Neither *tàitai* nor *xiǎojie* is appropriate, and using her given name might seem too familiar; he just says *nín hǎo*.

e. *àirén* 'spouse; wife; husband'. This is typical usage.

f. *zhēn bang*; *Bàng* is a noun meaning 'club' or 'cudgel', but in colloquial speech, it has come to function as an SV with the meaning 'good; strong'; cf. British English 'smashing'. The expression *zhēn bàng* is more common in certain regions and among certain age groups than others.

g. *chīdeguàn* 'in the habit of eating' ('eat-get-accustomed')

h. *jiàn* a measure word for 'luggage' (and, interestingly, for 'clothes' and 'business affairs' as well)

4.11 Food (1)

In China, meals are central to social life; however, learning how to read the menu and order meals takes a long time. Eating at Chinese restaurants overseas may give the impression that there is a set of basic dishes at the heart of every Chinese regional cuisine, but within China, menus start to seem infinitely variable. What is more, you will find that, rather than consulting the menu, Chinese customers are just as likely to base their orders on a conversation with the waiter about what is seasonal or fresh, or what the restaurant's specialties are. It is therefore necessary to incrementally build up competence about Chinese food, beginning with elementary categories.

The basic distinction in food is between *fàn* and *cài*. Both words have core and extended meanings.

fàn	'cooked rice'	→	staples
cài	'vegetables'	→	dishes; courses

Fàn, in its extended meaning, includes cooked rice, wheat, millet, and other grains that—at least in less affluent times—formed the main caloric intake. *Cài*, in its extended meaning, would normally have been vegetables, some dry or fresh fish, and, very occasionally, a small amount of pork. Now, of course, *cài* includes the vast array of dishes that can be served alongside the staples.

Any ambiguity between core and extended meanings can be eliminated through compounding.

báifàn; mǐfàn	'cooked rice' (as opposed to other staples)
qīngcài	'vegetables' (as opposed to other dishes)

Rice is the staple of southern China, where it is eaten cooked (*mǐfàn*) or ground into flour for noodles (*mǐfěn*) and dumpling wraps. In the north, wheat is the staple and forms the basis of wheat noodles (*miàn ~ miàntiáo*) and wheat dumpling wraps. At breakfast and lunch, Chinese often eat a rice gruel or congee (*xīfàn* 'watery rice' or *zhōu*), to which can be added various kinds of vegetables, meats, and sauces, as well as broken up *yóutiáo* 'fried dough sticks'.

miàn ~ miàntiáo	'noodles'
miànbāo	'bread' ('wheat-bun')
mǐfěn	'rice-flour noodles'
zhōu/xīfàn	'rice porridge; congee'
bāozi	'steamed stuffed buns'
jiǎozi	'dumplings'
guōtiē	'pot stickers'
yóutiáo	'fried dough sticks'
tāng	'soup'
dòufu	'tofu'
ròu	'meat'
yā⟨ròu⟩	'duck'
zhūròu	'pork'
yángròu	'lamb'
niúròu	'beef'
jī⟨ròu⟩	'chicken'
jīdàn	'chicken eggs'
hǎixiān	'seafood'
yú	'fish'
xiārén⟨r⟩	'shimp meat'
hǎishēn	'sea cucumber'

NOTES

a. In combinations, parts of these citation forms are often dropped. In most cases, it is the second element: *niúròu-miàn⟨tiáo⟩* 'beef noodles'. In some cases, it is the first: *niúròu-chǎo ⟨mǐ⟩fěn* 'beef fried rice-noodles'.

b. On a menu, unspecified *ròu* means 'pork'.

c. Many Chinese avoid eating beef because of Buddhist tradition and because of taboos about killing work animals.

d. *Xiā* is 'shrimp'; *rén⟨r⟩* is 'kernel'; so *xiārénr* is 'shrimp meat'.

e. Sea cucumber is a euphemistic name for a kind of slug that lives on the bottom of the sea; eaten fresh or dried, it is considered a delicacy.

Qīngzhēn xiānjī 'Muslim fresh chicken', *Kūnmíng* street stall

SHORT NARRATIVE A: *ZHŌNGGUÓRÉN ZUÌ XǏHUAN HĒ SHÉNME?*

Yǒu péngyou wèn wǒ Zhōngguó rén zuì xǐhuan hē shénme? Wǒ shuō chuántǒng de Zhōngguó rén xǐhuan hē chá huòzhě báikāishuǐ, kěshì xiànzài hěn duō Zhōngguó rén yě xǐhuan hē qìshuǐ, kělè hé niúnǎi. Zhōngguó nánrén yě xǐhuan hē píjiǔ. Qīngdǎo píjiǔ shi zuì yǒumíng de Zhōngguó píjiǔ. Wǒ yě xǐhuan hē píjiǔ, kěshì bù néng hē tài duō, yì píng jiù gòu le! Zǎoshàng, wǒ yě hē kāfēi, hē yì bēi wǒ jiù bú huì juéde lèi!

SHORT NARRATIVE B: *ZUÌ XǏHUAN CHĪ SHÉNME?*

Nà, Zhōngguó rén zuì xǐhuan chī shénme? Zhè hěn nán shuō. Yīnwèi Zhōngguó rén chī de dōngxi tài duō le. Kěyǐ shuō běifāng rén bǐjiào xǐhuan chī miànshí, jiùshì yòng xiǎomàifěn zuò de shípǐn; nánfāng rén ne, tāmen bǐjiào xǐhuan chī mǐfàn. Měitiān dāngrán chī qīngcài, yě chī yìdiǎnr ròu, xiàng zhūròu, jīròu, niúròu. Ménggǔrén yě tèbié xǐhuan chī yángròu. Zhōngguó rén yě cháng chī hǎixiān, xiàng yú, xiārénr, hǎishēn. Yě xǐhuan chī bāozi, jiǎozi; zhèi lèi dōngxi kěyǐ shuō shi Zhōngguó chuántǒng de kuàicān. Língshí ne, tǐng duō de! Yǒu niúròugānr, guāzǐ⟨r⟩, huàméi.

NOTES

a. *yǒu péngyou;* While English comfortably begins a sentence with an indefinite phrase such as 'a friend' or 'someone', Chinese favors the existential *yǒu* 'there is/are . . . ': *Yǒu rén wèn wǒ; Yǒu rén shuō . . .*

b. *chuántǒng* 'traditional'

c. *báikāishuǐ* 'boiled water' ('white-boiled-water')

d. *miànshí* 'cooked wheaten food'; In Mandarin, *shí* is a combining root that appears in compounds having to do with food, such as *shípǐn* and *língshí*, below. It is a cognate with Cantonese *sihk* 'to eat'.

e. *jiùshi* 'that is' (in this context)

f. *xiǎomài* 'wheat'; cf. *dàmài* 'barley', *yànmài* 'oats', *qiáomài* 'buckwheat'

g. *shípǐn* 'food; comestibles' ('food-product')

h. *Ménggǔ* Mongolia; cf. *Nèi Ménggǔ* 'Inner Mongolia'

i. *tèbié* 'special'; When used as an adverb, it has the meaning of 'especially'.

j. *zhèi lèi* 'this type'; particularly in the expression *zhèi lèi dōngxi* 'these sorts ~ categories of things'; cf. *zhèi zhǒng* 'this kind'

k. *kuàicān* 'fast food'

l. *língshí* 'nibbles; snacks' ('zero; incidental-food')

m. *niúròugānr* 'beef jerky'; measured with *yí dàir* 'a bag'

n. *guāzǐ⟨r⟩* 'sunflower seeds'

o. *huàméi* 'preserved plums'; measured with *yì bāo* 'a packet'

4.12 Pinyin: Initials *w* and *y*

Though pinyin syllables may begin with the vowels *a*, *o*, and *e* (*è*, *ān*, *ōu*, etc.), they do not begin with *i* or *u*. When medial *i* and *u* might occur at the beginning of a syllable, they are written *y* and *w*, respectively. Consider the following cases as examples.

duo, *shuo*, drop the C_i:	*uo*	→	*wo*
xie, *bie*, drop the C_i:	*ie*	→	*ye*

However, if *i*, *u*, or *ü* are the only vowels in a syllable (as in *nǐ*, *shū*, *nǚ*), then dropping the C_i would leave only the vowels *i*, *u*, and *ü*. If these were simply rewritten as *y* and *w*, you would end up with rather curious looking syllables like 'w' (*shu* → *u* → 'w') or 'wn' (*shun* → *un* → 'wn'). So in such cases, instead of changing *i* and *u* to *y* and *w* as before, *y* and *w* are added.

			As a syllable
ji, drop the *j*:	*i*	→	*yi*
jin, drop the *j*:	*in*	→	*yin*
jing, drop the *j*:	*ing*	→	*ying*
shu, drop the *sh*:	*u*	→	*wu*
xu, drop the *x*:	*u*	→	*yu*
jun, drop the *j*:	*un*	→	*yun*
xue, drop the *x*:	*ue*	→	*yue*

There are a few exceptions to this pattern.

jiu, drop the *j*:	*iu*	→	*you*	*yu* is taken (see above)
gui, drop the *g*:	*ui*	→	*wei*	no syllable 'wi'; rhymes with *ei*
zhun, drop the *zh*:	*un*	→	*wen*	no syllable 'wun'; rhymes with *en*

Exercise 7

By now, you should be familiar enough with the pinyin system to match it to the sound system of Chinese with a fair degree of accuracy. Here are two exercises to test your 'fluency'. The first gives the reading of seven notices observed on a subway system. The second gives the Chinese transliteration of English-language names of places, things, and people.

Try reading the following subway signs aloud. Glosses and translations are provided out of interest, but they also provide a guide to intonation.

(These phrases are not spoken, of course, but you might find a place in your conversation for the first and last.)

1. *Qǐng guānzhù yuètái de kòngxì.*
   'Mind the gap.' ('request mind platform DE gap')
2. *Qǐng wù suídì diū lājī.*
   'Don't litter.' ('request don't all-over discard trash')
3. *Búyào kàojìn chēmén.*
   'Don't lean on the doors.' ('don't be+close+to vehicle-door')
4. *Qǐng ràng chéngkè xiān xiàchē.*
   'Let passengers off first.' ('request let passengers first off-vehicle')
5. *Zhīfù zhèngquè chēzī, bùrán fùchū gèng duō.*
   'Pay the correct fare or risk paying more.' ('pay accurate fare or-else pay even more')
6. *Mén zhèngzài guān shí, qǐng búyào shàngchē.*
   'Please don't board when the doors are closing.' ('door in+process+of close time, request don't board-vehicle')
7. *Shēngmìng yào zhēnxī, xíngwéi yào fùzé.*
   'Embrace life, behave responsibly.' ('life need cherish, behaviour need responsibility')

Pronounce and then write the English names of the transliterated places, food items, and people in the lists below.

Names	Hint	English
Fóluólǐdá		
Yàlìsāngnà		
Mǎsàzhūsài		
Nèibùlàsījiā		
Éhài'é		
Élègāng	a U.S. state	
Zhījiāgē	a U.S. city	
Àidīngbǎo	a European city with a castle	
Hóngdūlāsī	a Central American country	

Ālāsījiā	
Àodàlìyà	
Bāxī	a South American country with rain forests
Dálāsī	
Xīn Ào'ěrliáng	a U.S. city famous for food and music
Bājīsītǎn	
Common nouns	
qiǎokelì or *zhūgǔlì*	sweet food
sānmíngzhì	common lunch food
hànbǎobāo	
qǐsī ~ zhīshì hànbǎobāo	
shālā	leafy vegetable
pīsà bǐng	fast food
Kěkǒukělè	
Màidāngláo	
Hànbǎowáng	*wáng* 'king'
People (Mainland usage)	
Shāshìbǐyà	
Suǒfēiyà Luólán	
Mǎlóng Báilándù	'Stella!'
Àosēn Wēi'ěrsī	
Gélìgāolì Pàikè	
Yīnggélì Bāomán	
Luósīfú	the longest-serving U.S. president
Gé'ěrbāqiáofū	
Shīwǎxīngé	'I'll be back!'
Pàwǎluódì	

4.13 Summary

Existence	*Zhèr yǒu xǐshǒujiān ma? / Yǒu, xǐshǒujiān zài hòutou.*
Location	*Zhèr fùjìn yǒu Zhōngguó fànguǎnr ma? / Yǒu liǎng ge.*
Born in . . .	*Tā shēng zài Běijīng, yě zhǎng zài Běijīng, kěshì xiànzài zhù zài Xī'ān.*
Clock time	*Xiànzài jǐ diǎn ⟨zhōng⟩ le? / Shí diǎn.*
	Wǒ wǎnshàng liǎng diǎn shuìjiào, zǎoshàng shí diǎn qǐlái.
Habitually	*Zhōngguó rén píngcháng jǐ diǎn chī zǎocān?*
Tickets	*Guìlín, jīntiān xiàwǔ 3:25, yìngzuò, yì zhāng.*
DE	*Shìjièbēi de xiāoxi; bù hǎotīng de yīnyuè*
	shēngrì de shēng, dàlù de lù; Tā shi IBM de.
No DE	*tā dìdi; lǎo péngyou; zhème duō xíngli*
Names	*Guìxìng? / Wǒ xìng Bái, jiào Bái Sùzhēn.*
Age	*Nín ⟨niánjì⟩ duō dà le? / Zhǐ yǒu shíqī suì.*
Sign	*Nǐ ⟨shi⟩ shǔ shénme de? / Shǔ mǎ de.*
Level	*Nǐ shi jǐ niánjí de xuéshēng? / Sān niánjí de.*
Major	*Zhuānyè shi shénme? / Shi wùlǐ.*
Department	*Nǐ zài něi ge xì? ~ Nǐ shi něi ge xì de?*
Zài + V	*Tā hái zài dúshū.*
Studying	*Tā zài túshūguǎn xuéxí.*
Titles	*Lǐ xiàozhǎng; Qián jīnglǐ*
Introductions	*Zhāng lǎoshī, wǒ gěi nǐ jièshào jièshào; zhè⟨i wèi⟩ shi . . .*
Nice to meet	*Jiǔyǎng, jiǔyǎng; hěn gāoxìng rènshi nǐ.*
Understand?	*Kàndedǒng ma? / Néng kàndǒng yìdiǎnr.*
Work	*Tā zài Chángchūn gōngzuò. / Tā gàn shénme huó ne?*
Used to doing	*Zhōngguó cài nǐ chīdeguàn ma?*
Rice, wheat	*Běifāng rén bǐjiào xǐhuan chī miàntiáo, nánfāng rén bǐjiào xǐhuan chī mǐfàn.*
Someone . . .	*Yǒu rén wèn wǒ . . .*

Exercise 8

Vocabulary practice. Incorporate each of the following words in a brief phrase that correctly demonstrates the word's meaning, e.g., *shàngwǔ* → *jīntiān shàngwǔ.*

juéde	*jièshào*	*fēicháng*	*zǎodiǎn*
yàoshi	*yǐjīng*	*yídìng*	*yígòng*
xiāoxi	*xiànzài*	*mǐfěn*	*máfan*
yìqiān	*yǐqián*	*qiánmiàn*	*mùqián*
shíchā	*zhuānyè*	*shàngwǔ*	*xiàwǔ*
duōshao	*dōu shì*	*zuǒbiānr*	*gànhuó(r)*
jiǔyǎng	*yángjiǔ*	*shàngbān*	*jīngcháng*
zhōngwǔ	*Zhōngwén*	*zhōngtou*	*zhōngbù*
bàngōngshì	*yánjiūshēng*	*jīchǎng*	*chǎngzhǎng*
niánjì	*mǐfàn*	*xīfàn*	*yěxǔ*

4.14 Rhymes and rhythms

First, a traditional rhyme for the (lunar) New Year which mentions several New Year customs, such as buying new clothes and setting off firecrackers.

Xīnnián dào, xīnnián dào,	('New-year arrives, new-year arrives,')
chuān xīn yī, dài xīn mào,	('wear new clothes, wear new hat,')
pīpī pāpā fàng biānpào!	('pipi papa set+off firecrackers!')

This next rhyme, which tells the story of life in a factory, from the workers' point of view, is an example of a popular genre rhyme known as *shùnkǒuliū*, a sort of oral political satire.

Èrlóu sānlóu, chángzhǎng shūjì;	('Second-floor, third-floor, factory-head secretary;')
sìlóu, wǔlóu, qīnqi guānxi;	('fourth-floor, fifth-floor, kin connections;')

gōngrén jiējí, dǐngtiān-lìdì,	('workers [social-]class, salt+of+the+earth,')
zhīzú chánglè, zán bù shēngqì.	('be+content+with+one's+lot, we not angry.')

NOTES

a. *shūjì* 'secretary of a political or other organization' ('book-note+down')

b. *dǐngtiān-lìdì* 'be of indomitable spirit' ('support-sky set+up-ground')

c. *zhīzú chánglè* 'be content with one's lot and be happy' ('know-enough happiness')

d. *zán*: a reduced form of *zámen*

Appendix 1: Courses of study and university names

COURSES OF STUDY

yǔyánxué	'linguistics' ('language-study')
wénxué	'literature' ('writing-study')
bǐjiào-wénxué	'comparative literature'
lìshǐ⟨xué⟩	'history'
rénlèixué	'anthropology' ('man-kind study')
yīnyuè	'music'
shāngyè	'business' ('business-occupation')
guǎnlǐ⟨xué⟩	'management' ('manage-study')
chéngshì-guǎnlǐxué	'urban planning' ('city-manage-study')
jiànzhù⟨xué⟩	'architecture'
jīngjì⟨xué⟩	'economics'
wùlǐ⟨xué⟩	'physics' ('things-principles')
huàxué	'chemistry' ('transformation-study')
shēngwù⟨xué⟩	'biology' ('life-matter')
yíchuánxué ~ jīyīnxué	'genetics' ('heredity-study' ~ 'gene-study')
dànǎo-rènzhīxué	'brain and cognitive science'
shùxué	'mathematics' ('number-study')
yīxué	'medicine'

Engineering:

gōngchéng⟨xué⟩	'engineering'
jìsuànjī⟨xué⟩ [Mainland]	'computer science' ('calculate-machine')
diànnăo⟨xué⟩ [Taiwan]	'computer science' ('electric-brain')
diànzĭ gōngchéng⟨xué⟩	'electrical engineering'
tŭmù gōngchéng⟨xué⟩	'civil engineering' ('earth-wood')
jīxiè gōngchéng⟨xué⟩	'mechanical engineering'
hángkōng gōngchéng⟨xué⟩	'aeronautical engineering'
hángkōng hángtiān⟨xué⟩	'aero-astro' ('aviation space+flight')
cáiliào gōngchéng⟨xué⟩	'material science' ('material engineering')

THE NAMES OF UNIVERSITIES

Most non-Chinese universities have transliterated versions of their names, e.g., *Gēlúnbĭyà Dàxué* 'Columbia University'. There are some exceptions; the Chinese names for Oxford and Cambridge universities are translations of their etymological meanings: i.e., *Niújīn* ('Ox-Ford') and *Jiànqiáo* ('Cam-Bridge'). The Cam is the name of the river that runs through Cambridge. MIT is also translated: *Máshěng Lĭgōng Xuéyuàn* ('Massachusetts Science Institute'). The names of Chinese universities often combine a location with *dàxué* 'university' ('big-learning'). Some university names can be shortened: e.g., *Běijīng Dàxué* → *Běi Dà*; *Táiwān Dàxué* → *Tái Dà*. Here, for reference, are the names of some other well-known universities.

Non-Chinese:

Kāngnăi'ěr Dàxué ~ Kāng Dà	'Cornell University'
Gēlúnbĭyà Dàxué ~ Gē Dà	'Columbia University'
Hāfó Dàxué	'Harvard University'
Yēlŭ Dàxué	'Yale University'
Pŭlínsīdùn Dàxué	'Princeton University'
Dùkè Dàxué	'Duke University'
Shĭtănfú ~ Sītănfú	'Stanford University'

Bókèlì Dàxué	'UC Berkeley'
Mìxīgēn Dàxué	'University of Michigan'
Míngdé Dàxué ~ Míng Dà	'Middlebury College, Vermont'
Lúndūn Dàxué	'London University'
Niújīn Dàxué	'Oxford University'
Jiànqiáo Dàxué	'Cambridge University'
Àozhōu Guólì Dàxué ~ Ào Dà	'Australian National University (ANU)'

Chinese:

Běijīng Dàxué ~ Běi Dà	'Peking University' (Beijing)
Qīnghuá Dàxué	'Tsinghua University' (Beijing)
Běijīng Shīfàn Dàxué ~ Běishī Dà	'Beijing Normal University'
Běijīng Hángkōng (Hángtiān) Dàxué ~ Háng Dà	'Beijing University of Aeronautics [and Astronautics]'
Rénmín Dàxué ~ Rén Dà	'People's University' (Beijing)
Nánkāi Dàxué ~ Nánkāi	'Nankai University' (Tianjin)
Nánjīng Dàxué ~ Nándà	'Nanjing University' (Nanjing)
Fùdàn Dàxué	'Fudan University' (Shanghai)
Jiāotōng Dàxué	'Shanghai Jiaotang' ('Communications') University
Zhōngshān Dàxué	'Sun Yat-sen University' (Guangzhou)
Guólì Táiwān Dàxué ~ Tái Dà	'National Taiwan University (NTU)'
Xiāng Gǎng Kējì Dàxué	'Hong Kong University of Science and Technology'
Xīnjiāpō Guólì Dàxué	'National University of Singapore (NUS)'
Nányáng Kējì Dàxué	'Nanyang Technological Institute (NTU)'

Appendix 2: The 50 most common surnames

It is useful to be familiar with the pronunciation of at least the most common surnames, so a list of the 50 most common surnames (including those already encountered) is provided below. Characters for each name (simplified/traditional) are included for reference, and each surname is exemplified by a Chinese person of some renown. The list is organized roughly by frequency. The first ten names alone constitute about 40 percent of all Chinese surnames in use. (The list is based on recent surveys, but since surname frequency changes, the list should not be considered definitive.)

Many Chinese residents of North America and the United Kingdom are of Cantonese background, so the varied English spellings of surnames there are frequently based on Cantonese pronunciation rather than Mandarin. To give some sense of this range, Cantonese pronunciations of the surnames are included on the far right. They are written in the Yale system of Romanization, which is more transparent than other commonly used systems of transcribing Cantonese. Cantonese has open syllables ending in a vowel or nasal, and closed syllables ending in a stop (-p, -t, -k). Open syllables have two registers, a high and low, each with three tones. In the Yale system, the high-register tones are plain (ā, á, and a, with 'a' standing in for all vowels); the low-register tones are marked with a final -h (*áh, ah,* and *àh).* With three additional distinctions in checked syllables, Cantonese can be said to have a total of nine tones. Actual English spellings of Cantonese names will vary. For instance, the spelling for the name transcribed as 'Wòhng' (which corresponds to both Mandarin *Wáng* and *Huáng*) is usually 'Wong'; spellings for 'Lòh' are 'Loh', 'Law', or 'Lowe'.

SURNAME	CHARACTER	NAME FROM HISTORY	CANTONESE
Lǐ	李	*Lǐ Sī* (3rd century BCE); chancellor to the Qin emperor	*Léih*
Wáng	王	*Wáng Ānshí* (1021–1086); poet and reformer	*Wòhng*
Zhāng	张/張	*Zhāng Xuéliáng* (1901–2001); Manchurian warlord, Republican general, and long-serving political prisoner	*Jēung*

SURNAME	CHARACTER	NAME FROM HISTORY	CANTONESE
Liú	刘/劉	*Liú Bāng* (256–195 BCE); first emperor of Han dynasty	*Làuh*
Chén	陈/陳	*Chén Yì* (1901–1972); PRC military commander	*Chàhn*
Yáng	杨/楊	*Yáng Guìfēi* (8th century); one of the four famous beauties	*Yèuhng*
Huáng	黄	*Huángdì* (trad. 2698–2598 BCE); the Yellow Emperor	*Wòhng*
Zhào	赵/趙	*Zhào Yuánrèn* / Chao Yuen Ren (1892–1982); well-known linguist who taught at U.C. Berkeley for many years	*Jiuh*
Zhōu	周	*Zhōu Ēnlái* (1898–1976); first PRC premier	*Jāu*
Wú	吴/吳	*Wú Sānguī* (17th century); general who 'let the Manchus in'	*Ngh ~ Mm(`)*
Xú	徐	*Xú Zhìmó* (1897–1931); poet and essayist	*Chèuih*
Sūn	孙/孫	*Sūn Yìxiān* / Sun Yat-sen (1866–1925), also called *Sūn Zhōngshān*; the 'Father of Modern China'	*Syūn*
Zhū	朱	*Zhū Yuánzhāng* (1328–1398); first Ming emperor	*Jyū*
Mǎ	马/馬	*Mǎ Yuán* (14 BCE–49 CE); conqueror of Vietnam in 42 CE	*Máh*
Hú	胡	*Hú Shì* (1891–1962); promoted vernacular writing	*Wùh*
Guō	郭	*Guō Mòruò* (1892–1978); author and academic who flourished in the early days of the PRC	*Gok*

SURNAME	CHARACTER	NAME FROM HISTORY	CANTONESE
Lín	林	*Lín Biāo* (1907–1971); once designated to succeed Mao	*Làhm*
Hé	何	*Hé Hòushēn* / Stanley Ho (1921–); wealthy entrepreneur, Macau's 'King of Gambling'	*Hòh*
Gāo	高	*Gāo Xíngjiàn* (1940–); French-Chinese novelist, critic, and artist who won the Nobel Prize for Literature in 2000	*Gōu*
Liáng	梁	*Liáng Qǐchāo* (1873–1929); early 20th-century intellectual	*Lèuhng*
Zhèng	郑/鄭	*Zhèng Hé* (1371–1433); the 'Three Jeweled Eunuch' (*Sānbǎo Tàijiān*) who led seven expeditions to the countries surrounding the Indian Ocean	*Jehng*
Luó	罗/羅	*Luó Chángpéi* (1899–1958); Chinese linguist who taught for many years at *Běijīng Dàxué*	*Lòh*
Sòng	宋	*Sòng Qìnglíng* (1893–1981); wife of *Sūn Zhōngshān* (Sun Yat-sen)	*Sung*
Xiè	谢/謝	*Xiè Jìn* (1923–); film director who directed *The Opium War* (*Āpiàn Zhànzhēng*), 1997	*Jeh*
Táng	唐	*Táng Yín* (1470–1523); scholar and artist of the Suzhou school	*Tòhng*
Hán	韩/韓	*Hán Yù* (768–824); Tang dynasty scholar and poet	*Hòhn*
Cáo	曹	*Cáo Cāo* (155–220); general from Three Kingdoms period	*Chòuh*

SURNAME	CHARACTER	NAME FROM HISTORY	CANTONESE
Xǔ	许/許	*Xǔ Xùn* (239–374); Taoist priest who performed miracles, slew dragons, and became one of the 'Four Ministers of the Heavenly Abode'	*Héui*
Dèng	邓/鄧	*Dèng Xiǎopíng* (1904–1997); post-Mao leader who set Chinese on the road to economic growth	*Dahng*
Xiāo	萧/蕭	*Xiāo Hé* (2nd century BCE); advisor to *Liú Bāng*, first emperor of the Han	*Síu*
Féng	冯/馮	*Féng Yǒulán* (1895–1990); wrote the two-volume *History of Chinese Philosophy* (1934)	*Fùhng*
Zēng	曾	*Zēng Yìnchuán* / Donald Tsang (1944–), current chief executive of the Hong Kong SAR	*Jāng*
Chéng	程	*Chéng Miǎo* (3rd century BCE); inventor of small-seal characters	*Chìhng*
Cài	蔡	*Cài Shùn* (1st century CE); one of the 24 exemplars of filial piety	*Choi*
Péng	彭	*Péng Zǔ* (2nd millennium BCE); pursued the elixir of life and became a Taoist saint	*Pàhng*
Pān	潘	*Pān Jīnlián*; 'the Golden Lotus', the female protagonist in the 17th-century novel *Jīn Píng Méi* ('Golden Vase Plum')	*Pūn*
Yuán	袁	*Yuán Shìkǎi* (1859–1916); first president of ROC	*Yùhn*
Yú	于	*Yú Yòurèn* (1879–1964); statesman and scholar, well known for his calligraphy	*Yúh*

SURNAME	CHARACTER	NAME FROM HISTORY	CANTONESE
Dǒng	董	*Dǒng Jiànhuá* / Tung Chee Hwa (1937–); first chief executive of the Hong Kong SAR	*Dúng*
Yú	余	*Yú Qiūyǔ* (1946–); Chinese author and public intellectual who writes a widely read blog	*Yúh*
Sū	苏/蘇	*Sū Shì*, known as *Sū Dōngpō* (1037–1101); poet, artist, and statesman	*Sōu*
Lǚ	吕/呂	*Lǚ Dòngbīn*; a Tang dynasty alchemist and scholar, transformed into one of the Eight Immortals (*Bā Xiān*)	*Léuih*
Yè	叶/葉	*Yè Míngshēn* (1807–1859); governor of Guangdong, known for resisting British demands before the outbreak of the Second Opium War	*Yihp*
Wèi	魏	*Wèi Jiǔ'ān*; occasional camel rider and author of this textbook	*Ngaih*
Jiǎng	蒋/將	*Jiǎng Jièshí* / Chiang Kai-shek (1887–1975); leader of the KMT and president of the Republic (in Taiwan) for almost 25 years	*Jéung*
Tián	田	*Tián Zhèn* (1966–); female rock singer from Beijing	*Tìhn*
Dù	杜	*Dù Fǔ* (712–770); renowned poet of the Tang	*Douh*
Dīng	丁	*Dīng Líng*, pseudonym of Jiǎng Bīngzhī (1904–1986); woman writer and political activist	*Dīng*

SURNAME	CHARACTER	NAME FROM HISTORY	CANTONESE
Shěn	沈	*Shěn Cóngwén* (1902–1988); pen name of author associated with the May 4th Movement	*Sám*
Jiāng	姜	*Jiāng Wén* (1963–); actor and film director, star of the 1992 TV serial *Běijīng Rén Zài Niŭyuē* 'A Native of Beijing in New York'	*Gēung*

Chinese speakers will often be able to tell from the English spelling of the surname the likely dialect grouping of the speaker. *Chan* as a spelling for what in Mandarin is *Chén*, suggests Cantonese, as noted above; but *Tan* suggests Hokkien. In Singapore, where Hokkien was the most common language before the success of the Speak Mandarin movement, *Tan* is still the most common surname in the telephone directory. Similarly, *Ng* is likely to be Cantonese, but *Goh*, Hokkien; both represent approximations to the regional pronunciations of Mandarin *Wú*.

Unit 5

Huó dào lǎo, xué dào lǎo, hái yǒu sān fēn xuébudào!
('live to old-age, study to old-age, still have three parts [of ten] study-not able to-reach')
—Said of a difficult course of study, such as learning Chinese

Unit 5 provides you with the language to talk about options ('or'), to express destination and purpose ('go to Shanghai to find work'), and to begin to talk about specific events in the past ('Yesterday, we took a trip to the Great Wall.'). Along the way, you will learn how to talk to children, talk about music and sports, and further elaborate on topics introduced earlier, such as food and cuisine.

Contents

5.1 Tone contrasts

Read the following sets aloud, focusing on the tones as well as the occasional tone shifts.

(1)	*Fēicháng mēn.*	(2)	*Mēnjíle.*	(3)	*Yǒu yìdiǎnr mēn.*
	Fēicháng máng.		*Mángjíle.*		*Yǒu yìdiǎnr máng.*
	Fēicháng lěng.		*Lěngjíle.*		*Yǒu yìdiǎnr lěng.*
	Fēicháng rè.		*Rèjíle.*		*Yǒu yìdiǎnr rè.*
(4)	*Juéde hěn mēn.*	(5)	*Mēnsǐle.*	(6)	*Hǎo mēn a!*
	Juéde hěn máng.		*Mángsǐle.*		*Hǎo máng a!*
	Juéde hěn lěng.		*Lěngsǐle.*		*Hǎo lěng a!*
	Juéde hěn rè.		*Rèsǐle.*		*Hǎo rè a!*

NOTES

a. *mēn* 'stuffy; close'; cf. *mēnrè* 'muggy'; contrast with related *mèn* 'bored'

b. *sǐ* 'to die'; SV*sǐle* 'SV to death', i.e., 'extremely'

c. *Hǎo* can function as an adverb with SVs, meaning 'very; so': *hǎo bàng* 'great'.

5.2 Or

5.2.1 Vocabulary

To begin this unit, here are some common and useful nouns (some of which have appeared earlier) and verbs.

Nouns:

nánde	*nánrén*	*nánzǐ*	*nánháizi ~ háir*
'males'	'men'	'man; male'	'boys'
nǚde	*nǚrén*	*nǚzǐ*	*nǚháizi ~ háir*
'females'	'women'	'woman; female'	'girls'
yánjiūshēng	*běnkēshēng*	*Kěkǒukělè*	*Bǎishìkělè*
'graduate student' ('research-student')	'undergraduate' ('root-section-student')	'Coca Cola' ('palatable-pleasant')	'Pepsi Cola' ('100-things-pleasant')
Zhōngguó cài	*wàiguó cài*	*kuàizi*	*dāochā*
'Chinese food'	'foreign food'	'chopsticks'	'knife and fork'

Verbs:

zhǎo	*yào*	*qù*
'to look for'	'to want'	'to go [to]'
xǐhuan	*yòng*	*děi*
'to like; prefer'	'to use'	'must; to have to'

5.2.2 The two uses of 'or'

In English, 'or' functions as a conjunction and sometimes has an inclusive meaning similar to 'and'.

> 'I drink tea or coffee in the morning, beer in the evening.' / 'Good for you!'
> 'Do you have any classes on Saturday or Sunday?' / 'No, none.'

However, 'or' also appears in 'disjunctive questions' in English, where it links alternatives. In this case, 'or' can be followed by a distinct pause.

'Will you have tea . . . or coffee?' / 'Tea, please.'
'Are you in the morning class . . . or the afternoon?' / 'The afternoon.'

In Chinese, the two uses of 'or'—the inclusive and the disjunctive—are expressed differently. The inclusive use is expressed with *huòzhě* (or *huòshì* or simply *huò*). As a conjunction, it can appear between nouns or noun phrases.

Jīntiān huòzhě míngtiān dōu xíng.	'Either today or tomorrow is okay.'
Bǎishìkělè huò Kěkǒukělè dōu kěyǐ.	'Pepsi or Coke, either one is fine.'
Wǒ zǎoshàng hē chá huòzhě kāfēi, wǎnshàng hē píjiǔ.	'I drink tea or coffee [in the] morning, [in the] evenings I drink beer.'

The disjunctive use of 'or'—the alternative 'or', which is typically (but not exclusively) found in questions—is expressed with *háishi* (which, in other contexts, means 'still'). Unlike *huòzhě, háishi* is an adverb, so it needs to be followed by a verb (as in example 2 below). However, when the verb would otherwise be *shì* (see example 1 below), *háishi* alone suffices. It is worth noting that *háishi shì* is never said.

(1)	*Tā shi Měiguórén háishi Zhōngguórén?*	'Is she American or Chinese?'
	Yěxǔ shi Měiguórén.	'Probably American.'
	Shi nǐ de háishi tā de?	'Are [these] yours or his [shoes]?'
	Dāngrán shi tā de, wǒ nǎlǐ huì yǒu zhème nánkàn de xiézi?	'His of course, how [on earth] would I have such awful looking shoes?'
	Nǐ shi běnkēshēng háishi yánjiūshēng?	'Are you an undergraduate or a graduate?'
	Wǒ shi èrniánjí de yánjiūshēng.	'I'm a second-year grad.'
	Sì ge háizi? Shi nánháir háishi nǚháir?	'Four children? Are [they] boys or girls?'
	Dōu shi nǚháir!	'[They]'re all girls!'

(2)	*Hē chá háishi hē kāfēi?*	'[Are you] drinking tea or coffee?'
	Chá hǎo, xièxie.	'Tea will be fine, thanks.'
	Yào chī Zhōngguó cài háishi chī wàiguó cài?	'Do [you] want to eat Chinese food or foreign food?'
	Wǒmen zài Zhōngguó, yīnggāi chī Zhōngguó cài!	'We're in China [so we] should eat Chinese food!'
	Nǐmen qù Běijīng háishi qù Shànghǎi?	'Are you going to Beijing or Shanghai?'
	Xiān qù Běijīng.	'First to Beijing.'
	Zhǎo Wèi lǎoshī háishi zhǎo Zhāng lǎoshī?	'Are you looking for Professor Wei or Professor Zhang?'
	Zhǎo Zhāng lǎoshī.	'[I]'m looking for Professor Zhang.'
	Nà, chīfàn, nǐmen xǐhuan hē píjiǔ háishi hē qìshuǐ?	'So, [with] a meal, do you prefer to drink beer or soda?'
	Wǒmen bǐjiào xǐhuan hē chá.	'We'd rather drink tea.'
	Chīfàn, nǐ píngcháng yòng kuàizi háishi yòng dāochā?	'[When] eating, do you usually use chopsticks or a knife and fork?'
	Zài Zhōngguó, wǒ dāngrán yòng kuàizi, kěshì zài zhèr, píngcháng dōu yòng dāochā.	'In China, I use chopsticks of course, but here, I usually use a knife and fork.'
	Guìlín shi zài nánbiānr háishi zài běibiānr?	'Is Guilin in the south or the north?'
	Guìlín zài Guǎngxī, zài nánbiānr.	'Guilin's in Guangxi, in the south.'

The response to an 'or' question may include a list of items. These may be juxtaposed, or they may be explicitly linked with *huòzhě* ~ *huòshì* ~ *huò*.

Chá kāfēi dōu xíng.	'Tea and coffee are both fine.'
Chá huòzhě kāfēi dōu xíng.	'Either tea or coffee will be fine.'
Lǐbàisān lǐbàisì dōu kěyǐ.	'Wednesday and Thursday are both possible.'
Lǐbàisān huò lǐbàisì dōu kěyǐ.	'Either Wednesday or Thursday is fine.'

Exercise 1

Paraphrase the following in Chinese.

1. Are you in the morning class or the afternoon?
2. Are you going today or tomorrow?
3. Either Coke or Pepsi is fine—it doesn't matter.
4. Do Koreans drink coffee . . . or tea in the morning?
5. Do you want to have a boy or a girl?
6. Do you prefer coffee or tea with breakfast? / Usually, either is fine, but today I'm tired, [so] I'll have coffee.
7. Are you in school or working? / I was in school, but now I'm working.

5.3 At the beginning of class

To show respect, students naturally stand when the teacher enters and greet him or her appropriately: *Wèi lǎoshī hǎo.* Then, still standing, the teacher asks for a count off: *yī, èr, sān, sì* . . . A dialogue similar to the one below then ensues. But first, some more vocabulary is necessary.

shuāngshù	'even number'	*dānshù*	'odd number'
bànr	'partner; mate'	*zuò bànr*	'act as partner'
dàjiā	'everyone (large family)'	*zěnme bàn*	'what to do (how manage)'

NOTES

a. *Shuāng* 'pair' can also be used as a measure word as in *yì shuāng kuàizi* 'a pair of chopsticks'.

b. The characters for *bànr* 'partner' (伴) and *bàn* 'half' (半) reflect the etymological relationship between the two words; however, neither is related to the homophonous *bàn* 'to do; to manage' (a verb), as in *zěnme bàn* (which is written 办).

Duōshao nánde, duōshao nǚde?

DIALOGUE A

Lǎoshī:	*Jīntiān yígòng yǒu duōshao xuéshēng?*
Xuéshēng:	*Yǒu èrshísì ge.*
Lǎoshī:	*Jǐ ge nánde, jǐ ge nǚde?*
Xuéshēng:	*Shí ge nánde, shísì ge nǚde.*
Lǎoshī:	*Èrshísì shi shuāngshù háishi dānshù?*
Xuéshēng:	*Shi shuāngshù.*
Lǎoshī:	*Dānshù hǎo háishi shuāngshù hǎo?*

Xuéshēng:	*Shuāngshù hǎo.*
Lǎoshī:	*Wèishénme?*
Xuéshēng:	*Yīnwèi shuāngshù, dàjiā dōu yǒu bànr.*

DIALOGUE B

Lǎoshī:	*Jīntiān yígòng yǒu duōshao xuéshēng?*
Xuéshēng:	*Yǒu shíjiǔ ge.*
Lǎoshī:	*Shíjiǔ shi shuāngshù háishi dānshù?*
Xuéshēng:	*Shi dānshù.*
Lǎoshī:	*Shi dānshù hǎo háishi shuāngshù hǎo?*
Xuéshēng:	*Shuāngshù hǎo.*
Lǎoshī:	*Wèishénme dānshù bù hǎo.*
Xuéshēng:	*Yīnwèi dānshù, yí ge rén méiyǒu bànr.*
Lǎoshī:	*Nà, zěnme bàn?*
Xuéshēng:	*Méi guānxi, Wèi lǎoshī kěyǐ zuò bànr.*

5.4 Food (2)

Unit 4 introduced staples and other basic categories of food (*miàntiáo, mǐfěn, tāng*) and some common meats and vegetables (*niúròu, xiārénr, dòufu*). The next step is to try to collate these ingredients and name the dishes accordingly. Typically, this will mean combining a meat or vegetable—or both—with a basic category of food. Ordering in this way will not always result in a well-formed menu item, for names can be idiosyncratic, but it should allow you to get meals with the ingredients you want while you continue to gain experience. In real life, it may be clearer to state the category first, and then repeat it with the ingredients: *chǎomiàn, chāshāo chǎomiàn; tāng, dòufu tāng*. Recall that some of the basic food names lose syllables in combination: *bāozi* → *chāshāobāo* rather than *chāshāobāozi*.

THE BASIC CATEGORIES OF FOOD FROM UNIT 4

(1) *fàn, chǎofàn, mǐfěn, miàn, chǎomiàn, tāng, tāngmiàn, jiǎozi, bāozi, zhōu ~ xīfàn*

(2) *zhūròu, niúròu, yángròu, yā, jī, jīdàn, yú, xiārénr, dòufu*

CONTAINERS (M WORDS)

yì wǎn niúròu tāng	*liǎng pán xiārénr chǎofàn*	*yì lóng / yì jīn bāozi*
'a bowl of beef soup'	'two plates of shrimp fried rice'	'a basket / catty of bao'
('one bowl beef-soup')	('two plate shrimp fried-rice')	('one steamer / catty steamed bun')

OTHER ITEMS

yúpiàn	*ròusī*	*báicài*
'slices of fish'	'shredded pork'	'cabbage'
('fish-slices')	('pork-shreds')	('white-vegetable')
jiǔcài	*shícài*	*gālí*
'scallions'	'seasonal vegetables'	'curry'
zhájiàng	*shuǐjiǎo*	*chāshāo*
'fried bean sauce'	'boiled dumplings'	'BBQ [pork]'

NOTE

Noodle dishes often come in two forms, one in which the noodles are dry and one in which they are in soup—'noodle soup'. What people actually say to indicate which one they want varies; the following options are quite colloquial.

⟨Yào⟩ gān de.	*⟨Yào⟩ tāng de.*
'I'd like [them] dry.'	'I'd like [them] with soup.'
('want dry one')	('want soup one')

It is a good idea to practice saying the names of dishes introduced in this and other units at the beginning of class, during the warm-up period. Three or four sessions repeating the names after the teacher and then responding freely to the question *Yào chī shénme?* will give you a basic repertoire, which can daily be built upon.

MODELS

xiārénr, dòufu, tāngmiàn, yì wǎn
yì wǎn xiārénr dòufu tāngmiàn } 'a bowl of shrimp bean curd noodle soup'

bāozi, zhūròu, jiǔcài, yì lóng *zhūròu jiǔcài bāo⟨zi⟩, yì lóng*	'a steamer of pork scallion steamed buns'
chāshāo, miàntiáo, gān de *chāshāo miàn, gān de*	'dry noodles with BBQ pork'

SOME TYPICAL DISHES

niúròu miàn	'beef noodles'
ròusī chǎomiàn	'shredded pork and fried noodles'
niúròu tāngmiàn	'beef noodle in soup'
gālí fàn	'curry and rice'
jīdàn chǎofàn	'egg and fried rice'
niúròu chǎofěn (~ *chǎomǐfěn*)	'beef and fried rice noodles'
jī zhōu	'chicken congee'
qīngcài tāng	'vegetable soup'
jiǔcài shuǐjiǎo (~ *jiǔcài jiǎozi*)	'leek dumplings'
chāshāo bāo	'roast pork buns'
zhájiàng miàn	'noodles with fried bean sauce (and pork)'

Exercise 2

Try ordering the following dishes.

1. a plate of curried fried rice
2. a bowl of congee with fish slices
3. a plate of BBQ pork and noodles, dry
4. a plate of BBQ pork and fried noodles, soup
5. two bowls of cabbage and some shredded pork soup
6. a plate of beef with rice noodles
7. a bowl of tofu soup
8. a steamer of cabbage and lamb dumplings
9. a plate of cabbage, shrimp, and rice noodles
10. a bowl of shrimp and noodles in soup
11. a plate of noodles with seasonal vegetables

DIALOGUE: ORDERING DISHES F is a *fúwùyuán* 'waiter'; G are four customers (*gùkè*) having dinner. Normally, the process of figuring out what to order would involve a perfunctory examination of the menu, followed by a discussion with the waiter about the specialties of the house, the types of fish in stock, what vegetables are fresh, etc. These customers have already decided what they want. They order the dishes by name rather than taking the descriptive approach seen in the last section.

F:	*Yào chī shénme?*	'What'll [you] have?'
G:	*Yào yí ge yúxiāng-qiézi, yí ge shāo'èrdōng, yí ge huíguōròu, yí ge sùshíjǐn, zài yào yí ge suānlàtāng.*	'[We]'ll have a 'fish-flavor eggplant', a 'cooked two winter', a 'double-cooked pork', a 'mixed vegetables', and also a 'hot and sour soup'.'

F:	*Suānlàtāng nǐ yào dàwǎn háishi xiǎowǎn?*	'Do you want a big bowl of hot and sour soup or a little bowl?'
G:	*Dàwǎn duō dà?*	'How big's the big bowl?'
F:	*Liù ge rén hē!*	'[Enough] for six to drink!'
G:	*Hǎo, yào dà de.*	'Okay, a big one.'
F:	*Hē shénme? Hē yǐnliào háishi hē píjiǔ?*	'What'll [you] have to drink? A beverage or beer?'
G:	*Chá jiù kěyǐ. Lǜchá.*	'Tea will be fine. Green tea.'
F:	*Hǎo, sì ge cài, yí ge tāng: yúxiāng-qiézi, shāo'èrdōng, huíguōròu, sùshíjǐn; dàwǎn suānlàtāng.*	'Okay, four dishes and a soup: 'fish-flavor eggplant', 'cooked two winter', 'double-cooked pork'; 'mixed vegetables' and a large bowl of 'hot and sour soup'.'
G:	*Hái yào báifàn.*	'And rice.'
F:	*Dàwǎn ma?*	'A big bowl?'
G:	*Kěyǐ.*	'That's fine.

NOTES

a. *Shāo'èrdōng* ('cooked-two-winter') is a vegetarian dish consisting of two winter vegetables such as *dōnggū* 'dried mushrooms' or *dōngsǔn* 'winter bamboo shoots'.

b. *huíguōròu* 'double-cooked pork' ('return to-pan-pork')

c. *sù* 'plain; simple; vegetarian'; cf. *chī sù* ~ *chī zhāi* 'be a vegetarian'

d. *shíjǐn* 'assortment of'; *sùshíjǐn* 'assorted vegetables'

e. *zài yào; zài* 'again', but here, 'in addition'

f. *yǐnliào* ('drink-material'); refers to non-alcoholic beverages—but not tea

g. *báifàn*; In China, rice is often ordered by the *liǎng* 'ounce'.

5.5 Expanding the V+*de* construction

5.5.1 Vocabulary

V + O:

chàng[gē]	*xiě[zì]*	*shuō[huà]*	*zuò[fàn]*
'to sing'	'to write'	'to speak; to talk'	'to cook'
('sing [songs]')	('write [characters]')	('say [speech]')	('make [food]')

N:

Yīngyǔ	*Hànyǔ*	*Zhōngguó huà*
'English'	'Chinese language'	'Chinese speech'

SV:

biāozhǔn
'be proper; correct; standard'

NOTES

a. Like *chīfàn*, when no other object is present or can be determined from the context, the verbs above usually appear with the generic objects indicated in brackets.

b. In southern China, *zhǔfàn* ('boil-food') and *shāofàn* ('heat-food') are also used for 'to cook'.

5.5.2 Commenting on abilities

Recall the earlier examples of the V+*de* construction.

Nǐ shuō+de hěn hǎo.	'You speak very well.'
Nǐ jiǎng+de bú cuò.	'You speak pretty well.'

Nothing can intervene between the verb *shuō* and +*de*, so an object has to be mentioned first, either alone or with repetition of the verb.

Nǐ Zhōngwén shuō+de hěn biāozhǔn.
Nǐ jiǎng Zhōngwén, jiāng+de hǎojíle.
Nǐ Hànyǔ shuō+de fēicháng hǎo.
Zhōngguó huà jiǎng+de hěn biāozhǔn.

The same construction can be applied to other verbs as well.

Hànzì xiě+de hěn hǎo.	'You write characters well.'
Nǎlǐ, xiě+de bù hǎo.	'Nah, I don't write well.'
Tā chàng+de hěn hǎo.	'She sings well.'
Tā chàng+de bú tài hǎo.	'He doesn't sing very well.'

Tā chànggē chàng+de zěnmeyàng?	'How does she sing?'
Tā chàng+de fēicháng hǎo!	'She sings really well!'
Wǒ zuòfàn zuò+de hěn chà.	'I'm a terrible cook.'
Nǐ zuò+de bú cuò!	'You cook pretty well.'
Wǒ xǐhuan chànggē, dànshì chàng+de bù hǎo.	'I like to sing, but I don't sing well.'
Nǐ tài kèqi, nǐ chàng+de bú cuò!	'You're too modest, you sing well.'
Wǒ xǐhuan zuòfàn kěshì zuò+de bù hǎo.	'I like to cook, but I don't cook well.'
Méi guānxi, wǒmen qù fànguǎnr chīfàn ba, wǒ qǐngkè.	'Never mind, let's go to a restaurant; I'll treat.'

5.5.3 *Huì* 'to be able'; *yìdiǎn⟨r⟩* 'a bit'

The response to someone praising your language ability is the modest:

Nǎlǐ, nǎlǐ ⟨shuō+de bù hǎo⟩.

To this, you can add a sentence with the modal verb *huì* 'to be able [of learned abilities]'.

Wǒ zhǐ huì shuō yìdiǎn⟨r⟩.	'I only speak a little.'
Wǒ zhǐ huì shuō yìdiǎndiǎn.	'I speak very little.'

Note that yìdiǎn⟨r⟩ 'a bit; a little' can appear between an action verb and its object.

Wǒmen chī yìdiǎnr fàn, hǎo bu hǎo?	'Let's have a bit to eat, okay?'
Hē yìdiǎn⟨r⟩ qìshuǐ ba.	'Have a soft drink.'
Zài zhèr kěyǐ mǎi yìdiǎn⟨r⟩ dōngxi.	'You can do a bit of shopping here.'

Contrast the use of *yìdiǎn⟨r⟩* directly after a verb (as part of the object) with the *yǒu yìdiǎn⟨r⟩* pattern that precedes SVs.

V *yìdiǎn⟨r⟩* O

Hē yìdiǎn⟨r⟩ chá ba.	'Why don't you have some tea.'

Subject *yǒu yìdiǎn⟨r⟩* SV

Zhè chá yǒu yìdiǎn⟨r⟩ kǔ.	'This tea's a little bitter.'

5.5.4 *Huì, néng* (~*nénggòu*), *kěyǐ,* and *xíng*

You have encountered a number of verbs all having to do with ability and likelihood. Although usage varies between regions, particularly between the Mainland and Taiwan, the basic differences are illustrated below.

A. *HUÌ*

'know how to; can'; typically used for learned abilities

Wǒ bú huì jiǎng Shànghǎihuà.	'[I] can't speak Shanghainese.'

'know about; be good at'; used as a main verb

Tā huì hěn duō shǎoshù mínzú de yǔyán.	'She speaks a lot of languages of minority peoples.'

'possibility' (often with a final 'emphatic *de*')

Jīntiān bú huì hěn lěng.	'It won't be too cold today.'
Bú huì de ba!	'No way!'
Tāmen huì yíng de!	'They're bound to win!'

B. *NÉNG ~ NÉNGGÒU*

'capable of; can'; ranging from physical ability to permission

Néng qù ma?	'Can you go?'
Wǒ bù néng hē báijiǔ.	'I can't drink 'white spirits'.'
Míngtiān wǒ bù néng lái shàngkè.	'I can't come to class tomorrow.'
Néng děng yíxià ma?	'Can you wait a bit?'

Néng hē yì jīn, hē bā liǎng . . . duìbuqǐ rénmín, duìbuqǐ dǎng!	'[If] you can drink a 'jin' [but] only drink eight ounces, you won't be able to face the people, you won't be able to face the party!'

C. KĚYǏ

'all right to; can'; ranging from possibility to permission

Kěyǐ jìnqù ma?	'Can [we] go in?'
Kě bu kěyǐ mǎi bàn ge?	'Can [one] buy a half?'
Túshūguǎn ⟨lǐ⟩ bù kěyǐ shuōhuà.	'[You are] not supposed to talk in the library.'

D. *XÍNG*

'to be okay; to do; to work'

Xíng has a meaning similar to *kěyǐ* or *néng*, but its grammatical behavior is different. *Xíng* is not a modal verb (that is, it cannot be followed by another verb); it is an ordinary verb that appears in predicate position (at the foot of the sentence).

	Qǐngkè chīfàn méi jiǔ bù xíng.	'You can't invite guests for a meal without [having] wine.'
Cf.:	*Chīfàn bù néng méi jiǔ.*	
	Xué Zhōngwén méiyǒu lǎoshī xíng ma?	'Can you study Chinese without a teacher?'
Cf.:	*Xué Zhōngwén méiyǒu lǎoshī, kěyǐ ma?*	

As the previous examples show, the expression *bù xíng* often corresponds to 'without' in English.

Qǐngkè chīfàn méi yú bù xíng.	'Having guests for a meal without [serving] fish won't do!'

Zài Měiguó chīfàn méi miànbāo bù xíng.	'In the United States, you can't have a meal without bread.'
Zài Fǎguó chīfàn méi jiǔ bù xíng.	'In France, you can't have a meal without wine.'
Zài Tàiguó chīfàn méi làjiāo bù xíng.	'In Thailand, you can't have a meal without hot peppers.'
Qù lǚxíng méi dìtú bù xíng.	'You can't go traveling without a map.'
Guò shēngrì méi dàngāo bù xíng.	'You can't have a birthday without a cake.'
Kàn yùndònghuì méi píjiǔ bù xíng.	'You can't watch a sporting event without beer!'
Méi jiǔ méi yú bù chéng xí.	'It takes wine and fish to make a feast!'

NOTE

chéng xí ('become feast')

Exercise 3

Paraphrase the following in Chinese.

1. She speaks very good Chinese.
2. I'm a lousy cook, but I love to eat Chinese food.
3. She speaks [Chinese] quite well, but she doesn't write very well.
4. You sing well. / Nah, not so well!
5. You speak [Chinese] very well. / No, I only speak a little!
6. Have some tea. / Thanks . . . This is great—what kind is it?
7. I find coffee a little bitter; I prefer tea.
8. You can't drink wine without a cup.
9. You can't eat Chinese food without chopsticks. (*kuàizi* 'chopsticks')
10. You can't drink coffee without milk.
11. You can't drink beer without peanuts! (*huāshēng* 'peanuts' ['flower-be born'])

Xiǎo péngyou, nǐ hǎo.

5.6 Talking to children

In China, you will find yourself in situations where you have to talk to children. In the following dialogue, you will strike up a conversation with the five-year-old child of some Chinese friends. You may have heard his or her name before, but you can't recall it, so you begin as follows.

Dà:	*Xiǎo péngyou, nǐ hǎo.*	'Hi, little friend.'
Xiǎo:	(to female) *Āyí, hǎo.*	'Hello, auntie.'
	(to male) *Shūshu, hǎo.*	'Hello, uncle.'
Dà:	*Xiǎo péngyou chī shénme ne?*	'What are [you] eating?'
Xiǎo:	*Chī táng ne.*	'Candy.'
Dà:	*Hǎochī ma?*	'Is it good?'
Xiǎo:	*Hǎochī. Gěi shūshu yì kē, hǎo bu hao?*	'Yes. [I]'ll give one to uncle, okay?'
Dà:	*Ò, xièxie. Xiǎo péngyou xǐhuan chànggē ma?*	'Ah, thank you. Do you like to sing?'
Xiǎo:	*Xǐhuan.*	'I do.'
Dà:	*Xǐhuan chàng shénme gē?*	'What song do you like to sing?'

Xiǎo:	*Zài xuéxiào wǒmen chàng 'Wǒmen shi Gòngchǎn-zhǔ yì jiē bān rén'.*	'At school we sing 'We're the ones who uphold Communism!''
Dà:	*Èi, hǎo gē! Kěyǐ gěi wǒ chàngchang ma? (~ Kěyǐ chàng gěi wǒ tīngting ma?)*	'Hey, nice song! Can you sing it for me?' (~ 'Can you let me hear it?')
Xiǎo:	*'Wǒmen shi Gòngchǎn-zhǔyì jiēbānrén . . .'*	
Dà:	*Ng, nǐ chàng+de hěn hǎo!*	'You sing well!'
Xiǎo:	*Chàng+de bù hǎo.*	'No, I don't.'
Dà:	*Hǎo, xiǎo péngyou, zàijiàn.*	'Okay, good-bye.'
Xiǎo:	*Āyí/Shūshu zàijiàn.*	'Bye, auntie/uncle.'
Dà:	*Zhēn kě'ài!*	'Cute!'

NOTES

a. *chī . . . ne*; The final *ne* conveys a tone of engagement or concern that is associated with ongoing actions otherwise marked with *zài* (cf. §4.7.4).

b. *táng*; cf. *tāng* 'soup' ('*soups* stay level', '*sugar* raises the pulse')

c. *kē*; an M for beads, beans, pearls, and even meteors and satellites

d. *Wǒmen shi . . .* ; S/he actually cites the first line. The title is '*Zhōngguó shàonián xiānfēngduì gē*', i.e., 'Song of the Chinese Young Pioneers'. The song is less likely to be heard in the schools these days.

e. *gòngchǎn* 'communist' ('common-production')

f. *-zhǔyì;* corresponds to English '-ism'; *zīběn-zhǔyì* 'capitalism'; *kǒngbù-zhǔyì* 'terrorism'

g. *jiēbānrén* 'successor' ('meet-duty-person')

h. *gěi*; root meaning 'to give', but also 'for'; cf. §5.7 directly below

i. *chàngchang*; repetition of the verb (without tone) takes the edge off the request: 'sing a little; just sing me a bit'

j. *zhēn* 'really; truly'; cf. *zhēn yǒuyìsi* 'really interesting' and *zhēn bàng* 'really super'

k. *kě'ài* ('capable-love'); cf. *kěpà* 'frightening' and *kěchī* 'edible'

5.7 Verbs, co-verbs, and serialization

jiāoshū	*gàosu*	*mǎi*	*mài*	*wèn*	*wèntí*
'to teach' ('teach-books')	'to tell'	'to buy'	'to sell'	'to ask'	'a question'

dǎ diànhuà	*sòng*	*shì⟨qing⟩*
'to telephone'	'present sth to sb;	'things [to do]'
('hit telephone')	escort sb somewhere'	

NOTES

a. *jiāoshū* 'to teach', with the generic object *shū* present when no other object is cited; *jiāo Zhōngwén* 'teach Chinese'. Contrast *jiāo* 'to teach' with the vocabulary you have learned for *jiào* with distinct falling tones: *jiào* 'to be named; to call', *bǐjiào, shuìjiào.*

b. *wèn* 'to ask a question', but *qǐng* 'to ask a favor'

c. *Sòng* parallels *gěi* in meaning—'to give [as a present]'; it also means 'to see someone off': *sòng tā qù jīchǎng. Sòng* and *gěi* also combine in the compound verb *sònggei* 'to send, present to', illustrated in later units.

d. *Dōngxi* are physical things; *shì⟨qing⟩* are abstract 'items of business'.

The dialogue with the child in the previous section presents an opportunity to introduce several functions (or meanings) of *gěi.*

A. *GĚI* AS A MAIN VERB Along with a number of other verbs involving transactions, *gěi* can take two objects, one that refers to the 'item' transferred (the direct object—DO), and the other to the person who gains it (the indirect object—IO).

gěi	*tā*	*yí ge lǐwù*	'give her a present'
sòng	*tā*	*yí ge lǐwù*	'present him with a gift'
jiāo	*tāmen*	*Zhōngwén*	'teach them Chinese'
wèn	*tāmen*	*wèntí*	'ask them a question'
gàosu	*tā*	*yí jiàn shìqing*	'tell him something'

The same pattern is common in English.

V	IO [person]	DO [thing]
give	them	an opera mask
teach	them	Chinese opera
buy	her	a ticket
sell	him	your robes

Be careful not to extend the pattern on the basis of English. For example, *mǎi* 'buy', which allows two objects in English ('buy her a ticket'), requires a different pattern in Chinese, introduced in subsection C below. There are other differences, too. In English, 'teach' and 'tell' can occur with single objects, but 'give' can not. In Chinese, all three can occur with a single object.

Wǒ jiāo tāmen.	'I teach them; I'm their teacher.'
Bié gàosu tā.	'Don't tell him.'
Wǒ gěi nǐ.	'I give [it] [to] you; it's yours!'

B. *GĚI* AS A CO-VERB MEANING 'FOR [THE BENEFIT OF]' In Unit 4, you encountered the phrase *gěi nǐ jièshào jièshào* 'introduce you to', or more literally, 'introduce [someone] for you'. The main verb is *jièshào*; the co-verb *gěi* precedes it, with the meaning 'for your benefit' rather than 'give'. Similarly, *gěi wǒ chàngchang*, in the previous dialogue, involves *gěi* functioning as a co-verb. Here are some typical examples; notice that *gěi* in its CV function always precedes the main verb.

Wǒ gěi nǐ zuò ba!	'Let me do it for you!'
Míngtiān gěi nǐ dǎ ge diànhuà, hǎo bu hǎo?	'[I]'ll phone you tomorrow, okay?'
Wǒ gěi nǐ xiě.	'I'll write it for you.'
Wǒ gěi tā mǎi dōngxi, tā gěi wǒ zuòfàn.	'I shop for her, and she cooks for me.'

C. *GĚI* AS THE SECOND VERB IN A SERIES As noted above, *mǎi* 'buy' does not permit the pattern with two objects, as demonstrated in subsection A. Instead, the purpose of the transaction has to be expressed by adding a phrase introduced by *gěi*.

mǎi lǐwù gěi tā	'buy her a present' ('buy present give her')

The two verbs, *mǎi* and *gěi*, appear sequentially—'buy' and 'give'—in a relationship that is sometimes called serialization. Here is a short dialogue that contrasts the co-verb and serialization patterns (subsections B and C, respectively).

Jiă:	*Míngtiān shi tā de shēngrì; wǒmen yīnggāi mǎi yí ge lǐwù gěi tā.*	'Tomorrow's her birthday; we should buy her a present.'
Yǐ:	*Mǎi shénme lǐwù?*	'What [sort] of present?'
Jiă:	*Tā shi wàiguó lái de; mǎi ge xiǎo jìniànpǐn gěi tā, zěnmeyàng?*	'She's a foreigner; how about we buy her a small memento?' ('buy a small memento to give to her')
Yǐ:	*Bú cuò. Dàn nǐ hěn máng, wǒ kěyǐ gěi nǐ mǎi.*	'Fine. But you're busy; I'll buy it for you.'

Serialization is quite versatile in Chinese. When the adult in the dialogue in §5.6 asked the child to sing the song for him, he used sentence (1) below, with a co-verb construction to indicate that he would benefit from the action ('sing for me'); but, as noted, he could also have used sentence (2), with a serialization to emphasize the purpose or result ('sing so I hear'). In the latter case, *gěi* might be translated as 'let' or 'allow'.

Co-verb:	(1) *Kěyǐ gěi wǒ chàngchang ma?*	'Can you sing [it] for me?'
Serialization:	(2) *Kěyǐ chàng gěi wǒ tīngting ma?*	'Can you let me hear [it]?'

There are other cases in which both a co-verb and a serialization construction are possible.

Co-verb:	*Wǒ gěi nǐ dǎ diànhuà, hǎo bu hǎo?*	'I'll phone you, okay?'
Serialization:	*Wǒ dǎ diànhuà gěi nǐ, hǎo bu hǎo?*	'I'll phone you, okay?'

Exercise 4

Compose a Chinese conversation based on the following English.

Jiǎ: She's leaving (*líkāi*) Hong Kong next week (*xià ge xīngqi*). We should give her a memento.
Yǐ: Yes, we should buy her something.
Jiǎ: What do you suggest?
Yǐ: How about a seal [chop]? (*túzhāng*)
Jiǎ: She probably already has a seal. I think we should get her a fan (*shànzi*).
Yǐ: I've got to go to *Xuānwǔqū* this afternoon—I'll get you one.
Jiǎ: Oh, that would be great—I have class from 1:00 to 5:00.
Yǐ: No problem, I often buy fans there.

Summary of *gěi* patterns

Verb	*Wǒmen gěi tā yí ge lǐwù, zěnmeyàng?*	'Let's give her a present.'
CV . . . V	*Wǒmen gěi tā mǎi yí ge lǐwù, zěnmeyàng?*	'Let's buy a present for her.'
V-O V-O	*Wǒmen mǎi yí ge lǐwù gěi tā, zěnmeyàng?*	'Let's buy her a present.'

5.8 Music and musicians

5.8.1 Singers and styles of singing

gē	*yì shǒu gē*	*gēshǒu*	*gēxīng*	*bǐjiào xǐhuan / zuì xǐhuan*
'song'	'a song' ('a M song')	'singer' ('song-hand')	'star singer' ('song-star')	'prefer' ('quite like / most like')

Māo Wáng	*Jiǎkéchóng*	*Jiékèxùn*	*Pàwǎluódì*	*Mài Dāngnà*
'Elvis'	'The Beatles'	'Michael Jackson'	'Pavarotti'	'Madonna'
('cat king')	('armor-shell-insects')			

yáogǔn⟨yuè⟩	*xīhā*	*juéshì⟨yuè⟩*	*xiāngcūn-yīnyuè*
'rock 'n roll'	'hip-hop'	'jazz'	'country music'
gǔdiǎn-yīnyuè	*míngē*		
'classical music'	'folk songs'		

NOTES

a. *Shǒu* is a measure word for songs and poems; this *shǒu* and *gēshǒu de shǒu* are homophones—words that are pronounced the same—but they are different words (written with different characters).

b. *zuì* 'most': *zuì dà* 'biggest', *zuì duō* 'most', *zuì nán* 'hardest', etc.

5.8.2 Dialogue: Musical preferences

Jiǎ:	*Nǐ zuì xǐhuan shénme yàng de yīnyuè?*	'What kinds of music do you prefer?'
Yǐ:	*Wǒ bǐjiào xǐhuan yáogǔnyuè hé xīhā.*	'I prefer rock and hip-hop.'
Jiǎ:	*Něi ge gēshǒu?*	'Which singers?'
Yǐ:	*Zhōngguó de ma?*	'Chinese [ones]?'
Jiǎ:	*Shì.*	'Yes.'
Yǐ:	*Xǐhuan Zhōu Jiélún, Èrshǒu Méiguì.*	'I like Zhou Jielun [and] Second Hand Rose.'
Jiǎ:	*Nà, Xīfāng de ne?*	'And Western ones?'
Yǐ:	*Xīfāng de ne, zuì xǐhuan Māo Wáng!*	'Western ones, I like Elvis!'
Jiǎ:	*Nà nǐ yě xǐhuan juéshì ma?*	'Do you like jazz too?'
Yǐ:	*Juéshì ne, hái kěyǐ, kěshi wǒ bù cháng tīng, tīngbuguàn.*	'Jazz, [I] quite [like it], but I don't often listen [to it], I'm not used [to it].'

5.8.3 Musical instruments

Talking about music often leads to questions about playing musical instruments. Traditional Chinese instruments include the *shēng*, a reed instrument, the *dí* 'flute', the *pípa* 'lute', and various kinds of *qín* 'stringed instrument'. Questions about traditional music or instruments can include the SV *chuántǒng* 'traditional'.

Jiǎ:	*Nǐ xǐhuan Zhōngguó chuántǒng yīnyuè ma?*	'Do you like traditional Chinese music?'
Yǐ:	*Nǐ shuō de shi shēng, dízi, pípá zhèi yàngr de yīnyuè ma?*	'You mean music such as the sheng, dizi, and pipa?'
Jiǎ:	*Jiùshì a.*	'Precisely.'
Yǐ:	*Ng, hái kěyǐ. Wǒ bù cháng tīng nèi yàngr de yīnyuè!*	'Yeah, it's okay. I don't listen to that kind of music much.'

NOTE

Note that *nǐ shuō de shi* ('you say thing is') corresponds to English 'you mean . . .'

Chàng+de hǎo, lā+de yě hǎo!

Words for modern instruments are mostly based on the traditional names (though *jítā* is a loan word from English).

gāngqín	*tíqín*	*héngdí*	*shùdí*	*jítā*
'piano'	'violin family'	'flute'	'clarinet'	'guitar'
('metal-qin')	('lift-qin')	('horizontal-flute')	('vertical-flute')	

Chinese does not have a single verb comparable to English 'to play' that can be used for any instrument (as well as for sports). Instead, verbs are chosen according to the particular musical gesture: *tán* 'to pluck; to flick; to strike', for instruments that are plucked or struck, such as the guitar, *pípa*, and piano; *lā* 'to pull' for bowed instruments, such as the violin; and *chuī* 'to blow' for wind instruments such as the clarinet or *dízi* 'bamboo flute'. However, the Chinese verb *huì* 'to be able [of learned abilities]', unlike its English counterparts 'can' or 'to be able', has the virtue of not requiring expression of the skill itself. The following sentence could, therefore, be literally translated as 'Can I ask what instrument you are able in?'

Qǐngwèn, nǐ huì shénme yuèqì?	'Can I ask what musical instrument you play?'
Wǒ huì tán diǎnr jítā, kěshì tán+de bú tài hǎo.	'I can play some guitar, but I don't play very well.'
Wǒ huì chuī lǎba, dànshì chuī+de bù hǎo.	'I play trumpet a bit, but not well.'

Exercise 5

Things change fast in modern China. But in the year 2000, at least, hotlines (*rèxiàn*), telephone numbers which allowed you to inquire about a subject for a small charge, were very popular in China. In the city of *Kūnmíng* (*zài Yúnnán*), you could dial a hotline number to get an explanation of your personality based on your color preferences; those who like red, for example, are warm, enthusiastic (*rèqíng*), and uninhibited (*bēnfàng*). Other lines allowed you to select a song and have it played over the telephone. Here are some of the selections. You can make your own choice as well as initiate a brief discussion with the operator along the following lines.

Jiă:	*Wei, wŏ xiăng tīng yì shŏu gē.*	'Hello, I'd like to listen to a song.'
Yĭ:	*Nĕi ge gēxīng?*	'Which singer?'
Jiă:	*Wŏ yào tīng Cuī Jiàn de ⟨gē⟩.*	'I'd like to listen to one of Cui Jian's.'
Yĭ:	*Cuī Jiàn de nĕi shŏu gē?*	'Which one of Cui Jian's?'
Jiă:	*Cuī Jiàn de Huāfáng Gūniang ba.*	'Cui Jian's 'Flower House Girl', is it?'
Yĭ:	*Èr líng jiŭ sān.*	'Number 2093.'
Jiă:	*Hăo, èr líng jiŭ sān.*	'Okay, number 2093.'

The songs of *Cuī Jiàn*, China's original rock and roll singer (actually a Chinese-Korean), as well as those of the others listed below, have slipped into the category of 'oldies' by now.

Number	Singer	Gender	Song
2093	*Cuī Jiàn*	男	*Huāfáng Gūniang* 'Flower House Girl'
2094	*Cuī Jiàn*		*Yīwú suŏyŏu* 'To Have Nothing at All'
2095	*Cuī Jiàn*		*Cóng tóu zài lái* 'Let's Take It from the Top Again'
2096	*Zhāng Xuéyŏu*	男	*Qíngwăng* 'Web of Love'

2097	*Zhāng Xuéyǒu*		*Nǐ lěng+de xiàng fēng* 'You're Cold as the Wind'
2098	*Wáng Fēi*	女	*Wǒ yuànyì* 'I'm Willing'
2099	*Wáng Fēi*		*Nǚrén* 'Woman'
2100	*Tián Zhèn*	女	*Yěhuā* 'Wild Flower'
2101	*Tián Zhèn*		*Zìyóu zìzài* 'Free and Easy'
2102	*Kē Yǐmǐn*	女	*Ài wǒ* 'Love Me'
2103	*Dèng Lìjūn*	女	*Yè lái xiāng* 'Fragrance in the Night'

5.9 Verbs of cognition

5.9.1 Knowing

Knowledge of facts is expressed by the verb *zhīdao* (with the second syllable often fully toned in the negative, *bù zhīdào*). In southern Mandarin, *xiǎode* is the colloquial equivalent.

Nǐ zhīdao ma?	*Nǐ xiǎode ma?*	'Do you know?'
Bù zhīdào.	*Bù xiǎode.*	'[I] don't.'
Zhī bu zhīdào?	*Xiǎo bu xiǎode?*	'Do [you] know (or not)?'

Tā wèishénme hěn jǐnzhāng? / Wǒ bù zhīdào. ~ Wǒ bù xiǎode.

Knowing someone, or being acquainted with someone or something, is expressed by a different verb in Mandarin: *rènshi*. (The same distinction is made in the Romance languages.) Contrast the two usages in the examples below.

Tā shì bu shi Yáng Lán?	'Is that Yang Lan?'
Wǒ bù xiǎode! Shéi shi Yáng Lán?	'I don't know. Who's Yang Lan?'
Tā shi Yáng Lán ma?	'Is that Yang Lan?'
Wǒ bù xiǎode, wǒ bù rènshi tā.	'I don't know, I don't know her.'
Shi Zhōngguórén ma?	'Is [she] Chinese?'
Bù zhīdao, wǒ bú rènshi tā.	'[I] don't know, I don't know her.'

NOTE

Yáng Lán used to work for CCTV (the PRC's state-sponsored television network) as a newscaster; she came to the United States to attend graduate school at Columbia University, then returned to China to become an immensely popular talk show host.

5.9.2 Understanding

A. *DǑNG* 'TO UNDERSTAND'

Dǒng ma? / Dǒng.
Dǒng bu dǒng? / Duìbuqǐ, wǒ bù dǒng.

Another word, *míngbai*, composed of *míng* 'bright' (also seen in *míngtiān*) and *bái* 'white', means 'to understand' in the sense of 'to get it'. Because understanding often comes as a breakthrough, both *dǒng* and *míngbai* are associated with the 'new situation' *le*.

Dǒng le ma? /	*Dǒng le.*	'I understand [now].'
	Chàbuduō le!	'Just about.'
	Jīběnshàng dǒng le!	'Basically, I do.'
	Duìbuqǐ, háishi bù dǒng!	'Sorry, I still don't get it.'
Míngbai ma? /	*Míngbai le!*	'[Now] I get it!'

Nǐ dǒng wǒ de yìsi ma? / Dǒng.	'Do you understand my meaning?' / 'I do.'
Nǐ liǎojiě wǒ de yìsi ma? / Ng, liǎojiě.	'Do you comprehend my meaning?' / 'Uh huh, I do.'

B. *KÀNDEDǑNG* The dialogue in Unit 4 began with the question in which the verbs *kàn* 'to look; to read' and *dǒng* 'to understand' are combined in a phrase mediated by *de* (which turns out to be written 得, like +*de*, 'so as to; get'): *Nǐ kàndedǒng ma?* A positive response would be *kàndedǒng*; a negative one would be *kànbudǒng*. *Tīng* 'to listen' may substitute for *kàn* if the stimulus is aural rather than visual (see chart below).

The relationship between the two verbs is one of action (*kàn*) and result (*dǒng*). The presence of the internal *de* or *bu* makes the construction 'potential' rather than 'actual', so the translation of *kàndedǒng* is not just 'to understand' but 'manage to understand'; similarly, *kànbudǒng* is 'not succeed in understanding'. The complete paradigm is as follows.

	POSITIVE		NEGATIVE	
Actual	*Kàndǒng le.* *Tīngdǒng le.*	'[I] understood [it].'	*Méi kàndǒng.* *Méi tīngdǒng.*	'[I] didn't understand [it].'
Potential	*Kàndedǒng.* *Tīngdedǒng.*	'[I]'m able to understand [it].'	*Kànbudǒng.* *Tīngbudǒng.*	'[I]'m not able to understand [it].'

Other examples of the potential construction encountered in earlier units include:

duìbuqǐ	'sorry (not worthy of facing)'
shuāibudǎo	'manage not to fall down'
chīdeguàn	'be in the habit of eating'
chībuguàn	'not be in the habit of eating'
tīngbuguàn	'not be in the habit of listening [to it]'
xuébudào	'not manage to learn it'

5.9.3 Reporting on questions

Verbs such as *zhīdao*, as well as *wèn* 'to ask', are often used to report on questions. In (formal) English, this has some interesting grammatical consequences, as shown below.

Direct speech (schematic)	Reported speech (actual)
I asked: "Where are you going?"	I asked where you were going.
We don't know: "Is he Chinese?"	We don't know whether/if he's Chinese [or not].
I don't know: "Why is she so nervous?"	I don't know why she's so nervous.

In formal English, reporting speech involves grammatical features such as agreement of tenses ('were going', not 'are going', in the first example), non-question word order ('where you were going' rather than 'where were you going'), and insertion of 'if' or 'whether' in 'yes-no' questions. Chinese, fortunately, does not require such contortions, as the following examples show.

A. *ZHĪDAO*

Direct speech	Reported speech
Wǒ bù zhīdào: "Tā wèishénme hěn jǐnzhāng?"	*Wǒ bù zhīdào tā wèishénme hěn jǐnzhāng.*
'I don't know: "Why is he so nervous?"'	'I don't know why he's so nervous.'

There is one constraint that needs to be noted, however: if the embedded question is a 'yes-no' question, then it must have the V-not-V form; it cannot be a *ma* question. The reason for this is that *ma* functions like the rising question intonation in English—it envelopes the whole sentence, not just a part of it. Some examples should make this clear.

Wǒmen bù zhīdào: "Tā shì Zhōngguó rén ma?"	'We don't know: "Is she Chinese?"'
Wǒmen bù zhīdào tā shì bu shi Zhōngguó rén.	'We don't know if she's Chinese (or not).'

Notice that in reported speech, the object of *zhīdao* always contains a question form, such as *shénme* or a V-not-V question.

There are times when *ma* does show up at the end of the sentence, but if it does, it goes with the 'higher verb', *zhīdao*, and not with the internal question.

Nǐ zhī bu zhīdào [tā shì bu shi Zhōngguó rén].
Or: *Nǐ zhīdào [tā shì bu shi Zhōngguó rén] ma?*

B. *WÈN* 'TO ASK [A QUESTION]' *Wèn* occurs in expressions such as *qǐngwèn* 'may [I] ask; excuse me' and *wèntí* 'question; problem' (*Yǒu wèntí ma?*). The root meaning of *wèn* is 'to ask [a question]'. Questions embedded after *wèn* have the same constraints as those after *zhīdao*; that is, they require the V-not-V form with 'yes-no' questions.

Tā wèn wǒ: "Nǐ shi Zhōngguó rén ma?"	*Tā wèn wǒ shì bu shi Zhōngguó rén.*
Tā wèn wǒ: "Nǐ shi shénme dìfang rén?"	*Tā wèn wǒ shì shénme dìfang rén.*

Notice that Chinese does not require repetition of the pronoun in a sentence like the first of the two above: 'He asked me if I was Chinese' (with both 'me' and 'I' in the English) is usually expressed as: *Tā wèn wǒ shì bu shi Zhōngguó rén* (with only one *wǒ*).

Exercise 6

Translate the following into English.

1. *Wǒ bù zhīdào tā de yàoshi zài nǎr.*
2. *Tā wèn wǒ yǒu méiyǒu hùzhào.*
3. *Wǒ bù xiǎode tā de guójí shi shénme.*
4. *Tāmen wèn wǒ xǐ bù xǐhuan Shìjiè Bēi.*
5. *Tā wèn wǒ jǐ diǎn chī zǎodiǎn.*
6. *Tā wèn wǒ shì bu shi běnkēshēng.*

How would you say the following in Chinese? Recall that *shì bu shi* 'is it the case that' is often used to question certain assumptions.

1. Do you know who *Bǎoyù* is? / Sorry, I don't.
2. I don't know whether *Bǎoyù* is hungry (or not).
3. Do you know why *Bǎoyù* is nervous?
4. He's nervous because he's going to see *Dàiyù*.
5. Do you know if *Bǎoyù* likes *Dàiyù*?
6. We don't know what *Bǎoyù's* surname is.
7. Did you ask them whether *Bǎoyù* was male or female?
8. I asked her whether she liked *Bǎoyù* or *Dàiyù* best.

NOTE

Jiǎ Bǎoyù and *Lín Dàiyù* are, respectively, male and female characters in the Chinese classic novel *Hóng Lóu Mèng* 'Dream of the Red Chamber'.

5.10 Destination

5.10.1 Going places: Some vocabulary

huíjiā 'return home'	*chéng lǐ* 'in town' ('town in')	*xiāngxià* 'the country'
wàiguó 'abroad' ('outside-country')	*jīchǎng* 'airport' ('airplane-area')	*Cháng Chéng* 'Great Wall' ('Long Wall')

5.10.2 Where to?

Destination may be expressed directly (1) after the motion verbs, *lái* 'to come' and *qù* 'to go': e.g., *lái Běijīng* 'come to Beijing'; *qù Běijīng* 'go to Beijing'. The same meaning can also be expressed prepositionally (2), with the destination placed before *lái* or *qù* (both usually untoned) as the object of *dào* 'to', or in some cases, *shàng* 'on'.

(1)	*Nǐmen qù nǎr ~ nǎlǐ?* *Wǒmen qù Běijīng.*	'Where are you going?' 'We're going to Beijing.'
(2)	*Nǐmen dào nǎr ~ nǎlǐ qu?* *Wǒmen dào Běijīng qu.*	same
	Nǐmen shàng nǎr ~ nǎlǐ qu? *Wǒmen shàng Běijīng qu.*	same

Though there may be stylistic reasons for choosing the direct pattern over the prepositional, the two patterns are essentially synonymous. The direct pattern accords with the order of verb and destination in regional languages such as Cantonese and Hokkien, and for that reason, it may be preferred by southern speakers (including Taiwanese). Of the two prepositional options, the *shàng . . . qu* pattern seems to carry a special nuance of 'setting off for some place', so it may be more common in the question than in the answer.

OTHER EXAMPLES

Tāmen qù shénme dìfang?	'Where are they going to?'
Wǒmen dào chéng lǐ qu.	'We're going into town.'
Wǒmen shàng jīchǎng qu jiē péngyou.	'We're off to the airport to meet some friends.'
Wǒmen huíjiā.	'We're going home.'

Notice that 'go home' is not expressed with *qù* but with *huí* 'return': *huíjiā.*

Jīntiān jǐ diǎn huíjiā? 'What time are you going home today?'

5.10.3 Going

Both *qù* and *zǒu* can be translated as 'to go'. They differ in that *zǒu* cannot take a specific object, while *qù* can. Also, *zǒu* can often be translated as 'to leave'.

	Wǒ gāi zǒu le.	'I should be off.'
But:	*Wǒ bāyuè bā hào qù Běijīng.*	'I'm going to Beijing on August 8th.'

To leave a place can be expressed by the verb *líkāi* (the first syllable is identified with the *lí* associated with *jìn* or *yuǎn*).

Wǒmen míngtiān líkāi Běijīng, qù Chángchūn.	'We're leaving Beijing tomorrow and going to Changchun.'

5.10.4 *Nǎr* ~ *nǎlǐ* as an indefinite

Like *shénme, nǎr* ~ *nǎlǐ* can also serve as an indefinite—in either the direct pattern or the prepositional.

Nǐ qù nǎr ~ nǎlǐ?	'Where are you going?'
Wǒ bú qù nǎr ~ nǎlǐ.	'I'm not going anywhere (in particular).'
Nǐ dào nǎr ~ nǎlǐ qu?	'Where are you going?'
Wǒ bú dào nǎr ~ nǎlǐ qu.	'I'm not going anywhere (in particular).'

5.10.5 Destination with other verbs

With the verbs *lái* and *qù*, the destination either follows the verb immediately without any mediation (*qù Běijīng*), or it is governed by *dào* 'to' and placed before the verb (*dào Běijīng qu*). However, with other motion verbs, such as *bān* 'to move [one's home]', *zǒu* in its meaning of 'to walk', *pǎo* 'to run', and *kāi* 'to drive', destination is placed after the verb, mediated by *dào* 'to; toward' (and sometimes followed ultimately by a toneless *lai* or *qu* to indicate direction toward or away from the speaker).

Wǒmen bāyuè bān dào Tiānjīn ⟨qu⟩.	'In August, we're moving to Tianjin.'
Bù néng kāi dào Guìlín, tài yuǎn.	'[You] can't drive to Guilin, it's too far.'
Nǐmen pǎo dào nǎr ⟨qu⟩?	'Where are you running to?'

The saying at the beginning of this unit also fits this pattern: *Huó dào lǎo, xué dào lǎo* '[If you] live to old age, [and] study to old age'. However, the last part of the saying, *xuébudào*, uses *dào* to express success (in the sense of reaching a goal), a function of *dào* that will be discussed in a later unit.

Coming and going

LÁI/QÙ		
UNMEDIATED	MEDIATED BY *DÀO*	MEDIATED BY *SHÀNG*
qù nǎr	*dào nǎr qu*	*shàng nǎr qu*
qù chéng lǐ	*dào chéng lǐ qu*	(*shàng chéng lǐ qu*)
lái Běijīng	*dào Běijīng lai*	(*shàng Běijīng lai*)

NOT *LÁI/QÙ*		
GENERIC OBJECT	SPECIFIC OBJECT, WITHOUT *DÀO*	V *DÀO* PLACE ⟨*LAI/QU*⟩
bānjiā 'move [house]'	*líkāi Běijīng*	*zǒu dào nàr* ⟨*lai/qu*⟩
kāichē 'drive [vehicles]'		*bān dào Shànghǎi* ⟨*lai/qu*⟩
huíjiā 'return [home]'		*kāi dào jīchǎng* ⟨*lai/qu*⟩

5.10.6 Specifying a time

With a comment about destination, you can mention a specific time, either a day of the week or a date. Recall the placement of time words—before or after the subject (if present), but always before their associated verb.

Nǐ xiànzài qù shénme dìfang?	'Where are you going now?'
Wǒ xiànzài qù shàngkè.	'I'm going to class now.'
Bāyuè sān hào wǒ qù Běijīng; wǔ hào qù Shànghǎi.	'I'm going to Beijing on August 3rd; and to Shanghai on the 5th.'
Wǒmen shíyuèfèn bānjiā.	'We're moving house in October.'
Bān dào nǎlǐ?	'Where are you moving to?'
Wǒmen bān dào Dōngchéng.	'We're moving to Dongcheng' ('east town').

Sān hào líkāi Zhènjiāng, wǔ hào dào Lìjiāng.	'[We]'re leaving Zhenjiang [in Jiangsu] on the 3rd, and [we]'ll get to Lijiang [in Yunnan] on the 5th.'
Wǒ shēng zài Shēnzhèn, zài nán biānr, shíjiǔ suì bān dào Běijīng lái, xiànzài zhù zài Běijīng.	'I was born in Shenzhen, in the south, moved to Beijing when [I] was 19, and now [I] live in Beijing.'

5.10.7 Inserting foreign words

Particularly in the early stages of studying Chinese, it is acceptable to insert English nouns into your conversation: *Wǒ qù* library / cafeteria / airport, etc. Foreign verbs, however, resist insertion into Chinese; instead they are recast as nouns attached to a general Chinese verb such as *zuò* 'to do; to make'. So 'reserve' might appear as *zuò yí ge reservation*. The main thing is to establish your credentials by producing the grammatical framework of the sentence—which includes the verb—with confidence.

Exercise 7

Explain that

you're going home at 6:00.
they're leaving Beijing tomorrow.
they're moving to the countryside next year.
they're going abroad.
you're going to the airport to meet someone.
you should be leaving, it's late.
you're not going anywhere this evening because you're so tired.
you're driving to the airport this afternoon—to meet some friends.
they'll leave *Chéngdū* on the 8th and get to *Lìjiāng* the next day (*dì-èr tiān*).

5.11 Purpose

5.11.1 *Kàn* 'to look at'

The verb *kàn*, whose root meaning is 'to look at', may, in combination with different objects, show a wide range of English translations.

kànshū	'to read'
kànbào	'to read the newspaper'
kàn diànyǐng ⟨r⟩	'to see a movie'
kàn diànshì	'to watch TV'
kàn Hóng Lóu Mèng	'to read *The Dream of the Red Chamber*'
kàn péngyou	'to visit friends'
kàn qīnqi	'to visit relatives'
kàn dìtú	'to look at a map'
kànbìng	'to see a doctor; to see a patient' ('look+at-illness')
kàn rènao	'to go where the excitement is' ('look+at-hubbub')

5.11.2 Other things to do

mǎi dōngxi	VO	'to shop' ('buy things')
zuò gōngkè	VO	'to do homework'
qǔ yīfu	VO	'to pick up [one's] clothes' ('get; fetch-clothes')
kāihuì	VO	'to hold / attend a meeting, conference' ('open-meeting')
gōngzuò	V	'to work' [also N 'a job']
gànhuór	VO	'to do things, to be working'
zuò shì⟨qing⟩	VO	'to do things'
duànliàn	V	'to exercise; work out; train'
yùndòng	V	'to exercise; to do sports'
zuò yùndòng	VO	'to do sports'

5.11.3 Reasons for going somewhere

The verb *qù*, with or without an explicit destination, may be followed by an expression of purpose; if the destination is present, then it precedes the purpose (as 'go' and 'going' do in English).

Wǒmen qù ⟨Běijīng⟩ kàn péngyou.	'We're going ⟨to Beijing⟩ to visit friends.'
Tā qù ⟨túshūguǎn⟩ zuò gōngkè.	'He's going ⟨to the library⟩ to do [his] homework.'

Purpose can be questioned by *zuò shénme, gàn shénme, gànmá,* all literally meaning ('do what'). The particle *ne,* associated with close engagement, may also appear, as in the following examples.

Nǐ qù túshūguǎn zuò shénme ⟨ne⟩?
Nǐ qù túshūguǎn gàn shénme ⟨ne⟩?
Nǐ qù túshūguǎn gànmá ⟨ne⟩?

The verb *gàn,* common as the ordinary word for 'do; make' in northern China, is avoided in polite circles in Taiwan and overseas communities because of sexual overtones. Also, the expresson *gànmá* often carries overtones of disbelief, particularly when followed by *ne*: *Gànmá ne?* 'What [on earth] are [you] doing?' A safe strategy is to use *zuò shénme,* but be prepared to hear other options.

5.11.4 *Qù* and purpose

In purpose clauses, the verb *qù* 'to go' may be repeated at, or postponed until, the end of the sentence (where it is usually toneless).

Tā qù mǎi dōngxi. *Tā qù mǎi dōngxi qu.* *Tā mǎi dōngxi qu.*	'She's going shopping.'
Qù kàn péngyou. *Qù kàn péngyou qu.* *Kàn péngyou qu.*	'[He]'s going to see a friend.'

Wǒ qù shàngkè. *Wǒ qù shàngkè qu.* *Wǒ shàngkè qu.*	'I'm going to class.'
Tā qù chéng lǐ mǎi dōngxi qu.	'She's going into town to shop.'
Wǒmen qù Sūzhōu kàn péngyou qu.	'We're going to Suzhou to visit friends.'

5.11.5 Intention

You can assert your intention or resolution to go somewhere (or do something) with the following verbs.

yào	*xiǎng*	*dǎsuàn*	*juédìng*
'to want'	'to think; to feel like'	'to plan; to intend'	'to decide'

USAGE

Q:	*Nǐ*	*yào* *dǎsuàn* *xiǎng*	*qù nǎr?* *dào nǎlǐ qu?* *qù shénme dìfang?*
		juédìng	*dào nǎlǐ qu le?*
A:	*Wǒmen bāyuè dǎsuàn qù Xīnjiāpō mǎi dōngxi.*	'In August, we're going shopping in Singapore.'	
	Wǒ yào dào Lúndūn qu kàn qīnqi.	'I want to go to London to visit [my] relatives.'	
	Xiàwǔ, tāmen dǎsuàn qù chéng lǐ mǎi lǐwù gěi yéye.	'They're planning to go into town this afternoon to buy [their] uncle a present.'	

Shí diǎn wǒ děi qù bàngōngshì kàn lǎoshī.	'At 10:00, I have to go to the office to see [my] teacher.'
Kěyǐ qù lóushàng zhǎo Chén lǎoshī.	'[You] can go upstairs and look for Professor Chen.'
Zámen qù wàitou kàn fēijī ba!	'Let's go out and look at the airplanes!'
Tāmen juédìng qù Táiwān kàn qīnqi.	'They've decided to go to Taiwan to visit relatives.'
Hěn duō rén dōu xiǎng qù Xiāng Gǎng zhǎo gōngzuò.	'Lots of people would like to go to Hong Kong to find work.'

SUBJECT	INTENTION	DESTINATION	PURPOSE	
Wǒmen	*dǎsuàn*	{ *qù chéng lǐ* / *dào chéng lǐ qu*	*mǎi dōngxi*	⟨*qu*⟩.
Tāmen	*xiǎng*	{ *qù túshūguǎn* / *dào túshūguǎn qu*	*kàn bào*	⟨*qu*⟩.
Tāmen	*juédìng*	*bān dào Běijīng qu*	*shàng dàxué*	⟨*qu*⟩ *le*.

5.12 In the past

5.12.1 Not having done something [yet]

As seen earlier, the non-occurrence of particular events, scheduled or expected, is regularly indicated by *méi* ⟨*yǒu*⟩ before the verb.

Wǒ hái méi xǐzǎo.	'I haven't washed yet.'
Tāmen hái méi zǒu ne.	'They haven't left yet.'
Tāmen hái méi líkāi Běijīng.	'They haven't left Beijing yet.'
Tāmen hái méi dào Shànghǎi.	'They haven't reached Shanghai yet.'

Hái méi kàn jīntiān de bào.	'[I] haven't read today's paper yet.'
Méi kàn Shìjiè Bēi de xiāoxi.	'[I] didn't read the World Cup report.'
Tāmen hái méi lái ne.	'They haven't arrived [here] yet.'
Tāmen méi qù Běijīng.	'They didn't go to Beijing.'
Tāmen hái méi juédìng ne.	'They haven't decided yet.'
Tāmen hái méi huíjiā.	'They haven't gone home yet.'

The negative construction with *méiyǒu* is generally only applicable to action verbs. Verbs such as *juéde* 'to feel', *zhīdào* 'to know', and *yào* 'to want', which express emotional or cognitive states, are less susceptible to a preceding *méi* ⟨*yǒu*⟩. Negation of such verbs with *bù* may often translate to the past tense in English.

Wǒ zuótiān bù shūfu—wǒ méi qù.	'I didn't feel well yesterday—I didn't go.'
Zuótiān méi qù ma?	'Didn't you go yesterday?'
Méi qù, tài yuǎn, bù xiǎng qù nàme yuǎn.	'No, I didn't, it was too far; I didn't want to go so far.'
Qùnián, wǒ bù rènshi tā; wǒ yě bù zhīdào tā gēge shi shéi.	'Last year, I didn't know her; nor did I know who her brother was.'

5.12.2 The position of *le*

Reporting the (past) occurrence of an event, that is, the positive version of sentences such as those cited above with *méiyǒu*, has also been shown in many earlier examples to involve the presence of *le* at the end of the sentence—after any object that is expressed.

Zhōumò nǐmen qù nǎlǐ le?	'Where did you go over the weekend?'
Wǒmen qù Cháng Chéng le.	'We went to the Great Wall.'
Jīntiān shàngwǔ nǐ dào nǎlǐ qu le?	'Where did you go this morning?'
Wǒmen dào chéng lǐ qù mǎi dōngxi qu le.	'We went shopping in town.'

However, *le* is not always in the final position of a sentence. Under certain conditions, it is also found between an action verb and its object, where it underscores the completion of the action. The most concrete manifestation of this meaning is found in sequences where the second event is conditional on the completion of the first; note that *le* in this position is written without a space after the relevant verb.

Nǐ jǐ diǎn huíjiā?	'When are you going home?'
Wǒ chīle fàn jiù huí jiā.	'I'm going home after [I] eat.'
Shénme shíhou mǎi piào?	'When do we buy our tickets?'
Shàngle chē jiù mǎi piào.	'Buy your tickets after boarding.'

Another manifestation involves the presence of what is often called a 'quantified object' after the verb. A quantified object is one containing a number and measure phrase, such as *liǎng ge*, or, as below, *yí tàng* 'a trip'. In such cases, if *le* is present, it will also be placed after the verb and before the quantified object, not at the end of the sentence.

Zhōumò nǐmen qù nǎlǐ le?	'Where did you go over the weekend?'
Wǒmen qù Cháng Chéng le.	'We went to the Great Wall.'
Wǒmen qùle yí tàng Cháng Chéng.	'We took a trip to the Great Wall.'

The difference in the meaning between the two options is subtle, but the grammatical choice is clear: if you choose *yí tàng* in your response, *le* follows the verb; if you do not—and if *le* appears—then it will be placed at the end of the sentence. This quantified object rule is important, and you should retain it for future reference. However, at this point, you will not be burdened with examples in which *le* is placed between verb and object; the examples in this lesson can be expressed quite naturally without use of measure phrases that constitute quantified objects.

One last point: Whether or not *le* appears in a particular sentence is better expressed as a tendency rather than a hard and fast rule. In general, where conditions are right (as, for example, in expressing one action as a condition of another), the tendency for the post-verbal *le* to be expressed is strongest: *Wǒ jīntiān chīle wǔfàn jiù huíjiā* 'I'm going home right after lunch today'. Sentence-final *le*, on the other hand, may be omitted rather more readily. In *Learning Chinese*, if *le* can be expressed without changing the meaning of the utterance, then it is expressed. You should pay attention to your Chinese-speaking friends to see if *le* appears where you expect it!

5.12.3 More time expressions

qùnián 'last year'	*shàng ge yuè* 'last month'	*shàng ge xīnqqī ~ lǐbài* 'last week'	*zhōumò* 'weekend'
jīnnián 'this year'	*zhèi ge yuè* 'this month'	*zhèi ge lǐbài ~ xīngqī* 'this week'	
míngnián 'next year'	*xià ge yuè* 'next month'	*xià ge xīngqī ~ lǐbài* 'next week'	

5.12.4 More examples of final *le*

Shàng ge yuè shàng nǎr qu le?	'Where'd [you] go last month?'
Shàng ge yuè wǒmen dào Shànghǎi qù kàn shūshu qu le.	'Last month we went to Shanghai to see [my] uncle.'
Zhōumò dào nǎlǐ qu le?	'Where'd [you] go over the weekend?'
Xīngqīliù wǒmen qù chéng lǐ mǎi shǒujī qu le. Xīngqītiān qù jīchǎng jiē péngyou le.	'Saturday, we went into town to buy a cell phone. Sunday, we went to the airport to meet some friends.'
Hùzhào yǐjīng qǔ le ma?	'Have you already picked up your passport?'
Yǐjīng qǔ le.	'Yes, I have.' [note *qǔ* vs *qù*]
Zuótiān méiyǒu kè, dào nǎr qu le?	'No class yesterday—where'd you go?'
Méi dào nǎr qù, wǒmen zài jiā lǐ zuò gōngkè ne.	'[We] didn't go anywhere, we stayed at home and did homework.'

The last sentence, in particular, serves to remind us that *le*, although associated with events that have happened, is not a past-tense marker.

Exercise 8

Paraphrase the following statements in Chinese.

1. On the weekend, we're going to visit the Great Wall; it's not far from Beijing.
2. No class tomorrow; we've decided to go to the country to visit *Mǎ Róng*'s uncle.
3. Don't forget your keys. / My keys, I already have, but I don't know where my umbrella is.
4. Where have they gone? / They've gone upstairs to look for a phone.
5. I haven't gone to get my visa (*qiānzhèng*) yet; I'm planning to go tomorrow.

Prepare a brief biographical sketch containing information such as the following.

> place of birth; place where you grew up; age when you moved to another place; where you live now; which university you are attending; which level

5.13 And

There is considerable disparity in the way English and Chinese express coordination. English makes broader use of coordinating conjunctions such as 'and'; Chinese often uses the equivalent of 'and' in a narrower range of grammatical contexts, and even there may leave the coordination unmarked.

Lìshǐ, shùxué dōu hěn nán!	'History and mathematics are both tough!'
Wǒ kāfēi, píjiǔ dōu bù hē, zhǐ xǐhuan hē chá.	'I don't drink coffee or beer, just tea.'

Explicit coordination is expressed with *gēn* (a word with a range of meaning that includes 'heel; follow; with; and') or *hé* (often pronounced, non-standardly, *hàn* by people from Taiwan). Both are only used to join nouns, pronouns, or, more generally, phrases.

Dàlǐ gēn Lìjiāng dōu zài Yúnnán de xīběi.	'Dali and Lijiang are both in the northwest of Yunnan.'
Míngtiān qù chéng lǐ kàn Wáng lǎoshī hé tā de xuéshēng.	'Tomorrow [I]'m going into town to see Professor Wang and her students.'
Nánde gēn nǚde dōu shuō+de hěn hǎo.	'The males and females all speak [it] well.'
Lǎoshī, fùmǔ gēn xuéshēng dōu děi qù.	'Teachers, parents, and students all have to go [there].'

Regardless of whether a conjunction is present or not, Chinese tends to use the adverb *dōu* to support coordination. *Dōu* occasionally anticipates upcoming material, but much more often it refers back to support already mentioned or implied material, which accounts for the order in the sentence: *Kāfēi píjiǔ wǒ dōu bù hē.*

Gēn and *hé* are not optional in settings that involve verbs or clauses, such as those illustrated below. If marked at all, such connections are indicated by adverbs such as *yě*.

Xuéshēng hěn jǐnzhāng, lǎoshī yě hěn jǐnzhāng.	'The students are nervous, and so are the teachers.'
Tāmen qù Běijīng kàn péngyou, mǎi dōngxi.	'They're going to Beijing to visit friends and shop.'

You should, therefore, be careful not to take your cue from English 'and'. Following are some other examples where English 'and' has no direct counterpart in the Chinese translation.

Hái hǎo; nǐ ne?	'[I]'m fine—and you?'
Gébì yǒu diànhuà, lóushàng yě yǒu.	'There are telephones next door and upstairs.'
Wǒ qī diǎn chī zǎodiǎn, bā diǎn shàngbān.	'I eat breakfast at 7:00 and start work at 8:00.'

5.14 Sports and scores

Table tennis (ping-pong), badminton, football/soccer (local clubs as well as European and other international clubs), basketball (Chinese and NBA), swimming, track and field, and motor racing (F1) are popular sports in China. If you choose your topics carefully, you can at least inquire about scores. Names of other sports and additional related conversational material appear in later units.

Begin with the verbs *yíng* 'to win' and *shū* 'to lose'; in order to avoid complications, use them only in the simplest of sentences, as demonstrated below.

Zhōngguó yíng le.	'China won.'
Bāxī shū le.	'Brazil lost.'

Scores are indicated with *bǐ* 'compare; than; to'. Thus, a basketball score might be 99 *bǐ* 98; football 2 *bǐ* 0. The scores of low-scoring sports can be questioned with *jǐ* 'how many': *jǐ bǐ jǐ*; high-scoring games with *duōshao*: *duōshao bǐ duōshao*. Finally, a simple way to mention the two relevant teams is to list them, separated by the conjunctions *hé* or *gēn*.

Zhōngguó hé Bāxī, shéi yíng le?	'China and Brazil, who won?'
Rìběn hé Tàiguó, Tàiguó shū le.	'Japan and Thailand, Thailand lost.'

Exercise 9

Translate the following into Chinese.

1. How about the U.S. and Mexico, who won?
2. The U.S. won, 2–1.

3. Did England win? / Yes, 3–1.
4. What was the score? / 98–92. Boston won. Boston's pretty good ('strong')!
5. 95 to what? / I'm not sure.
6. In ping-pong (*pīngpāngqiú*), China's number 1; the U.S. is number 1 in basketball (*lánqiú*).

Paraphrase the following in Chinese.

1. The tests are hard, and there's lots of homework.
2. I'm taking five courses and they're all hard!
3. Today's class has 12 men and 12 women.
4. Who won the Japan vs. Korea [match]? (*Rìběn* 'Japan', *Hánguó* 'Korea')
5. The library and cafeteria are air-conditioned (*yǒu kōngtiáo*), so we like to study there.

5.15 Dialogue: Who won?

Zhōu Shuǎng is a man in his forties who works in the foreign student office; *Zhāng Yīng* is the Chinese name of a younger woman, an undergraduate from abroad who has been studying at the university for a year. They run into each other just outside the cafeteria.

Zhāng:	*Zhōu lǎoshī, nín hǎo.*	'Professor Zhou, hello.'
Zhōu:	*Èi, Zhāng Yīng, nǐ hǎo.*	'Ah, Zhang Ying, hello.'
	Nǐ gāngcái zài lǐtou a?	'You were just inside?'
Zhāng:	*Shì a, gāng chīwán fàn.*	'Yes, we just finished.'
Zhōu:	*Xiànzài shàng nǎr qù a?*	'Where are you off to right now?'
Zhāng:	*Túshūguǎn.*	'[To the] library.'
Zhōu:	*Túshūguǎn a! Zuò gōngkè qù ma?*	'The library! [You]'re going [there] to do [your] homework?'

Zhāng:	*Bú shi zuò gōngkè, shi kànbào.*	'Not to do my homework, to read the paper.'
Zhōu:	*Ò, kànbào!*	'Oh, [to] read the paper!'
Zhāng:	*Shì, túshūguǎn yǒu kōngtiáo, bǐjiào shūfu.*	'Yeah, there's air-conditioning in the library, it's quite comfortable.'
Zhōu:	*Ng, jīntiān shì hěn rè!*	'Yes, it *is* hot today!'
Zhāng:	*Hěn rè, yě hěn mēn.*	'Hot and muggy.'
Zhōu:	*Zhōngwén bào nǐ kàndedǒng ma?*	'Are you able to read Chinese newspapers?'
Zhāng:	*Néng kàndǒng yìdiǎnr. Shìjiè Bēi de xiāoxi néng kàndǒng, méi wèntí!*	'I can read some. I can read about the World Cup—no problem [there]!'
Zhōu:	*Ò, Shìjiè Bēi. Zuótiān shi Zhōngguó hé Hánguó, nǐ kàn le méiyǒu?*	'Oh, the World Cup. It was China and Korea yesterday, did you watch it?'
Zhāng:	*Kàn le, dāngrán kàn le.*	'Sure, of course I did.'
Zhōu:	*Tài kěxī le, Zhōngguó shū le!*	'It's too bad, China lost!'
Zhāng:	*Ng, tài kěxī le. Búguò Zhōngguó bú cuò. Xià cì!*	'Yeah, a pity. But China's not bad. Next time!'
Zhōu:	*Nà, jīntiān shi Yīngguó hé Āgēntíng, shì bu shì?*	'Today it was England and Argentina, right?'
Zhāng:	*Shì, Yīngguó yíng le.*	'That's right, England won.'
Zhōu:	*Shì ma? Jǐ bǐ jǐ?*	'Is that right? What was the score?'
Zhāng:	*Yī bǐ líng.*	'1–0.'
Zhōu:	*Ei, bú cuò, Yīngguó hěn qiáng.*	'Hey, not bad, England's quite good.'
Zhāng:	*Hái kěyǐ, búguò Bāxī gèng qiáng, wǒ xiǎng.*	'They're not bad, but Brazil's better, I feel.'
Zhōu:	*Yīngguó hé Bāxī shi xià ge lǐbài ba?*	'England and Brazil are next week, right?'

Zhāng:	*Xià ge lǐbài'èr.*	'Next Tuesday.'
Zhōu:	*Nà míngtiān lǐbàiliù, méi kè, nǐ shàng nǎr qù?*	'Well, tomorrow's Saturday, no class; where are you going?'
Zhāng:	*Míngtiān bú dào nǎr qu, yěxǔ zài jiā lǐ xiūxi xiūxi, kàn yìdiǎnr diànshì. Dànshì xīngqītiān dǎsuàn dào Tiānjīn qù kàn péngyou.*	'I'm not going anywhere tomorrow, I'll probably just take it easy at home, and watch some TV. But on Sunday [we]'re planning to visit a friend in Tianjin.'
Zhōu:	*Nǐ zài Tiānjīn yě yǒu péngyou a?!*	'You have a friend in Tianjin as well?!'
Zhāng:	*Shì a, tā zài Nánkāi Dàxué dúshū.*	'Yes, she's studying at Nankai University.'
Zhōu:	*Wàiguó lái de ma?*	'Is [she] foreign?'
Zhāng:	*Jiānádà rén; Duōlúnduō lái de.*	'[She]'s Canadian, from Toronto.'
Zhōu:	*Tā yě huì shuō Hànyǔ ma?*	'She speaks Chinese too?'
Zhāng:	*Tā Hànyǔ shuō+de hěn bú cuò.*	'Her Chinese isn't bad!'
Zhōu:	*Kāichē qù ma?*	'Are you driving [there]?'
Zhāng:	*Bù, zuò huǒchē qù. Hǎo, Zhōu lǎoshī, wǒ děi cóng zhèi biānr zǒu le.*	'No, I'm taking the train. Okay, Professor Zhǒu, I've got to go this way.'
Zhōu:	*Hǎo, Zhāng Yīng, màn zǒu a!*	'Okay, Zhang Ying, take it easy!'

NOTES

a. *gāngcái* 'just now; before': *Gāngcái kěyǐ, xiànzài bù xíng.* 'Before was okay, but not now.'

b. *gāng* 'just; exactly'; *gāng dào* 'just arrived'; *Tā gāng chīguo wǎnfàn.*

c. *chīwán*; *wán* 'to finish' may follow almost any action verb: *shuōwán le; xiěwán le; hái méi kǎowán ne*

d. *kěxī* 'a pity' ('able-pity')

e. *xià cì*; *cì* 'time', a verbal measure word; cf. *zài shuō yí cì* 'say it again'

Yǒu méiyǒu Ōuzhōu Bēi de xiāoxi?

f. *qiáng* 'strong; powerful; better'
g. *xiūxi* 'to rest'; often reiterated as *xiūxi xiūxi*
h. *kāichē qù*, with *kāichē* acting as an adverbial, 'to go driving'; cf. *zǒulù qù*
i. *zuò huǒchē; zuò* 'to sit' corresponds to English 'to take'; cf. *zuò fēijī qù*
j. *cóng . . . zǒu*; 'to go this way' is expressed with *cóng* in Chinese

Exercise 10

Explain that

1. you are going to Beijing to visit friends.
2. you are not going anywhere tomorrow—you have a lot of homework.
3. you're off to class—Chinese class.
4. you have to go and pick up your [clean] clothes (*yīfu*) now.
5. you don't know what date they're going to China.
6. that's yesterday's [paper], today's is over here.
7. his wife's luggage is still on the plane.
8. you're going to the airport to fetch the luggage.
9. your teacher's outside.
10. you have lots of friends but none of them understands Chinese.

5.16 Pronunciation (final *r*; low tones)

5.16.1 Final *r* in standard Mandarin

A very few words in standard Mandarin always occur with a final *r*.

érzi	'son'
èr	'two'
ěrduō	'ear'

However, in the dialects of Beijing and other parts of the northern Mandarin-speaking area, a large number of words occur with an *r* suffix. Most of these are nouns: *kòngr* 'spare time'; *píngr* 'bottle', *wányìr* 'toys', *diànyǐngr* 'films', *ménkǒur* 'doorway', *xīnyǎnr* 'heart; cleverness', *wéizuǐr* 'bib', *xìngrénr* 'almonds', etc. The suffix appears with a few non-nouns as well, for example, *shùnshǒur* 'easily; without problem' and *wánr* 'have fun'.

One historical source for this, though probably not the only one, is suggested by the writing system, which writes this particular suffix with the *ér* of *érzi* 'son' (儿/兒). Supposedly, *ér* was originally attached to nouns in certain contexts as a diminutive or expression of familiarity, but with time, it came to have a much more abstract meaning, ultimately ending up as little more than a marker of familiar nouns. As noted above, hardly any verbs appear with the *r* suffix.

In some cases, the forms with and without *r* (which may also display a tonal shift) have distinct, though relatable, meanings.

mén	'door'	*ménr*	'way; knack'
kōng	'empty'	*kòngr*	'empty space; spare time'
dān	'unit'	*dānr*	'bedsheet; on one's own'
míng	'name'	*míngr*	'reputation; fame'

Southern speakers of Mandarin, who often regard the *r* suffix as a northern affectation, can, and do, avoid using it; instead of *yìdiǎnr* 'a bit' they will say *yìdiǎn*, instead of *kòngr* 'free time' they will say *kòng*, relying on only the tone (and context) to distinguish it from the level-toned *kōng* 'empty'. In reading, they will often treat the *r* suffix as a separate syllable, reading *mén-ér*, for example, instead of *ménr* [*mér*].

A. OTHER CASES OF FINAL *R* All the words cited above can be found with the [r] pronunciation indicated in dictionaries; for Beijing and other northern speakers, these pronunciations are standard. But not all usage of final *r* can be considered standard. Some speakers in the Beijing region, and in other parts of the north, lard their speech with final *r*. The following nursery rhyme—rather dated to be sure—in which every last word has the *r* suffix, illustrates this point.

Qióng tàitai

Qióng tàitair	*('poor wife')*
Bàozhe ge jiānr,	*('clutches [her] shoulders')*
chīwánle fànr	*('eat-finish-LE food')*
ràole ge wānr,	*('go+round-LE the corner')*
yòu mǎi bīngláng yòu mǎi yānr.	*('and buy betel and tobacco.')*

NOTE

Bīngláng (derived from the Indonesian/Malay word *pinang*) is the areca nut, the main ingredient in chewable betel quids that are popular in Taiwan, southern China, and in Southeast Asia. Chewing betel cleans the teeth, helps with digestion, and provides a pleasant sensation in the mouth and head. It also makes your saliva red and viscous—and leads to excess expectoration.

B. PRONUNCIATION You have probably observed that some of the words with final *r* look quite unpronounceable, particularly those ending in 'nr' or 'ngr' (*yìdiǎnr, yǐngr*). It turns out they are not pronounced as written in pinyin. As you already know, *yìdiǎnr* is actually pronounced [yìdiǎr]; similarly, *píngr* is pronounced [pyúhr]. The pinyin convention is to leave the syllables, to which the *r* is added, intact. In that way, the original syllable can be easily identified, and both versions can be listed together in a dictionary.

It would be difficult at this early stage to present all possible syllables with final *r* in the way that was done for other rhymes. Because these words are often regional, colloquial, or slang, relatively few are encountered in beginning textbooks. However, for reference, the following is a selection, organized by rhyme.

zìr [zèr]	*huàr*	*gàir* [gàr]	*bànr* [bàr]	*píngr* [pié^{n}r]
cír [cér]	*xiàr*	*wèir* [wèr]	*ménr*	*chóngr* [chó^{n}r]
shìr [shèr]		*kuàir* [kuàr]	*diǎnr*	*kòngr* [kò^{n}r]
pír [piér]		*huìr* [huèr]	*guǎnr* [guǎr]	*yàngr* [yà^{n}r]
yìr [yèr]			*gùnr* [guèr]	*huángr* [huá^{n}r]

Note how the last two columns are pronounced. When *r* is applied to a syllable with final *n*, the [n] sound is lost completely: *diǎn* → [diǎr]; *bàn* → [bàr]. When the *r* is applied to a syllable with final *ng*, however, the nasal endings survive as nasalization (indicated by the superscript 'n'), that is, the vowels are pronounced nasally: *kòngr* → [kò^{n}r]. These rules are hard to apply, so for now, we will focus on words with final *r* that are frequently encountered, like *diǎnr, yàngr, huìr,* and *kuàir.*

5.16.2 More than two low tones in a phrase

We have now learned enough low-toned words to encounter strings of more than two. Observe how the following are realized.

(1) *Yě hěn lěng.*	*Yé hēn lěng.* or *Yě* | *hén lěng.*
(2) *Wǒ yě hěn kě.*	*Wó yě* | *hén kě.*
(3) *Lǎo Lǐ yě hěn hǎo.*	*Láo Lī yě* | *hén hǎo.*
(4) *Wǒ yě hěn xiǎng xǐzǎo!*	*Wó yě* | *hén xiǎng* | *xízǎo.*

The second and fourth examples both have an even number of words (syllables). In such cases, the phrasing tends to be in pairs (as indicated) and the familiar tone shift takes place. But in the first and third examples, where the number of syllables is odd, there may be several options (as seen in the first example). Either the phrase is divided into two moras (*yě* | *hén lěng*), in which case the regular rule applies to the second, or, especially in fast speech, the three form a tonal unit, with the first rising (normally), the second staying high, and the third low: *Yé hēn lěng.*

5.17 Summary

OR	*Chá ⟨huòzhě⟩ kāfēi dōu xíng.*
	Nǐ shi guónèi hángbān háishi guójì de?
	Nǐ píngcháng yòng kuàizi háishi yòng dāochā chīfàn.
Q	*Nà, zěnme bàn?*
Food	*Liǎng pán xiārénr-chǎofàn.*
	Jiǔcài-bāo, yì lóng.
Duō?	*Dàwǎn duō dà? / Liù ge rén chī.*
V+*de*	*Tā chànggē chàng+de hǎojíle!*
Huì	*Zhǐ huì shuō yìdiǎndiǎn.*
Predications	*Jīntiān bú huì hěn lěng.*
A bit	*Hē yìdiǎnr chá ba.*
	Zhè chá yǒu yìdiǎnr kǔ.
Xíng	*Qǐngkè chīfàn méi jiǔ bù xíng.*
Kids	*Xiǎo péngyou chī shénme ne?*
VOO	*Wǒ xiǎng wèn tā yí ge wèntí.*
Gěi as CV	*Míngtiān gěi nǐ dǎ ge diànhuà, hǎo bu hǎo?*
VOVO	*Míngtiān shi tā de shēngrì, wǒmen yīnggāi mǎi ge lǐwù gěi tā.*
Music	*Nǐ zuì xǐhuan shénme yàng de yīnyuè?*
	Nǐ huì shénme yuèqì?
Know	*Bù zhīdào ~ bù xiǎode, wǒ bú rènshi tā.*
Dǒng	*Dǒng wǒ de yìsi ma?*
	Bù zhīdào tā shì bu shì Zhōngguó rén.
Go to	*Nǐ dào nǎr qu? ~ Nǐ qù nǎlǐ?*
Leave	*Wǒmen sān hào líkāi Běijīng, wǔ hào dào Lìjiāng.*
Move to	*Wǒ shēng zài Shāntóu, shíjiǔ suì bān dào Běijīng lái le.*
Purpose	*Hěn duō rén xiǎng dào Běijīng qù zhǎo gōngzuò.*
Go home	*Tāmen hái méi huíjiā.*
Sentence *le*	*Zhōumò wǒmen qù Cháng Chéng le.*
Verb *le*	*Shàngle chē jiù mǎi piào; Wǒmen qùle yí tàng Cháng Chéng.*

Sports	*Zhōngguó hé Bāxī, shéi yíng le?*
Score	*Jǐ bǐ jǐ?*
Can read?	*Zhōngwén bào nǐ kàndedǒng ma?*

5.18 Rhymes and rhythms

5.18.1 *Tiào shéng* 'skipping rope [rhymes]'

A. A TALE OF BETRAYAL

Jiāng Jiě, Jiāng Jiě, hǎo Jiāng Jiě,	('Sister Jiang, good Sister Jiang,')
tā wèi rénmín sǎ xiān xiě.	('she for people shed fresh blood.')
Pàntú, pàntú, Fǔ Zhìgāo,	(Traitor, traitor, Fu Zhigao,')
Nǐ shì rénmín de 'dà cǎobāo'.	('You are the+people DE 'great straw-bundle' ['good-for-nothing'].')

The story of Jiang Jie is well known in China. Jiang Jie was a communist operative who, not long before Mao's victory, was captured by the Kuomintang as a result of the treachery of Fu Zhigao. Her story was the basis for a revolutionary opera (1964), which in turn was the basis of a film of the same name, directed by Zhang Yuan (2004).

B. MORE HEROISM

Dǒng Cúnruì,	('Dong Cunrui,')
shíbā suì,	('18 years+of+age,')
cānjiā gémìng yóujīduì;	('take+part+in revolutionary guerrilla-force;')
zhà diāobǎo, xīshēng liǎo,	('blow+up blockhouses, sacrifice [self] LE,')
gémìng de rènwu wánchéng liǎo!	('revolution DE task complete-fulfill LE.')

NOTES

a. *yóujīduì* ('roving-attack-troops')

b. In song and poetry, *le* is often given the fully toned pronunciation of *liǎo*.

5.18.2 Something a little lighter

Yuèliàng zǒu, wǒ yě zǒu,	('Moon moves, I also move,)
wǒ hé yuèliàng jiāo péngyou,	(the moon and I make friends,)
dài lǐ zhuāng-zhe liǎng zhī dàn,	([my] pocket in is+filled+with two M eggs,)
sònggěi yuèliàng dāng zǎofàn.	(to present to the moon as breakfast.')

NOTES

a. *zhuāng-zhe* 'to be loaded with; to be packed with; to install'; *-zhe* is a verb suffix that, among other functions, turns actions ('to load') into states ('to be loaded with').

b. *sònggěi* 'to present to'

c. *dāng* 'to treat as; to regard as; to be'

Unit 6

Tiān bú pà, dì bú pà, zhǐ pà [wàiguó rén] shuō Zhōngguó huà!
'Nothing to fear from heaven, nothing to fear from Earth—the only thing to fear is [foreigners] speaking Chinese!'
—A self-deprecating phrase which, if you say it well, will get you accolades

Unit 6 is a little shorter than the earlier units, but it is still packed with interesting material. The main grammatical point that will be covered is the so-called *shi-de* pattern, used when talking about the circumstances of past events, often in complement with *le*: '*Where* did you meet?' '*When* were you born?' The construction leads naturally back for a deeper look at the V-*guò* pattern, as well as to questions of 'when', and to temporal clauses with 'before', 'after', and 'during'. The lesson also provides the language to describe people's appearance and to talk about their background and where they work.

Contents

6.1 Opposites

With SVs, opposites can be formed by negation: *duì* → *bú duì*. However, in many cases, there exists a word that can stand in for the negative phrase as a true opposite: *duì* 'right' → *cuò* 'wrong'. Occasionally, if they share a domain but are regarded as contrary, pairs of nouns can also be treated as opposites: *xuéshēng* and *lǎoshī*; *nánzǐ* and *nǚzǐ*; *gǒu* 'dog' and *māo* 'cat'. Exploration of opposites can reveal subtle cultural and linguistic differences. Chinese, for example, considers the opposite of *xīn* 'new' to be either *lǎo* 'old' [in the sense of 'former' or 'antiquated'] or *jiù* 'old' [in the sense of 'used' or 'dilapidated']. But *lǎo*, in the context of foods such as tofu, can also mean 'tough', opposite to *nèn* 'soft' (like baby's skin).

Ròu tài lǎo le.	'The meat's tough.'
Zhè dòufu hěn nèn.	'This tofu's quite soft.'

Shēng (*chūshēng de shēng, xuéshēng de shēng*) can mean 'raw; unripe' (as well as 'to bear; to be born') and, as such, is opposed to *shóu*, 'ripe; cooked'.

Rìběn rén hěn xǐhuan chī shēngyú.	'The Japanese like to eat raw fish.'
Yīngguó rén bǐjiào xǐhuan chī shóuròu.	'The English prefer well-cooked meat.'
Luóbo kěyǐ shēng chī, yě kěyǐ shóu chī.	'Turnips can be eaten raw, or cooked.'

NOTE

Shóu has a range of meanings, from 'ripe' to 'familiar' and 'experienced'. In certain contexts, and perhaps more by certain speakers, the word is also pronounced *shú* rather than *shóu*. The pronunciation *shú* seems to be more likely when the meaning is 'familiar', *shóu* when it is 'ripe' or 'cooked', though many dictionaries assert that *shóu* is simply more colloquial.

In Chinese, the term for 'opposite' is *xiāngfǎn* ('mutual opposition').

Rè de xiāngfǎn shi shénme?	'What's the opposite of "hot"?'
⟨Rè de xiāngfǎn⟩ shi lěng.	'⟨The opposite of "hot"⟩ is "cold".'
Dà ne, dà de xiāngfǎn shi shénme?	'And "big", what's the opposite of "big"?'
Ng, dà de xiāngfǎn yěxǔ shi xiǎo.	'Uh, the opposite of "big", I suppose, is "small".'
Gāo ne?	'And "tall"?'
Nà, gāo de xiāngfǎn shi ǎi; gāo de xiāngfǎn yě shi dī.	'Well, the opposite of "tall" is "short"; the opposite of "tall" is also "low".'

Below is a list of opposites with rough English glosses. A feel for their range and usage will have to wait until they have been encountered in different settings; but for now, you can practice pronunciation and start to get familiar with the words (SVs, as well as some nouns or noun phrases) by asking for, or responding with, their opposites.

Q: [ ] *de xiāngfǎn shi shénme?* A: [ ] *de xiāngfǎn shi* [ ].

LIST OF OPPOSITES

duō / shǎo 'many' / 'few'	*shàng / xià* 'above' / 'below'	*zài chéng lǐ / zài xiāngxià* 'in town' / 'in the country'	
gāo / ǎi 'tall' / 'short'	*gāo / dī* 'high' / 'low'	*cháng / duǎn* 'long' / 'short'	*guì / piányi* 'expensive' / 'cheap'

hǎo / huài 'good' / 'bad'	*kuài / màn* 'fast' / 'slow'	*pàng / shòu* 'fat' / 'thin'	*zuǒ / yòu* 'left' / 'right'
xiāng / chòu 'fragrant' / 'smelly'	*gānjìng / zāng* 'clean' / 'dirty'	*cōngmíng / bèn* 'smart' / 'stupid'	*nán / róngyì* 'difficult' / 'easy'

6.2 Describing people

hēi yǎnjing hēi tóufa huáng pífu, yǒngyǒng-yuǎnyuǎn shì lóng de chuánrén
('black eyes, black hair, yellow skin eternally be dragon's descendents')
—line from a popular song called *Lóng de chuánrén* 'Descendents of the Dragon'

Describing people involves a number of constructions. Most simply, an SV may suffice.

Tā hěn cōngmíng.	'She's very clever.'
Tā hěn kě'ài.	'She's quite cute.'
Tā yǒu diǎnr juè.	'He's a bit gruff.'
Tā yǒu diǎn tiáopí.	'She's kind of mischievous.'
Tāmen dōu hěn guāi.	'They're very well behaved.'
Tā bǐjiào pàng.	'He's kind of heavy.' ('fat')
Tā hěn shuài.	'He's good looking.'
Tā hěn piàoliang.	'She's pretty.'
Tā yǒu diǎnr hàixiū.	'She's kind of shy.'
Tā hěn kù.	'She's cool.'

NOTES

a. *juè* 'blunt' or 'gruff', a colloquial word

b. *tiáopí / guāi* 'naughty' / 'good'—words typically applied to children

c. *shuài*; The sense is 'controlled; unruffled; cool' and, hence, 'good looking'; *shuài* is usually applied to men. Women (as well as clothes and other beautiful things) are more often *piàoliang* 'pretty; beautiful', a word whose literal meaning is 'rinsed with light'.

In cases in which one aspect, or part, of a person is being described, the pattern is 'topic-comment', which often corresponds to a sentence with 'have' in English: e.g., *Tā yǎnjing hěn dà* 'She has big eyes' ('she eyes quite big').

TOPIC	COMMENT	
PERSON	PART	⟨ADV⟩ SV
Tā	*rén*	*hěn hǎo.*
Tā	*yǎnjing*	*hěn dà.*
Tā	*gèzi~gèr*	*hěn gāo.*

Tā	*rén*	*hěn hǎo.*	'He's very nice.'
Tā	*shēntǐ*	*bú cuò.*	'She's in good shape.'
Tā	*yǎnjing*	*hěn yǒushén.*	'She has 'sparkling' eyes.'
Tā	*tóufa*	*shi chángcháng de.*	'His hair's quite long.'
Tā	*gèzi*	*hěn gāo.*	'He's quite tall.'
Tā	*liǎn*	*hěn kuān.*	'She has a broad face.'
Tā	*pífu*	*hěn bái / hēi.*	'He has light skin / dark skin.'
Tā	*bízi*	*hěn gāo.*	'He has a large nose.'

Often, when describing some particular aspect of a person, the adjective is repeated.

Tā	*tóufa*	*chángcháng de.*	'Her hair is quite long.'
Tā	*yǎnjing*	*dàdà de.*	'He has large eyes.'
Ta	*gèzi*	*gāogāo de.*	'She's quite tall.'

When describing colors, the form with *sè* is often preferred over the root SV, and because the compound is a noun, it requires a construction with *shi.*

Tā ⟨de⟩ yǎnjing shi lánsè de.	'He has blue eyes.'
Tā ⟨de⟩ tóufa shi huángsè de.	'She has light brown hair.'

NOTES

a. *tā rén . . .*; *Rén* here has the sense of 'as a person', followed by attributes; *shēntǐ*, on the other hand, is the physical body.

b. *yǎnjing* 'eyes', with *qīngshēng* on the second syllable; contrast with *yǎnjìng* 'glasses' ('eye-mirrors'), with final falling tone

c. *yǒushén* 'sparkling' ('have-spirit')

d. *gèzi* 'height; stature'; also *gèr*

e. *bízi*; Broad or prominent noses are often described as *gāo* 'high' as well as *dà* 'big'.

f. *liǎn*; Faces are often described as *kuān* 'broad' (typical in northern China) or *cháng* 'long' and *shòu* 'thin' (more typical in southern China).

g. *pífu* 'skin'; People in China are often described in terms of skin tone. Light and dark skin are often simply described as *bái* 'white' and *hēi* 'black', respectively.

h. *tóufa*; The Chinese vary in how they describe non-black hair. Light brown is often *huángsè de* 'yellow'; darker may be *zōngsè de* (from *zōng* 'palm tree', a darkish brown color); blonds may be *jīnsè de* 'golden' or *jīnhuángsè de* 'golden yellow'.

6.2.1 Epithets

In English, it is possible to characterize someone as blond (using an adjective) or call someone 'a blond' (using the word as a noun). However, most adjectives do not have a corresponding epithet; there is no noun 'a tall' corresponding to 'to be tall'. In this respect, Chinese is the same. Sometimes, a nominal form can be produced instead of an SV, but the pattern is quite idiosyncratic. For example, although it is possible to say *tā bízi hěn gāo*, the alternative expression is usually *tā* ⟨*shi*⟩ *gāo bíliáng*⟨*r*⟩ 'he's high nose-bridged', i.e., 'he has a large nose', rather than just *tā* ⟨*shi*⟩ *gāo bízi* (though *tā* ⟨*shi*⟩ *dà bízi* 'he['s] big-nose[d]' is sometimes heard). Here are some other examples:

Description	Epithet
Tā gèzi ~ gèr hěn gāo.	*Tā* ⟨*shi*⟩ *gāo gèzi ~ gèr.*
Tā bízi hěn gāo.	*Tā* ⟨*shi*⟩ *gāo bíliáng*⟨*r*⟩.
Tā tóufa shi hēisè de.	*Tā* ⟨*shi*⟩ *hēi tóufa.*
Tā tóufa shi hóngsè de.	*Ta* ⟨*shi*⟩ *hóng tóufa.*
Tā tóufa chángcháng de.	*Tā* ⟨*shi*⟩ *chángcháng de tóufa.*
Tā yǎnjing dàdà de.	*Tā* ⟨*shi*⟩ *dàdà de yǎnjing.*
Tā gèzi gāogāo de.	*Tā* ⟨*shi*⟩ *gāogāo de gèzi.*

There is a nuance of difference between the two patterns. The first simply describes the person as tall, etc.; the second is more absolute, placing the person in a category of tall people: *Tā ⟨shi⟩ gāo gèzi* 'He's of tall stature'. The epithet pattern shades off to cases where a noun exists but not an adjective.

Tā shi tūtóu.	'He's bald.' ('bare-head')
Tā liúzhe húzi.	'He's got a beard.' ('leave-ZHE beard')

6.2.2 *Zhǎng +de*

Instead of just describing someone as *gāo* 'tall' or *piàoliang* 'pretty', Chinese often use the expression *zhǎng +de* '[grow up] to be'—with no final *le.*

Tā zhǎng+de zhēn shuài.	'He's [grown up] very handsome.'
Tā zhǎng+de hěn gāo.	'She's [grown up] very tall.'
Tā zhǎng+de hěn shòu.	'She's [grown up] very thin.'
Tā zhǎng+de hěn zhuàng!	'He's [grown up] very strong.'
Tā zhǎng+de yì tóu jīnfà.	'She's got a head of blond hair.'

Summary of descriptions

PERSON	PART	LINK	ATTRIBUTE	TYPE
Tā			{ *hěn gāo.*	SV
			yǒu diǎnr juè. }	
Tā	{ *rén*		*hěn hǎo.*	topic-comment
	gèzi }		*gāogāo de.*	
Tā		*zhǎng+de*	{ *hěn gāo.*	zhǎng+SV
			zhēn shuài. }	
Tā ⟨de⟩ tóufa		*⟨shi⟩*	*huángsè de.*	nominalized SV
Tā		*⟨shi⟩*	{ *gāo gèzi.*	nominal epithet
			hēi tóufa. }	

Exercise 1

Describe the following people, as indicated.

1. a sibling: tall; good looking; decent
2. a classmate: short; sparkling eyes; on the thin side
3. a German friend: brown hair; healthy; cute
4. your teacher: tall; black eyes; a bit overweight; gruff
5. an English friend: tall; dark skin; big eyes
6. the little boy next door: skinny; big eyes; mischievous

6.3 Verb + *guò*

When people hear you speaking Chinese, they are bound to ask you if you have ever been to China; if you have ever visited the Stone Forest (*Shí Lín*) in the southwest; if you have seen the terra-cotta figures (*bīngmǎyǒng* ['soldiers-horses-figurines']) in Xi'an; if you have eaten special Chinese foods like sea cucumber (*hǎishēn*) or shark's fin (*yúchì*); or if you've done any of a host of other things. As you know from the brief remarks in Unit 3, such questions, as well as their typical responses, make use of a verb suffix, *guò* (usually untoned in northern speech), placed directly after the verb: *qùguo*; *chīguo*; *kànguo*. The root meaning of *guò* is 'to pass; to cross over', and the use of *guò* in conventional expressions such as *Nǐ chīguo fàn le ma?*, where it has the sense of 'a regularly scheduled event has passed', is close to the root meaning. Its extended meaning (the 'have ever' meaning) is to signal that an event has happened at some time in the past (or over a period of time in the past) without saying precisely when it happened. For this reason, *guò* is sometimes referred to as an 'experiential' suffix; its general meaning is 'have ever had the experience of' or 'did ever have the experience of'.

6.3.1 *Guò* patterns

Responses to questions with *guò* (in the 'have ever' sense) retain the *guò* in negative responses as well as positive. The negative response is, like those with *le*, formed with *méiyǒu*.

Shàng ge xīngqī, nǐ shàngguo bān ma?	'Did you go to work [at all] last week?'
Méi shàngguo, bù shūfu.	'No, [I] didn't, [I] wasn't feeling well.'

It should be noted that speakers from southern regions, including Taiwan, tend to align the positive and negative responses, responding to the first with *yǒu* (with or without V-*guò*) and the second with *méiyǒu* (with or without V-*guò*).

Nǐ qùguo Táiwān ma?	'Have you [ever] been to Taiwan?'
+ *Yǒu.* ~ *Qùguo.*	'[I] have.'
– *Méiyǒu.* ~ *Méi qùguo.*	'[I] haven't.'

The V-not-V version of the question juxtaposes the positive with a final *méi⟨yǒu⟩* that can be regarded as a truncated version of the full negative, *méi⟨yǒu⟩ qùguo Zhōngguó* (as in the following examples).

Nǐ qùguo Zhōngguó méiyǒu?	'Have you been to China [or not]?'
Hái méi qùguo, kěshì hěn xiǎng qù.	'Not yet, but I'd really like to go.'

Shàng ge xīngqī, nǐ kànguo diànyǐngr méiyǒu?	'Did you see any films last week?'
Méi kànguo; shàng ge xīngqī yǒu hěn duō kǎoshì, bù néng qù kàn diànyǐngr.	'No; last week, [I] had a lot of exams, I couldn't go to [any] films.'

6.3.2 'Ever; never' and 'once; ever'

Two adverbs are particularly drawn to constructions with *guò*.

cónglái	'never'; used only in negative sentences; sometimes reduced to just *cóng*
céngjīng	'formerly; at some time; once; ever'; usually not used in negative sentences; often reduced to *céng* in writing

Wǒ cónglái méi chīguo hǎishēn. ‘I’ve never ever eaten ‘sea cucumber’.’

Nǐ shì bu shi céngjīng xuéguo Hànyǔ? ‘Have you ever previously studied Chinese?’

Bù, wǒ méi xuéguo. ‘No, I haven’t.’

The indefinite use of *shénme*, meaning ‘any’, is also common with comments about experience.

Shàng ge xīngqī nǐ kànguo shénme Zhōngguó diànyǐngr ma? ‘Did you go to any Chinese movies last week?’

Kànguo Wòhǔ Cánglóng. ‘[I] saw *Crouching Tiger Hidden Dragon.*’

FILMS

Wòhǔ Cánglóng — *Crouching Tiger, Hidden Dragon*

Dàhóng Dēnglóng Gāogāo Guà — *Raise the Red Lantern* (‘big-red lantern high hang’)

The following chart summarizes the two functions of *guò*: first, in its ‘experiential’ use (‘have ever’); and second, in conventional expressions involving regularly scheduled events. In the latter case, as the chart shows, it does not usually appear in the response.

Patterns with *-guo*

	QUESTION	RESPONSE
‘have [ever] eaten x’	*Chīguo huíguōròu ma?*	+ *Chīguo.*
	Chīguo huíguōròu méi⟨yǒu⟩?	– *Méi⟨yǒu⟩ chīguo. [Méiyǒu.]*
‘have eaten; did eat’	*Chīguo fàn le ma?*	+ *Chī⟨guo⟩ le.*
	Chīguo fàn le méi⟨yǒu⟩?	– *Hái méi⟨yǒu ⟨chīguo⟨fàn⟩⟩⟩ ne.*

6.3.3 *Xiē* 'several'

If you discover that someone has been to China, then you might want to know which places he or she has been to. *Něi ge dìfang* would mean 'which place'; but to ask 'which places', the M phrase (number + M) needs to be replaced by *xiē* 'several', as in the following example.

Nǐ qùguo Zhōngguó ma?	'Have you been to China?'
Qùguo, wǒ shi qùnián qù de.	'I have, I went last year.'
Ò, nà nǐ qùguo něi xiē dìfang?	'Oh, so which places did you go to?'
Qùguo Běijīng, Xī'ān, Shànghǎi; hái yǒu Guǎngzhōu, Chóngqìng.	'I went to Beijing, Xi'an, Shanghai; and also Guangzhou and Chongqing.'
Hěn duō ya!	'A lot!'

OTHER EXAMPLES

Nèi xiē shū dōu shì nǐ de ma?	'Are these books all yours?'
Zhèi xiē dōngxi dōu hěn guì.	'These things are all expensive.'

6.3.4 Times

Frequently, you will want to respond to a *guò* question with a number of times or occasions: *yí cì* 'once', *liǎng cì* 'twice', *dì-yī cì* 'the first time'. *Huí* (more stylistically informal than *cì*) is used in much the same way: *liǎng huí, sān huí. Cì* and *huí* are measure words, but because they measure verbal events (and are not associated with a following noun), they are called 'verbal measures'. Another common verbal measure is *biàn* 'once through' (as when repeating something).

Wǒ qùguo yí cì.	'I've been [there] once.'
Wǒ jiànguo tā jǐ cì.	'I've met her a few times.'
Wǒ chīguo hǎo jǐ cì le.	'I've eaten it a 'good many times' [so far].'
Wǒ láiguo yì huí.	'I've been here once before.'
Qǐng nǐ zài shuō yí biàn.	'Say it again, please.'

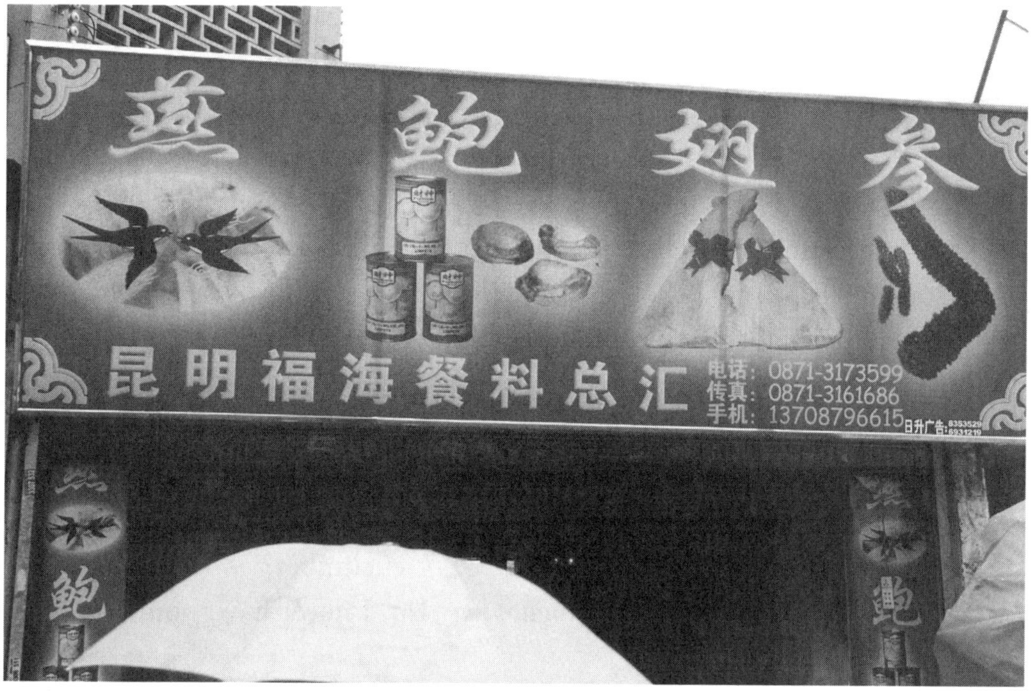

Shop specializing in *yànwō, bàoyú, yúchì*, and *hǎishēn, Kūnmíng*

Nǐ láiguo Běijīng ma?	'Have you been to Beijing before?'
Wǒ zhè shi dì-yī cì!	'This is my first time!' ('For me, this is first time!')
Dì-yī cì bú cuò, dànshì dì-èr cì gèng hǎowánr.	'The first time wasn't bad, but the second time was even more fun.'

NOTES

a. While *kàn* has a basic meaning of 'to look' (cf. *kànshū, kànbìng*), *jiàn* (cf. *zàijiàn* 'good-bye; see you again') suggests an encounter. The two may be combined as *kànjiàn* 'to see': *Kànjiàn le méiyǒu?* 'Did [you] see [it]?' Otherwise, *jiàn* suggests meeting, visiting, or catching sight of someone or something.

b. *Hǎo jǐ cì; Hǎo,* when used in this construction, creates an emphatic adverb.

c. *Zài* 'again' and *zài* 'be at' are, of course, different words.

6.3.5 Dialogues

FOODS

yútóu	*pídàn ~ sōnghuā*	*yúchì*
'fish head'	'preserved eggs'	'shark fin [soup]'

Other interesting foods include *yànwō* 'bird's nest [soup]' ('swallow nest'), *jiǎyú* 'soft-shelled turtle' ('shell-fish'), *yāzhēn* 'duck's gizzard' (more of a snack than a meal), *hóunǎo* 'monkey brain', and *xióngzhǎng* 'bear paw'. The last two are often talked about but rarely ever eaten.

DIALOGUE: SEA CUCUMBER

Jiǎ:	*Nǐ chīguo hǎishēn ma?*	'Have you ever had sea cucumber?'
Yǐ:	*Méi chīguo, cóng méi chīguo; nǐ ne?*	'No, I never have; you?'
Jiǎ:	*Wǒ chīguo hǎo jǐ cì.*	'I've had it quite a few times.'
Yǐ:	*Wèidào zěnmeyàng?*	'How does it taste?'
Jiǎ:	*Méi shénme wèidào, húaliūliū de. Lái yí ge chángchang ba.*	'There's no particular taste, it's 'slick'. Why don't [we] try one?'
Yǐ:	*Hǎo, fúwùyuán, qǐng lái ge cōngpá-hǎishēn.*	'Okay, waiter/waitress, please bring us an 'onion-braised sea cucumber'.'

NOTES

a. *wèidào* 'taste; flavor'

b. *huá* 'slippery'; *huáliūliū* 'slick; slippery'

c. *cháng* 'taste'; *chángchang* 'have a taste'; The word is homophonous with, but otherwise unrelated to *cháng ~ chángchang* 'often'.

d. Ways of hailing servers vary with time and place (as well as the age and status of both parties). On the mainland, people often call out with the very familiar *xiǎohuǒzi* 'young fellow' to youngish waiters. The safer path for a foreigner on the mainland is to use the term *fúwùyuán* 'service person', as in the dialogue. Older customers may simply call out *láojià* 'excuse me; may I trouble you'.

e. *Lái*, in the context of ordering food, means 'to cause to come', i.e., 'to bring'.

DIALOGUE: *SŪZHŌU*

Jiă:	*Qĭngwèn, nĭ shi nĕi guó rén?*	'May I ask which country you're from?'
Yĭ:	*Wŏ shi Zhōngguó rén.*	'I'm Chinese.'
Jiă:	*Nĭ shi Zhōngguó shénme dìfang rén?*	'Where in China are you from?'
Yĭ:	*Sūzhōu rén.*	'From Suzhou.'
Jiă:	*O, Sūzhōu; wŏ méi qùguo, kĕshì tīngshuōguo nèi ge dìfang.*	'Oh, Suzhou; I haven't been there, but I've heard of the place.'
Yi:	*Shì ma?*	'[That] so?'
Jiă:	*Dāngrán a, Sūzhōu hĕn yŏumíng, tīngshuō yŏu hĕn duō yùnhé, qiáo, lăo fángzi . . .*	'Of course, Suzhou's famous, [I] hear [it] has lots of canals, bridges, old houses . . .'
Yĭ:	*Shì a, 'Sūzhōu yuánlín' hĕn piàoliang. Wŏmen cháng shuō: 'Shàng yŏu tiāntáng, xià yŏu Sū Háng.'*	'Yes, Suzhou gardens are quite beautiful. We often say: "There's paradise above, and Su[zhou] and Hang[zhou] below." '

NOTES

a. *Sūzhōu*; An ancient city, west of Shanghai, close to Lake Tai (*Tài Hú*), known for its canals, stone bridges, and fine mansions. Until the growth of Shanghai in modern times, Suzhou was the most important cultural and administrative center of the region. Its earlier wealth is reflected in the great houses and gardens that belonged to merchants and officials. One of the best known has the quaint name of 'The Humble Administrator's Garden' (*Zhuō Zhèng Yuán*). Much of the old city has been obliterated in recent years by industrial growth and extensive building. *Hángzhōu* is another historically important city, southwest of Shanghai.

b. *tīngshuōguo* '[I]'ve heard [it] said'; cf. *tīngshuō* '[I] hear [that]'

c. *yùnhé* 'canal' ('transport-river'); The *Dà Yùnhé* is the ancient Grand Canal, whose southern terminus is at *Hángzhōu*. From Hangzhou, it runs north to the Yangtze–a little to the east of *Zhènjiāng*—then continues northeast toward *Bĕijīng*.

d. *qiáo* 'bridge'; *yí zuò qiáo, yí ge qiáo*

e. *huāyuán* 'garden' ('flower-garden'); cf. *gōngyuán* 'park' ('public gardens')

f. *fángzi* 'houses'; *yì suŏ fángzi* or *yí dòng fángzi*

g. *yuánlín* ('garden-groves'); a more formal term for gardens. Tourist brochures for Suzhou use the phrase *Sūzhōu Yuánlín* 'Suzhou Gardens'.

Dàyùnhé, Sūzhōu.

Exercise 2

Write out the following in Chinese.

1. Have you been to Beijing? / No, not yet, but my sister has; I'd like to go.
2. Have you ever eaten preserved eggs? / Never, but I'd love to try some.
3. Have you had breakfast yet? / Not yet.
4. Okay, let's go and have breakfast—we can order preserved eggs. / You eat preserved eggs for breakfast?
5. Of course, preserved eggs, rice gruel, pickles (*pàocài*), and noodles.

Write out the following in Chinese.

1. Have you been to the Stone Forest (*Shílín*)? / No, but I've heard of it.
2. It's about 125 kilometers southwest of Kunming (*Kūnmíng*). It's where the Sani people live (*Sāní zú*). / I'd like to go, but I have only three days, and I'm already planning to visit Dali (*Dàlǐ*) and Lijiang (*Lìjiāng*).
3. Never mind. Next time. You'll like Dali and Lijiang!

6.4 When; before; after

English and Chinese differ in the position of subordinating conjunctions, such as 'when', 'before', and 'after' in expressions like 'when you're in class', 'after eating', or 'before going to bed'. In English, such words appear at the beginning of the clause; in Chinese they appear at the end.

shàngkè de shíhou	'when [you]'re in class'
chīfàn yǐhòu	'after [you]'ve eaten a meal'
shuìjiào yǐqián	'before [you] go to bed'

The expressions involved have a number of forms.

	COLLOQUIAL	FORMAL	WRITTEN
When	*⟨zài/dāng⟩ . . . de shí⟨hou⟩*		*shí*
Before	*yǐqián*	*zhīqián*	*qián*
After	*yǐhòu*	*zhīhòu*	*hòu*

6.4.1 When

De shí⟨hou⟩ literally means 'the time of [having class]', 'the time of [having your bath]', etc.

shàng kè de shíhou	'while in class'
xǐzǎo de shíhou	'when bathing'
chīfàn de shí⟨hou⟩	'while eating'
zài Zhōngguó de shí⟨hou⟩	'when in China'
xiǎo de shíhou	'when [I] was young'
Kāichē de shíhou bù yīnggāi hē píjiǔ.	'You shouldn't drink beer when you drive.'
Kāichē de shíhou wǒ bǐjiào xǐhuan tīng màn yīnyuè.	'When I drive, I prefer to listen to slow music.'
Tā xǐzǎo de shíhou xǐhuan chànggē.	'She likes to sing in the bath.'

Měnggǔrén chīfàn de shíhou jīngcháng hē báijiǔ.	'Mongolians generally drink 'white liquor' with their meals.'
Nǐ zài Zhōngguó de shíhou qùguo xī'nán méiyǒu?	'When you were in China, did you visit the southwest?'
Qùguo, qùguo Kūnmíng, Dàlǐ, Lìjiāng.	'[I] did, I went to Kunming, Dali, and Lijiang.'
Nǐ Zhōngwén shuō+de hěn hǎo; nǐ shì bu shi céngjīng xuéguo?	'You speak Chinese very well; did you study it before?'
Nǐ tài kèqi, wo cóng méi xuéguo.	'You're too nice; no, I've never studied before.'

Additional nuances may be created by the addition of *zài* 'at' or *dāng* 'right at' at the beginning of the 'when' clause in conjunction with *de shí⟨hou⟩* at the end.

⟨Dāng⟩ tā huílái de shíhou, wǒmen hái zài xǐzǎo.	'When he got back, we were still in the bath.'
⟨Zài⟩ chīfàn de shíhou bù yīnggāi hē lěngyǐn.	'You shouldn't drink cold drinks with [your] meals.'

6.4.2 Before and after

Expressions equivalent to 'before' and 'after' are formed with the *yǐ* of *kěyǐ*, originally a verb meaning 'to take; to use'; hence *yǐqián* ('take as-before') and *yǐhòu* ('take as-after'). Now, however, the meanings have congealed into unitary subordinating conjunctions, with the first syllable often omitted in written texts. A more formal version of both words makes use of *zhī* (a word retained from Classical Chinese): *zhīqián; zhīhòu.*

Shuìjiào yǐqián bù yīnggāi hē kāfēi.	'You shouldn't drink coffee before going to bed.'
Chīfàn yǐhòu bù yīnggāi qù yóuyǒng.	'You shouldn't go swimming after you eat.'

The appendix at the end of this unit lists the more prominent dynasties of Chinese history. 'Dynasty' is *cháodài* in Chinese, which, in combination with a dynastic name, is reduced to *cháo*: *Tángcháo, Sòngcháo.* To help you learn the sequence of (main) dynasties, as well as to practice *yǐqián* and *yǐhòu*, you can ask questions and respond along the following lines.

Háncháo yǐqián shi něi ge cháodài?	'Which dynasty is before the Han?'
Nà shi Qíncháo.	'That's the Qin.'
Tángcháo yǐhòu ne? Tángcháo yǐhòu shi shénme cháodài?	'And after the Tang? What dynasty is after the Tang?'
Tángcháo yǐhòu shi Sòngcháo.	'After the Tang is the Song.'
Sòngcháo yǐhòu ne?	'And after the Song?'
Sòngcháo yǐhòu shi Yuáncháo.	'After the Song is the Yuan.'

NOTES

a. *Qíncháo* 'Qin dynasty' was the dynasty of *Qínshǐhuáng*, the emperor who is credited with first creating a single, unified China.

b. *Yuáncháo* 'Yuan dynasty' was the dynasty founded by the Mongol Kublai Khan (grandson of Genghis Khan).

6.5 When?

The phrase corresponding to the English questions 'when; what time' is *shénme shíhou*. However, particular segments of time can be questioned with *něi* or *jǐ*, as you have seen in earlier units: *něi nián* 'which year'; *něi ge yuè* 'which month'; *něi ge xīngqi* 'which week'; *něi tiān* 'which day'; *lǐbàijǐ* 'which day of the week'; *jǐ yuè* 'what month'; *jǐ hào* 'what day'. Like other time and place words, such questions generally appear after the subject and before the verb (or predicate).

Qǐngwèn, nǐ shénme shíhou qù Běijīng?	'May I ask when you're going to Beijing?'
Xīngqīliù qù.	'[I]'m going on Saturday.
Qǐngwèn, nǐ něi nián qù Lúndūn?	'May [I] ask when you're going to London?'

Wǒ dǎsuàn 2012 nián qù, Àoyùnhuì de nèi nián.	'I'm planning to go in 2012, the year of the Olympics.'

In regions where Cantonese influence is strong (including Malaysia, Singapore, and other parts of Southeast Asia), instead of the *shénme shíhou* of standard Mandarin, the expression *jǐshí* 'which time', based on the Cantonese, is often heard.

Tā jǐshí qù Jílóngpō?	'When is he going to Kuala Lumpur?'
Tā bú qù Jílóngpō, tā qù Mǎliùjiǎ.	'He's not going to Kuala Lumpur, he's going to Malacca.'

Exercise 3

Write a paragraph along the following lines. (Recall that *le* does not mark habitual or generic events.)

When I was in China, I didn't have much money. I ate noodles for breakfast, lunch, and dinner. I didn't eat seafood, and I've still never eaten bird's nest soup or soft-shelled turtle—all too expensive! In China, every day after I got up, I bathed, ate some noodles, and went to the university. I had classes from 9:00 to 12:30. I ate lunch at 1:00 in the cafeteria. While I ate, I often read the day's paper. In the afternoon, I did my homework.

NO TIME FOR . . . Expressions with *shíhou* (*shénme shíhou, shàngkè de shíhou*) involve specific periods of time. *Shíjiān*, on the other hand, is used for time in a more abstract sense. Here are some common examples.

Shíjiān dào le.	'Time's up; it's time.'
Zhījiāgē shíjiān	'Chicago time'
Shíjiān bù zǎo le.	'It's not early.'
Méiyǒu shíjiān chīfàn.	'There's no time to have a meal.'
Wǒ jīntiān méiyǒu shíjiān kànbào.	'I don't have any time to read the paper today.'

Exercise 4

Let it be known that you don't have time anymore to:

go swimming.	go into town to shop.
go see the Great Wall.	write a letter to them.
exercise.	ask them when they're going home.
phone them.	look for new restaurants.
buy a present for her.	listen to music.

6.6 Places of work

On the Mainland, the subdivisions of government organizations (including universities) are called *dānwèi*, usually translated as 'unit' or 'work unit'. In the socialist system, one's *dānwèi* provided social amenities from housing to schooling, as well as access to social services and to routes of legitimate advancement. Nowadays, though the term remains common, the importance of the *dānwèi* in the social and economic life of the Chinese is far less pervasive.

Tā zài nĕi ge dānwèi gōngzuò?	'Which is her work unit?'
Tā zài jīchăng gōngzuò, shi jīnglĭ.	'She works at the airport; she's a manager.'
Nĭ zài shénme dìfang gōngzuò?	'Where do you work?'
Wŏzài Hăidiàn de yí ge diànnăo gōngsī gōngzuò.	'I work in a computer company in Haidian.'

OTHER PLACES OF WORK

gōngsī 'company'	*gōngchăng* 'factory'	*zhèngfŭ-bùmén* 'government office'	*lǚxíngshè* 'travel agency'
yīyuàn 'hospital'	*zhĕnsuŏ* 'clinic'	*xuéxiào* 'school'	*xiăoxué* 'elementary school'
zhōngxué 'middle school'	*gāozhōng* 'high school'	*dàxué* 'university'	*băihuò-shāngdiàn* 'department store'

USAGE

Jiǎ:	*Wǒ jiārén dōu shi lǎoshī: wǒ bà zài dàxué jiāo gōngchéng; mā zài zhōngxué jiāo wùlǐ; mèimei zài xiǎoxué jiāo yīnyuè.*	'My family members are all teachers: Dad teaches engineering in college; Mom teaches physics in middle school; and my younger sister teaches music in an elementary school.'
Yǐ:	*Wǒjiārén dōu shì yīshēng: fùmǔ dōu zài Dì-yī Rénmín Yīyuàn gōngzuò, jiějie zài zhěnsuǒ gōngzuò.*	'My family members are all doctors: my parents both work at Number 1 People's Hospital, and my older sister works in a clinic.'

NOTE

yīshēng / *dàifu* 'doctor'; cf. *yīxué* 'medicine [as a field of study]'

Exercise 5

Provide Chinese sentences with the following information.

1. *Zhōu Shuǎng* works in a travel agency in *Kūnmíng.*
2. *Sū Ruì*, a teacher, works at the Number 6 Elementary School in *Xī'ān.*
3. *Wáng Jié* works in an automobile factory (*qìchēchǎng*) in *Chángchūn.*
4. *Jiāng Táo* is a director in an engineering company in *Zhèngzhōu.*
5. *Jiǎng Zhōngrén* works at the hospital in town.

6.7 Directions

So long as one accepts the fact that asking directions will provide little more than that—a direction—then asking directions can be a good way to engage strangers and confirm that you are at least heading in the right direction. Here are some basic phrases.

wǎng qián zǒu 'keep going straight' ('towards front go')	*wǎng zuǒ guǎi ~ zhuǎn* 'turn left' ('towards left turn')	*yìzhí zǒu* 'walk straight ahead' ('straight go')
cóng zhèi biānr 'this way' ('from this side')	*zài ~ dào⟨le⟩ dì-sān ge lùkǒu⟨r⟩* 'in three blocks' ('at ~ on reaching the 3rd intersection')	*hónglǜdēng* 'traffic light' ('red-green-light')
chēzhàn ⟨de⟩ duìmiàn 'opposite the station' ('station DE opposite')	*guǎi ~ zhuǎn ge wānr jiù dào le* 'just around the corner' ('turn a corner then arrive LE')	*jiù zài yòubiānr* '[it's] on the right' ('then on the right-side')

NOTES

a. *Wǎng* 'toward' (often pronounced *wàng*) is one of a number of directional co-verbs that include *cóng* 'from', *dào* 'to', *zuò* 'by; on', and *xiàng* 'to; toward'. The last is similar in meaning to *wǎng*, and in fact, *xiàng* could substitute for *wǎng* in *wǎng qián zǒu*. *Xiàng* also appears in the second half of the saying *Hǎohǎo xuéxí, tiāntiān xiàng shàng* 'study hard and advance daily.' In this saying, *xiàng shàng* literally means ('toward up').

b. For 'to turn', *guǎi* may be more common in the north, *zhuǎn* in the south.

c. *Duìmiàn* is another in the class of words known as position words; cf. *qiántou*, *zuǒbiānr*. Like them, the reference place precedes the position: *fángzi qiántou* 'in front of the house'; *fángzi duìmiàn* 'opposite the house'.

d. *zhuǎnwān⟨r⟩* 'to turn a corner; to make a turn'

e. *diàotóu* 'to turn around; to make a U-turn'

Xiānsheng, qǐngwèn, dìtiě . . . dìtiězhàn zài nǎlǐ?	'Sir, may I ask where the subway . . . the subway station is?'
Zài hónglǜdēng nàr wǎng zuǒ guǎi, yìzhí zǒu, dìtiězhàn jiù zài yòu biānr.	'Turn left at the light, go straight, and the subway station's on the right.'
Chēzhàn shì bu shi wǎng qián zǒu?	'Is the station this way?'
Shì, yìzhí zǒu, hěn jìn.	'Yes, straight ahead, it's quite close.'

Wángfǔ Dàjiē, wàng yòu zhuǎn!

Qǐngwèn, Tiāntán zěnme zǒu?	'May I ask how you get to the Temple of Heaven?'
Tiāntán . . . wàng nán zǒu, guò liǎng sān ge lùkǒu jiù dào le!	'The Temple of Heaven . . . go south, past two or three intersections and you're there.'
Guòle, guòle. Qǐng diào ge tóu.	'You've passed it; make a U-turn, please.'
Diào ge tóu? Hǎo, kěyǐ.	'Make a U-turn? Okay.'
Zài qiántou, zhuǎn ge wānr, jiù dào le. Hǎo, jiù zhèr. Tíng.	'Ahead, just around the corner. Okay, here. Stop.'

Exercise 6

Give directions, as indicated.

1. Number 5 High School: straight ahead for two blocks, on the left.
2. *Shìjiè Màoyì Zhōngxīn* ('World Trade Center'): turn left at the light, go a couple of blocks, it's opposite the train station.

3. People's Hospital: left at the second light, then it's on the right.
4. *Cháhuā Bīnguǎn* ('Camellia Guesthouse' in Kunming): on *Dōngfāng Dōng Lù*, opposite the stadium; straight ahead, through the next intersection and you're there.
5. Travel Agency: third floor, this way.
6. Meimei Department Store (*Měiměi Bǎihuò*): just around the corner, on *Huáihǎi Zhōng Lù*.

6.8 The *shi-de* construction

Reporting on an event (that has happened) is, under the appropriate conversational conditions, marked by *le*, either at the end of the sentence or directly after the verb. However, with the addition of a phrase designating location, time, or another kind of circumstance, there are two options: the *le* option, and the *shi-de* option. In the latter case, a *de* (written the same way as the possessive *de*, 的) is placed at the end of the sentence, and, optionally, the time or location (the latter always in its pre-verbal position) is highlighted by a preceding *shì* (usually unstressed, and therefore toneless).

le	*Wǒmen zài fēijī shàng chī le.*
shi . . . de	*Wǒmen* ⟨*shi*⟩ *zài fēijī shàng chī de.*

The two options are mutually exclusive: either you choose the *le* or the *shi-de* option, but not both. As noted in the previous section, biographical information can be provided in a matter-of-fact way without *shi-de*: *wǒ chūshēng zài Běijīng, yě zhǎng zài Běijīng*, etc. However, when the focus is more explicitly on the place, time, or other circumstance, then the *shi-de* pattern is required. In a typical context, an event is established with *le* or *guò*, but the follow-up questions utilize *shi-de*.

	Q	A	
(1)	*Nǐ qùguo Zhōngguó ma?*	*Qùguo.*	
	Něi nián qù de?	*Qùnián* ⟨*qù de*⟩.	(focus on when)

	Yí ge rén qù de ma?	*Yí ge rén qù de.*	(focus on with whom)
	Shénme shíhou huílái de?	*Wǔyuèfen huílái de.*	(focus on when)
(2)	*Chīfàn le méiyǒu?*	*Chī le.*	
	Zài jiā lǐ chī de ma?	*Zài cāntīng chī de.*	(focus on where)
	Hǎochī ma?	*Mǎma hūhū.*	

Similarly, when asking when or where someone was born, or where he or she grew up, the focus is not usually on the birth or childhood, which can be taken for granted, but on the time or location. If you ask a couple when or where they met or got married, the focus is particularly on time and place.

Wǒ ⟨shi⟩ 1946 nián shēng de.	'I was born in 1946.'
Wǒ ⟨shi⟩ zài Běijīng shēng de.	'I was born in Beijing.'
Wo yě ⟨shi⟩ zài nàr zhǎngdà de.	'And I grew up there, too.'
Wǒmen ⟨shi⟩ zài Duōlúnduō rènshi de.	'We met in Toronto.'
Wǒ ⟨shi⟩ zài Bālí shàng zhōngxué de.	'I went to high school in Paris.'

NOTES

a. As you may have observed, *zhǎng* and *zhǎngdà* differ in distribution: *zhǎngdà* does not usually occur before *zài*. So, the two patterns are *zài Běijīng zhǎngdà de* and *zhǎng zài Běijīng*.

b. The prototypical cases of the *shi-de* construction involve past events, so it is useful to regard that as a rule. Talking about where you live, for example, does not allow the *shi-de* pattern.

	Wǒ zài Jīntái Lù zhù, lí Hóng Miào hěn jìn.	'I live on Jintai Road, not far from Hong Miao.'
Or:	*Wǒ zhù zài Jīntái Lù, lí Hóng Miào hěn jìn.*	

In some respects, the *shi-de* pattern is similar in function (and to a degree, in form) to the so-called 'cleft construction' of English, which also highlights the circumstances (time, place, etc.) by using the verb 'to be' and the notional equivalent of *de*, 'that'. The English construction, however, is optional (or 'marked'); the Chinese—at least in the situations illustrated—is required.

We met at university.	→	It was at university that we met. *Wǒmen shì zài dàxué rènshi de.*

Notice the stress pattern of the English, with high pitch on 'uniVERsity', and low pitch on 'that we met', which is the part that can be taken for granted.

6.8.1 The position of objects

The position of *de* in the *shi-de* construction is complicated by the presence of an object. As a rule, the *de* of the *shi-de* construction is placed at the end of the sentence, but speakers in the traditional Mandarin-speaking regions of the north and northeast (as opposed to southern speakers, including those in Taiwan) tend to treat objects (that are not pronouns) differently. They place *de* before the object, rather than after it.

Non-northern regions:	*Wǒ* ⟨*shi*⟩ *zài Bālí shàng dàxué de.*	'I went to university in Paris.'
Northern regions:	*Wǒ* ⟨*shi*⟩ *zài Bālí shàng de dàxué.*	
Non-northern regions:	*Tāmen shi něi nián lái Běijīng de?*	'When did they come to Beijing?'
Northern regions:	*Tāmen shi něi nián lái de Běijīng?*	
With a pronoun:	*Wǒ shàng dàxué de shíhou rènshi tā de.*	'I met her when I was at university.'

In *shi-de* sentences, *de* before the object (*shàng de dàxué*) differs from *de* after the object (*shàng dàxué de*) only stylistically (or rhythmically); the two options are otherwise synonymous. The intrusive *de* is written with the same character (的) as the possessive, but does not function the same, though it is possible to construct a written sentence that is potentially ambiguous between the two (in speech, however, intonation is likely to distinguish them).

Attributive:	*Shi [zuótiān mǎi de] piào.*	'[That]'s the ticket we bought yesterday.'
Attributive or *shi-de:*	*Shi zuótiān mǎi de piào.*	
shi-de:	*Shì zuótiān mǎi piào de.*	'[We] bought the ticket yesterday.'

Exercise 7

Provide Chinese equivalents of the following statements.

1. He was born in *Xī'ān* but grew up in *Dàtóng.*
2. My father was born in 1943.
3. He met my mother in *Nánjīng.*
4. She was born in *Zhènjiāng.*
5. He went to college in San Francisco.

6.8.2 *Shi-de* in short

1. It highlights when, where, how, or other circumstances; it is frequent in follow-up questions.
2. It is generally used only when talking about past events.

Past:	*Tā shì qùnián qù de.*
Future:	*Tā 2012 nián dǎsuàn qù Yīngguó kàn Àoyùnhuì.*
Current:	*Tā zài Xī'ān shēng de, kěshì xiànzài zài Běijīng zhù.*

3. The *shi* is optional, but the *de* is required.
4. It generally places attention on a pre-verbal phrase. This means that if there is an option, as with location phrases (which can appear before or after verbs like *shēng* and *zhǎng*), then it is the pre-verbal option that will be selected.

Tā shi zài Běijīng shēng de, zài Běijīng zhǎngdà de, xiànzài yě zài Běijīng zhù.

The only obvious exceptions to the pre-verbal rule are purpose clauses. Recall that purpose usually follows destination in Chinese: *qù Běijīng mǎi dōngxi; dào chéng lǐ qǔ hùzhào qu*. There is no convenient pre-verbal option; yet purpose can be subject to the *shi-de* formula.

Nǐ shi qù mǎi lǐwù de ma?	'Did you go to buy presents?'
Shì, wǒ shi qù mǎi lǐwù de!	'Yes, I went to get some presents.'

Such sentences can be recast with final *qù* (recall the various options with purpose clauses), in which case the sentence looks more like a typical *shi-de* sentence, with *mǎi lǐwù* the focus of *shi*, and *de* following a verb, *qù*.

Nǐ shì mǎi lǐwù qù de ma?	'Did you go to buy presents?'
Shì, wǒ shi mǎi lǐwù qù de.	'Yes, I went to get some presents.'

5. When objects—other than pronouns—are present, *de* can be placed before them.

Wǒ ⟨shi⟩ zài Běijīng shàng dàxué de. ~ zài Běijīng shàng de dàxué.

Exercise 8

Provide a Chinese translation for the following conversation.

'Hello. I'm a student at [. . .]. My parents were born in Guangzhou, but I was born in the United States, in Chicago. I grew up in Chicago, but now, of course, I live in Boston. I have an older sister. She was also born in Guangzhou.'

'When did your parents come to the United States?'

'They came in 1982.'

'Do they still live in Chicago?'

'Yes, they do. They're coming to see me on Saturday.'

6.9 Dialogue: Where are you from?

Jiǎ is a Chinese student who has just met *Yǐ*, an overseas student who has been studying Chinese at *Qīnghuá Dàxué* in Beijing for the past year.

Jiǎ:	*Qǐngwèn, nǐ shi něi guó rén?*	'May I ask your nationality?'
Yǐ:	*Wǒ shi Jiānádà rén.*	'I'm Canadian.'
Jiǎ:	*Kěshì nǐ xiàng ⟨yí⟩ge Zhōngguó rén.*	'But you look like a Chinese.'
Yǐ:	*Wǒ fùqin shì Zhōngguó rén, mǔqin shì Měiguó rén, kěshì wǒ shēng zài Jiānádà. Nǐ qùguo ma?*	'My father's Chinese, my mother's American, but I was born in Canada. Have you been?'
Jiā:	*Méi qùguo, kěshì hěn xiǎng qù. Nǐ shi Jiānádà shénme dìfang rén?*	'I haven't, but I'd love to. Where in Canada are you from?'
Yǐ:	*Duōlúnduō, wǒ shēng zài Duōlúnduō, wǒ yě zhù zài Duōlúnduō.*	'Toronto, I was born in Toronto and I live in Toronto.'
Jiā:	*O, Duōlúnduō, wǒ nàr yǒu qīnqi.*	'Oh, Toronto, I have relatives there.'
Yǐ:	*Shì ma?*	'Really?'
Jiǎ:	*Wǒ tángxiōng zài nàr, shi yīshēng.*	'My cousin [older, father's side] is there—[he]'s a doctor.'
Yǐ:	*Nà, nǐ ne? Nǐ shì Běijīng rén ba?*	'And you, you're from Beijing?'
Jiǎ:	*Bù, wǒ shēng zài Xī'ān, yě zhǎng zài Xī'ān kěshì xiànzài zhù zài Běijīng.*	'No, I was born in Xi'an, and I grew up in Xi'an, but now I live in Beijing.'
Yǐ:	*Nǐ shi něi nián lái de Běijīng?*	'Which year did you come to Beijing?'
Jiā:	*Wǒ shi 1998 nián lái de. Wǒ fùmǔ hái zhù zài Xī'ān.*	'I came in 1998. My parents still live in Xi'an.'
Yǐ:	*Nà nǐ xǐ bù xǐhuan Běijīng?*	'So do you like Beijing?'

Jiā:	*Běijīng bú cuò, kěshì wǒ hěn xiǎng Xī'ān.*	'Beijing's not bad, but I miss Xi'an.'
Yǐ:	*Wǒ qùguo Xī'ān, Xī'ān hěn hǎowánr.*	'I've been to Xi'an, it's a great place to visit.'
Jiā:	*Nǐ shi shénme shíhou qù de?*	'When was it that you went?'
Yǐ:	*Wǒ shi qùnián qù de.*	'I went last year.'
Jiā:	*Xià cì qù, qǐng dào wǒ jiā lái wánrwánr.*	'Next time [you] go, you should come by my house.'
Yǐ:	*O, xièxie, nǐ tài kèqi.*	'Oh, thanks, you're very kind.'

NOTES

a. *tángxiōng* 'elder male cousin (on father's side)'; cf. *tángdì, tángjiě,* and *tángmèi. Táng* is 'a room' (cf. *yì táng kè*), 'the main house', or by extension, 'the clan'. The *táng* cousins all share a surname. The mother's side cousins are all *biǎo,* which means 'surface' or 'outside': *biǎoxiōng, biǎodì, biǎojiě, biǎomèi.*

b. *Qǐng dào wó jiā lái wánr* is a conventional phrase, equivalent to 'you must come by and see us'; often preceded by *yǒu kòng⟨r⟩ [qǐng dào . . .]* '[if] you have some free time . . .'

WÁNR *Wánr* is interesting not only for its pronunciation (one of the few common verbs with the *r* suffix), but also for its meaning. In dictionaries, it is glossed 'to play; to have fun; to play around with', but in many cases an appropriate translation is difficult to find. In the Chinese world, *wánr* is the counterpart of *gōngzuò* 'work'; in English, we sometimes place 'work' and 'play' in opposition as well. A better translation would be 'to have a good time; for some fun'. *Wán⟨r⟩* can also be a verb meaning 'to fool around with [for fun]': *wán diànnǎo* 'to play around with computers', *wán sàichē* 'to enjoy car races'.

Nèi ge dìfang hěn hǎowánr.	'That place is very interesting.'
Yǒu kòng⟨r⟩ qǐng zài lái wánr.	'If you have some time, come by again.'
Zánmen gàn shénme wánr ne?	'What shall we do for fun?'
Dǎ májiàng ba!	'Why don't we play mahjong?'
MIT xuéshēng hěn xǐhuan wánr diànnǎo.	'MIT students love to fool around with computers.'

NOTE

Qǐng zài lái wánr, with *zàijiàn de zài* (再), means 'again'.

Exercise 9

Provide Chinese paraphrases for the following.

1. There are a lot of large cities [*dà chéngshì*] in China.
2. Why are there so many people outside?
3. May I ask where you work?
4. I was born in Tianjin, but I live in Beijing nowadays.
5. When did you leave Tianjin?
6. We're going to Shanghai on the 18th.
7. My father's in Kunming—he's a manager for a computer company.
8. Next time you're in Kunming, please come by my house for a visit.

Write questions that would elicit the following answers.

1. *Wǒmen shì shàngge xīngqīsì lái de.*
2. *Zhōngwén kè, lǐbàiyī dào sì dōu yǒu, lǐbàiwǔ méiyǒu.*
3. *Xiàge yuè wǒ dǎsuàn qù Huángshān kànkan fēngjǐng.* ('scenery')
4. *Lóuxià yǒu diànhuà, lóushàng méiyǒu.*
5. *Wǒ hái méi qùguo, dànshì hěn xiǎng qù.*

6.10 Calling Michael Jordan

6.10.1 *Jiào* with two objects

The familiar verb *jiào* can take two objects and has the meaning 'to call someone something'.

Wǒmen jiào tā Chén lǎoshī.	'We call him Teacher Chen.'
Dàjiā dōu jiào tā lǎo fūzǐ.	'Everyone calls him 'the studious one'.'

Nǐ jiào tā shénme?	'What do you call her?'
Péngyou dōu jiào wǒ xiǎo Míng.	'Friends call me young Ming.'

A more colloquial form of this construction makes use of the verb *guǎn*, whose root meaning (as a verb) is 'to be in charge of'.

Wǒmen guǎn tā jiào lǎoshī.	'We call her 'teacher'.'
Tāmen guǎn tā jiào fàntǒng.	'They call him 'rice bucket'.' (i.e., 'big eater')

6.10.2 Finding out how to address someone

Frequently, when talking to someone with status, it may not be clear what form of address is appropriate. At such times, a direct inquiry will help, using the verb *chēnghu* 'to call or address', or, as is appropriate in this context, 'to be called; to be addressed'.

Jiǎ:	*Qǐngwèn, nín zěnme chēnghu?*	'Excuse me, sir/madam, how should you be addressed?'
Yǐ:	*Nǐmen jiào wǒ Yáng lǎoshī jiù hǎo le.*	'It's fine if you call me Professor Yang.'

6.10.3 Dialogue

People in China will often ask about foreign entertainers and athletes. Here, a Chinese youth (Ch) asks an overseas student (For) about a former American sports star.

Ch:	*Xǐhuan Màikè Qiáodān ma?*	'Do you like Michael Jordan?'
For:	*Shéi / shuí?*	'Who?'
Ch:	*Màikè Qiáodān, dǎ lánqiú de.*	'Michael Jordan, the one who plays basketball.'
For:	*O, ⟨Michael Jordan⟩. Tā de míngzi zěnme shuō? Qǐng zài shuō yí biàn?*	'Oh, Michael Jordan. How do you say his name? Would you mind saying it again?'
Ch:	*Màikè Qiáodān. Wǒmen dōu jiào tā 'Fēirén.'*	'Michael Jordan. We all call him the 'Flying Man'.'

For:	*Fēirén? Shénme yìsi?*	'Feiren? What does [that] mean?'
Ch:	*Zěnme shuō ne . . . tā xiàng niǎo ⟨yíyàng⟩, néng fēi.*	'How to say [it]—he's like the birds, he can fly.'
For:	*Ei, bú cuò. Dànshì tā tuìyì, bù dǎ lánqiú le.*	'Right! But he's retired, he doesn't play basketball anymore.'
Ch:	*Wǒ zhīdào, búguò tā háishi zuì bàng de!*	'I know, but he's still the best.'

NOTES

a. *dǎ lánqiú de* ('hit basketball one'); that is, 'the one who plays basketball'

b. *fēirén* ('flying-man'); Michael Jordan was also called *lánqiú-dàdì* ('basketball-great-emperor') in China. Other nicknames: Shaquille O'Neal was called *Shāyú* 'shark' (based on Shaq, of course); Kobe Bryant is mostly just called *Kēbǐ*.

c. *niǎo* 'bird'; alternatively, *tā xiàng fēijī* 'he's like an airplane'

d. *tuìyì* 'to leave [military] service', used here in the sense of 'to leave the profession'

This is a good time to mention some Chinese sports figures who are well known on the international stage.

NAME	SPORT, EPITHET	GENDER	ERA
Yáo Míng	*lánqiú yùndòngyuán (Xiūsīdùn Huǒjiàn)*	*nán*	current
Zhuāng Zédòng	*pīngpāngqiú guànjūn*	*nán*	late 1950s, early 1960s
Láng Píng	*páiqiú guànjūn*, known as *Tiělángtou*	*nǚ*	1980s
Chén Féidé	*wǎngqiú guànjūn*	*nán*	1990s
Liú Xiáng	*kuàlán xuǎnshǒu*	*nán*	current
Lǐ Nà	*wǎngqiú yùndòngyuán*	*nǚ*	current
Guō Jīngjīng	*tiàoshuǐ yùndòngyuán*, known as *Tiàoshuǐ Huánghòu*	*nǚ*	current
Fú Míngxiá	*tiàoshuǐ yùndòngyuán*	*nǚ*	current

NOTES

a. The terms *yùndòngyuán* 'athlete' and *xuǎnshǒu* 'contestant; athlete' ('select-hand') can be applied to everyone in the chart. Those who have won consistently have earned the epithet *guànjūn* 'champion' ('crown-troops') or *míngxīng* 'star' ('bright-star').

b. *Láng Píng* was known as the *Tiělángtou* ('iron-hammer') and *Guō Jīngjīng* has been called the *Tiàoshuǐ Huánghòu* ('diving-queen').

c. *Chén Féidé*; in English, Michael Chang

d. *kuàlán* 'to hurdle' ('cross-hurdle')

6.10.4 *Yíyàng* 'the same'

As observed in the previous dialogue, *xiàng* 'to resemble' is optionally followed by the expression *yíyàng* 'the same' ('one-kind') (cf. *jiu zhèi yàng⟨r⟩ ba, zěnmeyàng,* and a host of other phrases that make use of the root *yàng*). *Yíyàng* can be used independently of *xiàng*, with items to be matched connected by conjunctions such as *gēn* or *hé*.

Tā gēn wǒ yíyàng: wǒmen dōu shi yì niánjí de xuéshēng.	'He's like me: we're both first-year students.'
Tā hé wǒ yíyàng: dōu shì dúshēngzǐ.	'He's just like me: we're both only children.'
Nà nǐ shuō de hé tā shuō de bù yíyàng.	'Now, what you are saying isn't the same as what he's saying.'
Yí cì de cì hé yì huí de huí, yìsi chàbuduō yíyàng.	'The *cì* of *yí cì* and the *huí* of *yì huí* have roughly the same meaning.'
Guō Jīngjīng hé Fú Míngxiá bú shì yíyàng yǒumíng ma? Nà, zěnme zhǐ yǒu Guō Jīngjīng cái jiào 'huánghòu' ne?	'Aren't Guo Jingjing and Fu Mingxia equally well known? How come only Guo Jingjing is called 'the queen', then?'

NOTES

a. Observe the order of elements in the penultimate example: Topic (*yí cì de cì hé yì huí de huí*) followed by a comment (*yìsi chàbuduō yíyàng*). *Yìsi*—acting as the inner subject—narrows the scope of *yíyàng*.

b. Note the option of placing an SV after *yíyàng*: *yíyàng cōngmíng* 'equally intelligent', *yíyàng fāngbiàn* 'equally convenient'.

Exercise 10

Provide Chinese paraphrases for the following sentences.

1. He's very strict, so we call him 'the boss'.
2. She's my mother's sister, so we call her 'auntie'.
3. Because Mr. Chen's a director, people call his wife 'Madam' Chen.
4. Because he's rather old, we call him *lǎodàye*.
5. Although [*suīrán*] she's not a teacher, we still call her Professor Liao.
6. Excuse me, may I ask how we should address you? / It's okay to call me *Liáng Àimín* or Professor *Liáng*.
7. Their names are the same: they're both called *Lín Měi*.
8. They live in the same place.

6.11 Food (3)

Chinese dishes are variously named. Some are descriptive: *chǎojīdīng* ('stir-fried-chicken-cubes'); *zhàcài-ròusī-tāng* ('pickled-cabbage meat-shreds soup'). Others incorporate proper names: *Yángzhōu-chǎofàn* ('Yangzhou fried rice'), named after *Yángzhōu*, a city on the north shore of the Yangtze, east of Nanjing. Numbers are also common: *shāo'èrdōng* ('cooked-two-winters'), which are usually *dōnggū* 'winter mushrooms' and *dōngsǔn* 'winter bamboo shoots'. Finally, there are dishes with poetic or allusive names: *gǒubulǐ bāozi* ('dog-not-obey steamed buns'), a Tianjin specialty. Listed below are some other examples that can be practiced by repetition and incorporated into previous dialogues dealing with food.

máogū jīpiàn	('hairy-mushroom chicken-slices'), often listed on menus by its Cantonese name, *moogoo gaipan*.
tángcùyú	'sweet and sour fish' ('sugar-vinegar-fish')
Běijīng kǎoyā	'Peking duck'
Dōngpōròu	a rich pork dish, associated with the Song dynasty poet and statesman *Sū Dōngpō* [also named *Sū Shì*]

Qǐng zài lái ge mǎyǐ-shàngshù!

sānxiān-tāng	('three-fresh soup'); a soup with three fresh items, such as shredded pork, bamboo shoots, and chicken
máyǐ shàngshù	('ants climb-tree'); spicy ground beef sauce poured over deep fried 'beanthread' noodles; named for the small bumps that appear on the noodles
mápo dòufu	'hot and spicy bean curd'; a Sichuan dish with cubes of bean curd, minced pork, and spicy sauce
jiācháng dòufu tāng	'home-cooked bean curd soup'
zhūgān⟨r⟩tāng	'pig liver soup'

6.12 Summary

Opposites	*Cháng de xiāngfǎn shi duǎn.*
Descriptions	*Tā rén hěn hǎo, jiùshì yǒu diǎnr hàixiū.*
	Tā tóufa shi hēisè de.—Tā shi hēi tóufa.
	Tā zhǎng+de hěn piàoliang.
V-*guò*	*Tā cónglái méi qùguo Zhōngguó.*
	Nǐ chīguo gǒubulǐ bāozi ma?

SV+repeated syllable	*Húaliūliū de.*
Indefinite *shénme*	*Méi shénme wèidào.*
Times	*Wǒ yǐjīng jiànguo tā jǐ cì.*
	Qǐng zài shuō yí biàn.
When	*Shàngkè de shíhou bù yīnggāi shuō Yīngwén.*
Before	*Shuìjiào yǐqián bù yīnggāi zuò yùndòng.*
After	*Míngcháo yǐhòu shi Qīngcháo.*
When?	*Nǐ shénme shíhou néng qù qǔ hùzhào?*
No time	*Wǒmen méiyǒu shíjiān zuòfàn.*
Place of work	*Nǐ zài něi ge dānwèi gōngzuò?*
	Wǒ bàba zài dì-èr Rénmín Yīyuàn gōngzuò.
Directions	*Wǎng qián zǒu, dào dì-yī ge lùkǒu wǎng zuǒ zhuǎn.*
	Qǐngwèn, dìtiězhàn zěnme zǒu? (Zěnme qù dìtiězhàn?)
Shi . . . de	*Wǒ shì zài 1976 nián shēng de.*
	Tā zài Běijīng shēng de, zài Běijīng zhǎngdà de, yě zài Běijīng zhù.
	Nǐ shì něi nián lái de Běijīng?
Call me X	*Péngyou dōu jiào wǒ xiǎo Míng.*
How to address you?	*Nín zěnme chēnghu?*
The same	*Tā gēn wǒ yíyàng, dōu shì xué wùlǐ de.*

Exercise 11

Distinguish the following words (or compound parts) by using each in a short phrase that reveals its meaning.

yǐjīng	*jīngcháng*	*céngjīng*	*xiāngfǎn*	*yíyàng*	*kù*
cónglái	*huílái*	*méi lái*	*hěn guāi*	*sān kuài*	*kǔ*
yīnwèi	*yǐnliào*	*wèidào*	*jiào*	*qiáo*	*jiāo*
gōngsī	*gōngkè*	*gōngzuò*	*kǎoshì*	*gànhuór*	*biàn*

zhù	*qù*	*qǔ*	*yòu*	*yǒu*	*shíjiān*
zhǎng	*Zhāng*	*cháng*	*chàng*	*shàng*	*shíhou*
shòu	*shuō*	*shǒu*	*zuò*	*zuǒ*	*zǒu*

6.13 Rhymes and rhythms

Here is another *shùnkǒuliū*. This one was overheard at a meeting; again, no one wished to go on record, so it is cited anonymously—*yìmíng de* ('lost-name').

Néng hē yì jīn, hē bā liǎng:	('Can drink one jin [but] drinks eight ounces:')
duìbuqǐ rénmín,	('apologies to the people,')
duìbuqǐ dǎng.	('apologies to the party.')
Néng hē bā liǎng, hē yì jīn:	('Can drink eight ounces [but] drinks one jin:')
rénmín hé dǎng	('people and party,')
xīnliánxīn.	('heart-linked to-heart.')

NOTE

Recall that *jīn* is a Chinese measure equal to 1/2 a kilogram; a traditional *jīn* contains 16 *liǎng* 'ounces'. *Rénmín* are 'the people' and *dǎng* is 'the [Communist] Party'. *Xīn* is 'heart; feelings'.

Finally, something in the genre of animal adventure:

Chóng, chóng chóng, chóng

Chóng, chóng chóng, chóng fēi,	('insects . . . fly')
fēidào Nánshān hē lùshuǐ;	('fly-to South Mountain to+drink dew')
lùshuǐ hēbǎo le,	('dew drink-full LE')
huítóu jiù pǎo le!	('turn-head then run LE')

Newspaper kiosk, *Kūnmíng*.

Appendix: Chinese historical periods

Dates follow Wilkinson, 2000, pp. 10–12.

DYNASTY	PINYIN	DATES	NOTES
夏朝	*Xiàcháo* 'Xia Kingdom'	Before 1554 BCE	*Dà Yŭ* 'Great Yu', who controlled the floods
商朝	*Shāngcháo* 'Shang Dynasty'	1600–1045 BCE	*Shāng Tāng*, founder
周朝	*Zhōucháo* 'Zhou Dynasty'	1046–256 BCE	*Zhōu Gōng* 'Duke of Chou'

DYNASTY	PINYIN	DATES	NOTES
春秋	*Chūnqiū Shídài* 'Spring and Autumn Period'	770–476 BCE	*Kǒngzǐ* 'Confucius'
戰國	*Zhànguó Shídài* 'Warring States Period'	475–221 BCE	*Mèngzǐ* 'Mencius'
秦朝	*Qíncháo* 'Qin Dynasty'	221–207 BCE	*Qínshǐhuáng*, first emperor of Qin, unified a central China
漢朝	*Hàncháo* 'Han Dynasty'	202 BC–220 CE	*Liú Bāng*, founder *Hàn Gāodì* 'Great Emperor of Han'
三國	*Sānguó Shídài* 'Three Kingdoms'	220–280	*Cáo Cāo*, ruler of *Wèi* (north) *Zhū Gěliàng*, ruler of *Shǔ* (west)
隋朝	*Suícháo* 'Sui Dynasty'	581–618	*Suí Wéndì*, first emperor
唐朝	*Tángcháo* 'Tang Dynasty'	618–907	*Táng Tàizōng / Lǐ Shìmín*, first emperor
宋朝	*Sòngcháo* 'Song Dynasty'	960–1279	*Sòng Tàizǔ / Zhào Kuàngyīn*

DYNASTY	PINYIN	DATES	NOTES
元朝	*Yuáncháo* 'Yuan Dynasty'	1279–1368	*Yuán Tàizǔ / Chéngjí Sīhàn* (Mongol dynasty)
明朝	*Míngcháo* 'Ming Dynasty'	1368–1644	*Míng Tàizǔ / Zhū Yuánzhāng*
清朝	*Qīngcháo* 'Qing Dynasty'	1644–1912	*Kāngxī*, emperor from 1661 to 1722; *Qiánlóng*, emperor from 1736 to 1795
中華民國	*Zhōnghuá Mínguó* 'The Republic of China'	1912–	*Sūn Zhōngshān / Sūn Yìxiān* 'Sun Yat-sen', founder
中華人民共和國	*Zhōnghuá Rénmín Gònghéguó* 'The People's Republic of China'	1949–	*Máo Zédōng*, founder

Unit 7

Mǎn zhāo sǔn, qiān shòu yì.
'Pride incurs loss, humility reaps benefit.'
—Traditional saying, in Classical Chinese

For a learner, three ideal topics of conversation are food, language, and weather: food, because it is such a central part of Chinese social life; language, because it is so central to you, the learner, and because, like cuisine, it is a rich and entertaining subject; and weather, because it is pervasive yet circumscribed, and so relatively easy to talk about. In light of this, Unit 7 provides the linguistic basis for talking about language and weather. It also elaborates on a linguistic topic that has been touched upon earlier, that of verb combinations of the sort seen in *tīngdǒng* or *chībuguàn*. This is a complex topic that will be introduced incrementally. You will also learn ways to talk about duration ('for how long'), a topic that incorporates *le* patterns, and about means of travel ('alone'; 'by train'), a topic that incorporates the *shi-de* pattern. Finally, there are the usual jingles and rhymes, asides and annotations, and a long narrative in the form of a letter home.

Contents

7.1 Verb combos (1)

In Chinese, verbs often come in pairs, with the second verb completing or otherwise elaborating on the meaning of the first. Since such pairs are going to be a subject of prominence, we give them the catchy label of 'verb combos'. We will call the second verb of the pair by its traditional label of a 'verb complement'.

One particularly productive category of verb combos involves an action and a result: *tīngdǒng* ('listen-comprehend') → 'to understand [something heard]'; *kànjiàn* ('look-perceive') → 'to see'; *zuòwán* ('do-complete') → 'to finish doing'; *chībǎo* ('eat-full') → 'to eat one's fill'; *kàncuò* ('look-mistake') → 'to misread'; *dǎsǐ* ('hit-die') → 'to beat to death'. Such pairings often produce a cascade of relatable meanings, many of them expressed as independent verbs in English. Here, for example, are combinations based on *kàn* 'to see': *kàndào* 'to manage to see', *kàncuò* 'to mistake [something seen]', *kànjiàn* 'to see', *kàndǒng* 'to understand [visually]', *kànguàn* 'to be used to seeing', *kànwán* 'to finish reading', etc. Associated nouns (that, in English terms, would be called objects) often appear before the verbs: *Dì-liù kè yǐjīng xuéwán le.* '[We]'ve already finished studying Unit 6.'

Action-result verb combos have an important feature, one which has already been encountered in earlier units. With the insertion of positive *de* (得) or negative *bù*, they can be turned into 'potential verb combos', which convey the possibility or impossibility of the result.

Rìyǔ nǐ tīngdedǒng ma?	'Do you understand Japanese?'
Wǒ tīngbudǒng.	'No, I don't.'

You may wonder what the potential combo adds that is lacking in constructions with the verb *néng* 'to be able', which is already available. In fact, *néng* may appear, redundantly, with potential verb combos: *Néng tīngdedǒng ma? / Néng tīngdǒng yìdiǎnr.* However, while *néng* is common with single verbs (*bù néng qù*), the potential pattern is preferred for verb combos.

A few dozen verbs are particularly common as second members of verb combos, and some of these are very versatile–able to follow large numbers of verbs. *Wán*, for example, with the general meaning of 'to finish', combines with most action verbs to mean 'to finish V-ing': *zuòwán, xiěwán, shuōwán, dǎwán, chīwán, kǎowán, bànwán, tīngwán*, etc. Since verb combos are a large topic, they will be introduced incrementally. In this unit, we will introduce some 'phase complements', such as *wán* 'to finish', and some directional complements, such as *jìnlái* 'to come in [here]'.

7.1.1 Imminence

First, a short digression to take up the expression of imminence that will prove useful as a response to verb combos with *wán* 'to finish'. In China, when a train approaches a scheduled station stop, you are likely to hear the staff shout out the name of the place, followed by *kuài* ⟨*yào*⟩ *dào le* ('quick ⟨will⟩ arrive LE'): *Shíjiāzhuāng kuài* ⟨*yào*⟩ *dào le!* 'Almost at Shijiazhuang [in Hebei]!' The combination of *kuài* or *kuài yào* with a final *le* conveys the notion of 'about to; soon; almost'.

Kuài xiàkè le!	'Class is almost done!'
Kuài yào shàngxué le.	'School is about to begin.'

Tā kuài sānshí suì le.	'She's almost 30.'
Kuài sān diǎn le.	'It's almost 3 o'clock.'

7.1.2 Phase complements

The following examples contain verb combos in the potential form only when they are particularly apt. The topic of potential verb combos will be taken up again in the next unit.

A. *WÁN* *Wán* (完), as noted above, may combine with most activity verbs to mean 'to finish doing [something]'.

Jīntiān de bào yǐjīng kànwán le ma?	'Have you finished today's paper?'
Kànwán le.	'Yes, I have.'
Gōngkè yǐjīng zuòwán le méiyǒu?	'Have [you] finished [your] homework?'
Hái zài zuò ne.	'I'm still doing [it].'
Nǐmen kǎowán le méiyǒu?	'Are you done with the exam?'
Kuài kǎowán le.	'Almost.'
Shuōwán le méiyǒu?	'Has [he] finished talking?'
Hái méi ne, hái yǒu yí jù huà!	'Not yet, one more sentence!'
Dǎwán le ma?	'Are you done [with the phone]?'
Méiyǒu, hái méi dǎwán.	'Not yet, I'm still talking.'

B. *DÀO* *Dào*, with verbs that involve locomotion, introduces a destination: *bān dào* 'to move to'; *zǒu dào* 'to walk to'; *kāi dào* 'to drive to' (cf. §5.9.3). With other verbs, however, *dào* has the meaning of 'to succeed in; to manage to'.

Xiézi, wǒ yǐjīng mǎidào le.	'I've already purchased the shoes.'
Yào duōshao qián?	'How much were they?'
Nǐ yào wǒ zuò de, wǒ yídìng huì zuòdào.	'What you want me to do, I can certainly manage to do.'

Nǐ shàng cì yě shi zhème shuō.	'You said that last time.'
Kěshì zhèi cì yídìng zuòdedào!	'But this time I'll do it for sure!'
Zuótiān méi kàndào tā.	'I didn't see her yesterday.'
Tā shì bu shi yǐjīng zǒu le?	'Is it the case that she's left already?'
Zhǎodào le méiyǒu?	'Did [you] find [it]?'
Hái zài zhǎo ne.	'[I]'m still looking.'
Shuōdào zuòdào!	'No sooner said than done!'

C. *ZHÁO* The root meaning of *zháo* is 'to touch; to reach'. As a verb complement, it has a meaning very similar to that of *dào*; that is, 'to succeed in; to manage to', and in fact, with many verbs, *dào* often substitutes for it.

Hùzhào zhǎozháo ~ zhǎodào le ma?	'Did you manage to find [your] passport?'
Zhǎozháo ~ zhǎodào le. Xiètiān xièdì!	'I did–thank god!'
Zài Měiguó mǎidezháo ~ mǎidedào hǎishēn ma?	'Can you buy sea cucumbers in the United States?'
Yěxǔ zài Tāngrénjiē néng mǎidezháo ~ mǎidedào.	'I guess you can in Chinatown.'
Zuótiān wǎnshàng hěn rè, wǒ shuìbuzháo jiào.	'It was hot last night, I couldn't sleep.'
Nǐ yǒu méiyǒu kōngtiáo?	'Do you have air-conditioning?'

D. *HǍO* *Hǎo*, like *wán*, indicates completion, but as the core meaning of 'to be well' suggests, it has an added sense of 'properly; adequately; ready'.

Fàn yǐjīng zuòhǎo le.	'The food's ready.'
Hǎo, wǒmen lái le!	'Okay, we're on our way!'
Zuótiān wǎnshàng wǒ méi shuìhǎo.	'I didn't sleep well last night.'
Nà nǐ yīnggāi qù xiūxi xiūxi.	'Well, you should go and rest.'

Gōngkè zuòhǎo le méiyǒu?	'Have you done your homework properly?'
Chàbuduō le!	'Just about!'
Nǐ xiézi chuānhǎo le ma?	'Have you got your shoes on?'
Wǒ chuānbuhǎo.	'I can't get them on [properly].'

E. *BǍO* *Bǎo*, 'to be full', is found mainly with the verbs *chī* and *hē*. At the end of a meal (and sometimes in passing, as a greeting), Chinese will ask you if you've eaten enough; the answer is always positive, of course.

Nǐ chībǎo le ma?	'Have you had enough?'
Chībǎo le, xièxie.	'Yes, thanks.'

F. *CUÒ* *Cuò*, as a complement, indicates 'mistakenly': *kàncuò, tīngcuò, xiěcuò, dǎcuò*.

Nǐ nèi ge zì xiěcuò le.	'You've written that character incorrectly.'
Nà, yīnggāi zěnme xiě ne?	'So how should it be written?'
Ò, duìbuqǐ, wǒ rèncuò rén le; wǒ yǐwéi nǐ shi wǒ de yí ge tóngxué.	'Oh, sorry, I mistook you [for someone else]; I thought you were a friend of mine.'
Méi guānxi.	'No matter.'

NOTES

a. *Rènshi* is reduced to *rèn* in verb combos: *rèncuò*.

b. *yǐwéi* 'take to be the case; to think [mistakenly] that'; contrast with *xiǎng*

7.1.3 Motion verbs

Verbs of directed motion, such as *shàng* 'to move up', *xià* 'to move down', *jìn* 'to enter', *chū* 'to exit', *guò* 'to cross over', and *huí* 'to return', combine with [usually] untoned *lái* 'to come' or *qù* 'to go' to indicate direction toward or away from the speaker, respectively.

shàng	*shànglái*	'come up [here]'
	shàngqù	'go up [there]'
xià	*xiàlái*	'come down [here]'
	xiàqù	'go down [there]'
jìn	*jìnlái*	'come in [here]'
	jìnqù	'go in [there]'
chū	*chūlái*	'come out [here]'
	chūqù	'go out [there]'
guò	*guòlái*	'come over [here]'
	guòqù	'go over [there]'
huí	*huílái*	'come back [here]'
	huíqù	'go back [there]'

At this point, we will keep the contexts very simple and focus on getting used to the combinations. In some of the following examples, note the use of the final particles *a* and *ba* to signal heartiness and a suggestion, respectively.

IN THE ELEVATOR

Shàngqù a! Liù lóu.	'Up we go! Sixth floor.'
Xiàqù a! Yī lóu.	'Down we go! First floor.'

LOOKING DOWN THE STAIRS

Shànglái ba.	'Come on up [here].'
Xiàqù ba.	'Go on down [there].'

LOOKING UP THE STAIRS

Xiàlái a.	'Come on down [here].'
Shàngqù a!	'Go on up [there]!'

NOTE

Except in Hong Kong, where the first floor is the one above the ground floor (following British practice), *yīlóu* is the entrance floor in China. Basements are very rare in China, but if they do exist, they are usually called *dìxiàshì* ('ground-below-room'); cf. *jiàoshì* 'classroom' and *bàngōngshì* 'office'.

IN THE ROOM

Jìnlái ba?	'Why don't you come in?'
Chūqù ba?	'Why don't you go out?'

OUTSIDE THE ROOM

Jìnqù ba?	'Why don't you go in?'
Chūlái ba?	'Why don't you come out?'
Guòlái ba.	'Come on over [here].'
Guòqù ba.	'Go on over [there].'

7.1.4 Returning

Nǐ shi shénme shíhou qù de?	'When did you go [there]?'
Bāyuèfen qù de.	'In August.'
Shénme shíhou huílái de?	'When did [you] come back?'
Shíyīyuè.	'November.'
Wǒmen lǐbàiyī dǎsuàn qù Sūzhōu, lǐbài'èr huílái.	'We're planning to go to Suzhou on Monday, [and we'll] be back on Tuesday.'
Tāmen shi 1991 nián lái de, 1995 nián huíqù de.	'They came in 1991 and went back in 1995.'
Nǐ huíqùguo ma?	'Have you [ever] been back [there]?'
Tā shíbā suì lái de Měiguó, cóng méi huíqùguo.	'She came to the U.S. at 18, and she's never been back since.'

When a place other than 'home' is mentioned, it is usually placed after *huí* and before *lái* or *qù*.

Nǐ shénme shíhou huí sùshè qù?	'When are you going back to the dorm?
Nǐ shénme shíhou huí Běijīng lái?	When are you coming back to Beijing?

Return home, however, is expressed as *huíjiā*.

Jīntiān jǐdiǎn huíjiā?	'When are [you] going home today?'
Dàgài sān sì diǎn, xiàle kè yǐhòu.	'About 3 or 4 o'clock, after [I] get out of class.'

Exercise 1

Use appropriate gestures as you ask people to 'take a look'.

1. *Qǐng guòlai kànkan ba.*
   Guòqu kànkan ba.
2. *Qǐng shànglai kànkan ba.*
   Shàngqu kànkan ba.
3. *Qǐng xiàlai kànkan ba.*
   Xiàqu kànkan ba.
4. *Qǐng jìnlai kànkan ba.*
   Jìnqu kànkan ba.
5. *Qǐng chūlai kànkan ba.*
   Chūqu kànkan ba.
6. *Qǐng huílai kànkan ba.*
   Huíqu kànkan ba.

7.2 Connecting sentences

In earlier units, you encountered a category of words, called conjunctions, that indicate logical relations between clauses. Examples include *kěshì, dànshì, yīnwèi*, and *suǒyǐ*.

Wǒmen bù néng xiūxi, yīnwèi hái yǒu hěn duō gōngkè.	'We can't rest because we still have lots of homework.'

When the subordinate clause (that is, the *yīnwèi* clause) is placed first, the logical connection is often marked in the second clause as well (generally by another conjunction, but also by adverbs). Section 7.2 examines three such sets of paired connectors.

7.2.1 *Yīnwèi* 'because'

Yīnwèi is paired with *suǒyǐ*, the latter meaning 'so' or 'therefore' but often better left untranslated in English. In Chinese (unlike English), when only one of the two connectors is present, it is more likely to be the second–*suǒyǐ* rather than *yīnwèi*.

⟨Yīnwèi⟩ tiānqì hěn rè, suǒyǐ wǒmen dōu hěn lèi.	'Because the weather's hot, we're all quite tired.'
⟨Yīnwèi⟩ xiàxuě, suǒyǐ Wèi lǎoshī bù néng huílai.	'Professor Wei can't get back because it's snowing.'

Generally, conjunctions like *yīnwèi* and *suǒyǐ* precede the subject (*yīnwèi tiānqì . . .*); but when a single subject persists through the sentence, that is, when the rest of the sentence acts as a comment on the initial topic, then the subject may precede *yīnwèi*.

Tāmen yīnwèi qián bú gòu, suǒyǐ bù néng mǎi hěn duō dōngxi.	'They can't buy a lot of things because they don't have enough money.'

7.2.2 *Suīrán* 'although'

Roughly the same conditions apply to *suīrán . . . kěshì/dànshì* 'although . . . but'. Again, while English requires only the single conjunction 'although', Chinese often omits *suīrán*, leaving the only explicit signal in the second clause.

⟨Suīrán⟩ fùmǔ shì Zhōngguó rén, dànshì tā méi qùguo Zhōngguó.	'Although her parents are Chinese, she hasn't been to China.'
Suīrán dōngxi dōu hěn guì, kěshì nǐ kàn, háishi yǒu hěn duō rén yào mǎi.	'Although everything's expensive [there], there are still lots of people buying, as you can see.'
Tā suīrán gèzi bù gāo, kěshì tā lánqiú dǎ+de bú cuò.	'Although he's not tall, he's quite good at basketball.'

7.2.3 *Yàoshì* 'if'

The pair *yàoshì* ~ *rúguǒ* . . . *jiù* 'if . . . then' is a little different from the previous two pairs. In the first place, *jiù* is an adverb and, unlike *suǒyǐ* or *kěshì*, it must be placed directly before a verb (or another adverb). In addition, *jiù* (often toneless) is more likely to be omitted (with slight change of nuance) than *yàoshì* (or *rúguǒ*).

Yàoshì qián bú gòu, nǐmen jiù yòng xìnyòngkǎ.	'If [you] don't have enough money [cash], you can use a credit card.'
Nǐ yàoshì méi diànnǎo, kěyǐ qù wǎngbā fā e-mail.	'If you don't have a computer, [you] can go to an Internet café to send e-mail.'

NOTES

a. *gòu* 'be enough'; *qián bú gòu* 'not enough money'; *gòu le, gòu le* 'that's enough–fine'

b. *xìnyòngkǎ* 'credit card'

c. *diànnǎo* 'computer' ('electric-brain'); also *jìsuànjī* 'calculator; computer' ('compute-machine')

d. *wǎngbā* 'Internet café' ('net-bar'); cf. *shàngwǎng* 'access the Internet'

e. *fā e-mail* 'send e-mail'

Rúguǒ is a slightly more formal alternative to *yàoshì*.

Rúguǒ nǐ bù xiǎng qù, nà wǒ yě bù xiǎng qù.	'If you don't want to go, then I don't want to go either.'

Both *yàoshì* and *rúguǒ* can be buttressed by the phrase *de huà*, placed at the end of the clause (the *huà* of *shuōhuà*). The notion behind *de huà* is similar to English 'let's say', or simply 'say', used as a conditional in sentences such as 'say it rains . . . then we meet inside'.

Yàoshì nǐ yǒu diànnǎo de huà, wǒ zhèlǐ yǒu Zhōngwén ruǎnjiàn.	'If you [happen to] have a computer, I have some Chinese software here.'
Bù néng qù de huà, jiù dǎ ge diànhuà ba?	'If [by chance] [you] can't go, then phone, okay?'

Connecting clauses

⟨*yīnwèi*⟩	*suǒyǐ*	'because . . .'
⟨*suīrán*⟩	*kěshì* *dànshì* *búguò*	'although . . .'
yàoshi . . . ⟨*de huà*⟩	⟨*jiù*⟩	'if . . .'
rúguǒ . . . ⟨*de huà*⟩	⟨*jiù*⟩	

Exercise 2

Choose a pair of words to conjoin the following sentences.

1. *Màikè Qiáodān shi ge dǎlánqiú de. Tā bù zěnme ('so') gāo.*
2. *Tā hěn lèi. Tā bù néng gōngzuò.*
3. *Tā bú ràng* ('let') *wǒ kàn diànshì. Wǒ bú ràng tā tīng yīnyuè.*
4. *Zhōngwén kè hěn nán. Zhōngwén kè hěn yǒuyìsi.*
5. *Xuéshēng hěn duō. Lǎoshī hěn gāoxìng.*
6. *Méiyǒu bīngxiāng* ('icebox'). *Bù néng mǎi bīngqílín.*
7. *Tā shi zài Zhōngguó shēng de, zài Zhōngguó zhǎngdà de. Tā chībuguàn Zhōngguó cài.*
8. *Tā zài Hélán de shíhou cháng chī Zhōngguó cài. Tā chīdeguàn Zhōngguó cài.*
9. *Tā měitiān zǎoshàng dōu hē kāfēi. Tā háishi zǒng xiǎng shuìjiào.*

7.2.4 If . . .

The following conversation is, obviously, rather tongue-in-cheek, but it does give you a chance to practice 'conditionals'. *Jiǎ* is the straightman, *Yǐ* is the joker!

Jiǎ:	*Wǒmen mǎi yì tǒng bīngqílín, hǎo bu hǎo?*	'Let's buy a carton of ice cream, okay?'
Yǐ:	*Nà bù xíng!*	'No, we can't do that!'

	Yàoshì mǎi bīngqílín, wǒmen jiù méi qián mǎi cài le!	'If [we] buy ice cream, [we] won't have any money to buy food!'
	⟨Yàoshì⟩ méi qián mǎi cài jiù méi dōngxi chī ⟨le⟩.	'If [we] don't have money for food, [we] won't have anything to eat.'
	⟨Yàoshì⟩ méi dōngxi chī, wǒmen jiù méiyǒu jìnr ⟨le⟩.	'If [we] don't have anything to eat, we won't have any energy.'
	⟨Yàoshì⟩ méiyǒu jìnr, wǒmen jiù bù néng gōngzuò ⟨le⟩.	'If [we] don't have any energy, we won't be able to work.'
	⟨Yàoshì⟩ bù néng gōngzuò, jiù gèng méi qián le!	'If [we] can't work, [we'll] have even less money!'
Jiǎ:	*Dé le, dé le; nǐ bié shuō le–méiwán-méiliǎo.*	'Enough already! Don't say anymore–it's endless.'

NOTES

a. *Yàoshì* (or *rúguǒ*) may be omitted once the pattern is established. Similarly, once the pattern with 'new situation' *le* is established (*jiù méi qián mǎi cài le*), *le* might not reappear until the culminating sentence (*gèng méi qián le*).

b. *méiyǒu jìnr* or *méiyǒu jīngshén* 'without vigor, energy'; cf. *hěn yǒushén* 'lively'

c. *dé le*; This is the *dé* seen in the beginning of the multiplication table (*yī sān dé sān*, etc.), where it means 'to get'; *dé le*, then, means '[I]'ve got [it]', and by implication, '[That]'ll do'.

d. *méiwán-méiliǎo* ('not-finished not-complete')

7.3 Speaking languages

Language names are, for the most part, formed by the addition of bound nouns (such as *huà* 'words; talk; language' or *yǔ* 'language') to country names, or to the first syllable of country names: *Rìběn* → *Rìběnhuà*; *Rìběn* → *Rìyǔ*. General terms for 'foreign language' are formed in the same way.

wàiguóhuà	'foreign [spoken] languages'
wàiyǔ	'foreign languages'; *biéde wàiyǔ* 'other foreign languages'

7.3.1 Forms with *huà*

Huà 'speech' combines with full country names to form names of languages. These terms refer to the spoken language, typically forming objects of verbs such as *shuō* and *jiăng* 'to speak'.

Rìběnhuà	'Japanese'	*Yìdàlìhuà*	'Italian'	*Yìnníhuà*	'Indonesian'
Făguóhuà	'French'	*Tàiguóhuà*	'Thai'	*Yuènánhuà*	'Vietnamese'
Déguóhuà	'German'	*Yìndùhuà*	'Hindi'	*Miăndiànhuà*	'Burmese'

7.3.2 Compounds with *wén*

Wén 'written language', or 'language' in general, combines with either the first syllable of country names that end in *guó* (*Zhōngguó* → *Zhōngwén*), or with the full name of transliterated names (*Yìdàlì* → *Yìdàlìwén*) to form names of languages. The *wén* forms occur as objects to verbs such as *xué* 'to study', as well as with speaking verbs, such as *shuō* and *jiăng*.

Rìwén	'Japanese'	*Yìdàlìwén*	'Italian'
Făwén	'French'	*Hánwén*	'Korean'
Déwén	'German'	*Yìnníwén*	'Indonesian'
Yīngwén	'English'	*Zhōngwén*	'Chinese'

Not all languages have a version with *wén*; there is no word 'Tàiwén' for Thai, for example, nor 'Yuènánwén' for Vietnamese. In these cases, the *yŭ* forms are used.

7.3.3 Forms with *yŭ*

The addition of *yŭ* (from *yŭyán* 'language') to the first syllable of country names with *guó* (*Făguó* → *Făyŭ*), to historical names (*Rìběn* → *Rìyŭ*), or to full names (*Yìdàlì* → *Yìdàlìyŭ*) is quite regular, with the exception of *Hànyŭ* 'Chinese' (which uses the word for ethnic Chinese, *Hàn*).

Éyŭ	'Russian'	*Făyŭ*	'French'	*Hányŭ*	'Korean'
Rìyŭ	'Japanese'	*Yīngyŭ*	'English'	*Tàiyŭ*	'Thai'
Cháoxiănyŭ	'[North] Korean' (PRC)	*Yìdàlìyŭ*	'Italian'	*Táiyŭ*	'Taiwanese'

7.3.4 English

Because English is not just the language of England, the term *Yīngguóhuà* is not generally used for 'spoken English'. For similar reasons, the term *Měiguóhuà* is not used either. The following are the more usual expressions for 'English language'.

Yīngyŭ	*Tā bú huì jiăng Yīngyŭ.*
Yīngwén	*Zhōngwén, Yīngwén dōu huì, zhēn liăobuqĭ!*

The distinction between British English and American English can be expressed as *Yīngshì de Yīngwén* versus *Měishì de Yīngwén* (with *shì* meaning 'style' or 'type').

7.3.5 Chinese

The various names for the Chinese language differ according to country, or have different nuances (as noted in the Introduction).

Pŭtōnghuà	'ordinary language'; the formal name for Mandarin on the Mainland
Guóyŭ	'national language'; the formal name for Mandarin in Taiwan and for many residents of overseas communities
Huáyŭ	'language of the Hua'; the formal name for Mandarin in Singapore; *huá* is another ancient name for the Chinese
Hànyŭ	'language of the Han people'; used for Chinese language in general (including regional and historical varieties) on both the Mainland and in Taiwan

7.3.6 Exclamations

Even in a foreign language, you may have the urge to express an emotional reaction to an incident or situation. This is difficult territory, but below are some phrases for consideration. Some express pleasure at seeing something unusual, such as an athletic feat (*zhēn liăobuqĭ*); some register disgust (*zhēn ĕxin*) or impatience (*tăoyàn*). Still others show sympathy for the misfortune of others (*zhēn kěxī*). The plus or minus indicates, roughly, whether the phrase expresses a favorable or negative reaction. The general caveat about not relying too much on translation across languages holds even more strongly for phrases of this nature. As a learner, it is best to make use of phrases like these with caution, and carefully observe the contexts of their use.

Zhēn liǎobuqǐ!	(+)	'Amazing! Extraordinary! Outstanding!'
Zhēn bùdéliǎo!	(+)	'Amazing!'
Bùdéliǎo!	(–)	'How awful! Shocking!'
Liǎobùdé!	(–)	'Awful! Terrible! Outrageous!'
Hǎo/hěn lìhai!	(+)	'Pretty amazing!'
	(–)	'Formidable!'
Zhēn zāogāo!	(–)	'Too bad! What a pity!'
Zhēn dǎoméi!	(–)	'What bad luck! Shucks!'
Zhēn kěxī!	(–)	'What a pity!'
Zhēn kělián!	(–)	'How sad!'
Tǎoyàn!	(–)	'What a nuisance! What a pain!'
Máfan!	(–)	'What a lot of trouble! Bother!'
Zhēn ěxin!	(–)	'How nauseating! Gross!'
Bù hǎo yìsi!	(–)	'How embarrassing! I'm sorry! My apologies!'

NOTES

a. Unmodified, *bùdéliǎo* is a common response to something negative; if modified by *zhēn*, it may convey amazement.

b. Many of these expressions may also function in contexts other than exclamations. For example, both *bùdéliǎo* and *liǎobùdé*, mediated by *+de*, can also act as intensifiers with SVs: *hǎo+de bùdéliǎo*; *gāoxìng+de liǎobùdé*. *Liǎobùdé* can function as a modifier in a phrase like *yí jiàn liǎobùdé de dà shì* 'a matter of utmost importance'–where it does not sound particularly negative.

Exercise 3

Provide Chinese paraphrases for the following expressions.

1. He's a bit gruff.
2. Things are rather expensive here.

3. Have some ice cream!
4. I only speak a little Chinese.
5. Have some Chinese tea.

Provide Chinese paraphrases for the following miscellaneous remarks.

1. Amazing! She speaks three foreign languages!
2. If you are planning to work in Taiwan, then you should learn traditional characters (*fántǐzì*) as well.
3. It was so embarrassing! I invited them to dinner but couldn't find the restaurant.
4. Oh, what a pain! I left my passport in the dorm, so I'll have to go back and fetch it.
5. Gross! This toilet's filthy! And there's no toilet paper! What can we do? (*wèishēngzhǐ* 'toilet paper')

7.4 Dialogue: Language abilities

Yǐ is a foreign female student in China studying Chinese; *Jiǎ* is a middle-aged woman that *Yǐ* has just been introduced to. *Yǐ* is making an effort to be modest and deferential.

Jiǎ:	*Nǐ Pǔtōnghuà shuō+de hěn biāozhǔn!*	'You speak Mandarin very properly!'
Yǐ:	*Nǎlǐ nǎlǐ, nǐ guòjiǎng le.*	'Nah, you're too nice.'
Jiǎ:	*Nà, nǐ néng rènshi Hànzì ma? Néng xiě ma?*	'So, can you read Chinese characters? Can you write?'
Yǐ:	*Néng rènshi jǐ bǎi ge zì; yě néng xiě, kěshì xiě+de bù hǎo.*	'I can read a few hundred characters; and I can write, but I don't write well.'
Jiǎ:	*Duì a, Zhōngwén, tīng shuō bǐjiào róngyì, kěshì dú xiě hěn nán.*	'That's right; with Chinese, listening and speaking are relatively easy, but reading and writing are hard.'

Yǐ:	*Kě bú shì ma!*	'You said it!' ('Isn't [that] really the case!')
Jiǎ:	*Nǐ hái huì shuō biéde wàiyǔ ma?*	'Do you speak any other foreign languages?'
Yǐ:	*Wǒ yě huì shuō yìdiǎn Rìběn huà.*	'I speak a little Japanese as well.'
Jiǎ:	*Ò, Zhōngguó huà, Rìběn huà dōu huì shuō! Zhēn liǎobuqǐ!*	'Oh, [you speak] Chinese and Japanese! That's amazing!'
Yǐ:	*À, mǎmahūhū, dōu shuō+de bú tài hǎo.*	'Well, so-so, [I] don't speak them very well.'

NOTES

a. *Nǐ Pǔtōnghuà . . .*; *Nǐ de Pǔtōnghuà* is also possible, but Chinese prefer the topic-comment construction in this context, i.e., 'as for you, [your] Mandarin is . . .'

b. *biāozhǔn* 'to be standard'; Chinese often praise foreigners' language for being 'standard', meaning that they speak with the correct pronunciation, that is, the one taught in schools and heard in the media.

c. *guòjiǎng* 'to praise too much; to flatter' ('exceed-speak'); The phrase is a rather more formal response to flattery than *nǎlǐ*, and can be used when a person of higher status offers praise. The following *le* can be treated as part of the expression.

d. *rènshi Hànzì*; In Chinese, the ability to read is treated differently from the act of reading; the former is often expressed as *rènshi Hànzì*, while the latter is usually expressed as *kànshū*.

e. *tīng shuō dú xiě*; This is a set way for talking about the four skills: listening, speaking, reading, and writing.

f. *kě bú shì ma*; *Kě* (in its written form) is the same *kě* as in *kěyǐ* and *kěshì*, but here it is an ADV meaning 'really; indeed; surely' (cf. *Kě bié wàng le* 'Make sure you don't forget!'). A more literal translation of *kě bú shì ma* would be 'isn't that just the case!'

YǑU RÉN 'SOME PEOPLE' AND SIMILAR EXPRESSIONS It is useful to be able to answer 'yes-no' questions, such as *Zhōngguó rén xǐhuan hē kāfēi ma?*, with nuance, rather than simply 'yes' or 'no'. For this, the phrase *yǒu rén* 'there are people [who]; some people' is useful.

Yuèbǐng, yǒu rén xǐhuan, yǒu rén bù xǐhuan.	'Some people like moon cakes, some don't.'

Sìshēng, yǒu rén shuō+de hěn biāozhǔn, yǒu rén shuō+de bú tài biāozhǔn.	'[With] the four tones, some say them accurately, some don't.'

Yǒu shíhou or *yǒu de shíhou* 'sometimes; at times' are used in much the same way.

Yīnyuè ne, yǒu shíhou wǒ tīng yáogǔnyuè, yǒu shíhou tīng gǔdiǎn yīnyuè.	'Sometimes I listen to rock and roll, and sometimes I listen to classical music.'

When the meaning is 'some members of a particular group', then *yǒude* 'some [of them]' is used. Notice the topic-comment order in the next two examples.

Wǒmen bān de xuéshēng, yǒude shi běnkēshēng, yǒude shi yánjiūshēng.	'Some of the students in our class are undergraduates, some are graduates.'
Sìchuān, yǒude dìfāng hěn gāo, yǒude hěn dī.	'Some parts of Sichuan are high, some are very low.'

7.5 Dialogue: Tea and coffee

Yǐ is a Chinese student and *Jiǎ* is a foreigner.

Jiǎ:	*Ài, jīntiān yǒu diǎn⟨r⟩ lěng.*	'Gosh, it's a bit cold today.'
Yǐ:	*Hē ⟨yì⟩diǎn⟨r⟩ chá ba.*	'Have some tea.'
Jiǎ:	*Hǎo, xièxie.*	'Fine, thanks.'
Yǐ:	*Nǐmen Xīfāng rén bǐjiào xǐhuan hē kāfēi, duì ma?*	'You Westerners prefer to drink coffee, am [I] right?'
Jiǎ:	*Bù yídìng, yǒu rén xǐhuan, yǒu rén bù xǐhuan. Yǒu rén shuō kāfēi duì shēntǐ bù hǎo. Wǒ ne, wǒ zǎoshàng hē kāfēi, xiàwǔ hē chá. Bù hē kāfēi, wǒ méi*	'Not necessarily, some do and some don't. Some say coffee's not good for you. As for myself, I drink coffee in the morning [and] tea in the afternoon. [If] I don't have coffee, I can't wake

	jīngshen, dànshì hē tài duō, bù néng shuìjiào.	up, but [if I] have too much, [I] can't sleep.'
Yǐ:	*Yào bu yào fàng niúnǎi? Fàng táng ma?*	'Do you take milk? You take sugar?'
Jiǎ:	*Bú yòng le, bú yòng le. Hē kāfēi, wǒ fàng niúnǎi, yě fàng táng, dànshì hē chá, wǒ píngcháng bú fàng rènhé dōngxi.*	'No thanks. [When I] have coffee, I add milk and sugar as well, but [when I] drink tea, I don't usually add anything else.'
Yǐ:	*Wǒmen hē chá yǒu diǎnr xiàng nǐmen hē shuǐ yíyàng, shénme shíhou dōu xíng. Zài Zhōngguó, bù néng bù hē chá!*	'[When] we drink tea [it]'s a bit like you drinking water, [you] can drink it anytime. In China, [you] can't not drink tea!'
Jiǎ:	*Nà Zhōngguó rén bù hē chá hē shénme?*	'So [when] Chinese don't drink tea, what do they drink?'
Yǐ:	*Nà hěn nán shuō. Yěxǔ bù hē chá hē dòujiāng. Huòzhě qìshuǐ. Xiànzài nǚháizi hěn duō ài hē niúnǎi, rè niúnǎi.*	'That's difficult to say. I guess [if we] don't drink tea, we drink soybean milk. Or soda. [And] nowadays, women generally like to drink milk–hot milk.'
Jiǎ:	*Ài, wǒ zuì bù xǐhuan hē rè niúnǎi!*	'Gosh, I really don't like hot milk!'
Yǐ:	*Dànshi duì shēntǐ hǎo, duì ma? Duì pífu hǎo.*	'But [it]'s good for you, right? Good for the skin.'
Jiǎ:	*Hěn qíguài, Zhōngguó rén xiànzài hē niúnǎi chī miànbāo, Měiguó rén chī báifàn, hē chá. Zěnme shuō–shi 'guójìhuà'!*	'[It']s strange, nowadays Chinese drink milk and eat bread, Americans eat rice and drink tea. How do [you] say it–[it]'s 'internationalization'!'
Yǐ:	*Huòzhě 'quánqiúhuà'.*	'Or 'globalization'.'
Jiǎ:	*Ò, quánqiúhuà–hěn yǒu yìsi!*	'Aha, 'globalization'–interesting!'

NOTES

a. *duì* 'to be facing; to be correct; to be right'; cf. *duìbuqǐ*; In association with a stative verb, *duì* can also have a co-verb function roughly equivalent to 'to' or 'for': *duì shēntǐ bù hǎo* 'not good for the body; not good for [you]'. Notice the different word orders in the two languages.

b. *jīngshen* 'energy; vigor'; also an SV meaning 'animated'

c. *fàng* 'to put; to place'

d. *rènhé* 'any; any kind of', always followed by a noun

e. *shénme shíhou dōu xíng* ('whatever time all okay'); This is an additional example of the indefinite function of question words.

f. *nǚháizi*; also *nǚháir* 'girl' ('female-child'), but often used in the sense of 'young woman'. The ordinary word for 'woman' is *nǚrén* (parallel to *nánrén* 'men'), but just as 'woman' in American usage used to be avoided in favor of euphemisms such as 'lady' (cf. 'ladies' room'), so Chinese tend to use *nǚde* rather than *nǚrén* for 'women'. *Shàonián* ('young-years') is a 'youth'. Another word, *gūniang*, is sometimes used for 'young women' in poetic language or popular songs. Below are the first two lines of a popular folk song, originally from Taiwan, but now well known throughout the Chinese-speaking world.

Ālǐ Shān de gūniang měi rú shuǐ ya,	'Ali Mountain's girls are beautiful like water,'
Ālǐ Shān de shàonián zhuàng rú shān.	'Ali Mountain's boys are strong as mountains.'

g. *ài* 'to love'; On the Mainland, *ài* overlaps with *xǐhuan* 'to like'.

h. *guójìhuà* 'internationalization' ('international-ize'); *quánqiúhuà* 'globalization' ('complete-world-ize'). In modern Chinese, *huà* 'change' has come to have a word-forming function, as a suffix added to SVs and nouns to form verbs and nouns, much like '-ize' or '-ation' in English. Cf. *xiàndàihuà* 'modernize'; *sì ge xiàndàihuà* 'the four modernizations'.

Exercise 4

Rearrange the jumbled phrases below into grammatically correct sentences. To do this effectively, you need to take a deductive approach, projecting likely meanings from key words.

1. huì / xiě / bù yídìng / Pǔtōnghuà / de rén / shuō / néng / Hànzì
2. hěn duō / lèi / kǎoshì / tā / jīntiān / suǒyǐ / yǒu diǎnr / yīnwèi / yǒu
3. niúnǎi / yǒurén / yǐqián / hē / hěn shǎo / xiànzài / bù hē / yǒurén / Zhōngguórén / hē / kěshì

4. bù yídìng / Fǎguóhuà / tīngdedǒng / Yìdàlìhuà / huì / de rén / jiǎng
5. Yīngwén de / bù duō / huì shuō / hěn shǎo / yě / Yīngguó / Yīngguórén / dànshì / bù yuǎn / huì shuō / lí / Fǎguó / Fǎguórén / Fǎyǔ de
6. Zhōngguórén / dànshì / fùmǔ / tā / bú shì / yíyàng / Zhōngguórén zhēn hǎo / Zhōngwén / tā de / xiàng
7. kāfēi / chá / kěshì / hē / yǒurén / xǐhuan / yǐqián / zhǐ / xiànzài / Zhōngguórén / bù xǐhuan / hē / hē / yě xǐhuan / kāfēi

7.6 Alone or with others; conveyances

7.6.1 Accompaniment

A. TOGETHER WITH Earlier, it was noted that coordination (typically expressed by 'and' in English) is often left implicit in Chinese (*chá kāfēi dōu xíng*), but with nouns or noun phrases, coordination could be expressed explicitly with *gēn* (or, more formally, with *hé*).

Wǒ gēn tā shi tóngxué.	'She and I are classmates.'
Xīnjiāpō gēn Yìnní, shéi yíng le?	'Singapore and Indonesia–who won?'

Gēn (or *hé*) also commonly occurs with the phrases *yíkuàir* ('one-lump') or *yìqǐ* 'together; as a group'.

gēn tā yìqǐ qù *gēn tā yíkuàir qù* }	'to go [together] with him/her'
Yìqǐ qù, xíng ma?	'Would it be okay to go together?'
Wǒmen yíkuàir qù cāntīng chīfàn, hǎo bu hǎo?	'Why don't we go together and have a meal at the cafeteria?'
Gēn wǒmen yíkuàir qù, hǎo bu hǎo?	'How about going with us?'
Chīguo fàn le ma? *Hái méi ne.*	'Have you eaten?' 'Not yet.'

Lái gēn wǒmen yìqǐ chī ba.	'Come and eat with us.'
Hǎo, xièxie.	'Okay, thanks.'

B. ALONE 'Alone', in the question 'Did you go alone?', is often expressed in Chinese as *yí ge rén.*

Nǐ yí ge rén qù ma?	'Are you going alone?'
Shì, yí ge rén qù.	'Yes, alone.'
Nǐ yí ge rén qù hěn bù róngyì ba.	'It's not easy going alone is it?'
Méi guānxi, wǒ xíguàn le.	'It's okay, I'm used to it.'

Tā měitiān dōu yí ge rén zài cāntīng chī zhōngfàn.	'Every day she eats lunch all by herself in the cafeteria.'
Wǒ yě měitiān dōu yí ge rén zài cāntīng chīfàn.	'I eat on my own in the cafeteria every day too.'
Nà, nǐ wèishénme bù gēn tā yìqǐ chī ne?	'Well, why don't you eat with her?'
Yīnwèi wǒmen chīfàn de shíjiān bù yíyàng.	'Because we eat at different times.'

7.6.2 *Le* or *guò* → *shi . . . de*

As noted in Unit 6, the *shi . . . de* construction is often set up by a question about a previous event, containing *guò* or *le.* Here are some typical examples:

DIALOGUE 1

甲: *Chī le ma?*
乙: *Chī le, zài jiā lǐ chī de.*
甲: *Zìjǐ zuò de ma?*
乙: *Bù, shi mǎi de.*
甲: *Hǎochī ma?*
乙: *Mǎmahūhū.*

DIALOGUE 2

甲: *Chī le ma?*
乙: *Chī le, zài sùshè chī de.*

甲: *Sùshè yǒu cāntīng ma?*
乙: *Méiyǒu; shi wǒ zìjǐ zuò de.*
甲: *Ò, zìjǐ zuò de, yídìng hěn hǎochī.*
乙: *Hái kěyǐ.*

DIALOGUE 3

甲: *Chī le méi?*
乙: *Chī le, zài xiǎochīdiàn chī de.*
甲: *Gēn shéi yìqǐ qù de?*
乙: *Yí ge rén qù de.*
甲: *Xià cì, nǐ xiān lái zhǎo wǒ ba.*
乙: *Hǎo, wǒ huì lái zhǎo nǐ.*

DIALOGUE 4

甲: *Rènshi tā ma?*
乙: *Dāngrán, rènshi tā hěn jiǔ le.*
甲: *Shì ma?*
乙: *Shì, wǒmen shi zài xiǎoxué rènshi de.*
甲: *Xiǎoxué a?*
乙: *Shì, wǒmen shi zài Tiānjīn yìqǐ shàng de xuéxiào.*

DIALOGUE 5

甲: *Nǐ qùguo Zhōngguó méiyǒu?*
乙: *Qùguo.*
甲: *Něi nián qù de?*
乙: *Qù nián qù de.*
甲: *Yí ge rén qù de ma?*
乙: *Bù, gēn péngyou yìqǐ qù de.*

NOTES

a. *zìjǐ* '[one]self'; *zìjǐ zuò de [cài]; zìjǐ mǎi de*

b. *hěn jiǔ* ('very long+time'); cf. *hǎo jiǔ bú jiàn* 'long time no see'

c. *xiǎochīdiàn* 'snack bar; lunch room'

7.6.3 Ways of traveling

Conveyances and other means of transportation are often expressed by phrases placed before the verb, in the position of adverbs.

zǒulù 'to walk' ('walk-road')	*kāichē* 'to drive' ('drive-car')	*dǎ dí* 'to take a taxi' ('take taxi')	*qí zìxíngchē* 'to ride a bicycle' ('straddle bicycle')	*qí mǎ* 'to ride a horse' ('straddle horse')

zuò fēijī 'to fly; take a plane' ('sit airplane')	*zuò huǒchē* 'to take a train' ('sit fire-vehicle')	*zuò chuán* 'to take a boat' ('sit boat')	*zuò gōnggòng-qìchē* 'to take a bus' ('sit public-car')

NOTES

a. *zǒu* 'to leave; to go', but in combination with *lù* 'road; walk' it means 'to walk'.

b. *Dǎ dí* was formerly a Cantonese term, with *dí* derived ultimately from English 'taxi', but it is now the colloquial expression for 'take a taxi' in Mandarin.

c. *qí* 'to straddle; to ride'

d. There are three terms for bicycle: *zìxíngchē* ('self-move-vehicle'), *dānchē* ('unit-vehicle'), and *jiǎotàchē* ('foot-press-vehicle'). The last two are more commonly used in Taiwan.

e. *Zuò* occurs as a full verb in *qǐng zuò* and as a CV in *zuò fēijī*.

f. A note on word formation: As the examples ending in *chē* 'vehicle' show, Chinese often forms compounds by taking a generic base noun and adding specifying nouns to it: *qìchē* ('gas-vehicle') → 'car; automobile'; *huǒchē* ('fire-vehicle') → 'train'. In the same way, types of shoes are formed by adding nouns to the generic *xié*: *bīngxié* 'skates' ('ice-shoes'); *gāogēn⟨r⟩xié* ('high-heel-shoes'); *qiúxié* 'tennis shoes' ('ball-shoes'); *huǒjiàn-píxié* 'rocket shoes' ('fire-arrow leather-shoes'). The last are sharp-looking shoes with pointed toes that were specifically banned in China during the Mao era.

USAGE

Nǐ shì zěnme qù Zhōngguó de?	'How did you go to China?'
Dāngrán shi zuò fēijī qù de.	'Naturally, I flew.'
Nǐ shi zuò chuán qù de háishi zuò huǒchē qù de?	'Did you go by ship or by train?'

Zánmen dǎ ge dí qu, hǎo bu hǎo?

Zuò huǒchē qù de. Chuán tài màn le. ‘By train. Boat’s too slow.’

Nǐ píngcháng zěnme lái shàngkè? ‘How do you usually get to class?’
Wǒ píngcháng zǒulù lái, búguò jīntiān yīnwèi xiàyǔ, suǒyǐ wǒ shi kāichē lái de. ‘Usually, I walk, but today, because it’s raining, I drove.’

7.6.4 Time words

In earlier units, you encountered a number of time words; here, we enlarge the repertoire and present these words in a synoptic table. Recall that, unlike English, Chinese time words precede their associated verbs. Notice that the time words at the extremes–*nián* and *tiān*–form compounds, while those between form phrases with *shàng, zhèi*, or *xià* + *gè*.

BEFORE	PAST	NOW	FUTURE	AFTER
qiánnián	*qùnián*	*jīnnián*	*míngnián*	*hòunián*
	shàng ge lǐbài	*zhèi ge lǐbài*	*xià ge lǐbài*	
	shàng ge xīngqī	*zhèi ge xīngqī*	*xià ge xīngqī*	
	shàng ge yuè	*zhèi ge yuè*	*xià ge yuè*	
qiántiān	*zuótiān*	*jīntiān*	*míngtiān*	*hòutiān*

NOTE

Liǎng nián ⟨yǐ⟩qián 'two years ago' can often substitute for *qiánnián* 'the year before last'. The former, however, is not necessarily referenced to the present and could, for example, mean 'two years before then'. The same is true for *qiántiān* and the expressions with *hòu*: *hòutiān* 'the day after tomorrow' and *liǎng tiān ⟨yǐ⟩hòu* 'two days from now/then'.

7.7 *Cái* 'not until'

Cái is a common adverb, but its usage is sometimes confused by the fact that it generally corresponds to a negative in English, 'not until'.

Tāmen shi shénme shíhou qù de?	'When did they go?'
Qùnián bāyuèfen qù de.	'Last August.'
Shénme shíhou huílái de?	'When did they get back?'
Zuótiān cái huílái de.	'[They] didn't get back until yesterday.'

Notice the order of sentence elements: the conditions (often a time) come first, followed by *cái* in the normal position of an adverb before the associated verb, and then the result. If *cái* is defined as 'then and only then', rather than as 'not until', it will be easier to position correctly in the Chinese sentence.

Tā [sān diǎn zhōng] cái zǒu. 'She's not leaving until 3:00.'
('She [3:00] then+and+only+then leave.')

USAGE

Qǐngwèn, nǐ jǐ diǎn xiàkè?	'May I ask when you get out of class?'
Jīntiān yǒu kǎoshì, sān diǎn bàn cái xiàkè.	'There's an exam today, [so] we won't get out until 3:30.'
Nǐmen píngcháng jǐ diǎn shuìjiào?	'What time do you usually go to bed?'
Píngcháng wǎnshàng liǎng sān diǎn cái shuìjiào.	'[We] don't usually go to bed until 2:00 or 3:00 in the morning.'
Tā jiǔ diǎn bàn cái lái de, tài wǎn le!	'She didn't get here till 9:30, too late!'

Méi guānxi, míngtiān yě xíng.	'Never mind, tomorrow's okay too.'
Tāmen hái zài, míngtiān cái zǒu.	'They're still here, [they]'re not going until tomorrow.'
O, wǒ yǐwéi tāmen yǐjīng zǒu le.	'Oh, I thought [incorrectly] they'd already left.'
Nǐ shénme shíhou huíjiā?	'When are you going home?'
Wǒ chīle fàn yǐhòu cái huíjiā.	'I'm not going home until I've had a meal.'

Exercise 5

Paraphrase the following in Chinese.

1. Explain that she has a test today so she's not going home until 5:00.
2. Tell them that he doesn't go to bed until he finishes his homework.
3. Explain that you won't be going home until tomorrow.
4. Explain that you didn't know until now that she understood Chinese.

7.8 Duration

In earlier lessons, there have been many examples of 'time when' phrases: *jīntiān xiàwǔ; sān diǎn zhōng; shàngkè de shíhou*. Though there have been some examples of phrases that involve duration (*sān tiān, liǎng nián*), there have been no examples of duration in sentences. This section will introduce some sentence patterns that involve duration.

7.8.1 Units of time

Tiān and *nián* (which rhyme and form the extremes of the four units of time above the hour) are themselves measure words, so they are counted directly: *yì tiān, liǎng nián*. *Yuè* and *lǐbài/xīngqī*, on the other hand, are nouns, counted by *gè*. (*Yuè*, directly preceded by numbers, forms the names of the months: *yīyuè, èryuè*, etc.)

Q:	*Yì nián yǒu duōshao tiān?*	'How many days in a year?'
	Yí ge yuè yǒu jǐ ge xīngqī?	'How many weeks in a month?'
	Yì nián yǒu jǐ ge lǐbài?	'How many weeks in a year?'
	Yí ge xīngqī yǒu jǐ tiān?	'How many days in a week?'
	Yì nián yǒu jǐ ge yuè?	'How many months in a year?'
	Yí ge yuè yǒu duōshao tiān?	'How many days in a month?'
A:	*Yì nián yǒu sānbǎi liùshíwǔ tiān;*	'A year has 365 days;
	yí ge yuè yǒu sì ge xīngqī;	a month has 4 weeks;
	yì nián yǒu wǔshí'èr ge lǐbài;	a year has 52 weeks;
	yí ge xīngqī yǒu qī tiān;	a week has 7 days;
	yì nián yǒu shí'èr ge yuè;	a year has 12 months;
	yí ge yuè yǒu sānshí tiān huòzhě sānshíyī tiān.	a month has either 30 or 31 days.'

'Hour' is expressed as either *zhōngtóu* (originally 'bell; chime') or *xiǎoshí* ('small-time'). The first is consistently counted with *gè*, but the latter is variable, and can be counted with or withou *gè*.

zhōngtóu	*yí ge zhōngtóu, liǎng ge zhōngtóu*
xiǎoshí	*yí ⟨ge⟩ xiǎoshí, liǎng ⟨ge⟩ xiǎoshí*

It is important not to confuse *zhōng* 'o'clock' with *zhōngtóu* 'hours' or other cases of time-when and duration.

TIME-WHEN		DURATION	
liǎng diǎn zhōng	'two o'clock'	*liǎng ge zhōngtóu* *liǎng ⟨ge⟩ xiǎoshí*	'two hours'
liùyuè sān hào	'June 3rd'	*sān tiān*	'three days'
qīyuè	'July'	*qī ge yuè*	'seven months'
yījiǔjiǔsì nián	'1994'	*jiǔ nián*	'nine years'
sān diǎn shíwǔ fēn	'3:15'	*shíwǔ fēn ⟨zhōng⟩*	'fifteen minutes'

7.8.2 Duration in context

While 'time-when' phrases are placed prior to their associated verbs (*liù diǎn chī wǎnfàn; shí diǎn shàngkè*), duration phrases are placed directly after them: *qù yì nián* 'to go for a year'; *kàn yí ge zhōngtóu* 'to watch for an hour'; *xué yì nián* 'to study for a year'. Objects cannot intrude between the verb and the duration, and they must either be mentioned earlier (as with the verb+DE construction) or be placed after the duration: *kàn yì xiǎoshí ⟨de⟩ diànshì* 'to watch an hour's television' (which is homologous in structure to the English). In fact, objects often do not need to be mentioned at all; so, for the sake of presentation, they will be avoided in this lesson.

USAGE

(1)	*Nǐ zhù zài nǎr?*	'Where do you live?'
	Zài Lúwān.	'In Luwan [a district of Shanghai].'
	Zěnme lái shàngbān?	'How do you get [here] to work?'
	Zuò qìchē.	'By car.'
	Yào jǐ fēn zhōng?	'How many minutes does it take?'
	Dàgài sānshí fēn.	'About 30 minutes.'
(2)	*Míngtiān qù Lìjiāng ma?*	'[You]'re going to Lijiang tomorrow?'
	Shì, míngtiān zǎoshàng.	'Yes, tomorrow morning.'
	Zěnme qù?	'How are you going?'
	Zuò fēijī qù.	'[We]'re going by plane.'
	Yào jǐ ge xiǎoshí?	'How many hours does it take?'
	Chàbuduō yí ge bàn xiǎoshí.	'About an hour and a half.'
	Qù jǐ tiān?	'How many days are you going for?'
	Sān tiān, lǐbàisì huílái.	'Three days, [we]'ll be back on Thursday.'

Exercise 6

Compose a conversation along the following lines.

> Tomorrow you're going to Cháozhōu, right? / That's right, we leave at 7:00.

How are you getting [there]? / I'm driving.
How long will it take to drive? / About two hours, if the traffic is not too bad.
When will you be back? / Not until 9:00 in the evening.
So you'll be gone 12 hours in all. / Maybe longer!

7.9 More *le* patterns

The subject of duration leads quite naturally to some additional patterns involving the ubiquitous particle *le*. Recall that, earlier, you saw that *le* was interpreted differently according to whether it was associated with a state or with an action. The clearest cases involved SVs (*bú è le* 'no longer hungry') and V_{act} (*chīfàn le* 'have eaten'). It was also noted that *le* is sometimes attached directly to the verb, rather than to the sentence; thus, *xiàle kè jiù huíjiā*, where going home was conditional on getting out of class; and *qùle yí tàng Cháng Chéng*, with a 'quantified' object. These facts remain relevant for the new patterns that relate to duration.

SOME VOCABULARY RELEVANT TO DURATION

hěn jiǔ '[for] a long time'	*bù jiǔ* 'not long'	*duō jiǔ* 'how long'	*duō cháng shíjiān* 'how long a time'
bìyè 'to graduate' ('complete-enterprise')	*jiéhūn* 'to get married' ('tie-marriage')	*jiāoshū* 'to teach' ('teach-books')	*děng* 'to wait'

NOTE

Jiéhūn, *jiāoshū*, and *shuìjiào* are combinations of verb and object (VO), which means that, unlike two-syllable verbs such as *rènshi*, elements can intervene between the syllables. (*Bìyè*, it turns out, is interpreted by some speakers as a two-syllable verb and by others as a VO.)

7.9.1 Continuing action

When people ask you how long you have been studying Chinese, they are asking about action that has continued over a period of time. The assumption (signaled, in English, by a progressive verb form with an '-ing' ending) is that you began studying at some time in the past, and your study since, if not continuous, has followed right up to the present.

The situation can be envisioned as starting at a definite point in time and continuing to the present.

V_{act} *le*~~~~~~~~~~~~~~~~~~~~~~~~→ | *le* ⟨*xuéle yìnián le; kāile yí ge zhōngtóu le*⟩

The onset is signaled by *le* after the verb, and the connection with the current time is signaled by the final *le*. The order is 'V *le* duration *le*'.

Nǐ xuéle jǐ nián le?	'How many years have you been studying?'
Liǎng nián ⟨*le*⟩.	'Two years ⟨so far⟩.'
Nǐ yǐjīng zǒule jǐ ge xiǎoshí le?	'How long have you been walking so far?'
Sān ge xiǎoshí ⟨*le*⟩.	'Three hours ⟨so far⟩.'
Nǐ děngle duō jiǔ le?	'How long have you been waiting?'
Bàn ge xiǎoshí ⟨*le*⟩.	'A half hour ⟨so far⟩.'
Nǐ zài něi ge dānwèi gōngzuò?	'Which unit do you work in?'
Zài yóujú.	'In the post office.'
Zài nàr gōngzuòle jǐ nián le?	'How long have you worked there?'
Hěn jiǔ le–shí duō nián ⟨*le*⟩.	'A long time–over 10 years.'

NOTES

a. Multiples of ten (*shí, sānshí, liǎngbǎi*, etc.) are frequently followed by *duō* to express 'more than; over': *shí duō nián* 'more than 10 years'; *èrshí duō kuài qián* 'more than $20'; *yìbǎi duō ge xuéshēng* 'over 100 students'.

b. In the above example responses, the final *le* is sometimes left out, presumably because once a context has been established, speakers do not feel the need to reiterate the notion of 'so far'.

Objects cannot intrude between the verb (or verb-*le*) and the following duration phrase. Instead, an object is often mentioned earlier (with or without the verb).

xué Zhōngwén	'to study Chinese'
Nǐ Zhōngwén xuéle jǐ nián le?	'How long have you been studying Chinese?'
jiāoshū	'to teach'
Tā jiāoshū jiāole èrshí duō nián le.	'He's been teaching for over 20 years.'
děng tā	'to wait for him'
Wǒ děng tā yǐjīng děngle yí ge xiǎoshí le.	'I've been waiting for him for an hour already.'

RESTRICTIVE ADVERBS SUPPRESS FINAL *LE* One caveat: When asked how long you have been studying Chinese, you will often want to answer with a restrictive adverb such as *zhǐ* 'only'–'only six months', for example. It turns out that while English keeps the same form of the verb in both question and answer ('have been studying'), Chinese restrictive adverbs such as *zhǐ* 'only' (as well as *gāng* 'just', *gāngcái* 'a short while ago', and *cái*, 'only') seem to circumscribe the verbal event in such a way as to be incompatible with the final *le* (as indicated by the * below). To illustrate this point, the following is a typical dialogue.

Nǐ Zhōngwén jiǎng+de hěn hǎo! Xuéle jǐ nián le?	'You speak Chinese very well! How many years have [you] been studying [it]?'
*Zhǐ xuéle bàn nián *le.*	'[I]'ve only been studying half a year.'
Zhǐ xuéle bàn nián jiù shuō+de nàme hǎo, zhēn liǎobuqǐ!	'Only been studying half a year and [you] speak so well–that's amazing!'

7.9.2 Enduring states

If you ask friends how long they have known each other, or how long it has been since they graduated from college, you are asking about enduring states. By contrast to continuing action, enduring states involve an event (a marriage, an introduction, or a graduation, for example) that defines a new state that persists through a stretch of time. You can envision the situation as a definite point followed by a gap representing the passage of time.

event ------------------------- | *le* ⟨bìyè yì nián le; rènshi tā sān nián le⟩

The initial event will be expressed by a verb with associated subjects or objects: *wǒ rènshi tā, jiéhūn* 'to marry' ('tie-wedding'); *bìyè* 'to graduate' ('complete-enterprise'); *zài Zhōngguó*. Elapsed time will be expressed as a duration phrase, optionally introduced by *yǒu* 'to have': ⟨*yǒu*⟩ *sān nián*; ⟨*yǒu*⟩ *yí ge zhōngtóu*; and the connection with current time will be signaled by a final *le*. (However, the presence of a restrictive adverb such as *zhǐ* 'only' cancels the final *le*, as it did in *zhǐ xuéle bàn nián *le*.)

Tā jiéhūn ⟨yǒu⟩ èrshí duō nián le.	'He's been married over 20 years [so far].'
Wǒ bìyè yǐjīng ⟨yǒu⟩ liǎng nián le.	'I have been graduated for two years already.'
Tāmen zài Běijīng ⟨yǒu⟩ liù ge yuè le.	'They've been in Beijing for six months [so far].'
Nǐ rènshi tā ⟨yǒu⟩ duōcháng shíjiān le?	'How long have you known him [so far]?'
*Wǒmen zài Běijīng zhǐ yǒu liǎng ge yuè *le.*	'We've only been in Beijing for two months.'

The use of *yǒu* is optional, as indicated, though it is more often expressed in southern China or when an adverb such as *yǐjīng* is present (as in the second example above). *Yǐjīng*, interestingly, can appear before *yǒu*, before the duration phrase if *yǒu* is omitted, and also before *zài*.

Wǒ zài zhèr yǐjīng yǒu yì nián le.	'I've been here for a year already.'
Wǒ zài zhèr yǐjīng yì nián le.	'I've been here a year already.'
Wǒ yǐjīng zài zhèr yì nián le.	'I've already been here a year.'

A. INTERCHANGES INVOLVING ENDURING STATES

(1)	*Nǐ shi něi nián lái de?*	'When did you come [here]?'
	1997 nián.	'[It was] in 1997.'
	Na, nǐ yǐjīng zài zhèr liù nián le.	'So you've already been here six years [so far].'
	Shì a, liù nián le.	'Yes, six years [so far].'

(2)	*Nǐ zài Huáshèngdùn yǒu jǐ nián le?*	'How many years in Washington, D.C. [so far]?'
	Sān nián le. 2000 nián lái de.	'Three years [so far]. I came in 2000.'
(3)	*Nǐ zhù zài zhèr jǐ nián le?*	'How long have you lived here [so far]?'
	Shí nián le.	'Ten years [so far].'
(4)	*Qǐngwèn, nǐ shi jǐ niánjí de xuéshēng?*	'May I ask what year you are?'
	Sān niánjí de.	'A junior.'
	O, nǐ zài Běi Dà yǐjīng yǒu sān nián le.	'Oh, so you've been at Peking University three years already.'
	Shì, yǒu sān nián le.	'Yes, it's been three years [so far].'
(5)	*Nǐ rènshi tā jǐ nián le?*	'How long have you known her?'
	Yǐjīng èrshí duō nián le.	'More than 20 years already.'
(6)	*Nǐ zài Zhōngguó jǐ nián le?*	'How long have you been in China [so far]?'
	Sān nián le.	'Three years [so far].'
(7)	*Nǐ zài Zhōngguó jǐ nián?*	'How long were you in China?'
	Sān nián.	'Three years.'

The significance of the final *le* in the pattern is clear from the last two examples, (6) and (7). With *le*, the sentence is cued to the present; without it, it refers to time spent in the past. So, the sense of the final *le* is 'so far' or 'until now'.

B. OPTIONS Sometimes, situations that are objectively very similar can be viewed either as enduring states or as continuing actions. The different forms of the English verb in the following examples—'have lived' versus 'have been living'—reflect the same difference.

Wǒ zài Xī'ān ⟨yǒu⟩ sān nián le.	'I have been in Xi'an for three years.' (enduring state)
Wǒ zhù zài Xī'ān ⟨yǒu⟩ sān nián le.	'I have lived in Xi'an three years.' (enduring state)
Wǒ zài Xī'ān zhùle sān nián le.	'I have been living in Xi'an for three years.' (continuing action)

Wǒ xué Zhōngwén ⟨yǒu⟩ sān nián le.	'I've studied Chinese for three years.'
Wǒ Zhōngwén xuéle sān nián le.	'I've been studying Chinese for three years.'

C. TYPICAL VERBS While it is true that many events can be presented as enduring states or continuing actions, certain verbs are, because of their meaning, predisposed to one pattern or the other. The following verbs, for example, because they involve events that define a new state, are associated with the enduring state pattern.

jiéhūn	*Nǐmen jiéhūn ⟨yǒu⟩ jǐ nián le?*
bìyè	*Nǐ bìyè ⟨yǒu⟩ jǐ nián le?*
rènshi	*Nǐ rènshi tā ⟨yǒu⟩ duō jiǔ le?*
zài	*Nǐmen zài Běijīng ⟨yǒu⟩ duō cháng shíjiān le?*

Continuing actions involve the larger set of action verbs, including:

xué	*Nǐ xuéle jǐ nián le?*
děng	*Nǐ děngle duō jiǔ le?*
zhù	*Nǐ zài Shànghǎi zhùle duō cháng shíjiān le?*
gōngzuò	*Nǐ zài nàr gōngzuòle jǐ nián le?*

Fortunately, the two new *le* functions that have been introduced in §7.9, as well as those encountered earlier, are all frequent in the everyday exchanges that you are likely to encounter in your first year of learning Chinese. Your teachers and friends can use examples of them daily so that the choice of *le* versus *guo* or *shi . . . de*, on the one hand, or of one *le* versus two on the other, becomes more automatic.

Exercise 7

Compose dialogues along the following lines.

1. You write characters very well; how long have you been studying? / About two years.
   Have you ever been to China? / Sure; last year I was in Nanjing for two months.
2. How long have you been in Chengdu? / Only three weeks, I got here in June.
   How long are you staying? / I'm leaving on September 1st.
3. How long have you been studying [Chinese]? / A year.
   Only a year and you speak so well! / You're too kind! I really don't speak well at all!
4. How long have you known him? / For ages—over 20 years!
   Where did you meet? / We met at a bus stop in Hong Kong.

7.10 Weather

7.10.1 The seasons

Though not all parts of China enjoy distinct seasons, most parts do, and Chinese recognize four seasons (*sìgè jìjié* or, more concisely, *sìjì*). Names for seasons end with *tiān*.

chūntiān	'spring'
xiàtiān	'summer'
qiūtiān	'autumn; fall'
dōngtiān	'winter'

EXAMPLES

Běijīng, xiàtiān hěn rè, dōngtiān hěn lěng.	'[In] Beijing, summers are hot, winters are cold.'

Guǎngdōng, dōngtiān bù lěng, kěshi xiàtiān hěn mēnrè.	'[In] Guangzhou, the winter's aren't cold but the summers are hot and humid.'
Kūnmíng tiānqì fēicháng hǎo, sìjì-rúchūn.	'Kunming's weather is great–'four seasons like spring'.'

NOTE

The weather in Kunming, and Yunnan in general, is conventionally described as having *sìjì-rúchūn* ('four-seasons like-spring') or *sìjì-fēnmíng* ('four-seasons divide-clear'), that is, having four distinct seasons (though the latter can also apply to other places in China). Yunnan is also conventionally described as having *lántiān-báiyún* ('blue-skies white-clouds').

7.10.2 China's weather patterns

China's geographical configuration, with a vast continental mass to its north and west and a large body of water to the east, results in winters with cold air masses of high pressure over Mongolia and warmer air masses of lower pressure over the ocean, which retain heat longer. As the continental land mass heats up through the spring, the high pressure over Mongolia is relieved (as air expands), while the air over the ocean remains relatively more dense (as the water heats more slowly). These pressure differentials (high to low) give rise to the winds known as monsoons–*jìfēng* ('season-wind'). The winter monsoon brings cold, dry air from the north and northwest, resulting in cold and windy winters in the Beijing region, but little snow. The summer monsoon brings warm, moist air from the ocean that gives rise to heavy fog along the northeastern coasts, and humid weather inland.

The effect of the two monsoons is mitigated by mountain ranges, which protect the south from the cold, dry winter monsoon, and the north (and to some degree the northeast as well) from the moisture of the summer one. Rainfall in Beijing (in the north) varies considerably from year to year, but is heaviest in July and August. Southern regions, south of the *Jīnlíng* mountain range (which runs south of Xī'an and the Yellow River), have heavier rainfall, much of it between May and October. South of the *Nánlíng* range (which runs along the northern boundary of Guangdong province), the weather is subtropical with no real winter season. On the Tibetan plateau, however, the winters are long and summer is virtually nonexistent.

7.10.3 *Tiānqì* 'weather'

The most common word for 'weather' is *tiānqì*, composed of 'sky' plus *qì*. The root *qì* was noted earlier, when it was encountered in the word *kèqi* 'to be polite'. It is an important concept in Chinese physiology and medicine, and is familiar to English speakers as the first syllable in the word *qìgōng*, the name of the traditional system of breathing exercises that has become known in the West. *Qì* is sometimes translated as 'spirit' or 'essence'. It appears in a range of words having to do with weather (*tiānqì*, *qìhòu* 'climate'), mood (*qìfēn* 'ambiance', *qìpài* 'flair; design'), and breath or air (*qìduǎn* 'to gasp for breath', *shēngqì* 'to get angry', *qìqiú* 'balloon').

Jīntiān tiānqì zěnmeyàng?	'What's the weather like today?'
Lúndūn tiānqì bù lěng yě bú rè.	'The weather in London's neither [too] hot nor [too] cold.'
Zhōngguó běifāng de tiānqì bǐjiào gānzào, bù cháng xiàxuě, fēng hěn dà. Nánfāng de tiānqì bǐjiào cháoshī, chángcháng xiàyǔ.	'The weather in the north of China is quite dry, it doesn't often snow, [and] it's windy. The weather in the south is more humid [and] it rains a lot.'

Rather formal:

Zhōngguó běifāng de qìhòu hěn gānzào, yǔ shǎo shuǐ shǎo. Nánfāng shīrùn, yǔshuǐ-chōngpèi.	'The northern climate is dry, with little precipitation. The climate in the south is moist, with abundant rainfall.'

7.10.4 Rain and precipitation

Corresponding to English 'it's raining', Chinese has *xiàyǔ* ('falls rain'). English provides an 'ambient' subject, 'it', and treats 'rain' as a verb. Chinese, on the other hand, represents the same notion with a verb of motion, *xià*, and a noun, *yǔ*—the latter treated as an object of the verb. Other kinds of precipitation follow the same pattern: *xiàxuě* 'to snow' ('fall snow'), *xiàwù* 'to be foggy' ('fall fog').

(1)	*Nǐ kàn, xiàyǔ le / xiàxuě le!*	'Look, it's raining / snowing!'
(2)	*Zuótiān xiàyǔ le ma? / Xià le.*	'Did it rain yesterday?' / 'Yes, it did.'
(3)	*Yǐjīng xiàle yì zhěngtiān le / yì zhěngyè le.*	'It's been raining all day / night.'
(4)	*Wàitou zài xià dàyǔ.*	'It's raining heavily outside [right now].'
(5)	*Zuótiān xiàle yìdiǎnr xuě.*	'It snowed a bit yesterday.'
(6)	*Jiùjīnshān cháng xiàwù.*	'It's often foggy in San Francisco.'
(7)	*Běijīng cóng liùyuè dào bāyuè chángcháng xiàyǔ.*	'From June to August, it often rains in Beijing.'
(8)	*Dōngtiān shì hěn lěng, dànshì bù cháng xiàxuě.*	'The winters are quite cold, but it rarely snows.'

In cases involving amount, the V+*de* construction is often used.

(9)	*Zuótiān yǔ xià+de hěn dà.*	'Yesterday, it rained heavily.'

NOTES

a. *nǐ kàn*; Paradoxically, given the fact that Chinese frequently omits subject pronouns where English requires them, the equivalent of English 'look', used to beckon someone, is usually rendered *with* the subject pronoun in Chinese.

b. The final *le* in (1) suggests either that it is just starting to rain, or that the speaker is just becoming aware that it is raining; in (2), *le* reflects the end of an earlier phase (associated with V_{act}); in (3), final *le* confirms the fact that it was still raining at the time of speaking; in (5), *le* is conditioned by the quantified object, *yìdiǎnr*.

c. *zhěngtiān* ('whole-day')

d. *shì hěn lěng* 'it *is* cold [to be sure, but . . .]

e. *Zài* + V indicates the fact that the precipitation is ongoing.

7.10.5 Sun and wind

Weather reports often mention the sun as *tàiyáng*, literally 'the great yang'—where *yáng* is the male counterpart to the female *yīn*. While there is a regional word, *tàiyīn* 'the great yin' for 'moon', the standard word does not incorporate *yīn*; rather it is composed of *yuè* 'moon'—familiar as the word for 'month'—and *liàng* 'light': *yuèliàng*. Weather reports use *tàiyáng* in the slightly extended meaning of 'sunlight' or 'sunshine', but the word *yángguāng* is more specifically 'sunlight; sunshine'.

Wind is *fēng*; the semantic spread of the word *fēng* is interesting. It appears in compounds related to landscape (*fēngjǐng* 'scenery' and the geomantic practice known as *fēngshuǐ*), to personal bearing (*yǒu fēngdù* 'have poise'), to style (*fēngliú* 'notorious'—with the positive tone of 'renowned' for men, and the negative tone of 'common' for women), to custom (*fēngsú* 'social customs'), and to taste (*fēngwèi* 'flavor'). The wind is said 'to be big' (*fēng hěn dà*) or 'to blow': *guā fēng le* 'it's windy' ('blows wind'); *fēng guā+de hěn lìhai* 'the wind's blowing fiercely'.

Nánjīng měitiān dōu hěn rè, kěshì kànbujiàn tàiyáng.	'It's hot every day in Nanjing, but you can't see the sun.'
Běijīng chūntiān fēng hěn dà, tǔ hěn duō.	'In the spring in Beijing, it's windy and there's a lot of dust.'
Zuótiān tiānqì bú tài hǎo—fēng tài dà le.	'The weather wasn't very good yesterday—too much wind.'

7.10.6 Temperature and humidity

Winter temperatures in China show vast variation between the north and south. The mean January temperature for Beijing (in the northeast) is 4.6°C / 23.7°F, while Guangzhou (in the southeast) is 13.5°C / 56.3°F. Interestingly, mean summer temperatures in the north and south differ rather little. The mean July temperature for Beijing is 26.0°C / 78.8°F, while in Guangzhou it is 28.3°C / 82.9°F. Temperature (*wēndù*) is expressed in *dù* 'degrees' Celsius (*Shèshì*), rather than Fahrenheit (*Huáshì*). In the summer, most of the heavily populated regions of China are hot and humid *mēnrè* ('stuffy and hot') or *cháoshī* ('moist; damp'). The opposite is *gānzào* 'dry; arid' (in other contexts, 'dull; uninteresting').

Guǎngzhōu hěn mēnrè, báitiān sānshí dù, yèlǐ èrshíwǔ dù!	'Guangzhou is very humid, 30° in the daytime, 25° at night!'
Shèshì èrshísān dù shi Huáshì sānshíqī dù ba?	'23°C is 73°F, right?'

Wēndù shi duōshao?	'What's the temperature?'
Wǒ zuì bù xǐhuan mēnrè cháoshī de tiānqì.	'I hate hot and humid weather.'

7.10.7 *Yòu . . . yòu . . .* (又 . . . 又 . . .)

Yòu, with falling tone, has a core meaning of 'once again', but *yòu* reiterated before a pair of verbs—most commonly SVs—often translates as 'both . . . and' or simply 'and'.

Yòu kuài yòu shūfu.	'[It]'s fast and comfortable.'
Yòu lèi yòu jǐnzhāng.	'Tired and anxious.'
Yòu mēn yòu rè.	'Hot and humid.'

The following exercise has two parts. For the first part, you are asked to answer questions on the basis of *tiānqì yùbào* 'weather reports' from a number of Chinese cities presented in a table. For the second part, you are asked to write a weather report in Chinese for your area based on two examples provided.

Exercise 8

The table below shows weather conditions in major Mainland (*Dàlù*) cities (*chéngshì*). From it, you can read off temperature and cloud and rain conditions. Some of these (*zhuǎnyīn, duōyún*, etc.) will sound like what they are—weather report language; in context, though, this is acceptable. Answer the questions on the basis of the information contained in the national weather report.

Dàlù Tiānqì Yùbào

GUǍNGZHŌU	FÚZHŌU	KŪNMÍNG	HÀNKǑU	HÁNGZHŌU	SHÀNGHǍI
duōyún	*zhuǎnyīn*	*zhènyǔ*	*yǔtiān*	*duōyún*	*yǔtiān*
31 / 27	35 / 26	22 / 19	25 / 23	33 / 25	30 / 24

NÁNJĪNG	BĚIJĪNG	TIĀNJĪN	XĪ'ĀN	KĀIFĒNG	SHĚNYÁNG
zhuǎnqíng	*duōyún*	*zhuǎnyīn*	*yīntiān*	*qíngtiān*	*yǔtiān*
25 / 23	27 / 20	26 / 18	28 / 22	30 / 22	25 / 20

NOTE

A number of Mainland cities have *zhōu* as their second syllable: *Sūzhōu, Hángzhōu, Xúzhōu, Lánzhōu, Fúzhōu, Chángzhōu, Yángzhōu, Guǎngzhōu, Gànzhōu.* Before the modern era, *zhōu* was an important Chinese administrative unit, often translated as 'prefecture'.

duōyún	'cloudy'	*zhuǎn*	'to turn'
yīn	'overcast'	*qíng*	'clear'
zhènyǔ	'rain shower'	*yǔtiān*	'rainy day'
yīntiān	'overcast sky'	*qíngtiān*	'clear sky'

1. *Wèishénme měi ge chéngshì yǒu liǎng ge wēndù* (28/22)?
2. *Gēn zhuǎnyīn xiāngfǎn de shuōfǎ shi shénme? Gēn yīntiān xiāngfǎn de shuōfǎ ne?*
3. *Zhènyǔ hé yǔtiān yǒu shénme bù yíyàng? Duōyún hé yīntiān ne?*
4. *Nǐ juéde něi xiē chéngshì tiānqì zuì hǎo? Wèishénme?*
5. *Něi ge chéngshì tiānqì zuì chà? Wèishénme?*
6. *Nǐ juéde něi ge chéngshì lí Běijīng zuì jìn, něi ge lí Běijīng zuì yuǎn?*
7. *Něi xiē shi nánfāng de chéngshì, něi xiē shi běifāng de.*
8. *Nǐ juéde zhè shi dōngtiān de tiānqì yùbào háishi xiàtiān de tiānqì yùbào ne? Wèishénme?*

NOTE

shuōfǎ 'way of speaking': *gēn . . . xiāngfǎn de shuōfǎ* 'a way of saying the opposite of . . .'

Weather reports in Chinese newspapers, if they are not given in tabular form as above, are usually limited to a brief description of the skies, the wind velocity, and the high and low temperatures. The language is concise rather than colloquial, but otherwise fairly straightforward. Here are some actual examples, transcribed in pinyin (the Arabic numbers are in the original), with glosses added. The first is from a newspaper sold in Nanjing called *Yángzǐ Wǎnbào* 'Yangtze Evening News'. The second is taken, slightly edited, from the Internet. Following the model of these two reports, try writing a weather report (in Chinese) that is appropriate to your own district.

(1) ***Yángzǐ Wǎnbào*, 1999 *nián*, 7 *yuè*, 26 *hào***
Nánjīng shìqū tiānqì: jīntiān xiàwǔ dào yèlǐ duōyún,
('Nánjīng city-region weather: this afternoon to night cloudy')
míngtiān báitiān duōyún zhuǎnyīn yǒu zhènyǔ,
('tomorrow daytime cloudy becoming-overcast have showers')
piān dōng fēng 4–5 jí, wēndù 33°C–25°C.
('towards east wind 4–5 level, temperature 33°C–25°C')
(2) **Internet, 1999 *nián***
Běijīng: duōyún zhuǎnqíng, piān xī fēng 3 jí, wēndù 20°–24°.
('many-clouds becoming-clear, towards west wind 3 level, temp. 20°–24°')

Clouds over one of the *Sān Tǎ* 'Three Pagodas', *Dàlǐ, Yúnnán*

7.11 Dialogue: Talking about the weather (and finding the right words)

Jiǎ is a student from abroad, studying in China for the summer. *Yǐ* is from Nanjing.

Jiǎ:	*Jīntiān yǒu diǎnr rè, shì ma?*	'It's a bit hot today, isn't it?'
Yǐ:	*Duì, Nánjīng xiàtiān dōu shì zhèi yàngr, yòu rè yòu mēn. Chūntiān qiūtiān bǐjiào hǎo.*	'Yeah, summers in Nanjing are always like this, hot and muggy. Spring and autumn are better.'
Jiǎ:	*Suīrán hěn rè, kěshì měitiān dōu kànbujiàn tàiyáng! Zhèi yàngr de tiānqì, nǐmen zěnme shuō ne?*	'Although it's hot, you never see the sun! How do you talk about this kind of weather?'
Yǐ:	*Ng, zěnme shuō ne . . . yěxǔ kěyǐ shuō yǒu diǎnr huīméngméng de. Yě kěyǐ shuō wùméngméng de.*	'Yeah, what do we say? Perhaps [we] can say it's a bit 'gray'; or [we] can say 'misty'.'
Jiǎ:	*O, huīméngméng de; huòzhě wùméngméng de.*	'Oh, 'gray' or 'misty'.'
Yǐ:	*Shì.*	'That's right.'
Jiǎ:	*Huīméngméng de yǒu ge 'huī' zì, shì 'yīntiān' de yìsi, duì ma? Wùméngméng de yǒu ge 'wù' zì, shi 'yǒu wù' de yìsi. Kěshì zhèlǐ de tiānqì, yángguāng hěn qiáng, jiùshì kànbujiàn tàiyáng. Yǒu méiyǒu lìngwài yí ge cí?*	'*Huīméngméng* has the word 'gray' in it, meaning 'overcast', right? *Wùméngméng* has 'mist' in it, meaning 'misty'. But the weather here is bright, it's just that you can't see the sun. Is there another word?'
Yǐ:	*Ng, wǒ míngbai nǐ de yìsi. Yǒu diǎnr nán shuō. Wǒ xiànzài xiǎngbuchūlái hái yǒu shénme shuōfǎ. Yǐhòu zài gàosù nǐ, hǎo bu hǎo?*	'Yeah, I see what you mean. It's difficult to say. I can't think what other expression there is right now. I'll tell you later, okay?'

Jiǎ:	*Hǎo, xièxie nǐ. Cíhuì hěn bù róngyì!*	'Okay, thanks. Words are tough!'
Yǐ:	*Shì. Duì le, nǐ jiàqī dǎsuàn zuò shénme?*	'Right. Well, so, what are you planning to do over the break?'
Jiǎ:	*Wǒmen yào qù Kūnmíng.*	'We're off to Kunming.'
Yǐ:	*Kūnmíng, aiya, hěn yuǎn.*	'Kunming, wow, [that]'s far.'
Jiǎ:	*Wǒmen qù Kūnmíng yīnwèi nàr de tiānqì bǐjiào liángkuài, bù zěnme rè!*	'We're going to Kunming because the weather's cooler there, it's not so hot!'
Yǐ:	*Wǒmen cháng shuō Kūnmíng sìjì de tiānqì dōu xiàng chūntiān yíyàng—sìjì-rúchūn! Kōngqì yě hěn hǎo, yīnwèi hěn gāo—chàbuduō liǎngqiān mǐ gāo!*	'We often say every season in Kunming is like spring—'four seasons like spring'. The air's also nice because it's high—about 2,000 meters!'
Jiǎ:	*Liǎngqiān mǐ a, nà jiùshì liùqiān duō yīngchǐ. Shì hěn gāo! Tiānqì huì bu huì tài liáng?*	'2,000 meters! That's more than 6,000 feet. [That] *is* high! Will the weather [there] be too cool?'
Yǐ:	*Yèlǐ yǒu diǎnr liáng, kěshì báitiān dōu hěn hǎo. Cóng liùyuè dào bāyuè cháng xiàyǔ, kěshì tàiyáng yě hěn duō.*	'Nights are a bit cool, but days are fine. From July to August, it often rains, but there's also a lot of sun.'
Jiǎ:	*Kūnmíng dōngtiān zěnmeyàng?*	'How are the winters in Kunming?'
Yǐ:	*Dōngtiān yǒu diǎnr lěng, kěshì bú shì tài lěng.*	'Winters are a bit cool, but not too cold.'
Jiǎ:	*Nà nǐ ne, jiàqī nǐ dǎsuàn zuò shénme?*	'And you, what are you thinking of doing over the break?'

Yī:	*Wǒ bú zuò shénme, wǒ huì zài zhèr, xiūxi xiūxi.*	'I'm not doing anything [in particular], I'll be here, resting.'
Jiǎ:	*Nà yě hǎo!*	'That's good too!'

NOTES

a. *huīméngméng de; wùméngméng de;* In both cases, the tone on *mengmeng* varies; some say *méngméng* (as in the dialogue), others say *mēngmēng.* You can check to see what tone your friends use. There is uncertainty about how best to describe the kind of bright and hazy skies that dominate much of eastern China during the summer months. *Huīméngméng de,* built around the root *huī* 'gray', suggests 'overcast'; *wùméngméng de,* built around *wù,* meaning 'fog; mist', suggests 'misty'. Neither quite describes a sky that is just obscure—what in English might be called a hazy glare. In fact, the most appropriate description may simply be *hěn mēn,* which suggests not just muggy, but oppressive heat and humidity. The search for the right word can provide some interesting conversational opportunities for you.

b. *lìngwài* 'additional; another'; typically followed by a number expression: *lìngwài yí ge wèntí* 'an additional question'; cf. *biéde* 'other; another', followed by a noun: *biéde wèntí* 'other questions'

c. *cí* 'word', as opposed to *zì* 'character': *cíhuì* 'words; vocabulary'

d. *Chūlai,* seen as a verb combo in 7.1, can also appear as a suffix to verbs of perception and cognition, meaning, literally, 'figure out by V-ing': *xiǎngbuchūlai* 'cannot think up', *kàndechūlai* 'can recognize', etc.

e. V + *fǎ* 'way of V-ing': *shuōfǎ* 'way of speaking'; *kànfǎ* 'point of view'; *bànfǎ* 'way of dealing with [something]', etc.

f. *liáng* 'cool; cold'; *liángkuài* 'pleasantly cool'

g. *bù zěnme rè* 'not so hot', making use of the indefinite function of *zěnme;* cf. *bù zěnme gāo, bù zěnme shūfu*

h. *kōngqì* 'air; atmosphere' ('empty-air')

i. Chinese use the metric system: *mǐ* 'meter', *gōnglǐ* 'kilometer'. Traditional non-metric measures are sometimes prefixed with *yīng* 'English' to distinguish them from traditional Chinese measures: *yīngchǐ* 'feet'; *yīnglǐ* 'miles'.

j. *shì hěn gāo,* with *shì* providing confirmation, 'it is the case that'

k. *huì zài zhèr,* with *huì* here in the sense of 'likely to; going to'

7.12 Co-verbs (2)

In Unit 5, it was noted that *gěi* could function both as a verb (a main verb or one in a series) meaning 'to give' and as a co-verb (CV) meaning 'for [the benefit

Sunset through the haze, *Shànghǎi* (photograph by Jordan Gilliland)

of]'. In the latter case, it was placed before an associated verb, introducing the person who benefits from the verbal event: *Wǒ gěi tā mǎi dōngxi, tā gěi wǒ zuòfàn.* Now, we introduce two other CVs—*gēn* and *duì*.

The root meaning of *gēn* is 'to follow'. It was first encountered not as a verb, but as a conjunction in phrases such as *lǎoshī gēn xuéshēng*. Earlier in this unit, it also appeared in the phrase *gēn . . . yìqǐ*: *Gēn péngyou yìqǐ qù de* 'I went [there] with friends'. In both of these cases, it can be replaced by the slightly more formal *hé*. However, *gēn* also appears in association with certain verbs of communication and learning, where it often corresponds to English 'with; to' and where it is not synonymous with *hé*. This is its CV function. Here are some prototypical examples:

Nǐ gēn shéi xué Zhōngwén?	'Who do you study Chinese with?'
Gēn Zhāng lǎoshī.	'With Professsor Zhang.'
Tā gēn wǒ shuō:	'He said to me:'
Gēn nǐ jiè wǔ kuài, hǎo bu hao?	'Is it okay to borrow $5 [from you]?'
Kěyǐ, shí kuài yě kěyǐ.	'Sure; [you] can [borrow] $10.'
Tā cháng gēn fùmǔ yào qián.	She often asks her parents for money.

The root meaning of *duì* is 'to face; to be correct', and it appears in expressions such as *duìbuqǐ* 'sorry' ('face-not-worthy') and *duìmiàn* 'opposite' (*zài huǒchēzhàn⟨de⟩duìmiàn*). It may also function as a CV, subordinated to following SVs.

Yǒu rén shuō niúnǎi duì shēntǐ hěn hǎo.	'Some say that milk is good for you.'
Tīngshuō duì pífu tèbié hǎo.	'[I]'ve heard it's particularly good for the skin.'
Lǎoshī dōu hěn yán.	'The teachers are strict.'
Kěshì duì xuéshēng yě hěn hǎo.	'But [they]'re good to their students.'
Shì de!	'[That]'s true!'
Tāmen duì Zhōngguó fāngyán yǒu ~ gǎn xìngqù.	'They're interested in Chinese regional languages.'
Něi xiē fāngyán?	'Which ones?'
Guǎngdōng huà, Shànghǎi huà.	'Cantonese and Shanghainese.'

NOTE

Gǎn xìngqù ('feel interest') and the alternative, *yǒu xìngqù* ('have interest'), require the object of interest to be introduced with *duì*. *Yǒu* in the latter expression takes its regular negative—*méiyǒu xìngqù*.

Suīrán tā de zhuānyè shi huàxué, kěshì tā shuō duì huàxué měiyǒu xìngqù; xiànzài hěn xiǎng xué yǔyánxué!	'Although she's majoring in chemistry, she says she's not interested in it; now she wants to study linguistics.'

7.13 A letter home

The following is a letter from a student studying in China to a friend back home. It incorporates vocabulary and sentence patterns from the first seven units, and also introduces a few dozen new words, which are glossed in the notes that follow. It is written in a very colloquial style, as though spoken. Once you have practiced reading the passage aloud until you can read it with fluency and feeling, you should translate it carefully, making sure that you have accounted for everything and that the English reads naturally. Once you are satisfied with your translation, use it to back-translate into Chinese and see if you can retell the story with fluency.

Qīn'ài de Zhāng Yīng:

Nǐ hǎo. Wǒ xiànzài zài Běijīng! Fēijī shàng bú cuò, kànle liǎng ge diànyǐngr, tīngle hěn duō yīnyuè. Suīrán hěn yuǎn, yǒu yìdiǎnr bù shūfu, kěshì hěn yǒuyìsi. Wǒ shi yíyuè shíqī hào dào de. Běijīng Dàxué de Kǒng lǎoshī lái jiē wǒ. Wǒ zhù de sùshè zài Běijīng Dàxué, lí shàngkè de dìfang bù yuǎn. Sùshè hěn dà, yǒu liù qī ge dàlóu. Kěshì zhǐ yǒu wàiguórén néng zhù zài nàr; yǒu Ōuzhōu rén, Měiguó rén, Rìběn rén, yě yǒu Hánguó rén. Suīrán tāmen dōu dǒng Yīngwén, kěshì yīnwèi yǒude tóngxué shuō+de bú tài hǎo, suǒyǐ wǒmen zài yìqǐ píngcháng dōu shuō Zhōngwén, hěn shǎo shuō Yīngwén. Kàn nàme duō wàiguórén dōu zài nàr shuō Zhōngwén, Zhōngguó rén juéde hěn qíguài. Běi Dà de Zhōngguó xuéshēng yě yào gēn wǒmen shuō Yīngwén, suǒyǐ wǒmen shuōhuà de shíhou, tāmen gēn wǒmen shuō Yīngwén, wǒmen gēn tāmen shuō Zhōngwén. Báitiān wǒmen dōu chūqu shàngkè, chīfàn, zuò gōngkè, kěshì wǎnshàng huí sùshè lái. Zhōumò, wǒmen qù chéng lǐ pào zài kāfēiguǎnr, lěngyǐndiàn, xiǎochīdiàn. Běijīng chéng lǐ hěn rènao, wǒ hěn xǐhuan.

Běijīng dōngtiān shi cóng shíyī yuè dào èryuè. Fēicháng lěng, fēng yě hěn dà, kěshì bù cháng xiàxuě. Jīntiān shi qíngtiān, língxià wǔ dù, nà jiùshì Huáshì 23 dù. Yǒu diǎnr lěng méi guānxi, wǒ yǒu yí jiàn mián'ǎo—nà shì Zhōngguórén chuān de yīfu. Wǒ yě yǒu yì dǐng Měnggǔ màozi! Hěn nuǎnhuó! Zhōngguó péngyou dōu shuō wǒ xiàng ge qībāshí niándài de Zhōngguórén yíyàng. Tāmen bǐjiào xǐhuan chuān yǔróngfú.

Xià ge xīngqī yīnwèi shi Chūn Jié (jiùshì wàiguó rén shuō de Zhōngguó xīnnián), suǒyǐ Zhōngguó tóngxué dōu yào huíjiā guònián. Chūn Jié (jiùshì xià ge xīngqīsì), Lín lǎoshī qǐng wǒmen qù tā shūshu de jiā chīfàn. Tā shūshu shi Zhōngguó hěn yǒumíng de chúshī, zài Běijīng Dàfàndiàn gōngzuò. Wǒmen shi shàng ge xīngqī zài nàr rènshi tā de. Tā 60 duō suì, kěshì shēntǐ hěn hǎo, zhǎng+de hěn zhuàng, rén yě hěn hǎo. Tā zhù zài Wángfǔjǐng, Běijīng zuì rènào de dàjiē. Tā shuō zài nàr yǐjīng 25 nián le, suīrán yǒu diǎnr chǎo, kěshì tā bù xiǎng zhù biéde dìfang.

Nà, wǒ zài Běijīng yǐjīng sān ge xīngqī le, juéde hěn hǎo wánr. Hái méi qùguo Cháng Chéng. Yīnwèi měitiān dōu hěn máng xuéxí Hànyǔ, suǒyǐ yěxǔ děi děng fàngjià de shíhou cái néng qù biéde dìfang. Wǒ zhèi ge xuéqī shàng sì mén kè, měitiān dōu yǒu sān sì jié. Bān bú dà, dōu shì xiǎobān, suǒyǐ shuō Zhōngwén de jīhuì hěn duō ya. Zuòyè bù shǎo, měi ge xīngqī děi tīng lùyīn, xuéxí hěn duō Hànzì. Nà, wǒ zhǐ hǎo 'hǎohǎo xuéxí tiāntiān xiàng shàng'.

Zhù nǐ xīnnián kuàilè!

Nǐ de péngyou, — —.
2010.2.7

NOTES

a. *qīn'ài de* 'Dear . . .' ('intimate-love')

b. *Ōuzhōu* 'Europe'; cf. *Yàzhōu* 'Asia', *Àozhōu* 'Australia', *Fēizhōu* 'Africa', *Běi Měizhōu* 'North America', *Nán Měizhōu* 'South America'

c. *lěngyǐndiàn* ('cold-drinks-shop')

d. *pào ⟨zai⟩* 'hang out'; The original meaning of *pào* as 'steep; brew' [as of tea] has a colloquial extension meaning 'to dawdle; to hang around'. In some common phrases, it appears without *zài*: *pào jiǔguǎnr* 'to hang out at bars', *pào wǎngbā* 'to hang out at Internet cafés'.

e. *rènào* 'lively; buzzing with excitement'

f. *mián'ǎo* 'Chinese padded jacket' ('cotton-jacket') with M *jiàn*, for clothes

g. *chuān* 'wear' [clothes, but not accessories such as hats, belts, ties, etc.]

h. *Měnggǔ màozi* 'Mongolian hat' with M *dǐng*, for hats

i. *nuǎnhuó* 'to be warm; to feel warm' [of people or weather]

j. *qībāshí* '*qīshí, bāshí*'

k. *niándài* 'era; decade', as in *bāshí niándài* 'the 80s'

l. *yǔróngfú* ('down-filled-coat')

m. *Xīn Nián* 'New Year'

n. *guònián* 'pass the new year'

o. *Chūn Jié* 'The Spring Festival'—that is, the Lunar New Year

p. *chúshī* 'cook; chef' ('kitchen-teacher')

q. *fàndiàn* 'hotel'; Fancy hotels in China were historically associated with fine food, hence *fàndiàn* or *dàfàndiàn.*

r. *Běijīng Dàfàndiàn*; Considered the first modern hotel in Beijing, it is an interesting example of Soviet grand-style architecture. It was built in the 1950s to house foreign guests, and enlarged with a new wing in 1974, when it still towered over the low buildings of the area just east of Tiananmen Square in central Beijing.

s. *Wángfǔjǐng* ('prince's residence well'); the name of one of Beijing's most well known commercial streets.

t. *dàjiē* 'avenue' ('big-street')

u. *chǎo* 'to be noisy'

v. *fàngjià* 'to have time off; to take a holiday' ('put-leave of absence')

w. *Cháng Chéng* 'The Great Wall' ('long wall'); often known as the *Wànlǐ Cháng Chéng* ('10,000-li long-wall').

x. *jīhuì* 'opportunity'

y. *lùyīn* 'tape recording' ('record-sound'); also 'to make a recording'

z. *zhǐ hǎo* 'can only; have no choice but to; have to' ('only good')

a-a. *zhù* 'to wish; to extend blessings' (homophonous, but not synonymous, with *zhù* 'to live')

b-b. *kuàilè* 'happiness'

c-c. *Nǐ de péngyou* is the normal sign-off for personal letters; also *nǐ de tóngxué*, etc.

d-d. 2010.2.7; Note the contracting order of Chinese dating: year-month-day.

The phrase *hǎohǎo xuéxí, tiāntiān xiàng shàng* is said to have been spoken by (or perhaps repeated by) Mao Zedong, and often appears on school walls to urge children to work hard. *Hǎohǎo* is an adverbial (formed from the repetition of the SV) and can be translated as 'properly; well'; *xiàng shàng*, with CV *xiàng*, literally means 'towards above'; in other words, 'to make progress': 'Study hard and do well!'

Exercise 9

Paraphrase the following in Chinese.

1. Although the dorm's residents are foreigners, there are still many opportunities to speak Chinese. We spend our days out, talking to Chinese students, and we don't come home until quite late.
2. I came to Nanjing in November 2008, and now it's December 2009, so I've been living here for a year. I work at the Grand Hotel (*Gǔ Nándū Fàndiàn*), and I live there too, on the 16th floor. It's sometimes a bit noisy, but it's very comfortable.
3. We have class every morning from 9:00 to noon, but only four days a week. On Wednesday, we don't have any classes, so we often take the bus into town and shop and visit interesting places.

7.14 Pronunciation practice

Below are three sets of phrases to practice reading aloud. The first set consists of miscellaneous phrases and signs; the second, of disyllabic words with the *r* suffix; and the third, of titles of well-known Chinese films.

MISCELLANY

jūzhùqū	'residential district' ('reside-live-district')
zhíxiáshì	('direct-jurisdiction-city'); a city that is ruled directly by the central government
jiāotōng-shūniǔ	'communication or transportation hub' ('communication-pivot')
sīfǎjú	('judiciary-bureau')
ānquán-tōngdào	'emergency route' ('safety-route')
jǐnjí-chūkǒu	'emergency exit' ('emergency-exit')
shāngwù-zhōngxīn	'business-center'
gòuwù-zhōngxīn	'shopping center' ('buy-things-center')

Qǐng wù xīyān	'No smoking please' ('request don't draw+in-smoke')
yíngyè shíjiān	'business hours' ('operation hours')
Xiǎoxīn ménxì	'Mind the gap' ('careful door-crevasse')

COLLOQUIAL WORDS WITH THE *R* SUFFIX

huāpíngr [huāpyér]	'vase' ('flower-bottle')
húzuǐr [húzuěr]	'spout [of a kettle]' ('kettle-mouth')
xiǎoqǔr [xiǎoqǚr]	'popular ditty; song' ('little-tune')
dònghuàpiānr [dònghuàpiār]	'cartoon' ('move-drawing-film')
pūgàijuǎnr [pūgàijüǎr]	'bed roll; bed kit' ('bedclothes-roll')
chǒujuér [chǒujüér]	'clown'
qūqur [qüqür]	'cricket' [the insect, northern speakers]
dànhuángr [dànhuá^{n}r]	'egg yolk'

FILM TITLES Literal translations of those films whose English titles are not close to the Chinese are marked with *. You can add to the list by asking Chinese friends about films that are popular in China or Taiwan.

Huáng Tǔdì 'Yellow Earth' 1984
Hēipào Shìjiàn 'Black Cannon Incident' 1986
Hóng Gāoliang 'Red Sorghum' 1987
Dàhóng Dēnglóng Gāogāo Guà 'Raise the Red Lantern' 1991
Qiūjú Dǎ Guānsi (*Qiuju Sues) 'The Story of Qiu Ju' 1992
Xìmèng Rénshēng (*Theater-dream Human-life) 'The Puppetmaster' 1993
Bàwáng Biéjī (*The Conqueror Leaves His Consort) 'Farewell, My Concubine' 1993
Lán Fēngzheng 'Blue Kite' 1993
Huózhe 'To Live' 1994
Wòhǔ Cánglóng 'Crouching Tiger, Hidden Dragon' 2000
Huāyàng Niánhuá (*Flower-like Age) 'In the Mood for Love' 2000
Hé Nǐ Zài Yìqǐ 'Together' 2002

Yīngxióng 'Hero' 2002
Shímiàn Máifu (*Ten-sides Ambush) 'House of Flying Daggers' 2004

7.15 Summary

About to	*Kuài xiàkè le.*
V-*wán*	*Jīntiān de gōngkè hái méi zuòwán.*
V-*dào*	*Zuótiān méi kàndào nǐ.*
V-*zháo*	*Wǎnshàng hěn rè, shuìbuzháo jiào!*
V-*hǎo*	*Fàn yǐjīng zuòhǎo le.*
V-*bǎo*	*Chībǎo le, chībǎo le.*
V-*cuò*	*Nèi ge zì hǎoxiàng xiěcuò le.*
Cái	*Tā 1997 nián cái huílai de.*
Come back	*Nǐ shénme shíhou huí sùshè lái?*
V-*lai/qu*	*Qǐng guòlai kànkan ba.*
Because	*Yīnwèi tiānqì hěn rè, suǒyǐ wǒmen dōu hěn lèi.*
Although	*Suīrán fùmǔ shi Zhōngguó rén, dànshì tā méi qùguo Zhōngguó.*
If	*Nǐ yàoshì méi diànnǎo, kěyǐ qù wǎngbā fā e-mail.*
If	*Rúguǒ nǐ bù xiǎng qù, nà wǒ yě bù xiǎng qù.*
Say you . . .	*Bù néng qù de huà, jiù dǎ ge diànhuà ba.*
Exclamations	*Zhēn liǎobuqǐ!*
Other languages	*Nǐ hái huì shuō biéde wàiyǔ ma?*
Some	*Bù yídìng, yǒurén xǐhuan, yǒurén bù xǐhuan.*
Put	*Yào bu yào fàng niúnǎi?*
Together	*Gēn wǒmen yíkuàir ~ yìqǐ qù, hǎo bu hǎo?*
Alone	*Yí ge rén qù ma?*
Self	*Zìjǐ zuò de ma?*
Time/Duration	*liǎng diǎn zhōng / liǎng ge zhōngtóu*
Duration	*Huíjiā yào jǐ fēn zhōng?*
Continuous	*Zhōngwén xuéle jǐ nián le?*
Restrictive adverb	*Zhǐ xuéle sān ge yuè.*

Enduring states	*Wǒ rènshi tā yǐjīng yǒu èrshí duō nián le.*
Degrees	*Shèshì 23 dù shi Huáshì 73 dù ba.*
Yòu . . . yòu . . .	*Yòu kuài yòu shūfu.*
Gēn as CV	*Nǐ gēn shuí ~ shéi xué Zhōngwén?*
Duì as a CV	*Tā zhǐ duì diànnǎo gǎn xìngqù.*

7.16 Rhymes and rhythms

A schoolboy's ~ girl's lament

Dúshū rú dāng nú,	('Study-books like be slave,')
jiàn shī rú jiàn hǔ,	('see teacher like see tiger,')
Qín Huáng shāobújìn,	('Qin emperor burn-not-exhaust,')
shǐ wǒ yì shēng kǔ!	('make me one life bitter!')

NOTES

a. *Rú* is a more formal equivalent of *xiàng* 'resemble'.

b. *Shāobújìn* is a verb combo in the potential form.

c. *shǐ* 'to cause to'

The Qin dynasty (*Qíncháo*), 221–206 BCE, originated as a small kingdom in the west of what is now China. During the Zhou dynasty, it grew into a powerful kingdom that eventually conquered the surrounding kingdoms and created the first imperial dynasty, ruled by King *Zhèng*. The king styled himself *Shǐ Huángdì* 'First Emperor' and, aided by his minister, *Lǐ Sī*, consolidated his power through ruthless but effective political measures. These included the notorious (and probably exaggerated) 'burning of books' (*shāo shū*), the event referred to in the penultimate line of the rhyme. Under *Shǐ Huángdì*, walls built earlier to keep out non-Han peoples from the north were connected to make the original Great Wall (*Cháng Chéng*)—along a different route from the one seen today.

Huāmāo 'tabby cat'

Xiǎo huāmāo, shàng xuéxiào,	('little tabby-cat, attend school,')
lǎoshī jiǎng kè, tā shuìjiào:	('teacher give lesson, (s)he sleeps:')

yí ge ěrduo tīng, yí ge ěrduo mào,	('one ear listens, one ear blocked,')
nǐ shuō kěxiào bù kěxiào?	('you say funny or not?')

NOTE

kěxiào 'funny'; cf. *kě'ài* 'lovable' and *kěpà* 'fearsome'

Appendix: Question words

You have, by now, encountered most of the important question words of colloquial Chinese. You have also seen several cases of question words as indefinites. Here is a review:

SHÉI OR *SHUÍ*? 'WHO(M)'

Nà shi shéi?	'Who's that?'
Nǐ de lǎoshī shi shéi?	'Who's your teacher?'
Shéi shi nǐ de lǎoshī?	'Who [of these people] is your teacher?'
Wèn shéi?	'Who⟨m⟩ are [you] asking?'

Tā shi shénme rén ('what person') usually means 'what is she/he to you', and can be answered: *Tā shi wǒ de lǎoshī; tā shi wǒ shūshu.*

Indef: *Nǐ wèn shéi?* → *Wǒ bú wèn shéi.*

SHÉNME 'WHAT'

Shénme kǎoshì?	'What test?'
Tā xìng shénme?	'What's her surname?'
Nǐ jiào shénme míngzi?	'What's your name?'
Máng shénme ne?	'What're you busy doing?'
Nǐ shuō shénme?	'What did you say? What are you saying?'
shénme dìfang	'what place; where'
Nǐ shi shénme dìfang rén?	'Where're you from?'
shénme shíhou	'what time; when'
Nǐ shénme shíhou zǒu?	'When are you going/leaving?'

Shénme has a fairly common regional/colloquial alternative—*shá*—which is probably a telescoped version of *shénme*.

Tā gàn shá qù? = Tā gàn shénme qù?
Nǐ shi shá dìfang rén? = Nǐ shì shénme dìfang rén?

Indef:	*Nǐ xiǎng chī shénme?*	→	*Bù xiǎng chī shénme.*
	Shénme shíhou zǒu?	→	*Shénme shíhou dōu xíng.*

NĚI, NǍ 'WHICH; WHAT'

Nǐ shi něi wèi?	'Who are you?' / 'Who is it?'
Tā shi něi/nǎ guó rén?	'What's her nationality?'
Něi ge? / Nèi ge!	'Which one?' / 'That one!'

NǍR (NORTHERN, COLLOQUIAL), *NǍLI* (TAIWAN NEUTRAL, MAINLAND FORMAL) 'WHERE'

Nǐ qù nǎr ~ nǎli? Nǐ dào nǎr qù?	'Where are you going?'
Nǎli, nǎli!	'Oh, you can't mean it!'

Indef:	*Nǐ qù nǎr? / Nǐ dào nǎr qu?*	*Wǒ bú qù nǎr. / Wǒ bú dào nǎr qu.*

ZĚNME 'HOW; IN WHAT WAY'

Zěnmeyàng?	'How're [you] doing?' / 'How's [it] going?'
Zěnme bàn?	'What can be done about [it]?'
Zěnme shuō?	'How do [you] say it?'
Nǐ zěnme qù?	'How do [you] go [there]?'
Zhōngwén, zěnme shuō?	'How's [it] said [in] Chinese?'

Indef:	*Duō yuǎn?*	*Bù zěnme yuǎn, hěn jìn.*

DUŌSHAO 'HOW MANY; HOW MUCH'

Nǐ de diànhuà shi duōshao?	'What's your phone number?'
Yígòng yǒu duōshao?	'How many do [you] have all together?'
Duōshao qián?	'How much money?'

Indef:	*Yǒu duōshao péngyou?*	*Méiyǒu duōshao, zhǐ yǒu liǎng sān ge.*

JǏ 'HOW MANY; HOW MUCH' [EXPECTING RELATIVELY FEW]

Jǐ niánjí?	'Which level (year)?'
Jǐ hào?	'What day?' / 'What number?'
Jǐ ge?	'How many?'
Lǐbàijǐ?	'What day of the week?'

Cantonese-influenced Mandarin:

Tā jǐshí qù Jílóngpō? 'When's he going to Kuala Lumpur?'

Indef: *Xīzàng yǒu jǐ ge dàchéng?* (*Xīzàng* 'Tibet'; *dàchéng* 'cities') *Méiyǒu jǐ ge, zhǐ yǒu yī liǎng ge.*

Jǐ has an additional meaning of 'several':

Xīzàng yǒu jǐ ge dàchéng. 'Tibet has a number of large cities.'

DUŌ 'TO WHAT DEGREE; HOW'

Qǐngwèn, niánjì duō dà ⟨le⟩?	'May [I] ask what [your] age is?'
Tā duō gāo?	'How tall is she?'
duōjiǔ	'how long'
Nǐ xuéle duō jiǔ le?	'How long have you been studying?'
duōcháng shíjiān	'how long'
Tāmen zài Xīníng yǐjīng duōcháng shíjiān le?	'How long have they been in Xining?'

WÈISHÉNME 'WHY; HOW COME'

Nǐ wèishénme hěn máng?	'How come you're so busy?'
Hěn lèi a. Wèishénme?	'You're tired. How come?'

THE CHARACTER UNITS

Unit 8 第八課 DÌ-BĀ KÈ

名不正，则言不顺，言不顺，则事不成。
Míng bú zhèng, zé yán bú shùn, yán bú shùn, zé shì bù chéng.
('name not right then speech not clear, speech not clear then things not succeed')
—On the Rectification of Names, from the *Analects* of Confucius.

This is the first of the character lessons, in which you are introduced to the Chinese writing system, the form and function of characters, the principles of handwriting, the approach to reading adopted by *Learning Chinese*, and the characters for numbers, dates, surnames, pronouns, verbs, and enough function words to allow for some readable content. This lesson presupposes familiarity with the material in at least Unit 1.

8.1 General features of Chinese texts

8.1.1 Size

Regardless of complexity, characters are uniform in overall size, fitting into an imaginary rectangle along the lines indicated in the following example (written with simplified characters). For this reason, characters are also called *fāngkuàizì* 'squared writing'.

上海天气很热。 *Shànghǎi tiānqì hěn rè.*

8.1.2 Spacing

Compare the character and pinyin versions of the sentence above: though the convention is not always consistently followed, pinyin places spaces between words rather than syllables. Characters, however, are evenly spaced, regardless of word boundaries.

8.1.3 Punctuation

Modern Chinese writing makes use of punctuation conventions that are similar in form to those of English, though not always identical in function.

Periods, full stops:	。/ . The former is traditionally used, but the latter is becoming more common.
Commas:	, / 、 The latter is commonly used in lists separating enumerated items.
Quotes:	「 . . . 」/ ' . . . ' / " . . . " The first type is traditionally used, but the others are also common.
Proper names:	There is nothing comparable to a capital letter in Chinese. Proper names are usually unmarked, though, occasionally, they are indicated by a wavy underline.

Other punctuation will be noted as it is encountered.

8.1.4 Direction

Traditionally, Chinese has been written and read from top to bottom and from right to left. Major writing reforms instituted in the PRC during the 1950s not only formalized a set of simplified characters, but required them to be written horizontally, from left to right, like modern European languages. As a result, Chinese texts now come in two basic formats. Material originating in Taiwan and traditional overseas communities, or on the Mainland prior to the reforms, is written with traditional characters that are, with a few exceptions such as in headlines and on forms, arranged in vertical columns and read from right to left. Material originating in the Mainland, in Singapore, and in some overseas communities subsequent to the reforms of the 1950s is written with simplified characters arranged in horizontal rows and read from left to right, just like English and countless other languages.

A number of other writing systems originally adopted the Chinese convention of vertical writing, though most of these have also since shifted to a primarily horizontal configuration. Japanese writing remains vertical for the most part. Korean shifted to mostly horizontal a few decades ago. The Classical Mongolian script, still seen on some of the buildings in the National Palace Museum in Beijing and elsewhere, was written vertically on the Chinese model, but with columns moving left to right, not right to left. Nowadays, Mongolian is mostly written in the Cyrillic (Russian) script, horizontally and left to right.

8.2 The form of characters

Characters are the primary unit for writing Chinese. Just as English letters have several forms (such as g/g and a/a) and styles (such as *italic* and **bold**), Chinese characters also have various realizations. Some styles that developed in early historical periods survive to this day in special functions. For example, the Chinese traditionally use ink impressions made by seals or 'chops', mostly square-shaped and made from various types of stone, in lieu of signatures on documents and items of value. The names and other characters on such seals are usually, even now, inscribed in a version of the character script known as the 'seal script' (*zhuànshū*), first developed during the Qin dynasty (3rd century BCE). Other scripts include the 'grass script' (*cǎoshū*) and the 'running script' (*xíngshū*), impressionistic versions of the standard script that are still used in handwriting and art. As in other scripts, advertisers and designers may also modify the look of characters in a variety of different ways for their own purposes. Putting such variants aside, it is estimated that the number of distinct characters appearing in modern texts is between 6,000 and 7,000. Fortunately, about half that number will suffice to read most modern material, such as newspapers, academic writing, and popular novels. High total numbers of characters are to be found in the most comprehensive dictionaries, but these numbers are inflated by archaic characters and variants.

8.2.1 Radicals and phonetics

There are certain ameliorating factors that make the Chinese writing system more learnable than it might otherwise seem to be. One of the most significant is the fact that many characters have common constituents. Between two-thirds and three-quarters of common characters (cf. DeFrancis 1984, p. 110 and passim) consist of two elements, both of which can often also stand alone as characters in their own right. Historically, these elements were selected either for their sounds (hence the term 'phonetic elements', or simply 'phonetics'), or for their meanings (making them semantic elements, commonly called 'radicals'). Thus, 忘 *wàng* 'to forget' contains 亡 *wáng* as a phonetic element and 心 'heart' as a radical; 語 *yǔ* 'language' is composed of 吾 *wú* and 言 'language'. The significance of phonetics and radicals will be discussed in a later section. For now, it is enough to know that a few hundred simple graphs are the building blocks for a large number of compound graphs: for example, 亡 appears in 忙 and 氓; 心 in 志 and 忠; 言 in 謝 and 說; 吾 in 悟 and 晤. These 'root' graphs number in the high hundreds, and familiarity with them allows many characters to be learned as a pairing of higher-order constituents (such as 中 + 心), rather than just a complex composite of strokes (忠).

8.2.2 Simplified characters

As noted in the introduction, Chinese policy makers tried to make the writing system easier to learn by introducing the Chinese equivalent of spelling reform, i.e., reducing the number of strokes in complicated characters. Thus, 國 becomes 国 and 邊 becomes 边, with the simplified version generally modeled on variants that had long been current in handwriting or calligraphy, but not in print. The two sets of characters are usually referred to in English as 'traditional' and 'simplified', and in Chinese as *fántǐzì* ('complicated-body-characters') and *jiǎntǐzì* ('simple-body-characters').

For you, the learner, this simplification is a mixed blessing; while it ostensibly made writing characters simpler, it also made characters less redundant for reading. For example, 樂 and 東 ('music' and 'east', respectively) are quite distinct as traditional characters, but their simplified versions—乐 and 东—are easier to confuse.

As noted in the Introduction, *jiǎntǐzì* and *fántǐzì* should not be thought of as two distinct writing systems; many characters retain only one form (也 *yě*, 很 *hěn*, 好 *hǎo*), and of those that have two forms, the vast majority exhibit only minor differences: 说 / 説, 饭 / 飯. There are perhaps only three dozen relatively common characters with quite divergent forms, such as 这 / 這 and 买 / 買. Careful inspection reveals that even these characters often have elements in common. For native Chinese readers, the two systems represent only a minor inconvenience, on par with the discrepancies between capital and lowercase letters in the Roman alphabet (though, admittedly, on a larger scale). Generally, learners focus on one system for writing, but soon get used to reading in both. In this text, both sets are introduced, but most of the readings are based on the simplified set that is standard for the 1.3 billion people on the Mainland. In most major sections of the character lessons, there is at least one sample text or exercise written in traditional characters.

8.3 The function of characters

As noted in the Introduction, Chinese uses a system of writing that employs complex symbols (characters) to represent syllables of particular words, or syllables that constitute parts of particular words. For this reason, it is difficult to use Chinese characters to transcribe foreign names: 'Italy' can be incorporated into Chinese as *Yìdàlì* and written 意大利, but the usual meaning of the characters, 'meaning-be big-benefit' can only be dimmed by context, not completely suppressed.

In Chinese, different words with identical sounds (homophones) will usually be written with different characters.

sound	*jīn*	
meaning	‘today’	‘metal’
character	今	金

Such homophony is common in Chinese at the syllable level (as illustrated in the *shi* story, described in the Introduction). Here, for example, are common words or word parts that are all pronounced *shì*:

shì

是 ‘to be’ 事 ‘thing’ 室 ‘room’ 试 ‘test’

Except for certain high-frequency words (such as 是 *shì* ‘to be’), words in Mandarin are usually compound, consisting of several syllables: 事情 *shìqing* ‘things’; 教室 *jiàoshì* ‘classroom’; 考试 *kǎoshì* ‘examination’. At the level of words or compound words, homophony is relatively rare. In Chinese language word processing with pinyin input, typing ‘shiqing’ and ‘kaoshi’ (most input systems do not require tones) will elicit only a few options; and since most word-processing software organizes options by frequency, this usually means that the correct characters for *shìqing* and *kǎoshì* will often be produced on the first try.

shì

shìqing	*jiàoshì*	*kǎoshì*
‘thing’	‘classroom’	‘test’
事情	教室	考试

8.4 Writing

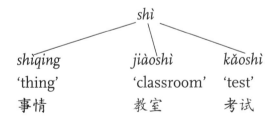

As noted in the Introduction, one of the most important pedagogical functions of learning to write Chinese characters is that it draws your attention to detail.

Characters are often distinguished by no more than a single stroke, or just a change in the orientation of a single stroke.

4 strokes:	天	夭	夫	犬	太
	tiān	*yāo*	*fū*	*quǎn*	*tài*
	'sky'	'goblin'	'person'	'dog'	'grand'
5 strokes:	白	申	田	甲	由
	bái	*shēn*	*tián*	*jiǎ*	*yóu*
	'white'	'to explain'	'field'	'A'	'from'

For the learner, there are also aesthetic and practical reasons for being able to write characters, over and above the contribution that writing makes to reading. Reasonable goals at the beginning level are to learn the principles of writing so that any character can be reproduced by copying, and to learn to write from memory a selection of representative graphs that can serve as the basis for future calligraphic endeavors.

8.4.1 Principles of drawing characters

There are many good websites that deal with the writing of Chinese characters. Some not only present the general principles of writing, but also allow the viewer to select characters and watch them drawn in animation, stroke by stroke. In this section, we will try to sketch out the basic principles of writing Chinese characters without using special graphics or non-text insertions and leave readers to browse the specialized websites for additional helpful information. (Cf. for example, yellowbridge.com, and the useful links listed in the appropriate sections of the Chinese Language Teachers Association website: clta-us.org.)

Calligraphic strokes are called *bǐhuà⟨r⟩* in Chinese. Strokes are drawn with a more or less fixed order and direction that are ultimately derived from calligraphic practices. This stroke order (*bǐshùn*) is considered important for both aesthetic and pedagogical reasons. Characters tend to look awkward if not drawn with the conventional order of strokes; and following the prescribed stroke order develops a tactile memory for characters that can act in support of visual memory.

A. FORM Characters are usually said to be formed from eight basic strokes, but because two of the 'basic' strokes' only appear appended to others (without the writing implement being lifted from the surface), they should really be regarded as basic components of strokes rather than actual strokes. All eight are illustrated below, with the names of each given on the far left. It is useful to be able to describe how a character is written by naming its strokes: *héng* + *shù* 'horizontal + vertical' for 十, *piě* + *nà* 'slanting down to the left + slanting down to the right' for 人. Chinese children often do this when they are learning to write, and we will do the same below when the general principles of stroke order are discussed.

To keep the presentation as clear as possible, the principles of drawing are illustrated by relatively simple characters. In most cases, it should be easy to identify the stroke in question.

The unitary strokes

NAME AND MEANING	DESCRIPTION	EXAMPLES IN CHARACTERS	
diǎn 'dot'	a very short stroke	小	热
héng 'horizontal'	a horizontal stroke	三	大
shù 'vertical'	a vertical stroke	十	中
piě 'cast aside'	a stroke that slopes downwards to the left	人	仁
nà 'press down'	a stroke that slopes downwards to the right	人	尺
tí 'raise'	a stroke that rises from left to right	打	汉

Extensions with gōu 'hook' and zhé 'bend'

NAME AND MEANING	DESCRIPTION	EXAMPLES IN CHARACTERS	
hénggōu 'horiz. + hook'	a horizontal stroke ending in a downwards hook	欠	买
shùgōu 'vert. + hook'	a vertical stroke ending in a leftwards hook	小	水
xiégōu 'slanted + hook'	a stroke that slants downwards to the right and ends in a upwards hook	氏	戈
héngzhé 'horiz. + bend'	a stroke that begins horizontal then bends to near vertical	夬	书
shùzhé 'vert. + bend'	an 'L' shaped stroke	世	凶

NOTES

a. The stroke *xiégōu* 'slant + hook' is always so called even though *nàgōu* 'slanting down to the right + hook' also looks like a reasonable name for it.

b. Sometimes a subcategory of the *piě* stroke, *duǎnpiě* 'short + slanting down to the left', is included in the list of basic strokes. Examples would be the top stroke of 千 or the top-left stroke of 午. Otherwise, these strokes are simply *piě.*

c. There are in fact some miscellaneous strokes that cannot be usefully analyzed in terms of the eight basics, e.g. *wāngōu* 'curved + hook', that appears, for example, on the left-hand side of the character 狗.

d. It is also quite common to combine three stroke components into a single stroke. The bottom stroke of 书 (shown above) consists of '*héngzhé* + *gōu*', i.e. 'horizontal with bend + hook'. In fact, in terms of frequency, bent strokes are more common with a final hook than without; cf. 儿, 也, 习.

B. DIRECTION In most cases, strokes are falling or horizontal, and left to right. Only one of the six unitary strokes rises—the one called *tí* (seen in the lower-left strokes of the two sample characters, 打 and 汉); only one flows leftwards—*piě*.

C. ORDER Though some useful generalizations can be made about the ordering of strokes within a character, it is not possible to reduce stroke order to a set of rules that would allow you to predict how to write any character. What the general principles listed below will allow you to do is make sense of the order and more easily recall the order once you have learned it. (Note that stroke direction and stroke order for individual characters are illustrated in Appendix 1.)

1. Left before right, top before bottom, top left to bottom right:

八	*bā* 'eight'	piě, nà
文	*wén* 'design'	*diǎn, héng, piě, nà*
地	*dì* 'place'	土 (slanted) then 也
三	*sān* 'three'	(upper) *héng*, (middle) *héng*, (lower) *héng*
火	*huǒ* 'fire'	*diǎn, piě, (duǎn)piě, nà*
早	*zǎo* 'be early'	日 then 十

2. *Héng* 'horizontal' before *shù* 'vertical', except *héng* as a final base stroke is held until after the vertical:

	十	*shí* 'ten'	*héng, shù*
	夫	*fū* 'person'	*héng, héng, piě, nà*
But:	土	*tǔ* 'soil'	*héng,* ***shù****, héng*
And:	王	*wáng* 'king'	*héng, héng,* ***shù****, héng*

3. Squares are drawn in three strokes, beginning with *shù* at the left, continuing with a *héng zhé* 'horizontal + bend' (sometimes ending in a hook), and closing with a bottom *héng*. (However, for innards, cf. number 4.)

口	*kǒu* 'mouth'	*shù, héngzhé, héng*

4. Outer before inner, except that the stroke closing a rectangle is drawn last, after the innards are filled:

月	*yuè* 'moon; month'	*piě, héngzhégōu,* (top) *héng,* (bottom) *héng*
问	*wèn* 'ask'	门 first, then 口

But:	日	*rì* 'sun; day'	*shù, héngzhégōu,* (middle) *héng,* (bottom) *héng*
And:	四	*sì* 'four'	*shù, héngzhégōu, piě, nà, héng*

5. Dominant strokes or components may override the left-to-right tendency.

小	*xiǎo* 'small'	*shù,* (left) *diǎn,* (right) *diǎn*
示	*shì* 'show'	*héng, héng, shùgōu,* (left) *diǎn,* (right) *diǎn*
迷	*mí* 'enchanted'	米 then 辶

6. With *diǎn* strokes ('dots'), an upper left-hand *diǎn* tends to be the first stroke of the character, and an upper right or inside *diǎn* tends to be the last stroke of the character. Both cases conform to the general left-to-right order of strokes.

First:	为	*wèi* 'for'	***diǎn***, *piě, héngzhégōu, diǎn*
	衣	*yī* 'clothes'	***diǎn***, *héng, piě, shùgōu, piě, nà*
Last:	玉	*yù* 'jade'	*héng, héng, shù, héng,* ***diǎn***
	戈	*gē* 'spear'	*héng, xiégōu, piě,* ***diǎn***

8.5 Presentation of characters

The reading and writing lessons in *Learning Chinese* are organized on the general principle that characters are best learned by encountering them many times in texts rather than in lists. Before characters can be read, however, they need to be recognized; and to be recognized, key features need to be noticed. In these lessons, characters are introduced in a large size, with information about number of strokes, pronunciation, general meaning, and form. This information is intended to give the characters some individuality and provide traction for the reading process. Sometimes, knowledge about the actual history of the character may account for, and therefore help to remember, its form. In other cases, the actual history of the character may be less helpful than a fanciful account. The notes that follow the introduction of each set of characters contain both actual and fanciful etymologies. Students, in any case, often make up their own stories to account for the form of characters. What is important is to find a way to link the shape of the character to the word it represents so that reading can proceed.

In the later sections of this lesson, and in other lessons, readings begin with words and phrases (with pinyin confirmation), then continue with short interactions, longer dialogues, and, when possible, narratives and stories. Once you find that you can read the material with confidence, you can consolidate by learning to write the graphs. Focusing on individual graphs will draw your attention to slight differences and prepare you for encountering new combinations.

NOTES

a. Since most words in Mandarin are compounds (of two or more syllables), characters generally represent parts of compounds rather than words as such. Sometimes combinational or historical information can suggest a general meaning for a single character in a compound: 明天 'bright' + 'day' for *míngtiān* 'tomorrow'. In cases where a particular character has no independent existence outside a compound, it may not be possible to give it a reliable meaning: 昨天 *zuótiān* '(? + day) yesterday'. (The same problems exists for the English word 'yesterday', which combines the word 'day' with the non-word 'yester'.) In such cases, if a general meaning can be inferred from other combinations, it will be placed in parentheses.

b. For characters with two forms, simplified and traditional, both forms are given, with the traditional form above the simplified. The reason for this order is that the simplified generally derives from the traditional. Once past the initial introduction, however, the focus is more on the simplified set, and when both are cited, simplified precedes traditional.

c. The order and direction of strokes for individual characters are provided in Appendix 1.

d. It is not crucial to know which radical a particular graph is classified under, but it is useful to recognize the most common radicals. The system of paired numbers written beneath the large-format characters that provide the introduction to each set is a practical way of doing this. The first number represents the number of strokes for the character's radical. The second number represents the number of remaining strokes in the character. (Traditionally, Chinese dictionaries are organized in this way, first by radical, then by number of strokes.) The sum of these two numbers is the total number of strokes for the character. When the second number is zero (as for 长 4 + 0 / 長 8 + 0), the character is itself a radical. In some cases, characters that have only one form have been assigned a different radical in the simplified set from that of the traditional; for example, 弟 *dì* 'younger brother', for which there is no traditional-simplified distinction, is assigned the radical 弓 in the traditional set (3 + 4), but 八 in the simplified set (2 + 5). In such cases, both numbers are given, with the traditional radical assignment first.

For the majority of cases, the numbering method makes it clear which element is the radical. However, when the radical is obscure, or the number of strokes for the radical happens to equal the number of strokes that remain (as is the case for 'six' below—2 + 2), the numbers will not indicate the radical with certainty. Knowing the radical assigned to a character was more important when dictionaries were organized by radical rather than pronunciation, as they tend to be now. Nowadays, it is enough to know the more common radicals, and the numerical system used herein will suffice to bring those to light.

e. Traditional characters would normally be written vertically, but for reasons of practicality, they too are presented in horizontal format herein.

f. Occasionally, new characters which have not been formally introduced in the character lessons are included in texts on the assumption that they can be identified from the context. Such material is underlined. When context is insufficient, new material is glossed in notes that follow.

g. As noted in the Introduction, a sensible policy toward the two character sets is to read both but write simplified.

SUMMARY Scan the **large-format** characters and the analysis and **notes** that follow to try to find a connection between each character and the word that it represents.

Remind yourself of the words and phrases that contain the new characters by covering up the pinyin with a pencil and reading the **phrases** section (§8.12.1). Then uncover the pinyin and check.

Making use of context, do the **readings** until you have a clear comprehension of the passage while reading it aloud.

Finally, complete the **exercises**, practice writing the characters until familiar, and review.

8.6 Numbers

一	二	三	四	五
1 + 0	2 + 0	1 + 2	3 + 2	1 + 3
yī	*èr*	*sān*	*sì*	*wǔ*
六	七	八	九	十
2 + 2	1 + 1	2 + 0	1 + 1	2 + 0
liù	*qī*	*bā*	*jiǔ*	*shí*

NOTES

The characters for 'one', 'two', and 'three' are obviously representational. The near left-right symmetry of the characters for 'four', 'six', 'eight', and 'ten' is not entirely coincidental. 四 seems to have represented a whole easily divided into two parts; an earlier form of 六 looked very much like that of 四 (with the two lower 'legs' of 六 matching the two inner strokes of 四). 八 (distinguished from 人 *rén* 'person' and 入 *rù* 'enter') is also said to have represented the notion of division (into two groups of four); and 十 represented a unity of the four cardinal directions with the center. Smaller multiples of ten are occasionally represented as unit characters, especially where space is at a premium: 廿 'twenty' and 卅 'thirty'. However, they are still read as if written 二十 and 三十.

Exercise 1

Practice reading the Chinese multiplication table.

The Chinese multiplication table is often called *jiǔjiǔ chéngfǎbiǎo* (九九乘法表) 'nine nines multiplication table' or the *jiǔjiǔ kǒujué* (九九口诀) 'nine nines rhyme' because in its traditional form it began with the nine-times table and descended to the one. Though nowadays it is usually recited upwards from one, it keeps another important feature of the traditional system in always reciting the smaller operand first: 3 × 7, never 7 × 3. In other words, the Chinese table has only half the entries of the standard American-British table. The six through nine-times tables given below illustrate. Note that when the product is only a single digit, the rhythm is preserved by adding 得 *dé* 'gets'; for similar reasons, the teens are often recited as *yīshí'èr*, etc., rather than just *shí'èr*.

六	七	八	九
一六得六	一七得七	一八得八	一九得九
二六一十二	二七一十四	二八一十六	二九一十八
三六一十八	三七二十一	三八二十四	三九二十七
四六二十四	四七二十八	四八三十二	四九三十六
五六三十	五七三十五	五八四十	五九四十五
六六三十六	六七四十二	六八四十八	六九五十四
	七七四十九	七八五十六	七九六十三
		八八六十四	八九七十二
			九九八十一

Practice reading telephone numbers.

Although telephone numbers are often written out in Arabic numerals on business cards, they do appear as characters in other contexts, with the exception of *líng* 'zero', which is more often written 'O'. Practice reading the following until you can do so fluently, with a good rhythm. Recall that, in the Mainland, 'one' in telephone numbers (as well as in other kinds of lists) is usually pronounced *yāo* rather than *yī*.

电话 / 電話 *diànhuà* 'telephone'		手机 / 手機 *shǒujī* 'mobile phone'		
(1) 六五九六	二九一八	一三五	O一七五	一四四三
(2) 四二七九	九四一五	一三九	三六二九	六九六四
(3) 五四二七	九四一五	一三九	二O三八	五八八二
(4) 五一六八	七二一九	一三O	二四六七	九九八五
(5) 八二二O	七四二六	一三五	一四四三	六四八八
(6) 二三八七	二七六二	O二九	二六六三	四一O九

8.7 Dates

In Unit 1, you learned the components of dates: *nián* 'year', *yuè* 'month', and *rì/hào* 'day'. It was also noted that dates, though spoken with *hào*, are usually written with *rì* 'sun; day'.

年	月	日	(号	/號)
1 + 5	4 + 0	4 + 0	(3 + 2)	(6 + 7)
nián	*yuè*	*rì*	*hào*	
'year'	'month'	'day'	'date'	

NOTE

The characters used for *yuè* and *rì* are representational, being squared-off versions of what were originally drawings of the moon and sun, respectively. On the other hand, *nián* is not obviously representational, so you might need to construct a made-up etymology for it, such as: 'A *year* contains four seasons; the first stroke (*piě*) stands for the winter, the three horizontal strokes (*héng*) are the growing and harvesting seasons (spring, summer, and autumn); the short fourth stroke (*diǎn*) marks the harvest, and the long vertical stroke (*shù*) represents the continuity of the year.' However, note that the short *diǎn* stroke on the third horizontal is drawn before the lowest horizontal, presumably following the stroke order principle of 'closing stroke last'. 号/號*hào* is placed in parentheses because it does not usually appear in written dates; its traditional form has 虎 'tiger' as radical.

Dates are frequently written using Arabic numerals, as in these examples, which could be taken from the banners of Mainland newspapers.

1999年7月26日
2002年2月11日
1998年5月7日

Interestingly, the traditional, 'lunar calendar' dates are often written out in full, with the numbers also represented by characters. The Chinese lunar calendar consists of 12 months of 29 to 30 days, plus intercalary months inserted every few years to make up the difference. The lunar New Year usually begins several weeks after the solar New Year. Lunar years are counted in cycles of 60, which accounts for all possible combinations of a set of 10 'stems' and 12 'branches' (i.e., 1–1, 1–2 . . . 1–11, 1–12, 2–1 . . . 10–12, etc.). Though the first lunar month has a special name (*zhèngyuè*), the rest are all written with number + *yuè*, just like the solar calendar months; *rì* is usually left out of lunar dates. The correspondence is as follows:

International dating:	1999年7月26日
Traditional Chinese:	己卯年七月 二十六
	jǐ mǎo

Most newspaper banners give dates in both forms. Even in traditional dates, *líng* 'zero' is usually written as o rather than with its complicated character 零.

Exercise 2

The following are all significant dates in Chinese history. Practice reading them aloud, and see if you can discover (or recall) the event that took place on each date.

一九四九年　十月　一日　　一九二一年　七月　一日
一九一九年　五月　四日　　一九八九年　六月　四日
一九四五年　八月　十五日　　一九一一年　十月　十日

In the spaces provided, write the following dates in Chinese.

November 23, 1949

April 18, 2003

February 15, 1994

October 19, 2001

8.8 Days

今天	昨天	明天
2 + 2　1 + 3	4 + 5	4 + 4
jīntiān	*zuótiān*	*míngtiān*
'today'	'yesterday'	'tomorrow'

NOTES

a. It is useful to distinguish simplex (non-compound) characters from compound. The latter contain parts that can themselves be characters: for example, 明 *míng* 'bright' is composed of the two graphs 日 *rì* 'sun; day' and 月 *yuè* 'moon; month'. While more common characters are often simplex, the vast majority are compound. The form of simplex graphs can often be classified as representational and thereby rationalized by a non-linguistic reference (e.g., 日 originated as a representation of the sun and 月 of the moon). Graphic elements are compounded, however, not to form new representations, but to combine linguistic elements of sound (phonetics) and meaning (radicals).

b. 天 *tiān* has the root meaning of 'sky; day', and it is said to be based on a drawing that represented the sky above Earth. 明 *míng* is composed of the characters for 'sun' and 'moon', and appears in compounds with the meaning 'bright' (cf. 'a bright tomorrow'). 昨 *zuó* is also a compound, combining the radical 日 *rì* 'sun' with the phonetic 乍 *zhà*.

Exercise 3

The list of days and dates below is out of order. Read the entries in numerical order, beginning with the numbers on the left. Though you would normally read the day out as *rì*, once you have read it, you can pass it on as information with *hào*: "*Dì-yī, míngtiān wǔyuè shí rì* (or *shí hào*)."

七：	今天	四月	二十日
三：	昨天	九月	十八日
六：	明天	三月	四日
二：	昨天	十二月	十七日
九：	今天	八月	二日
一：	明天	五月	十日
四：	今天	九月	二十五日
五：	明天	十一月	三十日
八：	昨天	六月	十四日
十：	今天	二月	九日

8.9 Surnames and pronouns

王	李	毛	周	白	林
4 + 0	4 + 3	4 + 0	2 + 6	5 + 0	4 + 4
wáng	*lǐ*	*máo*	*zhōu*	*bái*	*lín*
'king'	'plum'	'fine hair'	'circle'	'white'	'woods'

As shown, the characters that represent surnames also represent words with other meanings.

姓	她	他	也
3 + 5	3 + 3	2 + 3	1 + 2
xìng	*tā*	*tā*	*yě*
'surname⟨d⟩'	'she; her'	'he; him'	'also; too'

NOTE

姓 *xìng* 'surname⟨d⟩' and 她 *tā* 'she; her' both have 女 *nǚ* 'female' as a radical. (Early forms of 女 are said to depict a woman crouching or kneeling.) In 姓, 女 is combined with 生 *shēng* 'to be born', suggesting a notion such as 'children are born of women and given a *surname*'. 她 was created in relatively recent times as a counterpart to 他 (a contrast not represented in the spoken language). The right element of 他 and 她 was originally distinct from the graph 也, used to write the word *yě* 'also; too'. The modern identity is fortuitous, probably a result of scribal confusion, and causes confusion for students of the language. You will need to pay special attention to the characters 他, 她, and 也.

Exercise 4

Read the following sentences aloud (paying attention to tones), beginning with 'one' (and citing the number).

三	她姓毛。	七	他也姓周。
五	他姓李。	二	她姓王。
一	她姓白。	十	她也姓白。
八	他也姓林。	四	她姓林。
九	她也姓毛。	六	他姓周。

The following list is out of numerical order. Read it in order, and read out the surname and birthday (*shēngrì*), along the following lines.

"*Dì-yī ge:*	*⟨Tā⟩ xìng Wáng; ⟨shēngrì ne:⟩ yījiǔbā'èr nián, yīyuè sì rì* (or *hào*)"
六：	王；1946年8月23日
八：	李；1981年6月8日
三：	毛；1979年10月29日
九：	周；1966年2月30日
十：	白；1961年10月2日
十一：	林；1942年8月17日
二：	毛；1983年4月14日
一：	王；1982年1月4日
十二：	周；1976年11月21日

四：　　白；1959年9月21日
七：　　林；1967年3月16日
五：　　李；1951年11月7日

Use the data in the previous table as the basis for a conversation along the following lines.

Cue: *Dì-yī ge ne?*

Response: *Dì-yī ge: Xìng Wáng; shēngrì: yījiǔbā'èr nián, yīyuè sì hào.*

8.10 More pronouns and function words

我	你	們	不	嗎	呢
4 + 3 or 1 + 6	2 + 5	2 + 8	1 + 3	3 + 9	3 + 5
		们		吗	
		2 + 3		3 + 3	
wǒ	*nǐ*	*men*	*bù*	*ma*	*ne*
'I; me'	'you'	COLLECTIVE	NEG	Q	NE

NOTES

a. 我，你, and 们/們, like the other graphs used for pronouns (他 and 她) are compound, though only one of the parts of 我 can still be represented independently in the modern language—the right element is the graph 戈 *gē* 'spear' (looking more like a harpoon with its barbed tip down). Both 你 and 们/們 have a left element that is a vertical version of the graph 人 'person', known as *rénzìpáng* 'person at the side' (or the 'person radical'). The right elements, 尔 and 门/門, respectively, also appear independently (cf. next item).

b. 们/們 consists of the person radical plus 门/門 *mén* 'door', which is phonetic. 门/門 was originally a representation of a door with two leaves.

c. The graph 不, said to derive from a drawing of a bird, was borrowed to write *bù* not because of its form, but because of similarity of sound. A made-up etymology: '不 represents an arrow being shot at the ceiling—but *not* managing to pass through'.

d. The set in §8.10 is the first to include graphs that have both simplified and traditional forms: 们/們 and 吗/嗎. The simplified graphs are both based on traditional calligraphic forms, and they retain a holistic resemblance to the traditional form, even though the two share only a few strokes in common.

e. 吗/嗎 contains the graph 马/馬 *mǎ* 'horse' (originally a drawing of a horse) as a phonetic (in other words, used to indicate the similarity of its sound). The addition of 口 *kǒu* 'mouth; entrance' (but here suggesting 'colloquial') removes any ambiguity. Cf. 妈/媽 *mā*, the informal word for 'mother', which also makes use of 马/馬 as a phonetic with the graph 女 'woman; female' to disambiguate.

8.10.1 Reading

1. 他姓王。我也姓王。
2. 你也姓毛吗？/ 不，我姓王。
3. 他姓李吗？/ 不，他姓林。
4. 我姓王，他姓林，你呢？
5. 我姓周，他姓林，你姓王。
6. 我姓王，她姓白，你呢？
7. 我姓周，她姓林，你姓白吗？
8. 不，我姓林，你姓白吗？
9. 你们呢？他们呢？/ 我姓周，他们呢：他姓白，他姓李，她姓林。

8.11 SVs and associated function words

好 3 + 3	累 5 + 6	忙 3 + 3	餓 8 + 7 饿 3 + 7	冷 2 + 5
hǎo 'to be good'	*lèi* 'tired'	*máng* 'busy'	*è* 'hungry'	*lěng* 'cold'
很 3 + 6	還 3 + 13 还 3 + 4	熱 4 + 11 热 4 + 6	太 3 + 1	了 1 + 1
hěn 'very'	*hái* 'still'	*rè* 'hot'	*tài* 'too; very'	*le* LE

NOTES

a. SVs: 好 is composed of the female radical 女 and 子 *zǐ* 'child' (the latter without a phonetic function), often explained as the paradigm of a 'good relationship'. 累 includes 田 *tián* 'field' above and the radical derived from the graph for 'silk' below: 'a heavy and *tiring* burden for such a slender base'. 忙 combines the 'heart radical' (an elongated and truncated version of 心) and 亡 *wáng* as a phonetic element, and can be compared to 忘 *wàng* 'to forget' with the same elements configured vertically. 饿/餓 is composed of the element 饣/食, known as the 'food radical', and the phonetic element 我 *wǒ*. 冷 includes two strokes (*diǎn* and *tí*) on the left, forming the so-called 'ice radical', found only in a few graphs such as 冰 *bīng* 'ice'. The right element of 冷 is 令 *lìng*, a phonetic element also found in 零 *líng* 'zero'. The four strokes at the base of 热/熱 are a form of the 'fire radical' which, in its independent form, is written 火.

b. ADVs: The graph 很 is composed of the radical 彳 and the phonetic 艮 *gèn* (cf. 恨 *hèn*, 狠 *hěn*, 跟 *gēn*). 太 is 大 *dà* 'big' with an extra *diǎn*. The graph 还/還 is also used for the word *huán* 'to give back', which probably accounts for the presence of 辶 on the left, a radical associated with motion. The simplified version substitutes 不 not for its sound or meaning, but for its general shape, which serves to represent the complicated right-hand element.

c. 了 should be distinguished from 子 *zǐ*. In the traditional set, the radical assigned to 了 is the second stroke, the vertical hook; but in the simplified set, it is the first stroke, whose uncontorted form is 乙, a radical also assigned to 也.

8.11.1 Pronunciation practice

Cover the pinyin and check your pronunciation of the following phrases.

A. *JIǍNTǏZÌ* 'SIMPLIFIED SET'

三月 *sānyuè*	今天 *jīntiān*	也好 *yě hǎo*	姓王 *xìng Wáng*	昨天 *zuótiān*	我们 *wǒmen*
很累 *hěn lèi*	不饿 *bú è*	不好 *bù hǎo*	明天 *míngtiān*	还好 *hái hǎo*	姓毛 *xìng Máo*
你们 *nǐmen*	九月 *jiǔyuè*	二十日 *èrshí rì*	姓林 *xìng Lín*	明年 *míngnián*	她们 *tāmen*
你呢 *nǐ ne*	他们 *tāmen*	八月 *bāyuè*	很忙 *hěn máng*	不太累 *bú tài lèi*	冷吗 *lěng ma*
不冷 *bù lěng*	很热 *hěn rè*	九十 *jiǔshí*	不饿了 *bú è le*	好不好 *hǎo bu hǎo*	冷了 *lěng le*

B. *FÁNTǏZÌ* (INCLUDING GRAPHS THAT HAVE ONLY ONE FORM)

他們 *tāmen*	很熱 *hěn rè*	不冷了 *bù lěng le*	很餓 *hěn è*	明年 *míngnián*	我們 *wǒmen*
不熱了 *bú rè le*	餓不餓 *è bu è*	姓周 *xìng Zhōu*	你們 *nǐmen*	冷嗎 *lěng ma*	太好 *tài hǎo*

8.11.2 Dialogue

甲:　今天很忙也很累。
乙:　昨天呢？
甲:　昨天还好，不太忙，也不太累。

甲:　你们饿不饿？
乙:　不饿，还好！你呢？
甲:　我呢，我很饿。

甲:　今天很热!
乙:　昨天也很热！

甲:　今天冷了。
乙:　昨天呢?
甲:　昨天不太冷，还好。

甲:　我们很热。
乙:　我也很热！很热也很累！
甲:　我们也很累。

甲:　饿吗？
乙:　不太饿。我很累。你呢？
甲:　不累，还好。
乙:　饿不饿？
甲:　不饿了。
乙:　我也不饿。

8.12 Action verbs and associated function words

吃	飯	已	經	課	班
3 + 3	8 + 4	3 + 0	6 + 7	7 + 8	4 + 6
	饭		经	课	
	3 + 4		3 + 5	2 + 8	
chī	*fàn*	*yǐjīng*		*kè*	*bān*
'to eat'	'rice; food; meal'	'already'		'class; lesson'	'shift; class'

上	下	沒/没	有
1 + 2	1 + 2	3 + 4	1 + 5
shàng	*xià*	*méi*	*yǒu*
'on; upper; to go up'	'under; lower; to go down'	NEG	'to have'

NOTES

a. 吃 is a compound of 口 *kǒu* 'mouth' and the element 乞, independently pronounced *qǐ*. Hint: 'resembles teeth and tongue, used to *eat*'. 饭/飯 is a compound of the 'food radical' (whose independent form is 食) and the phonetic 反 *fǎn*. Hint: 'customer on the left with a cap on, with *food* on the right behind a sneeze shield'. 课/課 contains the 'speech radical' (言 in its independent form) and 果 *guǒ* 'fruit' as an imperfect phonetic element whose original phonetic connection to 课/課 has weakened due to changes in pronunciation. Hint: 'board on an easel in a *classroom*'.

b. Distinguish 已 *yǐ* from 己 *jǐ*, 巳 *sì*, and 乙 *yǐ*.

c. The right side of the traditional graph 經 is said to derive from the drawing of a loom used to represent the root meaning of *jīng*, the 'warp [of a loom]'. From the movements and result of weaving, the word derives meanings such as 'to pass through' or 'to regulate' as well as 'classic texts' [cf. English 'text' and 'textile']. The etymological meaning of the compound 已經 is harder to see, but probably derives from a notion of 'to complete the task'.

d. The traditional 沒 has the same number of strokes as 没 in the simplified set, so they are placed together above to save space. Both have the water radical on the left (three strokes, two *diǎn* and a *tí*, in contrast to a *diǎn* plus *tí* in 冷). In the simplified graph, the right side of the traditional character has been replaced by the independently occurring element 殳. 没/沒 is also used for the word *mò* 'to submerge', which probably explains the presence of the water radical.

8.12.1 Phrases

A. *JIǍNTǏZÌ* 'SIMPLIFIED SET'

吃饭 *chīfàn*	吃了 *chī le*	还没 *hái méi*	没有 *méiyǒu*	你呢 *nǐ ne*
上课 *shàngkè*	已经 *yǐjīng*	走了 *zǒu le*	下班 *xiàbān*	饭很好 *fàn hěn hǎo*
没有了 *méiyǒu le*	上课 *shàngkè*	没课 *méi kè*	明天 *míngtiān*	很累 *hěn lèi*
上班 *shàngbān*	还没吃呢 *hái méi chī ne*	已经吃了 *yǐjīng chī le*	走了没有 *zǒu le méiyǒu*	还没 *hái méi*

B. *FÁNTǏZÌ* 'TRADITIONAL SET'

熱了 *rè le*	上課 *shàngkè*	還好 *hái hǎo*	吃飯 *chīfàn*	已經走了 *yǐjīng zǒu le*
明天沒課 *míngtiān méi kè*	不太餓 *bú tài è*	你們 *nǐmen*	不餓了 *bú è le*	下課了 *xiàkè le*

8.12.2 Reading

A. *JIǍNTǏZÌ*

甲: 吃了吗?
乙: 吃了。你呢？
甲: 还没，我不饿。

甲: 吃了没有？
乙: 还没，你呢。
甲: 没有，我不饿。
乙: 我也不饿，今天太热了。

甲: 你吃饭了吗？
乙: 还没。你呢？
甲: 我已经吃了。

甲:　今天好不好？
乙:　还好。
甲:　吃饭了吗？
乙:　吃了。你呢？
甲:　我也已经吃了。

甲:　他们走了没有？
乙:　已经走了，上课了。
甲:　哦，上课了。

甲:　他吃了没有？
乙:　没有，太忙了。
甲:　他不饿吗？
乙:　不饿，还好。

甲:　他们已经上课了吗?
乙:　还没，他们还没有吃饭呢。
甲:　哦，没吃饭呢。
乙:　没有。

甲:　明天有没有课？
乙:　没有，明天十月一号。一号没课。
甲:　二号呢？
乙:　二号有，三号也有。

B. *FÁNTǏZÌ*

甲：　我今天很累！
乙：　吃飯了嗎？
甲：　還沒呢，太忙了。
乙：　餓嗎？
甲：　很餓。你呢？
乙：　我不餓，已經吃了。
甲：　李白呢，他已經上課了嗎？
乙：　他今天很忙，沒有上課。
甲：　你熱嗎？

乙：　熱！？我不熱，昨天很熱今天好了。
甲：　昨天很熱，今天也很熱。
乙：　今天還好，不熱。

Exercise 5

Fill in the blanks.

1. 我___没吃饭呢，你呢？/ 我___经吃了。
2. 今天很好，不___也不冷。 / ___天也很好。
3. 昨天不___冷，还好。 / 昨天很好，可是今天热___。
4. 我姓林，她___姓林。 / 是吗？你们姓林？我也___林。
5. 我昨天很忙，今天也很___。 / 明天___？
6. 吃___了没有？ / 吃___。

NOTES

a. 可是 *kěshì* 'but'
b. 是 *shì* 'to be the case'

8.13 On the street #1

This section appears regularly in the lessons to introduce you to words and phrases commonly seen on signs, notices, shop fronts, and billboards across China (as well as in Chinese communities throughout the world).

入口
rùkǒu
'entrance'
('enter-opening')

出口
chūkǒu
'exit'
('exit-opening')

雨水
yǔshuǐ
[on manhole covers]
('rain-water')

有限公司	銀行 银行
yǒuxiàn gōngsī	*yínháng*
'Co. Ltd.'	'bank'
('have-limit company')	('silver-shop')

NOTES

a. Left leaning 入 has, in earlier notes, been contrasted with right leaning 人 *rén*, as well as with balanced 八 *bā*.

b. 限 and 銀/银 are part of a phonetic set based on 艮 that includes 很 *hěn* 'very'.

c. 行 writes two (historically related) words: *háng*, with a number of meanings including 'shop; firm; row'; and *xíng* 'to go; to do; to be okay' (as in 还行).

Ideograms

Unit 9 第九課 DÌ-JIǓ KÈ

笨鸟先飞。
(笨鳥先飛。)
Bèn niǎo xiān fēi.
'The slow have to start early.'
('stupid bird first fly')

Unit 9 begins with a review of the traditional set of characters introduced in Unit 8 and a listing of common radical elements seen so far, along with their names. It goes on to introduce four sets of characters in the format established in the latter part of Unit 8, beginning with notes and information on the graphs, continuing with reading of compound words and phrases, and ending with readings in the form of dialogues or narratives. The unit ends with a discussion of character types, with some tonal sets presented in characters, and with the usual coda of real-life examples as seen 'on the street'.

9.0 Review

繁體字 *FÁNTǏZÌ* 'TRADITIONAL CHARACTERS'

甲: 今天很熱！

乙: 很熱！你吃飯了嗎?

甲: 還沒，我不餓，今天太忙了。

乙: 我也很忙。你累嗎？

甲: 今天好了，但是昨天很累。

乙: 小李已經上班了嗎？

甲: 已經上班了。

乙: 哦，上班了。

甲: 明天有課嗎？

乙: 沒有，你呢？

甲: 明天三十號嗎？... 沒有；三十號 沒有，一號有。

乙: 我呢，三十號有課，一號也有課！

甲: 你太忙了！

乙: 我們都很忙！

COMPOUND CHARACTERS As noted in Unit 8, a majority of characters can be resolved into two immediate constituents which, allowing for minor modifications, can stand alone as characters in their own right. The configuration of constituents can be horizontal (很), vertical (李), or one within another (国/國). The most recurrent of these constituents are the radicals; indeed, they serve as tags to classify characters into groups for purposes of retrieval (in dictionaries or filing systems, for example). Thus, compound characters with the radical 口 *kǒu* 'mouth; opening' can be grouped together: 吃，吗，喝，呢; or those with 讠/言 *yán* 'speech': 说/說，话/話，请/請，谁/誰。 Radicals are named based on either their position in the character or their meaning. Thus, 口 *kǒu* 'mouth; opening' on the left is called *kǒuzìpáng* ('mouth-character-beside') in Chinese, or the 'mouth radical' in English; 雨 *yǔ* 'rain', when it appears on the top of a graph (零), is called *yǔzìtóu* ('rain-character-on top') in Chinese, or the 'rain radical' in English. Here, for review, are some of the Unit 8 compound characters organized by radical.

NOTE

When the combining form of the radical cannot be printed on its own, the equivalent free form, if one still exists, is given in parentheses; if no free form is currently in use, the parentheses enclose a blank. The same is true for the column heading 'general meaning'; if no useful general meaning can be provided, the entry is left blank.

RADICAL CHARACTER	GENERAL MEANING	CHINESE NAME	EXAMPLES
木	'wood; tree'	*mùzìpáng*	林
		mùzìtóu	李
口	'mouth; opening'	*kǒuzìpáng*	吗/嗎，呢，吃
日	'sun'	*rìzìpáng*	昨，明
讠/言	'speech'	*yánzìpáng*	课/課
女	'woman'	*nǚzìpáng*	她，姓
(人)	'man; person'	*rénzìpáng*	他，你，们/們
(水)	'water'	*sāndiǎnshuǐ* ('three dots water')	没/沒
( )		*tóngzìkuàng* ("tong'-character-frame')	周，(同)
(辵)	'movement'	*zǒuzhīpáng*	还/還
饣/(食)	'food'	*shízìpáng*	饿/餓，饭/飯
(心)	'heart'	*shùxīnpáng* ('vertical-heart-beside')	忙
( )/纟	'silk'	*jiǎosīpáng* ('twisted-silk-beside')	经/經
(火)	'fire'	*sìdiǎnshuǐ* ('four-dots-water')	热/熱
彳		*shuānglìrén* ('double-stand-person')	很，得 (dé)

9.1 First set

是	男	的	女	第	小
4 + 5	5 + 2	5 + 3	3 + 0	6 + 5	3 + 0
shì	*nán*	*de*	*nǚ*	*dì*	*xiǎo*
'to be the case'	'male'	DE	'female'	ORDINAL	'small; young'

馬	陳	張	誰	這	都
9 or 10 + 0	3 + 8	3 + 8	7 + 8	3 + 7	3 + 8
马	陈	张	谁	这	
3 + 0	2 + 5	3 + 4	2 + 8	3 + 4	2 + 8
mǎ	*chén*	*zhāng*	*shéi ~ shuí*	*zhè ~ zhèi*	*dōu*
'horse' (surname)	(surname)	'to spread' (surname)	'who; whom'	'this'	'all; none'

押 *yā* 'pledge', pawn shop sign, Hong Kong

NOTES

a. 是 'to be the case', like 明 and 昨, assigns 日 'sun' as the radical (in this case combined vertically with 疋). One (made-up) account of the graph goes: 'the sun, over the horizon (the horizontal stroke) provides sustenance (*being*) through a pipe with a valve to mankind (人)'.

b. The graph 女, said to originate as a drawing of a woman, appears as a radical in 姓 *xìng* 'surname<d>', 她 *tā* 'she; her', and 好 *hǎo* 'good'. 男 is a compound graph, with the elements 田 *tián* 'field' and 力 *lì* 'strength' arranged vertically (looking vaguely like a *man* working in the fields). In colloquial speech, *nán* and *nǚ* appear in compounds such as *nánde* and *nǚde*, with *de* representing the possessive or attributive marker (i.e., 'the male one' and 'the female one').

c. 第 *dì* introduces the 'bamboo radical', which when appearing on top is called *zhúzìtóu* ('bamboo-character-on top'). The radical appears in graphs associated with bamboo (e.g., 筷子 *kuàizi* 'chopsticks') or with properties of bamboo, such as segmentation (节/節 *jié* 'segment; program') or splitting (笑 *xiào* 'laugh' [cf. 'to crack up']). The 'body' of 第 contains 弓 *gōng* 'bow', the same element that appears as the radical in the surname 张/張.

d. 小 should be distinguished from 少 *shǎo* 'few'. The stroke order is 'dominant' stroke (*shùgōu*), followed by left and right *diǎn* (cf. 你 *nǐ*).

e. The surname 马/馬 'horse' originated as a drawing of the animal and is used for its sound value in 吗/嗎 and 妈/媽, but is assigned as a radical in graphs used for words connected with horses, such as 驰/馳 *chí* 'to speed; gallop' or 骑/騎 *qí* 'to straddle; ride' (cf. §9.5.5 below). The graph 陈/陳, also a surname, contains the phonetic element 东/東 *dōng* 'east' and a radical called 'left ear': *zuǒ'ěrduō*. Its right-hand counterpart, seen in 都 *dōu*, is called *yòu'ěrduō* 'right ear' and is considered a different radical (and, in fact, has a different historical source character). 张/張, the last of the three surnames introduced in this set, contains the radical 弓 *gōng* 'bow' (seen in 第), and the phonetic 长/長 *cháng* 'long' or *zhǎng* 'to grow; be senior'.

f. The right-hand element of 谁/誰 (隹) is a phonetic, independently pronounced *zhuī* (cf. 推 *tuī* 'to push', seen in §9.7 below). 隹 with eight strokes will need to be distinguished from 住, with seven. The latter is the character for *zhù* 'to live', but it also occurs as a component of compound characters such as 驻 and 注. So remember: 隹 eight and 住 seven.

g. The element on the left of 这/這 (sometimes printed with two dots instead of one) is a left-side version of a more complex graph—辵—whose core meaning is 'stopping and starting'. As a radical, it is called *zǒuzhīr*, and appears in graphs such as 迎 *yíng* 'welcome' and 近 *jìn* 'near'. 言, which is given radical status when it appears on the left of the graph (or at the bottom), forms the core in the case of the traditional graph 這. Notice that, when it is a core element, 言 does not simplify to 讠 as it would if it were the radical; instead, the graph 文 *wén* 'language' (see §9.2 below) is used—这—presumably because its first two strokes match those of 言.

h. 者 *zhě* is the root element of a set that includes 都 *dōu*, 煮 *zhǔ* 'to boil', and 堵 *dǔ* 'to obstruct'. (Can you identify the radicals of each?) Though 都 apparently has only one form, it turns out that the element on the right (*yòu'ěrduō*), which is assigned as its radical, is written with three strokes in the traditional set, but only two in the simplified. A (made-up) account of the graph 都: '土 'earth' over 日 'sun', connected by a line (丿) to suggest *all, everything*, with the '3' at the right indicating *all* three states of matter.'

9.1.1 Phrases

是不是	男的	女的	第一	第三	很小
shì bu shì	*nánde*	*nǚde*	*dì-yī*	*dì-sān*	*hěn xiǎo*
小李	姓马	姓张	姓陈	谁的	这是
xiǎo Lǐ	*xìng Mǎ*	*xìng Zhāng*	*xìng Chén*	*shéi de*	*zhè shi*
都是	不都是	男女	我的	你们的	也是
dōu shì	*bù dōu shì*	*nánnǚ*	*wǒ de*	*nǐmen de*	*yě shì*

Exercise 1

Refer to the following list to answer the questions below.

第？个	姓？	男/女？	Comment
第四个	姓马	是男的	很饿，还没吃饭呢。
第七个	姓毛	是女的	不饿，已经吃饭了。
第一个	姓王	是女的	还没上课呢。
第九个	姓张	是男的	吃饭了，但是还没上班。
第二个	姓周	是女的	很忙，也很累。
第五个	小马	是女的	很累，还没上课。
第三个	小陈	是男的	昨天很累，今天好了。
第六个	姓白	是男的	今天没有课。
第八个	姓林	是女的	还没下班。
第十个	姓李	是女的	已经吃了，不饿了。

1	谁是第一个？	第一个是男的吗？
2	第二个是不是姓李？	第二个忙不忙？
3	第三个姓陈吗？	他今天很累吗？

4	第四个是男的吗？	他吃饭了没有？
5	第五个是不是小白？	她上班了吗？
6	第六个是男的吗？	他今天忙不忙？
7	第七个姓马吗？	她吃了没有？
8	第八个是女的吗？	她下班了没有？
9	第九个已经上班了吗？	他吃了吗？
10	第十个也吃了吗？	她姓陈吗？

9.2 Second set

學 3 + 13	生 5 + 0	老 6 + 0	師 3 + 7	點 12 + 5	兒 2 + 6
学 3 + 5			师 1 + 5 or 3 + 3	点 4 + 5	儿 2 + 0
xué	*shēng*	*lǎo*	*shī*	*diǎn*	*ér* → r
'study; school'	'pupil'	'old'	'teacher'	'point; bit'	'child; son' DIMINUTIVE

怎 4 + 5	麼 3 + 11	樣 4 + 11	對 3 + 11	難 8 + 11	中 1 + 3	文 4 + 0
	么 1 + 2	样 4 + 6	对 3 + 2	难 8 + 2		
zěn	*me*	*yàng*	*duì*	*nán*	*zhōng*	*wén*
'how'	INTERROGATIVE	'kind; type'	'correct; right'	'difficult'	'middle; China'	'script; language'

NOTES

a. A nonsense account of 學: 'a child *studying* from a blackboard on a stand; the backboard has two x's, each registered with strokes on the side'. The simplified character shows 'the successful *student*, with feathers in his cap'. Accounting for 生 'to be born; pupil' requires some ingenuity: 'three horizontals represent the three stages that follow *birth*—youth, maturity, old age; the first is marked (with a *piě* stroke) as the time of education'.

b. 老 is itself a radical (as indicated by the numerical designation 6 + 0), though it only occurs in very few characters. Distinguish 老 from the left-hand side of 都. For the former graph, think: 'an *elderly* person taking a rest under an awning'. 师/師, with the radical 巾 *jīn* 'cloth' (three strokes) for the traditional graph, and either 巾 or 丨 for the simplified, can be remembered with the following description: 'a *teacher* wearing a mortar board, standing before a podium covered by a cloth'. (The right-hand element of 师/師—the podium—has a clear top, unlike the graph 市 *shì* 'market; city', which has an extra stroke.)

c. In 點, 占 is the phonetic (cf. 店 *diàn* 'shop') and the radical is 黑 *hēi* 'black', with the four lower strokes, a combining form of the fire radical, hence: '*little* specks of soot'. The simplified graph preserves the phonetic element and the '*little* specks of soot'.

d. The root meaning of 儿/兒 is 'child', and the graph is said to have originally been a drawing of a child with a large head; the simplified form retains only the 'feet' (cf. compounds such as 儿子/兒子 *érzi* 'son' and 女儿/女兒 *nǚ'ér* 'daughter'). 儿/兒 is one source of the noun suffix '-r', seen in words such as *yìdiǎnr*.

e. 怎 and 昨 are members of a phonetic set based on the graph 乍 *zhà*. 麼 combines with 怎 and 什/甚 to represent the question words *zěnme* and *shénme*. The simplified form of 麼 substitutes a part for the whole: 麼 → 么. A made-up account: 'a shed (广), two trees (林), and a nose (么) sniffing them to find out *what* they are and *how* they got there', reduced to just 'a nose' in the simplified.

f. The traditional graph 樣 consists of 木 *mù* as the radical (*mùzìpáng*), 羊 *yáng* as the phonetic (without its stem), and 永 *yǒng*. It may originally have referred to a wooden mold or pattern, from which the meaning of 'type; kind' derived. The simplified graph pares the original down to just the radical and phonetic elements.

g. In both 对/對 and 难/難, the complicated left-hand elements are replaced in the simplified graphs with 又 *yòu*. In 难/難, 隹 *zhuī* is assigned as the radical, which contrasts with 谁/誰, where 讠/言 is the radical and 隹 is the phonetic. The left-hand side of the traditional graph for 難 includes 夫 *fū* inserted through a flattened 口.

h. 文 *wén* originally meant 'decoration' (and was probably a drawing of a design). It later came to mean 'written language', and is now often used for language in general. Later, the silk radical was added to the graph to form 紋 *wén* 'decoration', reflecting the divergence of the original connection between 'writing' and 'decoration'.

9.2.1 Compounds

学生 *xuéshēng*	老师 *lǎoshī*	一点儿 *yìdiǎnr*	一点点 *yìdiǎndiǎn*	有一点难 *yǒu yìdiǎn nán*	不对 *bú duì*
中文 *Zhōngwén*	不太难 *bú tài nán*	是学生吗? *Shi xuéshēng ma?*	怎么样 *zěnmeyàng*	三个 *sān gè*	日文 *Rìwén*
三个男的 *sān ge nánde*	没有女的 *méiyǒu nǚde*	难不难 *nán bu nán*	对不对 *duì bu duì*	陈老师 *Chén lǎoshī*	男的 *nánde*

9.2.2 Set 1 in *fántǐzì*

第一个是誰? *Dì-yī ge shi shéi?*	姓陳 *xìng Chén*	都是這樣 *dōu shi zhèiyàng*	小張，你好? *Xiǎo Zhāng, nǐ hǎo?*	都是 *dōu shì*
是第二个嗎? *Shi dì-èr ge ma?*	不是. *Bú shì.*	是誰的? *Shi shéi de?*	我的. *Wǒ de.*	小李很累. *Xiǎo Lǐ hěn lèi.*

Exercise 2

Answer the questions at the end of the exercise, taking your cue from the information given in the 'chart' below.

第一： 她姓毛，是女学生；今天有一点儿累。

第二： 他姓陈，是男学生；他有一点儿忙。

第三： 他姓张，是大学的老师；今天是第一天，他很忙。

第四： 她姓白，是小学 的老师；昨天很累，可是今天好了。

第五： 她姓林，是中学 的老师；今天没有课。

第六： 他姓周，是男学生；是张老师的学生。

第七： 他姓马，是男学生；今天有点儿饿，还没吃饭呢。

第八： 她姓王，女的；是老师，昨天是她的生日。

第九： 他姓林，男的；中文老师，还没上班。

第十： 她姓李，女的，学中文；中文不太难。

QUESTIONS

1. 姓马的是男的，对吗？
2. 姓毛的是不是学生？
3. 姓周的没有老师，对不对？
4. 姓张的是小学的老师，对吗？
5. 姓白的今天很累，对吗？
6. 姓林的已经上班了，对吗？
7. 姓马的今天怎么样？
8. 今天是王老师的生日，对吗？
9. 姓张的今天怎么样？
10. 谁是学生，谁是老师？
11. 姓林的是男的还是女的？
12. 老师是不是都是男的？

NOTES

a. 生字 *shēngzì* 'vocabulary' ('raw-characters')
b. 姓马的 *xìng Mǎ de [rén]* 'the one named Ma' (姓林的, etc.)
c. 小学 *xiǎoxué* 'elementary school'
d. 中学 *zhōngxué* 'high school'
e. 大学 *dàxué* 'university'
f. 生日 *shēngrì* 'birthday'
g. 还是 *háishi* 'or' (with choice questions)

9.3 Third set

高	緊	張	個	現	在
10 + 0	6 + 9	3 + 8	2 + 8	4 + 7	3 + 3
	紧	张	个	现	
	6 + 4	3 + 4	2 + 1	4 + 4	
gāo	*jǐn*	*zhāng*	*gè*	*xiàn*	*zài*
'tall' (surname)	'tight'	'to spread'	'individual'	'manifest'	'now'

起	來	看	報	以	前
7 + 3	2 + 6	5 + 4	4 + 8	2 + 3	2 + 7
	来		报		
	1 + 6		3 + 4	2 + 2	
qǐ	*lái*	*kàn*	*bào*	*yǐ*	*qián*
'to rise'	'to come'	'to look'	'report'	'take as'	'before; front'

但	可	那	哪	走
2 + 5	3 + 2	3 + 4 or 2 + 4	3 + 7 or 3 + 6	7 + 0
dàn	*kě*	*nà; nèi*	*nǎ; něi*	*zǒu*
'but'	'able'	'that'	'which'	'to walk; to leave; to go'

NOTES

a. 高 *gāo* can be used as a surname, but it is also a SV meaning 'tall'; think of the graph as representing 'a *tall* structure with a flat roof and a chimney'.

b. Recall the radicals 糸 (the 'silk radical') and 弓 (representing a bow under tension), both used in 紧张/緊張. Both graphs suggest 'tension' or 'anxiety'.

c. 个, the simplified version of 個 (固 *gù* with *rénzìpáng*) is an old handwriting variant that has been elevated to formal status in the simplified set.

d. 現 (like 班 and many other graphs) contains a radical that is virtually identical to 王 'king' (and a surname). Historically, however, it is the combining form (lacking the *diǎn* stroke) of a different character: 玉 *yù* 'jade' (found intact at the center of simplified 国 *guó* 'country'). Traditionally, the radical exemplified in 現 is called *yùzìpáng* 'jade character at the side', in recognition of its historical origins; but on the Mainland, at least, it is also called *wángzìpáng* 'king on the side', in recognition of its current form.

e. 起 contains 走 as a radical and 己 *jǐ* as a phonetic (cf. graphs such as 超 and 越 which are formed along the same lines). 來 was originally a drawing of a kind of cereal grain (cf. 麥 *mài* 'wheat', which is now differentiated from 來 by the lower radical element 夂). The meaning of 'to come' may represent a metaphorical extension (grain → sprouting → coming out); or the graph may have been borrowed to represent a near homophone.

f. 看 contains 手 *shǒu* 'hand' and 目 *mù* 'eye' (both of which had earlier forms suggesting drawings); hence 'hand over the eyes, *looking*'. 报/報 *bào* 'report; newspaper', with the right-hand component looking like 'a comfortable armchair where you might read the *paper*'.

g. 以 *yǐ* contains the radical 人. In the modern language, the syllable is a common 'bound form', occurring in words such as 可以 *kěyǐ* 'can' and 所以 *suǒyǐ* 'so'. But in the ancient language, it functioned as a verb with the meaning of 'to take'. So, 以前 'formerly' derives from 'to take as before'. In the simplified set, 以 is written with four strokes (2 + 2) rather than five.

h. 那 *nà* 'that' is formed with *yòu'ěrduō* 'right-ear' (or *yòu'ěrpáng*) as the radical (cf. 都). 哪 *nǎ*, the question word, has *kǒuzìpáng* as its radical.

9.3.1 Compounds

不高	姓高	很紧张	但是	不紧张	可是
bù gāo	*xìng Gāo*	*hěn jǐnzhāng*	*dànshi*	*bù jǐnzhāng*	*kěshì*
以前	现在	在哪儿？	三个	看报	起来
yǐqián	*xiànzài*	*zài nǎr?*	*sān gè*	*kànbào*	*qǐlái*
她们走了.	已经走了	紧不紧张？	在这儿	陈老师	九个
Tāmen zǒu le.	*yǐjīng zǒu le*	*Jǐn bù jǐnzhāng?*	*zài zhèr*	*Chén lǎoshī*	*jiǔ gè*

9.3.2 Set 2 in *fántǐzì*

老師	學生	怎麼樣	學中文	都很難	那樣
lǎoshī	*xuéshēng*	*zěnmeyàng*	*xué Zhōngwén*	*dōu hěn nán*	*nèi yàng*
有一點兒累	也很累	張老師	這樣	不對	
yǒu yìdiǎnr lèi	*yě hěn lèi*	*Zhāng lǎoshī*	*zhèi yàng*	*bú duì*	
不太難	男的	哪年	日文	生日	老王
bú tài nán	*nánde*	*něi nián*	*Rìwén*	*shēngrì*	*lǎo Wáng*

Exercise 3

Answer the questions at the end of the exercise, taking your cue from the information given in the 'chart' below. Note that the chart takes the form of lists: 'three students: one male, two female'. The questions (like your responses) have the form of sentences: 'The students are all female, right?'

第一： 三个学生，一个男的，两个女的；
他们都已经起来了， 可是还没看今天的报。

第二： 一个学生，一个老师，都是男的；
他们以前很累，但是现在好了。

第三： 两个老师，一个中文老师，一个日文老师；
他门已经下班了。

第四: 一个中文学生，没有老师；
中文很难，他很累。

第五： 四个学生，都很紧张；
都是陈老师的学生。

第六： 五个学生，两个老师；
学生很紧张，老师很忙。

第七： 一个男的，一个女的；
男的起来了还没吃饭呢；女的已经走了。

第八： 两个学生，一个对，一个不对；
一个是MIT 的，一个不是。

第九： 两个学生，一个姓张，一个姓高。
姓张的很紧张，可是姓高的还好。

第十： 十个学生，都是张老师的学生。
张老师的学生很忙也很累。

QUESTIONS

1. 第六个，学生，老师都很紧张吗？
2. 第二个，他们还是很累吗？
3. 第三个，那两个老师是中文老师吗？他们下班了没有？
4. 第八个，谁对，谁不对？
5. 第四个，学中文，没有老师，难不难？
6. 第十个，谁的学生都很忙很累？
7. 第五个，那 四个学生怎么样？
8. 第一个，学生都是女的，对吗？ 今天的报看了，但是昨天的 还没看，对不对？
9. 第七个，他们两个已经走了，对吗？已经上课了。
10. 第九个，姓高的是学生但是姓张的不是，是老师，对吗？

9.4 Fourth set

(甚)	麼	東	西	手	機
5 + 4	3 + 11	4 + 4	6 + 0	4 + 0	4 + 12
什	么	东			机
2 + 2	1 + 2	1 + 4			4 + 2
shén	*me*	*dōng*	*xī*	*shǒu*	*jī*
'what'		'east'	'west'	'hand'	'machine'

書	包	筆	車	子	傘	貴
4 + 6	2 + 3	6 + 6	7 + 0	3 + 0	2 + 10	7 + 5
书		笔	车		伞	贵
1 + 3		6 + 4	4 + 0		2 + 4	4 + 5
shū	*bāo*	*bǐ*	*chē*	*zǐ*	*sǎn*	*guì*
'book'	'pack; bundle'	'writing implement'	'vehicle'	'child' (with nouns)	'umbrella'	'expensive; worthy'

字	典	行	您
3 + 3	2 + 6	6 + 0 or 3 + 3	4 + 7
zì	*diǎn*	*xíng*	*nín*
'written character'	'records'	'to walk; to go; to be okay'	'you' (POL)

NOTES

a. Simplification is not a new process; it has been going on since the creation of the writing system. It continues even in the traditional set. The first character of 什麼, for example, is an older simplification of 甚 that substitutes the phonetically close 十 for the more complicated original, then marks it with *rénzìpáng*. The 台 of 台北 is another substitution that has gained currency in the traditional set as an alternative for the original 臺. Both simplifications have a long history, and have now gained acceptance in Taiwan and other traditional communities. Both can now be used in the traditional set.

b. 'East', in its traditional form of 東, shows 'dawn in the *east*, with the sun (日) coming up through the trees (木)'. The characters, 东西/東西, suggest that the compound is derived from 'east-west', i.e., the plane of existence, or 'where all things are' (though that is probably not the true etymology of the word). 東was employed as a phonetic element in 陳 *chén*, and the relationship remains in the simplified forms—东 and 陈.

c. 手 'hand', itself a radical (originally a drawing of a hand), has a rather different combining form, seen on the left of characters such as 报，把，拉，and 押.

d. The traditional version of the graph 机/機, with its complicated right-hand element, is more suggestive of the meaning 'machine' (cf. 飞机/飛機 *fēijī* 'airplane').

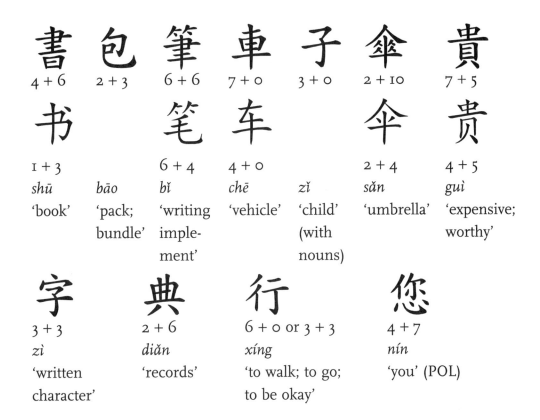

e. 書 consists of 聿 *yù* 'writing implement' and 曰, distinct from 日. The simplified graph represents the elevation of an old calligraphic variant. The traditional graph 筆 *bǐ* 'writing implement' also contains 聿, with the bamboo radical (a combining version of 竹 *zhú* 'bamboo'), since early writing implements were made out of bamboo. The simplified graph, 笔, substitutes 毛 *máo* 'hair' for 聿, not for its sound, obviously, but for the association with writing brushes that are made of hair. Finally, 包, whose root meaning is 'to wrap' or 'a bundle', looks like a *bundle*.

f. The traditional graph 車, originally an overhead drawing of a cart, is itself a radical (appearing in characters such as 輪，輛，軟); however, the simplified graph obscures the pictorial origin. The graph 子 *zǐ* (distinct from 字 *zì* 'written character') was originally a drawing of a child. If fully toned, it generally means 'young; child of; seed of': 王子 *wángzǐ* 'prince (king's son)', 天子 *tiānzǐ* 'emperor (son of heaven)', 松子*sōngzǐ* 'pine nut (child of pine)', 蝦子 *xiāzǐ* 'shrimp roe (child of shrimp)'. However, in its untoned form, 子 acts as a noun suffix, appearing with nouns that refer to familiar things from everyday life: 桌子*zhuōzi* 'table'; 椅子*yǐzi* 'chair'; 鼻子*bízi* 'nose'; 板子*bānzi* 'spanner; wrench'.

g. 伞/傘 remain relatively clear pictorial representations of the word they represent—*umbrellas*.

h. 贵/貴 introduces the important element贝/貝 *bèi*, a graph that is said to have originated as a drawing of a cowrie shell, used as currency along the southeast coast of China in ancient times. 貝 also appears as a radical in characters for many words involving transactions, such as 買*mǎi* 'to buy', 賣 *mài* 'to sell' and 寶 *bǎo* 'valuable' (all traditional graphs).

i. 字 *zì* 'written character' ('a child, 子, under a roof, studying *characters*'); 典 is said to be composed of 册 'classic books' on a stand, suggesting 'a *repository* of information'.

j. 行 is itself a radical in the traditional set (hence 6 + 0), but it is classified under 彳 in the simplified set (3 + 3). 行 is unusual in that it can be resolved into two independent characters, 彳 and 亍, which, at least in the modern language, only appear in the literary compound彳亍 *chìchù* 'to walk slowly'. The graph 行 represents two words: *xíng*, with a core meaning of 'street; walk', or, by extension, 'to be going, to work [of machines]' and 'to work, to be all right'; and *háng* 'row', or by extension, things that are arranged in rows, 'firm; business' (cf. 銀行 *yínháng* 'bank' ['silver-business']). The word *háng* has entered English historical writing from its Cantonese pronunciation as *hong*, meaning 'factory; warehouse'. 行 can combine with other elements placed internally, e.g., 街, 衎, 衡.

9.4.1 Compounds

我的伞 *wǒ de sǎn*	她的书 *tā de shū*	你的笔 *nǐ de bǐ*	手机 *shǒujī*	书包 *shūbāo*	什么 *shénme*
东西 *dōngxi*	车子 *chēzi*	字典 *zìdiǎn*	行李 *xíngli*	您好 *Nín hǎo.*	行吗 *Xíng ma?*
谁的书? *Shéi de shū?*	没有笔. *Méiyǒu bǐ.*	上车 *shàngchē*	贵姓? *Guìxìng?*	不太贵 *bú tài guì*	中东 *Zhōngdōng*
什么东西 *shénme dōngxi*	很贵 *hěn guì*	车子 *chēzi*	姓李 *xìng Lǐ*	手机不贵 *shǒujī bú guì*	没笔 *méi bǐ*

很緊張 *hěn jǐnzhāng*	可是 *kěshì*	三個 *sān gè*	現在 *xiànzài*	起來了 *qǐlái le*	走了 *zǒu le*
已經看報了 *yǐjīng kànbào le*	高老師 *Gāo lǎoshī*	現在好了. *Xiànzài hǎo le.*	還沒起來 *hái méi qǐlái*	不對 *bú duì*	

9.4.2 Set 3 in *fántǐzì*

看報 *kànbào*	以前 *yǐqián*	現在 *xiànzài*	在這兒 *zài zhèr*	在報上 *zài bào shàng*	起來 *qǐlái*
可是 *kěshì*	不對 *bú duì*	老高的 *lǎo Gāo de*	緊張 *jǐnzhāng*	還可以 *hái kěyǐ*	但是 *dànshì*
三個學生 *sān ge xuéshēng*	那樣 *nèi yàng*	在我這兒 *zài wǒ zhèr*	走了 *zǒu le*	昨天的報 *zuótiān de bào*	不高 *bù gāo*

9.4.3 Readings

A. A NARRATIVE (*FÁNTǏZÌ*) WITH QUESTIONS

王明是中文老師，有十二個學生。他們已經上課了。中文很難，但是學生都好，都行。今天九月一日，上學第一天。老師學生都很緊張，很忙，也很累。那兒有個學生姓陳，男的。小陳的中文很好。他也是王老師的學生。他今天沒有飯吃，很餓。 很餓上課不行， 對嗎？

QUESTIONS

1. 王明是學生嗎？
2. 老師有二十個學生，對嗎？
3. 他們上班了嗎？
4. 中文怎麽樣？
5. 王老師的學生怎麽樣？
6. 學生緊張嗎？
7. 姓陳的是男的嗎？
8. 小陳的中文怎麽 樣?
9. 他是誰的學生？
10. 不吃飯，上課，行不行？

B. A DIALOGUE

小马: 小张，你好。

小张: 小马，你好。今天怎么样？

小马: 很累，你呢？

小张: 我今天也有一点儿累—我没吃饭。你呢？你饿不饿？

小马: 我呢，不饿，我已经吃了。

小张: 好吃吗？

小马: 还行。好，那，我走了。

小张: 上课去吗？

小马: 不，今天没课。

小张: 好，那，明天见吧。

小马: 明天见。

Exercise 4

Answer the questions below by confirming the information in the following table.

第一	手机	高老师的	有一点贵
第二	毛笔	学生的	不太贵
第三	小车子	大学的	有一点儿贵
第四	书包	小李的	不贵
第五	中文字典	周老师的	不贵
第六	伞	李明的	好看，可是不贵
第七	书	小毛的	也不贵

QUESTIONS

1. 第一是什么东西？
2. 第一是谁的？
3. 毛笔贵不贵？
4. 学生有毛笔吗？
5. 小车子很贵，对不对？
6. 小李的东西是什么？
7. 周老师有什么样的字典？
8. 李明的伞怎么样？
9. 有书的姓什么？
10. 您贵姓？你是不是学生？

9.5 Form of characters

Traditionally, Chinese characters have been subdivided into six categories according to the way they are thought to have been formed. These categories are called the 六書 *liù shū* 'six scripts', and include graphs that are derived from drawings (such as 马/馬 *mǎ* 'horse', the earliest versions of which look much more like a horse), graphs that are formed as indications (such as 上 and 下, which represent meaning diagrammatically), or graphs that are borrowed or extended (such as 不, which was borrowed to represent a word of nearly identical sound).

Though the 'six scripts' are sometimes claimed to be descriptive, it actually requires considerable historical knowledge in order to decide in which category a graph belongs. For the beginner seeking a way to gain a foothold on the face of the written language by trying to rationalize relationships between the sound/meaning of a word and the form of its character, there are only two useful kinds of relationships. One is representational: the shape of the character suggests its meaning; for example, 上 'on', 下 'under', 中 'middle', and 心 'heart'. The other is phono-semantic, a rather awkward word that captures the fact that such characters were originally formed from a pairing of elements, one chosen for its meaning, and the other for its sound.

In the early stages of learning characters, it is useful to focus on the representational, or pictorial, qualities of characters in an attempt to provide some scaffolding for the memory; hence the use of real or made-up etymologies in the character notes. But, as noted in the Introduction, a large majority of characters originated as phono-semantic pairings. As you will see in Unit 10, almost all new characters are created on the phono-semantic model. Ultimately, knowledge of these elements—and particularly the phonetic elements—will prove to be the most important factor in correctly identifying characters and reading texts.

9.5.1 Representational characters

Characters that are not an amalgamation of other characters, such as 中, 马/馬, or 王, can be called 'simplex'. It is probably true that most simplex characters ultimately derive from drawings that relate to the original meaning of the graph. The following characters all have forms that can be rationalized fairly easily in terms of their meaning.

一	二	三	上	下	中	心	必	火	雨
yī	*èr*	*sān*	*shàng*	*xià*	*zhōng*	*xīn*	*bì*	*huǒ*	*yǔ*
'one'	'two'	'three'	'on'	'below'	'middle'	'heart'	'must'	'fire'	'rain'
米	木	月	山	凸	叉	弓	鱼/魚	鸟/鳥	伞/傘
mǐ	*mù*	*yuè*	*shān*	*tū*	*chā*	*gōng*	*yú*	*niǎo*	*sǎn*
'rice'	'tree; wood'	'moon'	'hill'	'convex'	'fork'	'bow'	'fish'	'bird'	'umbrella'

A particular graph can be viewed as representational regardless of whether the historical data support the notion. Thus, if you agree that 伞/傘 *sǎn* looks (even vaguely) like an umbrella, then you are regarding the graph as representational, and this image can help you to remember its meaning and form. Similarly, once the graph 心 *xīn* 'heart' is known, then 必 *bì* 'must; have to' can be viewed as representing the notion of obligation as 'a line crossing the heart'. Conversely, the pictorial origins of some graphs may have been obscured by historical change. The graph 象 *xiàng* 'elephant' may not look much like an elephant until someone makes the case for it, either by citing a more realistic earlier graph, or by drawing attention to a trunk, head, body, and tail in the modern character.

Beginning students show great skill in creating made-up etymologies (even for compound characters). Thus, the character 哭 *kū* 'to cry' is often seen as 'two eyes and a *tear*'; 电/電 *diàn* 'electricity' is seen as 'an appliance with an *electrical* cord running out the bottom'; or—to cite a more extreme case—会/會 *huì* 'to be able; capable' (among other meanings) is seen as Darth Vader, complete with helmet and breathing equipment—a man of impressive *capabilities*. While it is useful to find recognizable pictures in characters, this approach has its limits. There is not much to be said for, say, 皮 *pí* 'skin', 衣 *yī* 'clothes', or 豆 *dòu* 'beans'. They are simplex, and may well derive directly from representations, but their forms are difficult to account for without historical research—or a very creative imagination.

9.5.2 Additive characters–or blends

A small set of compound graphs can be interpreted as semantic blends, in which the meaning of the whole seems to be related to both its parts. Occasionally, as in the examples in section B, both meaning and sound are involved.

A. SEMANTIC BLENDS

尖 *jiān* 'sharp', composed of 小 *xiǎo* 'small' and 大 *dà* 'big'; i.e., 'wedge shaped'

忠 *zhōng* 'loyal', composed of 中 *zhōng* 'middle' and 心 *xīn* 'heart'

信 *xìn* 'believe; letter', composed of 人 *rén* 'person' and 言 *yán* 'language'

孕 *yùn* 'to be pregnant', composed of 乃 *nǎi* 'to exist' and 子 *zǐ* 'child'

好 *hǎo* 'to be good; well', composed of 女 *nǚ* 'woman' and 子 *zǐ* 'child'; i.e., 'goodness'

尿 *niào* 'urine', composed of 尸 *shī* 'body' and 水 *shuǐ* 'water'

屎 *shǐ* 'excrement', composed of 尸 *shī* 'body' and 米 *mǐ* 'rice; grain'

B. BLENDS OF SOUND AND MEANING (RARE)

甭 *béng* 'no need to', composed of 不 *bù* 'not' and 用 *yòng* 'use'

乒乓 *pīngpāng* 'ping-pong', whose graphs suggest a ping-pong table, but which also take their sound from the graph 兵 bīng 'soldier'

As with the simplex characters, students and teachers frequently ignore the historical facts and enlarge the category of blends with their own etymologies: 名 *míng* 'name' is composed of 夕 *xī* 'evening' and 口 *kǒu* 'mouth', explained as 'in the evening, you have to call out *names* to identify people'; the traditional graph for 東 *dōng* 'east' is composed of 日 *rì* 'sun' superimposed on 木 *mù* 'wood' (originally 'tree'), explained as 'sunrise through the *eastern* trees'; 杯 *bēi* 'cup' is composed of 木 *mù* 'wood' and 不 *bù* 'not', and explained as 'cups aren't made of *wood*' (a tongue-in-cheek example cited in T'ung and Pollard's fine textbook, *Colloquial Chinese*, one of a number of books to which this text is indebted).

9.5.3 Phono-semantic characters

Once your repertoire of characters begins to grow, it becomes more effective to relate characters not to things (their referents), but to each other. Thus, as noted earlier, once 马/馬 *mǎ* 'horse' is learned, it is then easier to relate it to 吗/嗎 *ma* the interrogative marker, 妈/媽 *mā* 'mother', or eventually to 蚂/螞 *mǎ* 'ant' and 码/碼 *mǎ* 'number'. The historical process that gives rise to such phonetic sets is borrowing followed by specification: 马/馬 is borrowed to write words similar in sound (mother, ant, number, etc.); then, to prevent confusion, the graph is further specified by the addition of a classifying character, or radical: 口, 女, 石, 虫, etc.

Many phonetic sets are quite regular, like the马/馬 set, or the following set based on 青 *qīng* 'green; young'.

請	情	晴	清	氰	蜻	鯖
qǐng	*qíng*	*qíng*	*qīng*	*qíng*	*qīng*	*qīng*
'to invite'	'feelings'	'clear'	'clean'	'hydrogen'	'dragonfly'	'mackerel'

In many cases, phonetic correspondences that were once regular have been obscured by historical changes in the language; such is the case for 饿/餓 and 我, or 陈/陳 and 东/東, where the pronunciation of members of the set (*è* and *wǒ*, in the first case, *chén* and *dōng* in the second) remains close (the tongue positions for 'd' and 'ch' are very similar) but no longer identical. Even the 'irregular' sets show patterns of correspondence, as illustrated by the set based on 重 below, which differ only slightly in terms of the initials *zh* and *d*.

重	種	踵	腫	動	懂	董
zhòng	*zhǒng*	*zhǒng*	*zhǒng*	*dòng*	*dǒng*	*dǒng*
'heavy'	'category'	'heel'	'swell'	'to move'	'to understand'	'to lead'

The common sound elements, the phonetics (重 above), are called *shēngpáng* in Chinese; the specifying elements, the radicals (禾, 月, 力, etc.) are called *bùshǒu*. As shown at the beginning of this unit, radicals do have concrete meanings (e.g., 言 'speech', 心 'heart', 日 'sun', 水 'water', etc.), and, initially, the selection of a particular radical to form a compound character would have been inspired by meaning. However, in many cases, the original impetus has been obscured by linguistic and cultural change. The presence of the water radical in 海 *hǎi* 'sea', 河 *hé* 'river', and 洗 *xǐ* 'to wash' reflects a connection with water, but its presence in 汉/漢 *hàn* 'Chinese', 温 *wēn* 'warm', and 活 *huó* 'to live' is harder to explain. Ultimately, the function of radicals in compound characters is one of differentiation (活 is not 适 or 括; 漢 is not 難, 嘆 or 艱) and classification (活 and 漢 are found under the water radical in indexes and dictionaries).

9.5.4 Character retrieval

Alphabetic writing systems, regardless of the regularity of their spelling, make use of relatively few symbols, so ordering titles in filing systems or words in dictionaries is a matter of alphabetization: establishing an order for the symbols and remembering it. For character writing systems, in which the number of symbols totals in the thousands, retrieval is much more problematic.

The most common method of ordering characters (and, ultimately, retrieving them) was suggested by the large number of compound characters that arose from the processes of internal borrowing (giving rise to shared phonetics) and specification (giving rise to shared radicals) described above. Compound characters could be grouped by radical, and then sub-grouped by the number of additional strokes. Thus, 請 would be categorized under the speech radical, 言, among those characters with eight additional strokes; 蜻 would be cateogrized under the insect radical, 虫, among characters with eight additional strokes, etc. Simplex characters that were themselves radicals (such as 言, 日, 气, 魚) would be listed at the head of their own set. Other simplex characters were brought into the same system by designating parts of their graphs—sometimes rather arbitrarily—to be radicals. Thus, 中, 北, 甲 (all simplex) are assigned the radical | (the vertical stroke called *shù*); 也 is assigned the radical 乙 (even though the character does not contain a stroke of that shape); 元 is assigned 儿, and so on.

Eventually, by Qing dynasty times, with the publication of the great Kangxi dictionary, the number of radicals was settled at 214, ordered by numbers of strokes for each. Students of the language who had to be able to look up characters efficiently, or search through indexes ordered by radical, came to know the radical chart virtually by heart. Because of their important classificatory role, and because they are stable (each character has only one assigned radical) and of fixed number, introductory textbooks have tended to focus on radicals (noting general meanings where possible), rather than on phonetic sets.

The radical system of retrieval is not the only one in use, but it remains one of the more popular systems for looking up characters in dictionaries or other reference works in cases where the pronunciation is not known. Adoption of the simplified set of characters was accompanied by some changes in the assignment of radicals that altered the arrangement and reduced the total number from the traditional 214. Dictionaries of the simplified set list from 188 to 201 radicals, depending on the dictionary.

The main difficulty in using the radical system is identifying the radical—particularly in simplex characters which are not themselves radicals and were assigned a radical to make them conform to the system. Nowadays, most dictionaries are organized alphabetically by the pinyin pronunciation of the first character, but they also contain lists organized by radicals that allow a user to look up characters when the pronunciation is unknown. Only one dictionary, *The ABC Chinese-English Dictionary* (cited under Further Reading) is organized by pinyin and word (rather than character), so that words are ordered uniquely, irrespective of the particular character of the first syllable. This dictionary proves extremely useful in looking up words that are overheard in speech.

9.5.5 An illustration

The couplet pictured below was observed on a shop door in the city of Zhenjiang, not far down the Yangtze River from Nanjing. It provides some good examples of phono-semantic characters. Despite being a product of the Mainland, the 'scroll' is written vertically in traditional characters, right to left: *Jùn jì ào chí*, etc. Each character contains the now familiar element 馬, but as a radical, not a phonetic, so the set of characters shows no particular commonality of sound. Rather, they all refer to types or attributes of horses.

The word-for-word glosses below are only very rough indications of meaning. Each set of four characters in a column forms a sentence consisting of an adjective and a noun, followed by an adverb and a verb. The sense is one of aspiration and hope.

	↓		↓			↓
驤	駿	*xiāng*	*Jùn*	(Adj)	'galloping'	'Outstanding'
駒	驥	*jū*	*jì*	(N)	'foal'	'fleet horse'
驩	驁	*huān*	*ào*	(Adv)	'joyously'	'proudly'
騰	馳	*téng.*	*chí,*	(V)	'soars.'	'races,'

The saying is not a well-known one; in fact, though they would get the gist of the meaning, many Chinese would be hard pressed to explain precisely the difference between a *jì* and a *jū* (the second characters of each vertical line).

Chinese encountering rare characters, such as these in the couplet, are quite likely to make use of the radical and phonetic elements to remind them of meaning and pronunciation, respectively. Students of the language require the

Front door, *Zhènjiāng*, near *Nánjīng*

hints even more. With some allowance for 馳, which needs to be referred to other compounds (池 *chí*, 弛 *chǐ*) rather than just the right-hand element 也 *yě*, the pronunciation of the phonetic elements alone matches the pronunciation of the compound characters in all features but tone. Thus, 驥 and 冀 are both pronounced *jì*; 驁 is *ào*, 敖 is *áo*; 驤 and 襄 are both *xiāng*, etc.

9.6 Miscellany

9.6.1 Tone sets

Read aloud from top to bottom, paying attention to the tones.

A. *JIǍNTǏZÌ*

老师	很好	再见	不热	很忙	不高
紧张	还好	看报	不累	很难	上班

B. *FÁNTǏZÌ*

緊張	還好	看報	不餓	很難	上班
老師	很好	再見	不熱	很忙	不高

C. OTHER COMBINATIONS

不忙	很好	不太累	忙吗？
不饿	很累	不太好	紧张吗？
不累	很忙	不太忙	饿吗
不紧张	很高	不太高	好吗
不高	很饿	不太饿	累吗

9.6.2 Set 4 characters in *fántǐzì*

沒有傘	沒有筆	還沒起來	書包	她的書	什麼
méiyǒu sǎn	*méiyǒu bǐ*	*hái méi qǐlái*	*shūbāo*	*tā de shū*	*shénme*
上車	字典	東西很貴	您好！	貴姓？	手機
shàngchē	*zìdiǎn*	*dōngxi hěn guì*	*Nín hǎo!*	*Guìxìng?*	*shǒujī*
那不行。	字典很貴	你的行李呢？	在這兒	看書	
Nà bù xíng.	*zìdiǎn hěn guì*	*Nǐ de xíngli ne?*	*Zài zhèr.*	*kànshū*	

9.7 On the street #2

歡迎光臨
欢迎光临
huānyíng guānglín
'Welcome [to you our] guests.'
('welcome bright-presence')

公話
公话
gōnghuà
'public telephone'
('public + speech')

推
tuī
'push'
[written on doors]

拉
lā
'pull'

空車/空车
kōngchē
('empty-vehicle')
[on taxis]

藥/药
yào
'medicine'
[sign for pharmacy]

押
yā
'pledge'
[sign for pawn shop]

Hong Kong shop sign (note the traditional graphs)

NOTES

a. The formal expression for welcoming customers, *huānyíng guānglín*, or thanking them, *xièxie guānglín*, is often written at the entrance to shops (on doors, walls, or floors).

b. Pay phones in China can be found on the street or in other public places. While they do accept coins, most customers make use of one of the many brands of phone cards that can be bought from newspaper stands and small shops (usually at 30–50 percent of face value). However, many people prefer using the ordinary telephones that small shops make available for public use. These are announced by small signs with 公話 or 公用电话 written on them. Normally, before making a call, you would let the shopkeeper know the type of call you will make (*shìhuà* 'local', *chángtú* 'long distance', or *guójì* 'international'—though the last are not always possible from shop phones). You are charged afterward, according to time and distance; fees are usually very modest.

c. 推 and 拉 contain the 'hand radical', a combining version of 手, called *tíshǒupáng* ('raise-hand-beside'). It is associated with words having to do with physical manipulation.

Unit 10 第十課 DÌ-SHÍ KÈ

三人行，必有我师焉。
(三人行，必有我師焉。)
Sān rén xíng, bì yǒu wǒ shī yān.
'[Even] a party of three will surely include one from whom I can learn.'
('[Among] three people walking, surely there+exists my teacher among+them')
—Confucius, *The Analects*

Unit 10 follows the format that is now fairly well established: a review section, then four sets of new characters, each with notes and a series of reading exercises designed to ensure that each character is encountered enough times and in enough contexts to make a memorable impression that can form the basis for further reading. The unit ends with a section on the creation of new characters that underscores the point that the Chinese writing system is not completely fixed, and that if there is a need for creating new characters, there are systematic ways to do so.

10.0 Review

FÁNTǏZÌ

馬:	你好，我是馬小東。
王:	哦，馬小東，我是王老師。
李:	王老師，您好，我是李明。

王: 李明，你好。

李: 還有他呢，他姓毛，叫毛明。

王: 毛明，你好。三個人了。你呢？

張: 我是張生明。

王: 張生明，你好。那好，歡迎你們來北京。

馬, 李, 張: 謝謝。

王: 你們很累吧。

馬, 李, 張: 不累，還好。

王: 餓嗎？吃飯了嗎？

馬, 李, 張: 不餓，在飛機上吃了。

王: 那，你們的行李呢？

馬, 李, 張: 在這兒，一二三四五。都在這兒。

王: 那好，我們走吧，上車吧。

馬, 李, 張: 好，好。

王: 今天有一點兒熱，你們熱嗎？

馬, 李, 張: 不熱，還好。

王: 行李，雨傘，書包呢？

馬, 李, 張: 都在這兒。

王: 好，那我們走吧。

RADICALS AND PHONETICS (SIMPLIFIED SET ONLY)

Review exercise: Character components

Try to recall characters from Units 8 and 9 that have the following characteristics:

1. two that contain the phonetic element 乍 (*zhà*)
2. two that contain the element 隹 (*zhuī*)
3. two that contain *zǒuzhīpáng*, the movement radical (whose independent form is 辵)
4. three that contain *kǒuzìpáng* (口), the mouth radical
5. two that contain *mùzìpáng* (木), the tree radical
6. one with *zuǒ'ěrduō* ('left-ear') as the radical, and one with *yòu'ěrduō*
7. one with *jiǎosīpáng* ('twisted-silk-beside'), and two with silk on the bottom
8. one with *sāndiǎnshuǐ* (the water radical), and one with the ice radical, *liǎngdiǎnshuǐ* 'two drops of water'

Review exercise: Character combinations (simplified graphs)

Add a character before or after the following characters to form a word or phrase.

1. 可__	5. __经
2. 学__	6. __报
3. 书__	7. __典
4. 中__	8. __以

10.1 First set

名	字	叫	地	方	美	吧
3+3	3+3	3+2	3+3	4+0	3+6	3+4
míng	*zì*	*jiào*	*dì*	*fāng*	*měi*	*ba*
'name'	'character'	'to be named; to be called; to call'	'place; region'		'beautiful; [USA]'	BA

國	英	過	氣	想	去	兩
3+8	3+5	3+9	4+6	4+9	2+3	2+6
国		过	气			两
3+5		3+3	4+0			1+6
guó	*yīng*	*guò*	*qì*	*xiǎng*	*qù*	*liǎng*
'country'	'hero; [England]'	'pass; ever'	'air; spirit'	'to think; to feel like'	'to go'	'two of'

NOTES

a. 名 contains the elements 夕 'evening' (originally a drawing of the setting moon) and the mouth radical 口; for mnemonic purposes, it might be helpful to think 'moon, low in the sky at evening, so you need to *call out your name* to identify yourself'.

b. 字 *zì* 'character' contains 子 *zǐ* 'child' as a phonetic; think 'a pupil under a roof, studying *characters*'. *Míngzi* is literally 'the name characters', i.e., the characters that form the name. Be sure to distinguish 字 from 子 and 了 *le*.

c. 叫 is composed of 口 'mouth' plus a component that resembles the Arabic numeral '4'.

d. 地 is the third character you have encountered with 也 as the right-side element (cf. 她 and 他). The presence of 也 in these characters seems to have resulted from orthographic confusion, and does not represent its use as a phonetic element. 地 contains 土 *tǔ* 'earth' as a radical, which is called *tǔzìpáng*. 方 'square; region' is common in compound characters, where it is assigned as the radical if it is the left-hand component, regardless of its phonetic function: cf. 放 *fàng* and 旅 *lǚ*. Its phonetic relevance is more consistent in other positions: cf. 防 *fáng*，房 *fáng*，and 访 *fǎng*.

e. 美 is a compound made up of 羊 *yáng* 'sheep; goat' (with its stem truncated) and 大 *dà* 'big'; the usual ordering of its strokes (with 大 beneath the truncated 羊) reflects that fact.

f. Like many of the other final particles (吗, 呢, 啊), 吧 is phono-semantic, with 巴 *bā* as a phonetic and 口 as a radical—the latter signaling the fact that these graphs represent spoken material.

g. The inner part of 國, 或 *huò*, is a phonetic element. The simplified 国 (a Japanese creation) has been formed with an entirely different inner constituent, 玉 *yù* 'jade', which has neither a semantic nor a phonetic connection to the word *guó*.

h. 英 contains 央 *yāng* as a phonetic; the radical is *cǎozìtóu* 'grass character on top', a combining form of the graph 艸 that appears in many characters representing plant names. 美 *měi* 'beautiful' and 英 *yīng* 'hero' are selected for the country names of *Měiguó* and *Yīngguó* (the United States and United Kingdom, respectively) both for sound and meaning. Students have observed the similarity of 英 to the shape of *Britain* (*cǎozìtóu* representing Scotland, etc.)—as well as to a muscular *hero's* body.

i. 過, with a phonetic element shared by 鍋 *guō* (a word that comes into English through Cantonese as a 'wok' or 'frying pan'), is simplified by substituting the non-phonetic (and semantically irrelevant but suitably simple) 寸 *cùn* 'inch' for the complicated 咼.

j. 氣 contains 气 as a radical, which is also found in characters for the gaseous elements, such as 氫 *qīng* 'hydrogen', 氖 *nǎi* 'neon', etc. The internal element in 氣 is 米 *mǐ* '[husked] rice', so the compound graph suggests '*steam* rising from rice as it cooks'. The simplified form simply omits the internal element. Contrast 气, with two upper strokes, and 吃, with only one—the other having been *eaten*.

k. 想 contains the elements 相 *xiāng/xiàng* as a phonetic (seen also in 箱子 *xiāngzi* 'trunk; box'), with 心 *xīn* 'heart' as a radical. 相, in turn, contains the basic components 木 'tree; wood' and 目 'eye', both pronounced *mù*.

l. 去 looks like a yacht 'skimming across the water, *going* from island to island'.

m. 两/兩 derives from a drawing of a balance (or pair of scales). The innards of the *fántǐzì* and *jiǎntǐzì* differ; the traditional has 入, which is also assigned as a radical, but the simplified has 人, which is not the assigned radical; instead, the first stroke of this character, the horizontal, is the assigned radical.

10.1.1 Phrases

名字	叫什么	地方	美国	美国人	走吧
míngzì	*jiào shénme*	*dìfang*	*Měiguó*	*Měiguó rén*	*zǒu ba*
英国	很想去	两个	天气	去过	有名
Yīngguó	*hěn xiǎng qù*	*liǎng gè*	*tiānqì*	*qùguò*	*yǒumíng*

好吧 *hǎo ba*	没吃过 *méi chīguo*	英国人 *Yīngguó rén*	姓方的 *xìng Fāng de*	看过 *kànguo*	不对 *bú duì*
哪国人 *něiguó rén*	那个地方 *nèi ge dìfang*	中英字典 *Zhōng-Yīng zìdiǎn*	天气好了 *tiānqì hǎo le*	英文 *Yīngwén*	姓名 *xìngmíng*

10.1.2 Short descriptions

1. 小白，女的，名字叫美文，中国人，去过美国；没去过英国，不过很想去。
2. 老高，男的，名字叫英明，美国人，去过中国，中文很好。
3. 周老师，男的，名字叫以天，中国人，昨天很紧张，现在好了。
4. 李四方，男的，中国来的，以前是小学的老师，现在是大学的。
5. 姓陈的，名字叫现中，英国的中国人，英文中文都很好；去过美国，很想上美国的大学。
6. 美国的天气，现在有的地方冷，有的地方热；中国呢，一样，有的地方冷，有的 地方热。英国呢?

Exercise 1

Answer the questions below, according to the information given in the chart.

	姓	名字	男/女	哪国人？	今天怎么样？	吃过饭了没有？
1.	王	美月	女	中国人	很累	还没吃过饭呢
2.	高	太白	男	中国人	很忙	已经吃过饭了
3.	陈	贵儿	男	美国人	现在好了	还没吃过饭呢
4.	周	班贵	女	美国人	很紧张	吃过了
5.	张	林生	男	中国人	很饿	还没吃饭呢
6.	毛	在中	女	英国人	不冷不热	吃过了
7.	林	明月	女	美国人	还好，不累	吃了

QUESTIONS

1. 姓高的名字叫什么？他是哪国人？他今天怎么样？他吃过饭了吗？
2. 第一个人姓什么，名字叫什么？是女的吗？是什么地方来的？她今天怎么样？她吃过饭了吗？
3. 陈贵儿是男的吧！是哪儿的人？他以前怎么样？现在呢？他吃过饭了没有？
4. 姓毛的名字叫什么？在中是不是他的名字？他是美国人吧。你去过那个地方吗？他今天怎么样？他很饿吧?
5. 第七个姓林，对吗？那，她的名字是什么？她是哪国人？她吃过饭了吗？她怎么样？
6. 那，第五个也姓林吗？是女的吗？ 是不是美国人？他饿不饿？他吃过了吗？
7. 是不是有三个女的四个男的？有没有姓王的？有姓马的吗？

10.2 Second set

北	京	南	西	安	海
2+3 or 1+4	2+6	2+7	6+0	3+3	3+7
běi	*jīng*	*nán*	*xī*	*ān*	*hǎi*
'north'/	'capital'	'south'	'west'	'peace'	'sea'

外	到	近	省	川	州
3+2	2+6	3+4	5+4	1+2	1+5
wài	*dào*	*jìn*	*shěng*	*chuān*	*zhōu*
'outside'	'to arrive; to'	'to be close'	'province'	'river'	'administrative division'

從	離	遠	邊	錯	部
3+8	8+10	3+10	3+15	8+8	3+8
从	离	远	边	错	
2+2	2+8	3+4	3+2	5+8	2+8
cóng	*lí*	*yuǎn*	*biān*	*cuò*	*bù*
'from'	'distance from'	'to be far'	'side'	'mistake; wrong'	'part'

NOTES

a. 北 could be said to resemble 'two people sitting back to back for warmth against the cold *north* wind'. 北 can be contrasted with 比 *bǐ* 'to compare; than', as in 比较 *bǐjiào*, in which the two parts are in line (and therefore easier to *compare*). The traditional set assigns the right-hand component as radical (2+3), but the simplified set ignores the larger constituents and assigns the vertical stroke on the left as radical (1+4).

b. 京 resembles 'a gateway in the wall around the *capital*, with a slit window and buttresses'. Chinese cities are oriented toward the south (the emperor sat with his back to the north); so 南 *nán* 'south', then, might be said to be a drawing of 'an elaborate *southern* city gate, with an observation tower, wide opening, and a barrier beneath'.

c. 西安 *Xī'ān* 'western peace'. Be sure to contrast 西and 四. 安 shows 女 under a roof, said to be 'an image of *peace*'.

d. 海 consists of 氵(the water radical) plus 每*měi* 'each; every' (most likely with a phonetic origin); this element is also found in other words, such as 悔 *huǐ* 'to regret'. 上海 'Shanghai' does not mean 'on the sea' (which would be *hǎishàng*) but 'rising to the sea'.

e. 外 is composed of 夕 *xī* 'evening' (seen also in 名) and 卜 'stick; divining rod'. Think of 'the wall of the house, with the moon setting *outside*'.

f. The right-hand element of 到 *dào* 'to arrive; to' is the 'knife-radical' (*dāozìpáng*), a combining form of 刀 *dāo* 'knife' that appears in characters for words having to do with cutting, as well as sharply demarcated events, such as 'arriving'.

g. 近 combines the movement radical with the phonetic element 斤 *jīn* (a Chinese unit of weight).

h. 省 has 少 *shǎo* 'few; little' over 目*mù* 'eye', the latter as a radical. 州 was originally a representation of islands or high ground in a river valley, but came to refer to towns or administrative centers that grew up in such places. It is therefore a common second element for cities, e.g., 广州/廣州 *Guǎngzhōu*, 苏州/蘇州 *Sūzhōu*, 杭州 *Hángzhōu* , 徐州 *Xúzhōu*. It is also used as a translation for 'state' in U.S. state names: 加州 *Jiāzhōu* 'California', 德州 *Dézhōu* 'Texas', 康州 *Kàngzhōu* 'Connecticut'. The original graph has been differentiated into 州 and 洲 (also *zhōu*), with the latter used as the second character in the names of continents, e.g., 亚洲/亞洲 *Yàzhōu* 'Asia', 欧洲/歐洲 *Ōuzhōu* 'Europe'. 川, which lacks the 'islands', shows just the river, and is an old word for 'stream', now associated only with the province of 四川, named for the four rivers which flow south through 四川 into the Yangtze River.

i. 從 has a core meaning of 'to follow; to obey' which is suggested by the two 人 in the upper right—which also form the basis of 从, the simplified form of the character.

j. 離 is a particularly complicated character with a total of 18 strokes. The simplified form (离) drops the traditional radical (隹) and assigns the first two strokes (on the top) as the radical. This element can be viewed as 'a diagram of a route, with the first two strokes and 'x' marking the starting point, the lower box and its contents marking the destination, and a line connecting the two indicating *distance*'.

k. 遠 is composed of 袁 *yuán* (a surname) as a phonetic; the simplified form substitutes a simpler phonetic 元 *yuán* (the unit of Chinese currency).

l. 邊 consists of the movement radical and a complex of three elements–自, 穴 and 方–on the right. The simplified graph is based on the last of these three elements.

m. 错/錯 consists of the metal (or 'gold') radical 钅/金 (cf. 钱/錢) and the phonetic element 昔, independently pronounced *xī*, but also found in 厝 *cuò* and 措 *cuò*, where its phonetic value is clearer. 错/錯 has an ancient meaning of 'grindstone', which accounts for the metal radical and suggests an evolution from 'burrs'–small imperfections–to 'errors'.

n. The left-hand component of 部 appears both on the left, as in 部 and 剖 *pōu* and on the right, as in 陪 *péi* and 倍 *bèi*; in either position, it generally has a phonetic function.

10.2.1 Phrases

北京 *Běijīng*	南京 *Nánjīng*	西安 *Xī'ān*	上海 *Shànghǎi*	西北 *Xīběi*
外国 *wàiguó*	到明天 *dào míngtiān*	从昨天 *cóng zuótiān*	很近 *hěn jìn*	北边 *běi biān*
四川 *Sìchuān*	南方 *nánfāng*	四川省 *Sìchuān shěng*	广州 *Guǎngzhōu*	广东省 *Guǎngdōng shěng*
外国人 *wàiguó rén*	从什么地方 *cóng shénme dìfang*	离这儿 *lí zhèr*	不远 *bù yuǎn*	南部 *nán bù*
不错 *bú cuò*	离北京 *lí Běijīng*	东北 *dōngběi*	东京 *Dōngjīng*	海边儿 *hǎi biānr*

Exercise 2

Answer the questions below, based on the information given in the following chart.

	姓	哪国人	什么地方	那个地方的天气	去过的地方
第八	毛	中国人	北京	有一点冷	英国
第二	林	中国人	上海	还好，不冷不热	—
第一	张	英国人	西北	不错	中国
第九	陈	美国人	南边	很热	英国
第三	白	美国人	东北	有一点冷	中国
第七	周	英国人	中部	很好，很热	美国
第四	李	美国人	北边	不太好	中国
第五	王	中国人	南京	昨天冷，今天好	—
第十	方	中国人	四川	有一点热	东京
第六	安	中国人	广州	很热	海外

QUESTIONS

1. 第一个人姓什么？ 是哪国人？ 什么地方来的？ 那儿的天气怎么样？ 他去过哪国？
2. 第二个人是谁？是什么地方来的？那儿的天气是不是很热？他去过外国吗？
3. 第三个姓什么？ 他是哪儿的人？ 那个地方的天气好不好？ 他去过英国吗？
4. 第四个是中国人吗？ 他是哪国人？ 那儿的天气怎么样？ 他去过中国吗？
5. 第五个姓什么？ 他是什么地方人？ 那个地方的天气怎么样？ 他去过外国吗？
6. 第六个是不是姓安的？ 姓安的是哪国人？ 那儿的天气有点儿热吧！ 姓安的去过外国吗？

7. 第七个姓什么？ 他是什么地方来的？ 那儿的天气很热吗？ 他去过美国吗？

8. 第八个姓毛吧? 是中国人吧? 什么地方呢？ 那儿的天气呢？ 他去过美国没有？

9. 第九个姓什么？ 是什么地方人？ 那儿的天气怎么样？ 他去过英国吗？ 英国天气怎么样？

10. 第十个姓方吗？ 他是中国什么地方来的？ 他去过外国吗？ 他去过的那个地方天气怎么样？

10.2.2 Set 1 in *fántǐzì*

美國 *Měiguó*	去過 *qùguo*	美人 *měirén*	天氣 *tiānqì*	不想去 *bù xiǎng qù*
英國 *Yīngguó*	什麼地方 *shénme dìfang*	天氣很熱 *tiānqì hěn rè*	兩個人 *liǎng ge rén*	叫什麼 *jiào shénme*
吃過了 *chīguo le*	哪國人 *něi guó rén*	天氣怎麼樣 *tiānqì zěnmeyàng*	起來了 *qǐlái le*	

10.3 Third set

别	忘	非	常	家	本
2+5	4+3	1+7	3+8	3+7	4+1
bié	*wàng*	*fēi*	*cháng*	*jiā*	*běn*
‘don’t; other’	‘to forget’	‘not’	‘often’	‘home; family’	(root; stem)

説	得	電	話	碼	裏
7+7	3+8	8+5	7+6	5+10	6+7
说		电	话	码	里
2+7		1+4	2+6	5+3	7+0
shuō	*+de; dé; děi*	*diàn*	*huà*	*mǎ*	*lǐ*
'to speak; to talk'	DE; 'must'	'electric'	'words; language'	(number)	'inside; in'

NOTES

a. 別 has the knife radical on the right (cf. 到 *dào* 'to arrive') and *lìng* 'other; in addition' on the left. The core meaning is 'separate', with the knife suggesting a line of separation; hence 'other' and 'don't'.

b. 忘 contains the same components as 忙, the heart radical and the phonetic 亡 *wáng*, but arranges them vertically rather than horizontally. If 亡 on the right side of 忙 is 'a container *busily* collecting things that need doing', then placed above the heart (忘), it represents 'those things you *forgot* to do'.

c. 非 is an older negative whose graph may represent two sides in opposition. 常 contains the cloth radical 巾 *jīn* (said to be a drawing of a handkerchief and also found in 帽子 *màozi* 'hat') and the phonetic element 尚 *shàng*, also seen in 裳 *cháng* or *-shang*, 廠 *chǎng*, and 當 *dāng*.

d. 家 contains 豕 (a graph derived from a drawing of a pig and representing modern *shǐ*, an archaic word for 'pig') placed beneath the roof radical, hence '*house* and chattels'.

e. 本 marks the stem or trunk of 木 *mù* 'wood; tree', hence its function as the measure word for books (一本书), and, by extension, 'root; origin' (本來).

f. 説 is sometimes printed as 說, with the upper right-hand strokes written as 八. 説, the verb, obviously needs to be distinguished from 話, the noun. The latter contains 舌 *shé* 'tongue' (protruding from 口, the mouth), thus implying 'words; language'. In many cases, you can be guided by the order of the words–说话/説話 (verb + noun)–but note that the reverse order can also appear in certain syntactic constructions: 中国话说得很好。/中國話説得很好 。

g. 得, pronounced *dé*, is a verb meaning 'to obtain'; untoned, it is the particle used in constructions such as *shuō+de hěn hǎo*; pronounced *děi*, it is a modal verb meaning 'have to; must'.

h. The form of the graph 裏 *lǐ* has a phonetic 里 *lǐ* inserted into 衣 *yī* 'clothing' (cf. 褒 and 哀); the original meaning was 'lining of clothes', hence 'inside'. The graph is also written 裡, with the same components organized horizontally—the clothing radical left of the phonetic. The simplified graph, 里, isolates the phonetic element, resulting in the same character used for both 'inside' and 'mile'.

Kūnmíng locksmith (电子配匙 *diànzǐpèi[yào]shì* 'electric match-key')

10.3.1 Phrases

别人 *biérén*	忘了 *wàng le*	别忘了 *bié wàng le*	非常 *fēicháng*	日本 *Rìběn*
家里 *jiā lǐ*	都忘了 *dōu wàng le*	别客气 *bié kèqi*	说得很好 *shuō+de hěn hǎo*	哪里 *nǎlǐ*
本来 *běnlái*	以前 *yǐqián*	现在 *xiànzài*	二三得六 *èr sān dé liù*	电话 *diànhuà*
号码 *hàomǎ*	非常好 *fēicháng hǎo*	三本书 *sān běn shū*	没有电话 *méiyǒu diànhuà*	我的家 *wǒ de jiā*
别说了 *bié shuō le*	马家 *Mǎ jiā*	说得不好 *shuō+de bù hǎo*	不想去 *bù xiǎng qù*	不太有名 *bú tài yǒumíng*

10.3.2 Set 2 in *fántǐzì*

上海 *Shànghǎi*	外國 *wàiguó*	海邊 *hǎi biān*	四川 *Sìchuān*	不遠 *bù yuǎn*	很近 *hěn jìn*
北京 *Běijīng*	英國 *Yīngguó*	四川省 *Sìchuān shěng*	南邊 *nán biān*	離這兒 *lí zhèr*	東北 *dōngběi*
不錯 *bú cuò*	還好 *hái hǎo*	從昨天 *cóng zuótiān*	到今天 *dào jīntiān*	北部 *běi bù*	中部 *zhōng bù*
從什麼地方 *cóng shénme dìfang*		廣州 *Guǎngzhōu*	東北邊 *dōngběi biān*	離西安很近 *lí Xī'ān hěn jìn*	

Exercise 3

Answer the questions that follow these dialogue pairs.

王:　你的伞，别忘了。
李：　不是我的，我没有伞。

白:　我的手机呢？
周：　在我这儿。别忘了。

毛:　你家离这儿很远吗？
林：　不太远，两里。

张:　你中文说得很好。
高：　哪里，说得不好。

马:　你的电话号码呢？
方：　家里：5-6021; 手机：13501 102130

安:　你是中国人吧?!
林：　不是，我是日本人，日本东京人。

高:　广州天气怎么样？
周：　七月八月非常热，一月二月不错，不冷也不热。

张:　你的书包，别忘了。
毛：　不是我的，我的在家里。

李:　这儿有没有电话？
王：　这儿没有；学生中心有一个，你可以从这边去，不太远。

张:　你的字典，别忘了。
马：　哦，太好了，上课没有字典不行。

QUESTIONS

1. 小李有没有伞？
2. 伞现在在哪里？
3. 小白的手机在哪儿？
4. 林家离这儿远不远？
5. 姓高的中文说得怎么样？
6. 姓方的有手机吗？号码呢？
7. 姓林的是中国人吗？东京在什么地方？
8. 广州天气怎么样？
9. 姓毛的，书包在哪里？
10. 学生中心离那儿远不远？
11. 学生中心有没有电话？
12. 上课，没有字典行吗？那，上班呢？

10.4 Fourth set

喝	渴	多	少	斤	百
3+9	3+9	3+3	3+1	4+0	5+1
hē	*kě*	*duō*	*shǎo*	*jīn*	*bǎi*
'to drink'	'thirsty'	'many'	'few'	'half a kilogram'	'hundred'

杯	酒	再	瓜
4+4	3+7	1+5	5+0
bēi	*jiǔ*	*zài*	*guā*
'cup'	'liquor'	'again'	'melon; gourd'

幾	塊	錢	見	茶
3+9	3+10	8+8	7+0	6+6
几	块	钱	见	茶
2+0	3+4	5+5	4+0	3+6
jǐ	*kuài*	*qián*	*jiàn*	*chá*
'how many'	'piece; dollar'	'money'	'to see; meet'	'tea'

NOTES

a. 喝 *hē* and 渴 *kě* share the phonetic element 曷 *hé*. 'To drink' is suggested by 口 'mouth', and 'thirst' by the water radical 氵.

b. 多少 is composed of the opposites 'many' and 'few'; the former consists of 夕 xī 'evening', and the latter is based on 小 *xiǎo* 'small' (from which it should be distinguished). For 多, duplication of 夕 suggests *many*.

c. 斤 was originally a drawing of an axe (now 斧 *fǔ*).

d. Be sure to distinguish 百 'hundred' from 白 'white; *surname*'.

e. 杯 is composed of 木 and 不. Despite the disparity in the modern pronunciation of 不 and 杯, the former probably originally had a phonetic function in the latter. Consider the following as a mnemonic device: '*Cups* are not made out of wood.'

f. 酒 is composed of the water radical 氵 and the phonetic 酉 *yǒu*. '*Liquor* as a liquid in a bottle with a cork; the horizontal dash at the bottom is sediment.'

g. A helpful description of 再 might be 'a plunger for setting off explosives and blowing up things which then have to be built *again*'. 見 has the same root as 現 *xiàn* (of 現在 *xiànzài* 'now'), the latter originally meaning 'cause to be seen; be manifest'.

h. 瓜 was originally a drawing of a *gourd* on the vine, and it appears as a radical in several words associated with gourds.

i. The radical for 幾 is the top left cluster of three strokes; and the character also contains 戈 *gē* 'spear' on the right (also used in 國). The simplified graph uses 几 *jī* 'stool; bench' (ignoring the tone) instead of the much more complicated traditional form.

j. 塊 is composed of 土, the earth radical, with 鬼 *guǐ* as a phonetic. 錢 is composed of the combining form of 金 *jīn* 'gold' with piled-up 戈 *gē* 'spears' at the right—'weapons guarding the *money*'.

k. 茶 is composed of the grass radical (on top) and a unique component on the bottom, resembling 'a shed, where *tea* from bushes (木) is drying'.

10.4.1 Phrases

喝什么	很渴	多少	不多	喝酒
hē shénme	*hěn kě*	*duōshǎo*	*bù duō*	*hē jiǔ*
不太渴	一百	喝茶	喝咖啡	一斤
bú tài kě	*yìbǎi*	*hē chá*	*hē kāfēi*	*yì jīn*
多少钱	不少	不喝酒	两杯	杯子
duōshǎo qián	*bù shǎo*	*bù hē jiǔ*	*liǎng bēi*	*bēizi*
西瓜	木瓜	三块钱	再见	南瓜
xīguā	*mùguā*	*sān kuài qián*	*zài jiàn*	*nánguā*
几块钱	三块钱	钱不多	明天见	几个老师
jǐ kuài qián	*sān kuài qián*	*qián bù duō*	*míngtiān jiàn*	*jǐ ge lǎoshī*
多不多	一块西瓜	一杯三毛	非常多	三百块
duō bu duō	*yí kuài xīguā*	*yì bēi sān máo*	*fēicháng duō*	*sān bǎi kuài*
三百不多	西瓜好吃	一斤八毛	两百	中国白酒
sānbǎi bù duō	*xīguā hǎochī*	*yì jīn bā máo*	*liǎng bǎi*	*Zhōngguó báijiǔ*

10.4.2 Set 3 in *fántǐzì*

書包別忘了。 *Shūbāo bié wàng le.*	非常熱 *fēicháng rè*	你的手機別忘了。 *Nǐ de shǒujī bié wàng le.*	非常累 *fēicháng lèi*
電話號碼 *diànhuà hàomǎ*	説得不錯 *shuō+de bú cuò*	筆還在家裏 *bǐ hái zài jiā lǐ*	日本 *Rìběn*
非常緊張 *fēicháng jǐnzhāng*	中國西南邊 *Zhōngguó xī'nán biān*	東西在家裏 *dōngxi zài jiā lǐ*	天氣不錯 *tiānqì bú cuò*
兩個東西 *liǎng ge dōngxi*	車子非常貴 *chēzi fēicháng guì*	從昨天到明天 *cóng zuótiān dào míngtiān*	非常餓 *fēicháng è*

已經吃飯了不過還是很餓。
Yǐjīng chīfàn le, búguò háishi hěn è.

説外國話很難。
Shuō wàiguó huà hěn nán.

他有個日本人的名字。
Tā yǒu ge Rìběn rén de míngzi.

已經起來了，但是還沒吃飯。
Yǐjīng qǐlái le, dànshì hái méi chīfàn.

Exercise 4

东西	几个?	几块钱 / 多少钱?
西瓜	一个	四块二一斤
冬瓜	一块	三块五分钱一斤
南瓜	一个	四块八毛五一个
茶	一杯	五块四毛一杯
咖啡	一杯	一杯二十五块钱
白酒	一瓶 (*píng*)	一百十五块钱
汉英字典	一本	二十八块钱
英汉字典	一本	三十二块钱
杯子	一个	十八块
手机	一个	一百二十五块钱
伞	一把 (*bǎ*)	二十二块
笔	一只 (*zhī*)	两块五毛钱
中文报	一份 (*fèn*)	一块二
英文报	一份	六块八毛钱

QUESTIONS

1. 西瓜好吃吗？ 多少钱一斤？ 那是不是有一点贵？
2. 英文，冬瓜怎么说？ 好吃吗？ 几块钱？ 一斤多不多?
3. 南瓜呢，美国南瓜很多，可是中国呢，中国也有南瓜吗？ 南瓜贵不贵？ 多少钱一个？ 你说一个南瓜有几斤？
4. 中国人喝茶，那美国人喝什么？ 你现在渴不渴？ 想喝一点 什么？
5. 一杯茶几块钱？ 那，咖啡呢，一杯几块? 咖啡更贵对吗？ 在美国咖啡也很贵吗？ 茶咖啡你都喝吗？
6. 美国一块钱是中国几块？ 你去过中国吗？
7. 你喝过中国白酒吗？ 好喝吗？ 白酒多少钱一瓶？
8. 美国人吃饭喝不喝酒？ 中国人呢？
9. 汉英字典多少钱？ 上课没有字典难不难？那，英汉字典呢？
10. 一杯茶几块？一个杯子几块？酒杯是不是更贵？ 茶杯呢？
11. 中国人说: '再见'，那美国人怎么说？
12. 中国人说：'你渴吗？想喝一点什么？' 美国人怎么说？
13. 伞在英国多少钱？ 那，伞在中国多少钱？
14. 看过今天的报了吗？ 在这儿，报多少钱？ 在中国呢？ 你看过 什么中国报吗？

10.5 Creating new characters

In English, new words are often 'dressed in old garments', by processes such as extension ('shuttle' extended from the part of a loom that shuttles back and forth to a spacecraft that shuttles back and forth) or compounding ('space' + 'ship' to 'spaceship'); sometimes, though, new fashions are introduced through processes such as coinage ('blooper'), borrowing ('sputnik'), or sound symbolism ('screech, blip'). In alphabetic languages, the result of each process can be written as easily as another; it is just a matter of rearranging letters.

Of the various options, Chinese makes greatest use of compounding to create new words. Thus, rather than borrowing the word 'laser' from English, Chinese creates a compound of 'excited' plus 'light': 激光 *jīguāng*. In the same fashion, specialized terms such as 'neutron' and 'proton' are built on the root 子 *zǐ* 'child', extended to mean 'particle': 中子 *zhōngzǐ* 'neutron' ('middle-particle'); 质子 *zhìzǐ* 'proton' ('substance-particle'). In each of these cases, the source of the word was probably written English; Chinese incorporates the meaning of each word, but not the original sound. However, there are times when Chinese borrows foreign words wholesale. Three common examples–*kāfēi* 'coffee', *shāfā* 'sofa', *tǎnkè* '[military] tank'–are all inspired by the pronunciation of English words. These words have to be assigned characters. Observing how this is done nicely illustrates traditional principles of character formation. There are two main options for creating new characters: utilize existing graphs solely for their sound: *shāfā* is written with 沙 *shā* 'sand' and 发 *fā* 'issue'; or form new graphs from a phonetic element and a radical: *kāfēi* is written with 加 *jiā* 'to add' and 非 *fēi* 'not', each marked with the mouth radical 口: 咖啡. In the examples that follow, it is the second option that is illustrated. The examples are drawn from two domains: words for atomic elements in the periodic table, and words that express sounds (onomatopoeia).

10.5.1 Atomic elements

The periodic table contains names of elements long known to Chinese science, such as 汞 *gǒng* 'mercury' (工 *gōng* 'work' over 水 *shuǐ* 'water'), 鉛 *qiān* 'lead', and the 'stony' elements listed in the third set below. Others, such as the gases and metals listed in the first two sets, are based on the English names. Regardless of the source, the elements are mostly written with characters created on strict phono-semantic principles, so that pronunciation can rely on the much more common characters acting as phonetic elements. The sets are marked by the choice of radical: 气 *qì* 'air' for gases, 金 *jīn* 'gold' for metals, and 石 *shí* 'stone' for silicon and other 'stony' elements.

ELEMENT	GRAPH	PHONETIC	RADICAL
Helium	氦 *hài*	亥 *hài*	气 'gas'
Neon	氖 *nǎi*	乃 *nǎi*	气 'gas'
Argon	氬 *yà*	亞 *yà*	气 'gas'
Thorium	釷 *tǔ*	土 *tǔ*	金 'metal'
Palladium	鏷 *pú*	菐 *pú*	金 'metal'
Uranium	鈾 *yóu*	由 *yóu*	金 'metal'
Silicon	硅 *guī*	圭 *guī*	石 'stone'
Phosphorus	磷 *lín*	鄰 *lín*	石 'stone'
Sulphur	硫 *liú*	流 *liú*	石 'stone'

10.5.2 Representing sounds—onomatopoeia

The representation of sound is an interesting source of innovation in any writing system. The list below includes a number of graphs taken from 'manga'-style Mandarin comics. (The Japanese term 'manga' is represented in Chinese as *mànhuà* 'comic; cartoon' ['unrestrained-drawing'].) Manga represents not only a genre in which the written language converges on the spoken, but one that is less subject to the usual prescriptions and constraints associated with writing and publication. Some of the characters listed below will not be found in Chinese dictionaries; indeed, some speakers may disagree about some of the examples provided below, both the pronunciation and the sound event that it represents. This is to be expected, for authors of manga are freer to create their own words and use the resources of the written language to represent them as they see fit. The interesting point is to observe how they use traditional phono-semantic principles of character formation to do so.

As befits the genre of 'anime', onomatopoeic words are usually drawn in highly stylized animated graphs whose very size and shape add to their intended effect. In the examples below, the radical element is consistently the mouth radical (口), which typically signals that the graph represents a sound. Because some of the graphs used to represent sounds in these examples do not occur in standard character sets, they are represented below as empty squares. In the original texts, they would have been drawn with a mouth radical added to the base phonetic graph.

ONOMATOPOEIC GRAPH AND PRONUNCIATION	PRONUNCIATION OF BASE PHONETIC	EQUIVALENT ENGLISH NOISE OR EVENT
啪 *pā*	拍 *pāi*	noise of hitting (slap, slam, pow)
啪嘞 *pālei*	拍,勒 *pāi, lè*	noise of something falling (crash)
噗通*pūtōng*	濮，通 *pú, tōng*	noise of something hitting water (plop, thud)
噗嗤*pūchī*	濮，蚩 *pú, chī*	noise of laughter, running water (tee-hee, tinkle)
嚓 *cā*	察 *chá*	noise of skidding (screech)
唧*jī*	即 *jí*	high-pitched sounds (squeak)
嘭 *pēng*	彭 *péng*	drumming noise (boom)
叮 *dīng*	丁 *dīng*	light metallic noise (ping)
噹 *dāng*	當 *dāng*	heavy metallic noise (bong)
叮噹 *dīng dāng*	丁, 當 *dīng, dāng*	noise of keys, money (jingle jangle)
呯叮 *pīngdīng*	平,丁 *píng, dīng*	noise of metal, bottle falling (clatter)
嚨 *lóng*	隆 *lóng*	reverberating noise (boing)
㕊*fú*	伏 *fú*	swishing noise (swish)
嗄 *shā*	夏 *xià*	hissing or whizzing noise (shh, hiss)
咔哒 *kādā*	卡,达 *kǎ, dá*	clicking sound (clip clop)
啵啵 *bōbō*	波 *bō*	rain drumming on the ground (pitter patter)

10.6 Miscellany

10.6.1 Set 4 in *fántǐzì*

喝酒 *hē jiǔ*	很渴 *hěn kě*	多少錢 *duōshǎo qián*	一斤四塊 *yì jīn sì kuài*
一百塊 *yìbǎi kuài*	南瓜很好吃 *nánguā hěn hǎochī*	再見，明天見。 *Zàijiàn, míngtiān jiàn.*	白酒 *báijiǔ*
幾塊錢 *jǐ kuài qián*	不多也不少 *bù duō yě bù shǎo*	多少學生 *duōshǎo xuéshēng*	茶杯 *chábēi*
喝一點酒 *hē yìdiǎnr jiǔ*	去過酒吧嗎 *qùguo jiǔbā ma*	喝太多不行 *hē tài duō bù xíng*	再說 *zài shuō*
酒杯 *jiǔbēi*	杯子裏有什麼 *bēizi lǐ yǒu shénme*	一杯兩塊五 *yì bēi liǎng kuài wǔ*	幾個老師 *jǐ ge lǎoshī*

Exercise 5

Distinguish the following characters by citing words or phrases in which each is used.

斤 - 今 - 近	在 - 再	美 - 没	钱 - 前
典 - 电 - 店	手 - 说	难 - 男	对 - 贵
不 - 还	我 - 饿	日 - 热	是 - 师
七 - 起	小 - 少	陈 - 车	伞 - 三
到 - 别	百 - 白	川 - 州	毛 - 笔
忙 - 忘	渴 - 可	一 - 以	本 - 杯

In the following compounds or phrases, provide the missing characters which have similar or identical sounds. See the examples that are partially done for you.

1. 车子	名___	6. ___女	不太难	11. ___以	很___
2. 一块___	以___	7. 号___	好___？	12. 英___	去___
3. ___有	___国	8. 一___儿	___话号码	13. 上课	很___
4. ___这儿不远	在家___	9. 姓___	一___钱	14. ___张	___天
5. ___经	可___	10. ___哪儿?	___见！	15. ___儿?	___儿!

10.7 On the street #3

当心扎脚 *Dāngxīn zhājiǎo* 'look out for sharp objects' ('look out-pierce-foot')

路标 *LÙBĪAO* 'ROAD SIGNS'

南京西路	*Nánjīng Xī Lù*	昌化路	*Chānghuà Lù*
北京西路	*Běijīng Xī Lù*	常德路	*Chángdé Lù*

NOTES

a. 路 *lù* 'road' contains 足 *zú* 'foot' as a radical.

b. 街 *jiē* 'street', not illustrated above, contains 行 *xíng* 'crossroads' as a radical.

航空公司 *HÁNGKŌNG GŌNGSĪ* 'AIRLINE COMPANIES'

中国航空公司	中国东方航空公司
中国北方航空公司	中国南方航空公司
中国西北航空公司	中国东方航空公司

Unit 11 第十一課 DÌ-SHÍYĪ KÈ

論(论)天下大勢(势)，分久必合，合久必分。
Lùn tiānxià dàshì, fēn jiǔ bì hé, hé jiǔ bì fēn.
'They say the momentum of history was ever thus: the empire long divided, must unite; long united, must divide.'
('speak+of sky-beneath great-power, divide long must join, join long must divide')

—The opening lines of 三国演义/三國演義 *Sānguó yǎnyì,* a title that is traditionally translated as *The Romance of the Three Kingdoms,* a popular historical narrative attributed to *Luó Guànzhōng* and dating to the 14th century. It deals with a period more than 1,000 years before the author lived, after the collapse of the Han dynasty (206 BCE–220 CE), when kingdom competed against kingdom and the heroes *Liú Bèi, Guān Yǔ,* and *Zhāng Fēi* swore brotherhood in a peach garden behind *Zhāng Fēi*'s farm (supposedly on the outskirts of modern-day *Chéngdū*). Part of their vow reads as follows. (Translations from Moss Roberts, *Three Kingdoms: China's Epic Drama by Lo Kuan-chung* [1976].)

不求同年同月同日生，但願(愿)同年同月同日死。
Bù qiú tóngnián tóngyuè tóngrì shēng, dàn yuàn tóngnián tóngyuè tóngrì sǐ.
'We could not help our separate births, but on the self-same day we mean to die!'
('Not choose same year, month, day born, but desire same year, month, day die.')

Unit 11 begins with some review material, including a narrative in traditional characters. This is followed by the usual four sets of characters, less than half of which have both traditional and simplified forms. The unit ends with (a) a review of those characters previously encountered that have two forms; (b) a section on business cards; and (c) a list of Chinese newspapers.

11.0 Review

FÁNTǏZÌ (See below for new words.)

李小山是南京大學的學生。她生在南京，也長在南京。南京在江蘇，在中國東部，在長江邊上，離上海不遠。那個地方很好，人口四五百萬，不大也不小。那兒的天氣還可以。七月到九月非常熱，常常下雨，可是一月到三月不怎麼冷，很舒服。李小山還沒去過外國，也沒上過英文課，可是她英文説得非常好，看英文書報也可以。那怎麼會這樣呢？很多人覺得學英文沒有老師不行。她説她沒有老師但是有很多外國朋友，有美國人，有英國人，有加拿大人，也有澳大利亞人。她説她可以看英文報紙，看英文書，看美國電視，這樣學。再説，她書包裏有一本很好的英文字典，有好字典就能學好！

生字表 *Shēngzìbiǎo* 'vocabulary list' ('raw-characters-table')
長/长 SV *cháng* 'long'; V *zhǎng* 'to grow; to grow up; N *zhǎng* 'head of; chief'

江	*jiāng* 'river'	江苏/江蘇	*Jiāngsū* (name of a province)
人口	*rénkǒu* 'population'	舒服	*shūfu* 'comfortable'
会/會	*huì* 'can; able to; likely to'	觉得/覺得	*juéde* 'to think; to feel'
朋友	*péngyou* 'friend'	电视/電視	*diànshì* 'television' ('electric-look at')
能	*néng* 'capable of'	万/萬	*wàn* 'ten thousand'
下雨	*xiàyǔ* 'to rain' ('fall-rain')	不怎么冷	*bù zěnme lěng* 'not so cold'

RADICALS AND PHONETICS

Review exercise: Character components

Try to recall characters from Units 8 through 10 that have the following characteristics:

1. three characters with the element 戈 *gē* 'spear'
2. two characters with 土 *tǔzìpáng* 'the earth radical'
3. two characters with 钅/金 *jīnzìpáng* 'the metal radical'
4. a second character with the radical called *bǎogài*, seen on top of 字
5. three characters that contain the element 目 *mù* 'eye'
6. two characters with the phonetic element 曷 *hé*
7. two characters with the radical 木 *mùzìpáng*

Review exercise: Character combinations (traditional graphs)

Add a character before or after (as indicated) to form a word.

1. ______瓜	6. 再______
2. ______川	7. 非______
3. 電______	8. 起______
4. 緊______	9. ______師
5. 上______	10. ______報

On the map provided, label as many places as you can in characters; add others in pinyin.

Review exercise: Character combinations (traditional graphs) (*Continued*)

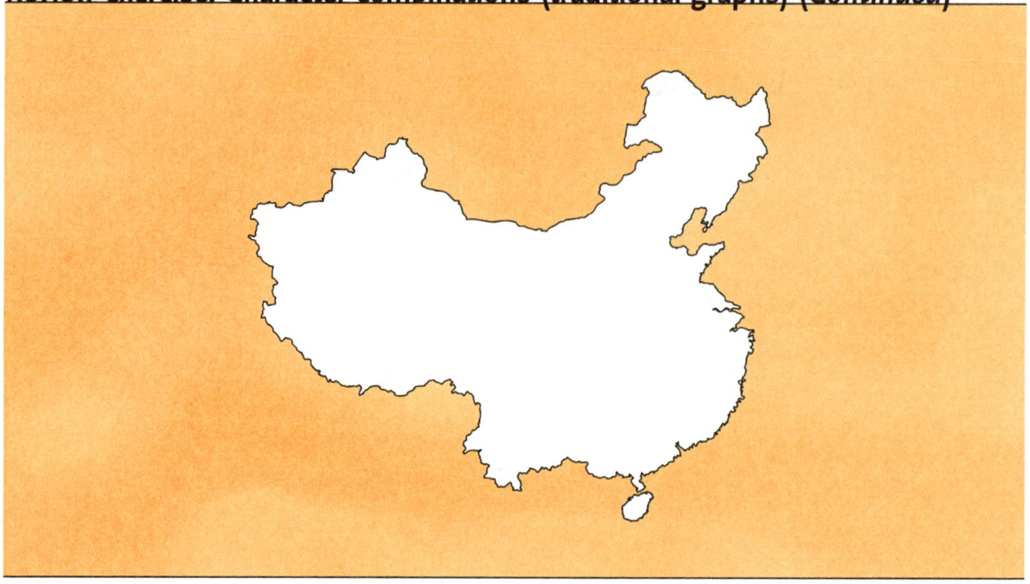

11.1 First set

衣服	舒	目	最	先	早
6 + 0 4 + 4	6 + 6	5 + 0	4 + 8	2 + 4	4 + 2
yīfu	*shū*	*mù*	*zuì*	*xiān*	*zǎo*
'clothing'	'stretch out'	'eye; see'	'most'	'first'	'early'

睡覺	洗澡	聽	買	晚
5 + 8 7 + 13	3 + 6 3 + 13	6 + 16	7 + 5	4 + 7
觉		听	买	
4 + 5		3 + 4	1 + 5	
shuìjiào/jué	*xǐzǎo*	*tīng*	*mǎi*	*wǎn*
'to sleep' 'be conscious of'	'to wash'	'to listen'	'to buy'	'late'

NOTES

a. 衣 (*clothes* billowing on the line) often appears as a radical at the bottom of graphs (e.g., 袋), at the top of graphs (e.g., 裔), or in its combining form 衤 *yīzìpáng* on the left side (e.g., 襯衫). It can also be split by an intervening phonetic element, as is the case with the traditional graph 裏 *lǐ* 'lining; inside', which inserts 里 into 衣.

b. 服 (a vanity *dress*er) has a broader range of meaning than 衣, that is, from 'clothes' to 'restraint' and 'submission'. The right-hand element is also found in报/報; contrast the right-hand element 反 that appears in 饭/飯.

c. You only encounter 舒 before 服 in the compound 舒服 'be comfortable'. The core meaning of 舒 is 'to unfold; to open up'; 服 is associated with clothing (cf.衣服), and by extension 'to be restricted; to submit'. Hence, 舒服 means 'to release from restrictions' or 'to be comfortable'. The radical in 舒 is 舌 *shé* 'tongue' (six strokes). The right-hand element is 予 *yǔ*, a formal word meaning 'to give', which looks like a broken version of 子. The 6 + 6 stroke designation represents the six strokes of the radical 舌 plus the four of 予and the remaining two on the left.

d. 目, originally a representation of an eye, is a common radical (called *mùzìpáng*), found in characters such as 睡, 省, 看, and 眼. The two radicals 目 and 木 are both pronounced *mù*.

e. The bottom element of 最 is 取 *qǔ* 'to get; to obtain', but the relationship is obscure. The top element is the horizontal 曰 *yuē* 'to say; to call', not the more familiar vertical 日 *rì* 'sun'.

f. 先 carries a meaning of 'first', so 先生 *xiānshēng* 'mister; sir' ('first born').

g. 早, with 日 'sun' above 十 representing the four quadrants; hence, 'the sun over the horizon, *early* in the morning'.

h. 睡, a compound of *mùzìpáng* and 垂 *chuí* 'to hang down; to droop' as a phonetic. 觉/覺 has two pronunciations: in combination with a leading 睡, it is pronounced *jiào* and treated as an object; when it precedes 得, it is read *jué* and makes up the core of a compound verb. So, 睡觉/睡覺 and 觉得/覺得.

i. 洗澡 contains two good phono-semantic graphs: 洗, which combines *sāndiǎnshuǐ* with 先, now only suggestive as a phonetic; and 澡, which combines the same radical with the phonetic element also found on the right side of 操 *cāo* and 躁 *zào*.

j. 聽 contains the radical element 耳 *ěr* 'ear', and the right-hand element of 德 *dé* (德国/德國 *Déguó* 'Germany'). The small 王 in the lower left corner was originally the element with a rising head stroke that appears in graphs such as 廷 *tíng* and 挺 *tǐng* (cf. 挺好的 *tǐng hǎo de*). The simplified form, 听, is an old variant, built on *kǒuzìpáng* and the imperfect phonetic 斤 *jīn*.

k. The traditional graph 買 contains 貝, originally a representation of a cowrie shell. Cowries are said to have been used as a form of currency in coastal regions, so the radical is associated with monetary transactions; c.f. 贵/貴 'to be expensive' and the traditional graph賣 *mài* 'to sell'. However, the simplified graph 买 (cf. simplified卖*mài* 'to sell') abandons the traditional radical completely and introduces the element 头 *tóu* 'head', whose only similarity to the traditional form is its legs—the two strokes at the bottom.

l. 晚 contains *rìzìpáng* and the element 免, independently pronounced *miǎn*.

11.1.1 Compounds and phrases

从前 *cóngqián*	本来 *běnlái*	目前 *mùqián*	衣服 *yīfu*	舒服 *shūfu*	水土不服 *shuǐtǔ-bùfú*
两本书 *liǎng běn shū*	日本 *Rìběn*	最近 *zuìjìn*	很远 *hěn yuǎn*	很晚 *hěn wǎn*	早上 *zǎoshàng*
最高 *zuì gāo*	先生 *xiānshēng*	我先去 *wǒ xiān qù*	睡了吗 *shuì le ma*	好听 *hǎotīng*	洗澡 *xǐzǎo*
早上 *zǎoshàng*	最大 *zuì dà*	晚上 *wǎnshàng*	买什么 *mǎi shénme*	觉得 *juéde*	觉得不舒服 *juéde bù shūfu*

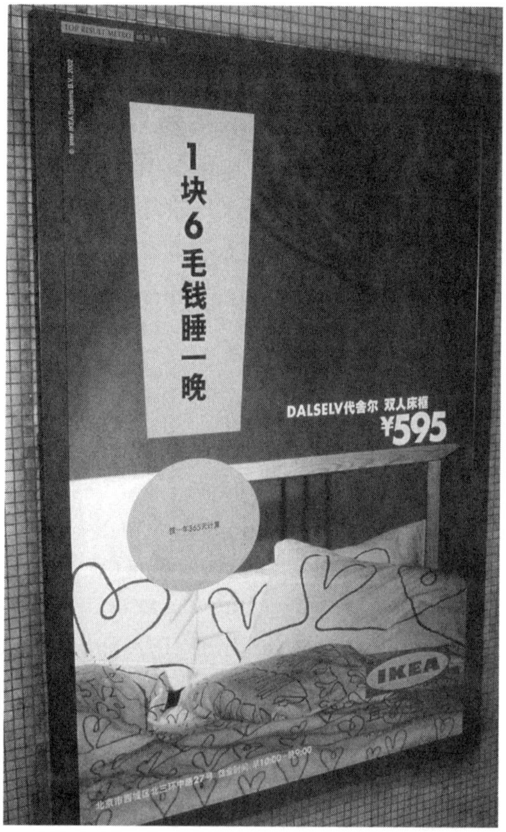

Ikea advertisement on the wall of a *Běijīng* pedestrian subway

11.1.2 Comment and response

1. 最近你觉得怎么样？ / 哎，昨天很不舒服，有一点累，不过今天好了。最近都是这样儿，一天很好，一天很累。

2. 哎，买衣服很难吧。 / 是很难。他想买的，我觉得不好看，我想买的他说不好看！
3. 你的行李多不多？/ 没有行李，东西不多，只有书包。
4. 他们都起来了吗？/ 都起来了，可是还没洗澡，也还没吃早饭呢。
5. 学中文没字典不行。 / 我有一本，可是不大，字不多。 / 那，最好买一本大的。
6. 明天没课，你想去哪儿？/ 明天是毛先生的生日，我们想去看他。
7. 这是你的衣服吗？/ 不，是张老师的，但是他已经走了。
8. 你渴不渴？ 喝一杯啤酒吧。 / 好，好，我喝 一点茶吧，中国茶吧。
9. 听说你们最近没有热水。 / 现在天气非常热，洗澡没有热水还可以，可是一月二月洗澡没有热水有一点不舒服。
10. 今天有一点儿冷，你们冷吗？ / 不冷，还好，很舒服。

NOTES

a. 哎 *ài* an interjection indicating surprise or dissatisfaction; composed of 口 as radical 艾 *ài* as a phonetic.

b. 不过 *búguò*, cf. 但是, 可是

c. 课 *kè* ‘course; class’; cf. 上课, 下课

d. 生日 *shēngrì* ‘birthday’

e. 啤 *pí*, composed of 口 as radical and 卑 *bēi* as a phonetic.

Exercise 1

The following table gives a list of suspects and indicates what they were doing at various times when crimes were committed. Stand by to give the information when asked.

	姓？	几月几号，几点？	在做什么？
(一)	毛先生	十一月八号，早上，七点十分	在洗澡
(二)	周小姐	十月十号，晚上，十一点四十分	在睡觉
(三)	陈老师	十二月二号，早上，八点	在吃早饭
(四)	张老师	八月二十四号，晚上，九点	在洗衣服

(五)	马太太	七月十九号，早上。八点二十分	在看报
(六)	林省长	一月三号，中午	在买东西
(七)	小白	三月二十号，晚上，很晚	在学中文
(八)	老李	六月二十八号，下午，五点多	在吃饭
(九)	王州长	八月八号，上午，十一点	在买西瓜

Ménkǒu, Tiānjīn

11.2 Second set

請	問題	機場	鐵	比較
7 + 8	3 + 8 9 + 9	4 + 12 3 + 9	8 + 13	4 + 0 7 + 6
请	问题	机场	铁	较
2 + 8	3 + 3 6 + 9	4 + 2 3 + 3	5 + 5	4 + 6
qǐng	*wèntí*	*jīchǎng*	*tiě*	*bǐjiào*
'please' ('invite')	'question' ('ask-topic')	'airport' ('machine-arena')	'iron'	'relatively' ('than-compare')

大	帽	清楚	姐	同
3 + 0	3 + 9	3 + 8 5 + 8	3 + 5	2 + 4
dà	*mào*	*qīngchu*	*jiě*	*tóng*
'big'	'hat'	'clear'	'sister'	'same; with'

NOTES

a. 请/請 contains *yánzìpáng* and the common (and reliable) phonetic element 青 *qīng*, seen also in the first character of 清楚 *qīngchu*.

b. 门/門 is a phonetic in some compounds, but assigned as a radical in others. In the traditional set, 問 is classified under the 口 radical, leaving 門 *mén* as a reasonable phonetic. The creators of simplified characters were more concerned with classification than history, so in the simplified set, 问 is classified under the 门 radical rather than 口.

c. Compound characters with the element 是 form a phonetic set whose members are pronounced similarly to *shì* or *tí*: thus 是 *shì* and [钥]匙 [*yào*]*shi* 'key', 题 *tí*, 提 tí, 惕 *tì*, 堤 *dī*. '*Sh*' and 't/d' sounds are actually quite closely articulated (a fact reflected by the pronunciation of the English suffix '-tion', in words like 'pronunciation'). We can thus assume that words with both *shi* and *ti/di* were pronounced very similarly in earlier times, and have since diverged. A similar process is reflected by the regional difference in the pronunciation of 'tea' as *chá* in Mandarin, but 'te' (which gives us 'tea') in Fukienese—pronunciations which have also evolved from a common source.

d. 场/場 is composed with *tǔzìpáng* and a phonetic element also seen in汤/湯 *tāng* 'soup' and 阳/陽 *yáng* 'sun; male principle'.

e. 鐵 contains *jīnzìpáng*; in the simplified graph, the complex right side is replaced with the simpler, but phonetically unmotivated 失*shī*: 铁. 铁/鐵 has only been encountered in the compound 地铁/地鐵.

f. Contrast 比 (lined up for *comparison*) with 北 (back to back to protect against the *north* wind). 较/較 has the element known as *chēzìpáng* 'vehicle at the side' as a radical and 交 *jiāo* as a phonetic, the latter also seen in 校 *xiào* 'school' and 狡 *jiǎo* (used in a compound meaning 'crafty'). The presence of *chēzìpáng* reflects the original use of the graph for a kind of carriage, which was then borrowed or extended to write the word for 'comparison'.

g. Contrast 大 with 太 *tài* and 犬 *quǎn*, the last being an ancient word for 'dog'.

h. 帽 consists of 巾 *jīn* 'cloth' as a radical (cf. 师) and 冒 *mào* as a phonetic.

i. 姐 *jiě* is composed of the radical 女 and the phonetic 且 *qiě*.

j. 清 is formed from the phonetic 青 *qīng*, cited in note (a) above, and the water radical; 楚 contains 疋, originally a phonetic element (cf. 胥 *xū*) but assigned as radical in the simplified set, and 林 *lín* 'forest'. (Note that 疋 differs only very slightly from the lower part of 是.)

k. Contrast 同 *tóng* with 周 *zhōu*, the latter containing the element 吉 *jí* within.

11.2.1 Compounds and phrases

请问	没问题	请坐	机场	铁路	比较好
qǐngwèn	*méi wèntí*	*qǐngzuò*	*jīchǎng*	*tiělù*	*bǐjiào hǎo*

机场很远 *jīchǎng hěn yuǎn*	比较贵 *bǐjiào guì*	大帽子 *dà màozi*	北大 *Běi Dà*	地铁 *dìtiě*	不清楚 *bù qīngchu*
小姐 *xiǎojie*	同学 *tóngxué*	买大的 *mǎi dà de*	不同 *bù tóng*	姐姐 *jiějie*	比较忙 *bǐjiào máng*
有问题吗 *yǒu wèntí ma*	我先走了 *wǒ xiān zǒu le*	车子不大 *chēzi bú dà*	我的同学 *wǒ de tóngxué*	大姐 *dàjiě*	太大了 *tài dà le*

11.2.2 Comment and response

1. 你的帽子，别忘了！/ 不是我的，是毛小姐的。她已经走了。
2. 有没有问题？ / 没有，都很清楚：从机场先去东长安街，在东长安街坐七号车，在北海下车。没问题。
3. 大连 [在东北] 有没有地铁？ / 没有地铁，有电车，大连的电车很不错，三十分钟，可以从大学到人民广场。
4. 请问，最近的地铁站在哪儿？/ 地铁站呢 . . . 在前边，离这儿不远，三分钟 — 很近。
5. 张老师，请问，您是什么地方来的？ / 我是大同人，大同在山西，离北京大概有三百公里，不是很远。
6. 马小姐，你去过大同吗？/ 没有，我家在南方，离大同很远。
7. 陈小姐今天好了没有？ / 她昨天觉得不太舒服，很累也很紧张，可是今天觉得比较好了。

NOTES

a. 长安 *Cháng'ān* ('long-peace'), ancient name for *Xī'ān*
b. 街 *jiē* 'street'
c. 坐 *zuò* 'to sit'
d. 大连/大連 *Dàlián* city in Liaoning province
e. 人民广场/廣場 *Rénmín Guǎngchǎng* 'People's Square'
f. 站 *zhàn* 'station; stand'
g. 大概 *dàgài* 'general; approximate'

Exercise 2

This exercise can be written out (in pinyin or characters) in a question/answer format. Alternatively, it can be practiced at home as the basis for a class exercise where one person asks the questions and another answers. In any case, both question and answer should be suitably contextualized by the addition of pronouns, polite phrases (e.g., *qǐngwèn*), etc.

Example:	*Èi, wǒ de màozi ne, wǒ de màozi zài nǎr?*
(Item 1)	*Nǐ de màozi … nǐ kàn, zài xiǎo Bái nàr!*
	O, xièxie.

	问题	在哪儿 etc.
1.	帽子在哪儿？	小白
2.	北京机场在哪里？	北京东北
3.	上海火车站在哪儿？	上海北边儿
4.	有没有电话？	学生中心
5.	谁有手机？	王老师
6.	地铁站在哪儿？	在前边，离这儿不远
7.	张小姐是不是你的老师？	是同学
8.	小林请你们去哪儿吃饭？	饭馆儿
9.	陈老师的家离这儿远不远？	离这儿很远，有三四公里。
10.	银行在什么地方？	火车站那儿有银行。
11.	北京大学离这儿远吗？	在北京西北,离这儿比较远。

NOTES

a. 火车站 *huǒchēzhàn* 'train station'
b. 中心 *zhōngxīn* 'center'
c. 饭馆儿 *fànguǎnr* 'restaurant'
d. 公里 *gōnglǐ* 'kilometer'
e. 银行 *yínháng* 'bank'

11.3 Third set

自	山	坐	孔	客	要
6 + 0	3 + 0	3 + 4	3 + 1	3 + 6	6 + 3
zì	*shān*	*zuò*	*kǒng*	*kè*	*yào*
'self; from'	'mountain'	'to sit'	'hole' (surname)	'guest'	'to want; to need'

飛	汽水	漢	長	籍
9 + 0	3 + 4 4 + 0	3 + 11	8 + 0	6 + 14
飞		汉	长	
1 + 2		3 + 2	1 + 3	
fēi	*qìshuǐ*	*Hàn*	*cháng; zhǎng*	*jí*
'to fly'	'carbonated drink' ('vapor-water')	'the Chinese' (name of river)	'long' 'to grow up; head of . . .'	'birthplace'

NOTES

a. Contrast 自 with 目 *mù* 'eye', 白 *bái* 'white', and 百 *bǎi* 'hundred'; 自行车 *zìxíngchē* 'bicycle' ('self move vehicle').

b. 山 was originally a drawing of a mountain. As a radical, it can appear at the top, at the bottom, or on the left (but not on the right) of a character, e.g., 岸 *àn* 'shore'; 岳 *yuè* 'high mountain'; 峨嵋山 *Éméi Shān* (in Sichuan).

c. 坐 (two people *sitting* on a mound of earth) should not be confused with the homophonous words/characters in 做飯 *zuòfàn* 'to cook' and工作 *gōngzuò* 'work'.

d. 孔 *kǒng* ('a gorilla on a building—King *Kong*') contains 子 as the radical, also seen at the top and bottom of graphs, e.g., 孟 *mèng* and 学 *xué*.

e. 客 is composed of a phonetic 各 *gè* (not 名) and *bǎogài* as a radical (cf. 字 and 家).

f. The top part of 要 is the combining form of 西 *xī*, rare as a radical.

g. 飛 (*flying* on two wings) contains 飞 (which forms the basis of the simplified character) and 升 *shēng* 'rise'. The traditional graph is classified as a radical even though it appears in very few characters.

h. 天气的气不是汽水、汽车的汽。/天氣的氣不是汽水、汽車的汽。气/氣 and 汽 represent specialized senses of what was originally a single root, much as the English spellings 'flour' and 'flower' derive from a single root.

g. The graph 水 is derived from a drawing that looks like flowing waters. Its left-side combining form appears in 汉/漢 *hàn*, originally the name of a river, later the name of a dynasty, and ultimately a name for the Chinese people.

h. 长/長 can also function as a phonetic element in characters such as 张/張 *zhāng*.

i. 籍 contains the bamboo radical (*zhúzìtóu*) at the top of the character, also seen in 第.

11.3.1 Compounds and phrases

自行车 *zìxíngchē*	自我 *zìwǒ*	山西 *Shānxī*	孔子 *Kǒngzǐ*	客人 *kèrén*	客气 *kèqi*
要几个 *yào jǐ ge*	山东 *Shāndōng*	飞机 *fēijī*	汽车 *qìchē*	长大 *zhǎngdà*	国籍 *guójí*
长江 Chángjiāng	汉字 *Hànzì*	汽水 *qìchē*	飞人 *fēirén*	姓孔的 *xìng Kǒng* de	要五毛 *yào wǔ máo*

11.3.2 Comment and response

1. 西安在山西，对吗？/ 不对，西安在陕西，我想。
2. 从南京到上海坐飞机行吗？/ 南京离上海很近，坐飞机太贵了，最好坐火车。
3. 我请你吃中饭，好不好？/ 你太客气了，我请你 吧。
4. 我 想去高州，今天还有没有去那儿的公共汽车？/ 今天没有了，明天上午有一班，下午也有一班。
5. 你看，来了一个客人！/ 客人吗？他不是客人，是我弟弟，他下课了。
6. 你通常怎么来上课？/ 走来。我没有自行车。
7. 他姓孔，名字叫大山，是山东人。/ 山东人？山东哪个地方？
8. 很多美国学生早饭、中饭、晚饭都喝汽水。/ 是吗？那，他们不喝汽水喝什么呢？
9. 你是什么国籍？/ 我有两个国籍，美国的国籍，还有英国的。
10. 汉字很多！/ 是，太多了！学一个，忘一个。

Exercise 3

Here is a list of contacts, their nationalities, their place of residence, and some locational information. Pass the information on (in written form or orally). Notice the novel use of some of the characters you have learned as surnames.

	姓		国籍	住的地方	在哪儿
1.	孔	先生	中国	北京东边	离机场不远
2.	英	老师	日本	东京东南边	离第一小学很近
3.	方	小姐	西班牙	南边	在海边
4.	周	太太	英国	西北	离我家不远
5.	伍	师傅	中国	文安县（河北）	离北京比较近
6.	同	省长	中国	西林县（广西）	离中山小学很近
7.	钱	经理	中国	同安县 (福建)	离福州比较远
8.	安	先生	加拿大	多伦多	离自行车公司很近
9.	边	市长	中国	常州 (江苏)	在高山中学前边儿

NOTES

a. 住 *zhù* 'to live'

b. 县 *xiàn* 'county'

c. 经理 *jīnglǐ* 'manager'

d. 福建 *Fújiàn* a province in southeast China

e. 福 *fú* 'good fortune; happiness'

f. 多伦多 *Duōlúnduō* 'Toronto'

g. 市 *shì* 'market; city'

11.4 Fourth set

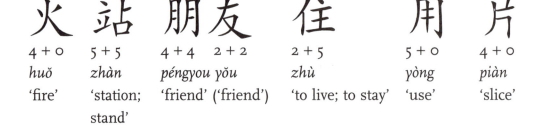

火	站	朋友	住	用	片
4 + 0	5 + 5	4 + 4 2 + 2	2 + 5	5 + 0	4 + 0
huǒ	*zhàn*	*péngyou yǒu*	*zhù*	*yòng*	*piàn*
'fire'	'station; stand'	'friend' ('friend')	'to live; to stay'	'use'	'slice'

Ài wǒ Nánjīng, jiànshè Nánjīng, měihuà Nánjīng, fánróng Nánjīng
'Love Nanjing, build Nanjing, beautify Nanjing, make Nanjing prosperous' (on a mailbox)

公	會	午	共	做
2 + 2	4 + 9	2 + 2	2 + 4	2 + 9
	会			
	2 + 4			
gōng	*huì*	*wǔ*	*gòng*	*zuò*
'public'	'to be able'	'noon'	'collectively'	'to do; to make'

NOTES

a. 火, originally a representation of flames, has a slightly compacted form when it appears on the side (炒) and a distinct combining form when used at the bottom (热/熱).

b. 站 contains 立 *lì* as a radical and 占 *zhān* as a phonetic. 占 appears in compound characters of two types: a 'zhan type' (e.g., 毡 *zhān*) and a 'dian type' (e.g., 点 *diǎn* and 店 *diàn*). Notice that the initial sounds 'zh' and 'd' are quite close.

c. In the traditional set, 月 as a component of compound characters represents two radicals: 月 *yuè* 'moon' and the otherwise more complex 肉 *ròu* 'meat; flesh'. 朋 *péng*, 有 *yǒu*, and 服 *fú* are traditionally assigned the moon radical; 脾 *pí* 'spleen' and 肺 *fèi* 'lungs', along with graphs for some other body parts, are traditionally assigned 肉. In the simplified set, the two are not distinguished, and all characters with the 月 component are listed together.

d. 友 contains 又 *yòu*, an element also found in the simplified versions of 難 and 漢 (i.e., 难 and 汉), where it serves the needs of simplification while obliterating the old phonetic relationship between the characters.

e. 住, with 主 *zhǔ* as a phonetic, should be distinguished from 隹 *zhuī* (with eight strokes) which functions as a phonetic in 谁/誰.

f. 用 appears very occasionally as a radical, such as in 甭 *béng* 'don't', a telescoped, colloquial version of 不用 *bú yòng*. 片 (a plane for making *slices*) is a radical that appears in a handful of graphs such as 版 and 牌.

h. 公 contains 八 *bā* and 厶 *sī*, the latter seen also in 私 *sī* 'personal'.

i. The traditional 會 has 曰 (not 日) as a radical. Earlier, we noted the similarity between 會 and the mask of Darth Vader—a man of impressive *capabilities*. The simplified 会 removes the mask and reveals 云 *yún* 'clouds'.

j. 午, said to have originated as a drawing of a sundial, is a phonetic in 许/許 *xǔ* (as in 也许/也許 *yěxǔ* 'probably').

k. 共 has 八, the legs, as a radical (cf. 典 with the same radical). The top of the graph looks like a container for placing things *all together*.

l. 做 consists of *rénzìpáng* and 故 *gù*. (Cf. the homophonous 坐 'sit' and 作 'work'.)

11.4.1 Compounds and phrases

火车 *huǒchē*	汽车 *qìchē*	自行车 *zìxíngchē*	车子 *chēzi*	做饭 *zuòfàn*	朋友 *péngyou*
名片 *míngpiàn*	住在哪里 *zhù zài nǎlǐ*	站起来 *zhànqǐlái*	不用了 *bú yòng le*	上午 *shàngwǔ*	用笔 *yòng bǐ*
火车站 *huǒchēzhàn*	住的地方 *zhù de dìfang*	用字典 *yòng zìdiǎn*	用中文 *yòng Zhōngwén*	好朋友 *hǎo péngyou*	站在那儿 *zhàn zài nàr*
公里 *gōnglǐ*	公共汽车 *gōnggòng-qìchē*	公用电话 *gōngyòng-diànhuà*	公话 *gōnghuà*	中午 *zhōngwǔ*	
下午 *xiàwǔ*	男朋友 *nánpéngyou*	会一点点 *huì yìdiǎndiǎn*	会下雨吗 *huì xiàyǔ ma*	一共多少 *yígòng duōshao*	午饭 *wǔfàn*

11.4.2 Comments

1. 你家离火车站很远吧！/ 不太远，只有三四公里，二十分钟就到了。
2. 我做饭做得不好！/你做得不错，这很好吃。
3. 对不起，我现在没有名片了，都用完了。
4. 字典，用一点点是可以的，可是用得太多不好。
5. 她的名片没有家里的电话号码，只有大学的。/ 那手机呢？
6. 今天一共有二十三个学生，大家都来了！/ 二十三个吗？那，有一个人没有朋友。
7. 这里有没有公用电话？ / 有，有两个，一个在门口那儿，一个在里边儿。
8. 我们明天晚上去西安，第二天早上七点到。/ 坐公共汽车去吗？
9. 我没有坐过火车，火车怎么样？/ 火车非常好，很舒服。
10. 你中文说得很好！/ 哪里，哪里，说得不好，只会说一点点！
11. 有朋友问我中国人吃饭喝不喝酒。/那，你怎么说呢？/ 我说请客，不喝酒不行。可是没有客人我们常常不喝什么酒。
12. 喝一点儿茶吧。/ 不用了，不用了，我还好。/ 别客气，喝吧！/ 好，那我喝 一点儿白开水。
13. 我们去吃一点儿东西，好不好？/ 现在不行，中午我还得去公共汽车站买票。

NOTES

a. 就 *jiù* 'then'
b. 用完 *yòngwán* 'used up'
c. 请客 *qǐngkè* 'to invite guests'
d. 白开水 *báikāishuǐ* 'boiled water'
e. 得 *děi* 'need'
f. 票 *piào* 'ticket'

Exercise 4

Write down the letters in the order that indicates how these jumbled sentences should be read.

1. (a) 我 / (b) 今天来北京看朋友 / (c) 生在大同 / (d) 现在还住在大同 / (e) 是大同人 / (f) 长在大同 / 。
2. (a) 就 [jiù] 问吧 / (b) 别客气 / (c) 有问题 / ！
3. (a) 已经会说一点常用的话了 / (b) 可是他们都没去过中国 / (c)他们都在学汉语 / 。
4. (a) 有一本 / (b) 也有个帽子 / (c) 那个书包里 / (d) 汉英字典 / 。
5. (a) 先生 / (b) 我姐姐的 / (c) 我朋友的 / (d) 老师 / (e) 是 / 。
6. (a) 很远吗 / (b) 请问 / (c) 公共汽车站 / (d) 离这儿 / (e) 师傅 / 。
7. (a) 起来洗澡 / (b) 坐地铁 / (c) 我们 / (d) 早上六点 / (e) 去上班 / (f) 十一点 / (g) 七点 / (h) 八点 / (i) 睡觉 / (j) 吃早点 / 。
8. (a) 说不难 / (b) 汉字 / (c) 中文 / (d) 但是 / (e) 太多了 /。

11.5 Traditional versus simplified characters

Of the 200 characters introduced in the first four character units, almost 70 have both traditional and simplified forms. For the majority of these 70 characters, the simplified and traditional differ minimally: e.g., 来/來, 贵/貴, 样/樣, 饿/餓, 伞/傘. Many, even if they lack many strokes in common, still retain a family resemblance: e.g., 马/馬, 学/學, 师/師, 问/問, 飞/飛, 电/電. Others are usually compounded and therefore more easily recognized: 什么/什麼, 紧张/緊張, 怎么样/怎麼樣. Only about 20 have sharply divergent forms, and these are among the most common: 个/個, 难/難, 点/點. Exercise 5 is a chance to review the more difficult pairs.

Exercise 5

Match the *jiǎntǐzì* on the left with the *fántǐzì* on the right by writing the appropriate number in the spaces provided.

热 ______	这 ______	1. 陳	14. 兒
对 ______	儿 ______	2. 過	15. 從
块 ______	边 ______	3. 對	16. 還
铁 ______	汉 ______	4. 機	17. 覺
听 ______	几 ______	5. 漢	18. 車
笔 ______	机 ______	6. 遠	19. 會
东 ______	过 ______	7. 筆	20. 鐵
书 ______	会 ______	8. 書	21. 熱
报 ______	远 ______	9. 這	22. 塊
陈 ______	难 ______	10. 買	23. 邊
车 ______	从 ______	11. 東	24. 難
觉 ______	买 ______	12. 幾	25. 聽
还 ______	长 ______	13. 報	26. 長

11.5.1 Comment and response, in *fántǐzì*

1. 學中文，我覺得學漢字有一點兒難，但是說話還可以。/ 請問，第一年你們學過多少漢字？
2. 請問，這兒有沒有個公用電話？/ 有，有兩個，一個在裏邊，一個在門口那兒。要不要用我的手機？別客氣！
3. 你想去買東西，最好坐地鐵去，地鐵比較舒服。/ 那，晚上很晚也可以坐地鐵嗎？
4. 你看，這是毛筆字，這不是。/ 毛筆字很好看，但是用毛筆很難吧？
5. 北京從六月到八月非常熱，從十二月到三月非常冷。/ 那幾月到幾月上學？

6. 現在在中國手機不太貴，一個月差不多一百塊。/哦，是不太貴。

7. 聽說在中國汽車不貴，也有人要買飛機。/問題是人太多了，車子也太多了，停車是個大問題。

8. 機場離這兒不遠，坐公共汽車四十分鐘就到了。/坐地鐵去也可以嗎？

9. 去東方書店，在這兒下車對不對？/對，在這兒下，你看前邊那四個字：東方書店。

10. 姓陳的也是從中國東北來的嗎？/對，他是長春人，家人還在那兒。

NOTES

a. 停車 '*tíngchē*' 'parking' ('put vehicle')
b. 四十分鐘 *sì shí fēn zhōng* 'forty minutes'
c. 就到了 *jiù dào le* 'arrived'
d. 書店 *shūdiàn* 'bookshop'
e. 長春 *Chángchūn*, the capital of Jilin province

11.6 Business cards

Business cards play an important role in Chinese etiquette, and this section provides three samples to show their typical design, and a glossary of words and phrases that will make it possible to read them. Cards are usually exchanged after introductions. They are individually presented with two hands to show respect, and then examined with some care. At a meeting, people will often place cards they have just received next to their place at the table for ease of reference. The card will include a title or rank and other important information for determining appropriate forms of address and other behavior.

周林 大中国地区销售经理 宝洁（广州）有限公司 中国广州市解放北路 986 号 以太广场 1–4 楼　　邮政编码 510040 电话：（8620）8669 8828 转 3386 传真：（8621）8666 2354 手机：13609727562 电子邮箱： 网址：

(男)
……经理
….有限公司
……路 986 号
….1–4 楼　　邮政编码 510040
电话：…………转….
传真：…………
手机：……..
电子邮箱：
网址：

北京大学 对外汉语教育学院
张舒　　　　　　　书记 　　　　　　　　　副院长 地址：北京，100871　北京大学 勺园二号楼 电话：86-10-62751916 传真：86-10-62757249 E-mail:

Duìwài Hànyǔ Jiàoyù Xuéyuàn
('Overseas Chinese Language Education Institute')
(女)　　　　　　书记
　　　　　　　　副院长

地址：…….　…………　二号楼
电话：………
传真：………

西安交通大学 王汉飞　　　　　　　工程师 地址：西安市咸宁路 28 号 能源馆 电话：（029）3267806（办） 传真：（029）2215891 邮编：710049

(男)　工程师

地址：…………………
电话：…………（办）
传真：…………
邮编：…..

Titles	教授		*jiàoshòu*	'professor'
	院長	院长	*yuànzhǎng*	'dean'
	副院長	副院长	*fùyuànzhǎng*	'vice dean'
	經理	经理	*jīnglǐ*	'manager'
	書記	书记	*shūjì*	'secretary'
	主任		*zhǔrèn*	'director'
	總裁	总裁	*zǒngcái*	'CEO'
	工程師	工程师	*gōngchéngshī*	'engineer'
	高級	高级	*gāojí*	'high level'
	有限公司		*yǒuxiàn gōngsī*	'Co. Ltd.'
Addresses	地址		*dìzhǐ*	'address'
	大街		*dàjiē*	'avenue; street'
	路		*lù*	'road'
	號	号	*hào*	'number'
	樓	楼	*lóu*	'building'
	二號樓	二号楼	*èrhàolóu*	'Building #2'
	大廈	大厦	*dàshà*	'(large) building'
	郵政編碼	邮政编码	*yóuzhèng biānmǎ*	'zip code'
Telephone, etc.	電話	电话	*diànhuà*	'telephone'
	辦	办	*bàn* (*bàngōngshì*)	'office'
	轉	转	*zhuǎn*	'(phone) extension'
	移動電話	移动电话	*yídòng diànhuà*	'mobile phone'
	傳真	传真	*chuánzhēn*	'fax'
	手機	手机	*shǒujī*	'cell phone'
	電子郵件	电子邮件	*diànzǐ yóujiàn*	'e-mail'
	電子郵箱	电子邮箱	*diànzǐ yóuxiāng*	'inbox'
	網址	网址	*wǎngzhǐ*	'Web address'
	信箱		*xìnxiāng*	'PO box'

11.7 On the street #4

甲 NAMES OF SOME MAINLAND NEWSPAPERS

青海日报	人民日报	西安晚报	北京日报
南京晚报	中国青年报	明报	大连日报
上海日报	扬子晚报	北京晚报	四川日报
海南日报	山西日报	南方日报	光明日报
南華早報	新京报	大同晚报	

NOTES

a. 人民 *rénmín* 'the people'; cf. *Rénmínbì*

b. 青年 *qīngnián* 'youth; young people'

c. 大连 *Dàlián*—在中国东北 (*Liáoníng*)

d. 扬子 *Yángzǐ*: the region around *Yángzhōu*, a city on the north side of the *Cháng Jiāng* ('Long River'), which gives its name to the lower stretch of the river, the *Yángzǐjiāng*. The English name of the river, the Yangtze, is, of course, based on *Yángzǐjiāng*.

e. 光明 *guāngmíng* 'light; bright'

f. 華(华) *huá* 'China; Chinese'

g. 新 *xīn* 'new'

乙 WARNINGS AND RESTRICTIONS

小心 (站台间隙)
Xiǎoxīn (zhàntái jiànxì)
'Be careful of (the platform gap)'

当心 (自行车)
Dāngxīn (zìxíngchē)
'Watch out for (bicycles)'

禁止(吸烟)
Jìnzhǐ (xīyān)
'(Smoking) prohibited'

严禁 (烟火)
Yánjìn (yānhuǒ)
'(Smoke and fire) absolutely prohibited'

请勿(入内)
Qǐngwù (rù nèi)
'Please do not (enter)'

危险
Wēixiǎn!
'Danger!'

NOTES

a. 禁 *jìn* 'to prohibit'

b. 严 *yán* 'be strict'

c. 勿 *wù* 'do not'

Unit 12 第十二課 DÌ-SHÍ'ÈR KÈ

早早儿睡晚晚儿起，又省灯油又省米。
(早早兒睡晚晚兒起，又省燈油又省米。)
Zǎozāor shuì wǎnwānr qǐ, yòu shěng dēngyóu yòu shěng mǐ.
'Early to bed, late to rise, saves you lamp oil, saves you rice.'
—Cited in Yuen Ren Chao, *A Grammar of Spoken Chinese*

The initial review section of Unit 12 includes instructions on how to talk about characters, such as asking about pronunciation, number of strokes, radical, etc. Following this are four sets consisting of characters for words that you have already encountered in core units 1–5. The final section includes the complex characters for numerals that you will encounter on currency and bills, a note on the 'five elements' (all of which function as radicals in compound characters), and, finally, the usual feature 'on the street'.

12.0 Review

A. CONVERSATIONS WRITTEN IN *JIǍNTǏZÌ* These conversations read across. Practice them until you can read each part fluently.

(1) 美国的钱叫美<u>金</u>，是吗？	在中国也叫美<u>元</u>。
那中国的钱叫什么？	叫<u>人民币</u>。

Notes to the epigraph are located at the end of the unit.

人民币有元角分吧。	是，元就是块，角就是毛，分就是分。
台湾也是人民币吗？	不是，台湾的是台币。
一块美金是八块多人民币吧。	不。现在 一块是七块多了。
那一百块人民币是十四块美金吧。	是，差不多十四块。台币呢，一块美金三十二块！

NOTES

a. 金 *jīn* 'gold; metal'
b. 元 *yuán* 'dollar'; also written 圓
c. 人民币 *Rénmínbì*
d. 角 *jiǎo* 1/10 of a *yuán*
e. 就是 *jiùshi* 'exactly'
f. 台湾 *Táiwān*

(2)	你有多少钱？	我这儿有两三百块。
	那不少。	也不太多。
	你的朋友有没有钱？	他们没有，他们都是学生。学生经常没有什么钱。
(3)	请问，你那一班一共有多少学生？	一共大概有二十个。
	二十个不少。中文课平常没有这么多。有几个老师？	只有一个老师。二十个学生是有一点儿多，但是不是太多，我想。
	老师一定很累！	在这个大学老师学生都很累。
(4)	请问，钱那个字为什么有个金字旁？	金就是钱。
	金是钱吗？那，块为什么是土字旁？土不是钱。	土是地，土地。
	钱币，美金，土地？	就是了。

NOTES

a. 大概有 . . . ; context should be enough to guess the adverb containing the unknown character. Recall the adverbs that allow you to hedge your bets: *yěxǔ, dàgài, kěnéng, chàbùduō*. Similarly, context will help you to guess, or recall, compounds (especially adverbs) beginning with 一. Options include: *yígòng, yídìng, yíkuàir, yíhuìr, yìdiǎn<r>*.

b. 旁 *páng* 'next to'

c. 土 *tǔ*; 土地 'land; soil'; cf. 土木 *tǔmù* 'construction' ('soil-wood')

B. NOW A FAMILIAR CONVERSATION WRITTEN IN *FÁNTǏZÌ*

兩個同學：王高飛，周中明；周中明在門口:

王: 誰啊？
周: 我是周中明。
王: 哦，小明，來來，請坐。
周: 好，哎，今天非常熱！
王: 嗯。那你喝一點兒什麼？ 有咖啡，有可樂，也有啤酒。
周: 不用了，不用了。
王: 你別客氣。喝吧！
周: 好。那，來一杯茶吧。
王: 可以。這茶很好，雲南的。
周: 是很好。
王: 你最近怎麼樣？忙嗎？
周: 今天不太忙，還好。我昨天有一點兒不舒服，可是現在好了。你呢？
王: 有一點兒緊張，功課很多，我也睡得不好。
周: 哎，學生都很忙很累！
王: 可不是嗎？！

NOTES

a. 门口/門口 *ménkǒu* 'doorway'

b. *Kǒuzìpáng* (口) is often found with interjections (at the beginning of sentences) such as 哦 *ò*, 哎 *ài*, and 嗯 *n ~ ng*; with exclamatory particles such as 啊 *a* and 吧 *ba*; and with borrowed words such as 咖啡 *kāfēi* 'coffee'.

c. Hint: 可樂 (可乐) and 啤酒 (啤酒) are drinks; 雲南 (云南) is a place.

Reading the news, *Kūnmíng*

C. RADICALS AND PHONETICS

Review exercise: Character combinations

Add a character (or two) to distinguish the following pairs:

1. ____毛____笔	2. ____周____州	3. ____年____午
4. ____生 住____	5. ____杯 林____	6. 忘____ ____忙
7. 小____ ____少	8. ____服____报	9. 洗____ 先____
10. ____文 这____	11. 地____ 她____	12. 汉____ ____难
13. ____有____友	14. ____陈 东____	15. 四____ 西____
16. 走____ 起____	17. ____呢 吃____	18. ____字____子
19. ____听____近	20. 省____ ____贵	21. 用____ 同____
22. 汽____ ____气	23. 公____ ____么	24. ____典____共
25. ____站____点	26. 几____ ____机	27. 自____ ____白
28. ____见 现____	29. ____过 还____	30. ____对____过

D. TALKING ABOUT CHARACTERS

Asking how to say it or how to write it:

水，火

Dì-yī ge zì, zěnme shuō?	'How do you say the first character?'
'Shuǐ'.	''Shui'.'
Dì-èr ge ne?	'And the second?'
Dì-èr ge shi 'huǒ'.	'The second is 'huo'.'

三塊四毛五

Zěnme niàn?	'How's [it] read?'
Ng, sān kuài.	'Hm, 'san kuai'.'
Hái yǒu ne?	'And what else?'
Sān kuài sì máo wǔ.	'San kuai si mao wu.'

小

'Dàxiǎo' de 'xiǎo' zěnme xiě?	'How do you write the 'xiao' of 'daxiao'?'

Asking about number of strokes (*bǐhuàr*):

元

'Yuán' zhèi ge zì yǒu jǐ ge bǐhuàr?	'How many strokes are in the character 'yuan'?'
Yǒu sì ge.	'There are four.'

我

'Wǒ' ne? 'Wǒ' yǒu jǐ ge bǐhuàr?	'And [in] 'wo'? How many strokes are in 'wo'?'
'Wǒ' yǒu qī ge.	''Wo' has seven.'

Asking about radicals (*bùshǒu*):

都

'Dōu' de bùshǒu shì shénme?	'What's the radical of 'dou'?'
'Dōu' shì yòu-ěrduō ~ yòu-ěrpáng.	''Dou' is the 'right ear'.'

很

'Hěn' zhèige zì de bùshǒu shi shénme?	'What's the radical of the character "hen"?'
Shì shuānglìrén ~ shuāngrénpáng.	'It's the "double man radical".'

12.1 First set

因	為~爲	樓	鐘	歲	喜歡
3 + 3	4 + 5 4 + 8	4 + 11	8 + 12	4 + 9	3 + 9 4 + 17
	为	楼	钟	岁	欢
	1 + 3	4 + 9	5 + 4	3 + 3	4 + 2
yīn	*wéi/wèi*	*lóu*	*zhōng*	*suì*	*xǐhuan*
'reason'	'be/for'	'building; floor'	'bell; clock'	'year; years old'	'to like' ('pleasure-joy')

工作	所~所	定	功	每	位
3 + 0 2 + 5	4 + 4	3 + 5	3 + 2	5 + 2	2 + 5
gōngzuò	*suǒ*	*dìng*	*gōng*	*měi*	*wèi*
'work'	'place; that which'	'fixed; settled'	'merit'	'each; every'	POL M

NOTES

a. The *wèi* of *wèishénme* is usually hand written as 為 in the traditional set (*why* a three-layered cake and candles?), which is classified under the radical 火 'fire'; but it is printed 爲, with radical 爫. The simplified form, which takes the first two strokes of the traditional handwritten form and then reduces the rest to two strokes, derives from calligraphic practices. With a falling tone, *wèi* means 'for [the sake of]'; thus *wèishénme* 'for what'. With a rising tone, it means 'to be; to do; by'. (The *wèi* of *yīnwèi* derives from the rising-toned word, but is now generally pronounced with a falling or neutral tone.) 因 *yīn* contains 大 *dà* 'big' confined inside a square (a big threat confined for a good *reason*).

b. 樓 contains the phonetic element 婁 *lóu*, also seen in 數, which has the unexpected pronunciations of *shǔ* 'to count' or *shù* 'number' (cf. 数学/數學). 婁 itself resembles a tall *building*.

c. 鐘 has 金 as a radical and 童 *tóng* as a phonetic element; originally it meant 'bell' of the sort that would ring the hours from a 钟楼/鐘樓 *zhōng lóu* 'bell tower', such as the fine one in *Xī'ān*. The simplified character provides a more exact phonetic element—中.

d. 歲 is composed of two characters—步 and 戌—with the first graph split into two, with one part appearing on the top, and the other in the middle. The simplified form is based on a non-standard but traditional graph with 山, rather than 止, on top.

e. 喜 'joy; happiness' (two mouths separated by a *joyful* smile) appears at weddings as 囍 'double happiness'. 歡 contains the phonetic element 雚, seen in 觀 *guān*, 灌 *guàn*, and 罐 *guàn*; in the simplified graph, this complex segment is reduced arbitrarily to 又 (cf. 难，汉).

f. 工 *gōng* is usually classified as a radical if it appears on the left (巧 and 项), even if it originally had a phonetic function (功 gōng, 巩 *gǒng*). When placed elsewhere in the graph, it has only a phonetic function: 汞 *gǒng*, 红 *hóng*. The graph looks like the cross section of a rail or girder—good for heavy *work*.

g. 作 consists of 乍 *zhà* as a phonetic, also seen in 昨天 and 怎么. The two characters 做 and 作 can both be translated as 'to do' or 'to make' in many contexts, and they are not always consistently differentiated in writing. 做 is more often an independent verb, and carries the meaning 'to do' as in 'to manufacture or produce' (做饭/做飯 *zuòfàn*) or 'to engage in' (做买卖/做買賣 *zuò mǎimài* 'to do business'). It can also mean 'to be' (做朋友 *zuò péngyou*, 做伴儿/做伴兒 *zuò bànr* 'to keep somebody company'). 作, on the other hand, is more common in compounds (工作) with meanings ranging from 'to compose' (作品 *zuòpǐn* 'works [of literature or art]', 作家 *zuòjiā* 'writer', 作诗/作詩 *zuò shī* 'to compose poems') to 'being [a member of a profession]', as in 作老师/作老师.

h. In both traditional and simplified script, *suǒ* may be written 所 (户 + 斤) or 所 (with a different first stroke). The original meaning of 所 is 'place', as in *cèsuǒ* 'outhouse' ('leaning-place'); the radical is 斤 *jīn*, originally a drawing of an axe (also in 近 *jìn* 'close'). The original meaning of 所 is barely evident from some of its most common uses, such as in the compound 所以 *suǒyǐ* 'so'.

i. 定 shows the 'roof radical' over the element seen at the bottom of 是. (Providing a roof *fixes* the location.)

j. 功 (功课) contains a phonetic 工 *gōng* plus 力 *lì* 'strength'.

k. 每 is the element found in 海 *hǎi* 'ocean', where it may once have been phonetic. It, in turn, contains 母 *mǔ* 'mother' and 人. (The *sea* 海 is the *mother* 母 of *each* 每 of us.)

l. 位 is the polite measure word, with 立 *lì* 'to stand; to set up'. (Stand out of *politeness*.)

12.1.1 Compounds and phrases

因为	为什么	楼上	楼下	大楼	五楼
yīnwèi	*wèishénme*	*lóushàng*	*lóuxià*	*dàlóu*	*wǔlóu*

三点钟	几岁	钟楼	八岁	喜欢	恭喜
sān diǎn zhōng	*jǐsuì*	*zhōnglóu*	*bā suì*	*xǐhuan*	*gōngxǐ*
欢迎	工作	做饭	所以	一定	功课
huānyíng	*gōngzuò*	*zuòfàn*	*suǒyǐ*	*yídìng*	*gōngkè*
每年	每天	这位	哪位	三位	不一定
měinián	*měitiān*	*zhè wèi*	*nǎ wèi*	*sān wèi*	*bù yídìng*

12.1.2 Short dialogues

甲: 请问，西京在哪里？
乙: 有一个北京，也有一个南京，东京（在日本），可是没有个西京。

甲: 你累不累？
乙: 很累。
甲: 为什么？
乙: 功课太多了。
甲: 明天呢？
乙: 明天还好，没什么课。
甲: 那，我们明天上山，好不好？
乙: 上山太难了，我们去游泳吧。天气这么热，游泳很舒服。

甲: 请问，三六号在这楼吗？
乙: 这是二楼，三六号在三楼，从这儿上吧。

甲: 我很饿。
乙: 为什么？
甲: 还没吃饭呢。
乙: 那，你吃吧。
甲: 没饭吃，只有一块西瓜。
乙: 西瓜不是好吃吗？
甲: 西瓜，瓜很少水很多。 我要个汉堡包，一个三明治。
乙: 这么晚，哪里有汉堡包？先吃那一块西瓜，明天再去吃比较多，好不好？

甲:　孔老师，这是我的好朋友，张小东。
孔:　张小东，你好，你好。
小东:　孔老师好。
孔:　张小东，你是哪国人？
小东:　我是西班牙来的。
孔:　哦，西班牙，我以前在西班牙工作过！
小东:　在那儿工作过!
孔:　是，在马德里。我很喜欢西班牙。
小东:　你在那儿几年。
孔:　不到一年，八个月。
小东:　会不会说西班牙话？
孔:　会说一点，可是说得不太好。

甲:　请问，这儿有厕所吗？
乙:　有，楼上有一个，楼下也有一个。

甲:　小东，我看你常常不吃早饭，只喝一点茶就去上课。你不觉得饿吗？
小东:　还好，我早上不喜欢吃东西，可是一定要喝一两杯茶。你呢，你平常都吃早点吗？
甲:　那不一定，可是不吃早饭上课我就觉得很累。
小东:　是吗？哦，那不行。

甲:　你的朋友已经上课了吗？
乙:　现在她不上学了，有工作了。每天很早上班，很晚下班，每天都很忙，所以每天都很累。
甲:　哎，很难，可是钱很多吧。
乙:　不少，所以每天也可以买东西。

学生:　这位是我的中文老师，王老师。
小丽妈:　王老师您好，我是小丽的妈妈。小丽说很喜欢你的课，现在她已经会说一点中国话。
王老师:　嗯，她是一个好学生，每天都来上课，每天都做功课。

NOTES

a. 游泳 *yóuyǒng* 'to swim'
b. 马德 *Mǎdé*—which city in Spain?
c. 汉堡包 *hànbǎobāo* 'hamburger'
d. 只 *zhǐ* 'just; only'

Exercise 1

Write down the letters in the order that indicates how these jumbled sentences should be read.

1. (a) 生在广州 / (b) 我在西安工作 / (c) 也常说广东话 / (d) 可是我是广州人 / (e) 长在广州 / 。
2. (a) 所以广东话 / (b) 她因为生在广州 / (c) 说得很好 / 。
3. (a) 很多人喜欢去那个地方 / (b) 离广州很远 / (c) 可是因为山多人少 / (d) 贵州在中国的西南边 / 。
4. (a) 每天都有很多功课 / (b) 汉字也多 / (c) 学中文很难 / (d) 生字多 / 。
5. (a) 下车 / (b) 因为我们有个朋友 / (c) 所以我们要在可可西里 / (d) 住在那儿 / 。
6. (a) 在饭馆吃饭 / (b) 在家里吃饭 / (c) 有人喜欢 / (d) 有人喜欢 / 。
7. (a) 可是 / (b) 我很喜欢喝咖啡 / (c) 每天都喝 / (d) 不一定 / 。

12.2 Second set

就	門	门	街	路	母	父
3 + 9 or 2 + 10	8 + 0	3 + 0	6 + 6	7 + 6	5 + 0	4 + 0
jiù	*mén*		*jiē*	*lù*	*mǔ*	*fù*
'then'	'door'		'street'	'road'	'mother'	'father'

爸	媽	應	該	後	頭	孩
4 + 4	3 + 10	4 + 13	7 + 6	3 + 6	9 + 7	3 + 6
	妈	应	该	后	头	
	3 + 3	3 + 4	2 + 6	1 + 5	3 + 2	
bà	*mā*	*yīnggāi*		*hòu*	*tóu*	*hái*
'dad'	'mom'	'should; ought to'		'back'	'head'	'child'

NOTES

a. Though there is no simplified form for 就 *jiù*, the two sets assign the character different radicals. In the traditional set, 尤—without the upper dot—is the radical; in the simplified set, the first two strokes are considered the radical. On the left is 京 *jīng* 'capital'. (After you've seen the capital, what *then*?)

b. 门/門, originally a drawing of a door with two leaves, is a radical in some characters (such as 開 'start; open', cf. *kāihuì*) and a phonetic in others, including 们/們 *men* and 问/問 *wèn* 'to ask'.

c. 街 consists of 圭 *guī* as a phonetic element enclosed within 行. The latter is said to have been a drawing of a crossroads (with the result looking like a grid system of *streets*).

d. 路 contains the radical version of 足 *zú* 'foot' (as in 足球 *zú qiú* 'football') and 各 *gè*.

e. The form of 母 (seen in 每) is said to be 女 with the addition of breasts. 妈/媽, like 爸, is formed on phono-semantic principles. 父 (*father* figure in collar and tie) is a radical in the more informal 爸, with 巴 as a phonetic element (cf. 吧).

f. 應 is classified under the radical 心 rather than the more obvious 广 (though the simplified graph is classified under the latter). 心 at least suggests some notion of intention ('should').

g. Both 孩 and 該 contain the phonetic element 亥 *hài* (whose bottom part looks like the numeral '4' over人).

h. 後 ('double-man' for *back*up), like 從 *cóng*, with which it is easily confused, has 彳 as a radical. 頭, originally 'head; chief' (hair-*head*-neck-shoulders, on the left), has evolved into a suffix in certain location words. Both 後 and 頭 undergo radical pruning in the simplified set, the former by substitution of the homophonous graph 后 and the latter by substitution of the novel graph 头.

12.2.1 Compounds and phrases

就是	三门课	门口	大街	就好了	父母
jiùshì	*sān mén kè*	*ménkǒu*	*dàjiē*	*jiù hǎo le*	*fùmǔ*
爸爸	妈妈	不应该	我该走了。	应该的	在后头
bàba	*māma*	*bù yīnggāi*	*Wǒ gāi zǒu le.*	*yīnggāi de*	*zài hòutou*

小孩儿 *xiǎoháir*	男孩子 *nánháir*	女孩儿 *nǚháir*	两个孩子 *liǎng ge háizi*	东长安街 *Dōng Cháng'ān Jiē*	北京路 *Běijīng Lù*
中山北路 *Zhōngshān Běilù*	上海西站 *Shànghǎi Xī Zhàn*	前门大街 *Qiánmén Dàjiē*	就这样儿 *jiù zhèi yàngr*	在后边 *zài hòubiān*	东四南大街 *Dōngsì Nán Dàjiē*

12.2.2 Comment and response

1. 中国人喜欢生男孩子还是生女孩子？/ 那很难说。最好有两个，一个男孩儿，一个女孩儿。
2. 大学的学生都应该学外国话吗？/ 那不一定，可是想去中国工作的学生应该学中文。
3. 我们是四个人，四个人吃几个菜？/ 四个人呢，四个菜一个汤就好。
4. 请问，厕所在哪儿？/ 这儿没有厕所，后头的大楼应该有。你去问问吧。
5. 请问，这是不是中山北路？/ 中山北路 在火车站后头，从这儿走。
6. 请问，这是北京路吗？/ 不，这是北门街。北京路在那边。那是青年路，再过去一点，后边就是北京路。
7. 在中国，以前只可以生一个孩子，两个不行。现在，有的地方，第一个孩子是女孩子，那你可以再生一个。/ 一男一女是最好。

Qǐngwèn, Tiān'ān Mén zài nǎr?

Exercise 2

Answer the questions based on the information in the following narrative.

小林友美的名字有四个字。为什么呢？因为她生在日本，也长在日本，是日本人，所以 有个日本人的名字。她妈妈 也是日本人，可是爸爸是在中国生的，是个中国人，会说中国话。1984年从中国来日本的，还是有中国的国籍，所以小林友美从小很想来中国看看中国怎么样，学一点中文。

爸爸妈妈说应该的，所以去年小林友美来中国想住一两年，现在在南京大学上学。在南大她上三门课：中文、英文、中国文学。文学很难，可是中文、英文不太难。中文课没有很多学生，只有十五个，七个男的，八个女的。上午 有大班，下午有小 班。中文老师姓李，没去过日本，也没去过美 国，可是 日文、英文都 说得很 好。

英文课、文学课学生更多，大概有五十多个。友美已经在中国六个月了，可是没有很多钱，一天五块美元就好了，不多也不少。她住的地方也没有很多东西。小林友美因为钱比较少所以还没去过很多地 方。她说七月因为没课，应该去看北京、上海、西安。我说应该的。

（一） 小林友美的名字为什么有四个字？
（二） 她是在什么地方生的？
（三） 哪年来中国的？
（四） 她为什么在中国?
（五） 她在中国哪个大学？
（六） 在那个大学大概已经几年了？
（七） 中文课学生多不多？ 英文课呢？
（八） 小林友美在中国去过的地方很多吗？
（九） 她哪门课有大班也有小班？

12.3 Third set

節	辦	總	菜	廁
6 + 7	7 + 9	6 + 11	3 + 8	3 + 9
节	办	总	菜	厕
3 + 2	2 + 2	4 + 5	3 + 8	2 + 6
jié	*bàn*	*zǒng*	*cài*	*cè*
'joint; (holiday)'	'to manage'	'total; always'	'vegetables; food'	'leaning building; (toilet)'

星期	系	城市	概	更
4 + 5 4 + 8	6 + 1	3 + 6 2 + 3	4 + 9	4 + 3 or 1 + 6
xīngqī	*xì*	*chéngshì*	*gài*	*gèng*
'week' ('star-period')	'system; department'	'city' ('wall-market')	'outline; approximate'	'change; more; even more'

NOTES

a. 節 has the bamboo radical (*zhúzìtóu*) supporting the core meaning of a joint of bamboo, giving rise to meanings such as 'segment; chapter; program; festival'. The simplified character is unusual in substituting the vegetation radical for the bamboo. Examples of festivals are provided in the 'Phrases and compounds' below.

b. 办/辦 *bàn* appears in 办公室/辦公室 *bàngōngshì* 'office' and contains 力 *lì* 'strength', enclosed by two 辛 *xīn* 'hardship; suffering' (boss and helpers ready *to work*), one of which is assigned as the radical. The simplified form reduces the two 辛 to dots; it should be distinguished from 为 *wèi/wéi*.

c. Adverbs: 總 contains the 'silk radical' 糸, which is lost in the simplified graph. Silk is associated with continuity (among other notions), thus the meaning 'always'.

d. Simplified 菜 differs from traditional 菜 only in having one less stroke in the *cǎozìtóu* 'grass on top' (cf. 英, 茶). The element under the radical, 采 *cǎi*, is phonetic.

e. 廁 (resembling an *outhouse*) loses its dot in the simplified graph, 厕. (The dot, along with a lot more, is also lost in the simplified graph for 'factory', 厂/廠 *chǎng*.)

f. 星 contains 日 *rì* 'sun' and 生 *shēng* 'to give birth', the latter originally phonetic. 期 contains 月 *yuè* 'moon' with 其 *qí* (independently used as a pronoun) as a phonetic. (*Weeks* are lunar quarters as 'born' by the sun's reflection.)

g. 系 contains the silk radical (suggesting a network or *system*).

h. 城市 is a compound of *chéng* 'wall' (typically made out of 土 *tǔ* 'earth'), which implies 'city', and *shì* 'market', which implies 'town'.

i. 概, which appears in the compound 大概, contains a central element similar to, but not quite the same as, the right-hand side of 很 *hěn* 'very'.

j. 更 *gèng* (a jaunty character, stepping forward with *even more* confidence) is classified under the radical 曰 *yuē* 'to say'.

12.3.1 Phrases and compounds

中秋节 *Zhōngqiūjié*	八月节 *Bāyuèjié*	学期 *xuéqī*	办公室 *bàngōngshì*	总是 *zǒngshì*	怎么办 *zěnmebàn*
节日 *jiérì*	青年节 *Qīngniánjié*	星期六 *xīngqīliù*	北京市 *Běijīngshì*	中国菜 *Zhōngguócài*	大白菜 *dàbáicài*
海菜 *hǎicài*	茶杯 *chábēi*	厕所 *cèsuǒ*	中文系 *Zhōngwénxì*	在哪个系 *zài nǎ ge xì*	大概 *dàgài*
最大的城市 *zuì dà de chéngshì*	更累 *gèng lèi*	更晚 *gèng wǎn*	水系 *shuǐxì*	山系 *shānxì*	

NOTES

a. 中秋节 *Zhōngqiūjié* 'Mid-Autumn Festival'

b. 海菜 *hǎicài* 'edible seaweed'

c. 青年节 *Qīngniánjié* 'Youth Day'

d. 水系 *shuǐxì* 'river system'

e. 山系 *shānxì* 'mountain range'

12.3.2 Readings

1. 明天是八月节。上课，学生应该吃月饼。/ 上午班有十八个学生，下午有十五个，那今天下午我们可以去唐人街买十七个月饼，一个人一半。

2. 请问，厕所在哪里？/ 厕所，那里有一个，在周老师的办公室那儿，门口前头。

3. 哎，已经十点钟，功课太多了。学中文的学生总是很忙很累。/ 对啊，不过中文老师不是更忙更累吗？/ 可不是吗！

4. 中国菜好吃可是难做。/ 不一定，好做的有，难做的也有。

5. 中文每天都有吗？/ 星期一到四都有，星期五没有。

6. 你是中文系的吗？/ 我不在中文系，我在文学系。

7. 北京是不是中国最大的城市？/ 最大的是上海。北京是第二，我想。

8. 你的伞呢？/ 哦，天啊，是不是忘在林先生的办公室了。你看，下大雨，没伞不行！

NOTES

a. 唐人街 *Tángrénjiē* 'the streets of the Tang people' is the conventional name for Chinatowns in large American and other cities.

b. Exclamations: 哎 *ài;* 哦 *ò;* 啊 *a*

c. 月饼 *yuèbǐng* 'moon cakes'

Exercise 3

(FÁNTǏZÌ) Write down the letters in the order that indicates how these jumbled sentences should be read.

1. (a) 想吃中國菜 / (b) 還是吃美國菜 / (c) 那 / (d) 今天晚上 / ？
2. (a) 所以 / (b) 沒有地方坐 / (c) 在她前邊 / (d) 她的辦公室裏 / (e) 我們都站 / 。
3. (a) 只喝咖啡 / (b) 不吃早點 / (c) 學生 / (d) 常常 / (e) 因爲很忙 / 。
4. (a) 都很忙 / (b) 學生 / (c) 可是 / (d) 老師更忙 / (e) 每天 / 。
5. (a) 起來 / (b) 晚上兩點 / (c) 睡覺 / (d) 早上十點 / (e) 我 / 。
6. (a) 到 / (b) 是 / (c) 兩點 / (d) 天文課 / (e) 晚上十一點 / (f) 星期四 / 。
7. (a) 吃中國菜 / (b) 可是 / (c) 我做得不好 / (d) 我最喜歡 / (e) 所以 / (f) 常常去飯館兒吃 / (g) 因爲 / 。

12.4 Fourth set

像/像	理	河	湖	江	肉
2 + 12 2 + 11	4 + 7	3 + 5	3 + 9	3 + 3	2 + 4
xiàng	*lǐ*	*hé*	*hú*	*jiāng*	*ròu*
'appearance'	'principle'	'river'	'lake'	'river'	'meat'

謝	開	考試	牛	羊	進
7 + 10	8 + 4	6 + 0 7 + 6	4 + 0	6 + 0	3 + 8
谢	开	试			进
2 + 10	1 + 3	2 + 6			3 + 4
xiè	*kāi*	*kǎoshì*	*niú*	*yáng*	*jìn*
'thanks'	'open, start'	'test'	'cow; beef'	'sheep; lamb'	'enter'

哥	兄弟	米	千	萬	眞
				4 + 9	5 + 5
				万	真
1 + 9	3 + 2 2 + 5	6 + 0	2 + 1	1 + 2	2 + 8
gē	*xiōng dì*	*mǐ*	*qiān*	*wàn*	*zhēn*
'older brother'	('brother') 'younger brother'	'rice'	'thousand'	'10,000'	'real'

NOTES

a. 像 consists of the person radical plus the phonetic 象 *xiàng*, said to derive from a picture of an elephant (the graph *resembles* an elephant), with the trunk at the top, a head, and a body with four legs and a complicated tail. The simplified graph differs from the traditional only in having the eighth stroke continue through the 'head' to form the 'neck'. 像 is often paired with 一样/様 *yíyàng*: 像中国人一样 'like a Chinese'.

b. 理 consists of the combining form of the 'jade radical' (玉), now often named for what it looks like—the 'king radical' (王). Cf. 裏 and 里, which share the same phonetic element.

c. 江, 河, and 湖 are all formed along regular lines, with phonetic elements (工 *gōng* , 可 *kě*, and 胡 *hú*) and semantic radicals.

d. 肉 (*meat* hanging in a locker) should be contrasted with 内 *nèi* 'internal' (市内 *shìnèi* 'within town'). 牛 *niú* and 羊 *yáng* form compound words with 肉 to give the names of meat.

e. 谢/謝 is a compound graph made up of the speech radical and 射 *shè*, which originated as a phonetic element (itself made up of 身 *shēn* 'body' and 寸 *cùn* 'inch').

f. 開 is yet another in the series of graphs with the door radical; the simplified graph isolates the inner component (that looks like an implement for *opening* bottles).

g. 考 is similar in form and, in fact, historically related to 老 *lǎo* 'old'. (The *old* set the *tests*.) 试/試 combines the speech radical and a phonetic 式 *shì*.

h. The element on the left of 進 (sometimes printed with two dots instead of one) is *zǒuzhī*, assigned as radical. It is the left-side version of a more complex graph, 辵, whose meaning is 'stopping and starting'. *Zǒuzhī* is also found in 迎 *yíng* 'welcome', 近 *jìn* 'near', and 送 *sòng* 'to escort'. The simplified character 进 makes use of the imperfect phonetic 井 *jǐng* 'a well'.

i. 兄 only appears in certain compounds, such as 兄弟 'brothers'. 哥 (with 可 *kě* as a phonetic) is a more versatile word used to mean 'older brother', in contrast to 弟弟 *dìdi* 'younger brother'.

j. 米 perhaps shows grains of *rice*. It appears in the traditional graph 氣 *qì*, which is often interpreted as '*vapor* rising from rice as it cooks'.

k. 千 seems to be based on 十 *shí* 'ten'. 萬 , with the vegetation radical, originally meant 'a very large number' or 'myriad', and was then applied to the largest root number (other than 亿/億 *yì* 'hundred million'). The simplified form (万) is an old simplification that should be distinguished from 方 *fāng*.

l. Both 眞 and 真 have existed in the traditional set as alternate forms; the latter is the usual handwritten graph, which has also been adopted in the simplified set. In the traditional set, 目 *mù* 'eye' is the radical (the look of *truth*, or perhaps *truth* on a pedestal); in the simplified set, the first two strokes are assigned as the radical.

12.4.1 Phrases and compounds

好像 *hǎoxiàng*	像飞机一样 *xiàng fēijī yíyàng*	西湖 *Xī Hú*	长江 *Cháng Jiāng*	青海湖 *Qīnghǎi Hú*	
进来吧 *jìnlái ba*	开水 *kāishuǐ*	开会 *kāihuì*	开车 *kāichē*	白开水 *báikāishuǐ*	
西江 *Xī Jiāng*	汉江 *Hàn Jiāng*	太湖 *Tài Hú*	请进 *qǐngjìn*	理工 *lǐgōng*	经理 *jīnglǐ*
谢谢 *xièxie*	很多考试 *hěn duō kǎoshì*	什么考试 *shénme kǎoshì*	牛肉 *niúròu*	羊肉 *yángròu*	

白酒 *báijiǔ*	羊毛 *yángmáo*	山羊 *shānyáng*	母羊 *mǔyáng*	米饭 *mǐfàn*
一千公里 *yìqiān gōnglǐ*	一千四百 *yìqiān sìbǎi*	四百万 *sìbǎiwàn*	真不错 *zhēn bú cuò*	真的吗? *Zhēn de ma?*

12.4.2 Dialogues

(一)

甲: 你有兄弟姐妹吗？
乙: 有个弟弟，十八岁了。
甲: 他在哪个大学上学？
乙: 在北大。最近非常忙，因为有考试。

(二)

甲: 她是哪个大学的？
乙: 南大。
甲: 南大？她不是天津人吗？
乙: 天津的南开大学也叫南大。
甲: 哦，有两个南大，南京的还有天津的。
乙: 是。

(三)

甲: 中国人最喜欢喝什么？
乙: 以前中国人最喜欢喝茶、喝白开水，可是现在很多人也喜欢喝可乐、牛奶、汽水。美国人呢？
甲: 美国人也喜欢喝汽水，像可口可乐、百事可乐，可是现在很多人也喝茶。
乙: 现在每个地方，每个国家有同样的东西，所以喝的都一样。

(四)

甲: 你说上海是中国最大的城市，那上海的人口是多少？
乙: 上海人口大概是九百万，有人说是更多，像一千五百万，不过那是上海东南西北地方加起来的人口。

(五)

甲：可以说中国南方人比较喜欢吃米饭，对不对？
乙：对，可是北方现在也吃很多米饭。
甲：他们也喜欢吃什么？
乙：那大家每天都吃一点肉，吃一点青菜，吃一点海鲜。

(六)

甲：我姓孔，叫孔大中。这是我的名片。
乙：哦，您是麻省理工学院的，那就是 MIT，对吗？MIT 很有名。我姓方，方现同，我的名片。
甲：谢谢，哦，经理，方经理，您好。常州人？我去过常州。
乙：你去过常州！很少有外国人去过常州！我在常州工作，可是不是常州人，我生在包头，在黄河边。

NOTES

a. 妹 *mèi*
b. 天津离北京很近
c. 可乐 *kělè*
d. 牛奶 *niúnǎi*
e. 百事可乐 *Bǎishì-kělè*
f. 海鲜 *hǎixiān* 'seafood'
g. 麻省理工学院 *Máshěng Lǐgōng Xuéyuàn*
h. 黄 *huáng* 'yellow'

Exercise 4

Practice presenting the information given in the table below. The titles are typical of forms: 出生地 *chūshēngdì* 'birthplace' ('exit-birth-place'); 年龄/年齡 *niánlíng* 'age'; 身份 *shēnfen* 'status'. New names are: 李爱华 *Lǐ Àihuá*; 周云 *Zhōu Yún*; and 毛大为 *Máo Dàwéi*.

姓名	出生地	年龄	身份	最喜欢的地方
林美	北京	35	在北大工作，是老师	北京的北海

王学英	南京	38	在南京的一个公司工作，是经理	云南的大理市
张英	广州	43	在机场工作，是经理	江西的三清山
小林友美	东京	19	在南大上学，是本科生	青海的青海湖
李爱华	英国	28	在汽车公司工作，是总裁	北京火车站
周云	西安	40	在饭馆工作，是大师傅	西安钟楼
毛大为	美国	21	在北大上学，中文系	长城

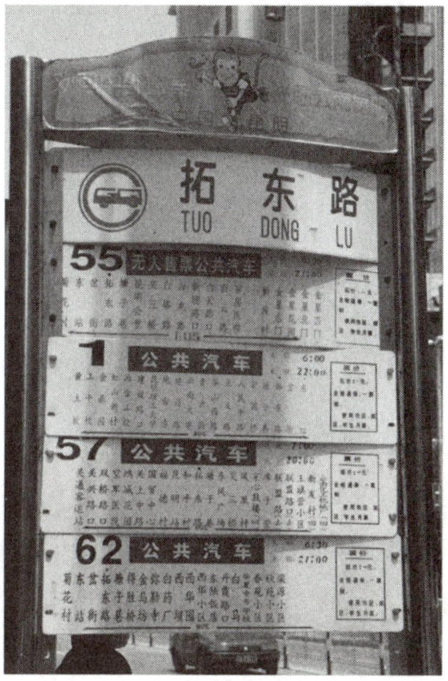

公共汽车站，昆明

12.5 Traditional characters

12.5.1 Comments

1. 因爲很高所以很清楚。
2. 公用電話在三樓。
3. 廁所在樓下，可以在這樓洗手。
4. 十點鐘上課，十一點下課。
5. 晚上一點鐘睡覺。

6. 她只有十五歲，不可以喝酒。
7. 喜歡吃中國菜嗎？我們去城裏吃晚飯，好不好？
8. 門口那兒有電話，市內的不用錢。
9. 上課不應該吃飯， 不應該喝汽水，不應該睡覺。
10. 電話在後頭，辦公室在二樓。
11. 今天星期幾？昨天是不是清明節？
12. 學生總是很忙很累。
13. 謝謝你們來機場接我們。
14. 今天幾點開門？
15. 開車不行，太遠。路也不好。
16. 請進，請坐，想喝一點兒什麼？
17. 住在這兒很貴，一個月一萬三千塊錢。
18. 你中文說得眞好，在什麼地方學的？

NOTE

市内 *shìnèi*, opposite of 市外

Exercise 5

Answer in 漢字 (either set) as much as possible; otherwise use pinyin.

1. 你是哪個大學的？ ______________________
2. 是學什麼的？ ______________________
3. 你的老師姓什麼？ ______________________
4. 功課多不多？ ______________________
5. 你是哪兒的人？ ______________________
6. 你有兄弟姐妹嗎？ ______________________
7. 他們也上大學嗎？ ______________________
8. 行李裏頭有什麼東西？ ______________________

9. 在你的大學，中文班多麼大？ ______________________

10. 你這個學期上幾門課？ ______________________

11. 你經常幾點吃早點？ ______________________

12. 大班好還是小班好？ 爲什麼？ ______________________

13. 請問，你在什麼地方工作？ ______________________

市中心的小河，安县，四川（离成都不远）

12.6 Formal numbers

FORMAL NUMBERS—KNOWN AS 大寫 *DÀXIĚ* ('BIG-WRITING') IN CHINESE On banknotes, checks, receipts, and occasionally even menus, a set of more complicated graphs for the numbers is used to prevent forgery or confusion. One rarely needs to write these, but it is obviously very useful to be able to recognize them.

一	二	三	四	五	六	七	八	九	十	百	千
壹	貳 贰	叁	肆	伍	陸 陆	柒	捌	玖	拾	佰	仟

Observe that some of the *dàxiě* numbers contain the ordinary graphs as phonetic elements, but, in other cases, a substitute phonetic is used. Thus, 玖 'nine' makes use of the element 久 *jiǔ*, normally used for a word meaning 'for a long time', while 陸 'six' is the character otherwise pronounced *lù* (as in *dàlù* 'continent; mainland').

FORMAL NUMBERS AS THEY APPEAR ON BILLS AND TICKETS

		How much?
Airport tax:	人民币玖拾圆整	______
Yangtze River Bridge at Nanjing:	票价柒元	______
Airport bus:	贰拾伍元	______
Hotel bill:	捌百壹拾圆整	______

NOTES

a. 人民币 *Rénmínbì* 'People's currency'

b. The graphs 元 and 圆 are both used to represent *yuán* 'dollar' (basic unit of currency). The core meaning of the first (元) is 'first; basic'. It has the advantage of being simpler, and is more common in ordinary usage. The practice of using it to write the basic unit of currency may have been influenced by its appearance in the term 元宝 *yuánbǎo* ('basic-treasure'), the name of the oval, boat-shaped ingots of gold or silver that were used for money in earlier times. 圆, with a basic meaning of 'round', is still used in more formal contexts, such as on the currency itself.

c. 整 *zhěng* 'entire'

d. 票价 *piàojià* 'ticket price'

12.7 The five elements

The 三字經 *Sān Zì Jīng* ('Three Character Classic') is a calligraphy primer (written in Classical Chinese) that also serves as an elementary guide to Chinese philosophy and history. It was written in the 13th century and was recited and copied by Chinese schoolchildren for many hundreds of years. Lines 65–68 read as follows:

曰水火	*Yuē shuǐ huǒ* ('say water fire')
木金土	*mù jīn tǔ,* ('wood metal earth')
此五行	*cǐ wǔ xíng,* ('these five 'agents'')
本乎數	*běn hū shù.* ('root in numbers')

Note that the first character—曰 *yuē* 'say'—which often begins quotations in Classical Chinese, is horizontal, while the character 日 *rì* 'sun; day' is vertical. 行 appears with a specialized meaning of 'agent', presumably derived from the core notions of the word, such as 'to go; to move; to act'.

In Chinese cosmology, 一 *yī* 'one' represents a pre-cosmic whole, which divided into the 二 *èr* 'two' that was the basis for the material universe (陰陽 *yīn/yáng* and other dualisms). 二, in turn, gave rise to the 五行 *wǔxíng* 'five agents': water, fire, wood, metal, and earth. The graphs that represent these words, shown below, are all frequently assigned as radicals in compound characters.

水	火	木	金	土
4 + 0	4 + 0	4 + 0	8 + 0	3 + 0
shuǐ	*huǒ*	*mù*	*jīn*	*tǔ*
'water'	'fire'	'wood'	'metal'	'earth'

As independent characters, none of these five has a simplified form. As elements within a character, however, they undergo varying degrees of accommodation depending on the position they occupy. For example, in the simplified set, 金 appears as 钅 when on the left but as a squat version of 金 when underneath. The combining forms are all illustrated below, with simplified on the left and traditional on the right (if the distinction is made):

	水	火	木	金	土
	↓	↓	↓	↓	↓
On the left:	江	炒	杯	钢/鋼	地
Underneath:	浆/漿	热/熱	案	鉴/鑒	坚/堅

12.8 On the street #5

Here are some more signs that are likely to be seen in Chinese communities, whether in China, Southeast Asia, or the Chinatowns of North America. This last group is usually called 唐人街 *Tángrénjiē* 'streets of the people of the Tang' (which was the current dynasty when the area around Guangzhou was first settled) or 漢人街 *Hànrénjiē* 'streets of the Han people'.

藥房
药房
yàofáng
'pharmacy'
('drug-store')

美容
měiróng
'beautician'
('beauty-appearance')

批發
批发
pīfā
'wholesale' ('batch-distribute')

施工
shīgōng
'construction [site]' ('carry + out-work')

營業時間
营业时间
yíngyè shíjiān
'business hours'

Yuán yī: Míngjiŭ pīfābù, Hūhéhàotè

NOTES TO THE EPIGRAPH

a. The addition of *-r* to certain adverbial expressions that involve repetition of stative verbs is often accompanied by a change in tone: *zăo* + *zăo* + *r* = *zăozāor*.

b. 省 *shěng* represents what, in the modern language, looks like two separate words: 'province' and 'economize; to save'.

c. As you would expect in a culture where rice is the staple crop, there are different words for rice at different stages of production: 稻 *dào* is the plant; 米 *mǐ* is the uncooked grain; 饭/飯 *fàn* is cooked rice.

Unit 13 第十三課 DÌ-SHÍSĀN KÈ

实事求是。
（實事求是。）
Shíshì qiú shì.
'Seek truth from facts.'
('[From] real-things seek what-is')
–The credo of the reformers in China, following the death of Chairman Mao in 1976

少说空话，多干实事。
（少說空話，多幹實事。）
Shǎo shuō kōnghuà, duō gàn shíshì.
'Shout fewer slogans and do more practical things.'
('less talk empty-words, more do real-things')
–A slogan

The typical written text in Chinese is, of course, not a dialogue; it is a narrative such as a story, notice, report, set of instructions, etc. However, with very few characters to work with, it is hard to write interesting narratives; until now, the narrative function has been served only by tables of data which can be read off. Otherwise, you have mostly been reading dialogues or short interactions. At this point, though, you have acquired enough characters to begin reading stories or specialized texts such as menus and weather reports. Unit 13, in addition to the usual four sets of characters and reading exercises, contains a simplified version of a traditional tale of filial piety, as well as a longer narrative about population. The unit ends with a discussion of animal radicals and an 'on the street' section that includes a typical form to be filled in with personal particulars.

13.0 Review

A. DIALOGUE

甲： 小张，你好，今天怎么样？
乙： 有点儿累，睡得不好，昨天晚上太热了！
甲： 嗯，是，最近非常热！我们应该在外头睡觉！
乙： 外头虫子太多了！那你呢？你最近怎么样？
甲： 最近啊，老样子，功课多，问题多。这个星期也有很多考试。
乙： 什么考试？
甲： 下午有中文的小考，可是明天有比较大的物理考试。
乙： 物理啊，物理很难吧？
甲： 物理有一点难可是中文更难，中文天天都有功课，天天还得学习汉字！
乙： 那你为什么要学中文？
甲： 我很喜欢学外语，想到中国去工作一两年。
乙： 是吗？那你得好好学习，去中国，应该会说一点儿中国话。你还有什么别的课?
甲： 今天还有生物。
乙： 生物每天都有吗？
甲： 星期一、三、五都有。
乙： 这个学期你一共上四门课吗？
甲： 是，四门，不多也不少。你呢？
乙： 我有六门。
甲： 六门啊，一定很累！
乙： 还好，还好，做学生的总是很忙、很累，不是吗？

NOTES

a. 虫子 *chóngzi* 'insects'
b. 物理 *wùlǐ*
c. 学习 *xuéxí*
d. 外语 *wàiyǔ*

B. DISTINGUISHING CHARACTERS

Review exercise

Distinguish the following characters by adding a syllable (or two) before or after each; this exercise can be spoken or written.

1.	喝	课	可	客	
2.	是	十	市	试	
3.	该	开	概	头	买
4.	喜	西	系	洗	
5.	还	孩	该	作	做
6.	门	问	们	开	

C. COMMENTS (*FÁNTǏZÌ*)

1. 你好像有個弟弟住在上海。 / 沒有，我弟弟住在北京。
2. 從我家到機場可以坐公共汽車，不到十五分鐘就到了。
3. 廣州在中國南邊，六七月天氣非常熱，很不舒服。
4. 這兒的東西有一點貴，你看：西瓜，一小塊四塊六毛錢。
5. 聽說他們昨天晚上喝了很多酒，所以今天沒有來上課。
6. 我的中國朋友說，我長得有一點像我爸爸，也有點兒像我媽媽。

北京市/北海

13.1 First set

愛	習	畢業	許	語	級
4 + 9	6 + 5	5 + 5 4 + 9	7 + 4	7 + 7	6+3
爱	习	毕业	许	语	级
4 + 6	1 + 2	4 + 2 5 + 0	2 + 4	2 + 7	3+3
ài	*xí*	*bìyè*	*xǔ*	*yǔ*	*jí*
'love'	'habit; practice; study'	'to graduate' ('complete-work')	'permission; to allow'	'language'	'level; year'

言	只	出	件	民	房
7 + 0	3 + 2	2 + 3	2 + 4	1 + 4	4 + 4
yán	*zhǐ*	*chū*	*jiàn*	*mín*	*fáng*
'language'	'only'	'exit'	(M word)	'the people'	'house'

NOTES

a. 愛 has 心 as a radical (*love* at the heart of the body, which shows the head, shoulders, and legs). The simplified character substitutes 友 (cf. 朋友) for the lower half (*love* among friends), and makes the top part (爪) the radical.

b. 習 has 羽 *yǔ* 'feathers' as a radical (*study* requires repetition, like overlapping feathers); the simplified graph substitutes part for whole (cf. 麼 → 么, 飛 → 飞).

c. 毕/畢 and 业/業 combine to form the compound meaning 'to finish school' or 'to graduate'. 毕, the simplified graph, substitutes the phonetic 比 *bǐ* for the top and reveals the central 十; 业, on the other hand, is a 'part for whole' substitution.

d. 许/許 (cf. 也许/也許) contains *yánzìpáng* and a phonetic 午 *wǔ* (cf. 中午); 语/語 (cf. 语言/語言) has *yánzìpáng* with a phonetic 吾 *wú*; and 级/級 (cf. 年级/年級) has *jiǎosīpáng* (the 'silk radical') and a phonetic 及 *jí*.

e. Note that 言 (*language* emitted from the mouth) is only simplified when incorporated as a left-hand component of a compound graph. 只 (*only* a moustache) consists of 口 and lower 八. 出 recalls 山, but is actually said to have been a drawing of plants bursting forth (bursting *out*).

f. 件 represents 'parts' and is a measure word for luggage, clothes, and items of business. The graph consists of *rénzìpáng* and *niú* 'cattle'—the latter unexplained.

g. 民 (cf. 人民) is assigned the radical 氏 in the traditional set and the unhelpful 乙 in the simplified. 房 (cf. 房子) is better behaved, consisting of 户 *hù* 'door; household' as a radical and 方 (cf. 地方) as a phonetic.

13.1.1 Compounds and phrases

爱人 *àirén*	学习 *xuéxí*	毕业了 *bìyè le*	爱你 *ài nǐ*	也许 *yěxǔ*	语言 *yǔyán*
汉语 *Hànyǔ*	英语 *Yīngyǔ*	几年级 *jǐ niánjí*	只有一个 *zhǐ yǒu yí gè*	出生 *chūshēng*	出去 *chūqù*
进来 *jìnlái*	一件行李 *yí jiàn xíngli*	人民币 *Rénmínbì*	房子 *fángzi*	三年级 *sān niánjí*	爱国 *àiguó*
只有三岁 *zhǐ yǒu sān suì*	三件衣服 *sān jiàn yīfu*	人民日报 *Rénmín Rìbào*	哪年毕业 *něi nián bìyè*	可爱 *kě'ài*	母爱 *mǔ'ài*
开业 *kāiyè*	工业 *gōngyè*	学业 *xuéyè*	作业 *zuòyè*	书房 *shūfáng*	文件 *wénjiàn*

NOTES

a. 开业 'to start an enterprise'

b. 工业 'industry'

c. 学业 'educational undertaking'

d. 文件 'a document; a file'

13.1.2 Reading

1. 这是我爱人，孔美；她是小学的老师。 / 孔美，您好。我们好像以前见过面，是不是？
2. 小朋友的帽子真可爱，可是有一点大。 / 不是我的，是我爸爸的。
3. 中国人常说："好好学习，天天向上"。 / 那是应该的。你好好学习，那你中文可以说得很好。
4. 请问，你哪年毕业？ / 2012 年。毕业以后，我想到中国去工作。
5. 四川最大的城市是什么？ / 也许是成都，成都人口大概是四百万。
6. 你已经毕业了吗？ / 还没，我现在是三年级的学生，明年就毕业了，还有一年。

7. 你还会说别的外语吗？/ 还会说一点儿日语，可是说得不好。
8. 那，方言是什么语言？/ 方言是地方的语言，像广东话，上海话。
9. 她多大了？/ 她只有二十六岁。她是1984年生的，十六岁就来北京了，现在住在北京东北边，离机场不远。
10. '件'那个字，为什么有人字旁，也有牛（牛肉的牛）？/ 那很难说，也许是因为'件'是一件衣服的件；衣服跟人一定很近，是人的朋友；牛也是人的朋友。所以件有人也有牛！/ 那怎么可以这样儿？

NOTES

a. 见过面 *jiànguo miàn* 'have seen [you] before; have met'
b. 成都 *Chéngdū* (capital of Sichuan province)

Exercise 1

Write down the letters in the order that indicates how these jumbled sentences should be read.

1. (a) 一天都在我的书房 / (b) 明天 / (c) 学习 / (d) 做作业 / (e) 我不到哪儿去
2. (a) 一点儿 / (b) 一，你得看 / (c) 今天的作业有两部分 / (d) 人民日报 / (e) 二，你得听 / (f) 广东话的录音 / (g) 一点儿
3. (a) 喝酒 / (b) 爱 / (c) 不应该 / (d) 开车的人
4. (a) 的外语 / (b) 我们大学 / (c) 学习一年 / (d) 都 / (e) 三年级的学生 / (f) 得到外国去
5. (a) 还有三个月 / (b) 现在是 / (c) 就毕业了 / (d) 她 / (e) 四年级的学生
6. (a) 家人就都 / (b) 现在都 / (c) 离开贵州了 / (d) 她在贵州 / (e) 可是两岁的时候 / (f) 住在四川 / (g) 生的

7. (a) 怎么那么好 / (b) 说得 / (c) 英文 / (d) 只有十四岁
8. (a) 有一两天 / (b) 就会忘了 / (c) 学语言 / (d) 不做功课 / (e) 很多 / (f) 就得天天学习

NOTE

录音 *lùyīn* 'recording'

Farmhouse, *Yúnnán*, between *Chǔxióng* and *Xiàguān*

13.2 Second set

麵	條	湯	餃	雞	蛋
11 + 9	4 + 7	3 + 9	8 + 6	8 + 10	6 + 5
面	条	汤	饺	鸡	
1 + 8 / 9 + 0	3 + 4	3 + 3	3 + 6	5 + 2	
miàn	*tiáo*	*tāng*	*jiǎo*	*jī*	*dàn*
'wheat flour; noodles'	'lengths'	'soup'	'dumplings'	'chicken'	'egg'

蝦	魚	奶	粥	炒	或者
6 + 9	11 + 0	3 + 2	6 + 6	4 + 4	4 + 4
虾	鱼				
6 + 3	8 + 0				
xiā	*yú*	*nǎi*	*zhōu*	*chǎo*	*huòzhě*
'shrimp'	'fish'	'milk'	'porridge; congee'	'fry'	'or'

NOTES

a. 麵 has 麥 *mài* 'wheat; barley; oats' as a radical and 面 *miàn* as a phonetic. (Whiskered 'wheat' is the source of *noodles*, served in a bowl.) Originally, both *mài* 'wheat' and *lái* 'come' were written with the graph 來, whose form is said to be a drawing of grain. At some point, the lower 夂 was added to 'wheat' to differentiate the two words. The simplified graph substitutes the part for the whole, resulting in the merger of what were two graphs in the traditional system, 麵 *miàn* 'flour; noodles' and 面 *miàn* 'aspect; facet' (as in 上面).

b. 條, a measure word for sinuous things such as rivers, roads, and some animals, with the lower right 木 *mù* (long *sinuous* branches) assigned as the radical. The rest of the graph, 攸 *yōu*, does not seem to have a phonetic origin. The simplified version omits the left-hand portion of the traditional graph, but assigns the top three strokes as radical (also seen in 处, 各, 夏).

c. 汤/湯 *tāng* consists of *sāndiǎnshuǐ* and the phonetic element seen in the 场/場 *chǎng* of 机场/機場. (The graph looks like noodles in *soup*.)

d. 饺 /餃 combines the food radical with a phonetic 交 *jiāo*.

e. 雞 has 奚 *xī* as a phonetic element (crest, head, body, and legs of a *chicken*) and 隹 'short-tailed bird' as radical. The simplified graph substitutes 又 for the complicated left-hand element, but then complicates matters by substituting one bird radical for another (隹 → 鸟).

f. 蛋 consists of 疋 *pǐ* above 虫 *chóng* 'insect' (as if laying an *egg*).

g. The following are all typical phonetic plus semantic characters (谐声字 *xiéshēngzì* 'concordant-sound-character'); 蝦 has 虫 'insect' as a radical and 叚 *jiǎ/xiǎ* as a phonetic, while its simplified counterpart has 虫 and 下 xià; 奶 has 女 and 乃 *nǎi*; 炒 has 火 and 少 *shǎo*.

h. 或 is a phonetic element in the traditional 國 *guó* 'country'. 者 is classified under 日 in the simplified set, but for obscure reasons, under 老 in the traditional set. 者 *zhě* has a phonetic function in 豬 *zhū* 'pig' and 都 *dōu/dū* 'all; both'.

i. The graph 粥 has the curious configuration of rice (米) between two bows (弓 *gōng* as in 张/張 *zhāng* and 弟 *dì*).

13.2.1 Compounds and phrases

面条	一条路	三条街	前面	后面
miàntiáo	*yì tiáo lù*	*sān tiáo jiē*	*qiánmian*	*hòumian*
汤面	清汤	一个汤	三个菜	白汤
tāngmiàn	*qīngtāng*	*yí ge tāng*	*sān ge cài*	*báitāng*
菜汤	油条	炒饭	炒面	鸡汤
càitāng	*yóutiáo*	*chǎofàn*	*chǎomiàn*	*jītāng*
鸡蛋	公鸡	母鸡	火鸡	王八蛋
jīdàn	*gōngjī*	*mǔjī*	*huǒjī*	*wángbādàn*
下蛋	一条鱼	金鱼	木鱼	面包
xiàdàn	*yì tiáo yú*	*jīnyú*	*mùyú*	*miànbāo*
虾仁	大虾	明虾	做得不错	一条鱼
xiārén	*dàxiā*	*míngxiā*	*zuò+de bú cuò*	*yì tiáo yú*
牛奶	奶茶	奶名	奶奶	鱼片粥
niúnǎi	*nǎichá*	*nǎimíng*	*nǎinai*	*yúpiànzhōu*
大米粥	小米粥	鸡粥	水饺	饺子
dàmǐzhōu	*xiǎomǐzhōu*	*jīzhōu*	*shuǐjiǎo*	*jiǎozi*
茶或咖啡	吃饺子	水饺或者包子	水饺还是睡觉？	
chá huò kāfēi	*chī jiǎozi*	*shuǐjiǎo huòzhě bāozi*	*Shuǐjiǎo háishi shuìjiào?*	

NOTES

a. 油条 *yóutiáo* ‘dough sticks’

b. 公鸡 *gōngjī* ‘rooster’

c. 母鸡 *mǔjī* ‘hen’

d. 火鸡 *huǒjī* ‘turkey’

e. 王八蛋 *wángbādàn* ‘son of a bitch’ (‘turtle egg’); *wángbā* ‘tortoise; cuckold; son-of-a-bitch’

f. 木鱼 *mùyú* ‘wooden fish’—a temple drum

g. 奶名 *nǎimíng* 'infant name'

h. 奶奶 *nǎinai* 'grandmother (paternal)'

13.2.2 Readings

1. 吃晚饭应该吃一点儿面包，应该喝一点儿酒，不对吗？/ 最好有啤酒或者白酒，有面包没有面包都行。
2. 中国人吃的东西太多了。可以说北方人比较喜欢吃面条；南方人比较喜欢吃米饭。/ 包子饺子，也许北方人南方人都喜欢吃。
3. 我们每天都吃一点青菜，也吃一点儿肉，像猪肉、牛肉、羊肉。/ 那你们不常吃海里的，像鱼、虾吗？/ 因为我们离海边很远，鱼、虾太贵了。一个星期吃一两次还可以。
4. 中国人吃早饭常吃面条或者吃粥，粥可以放很多不同的东西：像鱼片、青菜、虾仁、鸡肉。/ 吃粥就油条也行，对不对？
5. 请来一大碗白菜牛肉面、一个鸡蛋炒饭、还要二十个韭菜水饺。/ 要不要汤？
6. 我们是四个人，四个菜一个汤就好了。/ 要啤酒吗？我们这儿有扎啤。
7. 水饺六十个，还有鸡蛋汤，汤是大碗的吗？/ 大碗五个人吃可以。你们是九个人，两个大碗行。
8. 以前中国人很少喝牛奶，可是现在很多女孩子晚上喜欢喝一杯热牛奶，这样睡得比较好，比较舒服。/ 热牛奶！我最不喜欢喝热牛奶！

NOTES

a. 包子 *bāozi*

b. 猪肉 *zhūròu*

c. 放; a verb, with 方 as a phonetic

d. 虾仁 *xiārén* 'shrimp meat'

e. 就油条 *jiù yóutiáo* [here] 'with deep fried dough sticks'; *jiù* 'to go with'

f. 碗 *wǎn* 'bowl'

g. 韭菜 *jiǔcài* 'Chinese chives; scallions'

h. 扎啤 *zhāpí* 'draft beer'

Exercise 2

Practice ordering drinks and light fare from the following (limited) menu. Alternatively, write out five different orders.

饮料 *yǐnliào*

七喜	5.50元	瓶
可口可乐	6.00元	瓶
百事可乐	6.00元	瓶
鲜奶	8.00元	杯
咖啡	10.00元	杯
咖啡牛奶	12.00元	杯
中国茶	5.00元	壶
奶茶	6.00元	杯
矿泉水	6.00元	瓶
啤酒		
百威	18.00元	小瓶
五星	16.00元	大瓶
上海	16.00元	大瓶
青岛	14.00元	大瓶
扎啤	10.00元	大瓶
洋酒	25.00元	杯

小菜，点心

水饺	12.00元	笼
虾仁；羊肉白菜；韭菜猪肉；素菜		
面条（汤，干）		
鱼片炒面	12.00元	
虾仁炒面	12.00元	
牛肉炒面	10.00元	
鸡丝炒面	8.00元	

NOTES

a. 瓶 *píng*
b. 可乐 *kělè*
c. 百事 *bǎishì*
d. 鲜奶 *xiānnǎi* 'fresh milk'
e. 壶 *hú* 'pot; kettle'
f. 矿泉水 *kuàngquánshuǐ*
g. 百威 *Bǎiwēi* 'Budweiser'
h. 青岛 *Qīngdǎo* (city in Shandong province; also name of famous Chinese beer)
i. 笼 *lóng* 'basket; container; steamer' (*zhúzìtóu* as the radical and 龙 *lóng* as a phonetic)
j. 素菜 *sùcài* 'vegetarian'
k. 干 *gān* 'dry'

13.3 Third set

寫	時候	間	給	跟
3 + 12	4 + 6 2 + 8	8 + 4	6 + 6	7 + 6
写	时	间	给	
2 + 3	4 + 3	3 + 4	3 + 6	
xiě	*shíhòu*	*jiān*	*gěi*	*gēn*
'to write'	'time'	'space'	'to give'	'heel; with; and'

差	教	旁	和	否	妹
3 + 7	4 + 7	4 + 6	5 + 3	3 + 4	3 + 5
差					
3 + 6					
chà	*jiāo*	*páng*	*hé*	*fǒu*	*mèi*
'to lack'	'to teach'	'side'	'and; harmony'	'to deny'	'younger sister'

NOTES

a. 寫 is classified under the roof radical; the remaining graph contains portions that look like the top part of 兒 *ér* 'child' and the bottom of 馬 *mǎ* (thus, 'child under a roof *writing*, and drawing horses'). The simplified graph substitutes 与 *yǔ* for the complex interior (not for its phonetic connection, but for similarity of shape) and drops the dot on the top.

b. The first graph in 時候 consists of 日 *rì* 'sun' as a radical (*time* measured out by the sun) and a phonetic 寺 *sì* (also found in 詩 *shī* 'poem'). The simplified graph (时) obscures the phonetic connection. 候 is classified under 人 *rén* 'person', but the graph contains an extra vertical stroke (cf. 條 *tiáo*, which is classified under 木 *mù*), in contrast to the surname 侯 *Hòu*, without this stroke. 时/時 combines with 间/間 *jiān* 'time; space' to form the compound 时间/時間, often 'a period of time' rather than 'a point in time'. 间/間 is classified under the radical 门/門.

c. 给/給 contains the 'silk radical' 糹 (silk being associated with the *giving* of tribute and other gifts); 合 *hé* does not seem to have played a phonetic role.

d. 跟 is classified under the radical 足 *zú* 'foot' and contains the same phonetic element seen in 很 *hěn* and 银/銀 *yín* (cf. 银行的银).

e. In the course of its history, the original elements of the graph 差 (probably a configuration of hands) have been reformed into 工 *gōng* (under which the character is now classified) and 羊 *yáng* 'sheep', neither of which acts as a phonetic. The traditional form breaks the central stroke in two, but the simplified graph accepts the identification with 羊 and writes it as one. In other contexts, 差 can be pronounced *chā* (时差 shíchā 'jet lag; time difference'), *chāi* (邮差 *yóuchāi* 'mailman') or *cī* (参差 *cēncī* 'uneven').

f. 教 is sometimes written 敎 in the traditional set, with the first two strokes forming an 'x'. The form that is now standard in both traditional and simplified sets, 教, makes a historically false but mnemonically useful identification with 孝 *xiào* 'to be filial'. However, in its original form, the graph is said to show 爻 *yáo* above 子 *zǐ*, with the radical on the right called *fǎnwénr* or *fǎnwénpáng* 'back-to-front *wén*' (文). The same element also appears in 做 *zuò*, 效 *xiào*, and 數 *shù*.

g. 旁 has 方 *fāng* as a phonetic.

h. 和, itself actually a traditional simplification of a more complicated graph, contains 禾 *hé* 'grain; crops' (coincidentally homophonous with 和), also seen in 科 *kē* and 種 *zhòng*. (Grain in the mouth: a healthy diet promoting *harmony* and balance.)

i. 否, often used instead of the 'or not' part of the 'V-not-V' pattern in written communication, writes 不 over 口 to represent 'denial', i.e., 'not-V'.

j. 妹 has *nǚzìpáng* as a radical and 未 *wèi* as a phonetic. The radical marks the gender; the phonetic looks like *younger sister* in a skirt, arms extended.

13.3.1 Compounds and Phrases

写字 *xiězì*	写得不错 *xiě+de bú cuò*	时候 *shíhou*	没有时间 *méiyǒu shíjiān*	小的时候 *xiǎo de shíhou*
小时 *xiǎoshí*	买一件给他 *mǎi yí jiàn gěi tā*	房间 *fángjiān*	给你一本 *gěi nǐ yì běn*	应该给他 *yīnggāi gěi tā*
教书 *jiāoshū*	跟他们说中文 *gēn tāmen shuō Zhōngwén*	差不多 *chàbuduō*	写给你看 *xiě gěi nǐ kàn*	妹妹 *mèimei*
旁边 *pángbiān*	木字旁 *mùzìpáng*	是否请她 *shìfǒu qǐng tā*	教他中文 *jiāo tā Zhōngwén*	姐妹 *jiěmèi*
给他做饭 *gěi tā zuòfàn*	跟他学中文 *gēn tā xué Zhōngwén*	和她在一起 *hé tā zài yìqǐ*	跟她去 *gēn tā qù*	

13.3.2 Reading

1. 你汉字写得很不错。你学了几年了？/ 我只学了六个月。/ 你好像学得不错。
2. 学中文不太难，就是汉字有一点多，学一个忘一个。
3. 今天的考试是听写，看你们汉字写得怎么样。/ 老师，听写太难了，我们写字写得不好！
4. 我最近太忙了，没有时间吃饭睡觉。/ 那不行，太累的话那，你一定考得不好！
5. 上课的时候不可以说英文。/ 要是有个问题，可不可以用英文问？
6. 起来以后要是没有时间吃早点，那你最好喝一杯白开水。/ 我也得喝一杯咖啡，不喝咖啡，上课的时候一定很累，一定要睡觉。
7. 我是去年去的中国，跟我父母一块儿去的。/ 你在中国住了多长时间？
8. 小的时候，父母常常请我在客人面前唱歌，可是我长大了以后，不想在别人面前唱歌。/ 那也许你唱得很好听。
9. 你有没兄弟姐妹？/ 我只有个妹妹，她二十三岁，已经从大学毕业了，现在在市中心的第三中学教书。/ 哦，是个老师，跟你一样。

10. 我是否明天得给老师功课？/ 明天或者后天给她都行。
11. 火车站旁边儿有个小吃中心，你们可以在那吃早点。/ 小吃中心几点开门？我们差不多六点钟到，很早。
12. 这样儿好不好，我给你买菜，你给我做饭。/ 不错，可是我做的菜你不一定喜欢吃。

Exercise 3

Write down the letters in the order that indicates how these jumbled sentences should be read.

1. (a) 给他们 / (b) 所以 / (c) 因为 / (d) 他们下星期 / (e) 老师说 / (f) 离开北京 / (g) 我们应该买个小礼物
2. (a) 出去 / (b) 有考试 / (c) 买一点儿菜 / (d) 我今天 / (e) 你可不可以 / (f) 没有时间 / (g) 给我
3. (a) 所以她是 / (b) 她父母 / (c) 可是因为 / (d) 美国国籍 / (e) 是中国人 / (f) 她生在美国
4. (a) 好 / (b) 住在城外 / (c) 你觉得 / (d) 还是 / (e) 好 / (f) 住在城里
5. (a) 离开成都 / (b) 晚上 / (c) 他们 / (d) 第二天 / (e) 到上海 / (f) 八号
6. (a) 买东西 / (b) 我们 / (c) 昨天 / (d) 去了 / (e) 你上课 / (f) 的时候 / (g) 到城里
7. (a) 喝奶茶 / (b) 她像个美国人 / (c) 早上 / (d) 可是晚上 / (e) 像个英国人 / (f) 最爱喝咖啡
8. (a) 唱卡拉OK / (b) 去 / (c) 晚上 / (d) 跟朋友 / (e) 她常常

NOTES

a. 礼物 *lǐwù* 'gift; present'

b. 卡拉OK *kǎlā*OK 'karaoke'

13.4 Fourth set

醫	院	廳	館	煙	樂
7 + 11	2 + 7	3 + 22	8 + 8	4 + 9	4 + 11
医		厅	馆	烟	乐
2 + 5		2 + 2	3 + 8	4 + 6	1 + 4
yī	*yuàn*	*tīng*	*guǎn*	*yān*	*yuè*
'medical'	'yard'	'hall'	'office; tavern'	'smoke; cigarette'	'music'

音	吸	玩	病	左	右	店
9 + 0	3 + 3	4 + 4	5 + 5	1 + 4	1 + 4	3 + 5
yīn	xī	*wán*	*bìng*	*zuǒ*	*yòu*	*diàn*
'sound'	'to suck'	'to play'	'ill'	'left'	'right'	'shop'

NOTES

a. 醫 is composed of 医 *yī* (an enclosed 矢 *shǐ* 'arrow'), 殳 (originally, a kind of weapon) and 酉 *yǒu*, associated with concoctions; cf. 酒. The last, at least, are part of the practice of medicine. (Equipment and medicines in a *hospital* setting.)

b. 院 consists of *zuǒ'ěrduō* and 完 *wán* 'to finish' (as in 刚吃完 *gāng chīwán*).

c. 廳 is an obvious phono-semantic compound, with 广 ('shelter, covering') and 聽 *tīng*. The simplified form loses the upper dot (cf. 廁 → 厕, 寫 → 写). Note: 听/聽 but 厅/廳, the latter making use of the closer phonetic 丁 *dīng*.

d. 馆/館 *guǎn* contains *shízìpáng* (饣/食) and the phonetic 官 *guān*. (Food with tables at a *restaurant* or in a *hall*.)

e. The traditional 煙, with the radical 火 *huǒ* and 垔 *yīn* as a phonetic, was often handwritten as 烟 (with 因 *yīn* as phonetic); the latter is now the regular graph in the simplified set. A third, 'unofficial' graph, 菸 (with right-hand element 於 *yú*), is often used specifically for tobacco, especially on shop signs, for example 菸酒公賣 *yānjiǔ gōngmài* 'official purveyors of tobacco and wine'.

f. 乐/樂 *yuè* of 音乐/音樂 *yīnyuè* 'music' (also pronounced *lè* in 快乐/快樂 *kuàilè* 'happiness') shows 木 *mù* 'wood' on the bottom (wooden frame holding *musical* instruments). The simplified form, which keeps the frame but simplifies the top, needs to be distinguished from the simplified 东 *dōng* 'east': 乐 versus 东.

g. 音 is itself a radical in 韵 and 意. The graph looks like the whistle on a kettle, hence *sound*.

h. 吸 contains *kǒuzìpáng* and a phonetic 及 *jí*, also seen in 级/級 (cf. 年级 *niánjí*) and the simplified 极 *jí* (cf. *hǎojíle*). For smoking, the more colloquial word is 抽 *chōu* (with 由 *yóu* as a phonetic): *chōuyān* = *xīyān*.

i. 玩 contains 王 as a radical (玉) and 元 *yuán* as a phonetic. (It takes money (元) to have *fun*.)

j. The graph 病 (*ill* patient sprawled out on an operating table with tubes attached) introduces the 'illness radical', *bìngzìpáng*, also seen in 瘦 *shòu* 'thin' and 癌 *ái* 'cancer'. 病 contains 丙 *bǐng* as a phonetic (cf. 甲乙丙丁 *jiǎ-yǐ-bǐng-dīng*).

k. 左右 *zuǒyòu* ('left-right') (A mnemonic note: 工 bears a passing resemblance to the 'z' of *zuǒ* and 口 rhymes with *yòu*.)

l. 店 consists of 广 *guǎng* 'shelter' and 占 *zhān/zhàn*, which appears in phonetic sets that include *d*-types such as 点/點 *diǎn* or *zh*-types such as 站 *zhàn*. As noted earlier, because of changes in pronunciation over the centuries, graphs that share the same phonetic element have often diverged in sound. 方 *fāng* and 旁 *páng* are examples; so are 占 *zhān/zhàn* and 点 *diǎn*. However, though they are not identical in sound, they remain 'in touch': *fāng* and *páng* both have labial initials, and the initial sounds of *zhān/zhàn* and *diǎn* are both articulated behind the teeth with the tip of the tongue. So sets like these still provide useful hints for the identification of characters.

13.4.1 Compounds and phrases

医院 *yīyuàn*	医学 *yīxué*	医生 *yīshēng*	学院 *xuéyuàn*	很远 *hěn yuǎn*
好玩 *hǎo wán*	请来玩 *qǐng lái wán*	电影院 *diànyǐngyuàn*	住院 *zhùyuàn*	餐厅 *cāntīng*
饭馆 *fànguǎn*	菜馆 *càiguǎn*	一只烟 *yì zhī yān*	吸烟 *xīyān*	年级 *niánjí*
听音乐 *tīng yīnyuè*	民乐 *mínyuè*	西乐 *xīyuè*	看病 *kànbìng*	生病 *shēngbìng*
左右两边 *zuǒyòu liǎngbiān*	右边 *yòu bian*	前边 *qiánbian*	后边 *hòubian*	河边上 *hé biānshàng*
书店 *shūdiàn*	饭店 *fàndiàn*	酒店 *jiǔdiàn*	酒楼 *jiǔlóu*	小吃店 *xiǎochīdiàn*
肉店 *ròudiàn*	洗衣店 *xǐyīdiàn*	病房 *bìngfáng*	病人 *bìngrén*	有姓'院'的吗? *Yǒu xìng 'Yuàn' de ma?*

13.4.2 Readings

1. 请问去北京市第六医院怎么走？/ 那我不太清楚，离这儿不是很远，也许可以坐地铁。我是外地人，你问问她吧，她是北京人。
2. 北京市医院是不是北京最大最好的医院？/ 也许是最大的，可是不一定是最好的。
3. 昨天我很不舒服，所以到医院去了。/ 是不是因为昨天在街上的那家饭馆吃了生鱼？
4. 太累了，我今天不到哪儿去，在家里跟朋友在一起，听一点儿音乐，看一点儿电视。
5. 北京市的东北边，离市中心很近，有三个湖，一个叫北海，一个叫中海，一个叫南海。/ 对啊，我看过，南海可以从西长安街看到，北海可以从地安门西大街看到。
6. 毛泽东右边的那个人是谁？/ 那是周恩来。左边儿的是陈云。他们都在中南海开会。
7. 在这儿吸烟不行，要吸烟得到外头去。/ 好，明白。没关系，天气有点儿冷所以我不想出去。
8. 你来西安请到我家来玩。/ 您太客气了，我在西安的时候一定会来找你。
9. 餐厅在三楼，你可以从这儿上去。/ 谢谢，餐厅几点到几点开门？
10. 你喜欢什么样的音乐？/ 我比较喜欢古典音乐，可是有时候也听一点儿爵士。
11. 对不起，现在没有时间，我还得到城里去买几本书。/ 你到哪个书店去？给我买一本字典可以吗？

NOTES

a. 电视 *diànshì*
b. 陈云 *Chén Yún*
c. 关系 *guānxi*
d. 找 *zhǎo*
e. 餐厅 *cāntīng*
f. 古典 *gǔdiǎn*
g. 爵士 *juéshì*

13.5 A tale of filial piety

恣蚊饱血

晋朝的时候，有一个叫吴猛的人，他八岁的时候就非常孝敬他的爸爸妈妈。吴猛的家没有钱也没有东西；床上一个蚊帐也没有。热的时候蚊子很多，蚊子常常叮人，吸人身上的血，使人很不舒服。可是吴猛不把蚊子赶走，因为他怕要是他把蚊子赶走了，那么蚊子就会去叮他爸爸妈妈，他爸爸妈妈就会很不舒服。从这一点，我们可以知道，吴猛对他爸爸妈妈是多么孝敬啊！

NOTES

a. 恣蚊饱血 *zì wén bǎo xiě* 'license mosquitoes to fill up with blood'
b. 晋朝 *Jìncháo* 'Jin dynasty' (C.E. 265–420)
c. 吴猛 *Wú Měng*
d. 孝敬 *xiàojìng* 'to give respect to elders; to be filial'
e. 床 *chuáng* 'bed'
f. 蚊帐 *wénzhàng* 'mosquito net'
g. 蚊子 *wénzi* 'mosquito'
h. 叮 *dīng* 'sting; bite'
i. 身 *shēn* 'body'
j. 血 *xiě~xuè* 'blood'
k. 使 *shǐ* 'to make; to cause [somebody to feel something]'
l. 把 *bǎ* (highlights the affected object) i.e 蚊子.
m. 赶走 *gǎnzǒu* 'to drive [something or someone] away'
n. 怕 *pà* 'to be afraid of'
o. 知道 *zhīdào* 'to know'

13.6 One is enough (只生一個好) (*fántǐzì*)

魏老師，聽説您有四個孩子，三個已經大了，眞沒想到！在中國很少有人有這麼多孩子！中國以前在七十年代、八十年代不能生這麼多孩子，只能生一個。一家一個孩子，只生一個好！要是生兩個，就有問題了，孩子們不能上好學校，不能找好工作。爲什麼這樣兒呢？那是因爲中國人口太多。六十年代那個時候已經有七八億人口，現在是十三億。中國是世界上人口最多的國家。中國很大，跟美國差不多一樣大。雖然地方很大，但不一定每個地方都有很多人口，有的地方人口很少，有的地方人口很多。你們也許已經知道，人口最多的地方是東邊和東南邊，人口最少的地方是西邊和西北邊。

去過中國的人都知道中國城市裏人很多。以前中國人沒有很多錢，不能買很多東西，可是現在很多人都很有錢，可以買他們想要的東西，像車。有車可以去看朋友，可以去別的地方玩。可是因爲路上車很多，所以到哪裏去都很難。雖然現在中國人不像以前只能生一個孩子，現在可以生兩個孩子了，可是像你這樣生三四個很少很少。因爲他們知道，孩子太多，事兒就多，而且他們工作都很忙，沒有那麼多時間照顧孩子！

NOTES

a. 沒想到 *méi xiǎngdào* 'didn't expect [it]; surprisingly'
b. 年代 *niándài* 'the time of; decade of'
c. 能 *néng* 'able to'
d. 學校 (学校) *xuéxiào* 'school'
e. 億 (亿) *yì* 'hundred million'
f. 世界 *shìjiè* 'the world'
g. 雖然 (虽然) *suīrán* 'although'
h. 別的 *biéde* 'other'
i. 事兒 (事儿) *shìr* 'things; items of business'
j. 而且 *érqiě* 'moreover; but also'
k. 照顧 (照顾) *zhàogù* 'to look after'

13.7 Animal radicals

The graphs that form the radicals constitute a set of concrete images which have been extended metaphorically to classify basic notions in the Chinese lexicon (as, for example, 日 'sun' → day → time → awareness; 羊 'sheep' → sacrifice → goodness). Among the better-defined sets are those that involve animals, some of which have already been encountered. The main animal radicals are listed below, first in their radical form with the meanings they have (or had) as independent characters, then, on the lower line, in a sample compound character.

CITATION FORM	牛牜	(犬)	羊	(虎)	虫	豕	豸	隹
	niú	*quǎn*	*yáng*	*hǔ*	*chóng*	*zhū*	*zhì*	*zhuī*
	'cow'	'dog'	'sheep'	'tiger'	'insect'	'pig'	'reptile'	'bird'
EXAMPLE	物	犯	美	[处]/處	蚊	猪/豬	豺	[离]/離

CITATION FORM	马/馬	鱼/魚	鸟/鳥	鹿	鼠	龙/龍	龟/龜
	mǎ	*yú*	*niǎo*	*lù*	*shǔ*	*lóng*	*guī*
	'horse'	'fish'	'bird'	'deer'	'rat'	'dragon'	'turtle'
EXAMPLE	骑/騎	鲤/鯉	鸭/鴨	[丽]/麗	鼯	龚/龔	–

NOTES

a. 隹 is said to derive from a drawing of a bird with a short tail, but while it does occur in the graphs for a few birds (such as sparrow and pheasant), the usual radical with bird species is 鸟/鳥 *niǎo*.

b. Most of the animal radicals are quite complicated, reflecting their origins as drawings. The two graphs in parentheses, above, have combining forms quite distinct from their independent forms; the combining form for 虎 does not include the two lower inner strokes.

c. In some cases, the simplified form omits or otherwise alters the original radical and has, therefore, been reclassified; note 豬 → 猪, shifting from the 'pig' to the 'dog' radical. The three simplified graphs in brackets no longer incorporate an animal radical.

d. Some of the animal radicals are very rare in compound graphs. The last, 龜 *guī* 'turtle', does not appear in any compound graph in current use and is only included in the radical chart so it can classify itself and a few characters from past eras. 鼠 only appears in characters for a few rat-like animals, such as weasels.

It is interesting to observe the meanings of the compound characters to see how the concrete images play out over the written lexicon. 犬, for example, which is used to write the archaic word *quǎn* 'dog' (a word that has been replaced by 狗 *gǒu* in the modern language), is found (in its rather different combining form) not only in 狗, but also in characters for various kinds of primates (e.g., 猴子 *hóuzi* 'monkey'), other animals (狐狸 *húli* 'fox', 獅子 *shīzi* 'lion'), and in characters for words meaning 'violation', 'violence', 'craftiness', 'wildness', and (notably) 'independence': 犯 *fàn* 'to offend', 狂 *kuáng* 'crazy', 狡 *jiǎo* 'crafty', 猛 *měng* 'wild', 獨 *dú* 'solitary; independent'.

13.8 On the street #6

(甲) 上海机场的公共汽车站

机场五线
本站：浦东机场
下站：浦东大道
开往上海火车站

NOTES

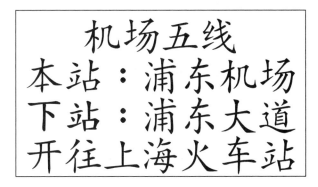

a. 线 *xiàn* 'thread; route; line'

b. 本 *běn* 'root; [here] this'

c. 浦东 *Pǔdōng*: a district in Shanghai which derives its name from being on the eastern bank of the *Huángpǔ* River. *Pǔdōng* is also the name of Shanghai's main international airport.

d. 道 *dào* 'road; way'

e. 开往 *kāiwǎng* 'going towards; bound for'

(乙) RESTROOMS

厕所	盥洗室	洗手间
廁所		洗手間
cèsuǒ	*guànxǐshì*	*xǐshǒujiān*
'toilet'	'lavatory'	'bathroom'

(丙) ADVERTISEMENT FOR KFC IN CHENGDU

李小鹏嘴子吃香辣鸡翅。

Lǐ Xiǎopéng zuǐzi chī xiānglà-jīchì.

('[name of Chinese gymnast] mouth eat fragrant-spicy chicken-wings.')

(丁) 身份证 *SHĒNFÈNZHÈNG* ‘IDENTITY CARD’ (‘STATUS-PROOF’)

This is an old version of an actual identity card, but it contains the sort of information requested by many other types of forms. It is followed by a blank version for you to fill out with your own particulars.

照 片	姓名 林美 性别 女 民族 汉 出生 1965年3月20日 住址 南京市南京大学31号楼206房间
公安局 公章	1996年11月30日签发 有效期限10年 编号 140202650320104

照 片	姓名 性别 民族 出生 住址
公安局 公章	2006年3月15日签发 有效期限10年 编号 140202 104

NOTES

a. 照片 *zhàopiàn* ‘photograph’

b. 性别 *xìngbié* ‘sex’

c. 住址 *zhùzhǐ* ‘address’

d. 公安局 *gōng'ānjú* 'public security bureau'

e. 公章 *gōngzhāng* 'official seal'

f. 房間/房间 *fángjiān* 'room'

g. 簽發/签发 *qiānfā* 'sign and issue'

h. 有效期限 *yǒuxiào qīxiàn* 'good for . . . [years]' ('effective-period')

Appendix 1 STROKE ORDER AND STROKE DIRECTION

The small numbers indicate the order of stroke; their position on the line shows the onset (and hence, the direction). (S) indicates a simplified character; (T) indicates a traditional character.

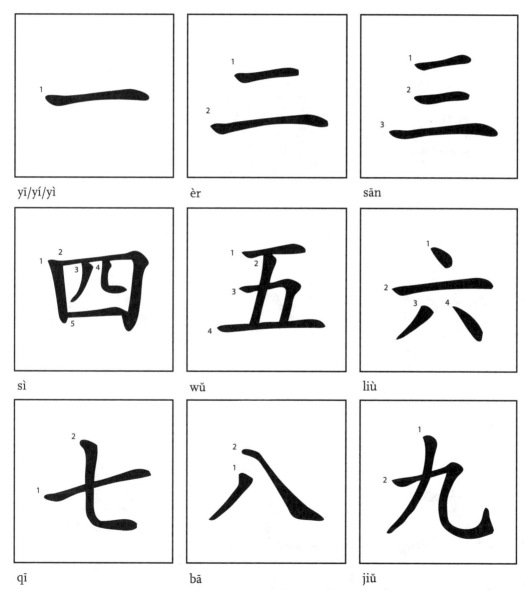

Unit 8

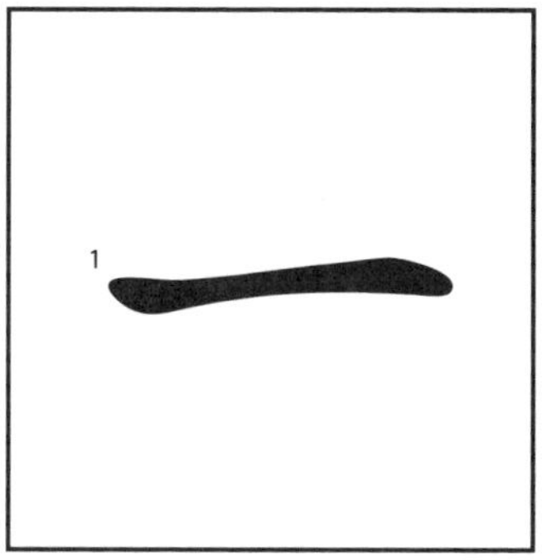

yī/yí/yì

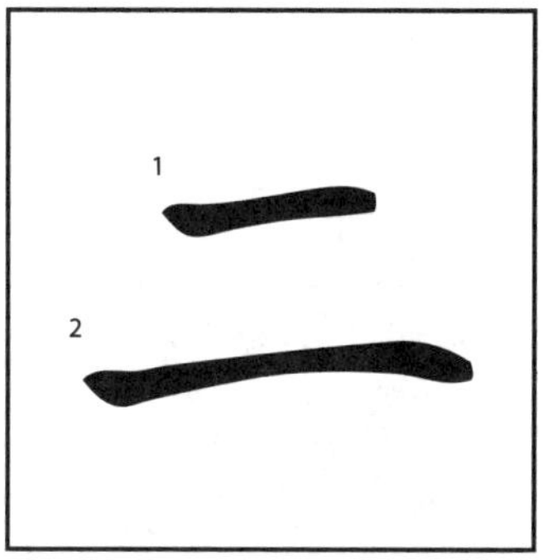

èr

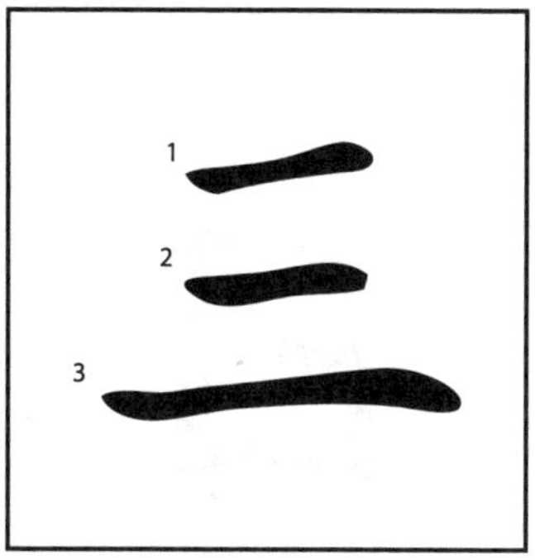

sān

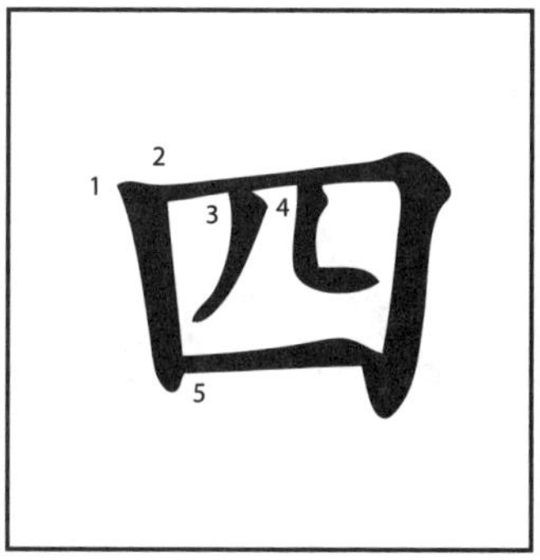

sì

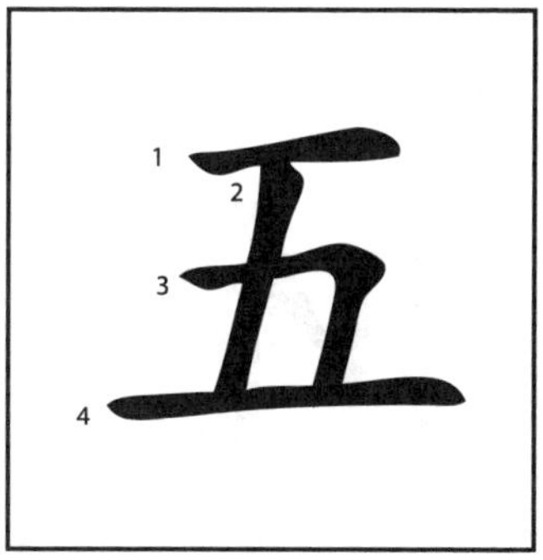

wǔ

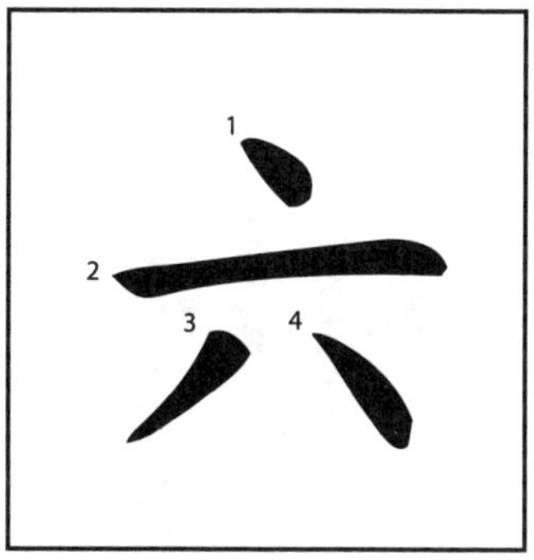

liù

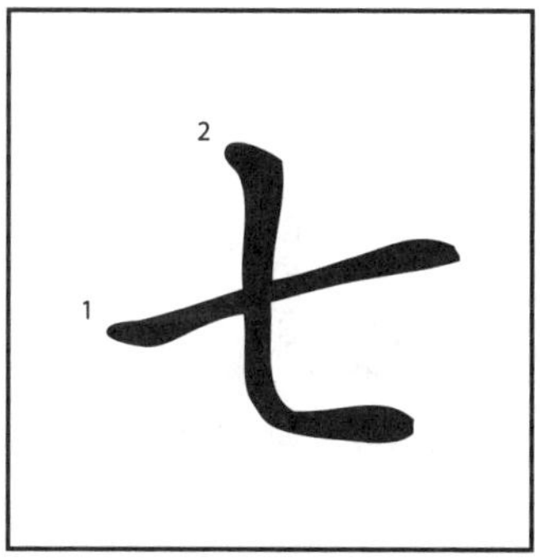

qī

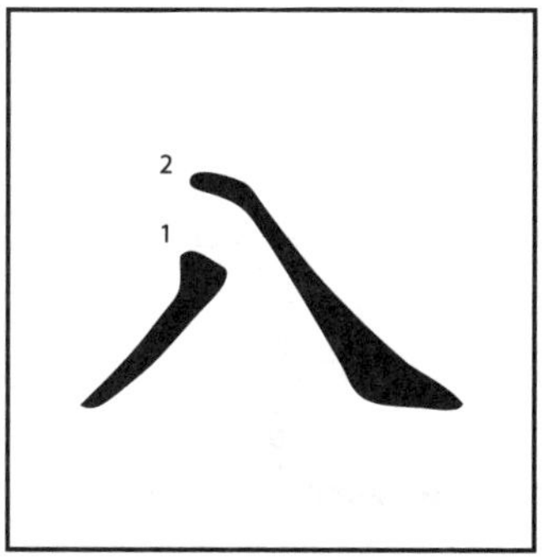

bā

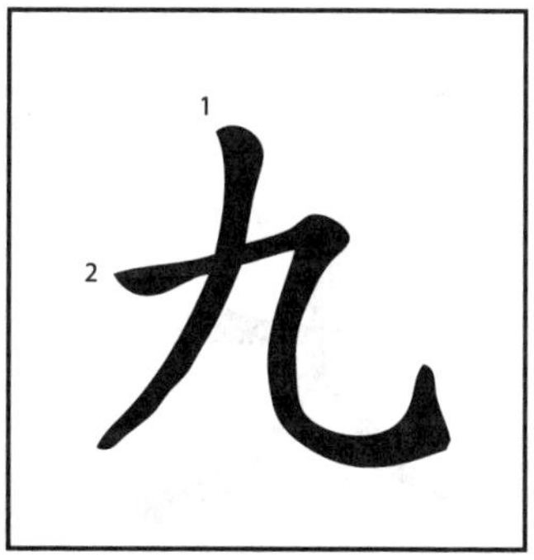

jiǔ

shí

nián

yuè

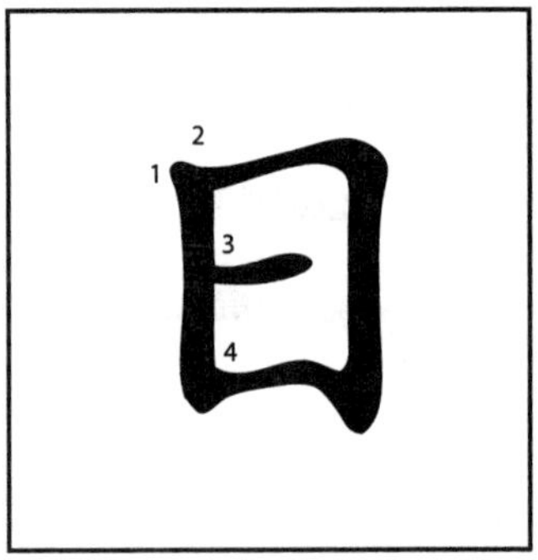

rì

hào (T)

hào (S)

míng

zuó

jīn

tiān

wáng

lǐ

máo

zhōu

bái

lín

xìng

tā

tā

yě

wǒ

nǐ

men (T)

men (S)

bú/bù

ma (T)

ma (S)

ne

hǎo

lèi

máng

lěng

hěn

hái (T)

hái (S)

le

è (T)

è (S)

tài

rè (T)

rè (S)

chī

fàn (T)

fàn (S)

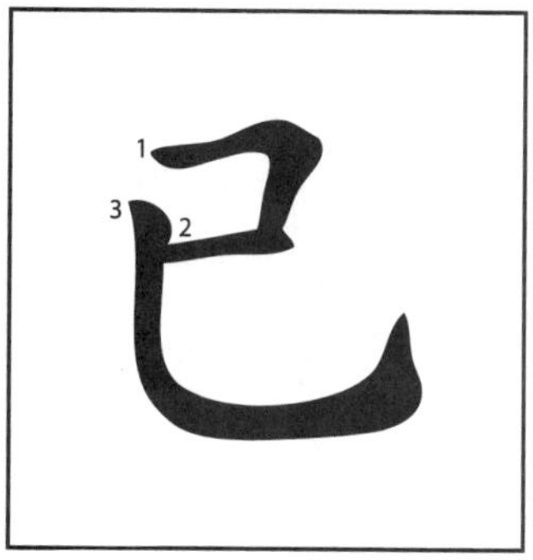

yǐ

jīng (T)

jīng (S)

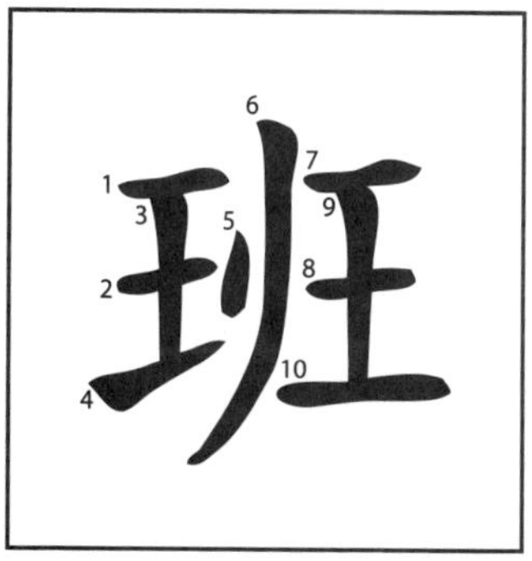

bān

kè (T)

kè (S)

shàng

xià

méi (T)

méi (S)

yǒu

Unit 9

shì

nán

de

nǚ

dì

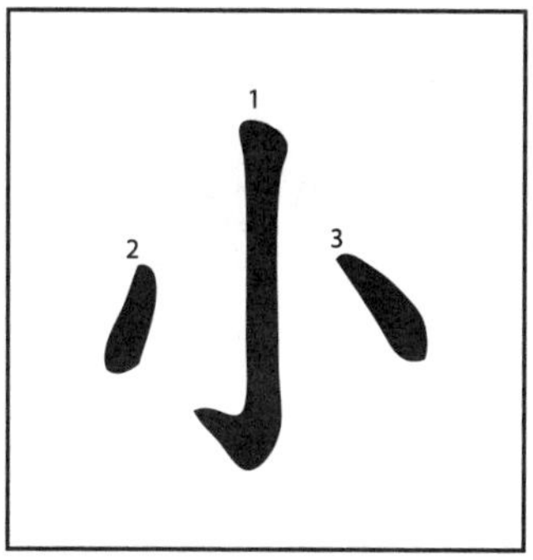

xiǎo

mǎ (T)

mǎ (S)

dōu

chén (F)

shéi/shuí (F)

zhāng (F)

chén (S)

shéi/shuí (S)

zhāng (S)

zhè/zhèi (T)

xué (T)

shēng

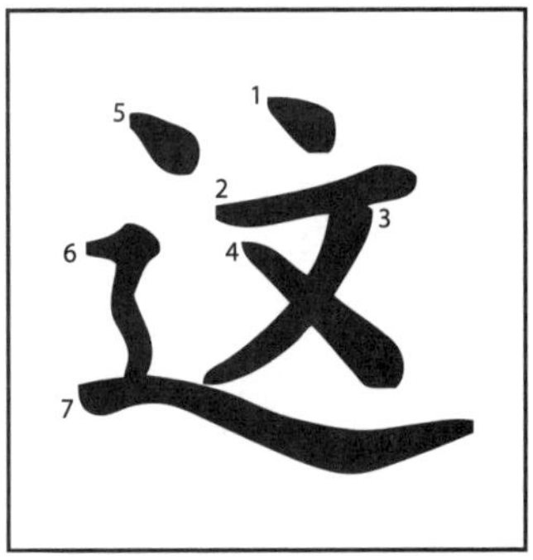

zhè/zhèi (S)

xué (S)

lǎo

shī (T)

diǎn (T)

ér/~r (T)

shī (S)

diǎn (S)

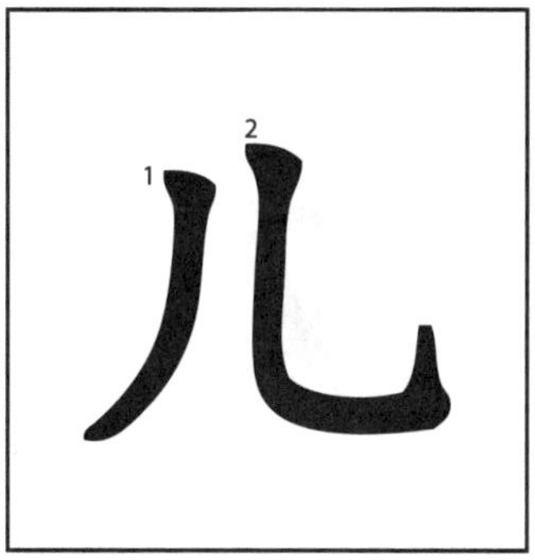
ér/~r (S)

zěn

me (T)

yàng (T)

gāo

me (S)

yàng (S)

zhōng

duì (T)

nán (T)

wén

duì (S)

nán (S)

jǐn (T)

gè/ge (T)

gè/ge (S)

jǐn (S)

yǐ

qián

xiàn (T)

xiàn (S)

zài

kàn

bào (T)

bào (S)

nà/nèi

dàn

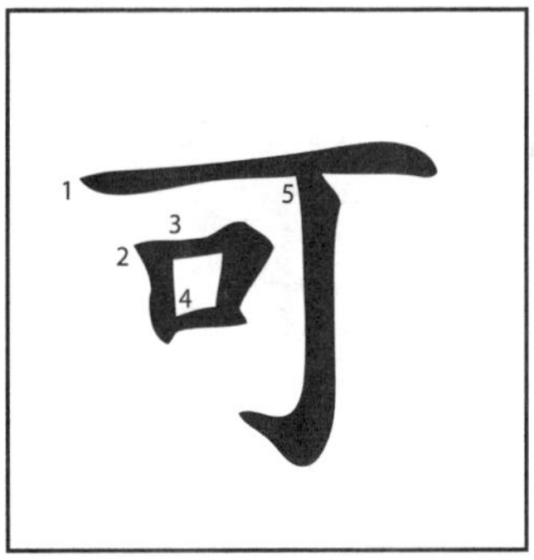
kě

nǎ/něi

shén (T)

shén (S)

dōng (T)

dōng (S)

xī

shǒu

jī (T)

jī (S)

shū (T)

shū (S)

bāo

bǐ (T)

bǐ (S)

zǒu

chē (T)

sǎn (T)

guì (T)

chē (S)

sǎn (S)

guì (S)

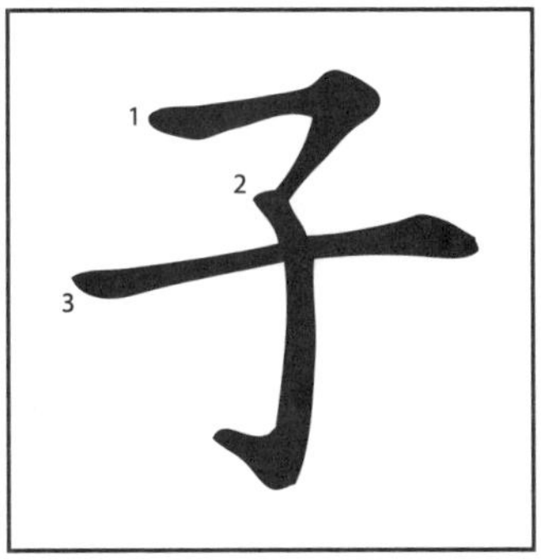

zǐ/zi

zì

diǎn

qǐ

lái (T)

lái (S)

xíng/háng

nín

Unit 10

měi

guó (T)

guó (S)

rén

yīng (T)

yīng (S)

jiào

míng

zì

ba

guò (T)

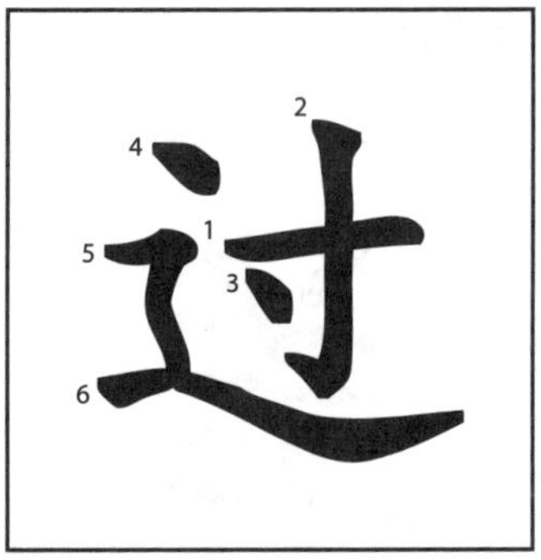

guò (S)

qì (T)

qì (S)

xiǎng

qù

dì

fāng

liǎng (T)

liǎng (S)

wài

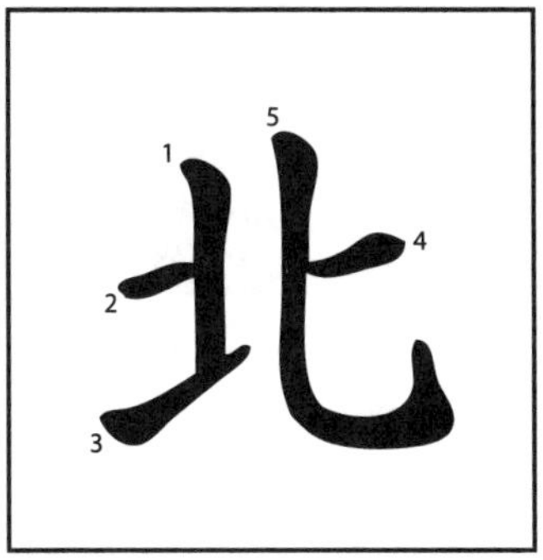

běi

nán

jīng

xī

ān

hăi

dào

jìn

shěng

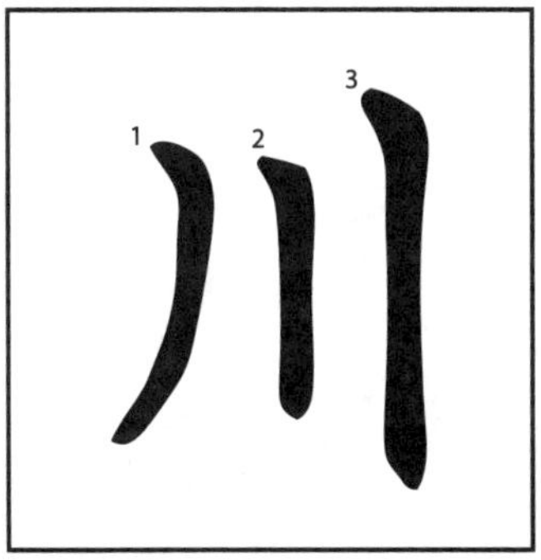

chuān

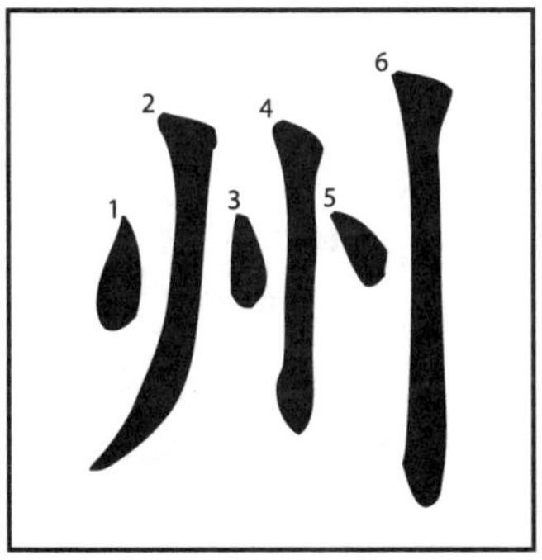

zhōu

bù

cóng (T)

lí (T)

yuǎn (T)

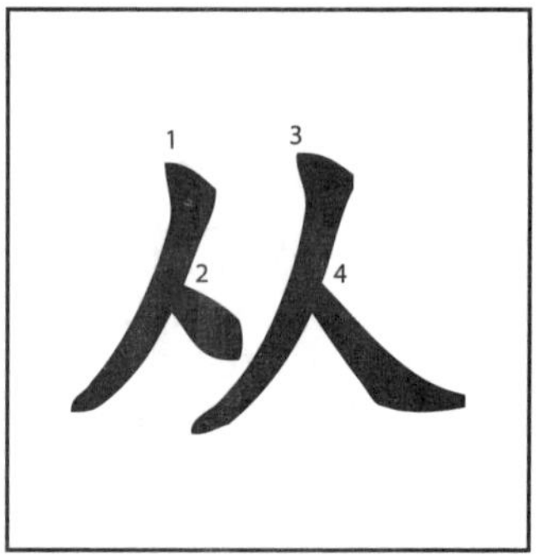

cóng (S)

lí (S)

yuǎn (S)

biān (T)

cuò (T)

bié

biān (S)

cuò (S)

wàng

fēi

cháng

jiā

běn

de/dé/děi

bǎi

diàn (T)

huà (T)

shuō (T)

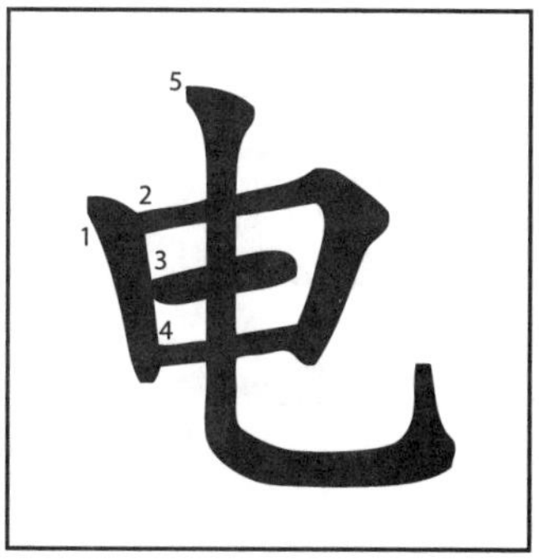

diàn (S)

huà (S)

shuō (S)

mǎ (T)

lǐ (T)

kuài (T)

mǎ (S)

lǐ (S)

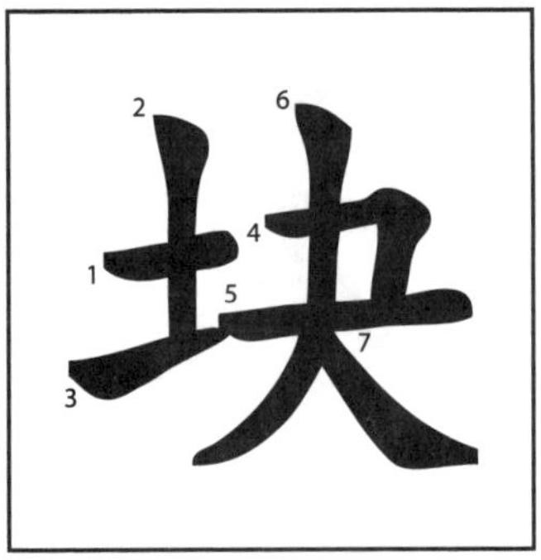
kuài (S)

qián (T)

chá (T)

kě

qián (S)

chá (S)

hē

zài

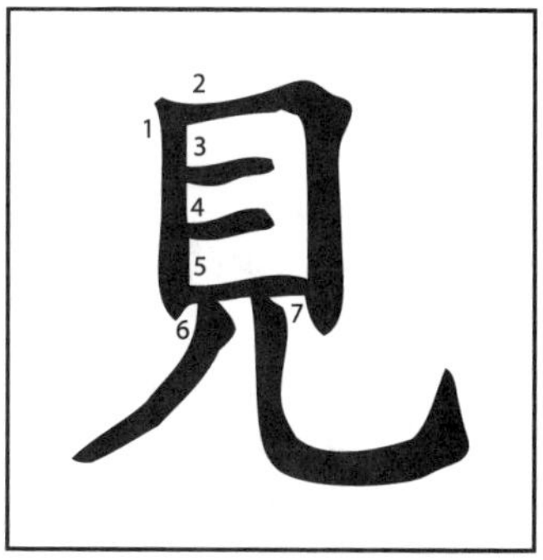

jiàn (T)

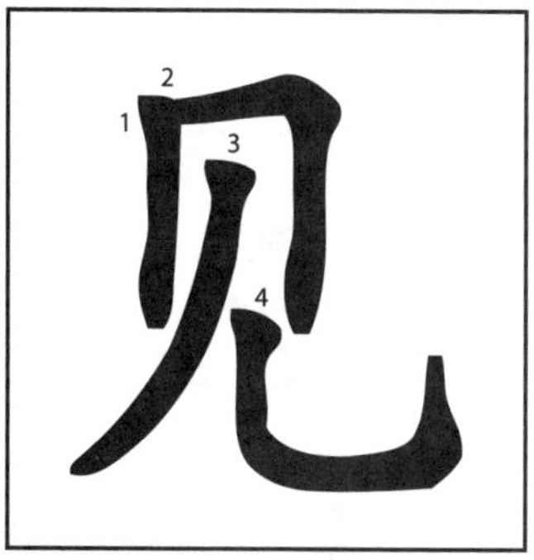

jiàn (S)

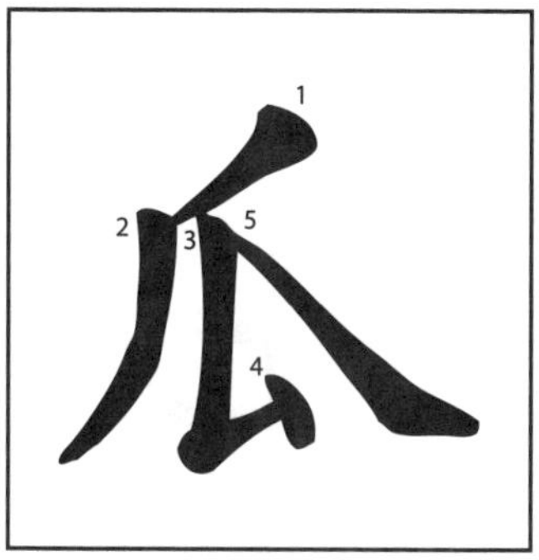

guā

jīn

bēi

jiŭ

duō

shăo

jĭ (T)

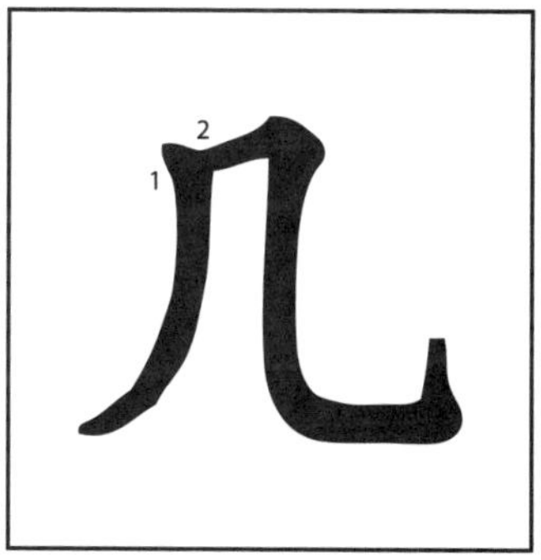

jĭ (S)

Unit 11

yī

fú

shū

mù

zuì

xiān

zǎo

xǐ

zǎo

shuì

jiào; jué (T)

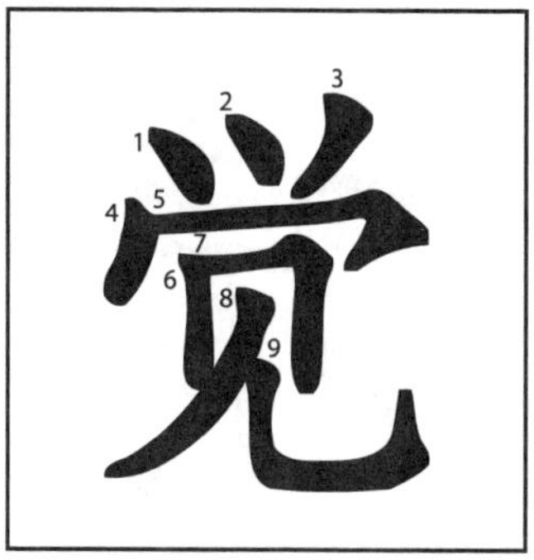
jiào; jué (S)

tīng (T)

tīng (S)

wǎn

mǎi (T)

mǎi (S)

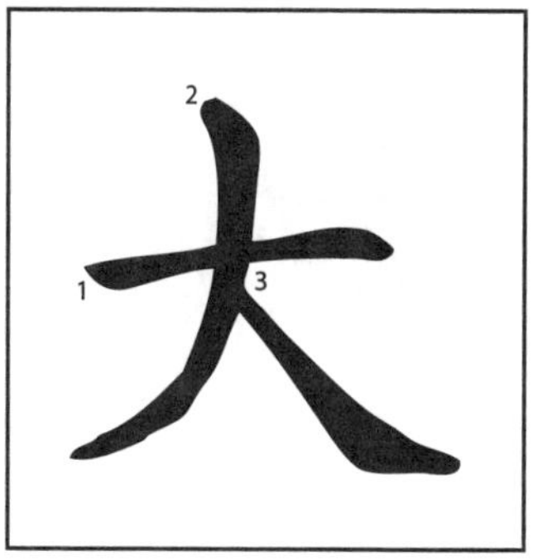
dà

mào

jiě

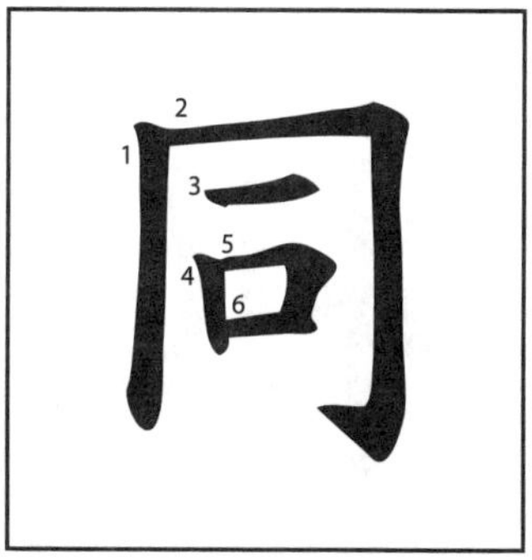
tóng

qǐng (T)

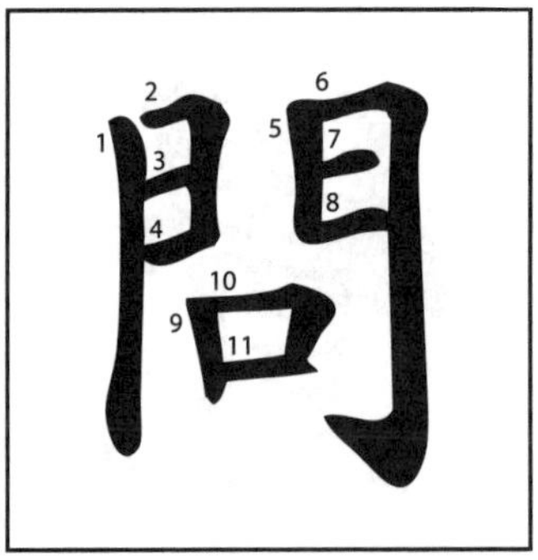

wèn (T)

tí (T)

qǐng (S)

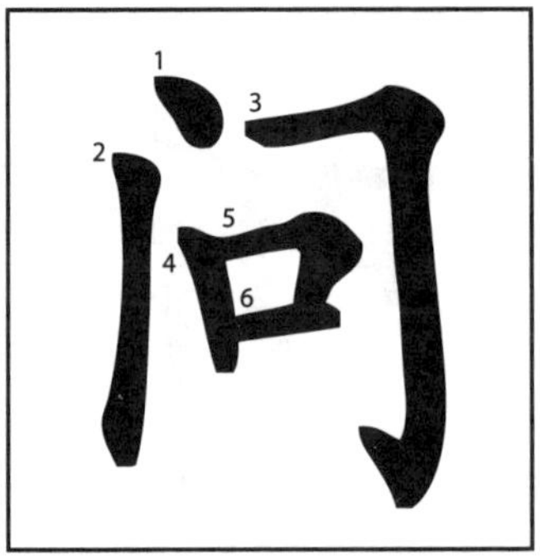

wèn (S)

tí (S)

jī (T)

chǎng (T)

tiě (T)

jī (T)

chǎng (S)

tiě (S)

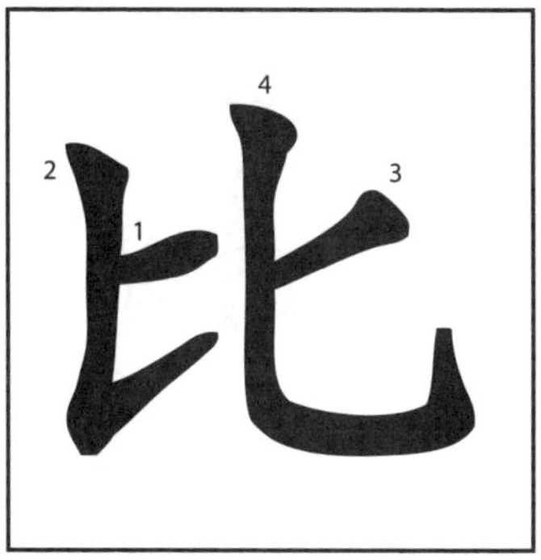

bǐ

jiào (T)

jiào (S)

qīng

chǔ

zì

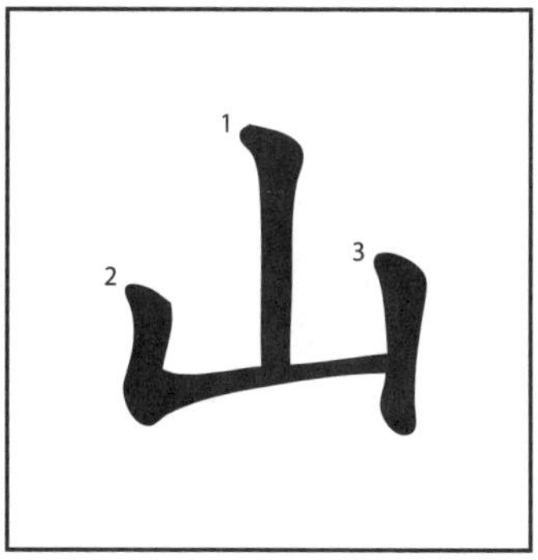

shān

zuò

kǒng

kè

qì

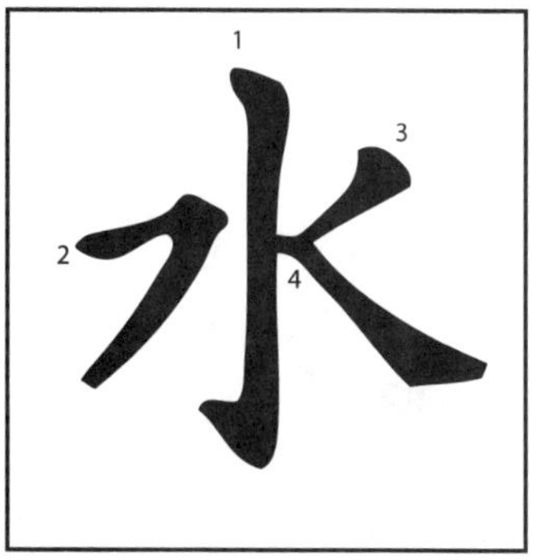

shuǐ

yào

fēi (T)

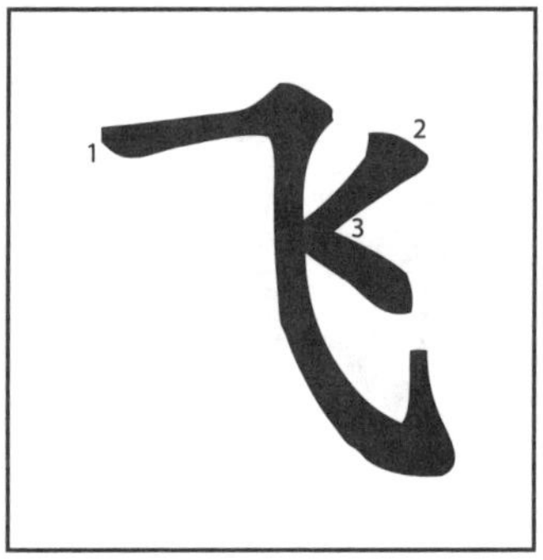
fēi (S)

hàn (T)

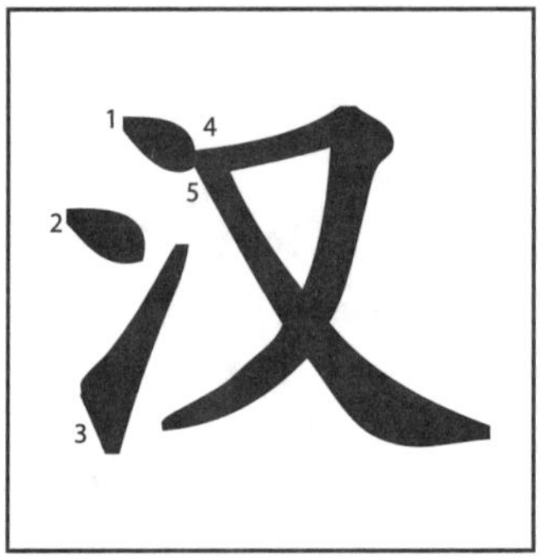
hàn (S)

jí

zhǎng; cháng (T)

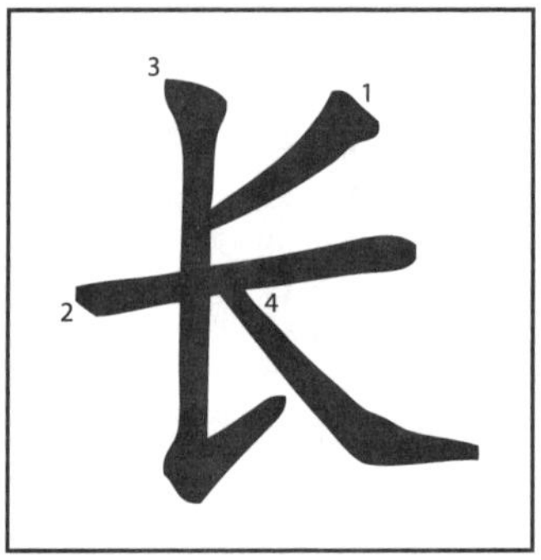
zhǎng; cháng (S)

huǒ

zhàn

péng

yǒu

zhù

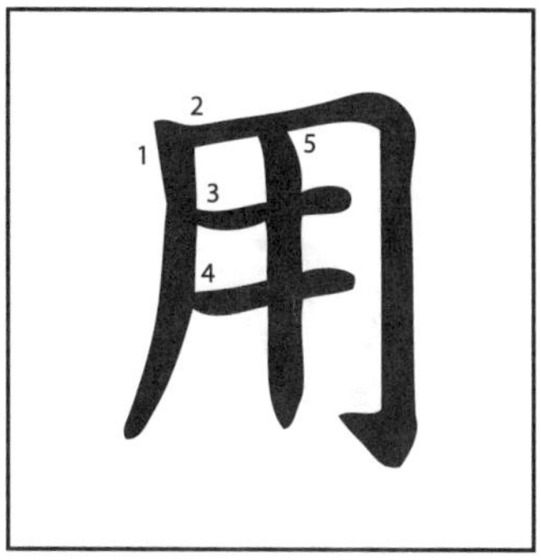

yòng

piàn

gōng

huì (T)

huì (S)

wǔ

gòng

zuò

Unit 12

yīn

wèi; wéi (T)

wèi; wéi (T)

wèi; wéi (S)

lóu (T)

lóu (S)

xǐ

huān (T)

huān (S)

zhōng (T)

zhōng (S)

suǒ (T)

suì (T)

suì (S)

suǒ (S) / (T)

gōng

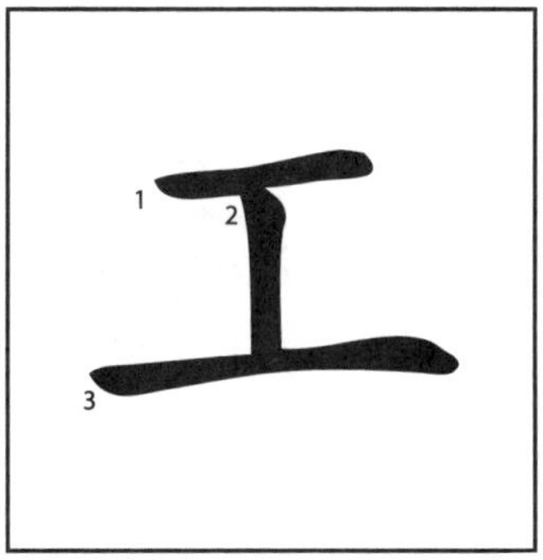

gōng

zuò

měi

wèi

jiù

mén (T)

mén (S)

jiē

fù

mǔ

lù

bà

mā (T)

mā (S)

dìng

xīng

qī

yīng (T)

gāi (T)

jié (T)

yīng (S)

gāi (S)

jié (S)

hòu (T)

tóu (T)

bàn (T)

hòu (S)

tóu (S)

bàn (S)

zǒng (T)

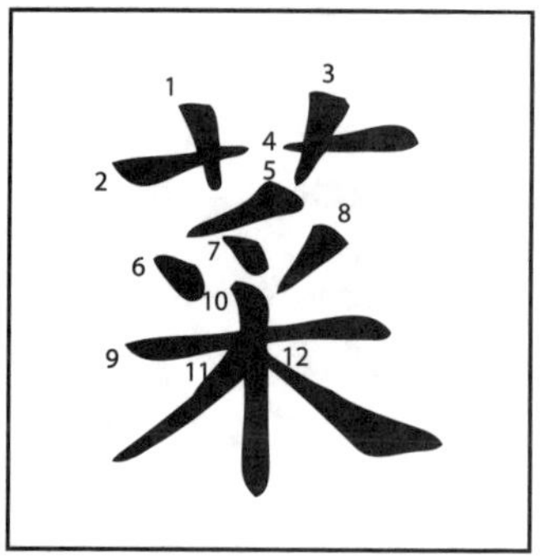
cài (T)

cè (T)

zǒng (S)

cài (S)

cè (S)

xì

chéng

shì

gài

gèng

hái

jiāng

hé

hú

niú

yáng

ròu

lǐ

xiè (T)

xiè (S)

kǎo

shì (T)

shì (S)

kāi (T)

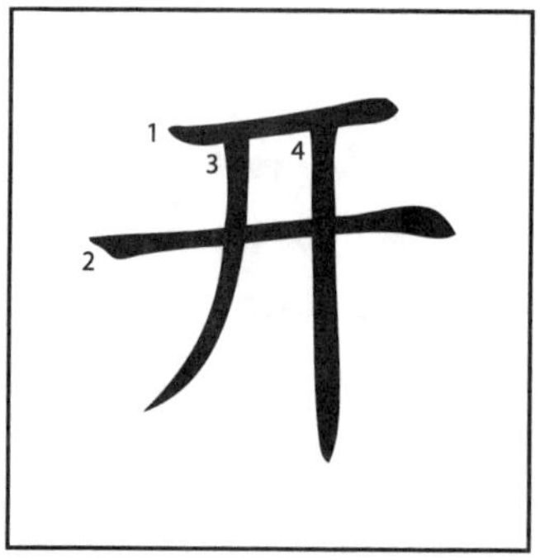
kāi (S)

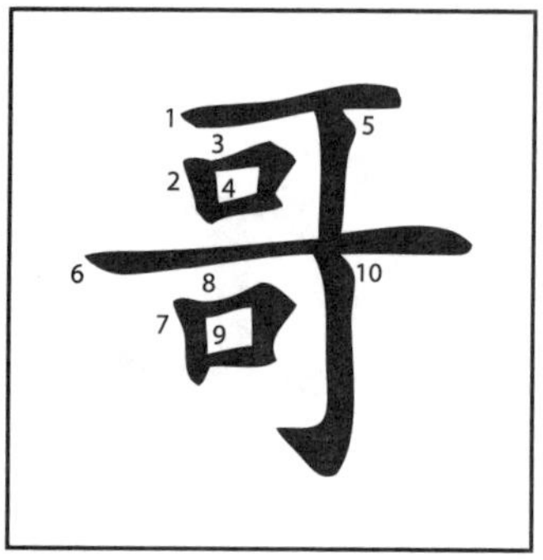
gē

jìn (T)

jìn (S)

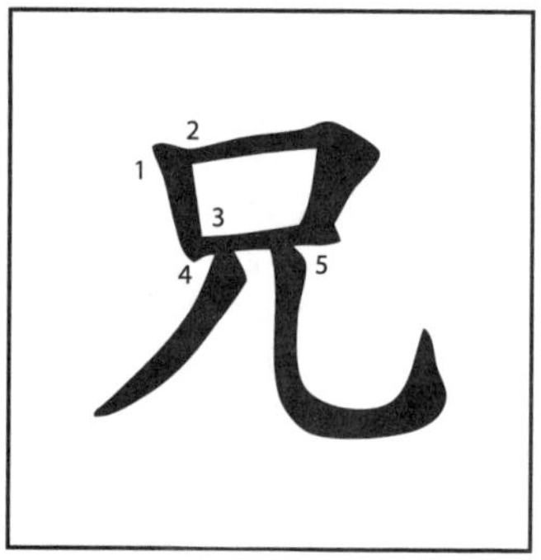
xiōng

qiān

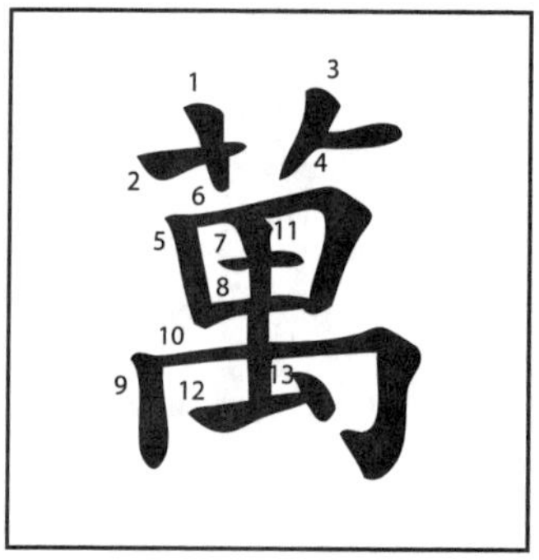
wàn (T)

wàn (S)

mǐ

zhēn (T)

zhēn (S) / (T)

xiàng (T)

xiàng (S)

dì

Unit 13

ài (T)

bì (T)

yè (T)

ài (S)

bì (S)

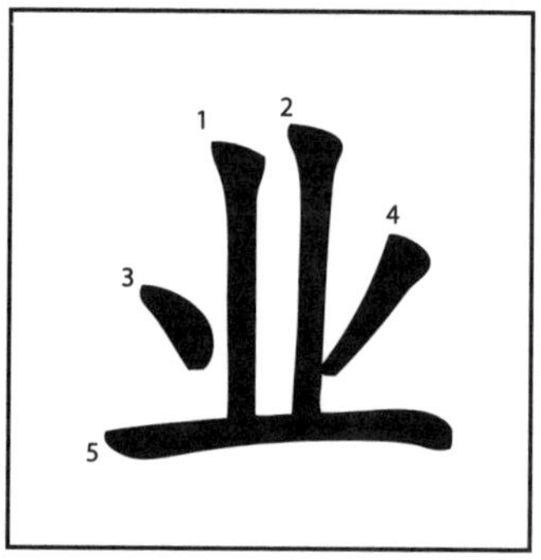
yè (S)

yán

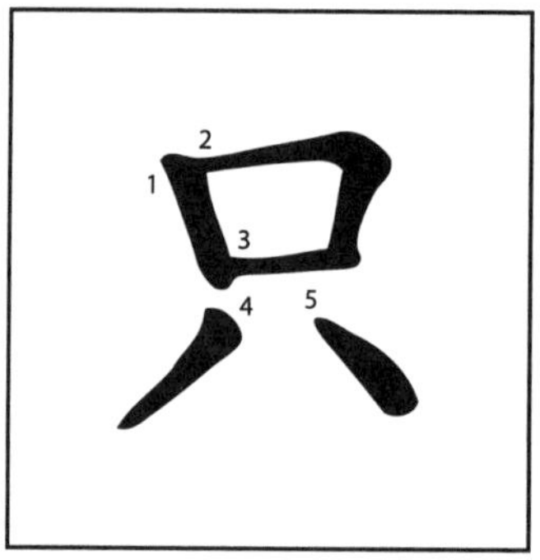
zhǐ

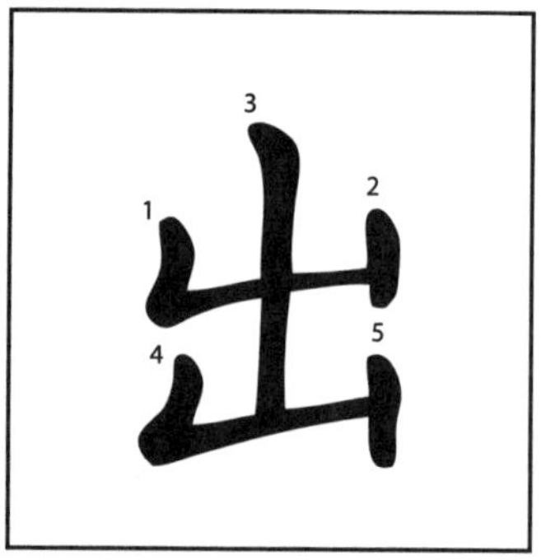
chū

xí (T)

xǔ (T)

yǔ (T)

xí (S)

xǔ (S)

yǔ (S)

jí (T)

jiàn

mín

jí (S)

fáng

chǎo

miàn (T)

tiáo (T)

tāng (T)

miàn (S)

tiáo (S)

tāng (S)

yú (T)

jī (T)

dàn

yú (S)

jī (S)

nǎi

xiā (T)

jiǎo (T)

huò

xiā (S)

jiǎo (S)

zhě

xiě (T)

shí (T)

hòu

xiě (S)

shí (S)

zhōu

jiān (T)

gěi (T)

páng

jiān (S)

gěi (S)

gēn

chà (T)

jiāo (T)

hé

chà (S)

jiāo (S)

fǒu

yī (T)

yuàn (T)

tīng (T)

yī (S)

yuàn (S)

tīng (S)

guǎn (T)

yān (T)

yuè (T)

guǎn (S)

yān (S)

yuè (S)

yīn

xī

wán

bìng

zuǒ

yòu

diàn

mèi

Appendix 2 A SAMPLE SCHEDULE FOR *LEARNING CHINESE*

The sample schedule provided below is based on courses that used pre-publication versions of *Learning Chinese* as the main textbook. These courses met four hours a week for thirteen weeks, for a total of fifty-two class hours. Courses meeting for more or fewer class hours can adjust the total number of assignments up (by adding hours from the schedules for the companion intermediate-level text) or down (by knocking off classes from the list below). The courses also covered both conversational and literacy skills, so these schedules make reference to both the core and character units of *Learning Chinese*.

The daily (that is, hour-by-hour) schedules provided indicate, in general terms, the material that should be studied *to prepare* for each class. While in most cases particular courses would have idiosyncratic features that would restrict the simple transfer of these schedules from one program to another, they should at least provide a useful guide to the pace and emphasis of typical courses, so they are included here for reference.

The audio clips that accompany *Learning Chinese* are not specifically referred to in the sample schedule. However, since they make reference to section and exercise numbers in the book, it will be easy to match them to the schedule. To access the audio clips, and for more information, visit the *Learning Chinese* website, **yalebooks.com/wheatley**.

Daily assignments for the first semester

The first fifty-two assignments cover a beginning semester. Each assignment is calculated to take no more than two hours. They involve reading or listening to sections of *Learning Chinese*, practicing, and ultimately internalizing samples of language material and doing exercises to monitor progress.

The first semester covers the following sections of *Learning Chinese*:

Preface and Introduction
Sounds and Symbols

Core Units	*Character Units*
Unit 1	Unit 8
Unit 2	Unit 9
Unit 3	Unit 10
Unit 4	

In class

In general, topics within a unit are previewed and practiced out of class so that they can be performed and fine-tuned in class, with further consolidation and progress following in overlapping waves. Most units culminate in a long dialogue that incorporates many of the points of grammar and usage. Students internalize these well enough to re-enact the scenario in class, and eventually use them as the basis for personalized dialogues. For courses that mix core lessons with character lessons, the alternation between the two allows one to be introduced while the other is being consolidated. With the character lessons, students practice the readings and exercises at home so that they can perform and respond to them with suitable fluency when they come to class.

Assignments

The daily assignments list relevant sections as a guide to progress through the textbook. How the material is presented depends on the teacher as well as the subject matter. Some classes will begin with a review of earlier material and then focus on current topics; others will begin with conversational practice and then shift to reading exercises; still others will introduce upcoming material. The assignments are milestones on the route.

The first one or two classes of the first semester are exceptional in that material is presented in class sight unseen, before it has been examined at home. By the third class, the items listed under each assignment should be done 'for that class', as indicated.

Abbreviations

Assignments make reference to sections as Unit 1.2.1 or simply 1.2.1, and to exercises as Unit 8 exs. 3, 4.

Classes 1–8 (to the practice test)

CLASSES 1 AND 2: In class, after dealing with curricular and administrative matters, you will find yourself in a totally Chinese setting where you will encounter your first conversational material 'sight unseen' and with hardly any (or no) explanation, so you will have to rely on mimicry and common sense. Topics include simple greeting and leave taking, basic questions and answers, and numbers (all anticipating Unit 1). In addition, you will be introduced to the tones and some of the other sounds of Chinese, and the system of transcription used to write them (anticipating the unit on Sounds and Symbols).

At home, read the prefatory material and the Goals and Methods section of the Introduction. Then read Sounds and Symbols up to the end of 0.3 (Initial consonants), doing exs. 1, 2, and 3 as you go. Finally, skip ahead to the beginning of Unit 1 and read up to the end of the section on pronouns (1.6). This homework will help you consolidate some of what you have been practicing, sight unseen, in the first two classes.

FOR CLASS 3: Read to the end of the Introduction, covering the sections on Basic geography and Linguistic background. Review through Sounds and Symbols 0.3 (Initial consonants), redoing exs. 1, 2, and 3. You should be able to list the 12 surnames in 0.2.5, and recite from memory the chart of initials in 0.3.1. Continue with 0.4 on the rhymes, focusing on those issues covered in exs. 4, 5, and 6. In Unit 1, review through 1.6 and do ex. 1. Skip to 1.10.1 and learn to recite from memory the first six 'tone combos'. Finally, preview the two rhymes in 1.12 at the end of Unit 1.

FOR CLASS 4: Review the Introduction and Sounds and Symbols so far. Then continue with Sounds and Symbols from 0.5 (Miscellany) to the end, doing the eight parts of ex. 7. In Unit 1, consolidate through 1.6 (Pronouns), then continue through 1.7 (Action verbs), including the mini-conversations in 1.7.5.

FOR CLASS 5: Review Sounds and Symbols well, redoing the exercises. You should be able to cite the examples of the tonal shift of *bu* in 0.5.3. Continue with Unit 1, sections 1.8 (Conventional greetings) and 1.9 (Greetings and taking leave). The 'closing phrases' under 1.9.5 need particular attention; practice them over and over again, as you would a difficult passage of music.

FOR CLASSES 6, 7, AND 8: Do Unit 1 exs. 2 and 3. Review all of the Introduction, Sounds and Symbols, and Unit 1 (referring to 1.11, the summary) for a practice test in Class 8. Make sure that you can write the material in pinyin with the proper tone marks.

Classes 9–18, to test #1

FOR CLASS 9: Begin Unit 8, the first character unit, by reading to the end of section 8.6. In 8.4.1, practice drawing the different types of strokes and the characters given, naming the strokes as you do so. (Write characters on appropriately ruled grid paper, if possible.) Learn to write the numbers in characters, and to recite the multiplication tables and telephone numbers (ex. 1). Look ahead to 8.7 (Dates) and 8.8 (Days). At the same time that you are learning character material in Unit 8, continue to consolidate Unit 1 material, which should also be practiced in class.

FOR CLASS 10: Review 8.7 (Dates) and 8.8 (Days), and continue with 8.9 (Surnames and pronouns). Do exs. 2, 3, and 4. (This is a good point at which to get instruction in Chinese word processing.)

FOR CLASS 11: Consolidate Unit 8 so far, and practice writing with correct stroke order (following the numbered strokes on the character sheets in Appendix I). Continue with section 8.10 (More pronouns and function words), doing the reading in that section.

As you consolidate Unit 8, begin the second core unit, Unit 2, doing section 2.1 (a pronunciation drill) and all the sections of 2.2 (Adverbs). Finally, preview the rhymes towards the end of the unit (2.13). (By this time, your teacher will have provided you with an appropriate Chinese name, and you will be spending some time in each class learning to read the pinyin representation of your classmates' Chinese names.)

FOR CLASS 12: Continue in Unit 8 with the third set of characters, 8.11 (SVs and associated function words), practicing the phrases (8.11.1) and the readings (8.11.2). Continue with Unit 2, section 2.3 (More SVs), doing ex. 1. Review and consolidate.

FOR CLASS 13: Complete Unit 8 with 8.12 (the last set of characters), practicing the phrases (8.12.1) and doing the reading (8.12.2), plus ex. 5. Study the last section (8.13), called 'On the street #1', which, as the heading suggests, introduces signs written in characters that are likely to be seen on the streets of Chinese cities. In Unit 2, study section 2.4 (Nouns and modification) and do ex. 2. Review the tone combos from Unit 1.10 and then practice the new tone combos from Unit 2.11.3. (Practice tone combos daily so you can eventually recite the examples from each tone category by heart.)

FOR CLASS 14: Consolidate the first sections of Unit 2, and continue through 2.7 (Location and existence), doing exs. 3, 4, and 5. Look ahead to the culminating dialogue in Unit 2.9 (At the airport). Review the characters in Unit 8 by regularly redoing selections of the 'phrases' and 'readings' and writing them out in phrases, etc.

FOR CLASS 15: Review 'Location and existence' (Unit 2.7) and continue with 2.8 (with special attention to 'Welcome' and 'Praise'); then prepare the long dialogue in 2.9 so as to be able to perform it in class with confidence. Do ex. 6; practice reading the airline names at the end of 2.9.

FOR CLASS 16: Finish up Unit 2 with sections 2.10 (Reflections) and 2.11 (Pinyin notes and practice). Continue to practice dialogue 2.9 (At the airport) until confident. Do ex. 7. Review pinyin, especially the rhymes, and practice saying the longer phrases involving welcome, thanks, praise, transition, etc. Prepare for test #1 in class 18, which will cover everything up to the end of Units 2 and 8.

FOR CLASS 17: Continue to review for test #1.

FOR CLASS 18: **Test #1**: You will be asked to distinguish tone combos, identify initials and common rhymes, produce material from Units 1 and 2 (in correct pinyin), and read material composed with the characters from Unit 8. (No writing of characters.)

Classes 19–31, to test #2

FOR CLASS 19: Begin Unit 9 by doing 9.0 (Review) and 9.1 (the first set of characters), including 9.1.1 and ex. 1; preview 9.2 (the second set). Continue to review Unit 2 material, and to practice the long dialogue in 2.9.

FOR CLASS 20: Continue with Unit 9 by working on 9.2 (the second set of characters) and doing ex. 2. Do a spot review of Unit 2, especially 2.7, 'Location and existence'.

FOR CLASS 21: Continue with Unit 9.3 (the third set), including 9.3.1 and 9.3.2, plus ex. 3. Review Units 1 and 2 tone combos and other pinyin material.

FOR CLASS 22: Continue with Unit 9.4 (the fourth set), including the readings and ex. 4. Preview Unit 3, sections 3.1 (a pronunciation drill), 3.2 (Amount), and 3.3 (Nationality), with special attention to the V + *guò* construction 3.3.4.

FOR CLASS 23: Practice the rote material in Unit 3: money (3.9.1), days of the week (3.10.2), dates (3.10.3), and rhymes (3.15). Finish the character unit 9.5 (Form of characters), 9.6 (Miscellany), and 9.7 (On the street #2).

FOR CLASS 24: Unit 3.4 (NSEW), including the three dialogues at the end of 3.4 and ex. 1. Keep practicing the rote material from Unit 3 and add 3.10.4 (Siblings).

FOR CLASS 25: Consolidate Unit 3 so far. Continue with 3.5 (Yes and no) and 3.6 (Thanks and sorry); skip to the pinyin practice (3.13). Continue to read and write characters regularly.

FOR CLASS 26: Unit 3, exs. 2 and 3; study 3.7 (Things to drink), doing ex. 4.

FOR CLASS 27: Do Unit 3, section 3.8 (Why; because; so) along with ex. 5, and section 3.9 (Money), with exs. 6 and 7. Review 3.10 (Other numbered sets) as well as Unit 3 so far.

FOR CLASS 28: Consolidate Unit 3 so far, doing ex. 8. Practice the last three tone combos (3.13.1).

FOR CLASS 29: Learn Unit 3.11 (Courses and classes); begin practicing the main dialogue (3.12). Do exs. 10 and 11. Review all 15 tone combos. Review the character lessons Units 8 and 9.

FOR CLASS 30: Review all of Unit 3, doing ex. 9; review Units 8 and 9 for test #2 in class 31.

FOR CLASS 31: Review again, focusing on the short dialogues at the end of 3.4 and 3.7 and the longer dialogue in 3.12. **Test #2** covers everything so far, that is, through Units 3 and 9.

Classes 32–44, to test #3

FOR CLASS 32: Begin Unit 10 with the review section (10.0). Practice naming the radicals; refer to the first section of the previous character lesson, Unit 9. Review earlier dialogues in the core units to increase fluency and confidence. These dialogues will form the basis of some of the conversational practice in the next few classes.

FOR CLASS 33: Continue with Unit 10, doing the first set of characters (10.1), along with the associated readings and ex 1. Continue to consolidate Units 3, 2, and 1.

FOR CLASS 34: Review the first set of characters in Unit 10. Preview Unit 4 material: 4.1 (Tone contrasts) and 4.2 (Existence and location), with particular attention to the new words for locations.

FOR CLASS 35: Do Unit 10.2 (the second set of characters), along with the readings and ex. 2. Study Unit 4, sections 4.3.1 and 4.3.2 to get familiar with clock time, then preview the mini-dialogues in 4.3.3 (Times of events [meals]).

FOR CLASS 36: Do Unit 10.3 (the third set), including ex. 3, and review the earlier sets (10.1 and 10.2). In Unit 4, consolidate the sections on clock time and meal times, and do exs. 1 and 2. Review the 15 tone combos.

FOR CLASS 37: Do the final character set of Unit 10, section 10.4, along with the reading practice and ex. 4. In Unit 4, continue with section 4.4 (DE revisited), doing ex. 3, and section 4.5 (Names in detail). Look ahead to sections 4.8.3 and 4.8.5, which deal with titles and forms of address. These can be practiced daily by greeting imaginary guests at the beginning of class.

FOR CLASS 38: Review all of Unit 10, redoing selections of the readings. In Unit 4, focus on 4.6 (Years) and 4.7 (Studying and working) and do ex. 4. Preview the long dialogue called 'On the bus to *Miányáng*' (4.10).

FOR CLASS 39: Unit 4: Look ahead to the rhymes (4.14); study all of 4.8 (Forms of address); do ex. 5. Practice greeting people with titles, e.g., managers, CEOs, film directors. Practice pinyin by doing ex. 7 in section 4.12. Continue to practice dialogue 4.10.

FOR CLASS 40: Do section 4.9, Introductions, and continue practicing the long dialogue (4.10). Prepare to perform the first half of the dialogue in class.

FOR CLASS 41: Work on improving fluency for dialogue 4.10. Study the section on food (4.11), and listen to the short narratives until you can follow easily. Review characters, as always, by reading and writing selections from the readings and exercises.

FOR CLASSES 42, 43, 44: Consolidate for **test #3** in class 44, which covers all material through Units 4 and 10.

Classes 45–52, through the oral interview to end of term

FOR CLASS 45: Review the main dialogues to improve fluency, beginning with 4.10 (On the bus to *Miányáng*), and continue to practice reading pinyin accurately and fluently.

FOR CLASS 46: In your assigned teams, write out and prepare conversational scenarios to perform impromptu, in class, and without notes.

FOR CLASS 47: Continue with class presentations.

FOR CLASS 48: Prepare for oral interviews, which will take the place at appointed times throughout the day (instead of class 48).

FOR CLASSES 49, 50, 51: Various activities and guests.

FOR CLASS 52: Chants, songs, and other activities.